HISTORY OF THE LABOR MOVEMENT
IN THE UNITED STATES
VOLUME IV

BY PHILIP S. FONER

History of the Labor Movement in the United States VOLUME I: *From Colonial Times to the Founding of the American Federation of Labor* VOLUME II: *From the Founding of the American Federation of Labor to the Emergence of American Imperialism* VOLUME III: *The Policies and Practices of the American Federation of Labor, 1900–1909*

A History of Cuba and Its Relations with the United States (2 vols.)
The Life and Writings of Frederick Douglass (4 vols.)
The Complete Writings of Thomas Paine (2 vols.)
Business and Slavery: The New York Merchants and the Irrepressible Conflict
The Fur and Leather Workers Union
Jack London: American Rebel
Mark Twain: Social Critic
The Jews in American History, 1654–1865
The Case of Joe Hill
The Letters of Joe Hill
The Basic Writings of Thomas Jefferson
The Selected Writings of George Washington
The Selected Writings of Abraham Lincoln
The Selected Writings of Franklin D. Roosevelt

HISTORY OF THE LABOR MOVEMENT IN THE UNITED STATES

— v. 4 —

VOLUME IV: *The Industrial Workers of the World, 1905–1917*

BY PHILIP S. FONER

INTERNATIONAL PUBLISHERS, NEW YORK

230570

331.88
F67

For this edition author has added
notes on pages 11, 146, 558

Fourth Printing 1980

1 0001 000 016 804

Dedicated to the Memory of
ELIZABETH GURLEY FLYNN

"*Is it not much better to even die fighting for something than to
have lived an uneventful life, never gotten anything and leaving
conditions the same or worse than they were and to have future
generations go through the same misery and poverty and degradation? The only people whose names are recorded in history are
those who did something. The peaceful and indifferent are forgotten; they never know the fighting joy of living.*"

—*From speech of* ELIZABETH GURLEY FLYNN, *Seattle,
January 28, 1917* (Industrial Worker, *February 3, 1917*).

Library of Congress Catalog Card Number: 47–19381
ISBN (Cloth) 0–7178–0094–6; (Paperback) ISBN 0–7178–0396–1

MANUFACTURED IN THE UNITED STATES OF AMERICA

CONTENTS

PREFACE

In his pioneer study of the I.W.W., published in 1919, Paul R. Brissenden wrote: "The public still knows little about the organization and its members. . . . The public has not been told the truth about the things the I.W.W. has done or the doctrines in which it believes. The papers have printed so much fiction about this organization and maintained such a nationwide conspiracy of silence as to its real philosophy—especially to the constructive items of its philosophy—that the popular conception of this labor group is a weird unreality."

Despite the appearance since 1919 of a number of valuable studies of the I.W.W. (and less valuable accounts, including novels and poems, which over-romanticize the organization), Professor Brissenden's statement is almost as applicable today as when he made it. In general, the letters "I.W.W." still conjure up the picture of a sinister internal enemy of American society, an organization of "bomb-throwing" hoboes who preached and practiced violence for no reason but to make trouble. Thus, a work published in 1956, *The Rocky Mountain Revolution* by Stewart Holbrook, sums up the history of the I.W.W. as a "great soaring saga of violence." And a review in the New York *Herald-Tribune* of June 12, 1955, summarizes Wallace Stegner's novel, *The Preacher and the Slave,* as follows: "Stark, unrelieved violence is the beginning, substance and end of Mr. Stegner's novel. If its swarming hoboes, bums and soapbox evangelists are not committing crimes in the name of the I.W.W. and the O[ne] B[ig] U[nion] which so alarmed the nation in the early days of this century, they are glorying in past depredations or planning future outbreaks." Robert G. Sherrill stated flatly in *The Nation* of March 9, 1964, that members of the I.W.W. "talked to their implacable employers: with fire, gunshot and dynamite." In *The Quest of the Dream,* published in 1964, John P. Roche writes that "romanticization of violence" was the dominant characteristic of the I.W.W.

No one would realize from these accounts that the I.W.W. made valuable contributions in the campaign to organize the unorganized (particularly the unskilled, the foreign-born, women, and Negro workers), spearheaded the fight for free speech, and pioneered in the battle for industrial unionism. Fortunately, the year 1964 also saw the publication of *Rebel Voices: An I.W.W. Anthology,* edited by Joyce L. Kornbluh, made up of articles, songs, poems, cartoons, and photographs from the Labadie Collection at the University of Michigan Library. But this work, despite its value in providing a true picture of the I.W.W., is not a history of the organization.

The present volume covers the history of the I.W.W. from its formation in 1905 to the eve of America's entry into World War I in 1917. While it does not encompass the entire life of the organization—indeed, on paper at least, the I.W.W. is still in existence—it does cover its most active period. The I.W.W. did important work after the United States entered the first World War—and this will be discussed in a subsequent volume—but its major concentration had to be on defense activities against government repression. After the war, the I.W.W. gradually sank into insignificance.

I had originally planned to include a chapter on the case of Joe Hill, but in view of the length of the present volume this proved impracticable. However, since the fiftieth anniversary of Hill's execution was approaching—he was shot to death by a firing squad in Salt Lake City on November 19, 1915—I decided to expand the chapter into a full treatment of the case, and it is being published as a separate book.

The names of many of the individuals appearing in this volume were spelled variously in the press. I have used the spellings that appeared most frequently.

The present volume is the second of a three-part study of the American labor movement from 1900 to 1917. The first in this series was volume three of the *History of the Labor Movement in the United States*. Published in 1964, it covered the policies and practices of the American Federation of Labor, 1900–1909, and of the immediate precursors of the I.W.W., the Western Federation of Miners and the American Labor Union. The third part in this series (Volume V of *History of the Labor Movement in the United States*) will deal with the A.F. of L., the Railroad Brotherhoods, and the Socialists, 1909–1917.

The files of the I.W.W. headquarters in Chicago have been scattered by fire, vandalism, and the action of government agents in the post-World War I onslaught on radical and nonconformist thought. However, there is a vast body of material related to the I.W.W. throughout the United States, and I have made every effort to make use of these sources. In the preparation of this volume I have had access to the correspondence of the A.F. of L. and to collections of manuscripts, newspapers, pamphlets, and unpublished and published studies in numerous libraries and historical societies.

I wish to thank the staffs of the Chicago Historical Society, Colorado State Historical Society, Forest History Society (St. Paul), Idaho Historical Society, Kansas Historical Society, Minnesota Historical Society, Wisconsin State Historical Society, Library of the U.S. Department of Labor, Library of the Department of Labour (Canada), Minnesota State Law Library, New York State Library, Washington State Library, Library of Congress, National Archives, National Bibliothèque (Paris), British Museum, Labadie Collection (University of Michigan Library), Tamiment Institute Library of New York University, the public libraries of the following cities: Akron, Boston, Chicago, Detroit, Denver, Edmonton (Canada), Eveleth (Minn.), Everett (Wash.), Bridgeport (Conn.), Hammond (Ind.), Hibbing (Minn.), Lawrence (Mass.), Minneapolis, New York, Paterson (N.J.), Philadelphia, Portland (Oregon), San Diego (Calif.), San Francisco, Schenectady (N.Y.), Seattle (Wash.), Skowhegan (Me.), Spokane (Wash.), Tacoma (Wash.), Utica (N.Y.), Vancouver (British Columbia), and the libraries of the following colleges and universities: Brigham Young, California, Catholic University of America, Chicago, Columbia, Dartmouth, Duke, Harvard, Idaho, Indiana, Iowa, Kansas, London School of Economics, Michigan, Minnesota, Missouri, Nebraska, New York, Oregon, Pennsylvania, Reed, State University of South Dakota, State College of Washington, Texas, Tulane, Washington State University, University of Washington, Wayne State, Wisconsin, Yale.

I wish to thank Professor Hyman Berman of the University of Minnesota for the opportunity to read his unpublished study of immigrant miners of the Mesabi Range. I wish also to thank Mrs. Louise Heinze, Director of the Tamiment Institute Library of New York University for valuable assistance in obtaining material through interlibrary loan. I owe a great debt of gratitude to the late Elizabeth Gurley Flynn, who not only permitted me to interview her at length, but read a draft of the entire manuscript and made valuable suggestions. Finally, I wish to express my gratitude to the Trade Union Committee for the Publication of Labor History for a grant which made publication of the present volume possible.*

PHILIP S. FONER

Croton-on-Hudson, New York
August 1965

---

* Since this volume was published, four additional studies of the I.W.W. have appeared: *The Wobblies* by Patrick Renshaw (New York, 1967); *Rebels of the Woods* by Robert F. Tyler (New York, 1967); *We Shall Be All: A History of the Industrial Workers of the World* by Melvin Dubofsky (Chicago, 1969), and *Bread and Roses Too: Studies of the Wobblies* by Joseph R. Conlin (Westport, Conn., 1969). Dubofsky's work is a full-length study of the I.W.W.; Renshaw's is a brief treatment of the organization; Tyler's is an analysis of the I.W.W.'s militant history in the Pacific Northwest, and Conlin's is a collection of essays dealing with such questions as whether or not the Wobblies were syndicalists and revolutions and whether or not they practiced sabotage. While these works (especially Dubofsky's) are useful, nothing in them has caused me to alter in any significant manner the text that follows.

Abbreviations Used in Footnotes and Reference Notes

AFL Corr.—American Federation of Labor Correspondence, American Federation of Labor Archives, American Federation of Labor Building, Washington, D.C. A small portion is presently stored at the Wisconsin State Historical Society.

GLB.—Samuel Gompers Letter-Books. Formerly stored in American Federation of Labor Building, Washington, D.C. At present stored at headquarters of AFL-CIO.

NA.—National Archives, Washington, D.C.

Pinkerton Reports.—Pinkerton Reports relating to the Western Federation of Miners, 1906–1907. From the Hawley and Borah Manuscripts, Idaho Historical Society.

Report by U.S. Commissioners of Conciliation.   .—Report by U.S. Commissioners of Conciliation William I. Fairley of Alabama and Hywell Davies of Kentucky on the Mesaba Iron Miners' Strike in Minnesota, June 2 to September 17, 1916, submitted October 28, 1916, National Archives.

Strikers' News.—*Strikers' News: Official Strike Bulletin of the Striking Iron Ore Miners of the Mesaba Range,* National Archives.

TIL.—Tamiment Institute Library of New York University.

TRP.—Theodore Roosevelt Papers, Library of Congress, Washington, D.C.

WS.—Scrapbooks of Clippings on the Wheatland Hop Field Riots, Wheatland, California, 1913–1915, University of California Library, Berkeley.

WSHS.— Wisconsin State Historical Society, Madison, Wisconsin.

CHAPTER I

Birth of the I.W.W.

By the summer of 1904, many progressive-minded elements in the American labor and Socialist movements were convinced of three basic principles: (1) the superiority of industrial unionism over craft unionism in the struggle against the highly integrated organizations of employers; (2) the impossibility of converting the conservative American Federation of Labor into a type of organization which would achieve real benefits for the majority of workingmen and women; and (3) the ineffectiveness of the existing organization of the industrial and radical type to build a movement which would organize and unite the entire working class. Clearly, in the eyes of these elements, a new organization of labor was necessary, one that "would correspond to modern industrial conditions, and through which they (the working people) might finally secure complete emancipation from wage slavery for all wage workers."[1] It was this conviction that led to the formation of the Industrial Workers of the World.

One of the men who led the way to this new development was Eugene V. Debs. From the time he had organized the American Railway Union on this basis in 1893, Debs advocated the industrial form of organization. He played a leading part in the formation of the American Labor Union. In 1902, and during the period between 1902 and 1904, his speeches and writings were full of references to the superiority of industrial unionism and the necessity of combining this principle with uncompromising action based upon the class struggle. His most important contribution in this period, and one of his chief theoretical works, was *Unionism and Socialism, A Plea for Both,* published in *Appeal to Reason* in 1904 and reprinted as a pamphlet shortly thereafter.

The study began with an analysis of the development of unionism. Debs then emphasized that modern industrial conditions required a modern type of unionism. "This is the industrial plan, the modern method applied to modern conditions, and it will in time prevail." But Debs was convinced that the A.F. of L. could not be quickly converted into a modern type of union, and that a new organization was necessary. Gompers and his lieutenants were completely wedded to the National Civic Federation philosophy of class collaboration. They refused to make any serious efforts to organize unskilled workers, especially Negro and foreign-born workers. They had frequently broken strikes by independent unions. They were unable to make any substantial gains in the face of the open-shop drive, and they absolutely refused to embark upon united economic or political action. They were, in short, committed to the continuation of capitalism with all of its evils. The Socialists inside the A.F. of L. had sought to change these policies through their educational programs. They had not only failed to accomplish their objective, but their outlook was even corrupting segments of the Socialist Party itself. Certain Socialist politicians, trying to win votes at elections from the conservative unionists, were deliberately trimming their own program to conform to the views of Gompers. There was, therefore, only one clear answer to this problem: a new revolutionary industrial union which would organize the unorganized and be "uncompromising" in its attempt to advance the cause of socialism.[2]

Debs' pamphlet did not impress the dominant elements in the Socialist Party leadership who still clung to the belief that the A.F. of L. would soon be transformed, by the education of its membership, into a revolutionary union. But it did arouse widespread discussion in radical circles. Debs' viewpoint was discussed at the Twelfth Annual Convention of the Western Federation of Miners held at Salt Lake City, during May and June 1904, and helped to crystallize the growing sentiments for a new, broad industrial union. The executive board of the W.F. of M. was instructed to take "such action as might be necessary" to bring the representatives of organized labor together to outline plans "for the amalgamation of the working class into one general organization."[3]

PRELIMINARY CONFERENCES

The resolve of the W.F. of M. gave impetus to the developing sentiment for a new labor organization. Dan McDonald, president of the American Labor Union, Clarence Smith, general secretary-treasurer of that union, George Estes and W. L. Hall, president and general secretary-treasurer of the United Brotherhood of Railway Employees, William E. Trautmann, editor of the *Brauer Zeitung,* official organ of the United Brewery Workers, and Father Thomas J. Hagerty, Socialist lecturer and editor, held informal discussions on the subject with W.F. of M. officials.[4]

In the organizational work leading to the establishment of the Industrial Workers of the World, Trautmann's role was a dominant one. For it was he who invited a group of radical labor leaders to a conference in Chicago in November 1904 to lay the groundwork for a new industrial union. The six who met in this preliminary conference were Trautmann, Clarence Smith, Father Hagerty, George Estes, W. L. Hall, and Isaac Cowen, American representative of the British Amalgamated Society of Engineers. All agreed the time had come to establish a new labor organization that, unlike the A.F. of L., corresponded to existing industrial conditions and would be the vehicle for the downfall of capitalism and the elimination of wage slavery. Several of those not present at this informal conference were kept informed of the discussions, and two of them, Debs and Charles O. Sherman, general secretary of the United Metal Workers' International Union, joined the others in an appeal for a larger meeting. The appeal, in the form of a letter dated November 20, 1904, was sent to 36 persons, inviting them to a secret conference in Chicago on January 2, 1905. The letter emphasized that the events of the past year had convinced the signers "that craft divisions and political ignorance were doomed to speedily end," and that they were confident in the ability of "the working class, if correctly organized, on both industrial and political fields, to take possession of and operate successfully for their own interests, the industries of the country." It continued: "We invite you . . . to discuss ways and means of uniting the working people of America on correct revolutionary principles, regardless of any general labor organization, past or present, and only restricted by such basic principles as will insure its integrity as a real protector of the interests of the workers."[5]

The invitation received widespread support in Left-wing circles. The W.F. of M. sent three delegates: Charles H. Moyer, W. D. ("Big Bill") Haywood, and John M. O'Neill, editor of the *Miners' Magazine*. From the Socialist Party came A. M. Simons, editor of the *International Socialist Review*, and "Mother" Mary Jones, an organizer for the United Mine Workers, but they participated in an unofficial capacity as individuals. Frank Bohn, a national organizer for the Socialist Labor Party and the Socialist Trade and Labor Alliance, was also present in an individual capacity and not as a representative of the party.*

Explaining that he was not able to attend the conference because the doctor had ordered him to rest and recuperate his strength, Debs wrote: "I keenly regret this for I had counted on being with you and in giving such assistance as I could to the work of organizing that is to be undertaken along new and progressive lines." But two of those invited refused

---

* Daniel De Leon, head of the S.L.P., was not invited. Perhaps there was fear that he would disrupt the proceedings, a tendency De Leon had already displayed frequently in the past and which he was to demonstrate again later. Another possibility is that De Leon was not yet identified as a supporter of industrial unionism; indeed, it was not until June 1905, at the first I.W.W. convention, that he endorsed the idea. (Donald Kennedy McKee, "The Intellectual and Historical Influence Shaping the Political Theory of Daniel De Leon," unpublished Ph.D. thesis, Columbia University, 1955, p. 14.)

to attend because of sharp disagreement with the purpose of the meeting. These dissenters were Victor Berger and Max Hayes, members of the National Committee of the Socialist Party. Berger did not even respond, but made his disagreement public in the *Social-Democratic Herald* in which he charged that the proposed new organization "will bring on a condition of strife in the labor world that will enable Samuel Gompers to keep industrial-union organization away for a much longer time than he would have been able to had the fight for it inside the A.F. of L. not been interfered with by impatient and short-sighted comrades." In a letter explaining his new refusal to attend, Hayes declared that the proposed new organization smacked too strongly of a revived Socialist Trade and Labor Alliance, and that he would not permit himself "to be dragged into any more secession movements or fratricidal wars between fractions of workers because they are not of one mind at this juncture." Instead, he preferred to "agitate *on the inside* of the organizations now in existence to dump conservatism overboard and prepare to take their places in the working class administration of the Co-operative Commonwealth." He was confident that this would be soon accomplished, for "the rank and file of the trade unions are awakening as never before, and as soon as even a good-sized minority become thoroughly class-conscious, the fossilized leaders will 'go up in the air.'"[6]

In the eyes of most of the men who attended the Chicago conference, to follow Berger's and Hayes' advice would not only be deluding themselves, but would also do an injustice and injury to the working class. Experience over many years had convinced them that the A.F. of L. leaders were misleading the labor movement, and they were not persuaded that the militant elements could change this situation by remaining inside the Federation.[7]

The absence of the leaders of the Right and Center wings of the Socialist Party at the conference foreshadowed the sharp conflict that was to arise later in the party over the attitude to be adopted toward the I.W.W. But at the time, the rejection of invitations by Berger and Hayes did not dampen the spirits of those who attended. Twenty-three persons were present in Chicago on January 2 when the secret conference was called to order by Trautmann. They represented eight different organizations: the American Labor Union, Western Federation of Miners, United Brotherhood of Railway Employees, Brewery Workers' Union, Switchmen's Union, United Metal Workers, Bakers' Union, and American Federation of Musicians. This was apart from the members of the Socialist and Socialist Labor parties, who were there as individuals.

The conference took on the name of Chicago Conference of Industrial Unionists, and elected William D. Haywood as its permanent chairman and George Estes, secretary. During the three days' session, plans for a new labor organization to be based on the principles of industrial unionism, working-class unity, and recognition of the class struggle were discussed and worked out. The result of the discussions was the adoption of the document known as the Industrial Union Manifesto.

INDUSTRIAL UNION MANIFESTO

The Manifesto pointed starkly to the displacement of human skill by machines and to the growth of capitalist power through concentration in the ownership of the tools of production, with the consequent disappearance of trade divisions among laborers, and sharpening class divisions and class antagonisms. While the worker, increasingly displaced by mechanical progress and deprived of his skill of craftmanship, was sinking into the uniform mass of wage slaves, his power of resistance was being broken by the perpetuation of outgrown, artificial craft divisions which only served the purpose of keeping the workers pitted against one another, thus weakening their resistance to capitalist tyranny. On the other hand, the capitalists had carefully adjusted themselves to the new conditions of modern industrial society, had wiped out all differences among themselves, and presented a united front in their war upon labor; and through employers' associations, brute force, injunctions and the use of military power, they sought to crush all efforts at resistance. At the same time, they concealed their more overt attacks on labor by such devices as the National Civic Federation through which they sought to hoodwink and betray those whom they would rule and exploit, depending for success upon the blindness and internal dissension of the working class. In short, the Manifesto emphasized, the employers' line of battle in the class struggle corresponded to the solidarity of mechanical and industrial concentration, while the workers' plan of battle still functioned along the lines of outmoded trade divisions.

"This worn-out and corrupt system offers no promise of improvement and adaptation. . . . [It] offers only a perpetual struggle for slight relief within wage slavery. It is blind to the possibility of establishing an industrial democracy, wherein there should be no wage slavery, but where the workers will own the tools which they operate, and the products of which they alone will enjoy."

Solidarity of the working class—the essential ingredient in achieving this goal—was impossible so long as craft was separated from craft; union men scabbed upon each other, engendering hatred of worker for worker; and unions discriminated against workers because of sex, creed or color— all resulting in delivering workers helpless and disintegrated into the hands of the capitalists. It was impossible so long as craft jealousy blindly attempted to create trade monopolies through prohibitive initiation fees, and so long as craft divisions fostered ignorance among the workers, thus dividing their class at the ballot box, as well as in the shop, mine, and factory. All this hindered the growth of class consciousness and fostered the erroneous idea of "harmony of interests between employing exploiter and employed slave."

Previous efforts for the betterment of the working class, the Manifesto continued, had proven abortive because they had been "limited in scope and disconnected in action." Then followed three paragraphs which stated the ideology of the new organization to be brought into being:

"Universal economic evils afflicting the working class can be eradicated only by a universal working class movement. . . . A movement to fulfill these conditions must consist of one great industrial union embracing all industries—providing for craft autonomy locally, industrial autonomy internationally, and working class unity generally.

"It must be founded on the class struggle, and its general administration must be conducted in harmony with the recognition of the irrepressible conflict between the capitalist class and the working class.

"It should be established as the economic organization of the working class without affiliation with any political party."

Other conditions were that (1) all power should rest with the collective membership; (2) all labels, cards, fees, etc., should be uniform throughout; (3) the general administration should issue a publication at regular intervals; (4) a central defense fund, to which all members should contribute equally, should be established and maintained.

All workers who agreed with the principles set forth in the Manifesto were invited to meet in convention in Chicago on June 27, 1905, "for the purpose of forming an organization of the working class along the lines worked out in the Manifesto."[8]

To push the meeting, an executive committee composed of W. D. Haywood, chairman; W. E. Trautmann, secretary; and A. M. Simons, W. L. Hall, and Clarence Smith was established. The chief duty of the committee was to attend to the distribution of the Manifesto. On the back of each printed copy was a charter classifying the industrial workers according to industry along with a statement entitled, "Industrial Organization of the Workers." This declared that a labor organization to correctly represent the working class had to have two requirements:

"First—It must combine the wage workers in such a way that it can most successfully fight the battles and protect the interests of the working people of to-day in their struggle for fewer hours, more wages and better conditions.

"Secondly—It must offer a final solution of the labor problem—an emancipation from strikes, injunctions and bull-pens."

This "emancipation" from "strikes" was evidently to be accomplished by a general strike which would bring about the end of capitalism, and usher in the new workers' state based solely on the economic organization of labor. For after urging the workers to study the printed chart classifying the industrial workers, the document stated: "Observe, also, how the growth and development of this organization will build up within itself—the structure of an Industrial Democracy—a Workers' Co-operative Republic—which must finally burst the shell of capitalist government, and be the agency by which the working people will operate the industries, and appropriate the products to themselves."[9]

Most of the ideas set forth in the Industrial Union Manifesto were not new. They had been stated over and over again by proponents of industrial unionism who had written many pamphlets and articles in radical journals describing the ineffectiveness of craft unionism in coping with modern tendencies in the industrial world. Debs had emphasized many of the same points in his pamphlet published only a few months before the Manifesto was drawn up. But Debs, like most other critics of existing conditions in the labor movement, had stressed the need for a new departure in labor organization on the political as well as the economic front. Trade union members had to be class conscious on the political field as well as the economic, and had to make use of the ballot box "not only to back up the economic struggles of the trades-union, but to finally wrest the government from capitalist control and establish the working class republic."

But the Industrial Union Manifesto made only a passing reference to the ballot box as part of its criticism of the craft form of organization, and emphasized that the remedy for current evils was through "the economic organization of the working class, without affiliation with any political party." In an interview three days after the secret conference, Trautmann was asked by a reporter for the Cincinnati *Post* if the lack of emphasis in the Manifesto upon the ballot box as a weapon of the labor movement in achieving immediate gains and the ultimate goal of socialism was a significant feature of the document. Trautmann replied that it was the "key" to the entire Manifesto, and that the sentence in the printed chart accompanying the Manifesto, beginning "Observe, also," and describing how the "Workers' Co-operative Republic" would be established by the industrial unions set forth the philosophic framework of the document. "The document," he declared, "is based on the same principles as organized labor in Continental Europe. The new labor organization is to be entirely free from party politics." And by the "same principles as organized labor in Continental Europe," he explained, he meant specifically the organization of labor under "revolutionary syndicalism."[10]

REVOLUTIONARY SYNDICALISM

It is possible to dismiss Trautmann's remarks as merely the statement of one individual. But it must be remembered that Trautmann played a dominant role in the events leading to the formation of the I.W.W. It was he, it will be recalled, who invited the radical labor leaders to the preliminary meeting of industrial unionists in November 1904. When this small group of key leaders decided to send a call to others to meet in Chicago the following January, Trautmann's name headed the list of signatures. The January session itself was called to order by Trautmann. When a committee was selected to draft the Industrial Union Manifesto, Trautmann was one of three chosen. That he "helped to frame" this document, he afterwards admitted with considerable pride. It was also he who was placed in charge of distributing the Manifesto and letters inviting union leaders, including foreign syndicalist leaders, to participate in the June meeting.[11] Trautmann's comment that the new labor organization to be established in June 1905 would be based on the principles of "revolutionary syndicalism" is, therefore, especially significant.

There are many definitions of syndicalism. William Z. Foster, an outstanding authority on the subject, defines it as follows: "In its basic aspects, syndicalism, or more properly anarcho-syndicalism, may be defined very briefly as that tendency in the labor movement to confine the revolutionary class struggle of the workers in the economic field, to practically ignore the state, and to reduce the whole fight of the working class to simply a question of trade union action. Its fighting organization is the trade union; its basic method of class warfare is the strike, with the general strike as the revolutionary weapon; and its revolutionary goal is the setting up of a trade union 'state' to conduct industry and all other social activities."[12]

It was in France that "revolutionary syndicalism" (or anarcho-syndicalism, as Foster correctly describes it) made its greatest headway. In general, it represented an amalgam of trade unionism, Marxism, and anarchism which began early in the 1890's when many anarchist workers entered the French trade unions and, once there, combined their ideas with those of the Marxists and the "pure and simple" trade unionists. It became definitely established as a movement by the turn of the century with the publication of important theoretical works. In 1901, *L'Avenir socialiste des syndicates* by Georges Sorel, the chief theoretician of "revolutionary syndicalism," was published as a book in Paris after being serialized three years earlier in *l'Humanité*. This work discarded political and parliamentary action, insisted that the state must be destroyed and never used as a means for achieving socialism, defended the general strike as the best method for bringing the new society into existence, and advocated an autonomous workers' movement based upon trade unions instead of political parties. Sorel also wrote a preface in December 1901 to Fernand Pelloutier's *Histoire des bourses du travail,* which was published in 1902. In this statement he insisted that parliamentary action led to compromises of the class struggle, praised Pelloutier for his theory of syndicalist decentralization based upon trade unions, and pointed out that the labor unions were to be the foundations of socialist society. The organization of the new social order upon the basis of trade unions was also one of the themes which Pelloutier stressed in the main body of the book.[13]

Although most of the syndicalist intellectuals took no part at all in trade union activities, their ideas made headway in French trade union circles and particularly attracted the attention of discontented Marxists. Workers who clung to a revolutionary interpretation of Marx and Engels believed that Socialist politics, particularly as practiced in parliamentary circles, violated the principles of the class struggle. They felt that the revolutionary flame of Marxism was slowly being extinguished by class collaboration and the insistence upon legality and evolutionary methods. They sought, therefore, an approach to socialism that would recapture the noncompromising interpretation of the class struggle which, they felt, lay at the heart of Marxism.

To these dissatisfied Marxists, the ideas of anarcho-syndicalism had a powerful appeal. The opposition to political action in general and parliamentary action in particular, and the advocacy of methods of "direct action," appeared to be a method of preserving the emphasis on the class struggle. Moreover, the anarcho-syndicalist concept of abolishing the state immediately after the revolution and basing the new society upon decentralized economic structures, filled in the void caused by the anti-political attitude of the anarchists. The economic organization thus replaced the political party as the agent for making the revolution. This it would do through the tactic of the general strike which, by bringing all production to a halt, would break the power of the capitalist class and enable the working class to take over industry. With immediate abolition of the state, the trade unions would then conduct production and form the centers of economic administration in the new social order. In short, the *syndicat,* or trade union, was to be a tool in the education of the working class, and a weapon in the continual war on the capitalist state. Every strike was viewed as a step toward a syndicalist seizure of power, and the workers would take their last step the day they enforced *la grève générale,* or the general strike.

In all of this there was no explicit need for violence. Indeed, a number of syndicalist theoreticians claimed that all that was meant was an effective utilization of the concept of passive resistance. The transition from the capitalist to the syndicalist state would be less a seizure of power than a ceding of it. How then, did syndicalists achieve such a reputation as a "revolutionary" force? The "revolutionary" label was due largely to those syndicalists who felt the need to supplement this theoretical abstraction with a more positive and practical program. The inclination toward violence was transmitted to syndicalism from the anarchism of Bakunin, and the varied definitions of such terms as "sabotage," "direct action," and even syndicalism itself. A striking illustration of this lack of precise definition was the many meanings accorded the word "sabotage." It might mean anything from the destruction of machinery in its most violent form, to the comparatively peaceful "slowdown." It might also mean the production of inferior goods, or more quaintly, working with such infinite care that the cost of production far exceeded the market value. Actually, sabotage in its more violent forms was disapproved of by the syndicalist theoreticians as being detrimental to working-class morality. The worker must be trained to take over and operate the plant, and anything that degraded or lessened his sense of dignity was "the direct negation of the ideal of self-governing industry." Yet syndicalism came to be associated with sabotage in all aspects.

The French syndicalists highly prized the militancy and aggressiveness of their rank and file and the spirit of "no compromise" with their natural enemy, the employer. This spirit of "no compromise" was to serve a dual purpose. It was to prevent the leadership from betraying working-class principles by falling into the pit of "bourgeois respectability"; and, also, it was the surest way, so the syndicalists argued, of preventing the working class from being duped by the capitalist class into thinking there could be any common identification of interests. The class struggle was paramount, and working-class solidarity was to be maintained by the spirit of "no compromise."

The backbone of the French labor movement, and the champion of syndicalism in France, was the *Confédération Générale du Travail* (C.G.T.). It had been formed in 1895 as the result of the amalgamation between two highly localized and loosely knit federations, the *Fédération des syndicats* and the *Fédération nationale des Bourses du Travail*. When the C.G.T. gave these two organizations a national coherence, it was not allowed to encroach on their essential localism. Each local *syndicat*, or *bourse*, regardless of number of its members, cast only a single vote in the C.G.T. Finances were largely under the control of the local organization and its contributions to the central organization were extremely small. Local organizations were seldom burdened by any system of benefits and therefore risked very little by militant strike policies. In this "the direct dependence of the movement on the rank and file" was assured and localization became "the essential basis of all effective working-class action." But, as the C.G.T. put it in 1905, "The affiliates composing the General Confederation of Labor must keep themselves separate from all schools of political thought."[14]

The revolutionary doctrine presented to the working class in France under the name of syndicalism was soon carried into Italy, Spain, and Portugal. As syndicalism developed in other countries, it developed new theories based on specific conditions in each country. But there existed a common belief in the need for a genuinely militant working-class movement. It was on this tenet that syndicalism presented a common front, and it was this, probably more than anything else, that won for syndicalism the appellation "revolutionary."

These then were the principles of "organized labor in Continental Europe" on which, according to Trautmann, the new revolutionary labor movement in the United States was to be based. All this, however, does not mean that the I.W.W. was basically the product of European ideas and influences. Although the influence of French syndicalism in the formative period of the I.W.W. was greater than has generally been assumed,* it is also true that the forces that brought the I.W.W. into being were the product of U.S. economic and political developments. As Louis Levine wrote in his article, "The Development of Syndicalism in America," published in 1913: "The forces which drove American toilers to blaze new paths, to forge new weapons and to reinterpret the meaning of life in new terms were the struggles and compromises, the adversities and successes, the exultation and despair *born of conditions of life in America.*"[15]

The theory of industrial unionism which the I.W.W. brought into sharp focus had no real intellectual basis in European syndicalism. It was, as we have seen in a previous volume in our discussion of the battle for industrial unionism inside the A.F. of L., of the Western Federation of Miners, and of the American Labor Union, essentially the product of the American environment. Even the seeds of an anti-political, anarcho-syndicalist tendency in the American labor movement had been planted in this country as far back as the 1880's, long before the I.W.W. came into existence.† Among the factors influencing its appearance was the existence of great masses of disfranchised immigrants and floating workers, the widespread corruption of American politics that turned workers away from it, the reactionary policies of the A.F. of L. which

---

* Professor Paul Brissenden is incorrect in stating: "It was only after 1908 that the *syndicalisme révolutionaire* had any direct influence on the revolutionary industrial-union movement here. Even then it was largely a matter of borrowing such phrases as *sabotage, en grième parlée*, etc." (*The I.W.W., A Study of American Syndicalism*, New York, 1919, p. 53.) The philosophic framework of the I.W.W. in the months prior to the first convention in June 1905 was constructed chiefly by Trautmann and Father Thomas J. Hagerty both of whom had been influenced by the anarcho-syndicalist movement abroad, and sought to advance in America the syndicalist ideas they had gathered from their contacts in Europe. Both men saw in the Chicago conference scheduled to meet in June 1905 the opportunity for the realization of their dreams. (*See* Trautmann's articles in *American Labor Union Journal*, Sept. 3, 1903; Sept. 24, Dec. 17, 1904; and *Brauer-Zeitung*, July 23, 1904; also Hagerty's articles in *Voice of Labor*, March, June, 1905 and in *Weekly People*, Feb. 18, 1905.)

† For anarcho-syndicalist tendencies in the American labor movement before 1900, *see* Philip S. Foner, *History of the Labor Movement in the United States*, vol. II, New York, 1955, pp. 100, 102, 213–14.

disgusted progressive unionists, and the growing conviction among Left-wing Socialists that neither reform legislation nor votes for socialism seemed to make much headway in gaining immediate benefits for the workers or bringing closer the day when the Socialist republic would be established. All of these factors, William Z. Foster points out, led to the erroneous conclusion that politics should be abandoned and all energy directed toward building the revolutionary labor union. The adherents of this view naively supposed that the workers, organized in "One Big Union," could, in the near future, call a general strike which would cause the end of capitalism, and then rule the new workers' state by trade-union organization alone.[16] All this, the history of the I.W.W. was to prove, was not as easy to achieve in real life as it was to put down in lengthy and stirring articles in journals and pamphlets.

RESPONSE TO CALL FOR JUNE CONVENTION

The Industrial Union Manifesto was distributed to all unions throughout the United States and to many in Europe from the temporary headquarters of the Industrial Union Movement of America in Cincinnati. In addition, it was published in every issue of the *Voice of Labor*, the *Miners' Magazine, Appeal to Reason, The People, International Socialist Review*, and a number of other radical journals. Special articles discussing the Manifesto, written by Trautmann, Hagerty, Haywood, A. M. Simons, Frank Bohn and others who had attended the January conference, appeared in these journals. Discussions of the Manifesto and the forthcoming convention were also conducted by a Speakers' Bureau established by the Industrial Union Movement which sent volunteers to address local unions in various parts of the country. George Speed was an especially active lecturer on the West Coast, and Joseph Gilbert, editor of the *Socialist Crisis* of Salt Lake City and a member of the Socialist Party National Committee, toured the mid-West and East for the Speakers' Bureau. The lecturers also assisted in forming Industrial Union Clubs in a number of cities.[17] While lack of funds appears to have limited the number of copies of the Manifesto that were distributed, it did receive widespread publicity.

The sponsors of the convention appeared to be satisfied with the reaction to their call; indeed, Hagerty predicted that, on the basis of the favorable response, "the Industrial-Union Movement . . . will, in fact, be the dominating union influence in this country within two years at the most." By the time this optimistic prediction appeared in March 1905, all of the A.L.U. national and international unions, except the W.F. of M., had already voted to take part in the Chicago convention. The W.F. of M. was to consider the question at its convention at Salt Lake City in May 1905. President Moyer recommended that the convention take immediate action on the Manifesto, and, if approved by that body, the matter should then be submitted to a referendum vote of the membership as to whether representatives should be sent to Chicago. He urged a positive endorsement of the Manifesto so that "the Western Federation of Miners will be the vanguard of any army that will lead them to industrial liberty." By a vote of nearly four to one, the delegates endorsed the proposed industrial union, and selected five delegates to attend the Chicago convention. (It was understood that the action was to be submitted to a referendum vote of the membership.) The miners were confident that this action would consolidate "all the forces of organization of labor in the economic field," and would put an end to the deplorable situation in which the members of the W.F. of M. were forced to go down to defeat time and again, despite their unselfish and unstinting support of the entire working class, because the obsolete form of craft organization of other workers compelled them "to fight alone an unequal battle against the combined forces of the capitalist class." The delegates proclaimed: "We can no longer fight alone . . . [but must] realign the forces of organized labor to weld them into a solid body."[18]

The action of the A.L.U. affiliates and the W.F. of M. caused no surprise in labor circles. But this was not true of the favorable response to the Manifesto by a number of A.F. of L. affiliates. Widespread publicity was given to the report of a committee appointed by the Schenectady Trades' Assembly, composed of A.F. of L. unions, to consider and make recommendations regarding the Manifesto. The report, submitted in April 1905, declared: "The motto of the industrialists is an open union and a closed shop, and your committee, believing that those principles contain the very essence of trade unionism, have no hesitation in commending them to this Assembly and to the Labor movement in general." Unions affiliated with the Trades' Assembly were urged to send delegates to the Chicago convention.[19]

An A.F. of L. organizer in Schenectady immediately informed Gompers of the recommendations, urged him to condemn the committee's stand as "Socialistic," and to take action instantly "to prevent any endorsement by the Locals affiliated with the Trades Assembly." Gompers needed no prodding on this subject. Once the existence of the Industrial-Union Movement was confirmed, he launched a series of scurrilous attacks on it. He denied that industrial unionism was the real purpose of the promoters of the June convention, insisting that the A.F. of L. allowed for industrial unionism wherever it was advisable or desired by the workers. The real, the only purpose was "to divert, pervert, and disrupt the labor movement" in order to promote socialism. The whole venture simply proved that "the trade-union smashers and rammers from without and the 'borers from within' are again joining hands."[20]

It was typical of Gompers that he should lump all Socialists together in one group, even though he was fully aware that those who favored the "boring from within" strategy did not approve of the Manifesto and the call for the Chicago convention. "The American labor movement would suffer great injury if any appreciable number of progressive trade unions should allow themselves to be misled into joining this movement," wrote Berger in his *Social-Democratic Herald,* "and we will not join it." He warned his comrades: "For us blindly to begin a fight with the American Federation of Labor at this time would be a crime against the trades unions and a fatal error in the Socialist propaganda."* Both Gompers and Morrison kept sending clippings to the A.F. of L. Executive Council from this and others of Berger's editorials which condemned the industrial-union movement, which stressed that not a single Socialist who believed in fighting for socialism at A.F. of L. conventions favored the movement, and which criticized Joseph Gilbert, National Committeeman, for "speaking and in other ways seeking to help the movement," a procedure that was "to the shame of the Socialists."[21] (Similar editorials by Max Hayes were also forwarded to the Executive Council.) But Gompers was determined to undermine the new movement by the old tactic of red-baiting, and it was much simpler for his purposes to label the pending conference a "Socialist plot" than to draw distinctions among different types of Socialists.

The A.F. of L. charge that disruption of the organized labor movement was the sole purpose of the June convention produced mixed reactions from its sponsors. Moyer did not deny the charge, but insisted that nothing could disrupt the labor movement more than had already been done by the A.F. of L., and if the new movement "which has for its object the amalgamation of the entire working class shall mean the disruption of the so-called labor movement of today, then I have no regret for the part I have taken in calling a congress for that purpose." But most of the participants in the January conference did not take so cavalier an attitude toward the "existing labor movement of today." To be sure, they believed that the A.F. of L. would have to go, since they were convinced that, as it was functioning, it was harmful to the interests of the organized workers and held out no hope for the unorganized who, after all, comprised 95 per cent of those gainfully employed. But they did not intend to conduct a wholesale or indiscriminate smashing of the local or national

---

* Writing to Morris Hillquit, Berger furiously demanded that Debs condemn the movement "in a decided and unequivocal manner or there will be war. If Debs stays with that crowd, he will lend them some prestige for a little while, but I am sure that would be the end of Eugene V. Debs." Evidently Berger felt that Hillquit did not take the matter seriously enough, for he wrote the New York Socialist leader "that the danger of a split on the industrial question is far more serious than you imagine, judging from letters from Debs and others." (Victor L. Berger to Morris Hillquit, March 28, April 28, 1905, Morris Hillquit Papers, Wisconsin State Historical Society. Hereinafter cited as WSHS.)

unions affiliated with the A.F. of L., as had been the objective of the Socialist Trade and Labor Alliance. Rather their aim was to take over the A.F. of L. affiliates and unite them with the new unions to be established out of the unorganized mass. A. M. Simons, who was a central figure at the January conference, stated that the idea was "to form a new central body, into which existing unions and unions to be formed could be admitted, but not to form rival unions." Ernest Untermann and others had hesitated to sign the Manifesto until they were convinced that "such an objective as that of the S.T. & L.A. was not anticipated."[22]

What the promoters of the June convention hoped for, in the main, was that once the industrial union was launched, the existing local and national unions would pry themselves away from the A.F. of L. and join the new movement. Not the smashing of existing workers' organizations, but the elimination of the A.F. of L. and the formation of an effective industrial type of unionism which would serve the interests of all workers, those already organized and the vast majority still to be organized—these were the goals.

The A.F. of L. leadership, however, continued to insist that the sole purpose of the pending convention was the destruction of the existing trade unions. This charge was broadcast on a mass scale. Thousands of leaflets containing reprints of Gompers' three editorials entitled, "The Trade Unions to be Smashed Again," were sent to local unions throughout the country. A.F. of L. organizers were ordered to drop all organizing work and concentrate all their energy on the campaign to convince the organized workers that the new movement sought only the destruction of their unions. "There is no better work which our special organizers can do right now than to counteract the effect of this proposed industrial movement," Gompers wrote on May 13, 1905.[23]

In their fury over the industrial union movement, the A.F. of L. leadership lashed out viciously against the organization believed to be mainly responsible for its launching—the Western Federation of Miners. In March 1905, the Executive Council declared that the W.F. of M. was repaying the A.F. of L.'s assistance in its eight-hour strike by taking "an active part in calling a 'Congress' for the purpose of forming another federation of organized workers of the country." It, therefore, called on its affiliated unions to make no further donations to the legal defense fund of the W.F. of M. which was being raised to assist in prosecuting pending Colorado court cases.[24]

Gompers was deluged with protests from city centrals and from local unions of many affiliated international organizations.[25] Actually, the Executive Council's intemperate attack on the W.F. of M. backfired, for it increased the determination of a number of A.F. of L. affiliates to send delegates to the Chicago convention. A. H. Cosselman, general secretary of the International Glove Workers' Union, urged Morrison to persuade the Executive Council to withdraw its circular on the. W.F. of M., pointing out that "since our locals have received the circular urging that no further contributions be made to the miners' defense fund, a great many of our members throughout the country (particularly those inclined toward Socialism) have become more disgusted than ever with the A.F. of L. and are using strenuous efforts to have their locals send representatives to the Convention at Chicago next June. I would consider it a great favor and believe it would be of special benefit to our organization if this question of continuing to send aid to the Western Federation of Miners were dropped altogether." Local No. 265 of the Journeymen Tailors' Union wrote to the Executive Council that "Gompers has more gall than we expected he had and if anything should lead us to look with favor on the industrial union movement it is this treacherous abandonment of a truly courageous union which has been fighting our battles as well as their own."[26]

Informed of this communication, John B. Lennon, general secretary of the Journeymen Tailors' Union, acted immediately. "If any of our Unions join that Organization in Chicago," he notified all locals, "they will certainly have to get out of the J.T.U.A. They will not be allowed to serve God and mammon both at one time." Daniel J. Keefe, president of the International Longshoremen, Marine and Transport Workers' Association, was another official who believed that the A.F. of L. represented "God" and the new union movement "mammon." He issued a circular to all locals in late April, stating: "You must not consider sending representatives to the Industrial Union conference at Chicago, June 27th, as they are opposed to the policy of our Organization and the A.F. of L."[27]

How many local unions affiliated with the A.F. of L. were intimidated by such tactics and prevented from sending delegates to the Chicago convention, even as observers, it is impossible to state. While a few simply ignored threats from their international officials or appeals from Gompers,* many local unions were prevented from acting favorably on the rising demand of the rank and file that their organizations be represented at Chicago to learn at first hand what the new movement had to offer the working class of the United States.

---

* Gompers tried to prevent the State Convention of the United Mine Workers of Illinois from sending a delegate to Chicago, but W. D. Ryan, secretary-treasurer of District No. 12, U.M.W., in Illinois, informed him that since the delegates were going "to listen and learn, and report their opinion of the meeting," the miners "did not see where any great harm would result from them sending representatives under such conditions." (Gompers to W. D. Ryan, May 13, 1905; W. D. Ryan to Gompers, May, 15, 1905, American Federation of Labor Correspondence, Washington, D.C. Hereinafter cited as *AFL Corr.*)

THE CHICAGO CONVENTION

Although Gompers bent every effort to prevent A.F. of L. locals from sending members to the Chicago convention, he himself dispatched a personal representative, Lee Grant, to observe and make confidential reports to him. Gompers paid him $50 for eight reports, covering the expenditure by listing it as payment for an article on the convention in the *American Federationist.*[28] Grant's first "confidential" report, dated June 27, 1905, began: "The 'first continental congress of the workers of the world,' as it was termed by W. D. Haywood in his opening address opened today with considerable noise." Haywood's dramatic words in calling the historic convention to order were:

"This is the Continental Congress of the working class. We are here to confederate the workers of this country into a working class movement that shall have for its purpose the emancipation of the working class from the slave bondage of capitalism. There is no organization, or there seems to be no labor organization, that has for its purpose the same object as that for which you are called together today. The aims and objects of this organization should be to put the working class in possession of the economic power, the means of life, in control of the machinery of production and distribution, without regard to capitalist masters. The American Federation of Labor, which presumes to be the labor movement of this country, is not a working-class movement. It does not represent the working class. There are organizations that are affiliated, but loosely affiliated with the A.F. of L., which in their constitution and by-laws prohibit the initiation of or conferring the obligation on a colored man; that prohibit the conferring of the obligation on foreigners. What we want to establish at this time is a labor organization that will open wide its doors to every man that earns his livelihood either by his brain or his muscle.... There is no man who has an ounce of honesty in his make-up but recognizes the fact that there is a continuous struggle between the two classes, and this organization will be formed, based and founded on the class struggle, having in view no compromise and no surrender, and but one object and one purpose and that is to bring the workers of this country into the possession of the full value of the product of their toil."[29]

Two hundred delegates representing 43 organizations were present in Chicago's Brand Hall when Haywood called the convention to order. Grant estimated, in his report to Gompers, that the delegates represented about 60,000 workers, but Charles O. Sherman of the Credentials Committee claimed that they represented 150,000, and Haywood put the figure at 300,000. Both Sherman and Haywood were probably counting union membership of delegates without authority to act for their organizations, and Haywood probably threw in the members of the Socialist Party as well.[30]

Grant's estimate was realistic. Of the 43 organizations represented, about half had instructed their delegates to affiliate with the new organization. Of this group, the Western Federation of Miners had 27,000 members—all real—while all the other organizations together had only 24,000, some probably paper ones. Apart from the W.F. of M., the other relatively large organizations which were ready to affiliate were the American Labor Union, claiming 16,750 members, including the United Brotherhood of Railway Employees with 2,800 members; the United Metal Workers with 3,000 members; and the Socialist Trade and Labor Alliance, with 1,450 members. Almost all of the other organizations were small labor groups. Sixty-one of the delegates represented only themselves, and 72 others came as sympathetic observers from organizations not ready to affiliate at once. Indeed, the majority of the delegates came merely to take notes and report back to their organizations.[31]

"On the whole from the standpoint of the American Federation of Labor the gathering is entirely satisfactory," Grant reported to Gompers at the end of the first day's proceedings. "As far as I have been able to learn . . . there are very few A.F. of L. locals represented." All told, only 16 A.F. of L. locals were represented,* and only five of these were prepared to affiliate: A tailors' local, two U.M.W. locals, a bakers' and confectionery workers' local, and a painters' and decorators' local. This, of course, did not include the Illinois District of the U.M.W. whose delegates attended as observers, nor individual A.F. of L. members who were there to watch. At the end of the second day, Grant wrote: "In the hall I met a goodly number of acquaintances who are members of unions affiliated with the A.F. of L. and who are socialists, but not one of them was there representing his union."[32]

The S.T. and L.A. had a larger number of delegates at the convention than did the W.F. of M., 14 as compared to five. But the larger representation did not mean, as some have alleged, that the convention was dominated by the S.T. and L.A. Regardless of the number of delegates present, the delegation from each organization had as many votes as the membership of that body. The five delegates of the W.F. of M. had a majority of the votes, and since two of these delegates, Moyer and Haywood, represented both the W.F. of M. and the A.L.U., they decisively held the balance of power. Together, the W.F. of M. and the A.L.U. outnumbered the others, ten to one, in voting power.

It is true, however, that some of the smaller organizations exerted an

---

* The Manifesto had been sent to local unions affiliated to the A.F. of L., and, in most cases, the international union headquarters were not approached. "Invitations are being sent to Local Unions affiliated with the I.L., & T.A.," Daniel J. Keefe, President of the Longshoremen's and Transport Workers' Union, wrote to Gompers on May 5, 1905, "requesting them to send Delegates to said Convention. They have not invited the general organization to be represented." (*AFL Corr.*)

influence far out of proportion to their numbers, largely because of the colorful personalities of individual delegates. Certainly, as we shall see, Trautmann, Hagerty, and De Leon carried great weight in the convention, but this does not mean, as has been frequently stated, that any of them, and particularly De Leon, dominated the proceedings.

Vincent St. John, prominent in the early history of the I.W.W., classified the groups represented in the convention into four principal categories: "Parliamentary socialists—two types—impossibilist and opportunist, Marxism and reformism; anarchist; industrial unionist; and labor union fakir." Paul F. Brissenden, in his pioneer study of the launching and early history of the I.W.W., questions this classification. He states that, at the time of the first convention, the direct-actionist, anti-political, anarchist group was not yet a prominent element. The only two groups who exercised influence, he holds, were the delegates associated with either the Socialist Party or the Socialist Labor Party. Still another authority, Marian D. Savage, in her work, *Industrial Unionism in America,* classifies the elements represented into three categories on the basis of tactics advocated: First, there were the members of the Socialist Labor Party who placed chief emphasis upon political action. Second, there were the members of the Socialist Party who were less doctrinaire than the members of the S.L.P., and who wished to subordinate political to economic action. The final group consisted of the anarchists, who stressed direct action instead of political action.[33]

One thing is clear: There were many shades of opinion represented in the convention which made the task of working out any unified program of action extremely difficult. But the diversity of viewpoints represented was at first overcome by the determination of leading personalities at the convention to achieve a harmonious atmosphere. Lee Grant was frankly disappointed that the first day's proceedings were not marred by factional strife. But in his report on the events of the second day, he wrote gleefully to Gompers: "The first scrap between the regular socialists and the De Leonites occurred on the floor today when A. M. Simons, a leading Socialist went after De Leon in a hot speech." Simons had, indeed, launched an attack on De Leon and the S.T. and L.A., warning of the danger of allowing the new organization to come under the control of the De Leonites. But he was speedily silenced. The majority of the delegates were in no mood for dire predictions.

Debs set the tone of the proceedings at this stage with an eloquent plea for harmony. He did not, however, refrain from criticizing elements within the convention. Addressing himself to De Leon and the delegates who were members of the S.T. and L.A., he admitted that he had long disagreed with their tactics. He did not belittle their principles and believed that they were sound on a number of basic issues, and that De Leon himself had made a number of valuable contributions to the working class, particularly in exposing the treacherous role of the "labor lieutenants of the capitalist class." But he insisted that their tactics were in need of considerable improvement. Specifically, their fault lay in their dogmatic approach, for they failed to "appeal to the American working class in the right spirit," and "are too prone to look upon a man as a fakir who happens to disagree with them." Their sin was fanaticism, and "fanaticism is as fatal to the development of the working class movement as is fakirism."

Nevertheless, Debs was optimistic that the convention's contending factions could find the means of reconciling their differences, "and begin the work of forming a great economic or revolutionary organization of the working class so sorely needed in the struggle for the emancipation." As for himself, he was ready "to take by the hand every man, every woman that comes here, totally regardless of past affiliations." Debs' eloquent appeal provided the cementing agency for the continuation of harmony. Amid great cheers, De Leon declared that he and Debs "had shaken hands over the bloody chasm of the past." He had come to the convention with an open mind and without any past grudges, except toward the capitalist class. He was ready to work with all those who would "plant themselves upon the class struggle."[34]

Another factor which held the heterogeneous group together was the bitter feeling against the "American *Separation* of Labor," as the A.F. of L. was to be referred to again and again during the convention. All were in agreement that they were not engaged in an attempt to set up a rival organization to the A.F. of L. This conception, said Haywood, was a mistake. "We are here for the purpose of organizing a *Labor Organization.*"

Apart from details such as adjustment of credentials and reading of the Manifesto, the first five days of the convention were taken up with an indictment of the A.F. of L. Three main counts were directed against the Federation:

(1) Its adherence to craft unionism, which limited unionism only to a small minority of the working class, the skilled "aristocrats of labor"; helped to stimulate "union snobbery"; created the "union scab" who continued to work at his particular trade when the men of an allied trade in the same industry were on strike; and rendered the working class helpless on the industrial battlefield.

(2) Its assumption of an identity of interests between employer and employee and its denial of the existence of the class struggle, concepts symbolized by the role of the A.F. of L. in the National Civic Federation where the labor lieutenants were tied up closely to the captains of industry.

(3) Its denial of the necessity of achieving socialism, its refusal to take the lead towards united political action on the part of the working class,

and the domination of the A.F. of L., by a small clique of dictatorial bureaucrats.

The majority of the speakers during the first five days agreed that there was no hope that the evils of the A.F. of L. could be eliminated by pursuing a "boring-from-within" strategy. The A.F. of L. had, in Debs' words, "long since outgrown its usefulness," and had "become positively reactionary, a thing that is but an auxiliary of the capitalist class" and was under capitalist control. True, it had the largest membership of any labor federation in the United States. But this did not impress the members of the convention. "The American Federation of Labor has members," Debs declared, "but the capitalist class does not fear the American Federation of Labor; quite the contrary. . . . There is certainly something wrong with that form of unionism which has its chief support in the press that represents capitalism; something wrong in that form of unionism whose leaders are the lieutenants of capitalism; something wrong with that form of unionism that forms an alliance with such a capitalist combination as the Civic Federation, whose sole purpose is to chloroform the working class while the capitalist class go through their pockets." Debs saw only one course open to those who wished to build a labor movement which would include all workers, advance their immediate interests, and ultimately abolish the capitalist system and establish in its place a Socialist republic: "There is but one way to effect this great change, and that is for the workingman to sever his relations with the American Federation and join the union that proposes on the economic front to represent his class."[35]

On the sixth day of the convention, the discussion of the preamble to the constitution of the new organization began,* and the friction which developed almost immediately revealed sharply the divergent views and conflicting ideologies of the heterogeneous elements present. It was the political clause, the second paragraph in the preamble, which provoked the conflict. As presented by Hagerty, secretary of the constitution committee, the first and second paragraphs read:

"The working class and the employing class have nothing in common. There can be no peace so long as hunger and want are found among the millions of working people and the few, who make up the employing class, have all the good things of life.

"Between these two classes a struggle must go on until all the toilers come together on the political, as well as on the industrial field, and take

* Hagerty is generally credited with being the author of the preamble. In the *Industrial Union Bulletin* (May 2, 1908), official organ of the I.W.W., he was referred to as "author of the 'preamble' of the I.W.W." Trautmann called the "preamble . . . the creation of one man . . . Thomas J. Hagerty" (*Industrial Union News*, Sept. 1913.) De Leon wrote: "The authorship of the Preamble alone will make immortal the name of Thomas Hagerty." (*Ibid.*, Oct. 1913.)

and hold that which they produce by their labor through an economic organization of the working class, without affiliation with any political party."[36]

The second paragraph represented a compromise in the constitutional committee between the anarcho-syndicalist ideas of Hagerty and Trautmann, embodying as it did their theories of non-political affiliations and direct trade union seizures and operation of industry, and the ideas of the Socialists, particularly De Leon, who favored political as well as economic action by the working class. Its confused nature was immediately objected to by Clarence Smith who charged that it did not "represent the principles and purposes of industrialism but represents a toadyism to three different factions in this convention. . . . It seems to me as if the paragraph is intended to be toadying to the man who does not believe in politics at all, the pure and simple trade unionist as we have come to call him; that it means a toadying to the Socialist, and also the anarchist, if you please." Smith wanted all references to political action deleted. His stand was immediately supported by a number of delegates who emphasized that what was contemplated was "primarily an economic organization based upon the conflict of classes," and demanded that all "that confusing language about political action at the capitalist ballot box" be stricken out, and that in its stead there be "a plain statement of what the working class is going to do on the economic field."[37]

On the other hand, A. M. Simons, while agreeing with Smith that the appeal made by the political clause was too vague, favored a statement clearly asserting a belief in political action, and especially "the principle of independent political action." On behalf of the Committee on Constitution, Hagerty rejected Simons' proposal. He made it clear that what the committee had in mind was that the members of the new organization could participate in politics, but that politics had nothing to do with political parties. Thus Russian workers were engaged in politics through their revolutionary strikes. The new organization would welcome workers who belonged to no party. As for himself, he did not believe that the working class needed any particular party to win its freedom. "The ballot box is simply a capitalist concession. Dropping pieces of paper into a hole in a box never did achieve emancipation for the working class, and to my thinking it never will achieve it." Hagerty's anti-political view was seconded by the anarchist, Lucy Parsons, wife of the famed Haymarket martyr, Albert R. Parsons.[38]

It was De Leon who played the role of compromiser between the two warring factions. He defended the political clause as submitted at great length, stating that it was a synthesis of the two class-conscious positions represented among the delegates: the "political Marxism" which he had, in the past, advocated, and to which he mainly adhered now, and the anarcho-syndicalist views for which Hagerty spoke and which he believed had important concepts to contribute. He acknowledged that he had changed some of his earlier beliefs, saying that he did not any longer adhere to an unlimited faith in political action under capitalism. It was necessary, he declared, to "gather behind that ballot, behind the united political movement, the Might which is alone able, when necessary to 'take and hold.'" For the first time in his career De Leon proclaimed that the process of taking possession of industry must be accomplished "through an economic organization of the working class," because "it is out of the question to imagine that a political party can 'take and hold.'" The real "Might" then of the workers was in a disciplined, class-conscious industrial organization. Its ultimate power would be held in abeyance but "if the capitalists should be foolish enough in America to defeat, to thwart the will of the workers expressed by the ballot, then there will be a condition of things by which the working class can absolutely cease production, and thereby starve out the capitalist class, and render their present economic means and all their preparations for war absolutely useless."[39]

De Leon's stand must have come as a distinct surprise to those who associated him with the exclusive reliance upon electoral procedures and parliamentary action to achieve socialism and who remembered how often he had declared that the trade union must be completely subordinate to the political party of the workers and serve only as a device for recruiting workers into that party. But those who had followed his editorials in *The People* as well as other articles in his journal knew that he had begun to question his earlier views, and that he had come increasingly under the influence of French syndicalism and the syndicalist views of Trautmann and Hagerty. It was not until December 1904 that De Leon became concerned with the concept of industrial unionism, and it was not until the spring of 1905 that he discussed the centrality of the trade union in the socialist movement.[40] But it was at the I.W.W. convention that he clearly defended both principles for the first time, thus throwing his influence behind the syndicalist forces at the gathering. To be sure, he did not completely abandon his support of the political-action elements, but his endorsement of the syndicalist doctrine was an important factor in the outcome of the controversy over the political clause in the preamble.

In the final vote, the controversial political clause, as proposed by the constitution committee, was sustained by a sizable majority. Yet the heated debate had clearly disclosed the delegates' conflicting views. "There is still a decided difference of opinion among the delegates on the question of the preamble," Lee Grant wrote to Gompers immediately after the vote was announced, "and I will miss my guess if the whole thing does not end in a fizzle."[41]

Grant did miss his guess. True, the conflicting feelings of the delegates continued to be expressed on a number of other issues. But this did not prevent them from adopting a constitution and various resolutions which reflected the class-conscious spirit of the majority of those present and their desire to create a revolutionary labor organization on industrial lines that had for its immediate purpose the organization of the entire working class for their immediate improvement under capitalism, and for its ultimate purpose the overthrow of the capitalist system.

When the delegates assembled in Chicago in June 1905, the general strike initiating the first Russian revolution was already under way, and its reverberations were heard in the convention hall. "You men and women," Lucy Parsons told the delegates, "should be imbued with the spirit that is now displayed in far-off Russia and far-off Siberia where we thought the spark of manhood and womanhood had been crushed out of them. Let us take example from them." Haywood said he hoped to see the new movement "grow throughout the country until it takes in a great majority of the working people and that those working people will rise in revolt against the capitalist system as the working class in Russia are doing today." Among the resolutions adopted by the delegates was one which hailed the "mighty struggle of the laboring class of far-off Russia against unbearable outrage, oppression and cruelty and for more humane conditions for the working class of that country," and concluded:

"Resolved, That we, the industrial unionists of America in convention assembled, urge our Russian fellow-workmen on in their struggle, and express our heartfelt sympathy with the victims of outrage, oppression and cruelty, and pledge our moral support and promise financial assistance as much as lies within our power to our persecuted, struggling and suffering comrades in far-off Russia."

Among the other resolutions adopted were: that an Educational Bureau, composed of a literature and lecture section, be established, since the new movement was to be "primarily an educational movement to show the workers that their interests are common in every part of the world . . . that the earth and all that the earth holds are theirs"; that the first day of May of each year be "designated as the Labor Day of this organization"; that the new organization enter into immediate relations with the International Bureau of those industrial unions which were based upon the class struggle, with headquarters at Berlin; that militarism was an evil force inimical to all workers, that it be condemned, and that membership be denied to anyone who joined the state militia or police.[42]

INDUSTRIAL WORKERS OF THE WORLD

The constitution committee proposed the name Industrial Workers of the World for the new organization. Coates offered the name Industrial

Union of America as a substitute, but Riordan of the W.F. of M. objected to the term "America," since it had been found that when the Western Labor Union changed its name to American Labor Union, it created ill feeling toward the organization in Canada, as "America" meant the United States to most Canadians. The suggestion of the constitution committee was adopted by a vote of 47,728 to 3,540.

The constitution, with its motto, "An Injury to One is the Concern of All," established the Industrial Workers of the World. Only wage-earners were eligible for membership in the new organization. Race, creed, color, and sex were made no bar to membership, and any immigrant with a valid union card was eligible for immediate membership. "Big Bill" Haywood, at the meeting ratifying the work of the convention, declared that although unions affiliated with the A.F. of L. discriminated against a worker who was a Negro or foreign-born, to the I.W.W., it "did not make a bit of difference whether he is a Negro or a white man. It does not make any difference whether he is American or foreigner."

Initiation fees and dues were made very low in order to facilitate, in one delegate's words, "the up-lifting of the fellow that is down in the gutter." "I do not care the snap of my finger whether or not the skilled workman joins this industrial movement at the present time," Haywood declared. "When we get the unorganized and unskilled laborer into this organization the skilled worker will of necessity come here for his own protection."

The constitution rejected time contracts in the trade agreements negotiated with employers because they prevented the workers from striking at any moment that appeared favorable to them and unfavorable to the employers. The presence of time contracts was also condemned because such agreements restricted the calling of sympathetic strikes, and encouraged the development of "union scabbing."

Under the I.W.W. plan of organization, the industries of the United States were divided on the basis of the products manufactured into 13 main industrial groups: "thirteen international industrial divisions subdivided into industrial unions of closely related industries in the appropriate organizations of or representation in the departmental administration." The departments of agriculture, mining, transportation, construction, etc., were further subdivided into industrial unions: agricultural workers, lumber workers, metal mine workers, marine transportation, railroad workers, railroad, canal, tunnel and bridge construction, shipbuilders, etc. At the bottom were the industrial unions with the shop as its smallest unit of organization. All the crafts within a shop would belong to the same local. Thus, in the mining department, all the men working in and around the mine as well as the clerks in the particular mine office would be organized into a unit. These units were to be organized into a department when the number of units were great enough to justify it.

Until that time the locals were to affiliate directly with the Chicago office. Mixed I.W.W. locals could be formed of workers living in the same locality and working in industries where there were no industrial unions.

Such divisions and subdivisions, although a recognition of the fact of separate interests of workers in different fields, were not regarded as barriers to solidarity, but as administrative divisions for purposes of convenience. The universal transfer was adopted to facilitate movement across divisional lines.

By the method of organizing all workers in any of the 13 groupings into one union, the I.W.W., it was argued, would have control of the workers who participated in the different phases of a particular manufactured product. Such control would increase I.W.W. bargaining power and, if necessary, also would increase the effectiveness of strikes.*

The officers provided for under the constitution were: A general president, a general secretary-treasurer, and a general executive board composed of these two officers and the presidents of the International Industrial Divisions. The General Executive Board was all-powerful, and was authorized to take up all questions which had not been fully settled by the convention. This was a considerable authority since many issues were left loosely unresolved. On the question of strikes, the Executive Board was given the authority to call any union out on strike during the period when any other I.W.W. union was involved in a strike situation.

The constitution was adopted by the vote of 42,719 to 6,998, and the convention then elected Charles O. Sherman, president; W. E. Trautmann, secretary-treasurer, and five members of the General Executive Board: Charles H. Moyer and John Riordan of the W.F. of M.; F. W. Cronin, Frank M. McCabe, and C. G. Kirkpatrick. Haywood, who had no official position in the I.W.W. at this time, although he was to play an important role later, retired as chairman of the convention. President Sherman assumed the chair, and at 1:20 P.M., July 8, 1905, "declared the first convention of the Industrial Workers of the World adjourned *sine die.*"[43]

Lee Grant immediately reported the news to Gompers, and noted that "the delegates were celebrating a little and most of them seem sanguine of success." He assured Gompers that "on the whole the entire affair has been satisfactory from the standpoint of the A.F. of L.," and he was convinced that the conflicting views expressed by the delegates would soon lead to major cleavages in the I.W.W.

This, as we shall see, was an accurate prediction. But even Grant had

* To a large extent, this plan of organization was based on a detailed illustration drawn up by Father Hagerty and published in the *Voice of Labor,* May 1905. While Gompers sarcastically labelled it "Father Hagerty's Wheel of Fortune," Hagerty boasted that it brought together "All workers of one industry in one union; all unions of workers in one big labor alliance the world over."

to admit that the final outcome was significant. Despite the differences among the delegates, despite the mixed elements present, despite the many irrational and half-baked ideas which were frequently voiced, some of which became fixed in the constitution, the convention had produced an entirely new organization of labor. As Grant admitted rather ruefully to Gompers: "The convention did better than I expected, for I hardly believed it possible that the delegates would agree among themselves long enough to adopt a Constitution or a name for the thing and they did both."[44]

Printed in tens of thousands of copies, the preamble to that constitution with its fiery first sentence, "The working class and the employing class have nothing in common," was to influence radical labor movements all over the world. And despite the many errors of theory and tactics associated with it, that name, Industrial Workers of the World (and especially its initials I.W.W.), was to make itself known throughout the world as the symbol of the American workers' indomitable struggle against ruthless capitalism.

CHAPTER 2

The Moyer, Haywood, Pettibone Case

The I.W.W. had barely come into existence when it was involved, together with the rest of the labor movement, in defending the victims of one of the worst frameups in American labor history—the Moyer, Haywood, Pettibone case.

THE ASSASSINATION

On the night of December 30, 1905, Frank Steunenberg, former governor of Idaho, was blown up by a bomb attached to the front gate of his home in Caldwell. Steunenberg had been elected as a Populist governor in 1896 and 1898 with labor support. But when bitter strikes broke out in the Coeur d'Alene mining district in 1899, Steunenberg, who had established close associations with corporate interests, betrayed the trust placed in him by calling for federal troops to break the strike. As a result, the influence of the W.F. of M. was effectively destroyed in Idaho. Almost immediately after the bombing, the Federation was blamed for the ex-governor's death. A. B. Campbell, an officer of the Mine Owners' Association, was reported to have asserted: "There is no doubt that Steunenberg's death was the penalty for his activity in doing his duty during the strike."[1] *Miner's Magazine* immediately rejected the charge, insisting that the W.F. of M. did not preach or practice anarchist principles:

"We recognize the assassination of Steunenberg is not a step forward in the march of organized labor toward the goal of economic freedom. . . . The murder of a man who may be looked upon by labor men as a tyrant . . . does not destroy one iota of the system that has given birth to industrial slavery." The leaders of the W.F. of M. announced: "We court the fullest investigation of rumors accusing the Western Federation of Miners of Governor Steunenberg's death."[2]

Soon the law-enforcement officers came up with a likely suspect. He was Harry Orchard (real name, Albert E. Horsley), itinerant miner and occasional W.F. of M. member, who had been in and around Caldwell for several weeks, posing as a sheep buyer. Orchard seemed to have wanted to be caught, for when detectives searched his hotel room they found crumbs of dynamite, plaster of Paris, and bits of twine—the very ingredients of the Steunenberg bomb.

On January 8, 1906, James McParland, head of the Denver branch of the Pinkerton Detective Agency, was employed by Governor Frank B. Gooding of Idaho as the chief investigator for the state.[3] McParland had been the key figure in the trials of the Molly Maguires (1877) as a result of which ten Pennsylvania miners were railroaded to the gallows, trade unionism in the anthracite regions set back for many years, and the cause of organized labor throughout the country injured. For many years, McParland worked for the Mine Owners' Association in Colorado to destroy the W.F. of M. Naturally, he saw in the bomb explosion an opportunity to apply the tactics that had been used so successfully against the anthracite miners in Pennsylvania. He set out to create the impression of a secret terrorist organization—the Western Federation of Miners—which constituted a menace to the welfare of the nation. On January 10, two days after he entered the case, McParland wrote that he was "almost sure" that Orchard was "the tool" of the W.F. of M. The following day, he wired his Denver office "to send me the pictures of Moyer and Haywood, and these today [Jan. 13], I showed the Governor and also showed him a group picture, showing all the members of the ex[ecutive] committee of the W.F. of M."[4] In short, even before he had met Orchard or conducted any investigation of the evidence, McParland had already concluded that the assassination should be pinned on the leaders of the W.F. of M., and Moyer and Haywood in particular!

At McParland's suggestion, Orchard was transferred from Caldwell to the state penitentiary at Boise where he was held in solitary confinement for ten days. Here, instead of being interrogated by local or state authorities, he was put under McParland's charge.

ORCHARD'S "CONFESSION"

McParland obtained a "confession" from Orchard. How he achieved this is revealed in McParland's hitherto unpublished reports of his two sessions with Orchard. His first meeting took place on January 22 and lasted three and one-half hours. McParland spoke first, developing a "line of thought." Just what this was, he neglected to mention in his report, but from his second report and from Orchard's response, it is clear that the Pinkerton manager told Orchard that he did not visit him to find out if he had assassinated Steunenberg. The state already had enough proof in its possession to hang him. The only way he could save himself was by squaring himself with the state through naming the leaders of the W.F. of

M. who had used him as a "tool" to carry out the assassination. After about 25 minutes, Orchard broke into McParland's presentation: "You speak your piece very well, but I don't know what you are getting at. I have committed no crime. I have heard and read over forty times just such talk as you have made, and there are instances where such talk has only made innocent men confess to crimes that they never committed and to implicate others who were also innocent. Talk about acting square with the state? I never heard tell of a man that did but that he afterwards paid the penalty." He had been advised by his attorney (Fred Miller) to say nothing relative to the case; he was innocent of any crime, and McParland was "simply wasting . . . time" in talking to him.

"I then cited to Orchard," McParland wrote, "cases in which the state witnesses went entirely free, and to put the matter more forcibly to him and to bring it home to the personal side of the present case, I cited and named personally the Molly McGuire state witnesses who saved their own necks by telling the truth, and especially Kelly, who, although he swore on the witness stand that he fired the first shot into Alexander McKes, exclaiming 'Dead dogs tell no tales,' went free."

McParland then told Orchard of "several other cases that I had personally handled wherein the state witnesses went free." He also kept reminding Orchard that his attorney would continue "to caution him to keep his lips sealed until such time as the inner circle of the W.F. of M. had him properly hanged." After assuring Orchard that he would use his influence to see to it that he got some exercise, McParland closed the interview. Orchard asked the Pinkerton "to be sure to call on him again."[5]

On January 25, McParland met Orchard for the second time. He found Orchard glad to meet him, and his manner "entirely changed" from what it had been on the first visit. McParland opened the conversation by asking Orchard if he had studied their first discussion, "and more especially the points wherein I suggested regarding the matter of State's witnesses." Orchard replied that he had "thought very little of anything except this matter." McParland then told Orchard that he had his "sympathy" since although he was a murderer, he was in reality "simply the tool of the Inner Circle."

After warning him again that the lawyers for the "inner circle" would assure him that he had nothing to worry about as long as he kept his mouth shut and would continue to do this "even up to the time when he would take his journey from the cell to the scaffold," McParland emphasized that if he followed this advice, "he would be convicted and eventually executed." Orchard then replied that he now had full confidence in McParland. "I know more about you than you suspect. I am well aware that if you made a promise to a man, no matter what crime he had committed, if he did his part, you have always seen that your promise was carried out." Orchard then asked McParland why if, as the

Pinkerton manager claimed, the state had positive proof of his guilt, it was necessary for him to confess. "What benefit would it be to make a confession?"

"To this I replied that he must remember at the very outset of our talk on Monday that I did not come there to find out whether he was guilty of the murder of Ex-governor Steunenberg or not, as we had positive proof of his guilt and would hang him upon the proof in our possession, but as he was but the tool of the power behind the throne, the Inner Circle, the hanging of him would be very little satisfaction . . . and if he would come up and make a full confession of all that he knew in this case the State would no doubt take care of him. To substantiate this fact I recited a number of instances which he knew of himself wherein men had become State's witnesses in murder cases and not only saved their necks but also eventually got their liberty."

McParland made it clear that the state would not be satisfied if Orchard mentioned just any names in his confession, and would, in this event, do nothing to save him from the gallows. He had specifically to name "those cut-throats known as the Inner Circle of the Western Federation of Miners. This being the case the State would gladly accept your assistance as a State witness and see that you are properly taken care of afterwards." Orchard replied that he understood McParland's point, but he was still worried lest even after serving the state of Idaho by naming the leaders of the W.F. of M., he would be tried in Colorado for crimes he was accused of having committed in that state where Idaho could not protect him.

"I told him," McParland reported, "that if he acted properly in this case we would get the leaders and that was all that the State of Colorado and the State of Idaho wished, and that I thought I could assure him he would not be prosecuted for any crime that he committed in Colorado. . . .

"He said, 'Now, there is another objection to my becoming a State witness. The people of the State would never be satisfied to allow me to go unpunished. The Governor has got to hearken to public sentiment and I know full well that the sentiment means that I be executed.' I told him that if he acted in good faith with the State that the sentiment that now existed would be reversed, that instead of looking upon him as a notorious murderer they could look upon him as a saver, not only of the State of Idaho, but of all States where the blight of the Inner Circle of the Western Federation had struck, and assured him that he need have no fear on that score. . . .

"This, I think, covered about the last objections of this man."

After a passing reference to "the moral side of this question," including the invocation of "an Allseeing and Divine Providence," McParland again assured Orchard that if he followed his advice he would "not be hung" whereas if he did not, "you will be hung in very quick order as the State is ready to prosecute as soon as Court convenes. After your conviction, when you see the noose dangling from the gallows you will then want to confess but you will be too late, as your testimony under those conditions will be of no importance."

Orchard had remained silent throughout this last statement, but when McParland spelled out just how "he could avoid the gallows," he walked over to the Pinkerton manager and said: "My God, if I could only place confidence in you. I want to talk. I ought to place confidence in you. You cannot live one hundred years longer. You certainly have not got to build a reputation as a detective and I am satisfied that all you have said is for my good." McParland immediately suggested that James H. Hawley, the chief counsel for the state, be called in and that Orchard talk to him. Orchard balked at this suggestion; he now trusted only McParland. "I know that you would not take the witness stand and testify as to one word that has passed between you and I here, nor would you add a word to what I have said. I have that much confidence in you." McParland assured him that he was right; he would not "take [the] witness stand at all, except that after he had made a confession that his testimony might require some corroboration on my part."

McParland ended his report of his interviews with Orchard on an interesting note: "I found that he prides himself on being very intellectual and I catered to his vanity in that respect all through this conversation."[6]

McParland, it is clear, came to see Orchard with the express purpose of getting him to name the leaders of the W.F. of M. as the men responsible for the assassination of ex-Governor Steunenberg, and this without having acquired the slightest evidence that this was the case. At no time before he visited Orchard did McParland divulge to the authorities any evidence he had against the leaders of the W.F. of M. Yet McParland did not ask Orchard who might have been associated with him in the assassination. He told Orchard, without having any proof of the charge, that the leaders of the W.F. of M.—the so-called "inner circle"—had hired him to do the job. Orchard was given a clear alternative: Either name the leaders of the W.F. of M. as the instigators of the assassination or hang! Name them and the states of Idaho and Colorado would see that Orchard was not made to pay for his crimes. (To be sure, McParland made a reference to the fact that he never really "guaranteed" Orchard his eventual freedom,[7] but everything he said during the two visits led Orchard to believe that this was part of the deal.) Orchard's own confession of guilt as the man who assassinated Steunenberg would not suffice; the state of Idaho and the Pinkerton Agency were determined to liquidate the leadership of the W.F. of M. and Orchard was to be used for that purpose. If there was any "tool" in the entire affair, McParland's reports reveal that Orchard was to be the "tool" of the drive to exterminate the leadership of the militant miners' union. Orchard, they also make clear, was primarily concerned with saving his own neck, and apart from the initial reference to the fact that he would be implicating innocent men if he followed Mc-Parland's "line of thought," his conversations with the Pinkerton manager revolved solely about how he could make sure that if he did what he was told, he could beat the noose.

McParland's reports on how he got Orchard to "confess" are probably not unique in the history of frameups. (Indeed, McParland even reveals that he used the same technique to frame the Irish miners executed in the Molly Maguire case.) What is unique is that these reports are at last made public, and it is possible to see the strategy used in the conspiracy to railroad the leaders of the W.F. of M. to their death.*

For four days, January 27, 28, 29, 31, 1906, McParland took down Orchard's statement. This was the sensational "confession." Explaining that he "owed it to society . . . to God and to myself," Orchard confessed to the murder of Steunenberg, and, at the same time, admitted participation in the killing of no less than 18 other men as well as numerous dynamitings during the past two and a half years. Every one of his crimes, Orchard claimed, had been commissioned by the "inner circle" of the W.F. of M. —which included the president, Charles H. Moyer, the secretary-treasurer, William D. ("Big Bill") Haywood, George A. Pettibone, a Denver businessman who was formerly an active member of the union and still semi-official advisor to the organization, and Jack Simpkins, member of the Executive Committee. All four men could be found in Denver, where the W.F. of M. made its headquarters.[8]

In subsequent interviews with McParland, Orchard kept embellishing his "confession" which, incidentally was never fully published. One gets a clear view of the distorted pictures he drew from the following report by McParland of one of his conversations with Orchard:

"In talking about the Industrial Workers of the World, he [Orchard] informed me when Haywood and Moyer returned from Chicago after organizing this order, Haywood explained the object of the order to him [Orchard] as follows: This order is something like a wagon. The officers are the hubs, and between each spoke is a union embracing all crafts or professions, even to bootblacks. The foundation or the anvil on which the hub turns is the emergency fund. Haywood went on to say when they had the order perfected and had all kinds of people, men and women, in it and got a few hundred thousand dollars in the emergency fund, there would no longer be any strikes. They would simply pick out men from the different unions whom they could depend upon and when

---

* In his 320-page book, *Debaters and Dynamiters: The Story of the Haywood Trial* (Cornwallis, Oregon, 1964), David H. Grover devotes just one sentence to McParland's interviews with Orchard. He writes: "McParland convinced Orchard that he had been 'used' by the 'Inner Circle' of the Western Federation who would now abandon him" (p. 63).

a demand was made on an employer and he refused to concede to the demand, they would simply remove him. Therefore there would be no more strikes and having no strike benefits to pay out, the emergency fund would soon be filled to overflowing and the employers or capitalists would soon learn that if the demand of their employes were not granted, they would be removed also their friends would be removed. Of course when Orchard made his first confession he explained this to me, but not so fully as he did today."[9]

The idea that the I.W.W. would achieve its goals by building an "emergency fund" of hundreds of thousands of dollars and use it to assassinate recalcitrant employers and capitalists was so absurd that anyone with the slightest acquaintance with that organization would have realized that Orchard was lying. But McParland who labeled all militant unionists as "anarchists" reported Orchard's statement as proof of a nation-wide plot to assassinate employers.[10]

THE KIDNAPPING

Orchard's "confession" was not immediately released. Even the prosecuting attorney of Caldwell was not told of the "confession" until February 9, and McParland noted that he (the prosecuting attorney) "did not seem to take any offense that this fact had been concealed from him up to the present time." Acting on McParland's advice, Orchard kept telling his lawyer that he was innocent.[11] Meanwhile, the state of Idaho indicted the four leading officials of the W.F. of M., named by Orchard, as accessories to the murder of Steunenberg. Simpkins disappeared and was never found. The other three were in Colorado, and extradition was a complicated procedure. As McParland noted after a conference with Governor Gooding and James Hawley, who served in the prosecution of the union men, "as to the method of procedure relative to extraditing Haywood, Moyer, and Pettibone from Colorado to Idaho": "Owing to the fact that neither of these three parties has been in Idaho during this conspiracy we cannot say that they are fugitives from justice, and we may have considerable trouble in extraditing them. However, we are perfecting plans by which we hope to get them into Idaho in a legal manner, where there is little doubt but that we can convict them."[12]

The "plans" adopted were simple: kidnap the three men! From Boise, Idaho, McParland wrote to Luther M. Goodard, associate justice of the Supreme Court of Colorado, who he felt was just the man from whom "to get the proper help that we wanted from the State of Colorado." Warning Goddard that his letter was "Strictly Confidential," McParland informed him that he had "unearthed the bloodiest crowd of anarchists that ever existed, I think, in the civilized world, not even excepting

Russia"; that "the outrages committed by the Molly McGuires in Pennsylvania were simply child's play when compared with the acts of these bloodthirsty assassins, and that it was through an act of Divine Providence that I have been enabled to get at the bottom of the conspiracy." Since the "conspiracy" was of great importance to Colorado as well as Idaho—indeed, to "all the western states where the blight of the Western Federation of Miners has taken root"—McParland asked Judge Goddard's cooperation in getting the W.F. of M. leaders moved from Colorado to Idaho.[13]

McParland, Hawley and party quietly traveled to Denver. Judge Goddard, presented with Orchard's "confession," arranged for McParland and Hawley to see Governor McDonald to get him to sign extradition papers. McParland, Hawley, and Goddard worked out the strategy whereby Moyer, Haywood, and Pettibone would be arrested, and speeded on a special train from Colorado to Idaho. No warrants would be served. The men would be simply picked up and forced to obey. McParland reported that it was decided to keep the Pinkerton Agency out of the forefront since "if a habeas corpus writ was served on the officers in charge of the prisoners while enroute through Colorado and Wyoming they would surely be discharged and we might get into trouble with the United States authorities, and as I would have to be present at the prosecution it became necessary to keep not only myself but the Agency in the background during the arrest and the conveying of the prisoners from Denver to the State of Idaho." He added coyly: "In order to clear myself particularly on this matter I never looked at the requisition papers, nor did I carry them to the Governor's office, but had Mr. Prettyman, one of the Ass't Superintendents, do that."[14]

Governor McDonald heard McParland relate for three hours "the substance of Orchard's confession." Then followed a discussion, in which a representative of the Mine Owners' Association of Telluride participated, as to how Moyer, Haywood, and Pettibone were to be arrested, and whether, as was the usual custom in Colorado, the extradition papers should be referred to the attorney general of the state. (After the meeting, Mr. Wells, the M.O.A. representative, informed McParland that the Association "would aise $25,000 or $50,000 if necessary to assist in the prosecution.") McParland objected to letting the attorney general see the paper since he was "liable to talk" and since his deputy, a former member of the W.F. of M., "is not removed very far from an anarchist." Although McParland and Hawley assured the Governor that "it would be death to the case to refer the papers to the Attorney General," they were not sure that he would be "willing to stand the roasting he would get from the *Rocky Mountain News and Times* for playing, as it were, the part of a kidnapper if he signed the papers without referring them to the Attorney

General."* They were overjoyed when the Governor picked up the papers and said: "I will sign them and the record will not go into the Secretary of State's office until some time next week, and I hope the prisoners will then be safely in Idaho."[15]

Arrangements were then made for the sheriff to obtain three carriages, and on Sunday morning, February 18, assisted by his deputies, arrest Moyer, Haywood, and Pettibone, and deliver them to a special train obtained from the Union Pacific Railroad. The menu for the train was prepared—"plenty of good chicken and ham sandwiches" and a case of beer for the men guarding the prisoners. The day selected for the arrests, Sunday, was carefully calculated, for the Denver courts would be closed and it would be impossible to obtain a writ of *habeas corpus*. Even then, it was planned that if lawyers for the three men tried to get in touch with them they should be given no information. McParland was still nervous that matters might be delayed and the W.F. of M. leaders get wind of the plot against them in which case "we would lose all."[16]

But the plan to arrest the three men simultaneously on Sunday morning had to be abandoned. Moyer had purchased a ticket for Lead, South Dakota, where he was going on union business. At 8 P.M. on Saturday night, February 17, Moyer went to the Union Depot and boarded the sleeper which was scheduled to leave at 1:30 A.M. Learning of this from a Pinkerton operative planted in the W.F. of M., McParland had Moyer arrested and placed in the county jail. "There is no doubt in my mind," he reported, "but Moyer was about to make his escape and the others would have followed possibly on Sunday."[17] Why if Moyer planned to escape, he boarded a train at 8 P.M. which would not leave for five hours instead of waiting until just before the train pulled out, McParland did not bother to discuss. At any rate, the original plans were entirely changed. Haywood and Pettibone had now to be arrested as quickly as possible and taken to the county jail. They were picked up and lodged in the jail. In none of the three arrests did the arresting officers, when requested by the prisoners, present a warrant. Later that evening, a member of the firm of Patterson, Richardson and Hawkins, lawyers for the W.F. of M., telephoned the county jail and inquired if Moyer, Haywood, and Pettibone were there. McParland jubilantly reported: "Jailer Duffy replied that they were not. From this it will be seen that the Sheriff carried out his instructions to the letter."[18]

To keep reporters from learning that a kidnapping was in the making, the prisoners were transferred to the Oxford Hotel, a few yards from the

---

* As predicted, the *Rocky Mountain News* of Denver denounced the whole "kidnapping conspiracy," saying editorially on February 19, 1906: "The manner in which the arrests were effected was repugnant to the spirit of the laws and constitution of this State and the *News* feels that the officials responsible for the proceedings merit the severest censure."

Union Depot, and at 6 A.M., the special train left with the prisoners aboard. The train whisked them to Boise, stopping at no towns enroute and taking on water and fuel only at way stations. The illegal journey ended at the Idaho penitentiary where the three W.F. of M. leaders were held in solitary confinement on the death row.

William Pinkerton, head of the Pinkerton Agency, wired McParland congratulating him for his "splendid work." Thanking him for the compliment, McParland replied:

"In connection with this matter would say that this evening ends the most strenuous week that I ever had in my life. Knowing the number of people that I had to take into my confidence here in Denver and that a slight leak from any one of them would be fatal to our plans, and that in order to secure perfect safety from legal attacks Sunday was the best day to start our special train and furthermore that it was absolutely necessary that the train travel through Wyoming in daylight as any person with a red flag could flag our train at night and cause us lots of trouble and eventually obtain these prisoners who would immediately be released under a writ of habeas corpus, it is hardly necessary for me to say to you that I have not slept very sound for the past week, and did not attempt to go to bed at all last night."[19]

Of course, the fact that the legal rights of three American citizens had been wantonly violated and that they had no opportunity to protest their seizure was not a reason for McParland's failure to sleep soundly. His only regret in the entire affair was that he could not send Pinkerton men on the special train. But he had swallowed his pride for the organization when advised by Colorado Supreme Court Justices Gabbart and Goddard that "the Agency and myself were of too much importance at the present time to get into trouble with either [the] United States or county officials enroute to Boise."[20]

Shortly after the prisoners were locked in the jail, the substance of Orchard's "confession" was released. On the same day, Steve Adams was arrested at Haines, Oregon. Orchard had implicated him as an accomplice in many of his crimes. Adams, too, subsequently made a "confession" corroborating the one that Orchard made but which he later repudiated. Although Adams was released from jail after he repudiated his confession, he was immediately rearrested and charged with the murder of two individuals he had related in part of his "confession." During his trial at Wallace, Idaho, Adams told how he had been persuaded to make his original "confession":

"After I was taken to Boise and put in the cell with Harry Orchard, I was taken to the office of the penitentiary and introduced to Detective McPartland [sic]. He told me about 'Kelley the bum' and other men who had turned state's evidence and had been set free . . . he kept me until 4 or 5 o'clock in the morning trying to make me confess. . . . Mc-

Partland told me he wanted to convict Moyer, Haywood, Pettibone, St. John, and Simpkins whom he called 'cutthroats.' If I did not help to convict them he said I would be taken back to Colorado and either hanged or mobbed. If I did help I would only be taken to Colorado as a witness. When we parted McPartland told me he was my friend. They put me back in the cell with Harry Orchard who talked with me about the need for backing up his story. I was frightened. The next day McPartland called again. I said I would do what he wanted me to do . . . when the confession was made McPartland led me on step by step and showed me all they wanted me to say. He told me that what I had said about the Tyler and Boule murders was only taken with the idea of making the strong chain of evidence to convict the officers of the Western Federation of Miners. He wanted the names of the officers of the Federation used as much as possible all through the confession. Two or three days later Warden Whitney brought the confession for me to sign."[21]

One has but to reread McParland's own reports of his discussions with Orchard prior to his "confession" to realize that Adams was describing accurately what had happened.

The jury divided seven to four for acquittal, and, therefore, Adams was found not guilty.* This came as a shock to Orchard, and McParland had to spend several hours convincing him that the fact that Adams' trial ended in a hung jury did not mean that his "confession" could not be used to corroborate Orchard's "confession." He claimed that "we had done better than expected. . . . Orchard picked up courage in learning this from me and felt good."[22]

McParland repeatedly had to keep Orchard's spirits up; the prisoner was often "morose." He urged Hawley to "visit Orchard occasionally so as to keep him in proper humor." On one occasion, McParland almost lost patience with Orchard, and he wrote to William E. Borah, assistant prosecuting attorney: "The trouble with Orchard is he has arrived at the stage that he does not realize that with the exception of Steve Adams he is one of the greatest criminals on earth. However, we must use him and I think it would be very well if you find time to make a trip to the penitentiary and have a little talk with him and get him on the right path. I wrote him a few days ago, but I must be very careful in writing letters to him because you can't tell what might happen. I have not heard from the Governor [Gooding] since I left Boise although I have written and asked him to drop down to the penitentiary and visit Orchard."[23] So the entire apparatus of the state of Idaho was mustered to keep "one of the greatest criminals on earth" on "the right path" to make sure that the plot against the leaders of the W.F. of M. went through as planned.

---

* Adams was rearrested and tried twice again, once in Colorado, but on both occasions he was acquitted. He was finally released.

LABOR AND SOCIALIST PROTESTS

Moyer, Haywood, and Pettibone were arraigned on February 21, 1906, after which a *habeas corpus* proceeding was instituted, as the arrested men claimed that their seizure was illegal. When the Idaho Supreme Court and the U.S. district court ruled against the three prisoners, the case was carried to the U.S. Supreme Court. The highest court ruled that the seizure had been illegal, but now that they were in Idaho's jurisdiction, there was no legal remedy. In a dissenting opinion, Justice Joseph McKenna said:

"Kidnapping is a crime, pure and simple. All the officers of the law are supposed to be on guard against it. But how is it when the law becomes the kidnapper, when the officers of the law, using its forms and exerting its power, become abductors? The foundation of extradition between the states is that the accused should be a fugitive from justice from the demanding state, and he may challenge the fact by habeas corpus immediately upon his arrest."[24]

Meanwhile, labor and progressive forces were not silent. The W.F. of M. had immediately charged that the illegal proceedings were the result of a conspiracy between state officials and mine owners to punish innocent men and destroy the militant union. The commercial press scoffed at this charge, and found the men guilty in lurid headlines and stories. But the American workers and their allies, especially organized labor and the Socialist Party, were quick to see the implications of the outrage in the West, and protests came quickly. On February 20, 1906, the I.W.W. distributed a leaflet headed: "Shall Our Brothers Be Murdered?" It charged that "the secret arrest, illegal deportation, and general criminal character of all the proceedings mark this as the first step to railroad these innocent men to the gallows, in the hope of thereby breaking up the radical working class organizations and putting an end to all resistance to tyranny." The arrest, it declared, was "the result of a conspiracy premeditated by the capitalist pirates of the West, led by the mine owners and backed by the Standard Oil Co." The leaflet called for "mass indignation meetings, not to pass meaningless resolutions, but to act as becomes men conscious of their rights and determined to maintain them." It urged the immediate launching of "a defense fund."[25]

On March 10, 1906, the so-called Kidnapping Edition of *The Appeal to Reason* came off the press, and was quickly distributed to trade unions, radical and liberal organizations throughout the country. It featured Eugene V. Debs' fiery appeal, under the head, "Arouse Ye Slaves!"

"Murder has been plotted and is about to be executed in the name and under the forms of law. Charles Moyer and William D. Haywood, of the Western Federation of Miners, are charged with the assassination of ex-Governor Frank Steunenberg, of Idaho, as a mere subterfuge to pounce upon them in secret, rush them out of the state by special train, clap them into the penitentiary, convict them upon the purchased, perjured testimony of villains, and then strangle them to death with the hangmans' noose. If they attempt to murder Moyer, Haywood and their brothers, a million revolutionists will meet them with guns."

On April 14, 1906, American newspapers carried the text of a telegram from Maxim Gorky, the famous Russian author and revolutionary, who had come to the United States to raise funds for his fellow revolutionaries in Russia. The telegram was addressed to Haywood and Moyer and read: "Greetings to you, my brother Socialists. Courage! The day of justice and delivery for the oppressed of all the world is at hand. Ever Fraternally Yours." To this greeting Haywood and Moyer replied from jail: "Brother: The class struggle which is worldwide, the same in America as in Russia, makes us brothers indeed. Convey our best wishes to fellow workers in your native land. We are with you in spirit. Accept fraternal greetings."[26]

The Chicago *Daily Socialist* of November 4, 1906, featured Jack London's brilliant article, "Something Rotten in Idaho," in which the Socialist novelist ridiculed Orchard's "confession," noting that "Colorado is a fertile soil for confessions," and pointed out that Moyer, Haywood, and Pettibone were in danger of dying for a crime they had never committed because they stood "between the mine owners and a pot of money."

"These men are leaders of organized labor. They plan and direct the efforts of the workingmen to get better wages and shorter hours. The operation of their mines will be more expensive. The higher the running expenses, the smaller the profits. If the mine owners could disrupt the Western Federation of Miners, they would increase the hours of labor, lower wages, and thereby gain millions of dollars. This is the pot of money."[27]

At the A.F. of L. convention at the end of 1906, Gompers denounced the outrage against constitutional rights, but made no recommendations for financial aid or for a campaign to secure justice for the victims of the frameup. In December 1906, the Executive Board of the Socialist Party asked Gompers to call a national conference of labor organizations, under the auspices of the A.F. of L., "to provide means of protection, methods of defense and channels of publicity on behalf of Moyer, Haywood and Pettibone." The request was accompanied by supporting petitions from leading officials of 17 national unions. Gompers, however, opposed the proposed action, explaining in a "confidential" memorandum to the A.F. of L. Executive Council that he doubted that the conference would "accomplish any good results for the men. It may indeed react to their detriment." Any action "should take the form that will have at least some assurance that it will be of a practical and tangible character. Agitation is one thing; tangible and practical results are another."[28]

This was typical Gompers' double-talk. Moreover, while rejecting a concrete proposal for much-needed action, he did nothing to propose anything "practical and tangible." In January 1907, the New York Central Federated Union, at a mass meeting, declared that Gompers and the A.F. of L. had still done nothing for the defendants, and announced that unless they soon "show their colors in this fight," it would be forced to conclude "that Gompers is too closely allied with the employers of the country." On the motion of the secretary of Local 144 of the Cigar Makers' Union, the C.F.U. called on the Executive Council to convene a national conference of labor unions to urge that President Roosevelt use his influence to obtain a fair and impartial trial.[29]

But the A.F. of L. leadership continued, in the words of the *Miners' Magazine,* "peddling hot air" as a substitute for "tangible action." During February and March, Gompers received scores of letters from international and local unions, central labor bodies, and Moyer-Haywood-Pettibone defense committees, asking what he was doing or would do to strengthen the defense campaign. But besides sending a form letter to all such inquiries stating that it was the "determination of the Executive Council to do anything and everything that it can to be helpful," the A.F. of L. leadership continued to do nothing. Finally, on March 18, unable to resist the pressure of the rank and file, the Executive Council issued a statement demanding a fair trial by an impartial jury before an unbiased judge, expressed confident belief in the innocence of the defendants, and assured them of "every assistance within our power to the demonstration of their innocence before the world." But when a week later the Central Labor Union of Indianapolis requested the Executive Council to send a member to the trial in order to obtain the fullest information, the request was filed and forgotten.[30] McParland, incidentally, reported gleefully that "we know Gompers is well aware the Inner Circle of the Western Federation of Miners is simply a crowd of murderers."[31]

While the A.F. of L. leadership remained inactive, the W.F. of M., the I.W.W., the Socialist Party and nearly the entire trade union movement was rallying to the cause of the defendants. Moyer-Haywood Conferences (defense committees) were formed in many large cities by individuals and groups representing the I.W.W., the S.P. and unions and central labor bodies affiliated with the A.F. of L. The letterheads of many of the conferences carried the slogan: "Death—can not—will not—and shall not claim our brothers." A defense fund estimated at $87,000 was raised by popular subscription.[32]

As the date for the trial of the W.F. of M. leaders approached, protest parades were held in every major city. In Boston, 50,000 unionists marched through the streets chanting: "If Moyer and Haywood die; if Moyer and Haywood die; Twenty million workingmen will know the reason why." A tremendous mass rally in San Francisco heard speakers declare that the defendants were framed because they fought for the eight-hour day and for higher wages for thousands of miners. Twenty thousand New Yorkers paraded from the East Side to 42nd Street's Grand Central Palace "where they cheered, wept and hooted" as John Chase, Morris Hillquit, and others condemned the frameup. The audience of 8,000 joined in singing to the tune of "Hold the Fort":

> *"When you look upon your babies 'round your hearthstone bright.*
> *Think of Haywood's tear-faced daughter, think of her tonight.*
> *Make a vow to God in Heaven, to that God on high,*
> *That these boys in Idaho by Greed shall never die."*[33]

A Pinkerton agent, operating inside the Socialist Party, attended the meeting, and reported to the Agency that representatives of the building trades, cigar makers', brewers', and typographers' unions were present, with "the East Side Sweat Shop employees predominating." He reported, too, that Isaac Cowen, one of the speakers, declared: "Do you realize that no one of you are safe from the attack of these blackguard Pinkertons, who will swear to anything for a money consideration."[34]

On the eve of the trial, President Roosevelt stated that Haywood and Moyer were "undesirable citizens." Roosevelt's hostility to the defendants is revealed in his correspondence. He showed no concern over the illegal way in which the three unionists had been seized and taken out of Colorado. He accepted the idea that there was a conspiracy on the part of the W.F. of M. to assassinate those opposed to the union. "I think that the Western Federation of Miners is a body just like the Molly Maguires of Pennsylvania," he told Lyman Abbott, editor of *The Outlook*. "That there are a number of good, honest, and stupid men in the ranks I have no doubt, just as I have no doubt that this was true of the Molly Maguires; but the moving spirit is to be described as representing 'a revolt against economic and social injustice' only in the sense that we thus describe a band of road agents who rob a coach."[35] On May 9, 1906, McParland reported that Brigadier-General Hale had visited Roosevelt and had been asked if he knew the Pinkerton manager personally. Hale, who was a neighbor and friend of McParland, had recommended him highly. "To this the President replied: 'I am very glad to hear you speak in that way as such persons as I have talked to who know McParland give him the same character.'" McParland was happy; he felt that "an appeal to the President by the Western Federation of Miners would get a cold reception.[36]

These Rooseveltian views, though reflecting the President's hostility to militant trade unionism, were at least private. But when he denounced Haywood and Moyer as "undesirable citizens," the President was molding opinion on the eve of a trial in which their lives were at stake. Labor and Socialist groups immediately attacked this characterization of the men facing trial. Debs (who had also been named an "undesirable citizen") accused Roosevelt of improper action and charged that he was conniving at the legal murder of the two labor leaders. Haywood agreed. In a statement to the press, he declared: "The President says that I am an 'undesirable citizen," the inference being that as such, I should be put out of the way. His influence is all-powerful, and his statement coming, as it does, on the eve of my trial for my life, will work me irreparable injury, and do more to prevent a fair trial than everything that has been said and done against me in the past." A delegate to the New York Central Federated Union proposed that "instead of the Statue of Liberty put up a statue of President Roosevelt in the harbor dressed as a Russian Cossack." The Chicago Federation of Labor passed resolutions condemning the President for "usurping prerogatives which neither the law nor the constitution of the United States gave to him." Delegates from the Federation of Labor, the Socialist Party, the I.W.W., and many other groups joined in a huge protest parade in Chicago. Among the banners carried by the demonstrators were ones which proclaimed, "I am an undesirable citizen, but Teddy Roosevelt wants my vote," and "To be loyal to the workers is to be undesirable." Most of the marchers wore buttons bearing the inscription, "I am an Undesirable Citizen."[37]

John H. Brinkman, president of the Washington (D.C.) Central Labor Union, summed up the attitude of organized labor: "We condemn President Roosevelt for the utterances he has made respecting these people, and we cannot view it as other than an attempt from the Chief Magistrate of this great republic to influence a jury before whom these men will be tried." This view continued to prevail even after Roosevelt, in a letter to the Cook County Moyer-Haywood Conference, denied that he had intended to influence the court, but repeated and defended his remark that the men on trial were "undesirable citizens."[38]

HAYWOOD TRIAL

The long-awaited trial began in the Ada County courthouse in the town of Boise, Idaho, on May 7, 1907. Haywood, whom the state deemed the most guilty of the three defendants and about whom McParland is alleged to have said, "Haywood is too dangerous an agitator, he must be done away with,"[39] was the first to be prosecuted. Moyer and Pettibone would be tried separately later on. For the next three months, the attention of the nation and that of many other nations was focused on the dramatic scene in Idaho.[40] For, as one newspaper correctly editorialized: "It is not merely that Moyer and Haywood are on trial at Boise. A great labor organization is on trial. If Moyer and Haywood are found guilty, if it is shown that the Western Federation of Miners did conspire to assassinate a state governor who was unfavorable to labor, then organized labor will receive its bitterest blow."[41]

The prosecution was headed by James H. Hawley of whom it was said, "Jim Hawley has defended more men and got them acquitted and prosecuted more men and got them convicted than any lawyer in America." Hawley's associate counsel was William E. Borah, Idaho's most prosperous lawyer who had been elected to the U.S. Senate only four months before the trial began. Less than a month before the trial opened, a federal grand jury, meeting in Boise to investigate land frauds in Idaho, returned indictments against several persons including Borah. Borah called in the Pinkerton Agency to investigate the witnesses who would testify in the trial. He told Operator No. 19 that he had "reason to believe that [N.M.] Ruick [the U.S. District Attorney] was paid $15,000 by the Western Federation of Miners to secure his (Senator Borah's) indictment in retaliation for the part he took in the trial of Haywood."[42]

Clarence Darrow, whom *The New York Times* deprecatingly described as "the Socialist lawyer from Chicago" headed the defense counsel. (McParland informed Governor Gooding that "Darrow and his wife are free lovers as well as Socialists."[43]) Already well known as a champion of labor, Darrow had defended Debs after the Pullman strike, and had advanced the case of the United Mine Workers before a Federal mediating board after the coal strike of 1902. Darrow was assisted by Edmund Richardson, general counsel for the W.F. of M.

One of the members of the defense counsel's staff was a man whose function was described by Governor Gooding in a letter of April 10, 1907, to President Roosevelt: "I am sending you several reports of No. 21— secret operative of the Pinkertons—who has been in the employ of the state for more than a year last past. He has reported to me every day, and I have absolute confidence in him. His work has been of extreme value to us. *He has so fully gained the confidence of the attorneys for the defense that he has been put in full charge of the work of polling the county, for the jury that will try the Heywood [sic] case next month.*"[44] Among other duties, the Pinkerton agent was in charge of investigating the backgrounds of people on the jury list for the defense. His responsibility was to uncover any factor that might prejudice the prospective juror against the defendant. He regularly sent reports to McParland listing the names of the people on the jury list the defense counsel preferred to have serve on the jury thus enabling the prosecution more easily to challenge them.[45]

In short, the governor of the state of Idaho, as an ally of the mine owners, had planted a spy to sabotage the work of the defense, and President Roosevelt, who had assured the Chicago trade unionists that he favored a fair trial for the defendants, did not reveal this information nor even rebuke the governor! Just as he had not been shocked by the way in which the three men had been taken out of Colorado, Roosevelt was not disturbed by the planting of a Pinkerton agent on the defense staff.

As his own and McParland's reports reveal, No. 21 kept the Prosecution fully informed of the strategy to be used by the defense, the witnesses to be called and what their general testimony would be, and the plans to "secure evidence to rebut Orchard's testimony."[46] Nor was No. 21 the only Pinkerton agent doing such work. On April 26, 1906, McParland reported some information gathered by an operative working inside the W.F. of M., and added: "In connection with this report would say that in following up the reports of No. 20 at Boise while I know him to be a painstaking, hard working operative and it may be possible that he is getting all the information that is to be secured in Boise, be that as it may, I have concluded to withdraw this operative and replace him with another operative *who is also a member of the Western Federation of Miners in good standing and well thought of.*"[47]

The prosecution rested its case on the testimony of Harry Orchard, and during six days on the stand, he described how he had killed 19 men, including Steunenberg, at the behest of Haywood and other members of the W.F. of M.'s "inner circle." But despite McParland's intensive and widespread efforts, the state could not produce a witness to corroborate Orchard's fantastic story of his conspiring with Haywood. Beyond his own word, there was only the flimsiest of circumstantial evidence to suggest this. Even Judge Fremont Wood, though refusing out of fear to throw the case out of court on the ground that there was no evidence corroborating Orchard's testimony, conceded later that "there was very little legal corroboration upon which a verdict of guilty could be justified."[48]

The defense set out to prove that Orchard lied to save his own skin, and presented witnesses who portrayed him as a bigamist, a drunken gambler, a pathological liar, and a police informer. It was brought out—indeed, Orchard openly admitted it—that he had a constant association with McParland, and it was clear that he had been carefully coached by the Pinkerton manager, although the fact that the defense did not have access to McParland's reports on how he got Orchard to "confess" hampered its case. It also turned out that he had been in the pay of detectives employed by the Mine Owners' Association when he first met Haywood—they had, in fact, paid for his trip to Denver—and had been seen in their company several times before the Independent Depot explosion in which 14 miners had been killed and many others maimed. Orchard claimed that he had been hired by Haywood to blow up the Depot, but it emerged that he was actually an assassin hired by the Pinkertons who were working for the Mine Owners' Association. Although the defense's attempt to present evidence to show the existence of a great counter-conspiracy to destroy the W.F. of M. was ruled out, Orchard's testimony under cross-examination established this fact. The defense also argued that Orchard killed Steunenberg out of revenge; that he had been forced to sell his one-sixteenth interest in the Hercules Mine at Coeur d'Alene for $300, thus losing the chance of becoming a millionaire, as a result of Steunenberg's actions in the labor struggles of 1899. McParland, who learned in advance "through a reliable source" that the defense was going to raise this fact "to show . . . the reason why Orchard killed Ex-Gov. Steunenberg" was exceedingly worried over the effect it would have on the jury.[49]

In late July 1907, the case drew to a close. Darrow was convinced that the verdict, despite the total absence of corroborative evidence, would be guilty and that the trial would end in a hanging. He decided to throw everything in his speech to the jury. The most eloquent courtroom pleader of his time was never more effective. In his summation, Darrow kept hammering away at the idea that what was involved was not the life or death of Haywood—but the conspiracy of the Mine Owners' Association to murder the Western Federation of Miners:

"If at the behest of this mob you should kill Bill Haywood, he is mortal, he will die, but I want to say that a million men will grab up the banner of labor where at the open grave Haywood lays it down, and in spite of prisons or scaffold or fire, in spite of prosecution or jury or courts, these men of willing hands will carry it to victory in the end."

Darrow told of the life of the miners before the advent of the W.F. of M.—of the long days, the dangerous working conditions, and the starvation wages paid by the rich mine owners. But the union had changed all that: it had built stores, libraries, hospitals, and union halls; supported the sick, buried the dead, cared for widows and orphans. Darrow spoke of the labor spies who infiltrated the union and deliberately sought to weaken it—Orchard was part of this conspiracy. He described, too, the violence of the state authorities—the brutalizing tactics of the militia, the suspension of legal rights, the confinement of arrested strikers in crowded, filthy "bull pens," and the mass deportations across state lines. When all lawful means of resistance failed, a union had no choice but to retaliate with violence. "Labor unions," Darrow said, "are often brutal, they are often cruel, they are often unjust . . . I don't care how many wrongs they commit. I don't care how many brutalities they are guilty of. I know their cause is just."

After two days, his speech came to an end. In a weak, hoarse voice, he closed on a note of the most moving eloquence:

"I speak for the poor, for the weak, for the weary, for that long line of men who, in darkness and despair, have borne the labors of the human race. Their eyes are upon you twelve men of Idaho tonight. If you kill Haywood your act will be applauded by many. In the railroad offices of our great cities men will applaud your names. If you decree his death, amongst the spiders of Wall Street will go up paeans of praise for these twelve good men and true. In every bank in the world, where men hate Haywood because he fights for the poor and against the accursed system upon which the favored live and grow rich and fat—from all these you will receive blessings and unstinted praise. But if your verdict should be 'not guilty' in this case, there are still those who will reverently bow their heads and thank these twelve men for the life and reputation you have saved. Out on our broad prairies where men toil with their hands, out on the broad ocean where men are tossed and buffeted on the waves, through our mills and factories and down deep under the earth, thousands of men and women and children—men and children weary with care and toil— these men and these women will kneel tonight and ask their God to guide your hearts—these men and these women and these little children, the poor, the weak, and the suffering of the world, are stretching out their helpless hands to this jury in mute appeal for Bill Haywood's life."[50]

Darrow concluded his address—one of the most eloquent ever heard in a courtroom—late in the evening of July 27. Early the next morning, the case went to the jury. After 20 hours of deliberation, the jury brought in a verdict of "Not Guilty."[51] The labor movement had won what Debs called "one of the greatest legal battles in American history." It had cost the W.F. of M. and the entire labor movement a good deal of expense and time, but it had been worth it. To the Seattle *Socialist* there was "one good effect of the Haywood trial." "It has drawn the curtain and labor has an unobstructed view of the Class Struggle."[52]

Although Haywood was set free, the state brought Pettibone to trial, but in January, 1908 he was also acquitted.[53] Moyer was never tried. Despite McParland's repeated assurance that he would save his neck if he did as he was told, Orchard was sentenced to die by hanging. But his punishment was commuted to life imprisonment. He died in prison in 1954 at the age of 88.

"Verdict Not a Surprise," was the heading of the lead editorial in the Bridgeport *Post* of July 29, 1907. "The verdict of not guilty brought in by the jury in the Haywood case," it declared, "will not surprise those who have carefully followed the evidence. The state clearly failed to prove, beyond a reasonable doubt, that Haywood was connected with the killing of a former governor of Idaho." To President Roosevelt, as to the Mine Owners' Association, most officials of Idaho and Colorado, and the Pinkerton Agency, the verdict came as a bitter disappointment. "There has been a gross miscarriage of justice, to my mind, out in Idaho in the acquittal of Haywood," Roosevelt wrote to Whitelaw Reid, American Ambassador to England. "It is not a pleasant matter from any stand-point."[54] But from the standpoint of the American labor movement, it was indeed a most "pleasant matter."

CHAPTER 3

The I.W.W., 1905-1907

REACTION TO FORMATION OF I.W.W.

The launching of the new industrial union aroused a mixed reaction in trade union and Socialist circles. Gompers, his earlier apprehensions relieved by reports from A.F. of L. observers at the Chicago convention, could not restrain his joy. He promptly informed the Executive Council of the "absolute failure of the Chicago gathering to cause even a ripple upon the minds of our fellow trade unionists." He had learned that "even those who were enthusiastic for the movement are all at sea as to what they shall do, and have lost heart." In a circular to the labor movement, Gompers tried to cover the "august gathering" with ridicule. "The mountain labored and brought forth a mouse, and a very silly little mouse at that." He characterized the I.W.W. plan of organization as "fantastic," and prophesied that "the future . . . will record the Chicago meeting as the most vapid and ridiculous in the annals of those who presume to speak in the name of labor, and the participants in the gathering as the most stupendous impossibilists the world has yet seen."[1]

The only thing that seemed to worry Gompers was that all Right-wing and most Center elements in the Socialist Party echoed the charges of the A.F. of L. leaders against the I.W.W. For these attacks on the new industrial union were coupled with appeals to the Socialist rank and file not to antagonize the A.F. of L. by supporting "a dual union movement," but to bore steadily within the Federation and transform the A.F. of L. members into Socialists. "There is one result, however, of the [Chicago] gathering," Gompers wrote to John B. Lennon, "which I feel we will have to meet, and that is that the Socialists will more thoroughly concentrate their efforts in the Federation of Labor to try to capture it."[2]

Actually, precisely the opposite happened, for one of the main results of the launching of the I.W.W. was that the conservative leaders of the A.F. of L. gained a tighter control over the affairs of the Federation. A number of Socialists who had been combatting the Gompers' leadership most vociferously inside the A.F. of L. dropped away from the Federation into the new industrial union, while those who remained increasingly worked hand-in-glove with the Gompers' leadership.

The Left-wing of the Socialist Party voiced its approval of the outcome of the Chicago convention, and announced its support of the new industrial union. Simons wrote that "the convention . . . makes the beginning of the end of Civic Federation and craft war in the American labor movement." Debs regarded it as "the greatest labor convention" he ever attended because the delegates agreed "upon the great vital principle of uniting the working class upon the economic field in a revolutionary organization recognizing and expressing the class struggle."[3] He toured the East and Middle West in the fall of 1905, organizing for the I.W.W., addressing meetings of steel and meat-packing workers in Chicago, needle-trades workers in New York and mass meetings of various types of workers in a number of cities. "The year now drawing to a close," he declared on November 24, "will be memorable in the annals of labor because of the organization of the Industrial Workers of the World." He emphasized that the supreme need of the working class was to "unite and act together economically and politically" so that its members could "overthrow the capitalist system and emancipate themselves from wage slavery." Since the I.W.W. was based on these postulates, "the revolutionary movement of the working class will date from the year 1905." Debs called on the workers to "sever your relations with capitalist unions," and join the I.W.W. He urged all workers to memorize the preamble to the I.W.W.'s constitution, and use it as a guide in their activities.[4]

Debs' public appeal to the workers to cast their lot with the I.W.W.* infuriated the Right and Center Socialist leaders. Max Hayes, Morris Hillquit, Abe Cahan of the New York *Forward,* Victor Berger, Fred Heath, and W. J. Ghent, all joined in criticizing Debs on the ground that his action would seriously impair the movement to achieve industrial unionism within the A.F. of L. The Federation, they maintained, had been moving in its own way toward an industrial form of organization, and the activity of the Socialists in founding and supporting the I.W.W. was destroying this development. Nevertheless, there was still a good chance that the A.F. of L. could be captured by the Socialists, and Debs could help this cause by refraining from attacking the Federation.

Debs was also accused of injuring the Socialist Party by allying himself with Daniel De Leon who was "an enemy of Socialism and a prevaricator and slanderer," a "humbug Professor and all around adventurer" who led in causing "internal strife and disruption in the labor movement." Pictures

---

* In February 1906 Debs qualified his previous statements urging workers to withdraw from the A.F. of L. and join the I.W.W. with the observation: "No man is expected to join the Industrial Workers of the World to whom it means the loss of his job." (*The Industrial Worker,* Feb. 1906.)

showing Debs and De Leon warmly shaking hands before the former's speech in favor of the I.W.W. at Grand Central Palace in New York City on December 10, 1905, were published in the Cleveland *Citizen,* the New York *Forward,* and the Milwaukee *Social-Democratic Herald* with the caption: "Beware of the enemy of Socialism—a warning to Comrade Debs."[5]

Debs hit back sharply at his critics. He denied that the Right-wingers could convert the A.F. of L. into "a clean industrial union." "To talk about reforming these rotten graft-infested [A.F. of L.] unions, which are dominated absolutely by the labor boss, is as vain and wasteful of time as to spray a cesspool with attar of roses." He denied that the I.W.W. would split the labor movement, for a glance at the A.F. of L. demonstrated that it was already sharply divided by a factional struggle for power. He denied that he was injuring the Socialist Party by his friendly relations with De Leon. "De Leon is sound on the question of unionism," Debs wrote in the autumn of 1905, "and to that extent, whether I like him or not personally, I am with him." He praised De Leon for devoting considerable space in the *Daily* and *Weekly People* to the activities and prospects of the I.W.W., for urging his followers in the S.L.P. and the S.T. and L.A. to exert themselves to the utmost in its behalf, and for delivering several speeches in a number of cities to help gain members for the new industrial union. Anyone in the United States who believed in the doctrines of Karl Marx, Debs insisted, had to throw his full support behind the I.W.W.[6]

This Debs did. Throughout the first year of the I.W.W.'s existence, he rendered it wholehearted support. The initial number of *The Industrial Worker* (January, 1906), official organ of the I.W.W., published at Joliet, Illinois, featured Debs' article "Industrial Revolutionists" in which he hailed the I.W.W. as a "revolutionary economic organization" which had "come at the right time" and had a "stupendous mission" to fulfill. The April 1906 issue carried Debs' assurance to members of the I.W.W. that if they did their best, "victory will be with the Industrial Workers of the World." In the July 1906 issue, Debs once again announced his belief in the need for the I.W.W.: "Never was an organization more timely, or better adapted to the pressing needs of the time."

I.W.W. INROADS ON A.F. OF L.

A month after the I.W.W. was launched, Gompers told a Pittsburgh audience that the new union had "died aborning," and that the A.F. of L. had nothing to fear from the organization. "The whole scheme . . . went up in thin air." It was inevitable that it should do so, he commented, for the "scheme" of industrial organization embodied in the I.W.W. went counter to basic trade union principles. If the trade union movement was based on this "scheme," "the tinker, the tailor, and the candlestick maker would legislate upon every minute detail affecting the interests of the workers."[7]

However, many members of the A.F. of L. viewed the industrial-union idea differently, and soon Gompers was to learn that for an organization that had "died aborning," the I.W.W. was attracting the interest and attention of important elements within the Federation.

"I am in receipt of several letters from our representatives in Buffalo setting forth that the [Industrial] Workers of the World are making headway among the workers of that city," James O'Connell, president of the International Association of Machinists, wrote to Gompers on October 26, 1905. "There are a number of other places, too, where the [Industrial] Workers of the World are making apparent headway, namely, Schenectady, N.Y., Newport News, Va., Cleveland, Ohio, Detroit, Mich., Rochester, N.Y., Chicago, Ill., Milwaukee, Kenosha, Racine, Oshkosh, Wisc., and many other places. It appears to me that it would be a good idea if a circular letter was addressed to the organizers of the A.F. of L., calling their attention to this effort that is being made by the [Industrial] Workers of the World and outline some sort of a policy so that the organizers might take hold of the work a little more energetically."[8]

Other reports submitted to Gompers around this time emphasized that some A.F. of L. unions were losing members to the I.W.W., especially among the brewers, machinists, meat cutters and butchers, shoemakers, textile workers, stogie makers, and mine workers. By the end of 1905, Max S. Hayes wrote in "The World of Labor" column of the *International Socialist Review* that "the I.W.W. appears to be gaining strength in New York, Chicago, and smaller places, especially in the West. A national officer of the brewers told me a few weeks ago that the rank and file in many parts of the country are clamoring to cut loose from the Federation and join the Industrialists. . . . Still another national officer, a Socialist by the way, said he had visited the little city of Schenectady, N.Y., recently and found the machinists, metal polishers and several other trades unions in open revolt against their national organization and going into the camp of the Industrial Workers. Some of the garment working crafts and textile workers are also affected."[9]

O'Connell's appeal to Gompers calling for energetic action to stave off additional inroads among A.F. of L. members by the I.W.W. was echoed by others. An organizer for the United Mine Workers from Missouri wrote: "I think it imperative at the present time for the American Fed. of Labor to act, if it is going to act with reference to the growing influence of the Industrial Workers in this state. If you do not, there is real danger that we will lose many members to the Industrialists. Special organizers should be sent at once into the field to combat the influence of these dangerous elements."[10]

The request for special organizers came from various parts of the country, and it was useless for Gompers to try to convince the correspondents that the I.W.W. had simply gone up "in thin air." Instead, he replied: "I am sure that I am quite within the bounds of truth, when I say, that if I had a million dollars now at my command, I would comply with the constant requests which are being made to this office for the appointment of special organizers to meet the threat of the so-called Industrial Workers. Indeed, I could use every penny of it in carrying on organization work, but our funds for this branch of work are limited, and as a consequence, we will have to find other means to combat the forces of our enemies who are preaching disintegration and division." The method hit upon by the A.F. of L. leadership was to issue a notice to central labor bodies to expel all delegates who were, in any way, associated with the I.W.W. This action, however, did not meet with wide approval. "I found a very strong sentiment against unseating the delegates to the Trades Assembly who had joined the I.W.W.," James F. Valentine, president of the Iron Molders' Union of North America, wrote to Gompers from Schenectady, New York. "There is considerable dissatisfaction among the rank and file of the local unions connected with the Assembly due to the demand that the Assembly expel these delegates. They feel that the I.W.W. people are doing something for the workers, which is more, they tell me, than can be said of the A.F. of L. organizers. I am convinced from a study of the situation in Schenectady that we need better organizers and fewer expulsion orders."[11]

The Central Labor Union of New Bedford, Mass. flatly refused to expel the I.W.W. union of textile workers organized in that city in the fall of 1905. "To make matters worse," John Golden, president of the United Textile Workers of America, informed Gompers in March 1906, "the President and Secretary of the Central Labor Union have stated that the Industrial Workers of the World deserve to be represented because they are organizing textile workers who have been neglected by our union. It is clear that we have an unscrupulous enemy to deal with." A month later, Golden reported that the I.W.W. union was still represented in the New Bedford Central Labor Union, and he urged Gompers to "go into that city and organize a new central body."

J. J. Windell, president of the Yonkers, New York, Federation of Labor bluntly informed Gompers that the organization would not honor his order demanding that it expel the I.W.W. Butchers' Union. "They are true union men, clear through, and are among the best workers we have in the cause of unionism in this city. As an evidence of their temper— when the motion was made to seat the I.W.W. delegates, the president at the time refused to entertain it. His decision was appealed from and the organization voted *unanimously* in favor of the Butchers. While I recognize the necessity for discipline and obedience to headquarters, I must tell you frankly that it would do far more harm to the cause of unionism to force us to unseat the Butchers than to forget that they are affiliated with this body."[12]

Part of the reluctance of these and other central bodies to expel I.W.W. delegates arose from the assistance A.F. of L. unions obtained from I.W.W. members during strikes. In Cleveland, the I.W.W. bricklayers went out in a sympathy strike with A.F. of L. hodcarriers, "and refused an offer of ten percent increase in wages and a closed shop contract, if they would desert the building laborers." In Newark, New Jersey, I.W.W. shoemakers refused to work with strikebreakers brought in to defeat A.F. of L. strikers. In Schenectady, New York, I.W.W. metal polishers voted to stay out of the plant until the striking A.F. of L. engineers won their battle. Such examples of working-class solidarity stood in sharp contrast to the policy of several A.F. of L. unions whose officials engaged strikebreakers to take the places of I.W.W. strikers, and placed boycotts against goods made in factories where I.W.W. members were employed. In Youngstown, Ohio, the tinners and slaters, heretofore divided in four crafts, joined the I.W.W. and struck. The employer wired the A.F. of L. for scabs, and these were sent despite the protest of the local painters. The International Association of Machinists, the United Brotherhood of Carpenters and Joiners, and the United Cloth Hat and Cap Makers ordered firms which had agreements with these unions to discharge all I.W.W. members.[13]

It is true that the I.W.W. was not reaching into new fields and developing new unions. Instead, it concentrated almost exclusively during its first year of existence in forming unions in industries in which A.F. of L. unions already existed to a lesser or greater degree, thus immediately bringing down upon itself the charge of injecting the evils of dual unionism in these industries. In the case of the struggle between the United Cloth Hat and Cap Makers and the I.W.W., the Industrial Workers gained the reputation of carrying dual unionism to the point of union destruction. In Detroit, the cap makers sympathetic to the I.W.W., led by Lazarus Goldberg, a cutter who was an ardent admirer of De Leon and a member of the S.L.P., joined the mixed local of the I.W.W. which had been organized in that city. In October 1905, the cap makers walked out of the Detroit Cap Co., the biggest in the city and one with which the A.F. of L. union had practically a closed-shop agreement, demanding that two of their members, who had revealed I.W.W. sympathy and had criticized the A.F. of L. union and its officers, be discharged. Their argument was that because of their attitude, these two men were non-union men, and the union permitted the union workers to quit when nonunion men were employed. The I.W.W. mixed local replied by accepting these two as members.

When the Detroit Cap Co. demanded that each worker sign an

individual contract with the company and post a $25 bond to guarantee that he would remain with the company until May 1906, the union rejected the proposal. On November 27, 1906, the men were locked out, and the union responded with a strike. But the cutters, led by Lazarus Goldberg and two other I.W.W. members, refused to go out with the men. "The question," noted the Detroit *Times* of December 1, 1905, "whether the I.W.W. are organized to act as strike-breakers or as a bona fide labor organization has been raised in the Cap Makers' strike." Five days later, it commented: "This is the first real controversy that has arisen between the two national organizations, the A.F. of L. and the I.W.W., and it is being watched with interest by the entire labor movement."

Realizing that its prestige was challenged, the I.W.W. finally declared that its members would not be allowed to work as strikebreakers and informed the Cap Makers' Union that it would leave the decision and time of calling out the I.W.W. members in the hands of the A.F. of L. organization. I.W.W. cap makers who refused to aid the union were expelled. But the strike of 80 men had been so weakened by the conflict between the A.F. of L. union and the I.W.W. that it ended on February 19, 1906, in a total defeat for the workers. Not only was the strike lost, but the Detroit union was destroyed.[14]

In certain instances the I.W.W.'s appeal met with quick response from the members of A.F. of L. affiliates only because the workers had become disillusioned with the conservative policies of these unions. Moreover, the I.W.W. brought with it a spirit of militancy and vitality which had been lacking in these unions, and spread the idea of unionism to workers who had not been affected by the idea before.

The International Ladies' Garment Workers' Union is a case in point. At its birth in June 1900, the I.L.G.W.U. had only 2,310 members in seven locals. Growth in the next two years was rapid as a result of the militancy of the workers which was expressed in the winning of 158 out of the 189 strikes conducted in this period. By 1904 there were 5,400 members in 66 locals in 27 cities. But after 1904, the union's growth was exceedingly slow. This was partly due to the general open-shop drive, but, in a large measure, it was the result of the leadership's cautious policy, patterned on the A.F. of L. to which it was affiliated. "They [the leaders]," writes Louis Levine, historian of the I.L.G.W.U., "continuously pointed to such craft unions as that of the cigar makers, as a model to be copied. . . . There was a definite desire to restrain the workers from striking often. Organization and preparation were the main slogans. High dues were advocated as a means of building up a strong treasury. A system of sick-and-death, strike and out-of-work benefits was recommended to the local unions. Boycotts were advocated and used. But above all, faith was pinned to the union label." It was hardly to be expected that the Socialist-minded membership, including the revolutionary elements from Russia who had entered the garment industry in increasing numbers after 1903, would be satisfied with such a conservative policy. The immigrants who had participated in the militant activities of the Jewish Bund in Russia, helping to organize the Jewish workers and leading them in strikes for the improvement of working conditions, were quickly dissatisfied with the policies of the A.F. of L. "If this new immigrant group had sympathies for any branch of the American labor movement," notes Martin A. Cohen in his unpublished study, "Jewish Immigrants and American Trade Unions," "they were for the Industrial Workers of the World." The same could be said for many Italian workers in the industry who were attracted by the fact that the I.W.W. invited all workers to join on an equal basis with dues and initiation fees low enough not to bar any worker from the ranks of organized labor.[15]

I.W.W. unions, composed of workers who had become disillusioned with the I.L.G.W.U. and of workers who had not been unionized, were established in Cleveland, Boston, Chicago, St. Louis, and, of course, New York, the heart of the industry. In the last-named city, the various craft unions were combined into an industrial union, Local 59, I.W.W., with the cloak makers comprising Branch 3, the pressers Branch 6, the white-goods workers Branch 12, and the ladies tailors Branch 10. Local 59 and its branches conducted a vigorous campaign against the "false principles of the American Federation of Labor" by which "one group of workers is led to believe that it is superior to and can get along without the aid of the less skilled or poorer paid workers in the same industry." The reference was especially meaningful in the cloak industry because the English-speaking, highly skilled cutters were a conservative and craft-conscious group who looked down upon the less-skilled immigrant Jews and Italians, and refused to assist them in their struggles to organize. The I.L.G.W.U. leadership based itself upon the skilled, whereas the I.W.W. deliberately sought to build its strength among the rest of the workers, the majority in the cloak industry, and through them to unionize shops which had not been organized before. Through the course of the class struggle, the I.W.W. believed the highly skilled and the less-skilled workers in the industry could be united. Hence they advocated the "recognition of the class struggle in the shop every day and the uniform organization of all branches of the clothing industry into one grand industrial body" which would affiliate with similar "grand industrial bodies" in other industries thereby "uniting the entire working class."[16]

In the course of 1905-06, the I.W.W. succeeded in organizing many shops which had not been reached before, and had it not been plagued by internal conflicts, it could have become the dominant factor in the ladies' garment industry. But these conflicts eventually drove most of the locals back into the I.L.G.W.U. Nevertheless, when they did return, they brought with them the ideas of industrial unionism and a spirit of militancy which helped to rejuvenate the International.

THE RUSSIAN REVOLUTION

One reason for I.W.W. prestige among the garment workers, many of whom had a revolutionary background in Russia, was its fervent support of the Russian Revolution. In October 1905, a general strike paralyzed Russia; the government capitulated, promulgating the Tsar's Manifesto which promised civil liberties and conferred legislative authority upon the elective Duma conceived originally as a purely advisory assembly. But the liberal bourgeoisie was frightened by the revolutionary trend, and gradually moved to make peace with the Tsar. Only the workers kept the revolutionary struggle alive. In December an armed insurrection of Moscow workers lasted eight days but was drowned in blood by loyal troops.

Despite its limited resources, the I.W.W. responded eagerly to a call of the International Socialist Bureau in Brussels, Belgium, for an international demonstration on January 22, 1906, to support the Russian workers on strike and raise funds to assist them. Mass meetings sponsored by the I.W.W., often in conjunction with local members of the Socialist Party, took place in several cities on that day. President C. O. Sherman, A. M. Simons, and William E. Trautmann addressed a mass meeting in Chicago, and hailed the Russian Revolution as "the greatest struggle for human liberty ever witnessed in the annals of history."[17]

The general strike, in the opinion of the I.W.W. at that time, had proven its value in Russia;* indeed, the Russian Revolution had demonstrated the validity of the I.W.W. doctrine that struggle on the economic front was all-important and must be fully developed before political action could be effective:

"What was it that happened in Russia? The workers quit work—tied up the railways, closed the shops, shut down the mills and suspended profit-making in general. With what result? Business was alarmed and government compelled to make what, to autocrat and aristocrats, were revolutionary concessions. It was a struggle in the economic field. It is likely to win more than any battle with ballots has done for any people in the world. The Russians are better fitted than before to conduct a triumphant political campaign and secure control of the government."[18]

The principles of industrial unionism had been vindicated in Russia:

---

* This did not mean that the I.W.W. felt that the time was ripe for a general strike in the United States. "Unless we are trying to deceive ourselves and hold out a false hope to others, we will confront the facts squarely. The working class has neither a political nor economic organization powerful enough to undertake a general strike." (*The Industrial Worker*, Feb. 1906.)

"Industrial Unionism is solidifying the Russian workingman." The majority of the revolutionary workers in Russia were the unskilled, and only through industrial unionism could they have been organized in the revolutionary struggle. "When would Gompers and his clumsy federation ever stir Russia to arms?" The proletariat of Russia, recognizing the class struggle and organized industrially, was "the directing and dominating power of, in fact, is the revolution. The sun of the socialist republic will first cross the horizon of the Slavic empire."[19] Even after the revolutionary tide in Russia had receded and the Tsarist government withdrew its concessions and greatly curtailed the power of the Duma, the I.W.W. continued to voice its faith in the ultimate triumph of the revolutionary cause and to render it support. The I.W.W. welcomed Maxim Gorky who had come to the United States to raise funds for the continuation of the revolutionary struggle in Russia. And when sponsorship of Gorky's meetings was abandoned by leading American liberals because it was discovered that the actress who had accompanied the Russian author to the United States as his wife was not married to him, the I.W.W. proudly announced that it would sponsor the meetings: "Gorky stands out clearly in the life of the Russian people for exactly what the Industrial Workers advocate in America. . . . We welcome Maxim Gorky to America as a representative Industrial Unionist, as a missionary of order throughout the land."[20]

I.W.W. GROWTH

Although there is no record of outstanding organizational results during the I.W.W.'s first year of existence in mass production industries, on the farms, and in the lumber camps, members of the new unions were not entirely inactive in these areas. The Metal and Machinery Department's growth to 3,000 members in March 1906 was largely the result of organizational activity in the General Electric plant at Schenectady, New York, which city was soon known as "one of the strongest centers of Industrial Unionism." Apart from the workers in the G.E. plant, the I.W.W.'s Metal and Machinery Department organized Italians who were not permitted to join the A.F. of L.'s Crane Runners' Union on the ground that they were "guineas."[21]

In Crescent City, Oregon, the sawmill workers and woodsmen were solidly organized in the I.W.W. They displayed their labor solidarity by helping the Sailors' Union of the Pacific win a strike against the leading lumber company in the city. After the strike was over, the boats carrying lumber from Crescent City were manned by union sailors.[22]

Without the flair for dramatic action which was later to characterize the organizing activities of the I.W.W., these early efforts went practically unnoticed in the press. But the I.W.W. was proud that its opposition to race prejudice in the labor movement was noticed in the *North American Times,* a Japanese newspaper, published in Seattle, which announced:

"A few days ago, two men who represent the Industrial Workers of the World called on the Times office, informing us that they are proposing to hold a mass meeting of laborers . . . on May 20th [1906]. . . . The special feature of the gathering is that every worker, no matter whether he is Japanese or Chinese, is invited. Here he can raise his voice and express his opinion. . . . At this juncture we urge upon our brothers from Japan to consider the matter earnestly and those who believe in it should join it at once. This new organization does not exclude you as others do, but they heartily welcome you to join. Don't lose this chance."[23]

From the birth of the I.W.W. to September 17, 1906, the date of the opening of the second convention, 384 locals were organized in the United States and Canada. Included among them were locals of the Socialist Trade and Labor Alliance which had installed their members in the I.W.W. immediately after the founding convention. (Most of these locals were in textile centers such as Paterson, Lawrence, Providence, and New Bedford, and others were in Newark, New York City, Brooklyn, and Detroit.) The membership of the I.W.W. at the time of the second convention is not easy to determine with any degree of accuracy, varying widely from Secretary Trautmann's optimistic statement in his report to the convention of 60,000 members (including 27,000 in the W.F. of M.) to Professor George Barnett's estimate of 10,400. Vincent St. John, who later replaced Trautmann as I.W.W. secretary-treasurer, asserted flatly that "the *average* paid-up membership *with the W.F. of M.* for the first year of the organization was 14,000 in round numbers."[24]

Whatever the membership figures may have been, three things are clear: (1) The I.W.W. during its first year of existence, drafted its membership mainly from established unions which were affiliated with the A.F. of L.; (2) the majority of these members soon left the I.W.W. and the locals to which they belonged either broke away or simply expired—victims of the intense factional feud that wracked the early I.W.W., and (3) certain A.F. of L. national unions, such as the Brewers, and local unions of the Machinists, Lathers, and the Carpenters showed some sympathy for the I.W.W. shortly after the founding convention, and some even predicted early affiliation, but none of them joined the organization. This was partly due to opposition of the national leaders of the organizations to the I.W.W.—an opposition which in the case of the Machinists threatened expulsion of all I.W.W. sympathizers; partly because of the failure of the I.W.W. to prove that it could accomplish much in the way of organization outside of the distribution of literature; and partly because of the sectarian, dual-unionist policies pursued by many I.W.W. leaders. In any case, in most communities, the I.W.W., during its first year of existence, was not an industrial union but a propaganda group trying to instill and spread the idea of industrial unionism. In this respect, it did achieve some success. In Detroit, for example, the Federation of Labor adopted a plan for organizing workers into industrial unions. John J. Scannell, Federation secretary and originator of the plan, acknowledged that the existence of the I.W.W. had influenced him in developing the idea: "I believe this proves that a revolution is going on in the A.F. of L., which will result in time in a complete industrial form of organization. If that is true, there is no necessity for the organizations breaking away from and disrupting the federation by organizing the I.W.W., because as fast as the conditions demand the change, the federation will conform to it."[25]

I.W.W. LEADERSHIP

From the outset the I.W.W. was plagued by a lack of capable leadership. President Sherman drained the small treasury* in useless travel and operating expenses, and his ridiculously optimistic "Notes from the Field" predicting membership in the hundreds of thousands by the second convention were probably more to justify his expenditures than to present a realistic picture of the problems facing the new organization.[26] An honest and sincere official, Executive Board member John Riordan, formerly of the American Labor Union, tried to put a stop to the drain on the treasury by the president, but fresh from the mines, he lacked the necessary experience to cope with the problem. He sent Trautmann Sherman's expense vouchers with the comment "for graft" written across the face, but the secretary-treasurer, busily roving around the country, had no time to examine the problem, and simply sent the vouchers through with instructions that they be paid. (Sherman spent over $7,000 for travel and operating expenses within a few months. His salary was $150 a month.) Another evidence of "graft" was Sherman's connection with the Fraternal Supply Co., a firm in which he was a partner and which sold badges, ribbons, and the like for the use of lodges and unions. Full pages of *The Industrial Worker* were devoted to appeals to locals and members of the I.W.W. to send in orders to the Fraternal Supply Co. for badges and banners. On March 11, 1907, P. A. Kirby, Sherman's partner in the company, charged in a sworn affidavit that after the formation of the I.W.W., "the business of the Fraternal Supply Company was considerably increased; that the said Sherman being President of the Industrial Workers of the World and continuing his connections with

* The I.W.W. started with a treasury of $817.59 which was transferred to the new organization by the American Labor Union after it ceased operations. (Fred Thompson, *The I.W.W.: Its First Fifty Years, 1905-1955*, Chicago, 1955, p. 23.)

this affiant in the Fraternal Supply Company, thereby participating in its profits, was not content with a fair or moderate profit on goods sold to the Industrial Workers of the World, but insisted that this affiant should charge unfair and exorbitant prices."[27]

The absence of capable officials during the formative year might not have been so serious had not the I.W.W. been deprived so early in its career of the services of two of its most experienced and influential personalities—Charles H. Moyer and "Big Bill" Haywood. The imprisonment of Moyer, an I.W.W. Executive Board member, and Haywood, a member of the Mining Department, was a serious blow to the new organization. For one thing, Moyer and Haywood could have exercised a restraining influence on Sherman's excessive expenditures and graft, and given the struggling organization the steadying influence it so sorely needed. (Indeed, before he was removed from the scene, Moyer had sharply criticized Trautmann for continuously being absent from headquarters, urged him to stay at the national office, and charged him with keeping a closer eye on the treasury.) For another, the jailing of Haywood drastically affected the I.W.W.'s organizing drive, for he was the organization's most militant and aggressive organizer. Moreover, the frameup caused the I.W.W. to suspend nearly all its organizing work and devote itself exclusively to raising support and funds for the defense. To be sure, for a new organization barely starting out on its career, the I.W.W. accomplished miracles in arousing public and financial support for the indicted men, and its tremendous activity in their defense made the name of the organization known to thousands of workers throughout the country who might not otherwise have learned of its existence. (The April 1906 issue of *The Industrial Worker,* almost entirely devoted to the case, received a wide circulation in labor circles.) But the Western Federation of Miners actually benefited more from this publicity than did the I.W.W. In many cities, the I.W.W. and A.F. of L. unions jointly sponsored defense meetings, but usually no mention was made of the I.W.W. in these protests, only the W.F. of M. membership of the indicted men being stressed. The fact that Moyer and Haywood were also members of the I.W.W. was usually ignored.[28]

The celebrated case, however, had a temporary welding effect on the I.W.W., uniting all elements in the organization around a common cause. But underneath an internal battle had been brewing, and it soon came to the surface.

Opposition to President Sherman had been mounting within the I.W.W. throughout the first year of its existence. His extravagant expenditure of funds had especially antagonized the poorer and less-skilled workers in the organization. On top of this, there was a growing impression that a conspiracy was being engineered by Sherman and his associates from within and without the I.W.W. to wreck the new industrial union or, at least, to divert it from its revolutionary course. There were several groups charged with being involved in this conspiracy. Trautmann accused the A.F. of L. leadership of having planted Sherman and a number of his followers inside the I.W.W. in order to direct the new organization along conservative lines. He charged further that Victor Berger and a group of conservative elements in the W.F. of M., who had assumed greater influence in that union while Moyer and Haywood were in prison, were also engaged in the conspiracy with Sherman. Specifically, John O'Neill, editor of the *Miners' Magazine,* James Kirivan, acting secretary of the W.F. of M., Berger, and Sherman were accused of having conferred in Denver on February 1, 1906, with the purpose of driving "the radical elements" out of the I.W.W.

Just how much truth there was to these charges is difficult to determine. O'Neill flatly denied the accusation and even offered a $500 reward to anyone who could prove the truth of it.[29] Berger and Sherman ignored the conspiracy charge.

Certainly there is no evidence of Trautmann's charge that the A.F. of L. had planted Sherman and his associates inside the I.W.W. to control the organization. But there is considerable evidence that Sherman had little interest in or sympathy for the basic principles of the I.W.W. As general secretary of the United Metal Workers' International Union, he had advocated the principle of "conciliation and arbitration between the employer and employee," and his difference with the A.F. of L. leadership had arisen primarily because the Executive Council refused to prevent the Bridge and Structural Iron Workers from interfering with the Metal Workers' jurisdiction. On November 7, 1904, on the eve of the A.F. of L. convention, Sherman wrote to Morrison: "I have no difference with you or Brother Gompers that cannot be settled once the correct attitude is adopted towards the vicious efforts of the Bridge and Structural Iron Workers to raid our organization and take over our jurisdiction. I am ready to support you and Brother Gompers for re-election if you will not be wanting in our behalf." On February 15, 1905, Sherman assured Morrison that a report that he was "connected with the movement to launch a new labor organization was without foundation." Two days later, it was announced that Sherman was associated with the Congress to be held in Chicago on June 27, 1905.[30]

All this, of course, was not known to the delegates at Chicago who elected Sherman president of the I.W.W. mainly because he had no connection with either the Socialist Party or the Socialist Labor Party. But within the next few months there was increasing evidence that Sherman was intent on basing the I.W.W. on the more highly skilled workers, that he showed little interest in the unskilled workers, and that, together with the conservative elements in the W.F. of M., who were on the I.W.W. General Executive Board and with Socialist Party leaders, he was bent on converting the new industrial union into a replica of the A.F. of L.[31]

SECOND I.W.W. CONVENTION AND FIRST SPLIT

It has been suggested that if the second convention had been held in May, as originally scheduled, while the spirit of unity created by the Moyer-Haywood defense was still prevalent, the internal struggle might have been "ironed out."[32] While this is highly doubtful, the two postponements of the convention—first to June 27 so that the W.F. of M. could convene beforehand and be installed and then to September 17 until after the trial of the officials of the miners' union—gave additional time for the internal conflict to emerge even more sharply.

The second convention had barely opened at Chicago's K.P. Hall on the morning of September 17, 1906, when the conflict within the ranks of the I.W.W. flared into the open. The Trautmann–De Leon–St. John faction accused Sherman of high-handed usurpation of authority in personally appointing a credentials committee to determine who had a right to vote rather than allowing the committee to be selected by a majority vote of those present. Days of wrangling followed over the decision of the credentials committee as to who should be seated, during the course of which the convention moved to a larger hall after De Leon's charge that Sherman had deliberately hired a small hall so that he could control the gathering. Sherman and his followers were also accused of deliberately delaying the convention to starve out the majority of the "revolutionist" or "wage-slave" element who, coming from local unions which paid their representatives nothing but mileage, were without means of support. A motion was introduced to provide $1.50 a day for any delegate who was without the necessary expense money. Sherman held this to be in violation of article VI, section 8 of the constitution which provided that "the expense of delegates attending the convention shall be borne by their respective organizations." Thereupon De Leon moved that this section of the constitution be suspended during the meetings of the convention. This was accepted by the delegates.

In an interview in the Chicago *Record-Herald* of October 7, 1906, Sherman explained the real reason for his opposition to the motion: "We believed we could starve them out by obstructive tactics." Now that Sherman could not "starve them out," the delegates proceeded to the work of the convention. A proposal to abolish the office of the president was introduced as an amendment to the constitution,* and, when it was

---

* The proposal had first been advanced at a pre-convention conference of 16 I.W.W. locals in Chicago which unanimously voted that "the office of president of a class-conscious organization is not necessary. The rank and file must conduct the affairs of the organization directly through an executive board or central committee."

carried, De Leon immediately pointed out that since there was no longer a president, the convention should elect a chairman. Vincent St. John was elected to the position. Speaking to the delegates after he was deposed from his office, Sherman charged that his ouster was the result of a plot by De Leon and the S.L.P. to control the I.W.W., and warned that "their tactics are suicide to the movement." De Leon denied Sherman's accusation. He justified the president's ouster on the ground that the I.W.W. had to be purged of its opportunistic, non-revolutionary elements so that it could "continue its work as the revolutionary economic organization of the working class of America."[33]

The De Leon–Trautmann–St. John faction, with De Leon masterminding its operations, was now in control of the convention. But ex-president Sherman and the majority of the Executive Board members refused to yield control of the general headquarters of which they had taken possession and continued to control with the assistance of hired detectives. A battle for the headquarters followed, but when Sherman called in 21 Chicago policemen to help him and his followers, the De Leon–Trautmann–St. John faction had to give in. The deposed president and the old Executive Board now had possession of the general office and all the books, records, papers, lists of local unions, and other property of the organization. The new leadership of the I.W.W. controlled the organization, but "were obliged to begin work . . . without the equipment of so much as a postage stamp." There was exactly seven cents left in Trautmann's hands.[34]

Sherman and his followers were later forced to surrender the headquarters as a result of a court order which upheld the convention and its actions and declared that Sherman's acts "were illegal." Despite the decision, Sherman continued to conduct a separate I.W.W. of his own in Joliet, Illinois, from where he announced he would set out to "push forward and build up the Industrial Workers of the World." But apart from competing for allegiance for members in a few areas where the I.W.W. had some strength and continuing to blast the delegates to the second convention as "the beggars," "the coffee and doughnut brigade," and "the Brigade of the Hungry," Sherman's organization did nothing and it never amounted to anything.[35]

The alliance at the 1906 convention between De Leon on the one hand, and St. John and Trautmann on the other, had successfully dislodged the conservative forces. But on a number of other issues at the convention, these different elements did not see eye-to-eye. St. John and Trautmann, leading the anti-political action, pro-syndicalist delegates,

---

Reprinting the text of the pre-convention conference in the *Miners' Magazine,* John O'Neill commented sarcastically: "There is a vast difference between being class-conscious and being class-crazy." (Sept. 6, 1906, pp. 1–2.)

sought to delete the words "political as well" from the second paragraph of the I.W.W. Preamble which read: "Between these two classes [the working class and the employing class] a struggle must go on until the workers come together on the political as well as on the industrial field. . . ." But De Leon opposed the move, and the constitution committee, dominated by his followers, recommended that the "Preamble remain as it now stands." A heated debate followed. The pro-syndicalist delegates emphasized that it was necessary for the I.W.W. to concentrate entirely on economic activity because "all politics outside of this organization is capitalist politics." Moreover, it was a waste of time to vote at capitalist-controlled ballot boxes because the total votes released for the candidates "do not comply with the votes that you put in the ballot box." These were rather weak arguments for the pro-syndicalist position, and De Leon and his followers had little difficulty in demolishing them.[36]

Had Trautmann and St. John, the theoretical leaders of the anarcho-syndicalist elements, openly attacked De Leon's position, the controversy might have created still another split at the convention. But they were not prepared at this time to throw down the gauntlet on the political issue. Instead, they chose to effect a compromise with De Leon. They agreed to support the constitution committee's recommendation that the "Preamble remain as it now stands," in return for De Leon's support for a resolution submitted by St. John on behalf of the Mining Department which called for a referendum of the membership on the question: "That the Industrial Workers of the World does not desire the endorsement of any political party, neither will the Industrial Workers of the World endorse any political party."[37] The resolution was approved by the convention as was the constitution committee's recommendation that the Preamble remain unaltered.

Although the outcome was a compromise, it was clear that there was a strong feeling among the delegates against political action. This was reflected in the approval of a resolution which ordered the Denver local to withdraw support for W. D. Haywood who, although in prison in Idaho awaiting trial, was running for governor of Colorado on the Socialist Party ticket. Local 125 was instructed "to withdraw its endorsement and keep within the provisions of the Preamble and Constitution of the Industrial Workers of the World." Likewise, John O'Neill, who had endorsed the Socialist Party of Pennsylvania in the *Miners' Magazine,* was censured as being guilty of "insubordination" against "the objects and aims of the I.W.W. in general and the Mining Department in particular." Following these acts, the convention inconsistently adopted a resolution recommending that Good and Welfare Committees in local unions devote "at least ten minutes . . . to the discussion of economic and political questions at each meeting."[38]

The discussion at the convention proved that although the issue of political action was not yet strong enough to split the I.W.W., the matter was far from settled. Neither side had really abandoned its position. De Leon made it quite clear after the convention that he expected the I.W.W. to ally itself with the S.L.P. and endorse that party as its "political reflex."[39] The anti-political-action element, led by Trautmann and St. John, likewise made it evident that they were not really satisfied with the fact that the only change made in the Preamble at the 1906 convention was the inclusion of the statement that the I.W.W. would not endorse nor desire the endorsement of any political party. As future conventions would show, they were determined to eliminate any and all references to political action from the constitution.

OTHER ISSUES AT 1906 CONVENTION

Other matters discussed at the second convention showed the drift toward an anarchist ideology. The resolutions committee refused to recommend the adoption of sick and death benefit funds because such features were "not among the aims, purposes and objects of the industrial union movement." Anything which lessened the worker's class consciousness, mitigated his recognition of the class struggle, and had the effect of "dimming" his understanding that "unless he overthrows the system of capitalist exploitation, he will always be a wage slave," was not acceptable.[40] Here was "class craziness" with a vengeance!

Nevertheless, a few sound notes were struck at the convention. It was agreed that special efforts should be made to organize the "farm wage slaves," using the lumber workers, among whom the I.W.W. had already made some headway, as a wedge to reach the farm laborers, and building closer cooperation between the farm and forest workers with "the wage slaves of the industrial centers." It was also agreed that a more aggressive organizing policy be adopted towards reaching the immigrant workers with the I.W.W. message. "The literature of the Industrial Workers of the World," said Secretary Trautmann, "should be distributed in different languages in the various emigration ports in Europe and central bureaus be established . . . in American harbors, and be opened to the immigrants, and information should be furnished them [as] to how they could . . . participate in the struggles of organized labor." Although nothing was done along the lines of Trautmann's suggestion to facilitate the organization of foreign-born workers, with their wide variety of languages, traditions, and customs, the convention voted to issue literature in many foreign languages, and to allow wage-earners of a given nationality "to form unions of their own in the respective industries in which they are employed and where there are not enough to form unions of that kind, the parent unions shall allow the [non-English speaking] members . . . to have branch meetings for educational purposes." A special inducement was also offered to women and young workers through the adoption of a resolution "to remit for female members, ten cents per member per month to the union, the same to apply to juniors."[41]

On October 3, 1906, the second convention of the I.W.W. adjourned. De Leon, who made the closing speech, touched on a matter of no small concern to the organization—the fact that the delegates of the Western Federation of Miners, the backbone of the I.W.W., had bolted the convention after the deposition of President Sherman. But he hastened to assure the remaining delegates that there was no real reason for discouragement. Numbers alone would not assure the overthrow of capitolism. The "earnest, the resolute, the revolutionary men" had only to pursue "that firm line of agitation that proceeds alone from well established knowledge," and "the emancipation of the working class," under the leadership of the I.W.W., "would inevitably follow."[42]

W.F. OF M. LEAVES I.W.W.

On June 6, 1906, at its 14th annual convention, the W.F. of M. had gone on record as being an integral part of the I.W.W., and announced that it would "do everything possible to build up the I.W.W. throughout the country." Six months later, the union was torn apart over the question of whether or not to remain affiliated with the I.W.W. For over a year after the second I.W.W. convention, which the W.F. of M. membership overwhelmingly condemned in a referendum vote, the wrangling over this issue continued. Although Moyer and Haywood were still confined to their prison cells in Idaho, they joined in the debate by means of correspondence. Both were vigorously opposed to De Leon, condemned his role in splitting the I.W.W. at the 1906 convention, and accused him of deliberately provoking the split in order to gain control of the new industrial union and convert it and its affiliated unions into an appendage of the S.L.P. While Haywood condemned Sherman as well, he felt that the abolition of the office of president and the installing of a different system of administration was both unconstitutional and unnecessarily harsh. The evils of "Shermanism" could have been eliminated "without a division or any internecine trouble among the rank and file."[43]

Although connection between the W.F. of M. and the I.W.W. almost ceased after January 1907, neither Moyer nor Haywood wanted the miners' union officially to leave the I.W.W., and largely as a result of their influence, even while confined in prison, the 1907 W.F. of M. convention did not vote for immediate withdrawal. Instead, a compromise was proposed which called upon the W.F. of M. to invite "the contending factions of the Industrial Workers of the World, the United Brewery Workers, and all other labor unions ready to accept the principles of industrial unions as set forth in the manifesto issued by the conference of industrial unionists at Chicago, January 2, 1905, to meet the Western Federation of Miners in a convention at Chicago, to convene October 1st, 1907, for the purpose of re-establishing and strengthening the Industrial Workers of the World." With an amendment providing for democratic control of the new organization by the initiative and referendum, the proposition was carried.[44]

But this effort at reconciling the two factions in the I.W.W. and at reorganizing it on a reunited basis came to naught. The I.W.W. leadership immediately branded the W.F. of M. action as a "reactionary peace proposal," pointed out that the Sherman faction was now really out of the picture, and that the only organization worthy to bear the name, "Industrial Workers of the World," was the one sanctioned by the 1906 convention. Nevertheless, the W.F. of M. Executive Board decided to go ahead with its plan and issued a call for a unity conference in Chicago on April 6, 1908. The I.W.W. dismissed the call, condemned the W.F. of M. Executive Board for addressing the invitation "to officers of both factions of the I.W.W.," and again pointed out that "there is but one I.W.W. in existence now or any time that has claim to the name."

The W.F. of M. dropped the plan for unification, and at the 16th annual convention in 1908, all connection with the I.W.W. was broken off.[45]

SOCIALISTS AND THE I.W.W.

The serious rift in the W.F. of M. over the question of affiliation to the I.W.W. was cited by the Center-Right Socialists as proving their earlier charge that the new union would only succeed in disrupting the existing unions. Even some former Socialist supporters of the I.W.W. either turned cool to the organization or bitterly attacked it. Debs, for example, never wavered in supporting the principles of revolutionary industrial unionism, and although he did not attend the I.W.W. second convention, he had sent a telegram congratulating the organization and wishing "success to their deliberations." But Debs had begun, even before the 1906 convention, to devote less and less activity in behalf of the I.W.W., for he had become increasingly concerned by reports that "active workers in the Socialist Party all over the country have suddenly grown lukewarm in the effort to build up a political organization and are enthusiastically proclaiming the advantages of industrial unionism." To be sure, Debs himself had encouraged this tendency when he had emphasized in his speeches that the new union would achieve the "complete emancipation" of the working class from capitalism, and would "develop the embryonic structure of the cooperative commonwealth."[46] But Debs' working-class instinct caused him to see that this approach led to a complete underestimation of the party, and he consequently lost a good deal of his earlier enthusiasm for the I.W.W. The unfortunate battle between the I.W.W. and the W.F. of M. only served to further dampen his enthusiasm.

However, Debs refrained from publicly attacking the new industrial union. Not so, however, A. M. Simons who now became one of the bitterest Socialist opponents of the I.W.W. Writing in the *International Socialist Review* following the 1906 convention, he charged that "De Leon is . . . doing the work of a capitalist spy [even if] not getting the pay." In the eyes of the Center-Right Socialists, however, there was one consolation. The split between the W.F. of M. and the I.W.W., on top of the split at the 1906 convention, guaranteed the imminent dissolution of the new union. This was an opinion widely shared. The Detroit *Times* reported the fact that "the Socialist Labor Party had captured the (I.W.W.) convention," and that it was "the opinion of a great many that this would kill the I.W.W. movement which, only a year ago, threatened the very life of the American Federation of Labor."[47]

The I.W.W., however, disputed these gloomy predictions. In its first issue, March 2, 1907, the *Industrial Union Bulletin,* now the official organ of the I.W.W., announced that its appearance was an answer to the "undertakers" who had the I.W.W. "dead and prepared for interment six months ago." The 1906 "house-cleaning," it insisted, had enabled the I.W.W. to move ahead to accomplish its mission. "The future of the organization is bright and promising."

Events would soon prove who was correct: the "undertakers" or the supposed "corpse."

CHAPTER 4

The I.W.W., 1907-1909

The upheaval of 1906 had deprived the I.W.W. of its strongest affiliate, the W.F. of M., and this, together with the defection of the Sherman contingent, left the organization with fewer than 6,000 members. Nevertheless, the I.W.W. was still alive. On August 8, 1907, Gompers sent an urgent memorandum to a number of international presidents cautioning them not to be taken in by reports that "the Industrial Workers of the World are dead and buried. In this connection, I desire to call attention to the very persistent work of organizing that is being prosecuted by the Industrial Workers of the World. I make mention of this because I think it necessary that something should be done in the near future to check the growth of this Dual movement."[1]

PROGRESS IN ORGANIZATION

Despite its straitened financial status, the I.W.W. made a real effort after the second convention to organize the foreign-born workers. Circulars and pamphlets were issued in a number of languages, and in the summer of 1907, the *Industrial Union Bulletin* announced that this educational campaign was producing results, especially among Polish workers who were said to be "taking to the I.W.W. as a duck takes to water." Foreign-language branches were increasingly established, such as the Hungarian branch of the Metal and Machinery Workers' Industrial Union, L.U. No. 113—there was also an English-speaking branch—and the French-speaking branches in the textile industry. Jewish and Italian organizers were appointed, although lack of funds prevented the organization from filling requests for other organizers of these nationality groups. The Italian Socialist Federation and its local branches urged their members and all Italian workers to join the I.W.W., and its journal, *Il Proletario,* became an official organ of the industrial union. *La Propaganda,* a weekly Italian paper was started in Chicago. In San

Francisco, *The Revolution,* a Japanese-language paper, opened its columns to the I.W.W. and aided the organization in translating its literature into Japanese. In the same city, two Chinese Socialists translated I.W.W. literature into Chinese. The I.W.W. also issued a pamphlet entitled, "Japanese and Chinese Exclusion or Industrial Organization, Which?" It presented the following "Cold Facts for Consideration by the Working Class."

"1. The Japanese and Chinese are here.

"2. Thousands of them are wage workers.

"3. They have the same commodity to sell as other workers—labor power.

"4. They are as anxious as you, to get as much as possible. This is proven by the fact that they have come to this country. For what? To better their conditions."

The pamphlet concluded: "We the Industrial Workers of the World have organized the Japanese and Chinese in lumber camps, on the farms, mines and railroads, and the United Mine Workers of America have organized Japanese in the coal fields of Wyoming. This is proof that they can be organized."[2]

In May 1907, the I.W.W. established relations with the Roumanian Syndicalist General Commission at Bucharest with the aim of increasing "international solidarity and . . . to enable us to bring before the workers of Roumania, Transylvania, etc., the conditions in America and the respective relations of the A.F. of L. and the I.W.W. to the international labor movement."

"In this way the workers intending to emigrate to America will know where they rightly belong and will not be confronted with exorbitant initiation fees for the privilege of becoming or remaining part of the labor movement, and even after they get inside the wall, to be serving the master class.

"The Industrial Workers of the World accepts anyone presenting a membership card from any labor organization from other countries without any initiation fee. The A.F. of L. is fighting against Chinese, Japanese, and the Southern European races calling them 'undesirable' class of immigrants; and is agitating for laws to bar them from America.* The I.W.W. extends a fraternal hand to every wage-worker, no matter what his religion, fatherland, or trade."

The Roumanian Syndicalist General Commission welcomed "with great pleasure" the I.W.W. proposal, and asked for "a clear and precise report" of what was expected of it "so that we may be able to communi-

---

* At its 1907 convention, the I.W.W. condemned the A.F. of L. for participating in outbreaks against Asian workers. These "outbreaks . . . serve to divide the workers" (*Industrial Union Bulletin,* March, 16, 1907; *Proceedings, 3rd Convention, I.W.W.,* Chicago, 1907, Report No. 7, p. 9.)

cate it to our Hungarian comrades and to publish it in our official organ."[3]

In Lynn, Haverhill, and Brockton, Mass., I.W.W. locals were organized among the shoe workers, and among the textile workers in Paterson and Hudson County, N.J., Providence and Woonsocket, R.I., Lawrence, New Bedford, and Lowell, Mass. By March 1907, the I.W.W. boasted of 1,000 members in Local No. 152, Silk Workers' Industrial Union of Paterson, and predicted that "we have a splendid opportunity to organize the entire silk industry." The militancy of the foreign-language branches in Paterson was frequently referred to in the *Industrial Union Bulletin,* and special tribute was paid to the women members of the local union:

"It is very encouraging to see the splendid stand taken by the girls and women in these [silk] mills. They grasp the situation and perform their part in a very practical and creditable manner; and it must be said further, to their credit, that when anything is suggested that savors of exploitation of the union by officers or committeemen in the pure and simple graft fashion the women point out its tendency and oppose it with an insight and honesty that is fine to see."[4]

The I.W.W. felt sufficiently strong in the textile industry to issue an official call in the name of the General Executive Board for the "First Convention of Textile Workers" to be held on May 1, 1908, in Paterson. ..a the call (printed in English, French, German, and Italian), the claim was made that "over 5,000 textile workers have already been organized into the Industrial Workers of the World." The 22 delegates representing seven textile workers' unions (and a delegate from the United Brotherhood of Tailors) set up the National Industrial Union of Textile Workers, which was to function as a subdivision of the "Department of Textile and Clothing Industries," and was to be composed of wage workers of all branches of labor employed in the production of textile fabrics. Before adjourning, the convention sent fraternal greetings to the Textile Congress meeting in Vienna.[5]

I.W.W. STRIKES

Strikes conducted by the I.W.W. between the second and third convention were much more successful than those in the first year of its existence, most of which were lost. In his report to the third convention, Trautmann noted that out of 24 strikes involving 15,500 members, only two were "flat failures" (the strikes of restaurant workers of Tonopah and of the Detroit car foundry workers). . . . All other strikes ended either in compromises, or in the complete attainment of what the strikes had been inaugurated for."[6] Granted that all statements by I.W.W. officials regarding gains in membership or victories in strikes must be taken with a grain of salt, yet it is true that there were some significant victories. Moreover, some of the characteristics that were later to be commonly associated with I.W.W. struggles made their appearance. One was the prominent role played by the foreign-born strikers.

This was best illustrated in the five-week strike conducted by Local No. 113 (Metal and Machinery Workers' Industrial Union) against the American Tube and Stamping Co. of Bridgeport, Conn. (Local No. 113 was divided into two branches: No. 1 composed of Hungarian and other foreign-born workers, most of them unskilled, and No. 2 of English-speaking and mainly skilled workers.) The strike began on July 15, 1907, when the company declared that the night shift workers at the West End plant would have to work continuously instead of changing with the day shift, once a month. Although the majority of those who quit were Hungarians, many English-speaking workers in the plant joined the walk-out and by the end of the day over 600 workers were on strike. A committee representing the strikers presented A.T. & S. Co.'s president Frank A. Wilmot with demands drawn up with the assistance of Samuel J. French, I.W.W. organizer. These called for a 15 per cent wage increase for the day and 20 per cent for the night shift above the average wage of from $7 to $10 a week; time and a half for all work after eight hours (later changed to ten hours); restoration of the old plan of alternating day and night shifts; no discrimination against the strikers because of their affiliation with the I.W.W. Later, another demand was added—that a shop committee, selected by the workers for the purpose of adjusting any disputes over piece work, wages or minor grievances, be recognized and dealt with by the company.[7]

President Wilmot rejected the demands, and expressed regret that the Hungarians, whom the company heretofore had regarded "as a race reasonably amenable to the laws of the country and as a whole calculated to make as large a proportion of good citizens as those coming here from other foreign countries," should let themselves become "tools" of "anarchistic and socialist agitators from other states." He threatened to move the company's plant from Bridgeport if the strikers did not immediately return to work, warning that "The property owners and store keepers of this district . . . would eventually experience a considerable loss in trade and depreciation of values in real estate. If the plant was moved hundreds of this district would have to seek employment elsewhere, and would move to more convenient districts. I understand many Hungarians own property in 'Little Hungary,' as it is called in this district."[8]

This threat did not work. Not only was the West End plant shut tight, but by July 19, the East End plant was also closed down as workers there joined the strike. "That the company is in no condition to cope with the situation," the Bridgeport *Post* reported, "is demonstrated by the fact that all business in the West and East side plants is at a standstill."[9]

On the morning of July 20, as the strikers lined up in their daily "silent demonstration" outside the struck plants, circulars were distributed among them by company representatives. Printed in Hungarian, they contained a statement, signed by President Wilmot, in which the company offered $1,000 to the children of the strikers, provided they returned to work, the money to be distributed by the pastors of the four Hungarian churches. The circular also warned the Hungarian strikers that "600 American speaking workers are ready to step into the places of the strikers at a moment's notice." But this strikebreaking maneuver also failed. "Almost as quickly as the contents of the handbills were known to the men," the Bridgeport *Post* reported, "matches were applied to the papers and they were burned."[10]

Not only were the English-speaking and Hungarian branches of the I.W.W. united in the strike, but, on the second day, the members of the A.F. of L.'s International Association of Machinists, despite the opposition of their officials, joined the strike. "Officers of the International Machinists local in the city today," reported the Bridgeport *Post* on July 17, "expressed themselves as greatly surprised that the International men had entered into the strike with the Industrial Workers as they had just been granted the 54-hour week." (On the previous day, one of these officers had told a *Post* reporter: "You can say for me that the I.A.M. are not mixed up in this strike."[11]) The company was also surprised since a major reason for granting the machinists a 54-hour week was to keep them from joining the unskilled, foreign-born workers in their battles. But Samuel J. French was not surprised. As he explained to the press: "The mistake on Mr. Wilmot's part was that he did not realize the educational influence of an organization of the I.W.W. stamp, which teaches industrial unity on the principle that an injury to one worker of whatever craft or race is an injury to all others of all crafts or races in the industry and uses printers' ink profusely in its efforts. His natural contempt for the intelligence of his 'cheap help' evidently led him to believe that an attempt to play the day and night shifts against one another would destroy this unity rather than more firmly establish it. President Wilmot naturally fails to understand how tool makers can have sufficient intelligence to stand for industrial unity with their more poorly paid fellow workers."[12]

All who commented on the strike stressed the unflinching dedication of the Hungarians. "The feature of the greatest interest connected with the strike," went one account, "was the splendid manner in which the Hungarian workers, members of the I.W.W., stood by their principles and without understanding any speakers, except those in their own tongue,* fought out the battle against a powerful corporation and opposed

---

* The Bridgeport *Post* of July 19, 1907, reported that organizer French communicated with many of the strikers "through his lieutenants who speak the languages of the foreign workers." It also reported that "a young I.W.W. lady or-

any compromise of their position."[13] Even Stewart Reid, A.F. of L. organizer in New England, was impressed, and informed Gompers that "the devotion of these Hunks to the dual union is pathetic. They sit at strike meetings listening to speakers whose speeches they cannot understand and join in the applause at the end louder than any of the others. These people still have to learn that they can get nothing of real value from a ridiculous organization like the Industrialists." Yet Reid did not permit his grudging admiration for the Hungarian strikers (mingled with a typical use of the derogatory term "Hunk") to stop him from ordering the I.M.A. local to follow the advice of their leaders and cease supporting the I.W.W. strike. He was turned down, however, and was informed that when the machinists had gone out on strike during the previous spring, they had been assisted by the I.W.W. local. The machinists told Reid that while their leaders had forgotten, they would not betray the men who had helped them. "I am leaving Bridgeport," Reid wrote to Gompers in disgust on August 22, 1907. "It looks like the Industrialists will be able to claim a victory here, although how long they will hold on to what they have, is a big question.* The machinists here are a rather poor lot, and I am quite happy to get away from them."[14]

The victory had come on August 17. The strikers voted to return to work after the company had agreed, in a conference with a committee of Hungarian businessmen, to restore the alternating day and night shifts, the ending of which practice had originally caused the strike, to arbitrate the wage question, to recognize a committee of shop employees, and to discharge anti-union foremen. Wages were raised as a result of the arbitration and the foremen were discharged. French attributed the victory to "the educational and disciplinary influence of the Industrial Workers of the World," and paid a special compliment to "the Hungarian working people of the West End for their intelligent susceptibility to these influences."[15]

On January 24, 1907, the Somerset *Reporter,* a weekly published in Skowhegan, Maine, carried the following news: "At about two thirty, Monday morning [Jan. 21], the employes of the Marston Worsted Mills, to the number of 225, united in a strike, leaving the various departments where they were employed and quitting the buildings and grounds." Trouble had been brewing at the plant since the discharge of one of the

---

ganizer, named Elizabeth Gurley Flynn," was assisting French in his work. Miss Flynn, who was seventeen in August, spent the summer months of 1907 speaking during the day to the strikers and at night at street meetings to collect money for the strike. This was her first strike activity. (Interview with Elizabeth Gurley Flynn, January 31, 1964.)

* Reid shrewdly touched as early as 1907 on a weakness that was to characterize the I.W.W. throughout most of its history—the failure to hold on to gains in strikes and consolidate their victories.

sewers, Miss Mamie Bilodeau, a militant member of Pioneer Local No. 379, I.W.W. The local had demanded a ten per cent wage increase at the beginning of the year, but had settled for a five per cent increase and the promise of an additional five per cent in July if the season was profitable. It appeared that management was out to rid the plant of active union members and rescind the wage increase. Hence when the company notified 26 weavers, also members of the I.W.W., that there was no longer any work for them, the entire working force struck. As the Somerset *Reporter* explained: "Industrial Workers of the World (Local No. 379) takes in practically all the help in the mill, both men and women. As all, or nearly all the hands are members of the organization, when the weavers were given their notice the rest of the help left." The workers struck as a body, "even the man in the boiler room who blew off the steam and pulled his fires, shutting down the plant absolutely."[16]

Within the week French arrived from New York to assist the strikers. A letter was drafted and addressed to the company demanding the reinstatement of all employed at the mill on January 7; abolition of the fining system in the finishing room; discharge of the overseer of the finishing room; settlement of minor grievances, and recognition of a committee of employees to aid in the adjustment of grievances. The response of management was blunt: "There is nothing in your requests that the mill can grant." Upon receiving this reply, the strikers unanimously resolved: "That this note be stored in the archives of Local 379 for the benefit of some future historian of Skowhegan labor troubles."[17] Along with it, it might have stored the comment by the Somerset *Reporter* that the strikers were made up of "a coterie of individuals who have come to us from other manufacturing centers in none of which they have had anything but a temporary residence."[18] Since the ranks of the strikers consisted of long-time residents of Skowhegan, it is obvious that the *Reporter* knew little about the town's working class.

With the plant completely shut down, the company would have been forced to settle early in the strike. But on February 7, the Somerset *Reporter* published a notice, at the request of the company, which management believed would force the strikers to surrender. This was a letter addressd to the employees of the Marston Worsted Mill by John Golden and Albert Hibbert, president and secretary-treasurer, respectively, of the A.F. of L.'s United Textile Workers. The letter warned the strikers against "the so-called 'Industrialists'" who "had no standing whatsoever so far as the recognized trade union movement is concerned, as exemplified by the American Federation of Labor," and whose sole policy was to pull workers out on strike "on the most flimsy pretext, knowing full well at the time they have not a dollar practically speaking to assist the people they have forced out on the street." The U.T.W. officials advised the strikers "to return to work before it is too late, and if they desire to belong to a union, organize one that will have a legitimate affiliation with the recognized trade union movement of the country." But should the strikers "fail to take advantage of this advice," the U.T.W. would not hesitate to "supply the firm" with workers to replace those on strike. These would not be "Scabs," but "Union men and women, who, while standing out for their own rights, will not lose sight of the fact that other people have rights also that must command respect and consideration at their hands."

The Somerset *Reporter* described the letter as "self explanatory." It was! The officials of the U.T.W. were publicly offering to assist the company break a strike in which every worker employed at the plant was involved, a strike called by the workers themselves without the knowledge of the national office of the I.W.W., which sent in an organizer to assist the strikers only after the workers had walked out. Any hope that management had that this letter would break the strike soon disappeared. The picket line surrounding the plant continued throughout the bitter winter when the thermometer ranged from zero to 44° below. In the face of the strikers' determined stand, the company found it impossible to take advantage of Golden's offer to fill the plant with "union scabs."[19]

On April 23, the strikers won a complete victory. The terms, as published in the press, were: Reinstatement of all workers discharged without discrimination; abolition of the fining system in both the finishing and weaving room; a day's pay for all work instead of piece work, and recognition of a shop committee to be elected by the local which was to meet with the company every two weeks to settle grievances. In July, the second five per cent increase in wages was granted by the company.[20]

The "sit-down" tactic was introduced by the I.W.W. on December 10, 1906, in the strike of the General Electric Industrial Workers' Union of Schenectady, N.Y. When the General Electric Co. refused to reinstate three discharged draftsmen, members of the I.W.W., 3,000 I.W.W. workers at the plants struck in what was called "regular syndicalist fashion." "At 2 o'clock the members of the I.W.W. quit work, but remained in the shops," reported the Schenectady *Union*. "They did not walk out," observed another paper, "but remained at their places, simply stopping production."[21] How long they remained in the shops without working is difficult to determine. The contemporary press carried no further report on the sit-down phase of the strike, but years later, an I.W.W. member who interviewed some of those engaged in the sit-down, wrote: "The sitdowners stayed in the plant 65 hours receiving food and drink from outside friends."[22]

Condemned for shutting down the entire works because of the grievance of three members, the strikers' press committee replied that although the I.W.W. at General Electric was composed of craft locals, it operated according to the principles of industrial unionism: "The case is clearly one of discrimination against three members of the I.W.W., and as such the question of numbers discriminated against does not enter into the matter. For the simple reason that if discrimination is permitted in one case, who then can feel he is protected? The principle of organization is that protection reaches down to the last man."[23]

"The action of the strikers has crippled the works," reported the Schenectady *Union*. "At the power plant nearly all of the employes were I.W.W. men and when they left, it was necessary for the officials of the company and technical students to operate it."[24] But the strikers were unable to win the support of the A.F. of L. Trades' Assembly which ordered all members of its affiliated unions to continue working for G.E. "We do not recognize the Industrial Workers of the World as a bona-fide labor organization, or its members as union members," the A.F. of L. body informed the press. "As to any individual organization affiliated with the American Federation of Labor going out in sympathetic strike, such action would result in the forfeiture of its charter."[25] It was clear that the strike could not succeed, and on December 20, even though the company still refused to rehire the discharged draftsmen, the I.W.W. members called off the strike and voted to return to work.[26]

The strategy used in the Portland, Ore., sawmill workers' strike in March and April 1907 was so startling that it commanded attention all over the country. On March 1, 1907, workers in one of Portland's mills walked off their jobs and a strike was on. Unorganized and practically unled, the men had asked for higher wages and having been turned down, they walked out. But the I.W.W. members had not been unprepared and before long they had taken over leadership of the strike and had organized a flourishing group in Portland. W. J. Yarrow, Portland leader of the I.W.W., told the *Oregonian*: "This situation [the strike] is not the product of a day's work. We have been working along the line of organizing workmen in the lumber mills on the Coast for the last ten weeks and we are now in a position to control the organization."[27]

The agitation at the mills took effect, and the natural result followed —a strike. By March 7, the strike was well under way. Portland's four largest mills and many of the smaller ones were closed, and the I.W.W. was recruiting members rapidly. Mass picket lines surrounded plants which were still operating, and the men were called out, many of them being signed up on the spot. On March 7, the *Oregonian* reported: "Late yesterday afternoon a delegation of more than 200 of the strikers went to the yards of the Inman-Poulsen Company and induced 47 of the members of the night shift to leave the yards. A procession was formed and the new recruits were marched to the union headquarters . . . where they signed the membership roll of the Industrial Workers of the World."

Commenting editorially on this news report, the *Oregonian* noted: "Where the A.F. of L. has failed, the I.W.W. at one leap is succeeding. The federation is slow to organize unskilled workers, the I.W.W. is quick to do so. This is why the sawmill men are joining the numerically weaker organization."[28]

The I.W.W. hired an excursion boat to make it easier to visit mills in the area, inviting men to join them on strike. Notices were sent to all cities in the Northwest advising workers to stay away from Portland because a strike was on, and committees from the I.W.W. met each incoming train to "take in charge all laborers arriving in the city."[29] On March 8, the *Oregonian* reported: "Today, at the end of the first week of the saw-mill laborers' strike, the lumber industry of Portland is completely paralyzed. Not a pulley is revolving at any of the four big mills, and two of the smaller concerns are temporarily out of business. Fifteen hundred men are idle. A man could hardly throw a brick in the north end this morning without hitting a man with a ribbon on his coat. As fast as the mill laborers are organized they are given red ribbons and told to wear them."

On the same day, March 8, the *Oregonian* described a curious meeting of the strikers: "Strikers last night formulated their demands, which embraces a minimum schedule of $2.50 for nine hours' labor for all mill workers. In box factories the minimum wage for box nailers is fixed at $3, for the nine-hour day with an increase of 25 cents per day for all other employes." This meeting took place a week after the walkout, yet up to this point no demands had been formulated by the strikers. The strategy, which was to be used often in I.W.W. strikes in the Northwest lumber industry,[30] was based on the idea of presenting the employers with demands when the strike was in full swing and when they could see that they were dealing with a powerful movement. On March 8, the *Oregonian* reported that "the ultimatum of the strikers will be presented mill owners today and if advanced wages are not granted the Industrial Workers of the World threaten to declare a general strike."

The mill owners replied by locking out the strikers, and stating emphatically that they were used to dealing with their workers directly and were "not prepared to substitute the new order of things." The employers denounced the strike as an "imported disturbance not incited by the laboring men themselves . . . but because they have been unduly intimidated by influences that are directing the strike." Yet if there was any "disturbance," it was only in the minds of the employers. On March 12, with the walkout already in progress 11 days, the *Oregonian* noted that it "has been the most orderly one that Portland has ever seen. With 2300 men out [of a total of 2500 mill workers in Portland], and the strike headquarters . . . surrounded by saloons, there has been no drunkenness or violence and only one arrest. This was on the charge of refusal to move on when directed to do so by an officer. The men are directed by the strike leaders to preserve order and the peaceful conduct of the strikers is causing surprise."[31]

The I.W.W. made immediate efforts to gain as many allies as possible. Many of the craftsmen in the city were mobilized to aid in the struggle, and longshoremen, carpenters, bricklayers, and others also lent their help. Miss Nina Wood, I.W.W. organizer, helped to set up a woman's brigade in aid of the strikers. Support came from loggers, and contributions of money from unions and sympathizers all over the country, including a large donation from the W.F. of M., were reported in the Portland press. "Not one of the striking men will go hungry or lack for a place to sleep," W. J. Yarrow declared. "In this fight we have the backing of the Industrial Workers of the World throughout the country and we will have all necessary funds with which to wage our fight. We have arranged to care for the strikers through the medium of a soup house and ample bunking accomodations. We will stand together in insisting that the increase in wages is granted. We are not only in the fight to win, but we will win."[32]

The hard-hit employers received valuable support from the A.F. of L. Labeling the I.W.W. "socialistic," the Portland Federated Trade Council announced that it would not endorse or in any way support the strike. Furthermore, C. H. Gram, president of the Oregon Federation of Labor, declared in an interview with a reporter that the "Federation was not only not in sympathy with the striking millhands, but would fail to lend the strikers any assistance while they were affiliated with the Industrial Workers of the World because that organization was recognized as an agency for disrupting the Federation." In answer, the I.W.W. published and distributed a circular which went in part:

"Mr. Gram says that the Industrial Workers of the World was started for the purpose of disrupting the American Federation of Labor. Nothing could be further from the facts, and this statement is a malicious lie and could only be hatched in the brain of a labor faker. . . . No, fellow workers, we have nothing against any man who has to work for wages, which includes the rank and file of the A.F. of L., but we have something against liars and fakers of the Gram type. Moral support and flowery resolutions count for nothing in time of strikes. It is action that counts. . . .

"He [Mr. Gram] cannot come into the Industrial Workers of the World, as we do not tolerate labor fakers any longer than the time it takes to fire them out, a job which we had to do at our last convention.

"Trusting that no union man will haul or handle in any manner the product of the sawmills and box factories. . . ."[33]

The dispute between the A.F. of L. and the I.W.W. undoubtedly damaged the strike. The attack on President Gram gave the Federated Trade

Council and the Federation of Labor the excuse for threatening expulsion for any A.F. of L. local union which assisted the strike, and a number of A.F. of L. members indicated that the circular had diminished their sympathy for the strikers. Gram himself pointed this out in a letter to Gompers which enclosed the I.W.W. circular. "The dual unionists have overplayed their hand this time," he wrote, "and we should have no difficulty convincing our people that support for the Industrialists is treachery to the true labor cause." That this was no vain boast is revealed by the following report in the *Oregonian:* " 'Until this time,' said a member of the Federation of Labor last night, 'the members of our organization have expressed great sympathy for the striking mill hands and have hoped that they might win in their contentions for better wages and a shorter workday, but the publication of such circulars . . . will not conduce to a promotion of this feeling of sympathy or enlist from us a more active co-operation.' "[34]

The strike lasted 40 days before it was called off by the I.W.W. The organization claimed that since most of the strikers had secured work elsewhere through the services of the I.W.W.'s free employment office, there was no point in continuing the struggle. Still, it claimed victory on two grounds: (1) "The mill owners were forced to pay the scale and later on will be forced to grant the hours," and (2) "From the standpoint of industrial unionism the strike has been a great success. Thousands of men have been educated and the organization greatly strengthened."[35] Had not the A.F. of L. scabbed on the strike, the I.W.W. declared, it would have gained an even greater victory.

The contemporary press questioned the I.W.W. claim of a victory, contending that the strike was lost largely because of the dispute with the A.F. of L., though some concessions, such as slightly improved wages for some of the workers, were gained. But it was generally conceded that, in the larger sense, the first important I.W.W. action in the Northwest was spectacularly successful. As Vernon H. Jensen puts it: "Although in one sense the strike was lost, it brought the organization to the attention of the public besides securing improvements in wages and conditions."[36] On March 31, 1907, the *Oregon Journal* ran a feature article by John Kenneth Turner entitled, "Story of a New Labor Union" which aroused widespread attention in the Northwest, and when reprinted in the press throughout the country and circulated as a leaflet by the I.W.W., created considerable discussion in other parts of the nation as well:

"Portland has just passed through her first strike conducted by the Industrial Workers of the World, a new and strange form of unionism which is taking root in every section of the United States, especially in the West. The suddenness of the strike and the completeness of the tie-up are things quite unprecedented in this part of the country. These conditions did not merely happen—they came as direct results of the peculiar form and philosophy of the movement that brought the strike into being. . . . Wherever the Industrial Workers of the World are organized they can paralyze industry at almost the snap of a finger. It is the way they work. . . .

"There is no workman so poor, old or unskilled but what the Industrial Workers will organize him gladly. It makes no difference if he is white, black or yellow. As long as he works for wages he will be taken in and will receive the same consideration as the strongest and most skilled. . . .

"If you are a business man, or if for any reason you consider that the business interests of the community are your interests, you should choose the American Federation of Labor. The Industrial Workers of the World have no respect for business interests. But if you are looking for a form of organization best calculated to paralyze a given industry in the briefest possible time, you should choose the Industrial Workers of the World."[37]

Whatever the exact nature of the immediate outcome, the Portland strike resulted in bringing the name of the I.W.W. to the attention of workers of the Pacific Northwest, and, in the words of Vincent St. John, "gave much impetus to the I.W.W. agitation in the western part of the United States." A report from Seattle in the *Industrial Union Bulletin* stated: "The Portland strike of the I.W.W. is talked about in all labor circles, and as such, shows conclusively to the worker that there is only one kind of organization worthy of serious consideration—industrial unionism."[38]

It was, however, at Goldfield, Nevada, in the years 1906–08 that the I.W.W. made the first real test of its principles of revolutionary industrial unionism.

Although the miners at Goldfield had been organized for over a year in the W.F. of M. when the I.W.W. was launched, the town workers were still mainly employed in open shops. The only A.F. of L. unions were those of the carpenters and printers; although feeble attempts had been made to organize the other workers into a Federal Union, this had come to very little. Early in 1906, the unorganized workers at Goldfield were unionized and brought together in a body which became known as Local No. 77 of the I.W.W. Local 77 absorbed the old federal union, and later amalgamated with the W.F. of M., Local No. 220, thereby creating a "mass" union which included practically all the wage earners in the community. "In the organization," the I.W.W. official journal boasted, "were miners, engineers, clerks, stenographers, teamsters, dishwashers, waiters—all sorts of what are called common laborers." It announced that the I.W.W.'s slogan, "An injury to one is an injury to all," would be put into effect the moment any group of members were attacked by the employers.[39]

The power of the "mass" union soon made itself evident. In a series of swift strikes, miners won a wage scale of $5.00 for eight hours for all skilled labor and for all underground work, and $4.50 for unskilled labor. Bakers secured $8.00 and board for an eight-hour day; dishwashers, $3.00 and board for an eight-hour day; restaurant and hotel employees, $3.00 to $5.00 and board for an eight-hour day; clerks, $5.00 for a ten-hour day, and bartenders, $6.00 for an eight-hour day. In addition to improvements in wages and hours, the union won complete job control by the workers. Even the Goldfield *Gossip,* a bitter opponent of the I.W.W. union (advocating that all members be "hanged . . . to telegraph poles.") admitted that as soon as the industrial union entered Goldfield, "its advantage to the workers, to the men and women for example, who were employed as waiters at restaurants, was immediately apparent. Where these men and women had previously been called upon to work for twelve or fifteen hours a day for a small wage, they found themselves, as members of the I.W.W. commanding a higher wage, enjoying a union scale, and working only eight hours a day."[40]

"Radicals," "Agitators," "I-Won't-Works," "Hydrophobias," "Anarchists," "Trouble breeders," were some of the milder epithets applied to the leaders of the I.W.W., especially Vincent St. John who came to Goldfield, in November 1906. The employers and their hired press were especially infuriated by a demonstration held by the I.W.W. union on January 20, 1907. The date was chosen in commemoration of "Bloody Sunday" in St. Petersburg, Russia, January 22, 1905. But a chief purpose of the meeting was to protest the imprisonment of Moyer, Haywood, and Pettibone. By order of the union all mines and leases were closed, and even all restaurants and saloons for two hours during the parade, which had over 3,000 union members, headed by the newsboys, all wearing tiny red flags. It was the largest demonstration ever seen in Goldfield. At the close, Vincent St. John made a stirring speech and a series of resolutions were passed with great enthusiasm. One denounced the imprisonment of the three labor leaders, labeled the Supreme Court as the tool of corporate greed, and demanded that its members be elected by popular vote. Another sent "true revolutionary greetings" to the working class of Russia, Poland, and Finland, and closed: "We have no enemy but the capitalist class! Our country is the world! Our flag is the banner that is dyed red with the Martyr's blood of our class! Down with capitalism!"[41]

To meet these alarming developments, a Committee of Safety and the Goldfield Business Men's and Mine Operators' Association were established in March 1907. The employers' association quickly hit on the tactic of trying to split off the miners from the rest of the amalgamated union. In this work, the employers' association had the full cooperation of the state and local A.F. of L. officials. A.F. of L. organizers moved into Goldfield for the sole purpose of luring members from Local No. 220 whose organizing tactics were denounced as "out of reason in sane unionism." In

March 1907, Grant Hamilton, A.F. of L. organizer, wrote to Gompers from Goldfield:

"I arrived here a week ago, and have been actively engaged ever since in addressing two or three meetings every night. You are no doubt aware that this is a stronghold of the I.W.W. I am sorry to report that they have had considerable success here thus far, having organized most of the workers in the region. They have won victories by their tactics of terror, but even some of our members seem to feel that since these tactics get results, we, too, ought to adopt them. There are, however, some more sensible people even in the I.W.W. union, especially among the miners, and I hope to convince them that these tactics will only hurt them in the end and that they can best help themselves by joining a level-headed organization. I am informed that no obstacles would be put in the way of these men becoming members of the A.F. of L. because the mine owners do not want the I.W.W. to gain a real foothold here. With the miners separated from the rest, it would be an easy matter to get the other working men into line."[42]

The Goldfield papers hailed the arrival of the A.F. of L. organizers. "As a labor organization representing the best ideals and methods, we welcome them," declared the Goldfield *Chronicle*.[43] But the A.F. of L.'s efforts to break up the amalgamated union had no noticeable success. Vincent St. John wrote from Goldfield late in March 1907: "The situation is in our hands. . . . All efforts to disrupt us by the Mine Owners', Citizens' Alliance and the A.F. of L. are failures. Victory is ours to date."[44]

The employers' association now took more direct action by locking out the miners and other members of Local 220. Then, in a public statement, it declared that "conditions are becoming intolerable through constant and unreasonable agitation on the part of the leaders of an organization known as the Industrial Workers of the World," and pledged themselves "to absolutely refuse to employ any man in any capacity who is a member of the Industrial Workers of the World." At the same time, however, they announced they would recognize "any miners' union that is independent of the I.W.W., [and that] other business interests and industries will recognize and employ members of separate craft organizations not affiliated with or under the jurisdiction of the Industrial Workers of the World." They announced further "that this action is irrevocable," urged the miners to separate from the I.W.W. and "thus preserve their honor and manhood," and assured the miners that they had no intention of modifying or changing "in any way the present conditions or wages or hours" in effect in the camps.[45]

The employers' strategy was based on the knowledge that relations between the national W.F. of M. and the national I.W.W. had deteriorated since the I.W.W. convention in Chicago, that dissension had been developing in the miners' union on this question, and that conservative members of the W.F. of M. in Goldfield were anxious to dissociate themselves from the more radical I.W.W. members. The Goldfield correspondent of the Chicago *Journal of Finance* wrote: "If this program [of the employers' association] is carried out it will leave Acting President [Charles] Mahoney of the Western Federation of Miners in charge of the situation. . . . His enmity to the I.W.W. is not concealed."[46]

The conservatives in the W.F. of M. made an effort to have the miners and town workers meet separately, thereby hoping to end the influence of the more radical I.W.W. members in the affairs of the miners. Over the opposition of the town workers and many miners, they forced the two groups in Local 220—the miners and the town workers—to divide. As soon as the split became official, the mine owners agreed to end the lockout, recognize the miners' union and establish the same hours and wages that had existed prior to the lockout. But they continued to lock out I.W.W. members, and filled their places with scabs furnished by the A.F. of L.[47]

The W.F. of M. accepted the employers' terms and the mines resumed operation on April 22, 1907. Soon enough, however, the miners discovered that, having succeeded in splitting off the miners from the rest of the workers in Goldfield, the employers would now seek to destroy the W.F. of M. The mine owners deliberately provoked the break with the union by announcing that, owing to the financial panic that had started in October 1907, they would not pay wages in cash but only in cashier's checks and company scrip. The miners then resolved that "all members of this union refuse to work for any employer who will not pay the wages of his men in legal tender or satisfactorily guarantee the paper issued in lieu of the same." When the mine owners refused to guarantee the paper issue, the miners walked out on November 27. The businessmen, newspapers, and the A.F. of L. unions immediately lined up on the side of the operators.[48]

Throughout the months of struggle following the formation of Local 220, Goldfield had been an armed camp. Armed guards, furnished by the Business Men's and Mine Operators' Association, had patroled the streets.* But to smash the miners' union, the employers needed more than their own private army. Nevada, however, had no militia, so Governor John Sparks, after consultations with the mine owners, mine operators,

---

* In self-defense union leaders and members also went about armed. Vincent St. John carried a gun with him when he was attacked by a company agent, but he could not draw it quickly enough. He was shot in both hands, and his right hand was permanently crippled as a result. (*Industrial Union Bulletin,* Nov. 16, 1907.) An armed battle between Morrie R. Preston, officer of the union, and John Silva, a restaurant owner whose place was being picketed, resulted in Silva being killed. Although Preston shot in self-defense after Silva had raised his gun toward him, he was sentenced to 25 years in the State penitentiary. He was released on parole in

and mill operators, sent a telegram to President Roosevelt requesting Federal troops. The President assured Governor Sparks that he was prepared to send a detachment of troops, but he must first have a description of the conditions that would justify the Federal government in acting. The Governor, having been shown the path to follow, immediately wired: "At Goldfield . . . there does now exist domestic violence and unlawful combinations and conspiracies . . . unlawful dynamiting of property, commission of felonies, threats against the lives of law-abiding citizens, the unlawful possession of arms and ammunition, and the confiscation of dynamite and threats of the unlawful use of same by preconcerted action."[49]

In response to this telegram, and without even bothering to consult other sources which contradicted it, such as newspaper reports that the miners were keeping the peace in every way, President Roosevelt sent federal troops to Goldfield. When the troops arrived the mine operators went into action. They cut the wage rate from five to four dollars per day, and forced each worker to sign a "yellow dog" contract, in which he had to swear that he was not and would not become a member of the union while in the company's employ. Other industries in the vicinity also took advantage of the existing conditions to lower wages and smash unionism. Thus under the cover of federal protection, the mine owners and other employers in Goldfield set out to make the area an open-shop center.

Trade unions throughout the country deluged the White House with protests, condemning Roosevelt for sending troops when there was not the slightest evidence of violence. In the House of Representatives Isaac Sherwood of Ohio was greeted with applause when he said: "The President like the Secretary of War had a labor record that needs extensive patching to make it presentable. . . . Contrary to all precedent, contrary to law, in order to aid the mine owners to crush out the miners' union, the President called out the United States troops." An Iowan complained to Senator Jonathan Dolliver of that state that "it appears to a great many people that the federal troops are now being used for the benefit of the mine owners in the settlement of strikes." The miners themselves accused the President of having been motivated "by personal hatred against the Western Federation of Miners and its officers."[50]

Roosevelt was forced to appoint a commission to investigate the need for troops, and its report blasted Governor Sparks and the mine operators. As for the Governor's request for troops, it declared: "Our investigation so far completely has failed to sustain the general and sweeping allegations in the Governor calling for troops, and the impression as to con-

---

1914 after serving seven years. The Board of Parole Commissioners in voting the parole stated that he was convicted on testimony that "was perjured." (*Solidarity*, June 6, 1914.)

ditions here given in that call is misleading and without warrant." The demand for troops, it continued, was part of the plot to destroy the miners' union and reduce wages, but the mine operators "feared to take this course of action unless they had the protection of Federal troops, and that they accordingly laid a plan to secure such troops, and then put their programme into effect."[51]

Unfortunately, this unusually frank report was of little assistance to the miners' union, for, under the protection of the federal troops, the operators had been able to fill the mines with scabs. Moreover, despite the Commission's report, President Roosevelt did not withdraw the troops. Instead, they were permitted to remain "for a reasonable length of time" until the Nevada legislature had established a state militia. The legislature was called into special session and speedily passed a "State Police Bill." The local W.F. of M. and I.W.W. jointly adopted a resolution which condemned the establishment of a "state militia" as being "inimical to the interests of state sovereignty [and] . . . a relic of antedeluvian, fossilized, fiendish barbarism. . . . We raise our voices in protest [against] creating the organization as legalized, uniformed murderers, misnamed or called, under the disguise of the state militia."[52] But the joint action of the two organizations came too late in the struggle to save the strike.

On January 30, 1908, after the police bill had been approved by the Governor, the operators, now assured of continued protection for the scabs, posted regulations at each mine which eliminated the I.W.W. and W.F. of M. from employment, and insured an open-shop policy. The strike petered out, and when the miners went down to defeat, unionism in Goldfield for all workers sank into oblivion.[53]

Despite the tragic final outcome for both the W.F. of M. and the I.W.W., doubly tragic because it was hastened by the internecine war that had developed between the two organizations, the achievements of the I.W.W. in Goldfield during the years of 1906 and 1907 proved that far from being dead the organization was capable of organizing an entire locality. "We proceeded," the I.W.W.'s official journal declared proudly, "without force, without intimidation, without deportations, and without murder, to organize all wage workers in the community."[54]

THIRD I.W.W. CONVENTION

The third convention of the I.W.W. met in September 1907. Although over 900 locals had been organized since the I.W.W. was launched, there were only about 200 in existence, representing a total membership of about 6,000. Of these only 74 local unions were represented by delegates—53 in number—the others being too poor to send delegates. Financially, the organization was "in the red"; Secretary-Treasurer Trautmann revealed that for the period from October 1906 to August 1907, receipts were $30,050.75 and disbursements, $31,578.76. He hoped, however, to collect enough money due from local unions after the convention to wipe out the deficit.[55]

Naturally, whatever interest was aroused by the third convention in the press was concentrated entirely on the question as to whether the factions which had won out over Sherman in 1906 would split apart.[56] It had been taken for granted in 1906 that sooner or later there would come a show-down between the De Leon faction and the one led by St. John and Trautmann. Certainly there were signs even before the third convention that the alliance was beginning to weaken. The official organ of the I.W.W. noted with displeasure early in 1907 that in the discussion in the columns of *The People* during the months November 1906 to February 1907, consisting of 13 letters to the paper with answers by De Leon, the editor, the S.L.P. leader attacked those in the I.W.W. who opposed political action, and warned that "the rejection of political action would throw the I.W.W. back upon the methods of barbarism." But, in the main, the I.W.W. journal treated De Leon with a good deal of respect during this period. The March 9, 1907, issue featured the text of De Leon's speech in Chicago under the auspices of the I.W.W., and particularly emphasized his statement that "It is folly to contend that the Republic of Labor can be set up or maintained without the union, and those who talk of political action simply, unsupported by the industrial organization are wrong." It observed editorially that De Leon now realized that "such economic organization (industrial unions) must be supreme and separate from the political movement." Insofar as he now understood the truth of this doctrine, De Leon was proving himself to be "a profound economist and student of industrial relations." Nevertheless, the *Bulletin* made it clear that praise of De Leon did not mean that the I.W.W. was subservient to the party he headed.[57]

As was to be expected then, the tone of the third convention was "one of harmony." The only controversy rose over the political clause of the Preamble, and though the debate was lengthy, it was not bitter. A motion was again introduced by the direct-actionists to delete from the Preamble the exhortation to workers to "come together on the political . . . field." Bu De Leon spoke out vigorously against the proposal, and the majority of the delegates upheld his position. The motion was defeated over-whelmingly, 113 to 15.[58] In its "Reflection on the Third Annual Convention," the *Industrial Union Bulletin* hailed the fact that there had been a complete absence of the "destructive tactics of the (1906) assembly," attributed this to the fact that it "was a gathering typically working-class and loyal . . . to the workers," and concluded that there could no longer be any doubt of the stability of the organization. "Its future is full of promise."[59]

ECONOMIC CRISIS AND THE UNEMPLOYED

Barely was this prediction made early in October 1907, when a severe financial panic hit the country. In the last week of October, the New York stock market crashed, and several banks closed. The succeeding depression of 1907–08 hit the working class severely. "There are 184,000 men out of work in New York City alone," a labor paper estimated in the spring of 1908. "There are at least 75,000 out of work in Chicago. There are 30,000 out of work in St. Louis. There must be more than 500,000 unemployed in the whole country on the most conservative estimate." The wages of those working were cut from 15 to 50 per cent.[60]

The crisis nearly wiped the I.W.W. out of existence. The depression had a particularly serious effect on the unskilled and semi-skilled workers who made up the bulk of the I.W.W. membership. *Il Proletario* and other foreign language I.W.W. papers were forced to suspend publication. From August 8 to December 12, 1908, the *Industrial Union Bulletin* appeared fortnightly instead of weekly, suspended publication temporarily between December 12, 1908, and February 20, 1909, and ceased publication with the March 6, 1909, issue. I.W.W. locals dissolved by the dozens and the general headquarters in Chicago "was the only maintained by terrific sacrifice and determination." The hope of collecting money due from local unions, expressed at the third convention, vanished; before collections could be arranged, the general secretary explained, "the industrial panic struck the country with all its force, and the misery following in the wake of that collapse, was mostly felt in places where the Industrial Workers of the World had established a stronghold." As a result, the revenue for December 1907 was not more than half of what it had been the year before.[61]

Fighting for its very existence, the I.W.W. virtually suspended organization of workers into unions and gave up its strike activities. However, it boasted that it was winning support of large sections of the working class because of its activity on behalf of the unemployed. However, there was some dispute within the I.W.W. whether the organization should even be involved in fighting for immediate relief for those out of work. There were those, for example, who adhered to the theory that "immediate demands" to solve the unemployment problem, such as shortening the work day or providing public works, were a waste of time, and that the only answer was for the workers to take over and operate the industries.[62] The *Industrial Union Bulletin,* on the other hand, emphasized the need for a mass campaign for a shorter work day through economic action. "We do not share the view that the unemployed can be entirely eliminated under the capitalist system. But that unemployment can be greatly reduced in volume by the action of an economic organization in shortening the work day and dividing up the work at hand, goes without much argument."[63] The editorial was entitled "Special Agitation For a Shorter Work Day." But the I.W.W. was scarcely in a position to do much in this direction. Most of its energy was spent in leading the unemployed in local demonstrations.

In January 1908, the I.W.W. in St. Louis led 600 marchers to the City Hall to demand work from the government. In the same month, meetings and parades of the unemployed were organized by the I.W.W. in Chicago and Boston.[64] In February, Local No. 196 led a successful demonstration in Youngstown, Ohio, for work for the unemployed on public improvements. The Youngstown *Daily Vindicator* reported: "The board of service was swamped by men, led by the Industrial Workers of the World, asking for employment, and the board has agreed to act. The men will be employed in three-day shifts as long as there is not sufficient work to give all steady jobs. As soon as possible a larger gang will be put to work grading the new road."[65]

The New York Propaganda League, organized by the I.W.W. on April 21, 1908,* carried on systematic agitation for unemployment relief throughout the city at open-air meetings. Speakers in English, Yiddish, and Italian, including 18 year-old Elizabeth Gurley Flynn, addressed the meetings on the need for organization to end a system which doomed so many workers to starvation in the midst of plenty. Miss Flynn also addressed an unemployed demonstration, organized by the I.W.W., at Philadelphia's City Hall Park in August 1908, after the industrial union had been barred from the Unemployed Council by the A.F. of L.'s Building Trades' Unions.† Even the Philadelphia *Press* had to report the fact "there were more unemployed at the City Hall Plaza yesterday to hear speakers representing the Industrial Workers of the World than have ever attended a demonstration in this city in recent years."[66]

When the I.W.W. mobilized the unemployed of Los Angeles to de-

---

* The League was formed solely for propaganda, and a worker who joined it did so for the sole purpose of taking an active part in the work of propaganda. If he wished to join the I.W.W. proper, his application would be referred to the local union of his industry, already in existence, or to the district organizer.

† Miss Flynn delivered her first public speech on January 31, 1906, at the age of 16 before the Harlem Socialist Club. She joined the I.W.W. in 1906, becoming a member of Mixed Local No. 179, in New York City. Thereafter, she was in constant demand as a speaker. Referring to a speech she delivered in Duluth in November 1907, the *Industrial Union Bulletin* called her "The Girl with a Mission": "Elizabeth Gurley Flynn is nothing if not earnest. Socialistic fervor seems to emanate from her expressive eyes, and even from her red dress. She is a girl with a 'mission,' with a big 'M.' " On March 15, 1908, the Los Angeles *Times,* under the heading, "Most Bloodthirsty of Agitators Are the She-Dogs of Anarchy," wrote: "E. G. Flynn is said to be only 17, but her power of speech has won her spellbound audiences all over the eastern cities. . . . Never has she advised violence. But the teachings of the young girl are so intensely radical, and her demand for action so vehement that she is assured of a royal welcome from any audience of extremists."

mand a public works program, the police commissioner ordered a halt to street meetings to advance this campaign. When the I.W.W. defied the order, its leaders were arrested and jailed. However, the city and county authorities were forced to appropriate money for a public works program.[67]

In Seattle, where thousands of workers were reported to be "starving" by the winter of 1908, the I.W.W. and the A.F. of L. cooperated in the unemployed movement. On January 20, 1908, a huge parade of the unemployed took place in that city under the joint auspices of 24 I.W.W. and A.F. of L. locals whose delegates had previously met to arrange the demonstration. The City Council, responding to the pressure, appropriated $3,000 to build roads and establish camps outside of the city. Unemployed were to receive board and lodging and 25 cents per day.[68]

Out of the distressed economic conditions and unemployed struggles of the Northwest emerged one of the great songs of the I.W.W. A dispatch to the *Industrial Union Bulletin* from Spokane tells the story:

"There are so many hundred idle men in this country that many around the headquarters have little to do but study the question, compose poetry and work up songs for old tunes. It might be of interest to some to know about the program that has been followed out in this city for a few weeks and which has its effect. Among the I.W.W. membership there are a few good singers as well as jaw-mouths, and their genius has been expressed in the following composition and the rendition at street meetings as well as in the hall" and the song follows:

Hallelujah I'm a Bum!
  (Air: Revive Us Again.)

O, why don't you work
As other men do?
How in hell can I work
When there's no work to do?

  (Chorus)
Hallelujah! I'm a Bum!
Hallelujah, bum again,
Hallelujah! give us a hand-out,
To revive us again!

O, I like my boss.
He's a good friend of mine,
That's why I'm starving
Out in the bread-line!

(Chorus)
I can't buy a job,
For I've not got the 'dough.'
So I ride in a box car
And am a hobo.
(Chorus)

The words to the song appeared for the first time in the *Industrial Union Bulletin* of April 4, 1908. A month later, a dispatch from Spokane reported that it was "now being sung not only here, but also in the surrounding towns and camps, by those who, having heard it here, are now scattered after the deplorable 'job.' This song is not scientific in the strict sense, but it is not without its effect in keeping alive 'the holy flame of discontent.' "[69]

Out of the economic crisis in the Northwest emerged not only a song that was to exert an influence on the course of the I.W.W. but also a new type of worker who was to play an important role in the organization. "We are confronting a new condition in the labor movement in the northwest," wrote J. H. Walsh from Spokane in July 1908. "Every train in this country is loaded with dozens of 'hoboes' (working men looking for jobs), and in some instances there are hundreds in place of dozens. . . . The men coming to the headquarters report the same news day after day, and that is that this unemployed army is getting larger and larger." I.W.W. organizers at Spokane, Seattle, and Portland met the trains as they came into the city; handed out leaflets to the "hoboes" inviting them to the I.W.W. halls, signed them up into the union, and led them in demonstrations for relief and work. Other "hoboes" who had been jailed as vagrants were approached in the same way as soon as they were released from prison. "We are meeting with great success in reaching these unemployed as they come in on the trains or out of jail," an I.W.W. organizer wrote from the Northwest. "We don't propose to form a 'Coxey's Army' to march to Washington, but we do propose to form a militant army to march to the local authorities for jobs, 'ham-and-eggs,' and 'pork-chops.' "[70]

This was the element that played so important a role in the second and most serious internal struggle in the I.W.W.'s career. It came at the fourth convention in 1908.

THE FOURTH CONVENTION AND THE SECOND SPLIT

In 1906, after the delegates to the second convention of the I.W.W. ousted the president, a number of industrial unionists from the Socialist Party withdrew from the I.W.W. Then when the W.F. of M. broke off all connection with the I.W.W., still more members identified with the

Socialist Party withdrew. And when A. M. Simons and Eugene V. Debs were no longer connected with the I.W.W., many other rank and file I.W.W. members who were also members of the Socialist Party quit the industrial union.

One effect of the departure of many Socialist Party members was to strengthen the position of the direct-action, anarcho-syndicalist element in the I.W.W. Most of these elements now held the Socialist Party and all its work in contempt. For one thing, they felt that the party was a worthless reform movement run by "sky pilots" (ministers), lawyers, politicians, editors, and small businessmen, or, as Trautmann expressed it, "the bourgeois element of lawyers and intellectual swaggerers."[71]

Then again, what the I.W.W. called the "lying report" of the S.P. delegation to the International Socialist and Labor Convention at Stuttgart in August 1907 had deepened its contempt for the leadership of the party. Morris Hillquit and A. M. Simons—S.P. delegates to the Stuttgart convention—attacked the I.W.W. for dividing the workers and recommended endorsement only of "boring within the A.F. of L." In reply, F. W. Heslewood, speaking for the I.W.W., accused the Socialist Party of being merely a "vote-getting machine . . . [which] will stoop to anything and *go to any length to secure votes*. They have defended a lot of scab unions of the A.F. of L. in California, have endorsed resolutions condemning the Japanese and asking for their exclusion from America, although we find that the Japanese, with very little education in revolutionary unionism, make better union men than the sacred contract scab of the A.F. of L." The so-called "neutrality" of the S.P. in its relations with labor organizations, he charged, boiled down to support of the "agents" of the capitalist class. Essentially, "neutrality" towards trade unions was "equivalent to neutrality towards the machinations of the capitalist class."[72]

The stand taken by the Socialist delegates at the 1907 A.F. of L. convention and by the Socialist Party at its May 1908 convention only confirmed the I.W.W.'s view of the party. At the 1907 A.F. of L. convention, when Gompers presented the facts of N.A.M.'s attempt to bribe him, Berger arose and promised that the Socialist delegates would vote to make Gompers' re-election unanimous, and that he himself would second the nomination. He proudly reported that the declaration was followed by "a storm of applause such as has been rarely heard in any convention." Even though Gompers effectively crushed Berger's effort to conduct a discussion of socialism on the usual ground of "no politics in the A.F. of L.," the Wisconsin Socialist felt that the applause that greeted his declaration of support for the A.F. of L. president was proof that "a *common basis* was found for united *action* for the Socialist trade unionists and the so-called 'Pure and Simplers.'" To the I.W.W. it simply proved that the Socialists had surrendered even the pretense of struggle to oust the A.F. of L. bureaucracy.

At the 1908 Socialist Party convention, which met in Chicago May 10–17, attacks by the Center and Right on the I.W.W. for its extreme radicalism were coupled with demands that Socialists "bore from within" the A.F. of L. rather than join the I.W.W. The side-stepping of the issue of craft versus industrial unionism and the refusal to endorse the latter, the passage of a resolution favoring the restriction of immigration, and of a constitutional amendment restricting party membership to those who advocated "political action as a weapon of the working class" by providing for the expulsion of any member who opposed such action—were all concrete proofs to the militants in the I.W.W. that the Socialist Party was in no sense of the word a genuinely revolutionary movement. And the fact that the Center and Right publicly proclaimed that the party had given up revolution for reform still further convinced the direct-actionists in the I.W.W. that there was no room in the industrial union for the Socialist Party ideology.[73]

Meanwhile, an argument over economic theory was taking place in the I.W.W. between the De Leonites and those who opposed their view. The issue involved was whether a rise in wages caused a rise in prices. The De Leonites contended that a rise in wages did cause a rise in prices, and coupled this with the argument that this demonstrated that workers could not improve their conditions in organizing to increase wages, but must take only revolutionary action to abolish the wages system. Their opponents in the I.W.W. contended that a rise in wages caused no rise in prices, basing their argument on the Marxian theory of value and on the arguments advanced by Marx in *Value, Price and Profit*. To this they added the contention: "If a rise in wages caused a rise in prices, employers would welcome instead of oppose wage increases and would lose rather than gain by wage-cuts." To accept De Leon's viewpoint, they argued, was to accept the idea that "the union is of no or only secondary importance."[74]

The ideological dispute was carried on in the columns of the *Daily* and *Weekly People* and the *Industrial Union Bulletin*. James Connolly, recently arrived from Ireland where he fought the S.L.P. for attempting to control the unions, was a chief opponent of the De Leon theory. Writing in the *Industrial Union Bulletin* of October 26, 1907, Connolly argued in favor of the theory that wages did not cause a rise in prices:

"This fact of our common everyday experience is in striking confirmation of the theory of Marx, as you will find it stated, for instance, in *Value, Price and Profit, viz.,* that the market price of labor (wages) is determined by the value (price) of the necessaries of life. On the other hand, the contention of our opponents on this matter—the contention that a rise in wages is offset by a rise in prices—is best crystallized in the formula that wages determine prices, a theory that Marx . . . calls 'antiquated and exploded' . . . an 'old, popular and wornout fallacy.' Thus economic science, based upon and in alliance with the facts of life, emphatically refutes the contentions of the writers of Marx's day as well as those of the charlatans of our day who revamp the same arguments to prove the same point."

At the same time, the direct-actionist I.W.W. leaders, St. John and Trautmann, were growing more and more irritated by De Leon's continued use of the *People* to advance the principles of political action and to attack those in the I.W.W. who opposed such action.* (An article in the *Daily People* of March 13, 1908, entitled "Political Action," and denouncing those in the I.W.W. who opposed it, especially aroused the resentment of the direct-actionists.) In November 1907, directly after the third convention, the I.W.W. General Executive Board was already considering the charge that the *Daily People* was being used against the industrial union, and that De Leon was plotting to dominate the I.W.W. and convert it into an appendage of the S.L.P. De Leon and his lieutenant, Rudolph Katz, heatedly denied the charge, and the controversy over this issue between them and Trautmann and other anarcho-syndicalists filled issue after issue of the *Industrial Union Bulletin*. Naturally, the discussion was replete with long analyses of the virtues and defects of political action and with long quotations from various theoretical writings on capitalism and socialism to buttress the differing points of view. The "letters to the editors" columns of the *Bulletin* were preempted for several months by adherents and opponents of De Leon and the S.L.P.[75]

By the spring of 1908, this interminable squabble had thoroughly disgusted rank and file elements in the I.W.W., especially those in the Pacific Northwest, who felt that the endless controversy over De Leonism was interfering with the all-important task of organizing the unorganized. "Why does the I.W.W. not grow faster?" these elements asked, and they answered: "Too many political squabbles fill the *Bulletin,* taking away valuable space from organizational activity. The *Bulletin* should not be used for anything but the propaganda for industrial unionism." "Clear the deck for more constructive work," went the appeal from the Northwest, "for more organizing." Again: "There is enough work in this northwest country in the line of organizing, at the present time, to employ an army of organizers." F. W. Heslewood, who had formerly worked

---

* Joseph J. Ettor, who was soon to become one of the leading organizers of the I.W.W., maintained that many non-S.L.P. members of the I.W.W. were also angered by the fact that S.L.P. members propagandized for both organizations at the same time. "One night they would urge from the soapbox support of the S.L.P. and the next night that of the I.W.W. It was a familiar custom of theirs to pin the I.W.W. button on one lapel and the S.L.P. button on the opposite lapel of the same coat. Taking into consideration, right or wrong, the prejudices of the average unionist against the S.L.P. we can readily surmise how much attraction that sort of propaganda held for the average unionist towards the I.W.W." ("The Light of the Past," *Industrial Worker,* July 7, 1945.)

closely with De Leon, summed up the viewpoint of the I.W.W. members in the Northwest when he wrote:

"I hope that you won't print any more of that junk about De Leon, Katz, etc., as the great majority of the members do not belong to the S.L.P. and the continual harping about these things will do more harm than good. Tell them there is too much to do to bother with such small matters, and if they don't like it go to hell, or some other place. It costs more to be eternally getting out these petty charges than the whole bunch of these political fanatics are worth. The I.W.W. has no political affiliation, and that settles it, and any more of this damn dope about De Leon or S.L.P. will be very obnoxious to me and to hundreds of others that are the life of the I.W.W."[76]

The *Bulletin* rebuked Heslewood and others like him for dismissing significant theoretical questions so casually. Quoting Karl Marx on the necessity of emphasizing theory in educating the working class, it commented: "Although it [the devotion of so much space in the *Bulletin* to a discussion of political issues] may retard the growth of the I.W.W., it is safer if the slow groundwork is done perfectly and future work thereby secured." At the same time, the *Bulletin* conceded that its critics were justified in their major complaint, and that it was time to concentrate on organizing the unorganized. It appealed to the "S.L.P. comrades" to put a stop to discussions of the political question and recognize that "the duty of the hour demands the upbuilding of economic organization." If De Leon, it noted, could "repudiate sectarian methods," and realize what was happening within the I.W.W., he would quickly understand the value of the *Bulletin's* advice to the S.L.P. A new element, it pointed out, had entered the I.W.W., composed largely of farm hands, loggers, sailors, unemployed, and other migratory workers—in short, "the Honorable and Ancient Order of Overalls Wearers." These men, unable to vote in national or local elections because they never stayed in one place long enough to fulfill voting requirements, and suspicious of politics because of their bitter encounters with the law, were opposed to all "ballot-box politics." They were interested at present only in what they regarded as a real revolutionary program—a program of economic action. If De Leon were wise, the *Bulletin* observed, he would postpone the whole discussion of political action, and join with this new element in building the I.W.W. by concentrating, for the time being, entirely on what this new element called "the real constructive work of organizing the wage workers industrially."[77]

De Leon had only to read the dispatches from the Northwest to understand that the *Bulletin* was accurately describing the characteristics of this element in the I.W.W. A typical dispatch read: "I have seen for some time that the workers of the northwest who carry their homes on their backs will have some difficulty in emancipating themselves at the ballot box, and especially so when they have to move about twice a month and leave the counting to some Citizens' Alliance disciple or the Mine Owners' Association." But De Leon was not one to take advice readily, and, in addition, he had only contempt for the new element in the I.W.W. whom he regarded as "bums" rather than workers. Possessing a supreme confidence in himself and his views, highly impatient with those who could not see matters in the same light as he saw them, he continued to hammer away in the *Daily* and *Weekly People* on the all-importance of developing the "political reflex" of the I.W.W., making it unmistakably clear that this meant helping to build the S.L.P.[78]

Thus the attempt of the *Industrial Union Bulletin* to stave off a split in the I.W.W. failed.

"I.W.W. Red Special Overalls Brigade," read a headline in the *Bulletin* of September 19, 1908. The article by J. H. Walsh vividly described the experiences of the delegation to the 1908 I.W.W. convention from the West, numbering 19 men and one woman, a group of "red-blooded working stiffs" who had "beat their way" from Portland to Chicago, holding propaganda meetings en route featured by singing sessions. The "Overalls Brigade" arrived in Chicago in time for the opening of the convention. They immediately joined forces with St. John and Traut-mann to gain complete control of the convention and oust Daniel De Leon and his followers. The direct-actionists were determined to eliminate De Leon's ideological influence within the I.W.W., and the "Overalls Brigade" was anxious to get rid of an influence which, by creating endless bickering over terminology and procedure on issues which they considered unimportant was, they felt, holding back the organization activities of the I.W.W. The tactic they used to oust De Leon was to deny him a seat at the convention on the flimsy ground that "he is not a member of the local of the industry in which he is working, such local being in existence." The technicality was that De Leon was a delegate, as he had been at previous conventions, from the Office Workers' Local Union, when, as an editor, he really should have been assigned to the Printing Workers' Local Union.

The Credentials Committee, dominated by St. John and his followers, reported in favor of barring De Leon. The latter's supporters challenged the recommendation on the ground that De Leon had proved his devotion to the working class, and whatever his personal faults, he had given impetus to the movement for industrial unionism by his writings and speeches on the subject, had effectively demonstrated the weaknesses of the craft union form of organization, and had exposed, better than anyone else, the treacherous role of "the labor lieutenants of the captains of industry," the so-called labor leaders—the labor fakers. Moreover, they claimed that the protest against him "was not brought in good faith and other motives were behind the whole procedure." In his own defense,

De Leon argued that the issue at stake in the move to bar him from the convention was his opinion "as regards to the correct structure of an industrial union." He reviewed his efforts since the founding of the I.W.W. to establish "the theory that political and economic organizations are necessary for the task of emancipating the workers." Because he understood that political action was civilized and gave dignity to labor, he had been obliged to fight "against the advocates of physical force within the organization." This had gained him the enmity of the direct-actionists who now sought to expel him. He warned, in closing his defense, that repudiation of the policies he had affirmed would mean the eventual destruction of the I.W.W.

St. John, chairman of the convention, answered De Leon. He was unable to see how a revolutionary movement "would be successful as long as ideas such as advocated by the protestee [De Leon] are adhered to by masses of workers." Labor political action pleased the capitalists for it presented them with no danger to their privileges. It was a danger, however, to labor, for it wasted their efforts in an activity that could not gain them their emancipation. De Leon's ideas and actions, St. John insisted, were "at variance with the adopted principles of industrial union-ism," and would, if followed, change the I.W.W. from a revolutionary organization into a mere political vehicle for De Leon's personal ambi-tions. Therefore, the delegates should assume their "duty to the revolu-tionary working class and establish the principle that the organization is supreme, the individual only but a part of the whole. The protestee has placed himself above the organization, and pointed out a road that inevitably must lead to disaster." For these reasons, St. John concluded, he should not be followed, nor allowed "to take a seat as delegate to this convention."[79]

The motion to adopt the recommendation of the Credentials Com-mittee and refuse to seat De Leon as a delegate was carried by a roll call vote of 40 against 21. Following his ouster, De Leon and his supporters withdrew from the convention and made plans to set up their own organization with headquarters in Detroit which would be "true to the principles of the Industrial Workers of the World."[80]*

* From the fourth annual convention in 1908 until 1915 there were two Industrial Workers of the World—one in Detroit and one in Chicago. The "yellow" I.W.W., as the Detroiters were called, represented Daniel De Leon and a group of his faith-ful followers. The "red" I.W.W. of Chicago, led by St. John, Haywood and Traut-mann, represented the element that gained complete control of the organization at the 1908 convention. (In 1913 Trautmann resigned from the Chicago I.W.W. and applied for membership in the Detroit I.W.W.) The Detroit faction strenuously maintained that they were the real I.W.W., and in all of its propaganda, the De-troit I.W.W. emphasized that it stood for "civilized" labor activity as opposed to the anarchistic, direct-action methods of the Chicago I.W.W. "We propose to win by intelligence, not brute force," declared the *Industrial Union News,* its official

With De Leon and his followers out of the way, St. John, Trautmann and their followers moved to make it clear that the I.W.W. would thereafter have no truck with any kind of politics or politicians. They called immediately for action to expunge from the Preamble all references to political action.[81] But even without De Leon's presence, there still remained some feeling that the political clause should be retained. It is significant that the constitution committee's majority report favored retaining the Preamble without any change, while it was the minority report which recommended the elimination of the political clause.

In the subsequent debate on the report, it became clear that not all who favored De Leon's ouster were opposed to political action under any circumstances. Delegate Sauer, speaking for the majority report, argued that though he had favored the ouster, the elimination of the political clause would only increase opposition to the I.W.W. among those who should be its allies. "If changes are made there will be more squabbles with the members of the Socialist Party and the Socialist Labor Party." He was supported by Delegate Heslewood who asserted that though he had opposed De Leon, he did not favor the change. Pleading for keeping the Preamble intact, he stated he "did not care to be called a dynamiter, and the changing of the preamble by taking out the word 'political' will inevitably give somebody a chance to denounce the I.W.W. as an anarchist organization. Let the preamble stand at least for the time being." His view was seconded by Delegate J. J. Ettor who also urged that the Preamble be kept unchanged "for the time being," and that the question be put to a referendum of the rank and file.

The spokesmen for the minority report were vigorous in denouncing the old Preamble. Delegate Axelson contended that "rag-chewing will never cease in meetings and the council of the I.W.W. as long as the present

---

organ in May 1912. The Detroit I.W.W. would rather lose a strike than win by having "one drop of human blood spilled." It called upon the workers to "come together on the political and industrial fields."

The Detroit I.W.W. was rarely more than another propaganda organization of the S.L.P. In 1912 and 1913, when it reached its peak, it claimed a membership of close to 11,000. But when it is realized that in this figure are included 7,000 or 8,000 silk weavers in Paterson who only rallied temporarily to the Detroit I.W.W., the failure of the group to appeal to those outside of the S.L.P. is obvious. In September 1915, at its eighth convention, the Detroit I.W.W. renounced the title of I.W.W. and changed its name to the Workers' International Industrial Union. But the W.I.I.U. never recruited a larger membership than had the Detroit I.W.W., and it never conducted a strike of any importance. In 1925, the remnants of the W.I.I.U. voted to dissolve, bequeathing the assets and membership to the Socialist Labor Party. (*Industrial Union News,* Jan. 1912–Jan. 1916; H. Kuhn and Olive H. Johnson, *The Socialist Labor Party,* New York, 1931, pp. 80–81; John J. Murphy, "The Workers' International Industrial Union," unpublished M.A. thesis, Columbia University, 1921, pp. 32–40.)

confusing reference to political action is expressed in the preamble." "Show me," he asked, "where political action has accrued to the benefit and where it can benefit the working class?" Delegate Thompson asserted that "the harping on the necessity and importance of political action turns the workers away from the I.W.W. and instils in their minds the belief that relief and salvation can be expected from the capitalist class and their political agencies." He insisted that the minority report was based partly on Karl Marx's writings, and, as for the cry that the proposed change would bring down the charge of "anarchy" on the I.W.W., he asked: "Where can there be 'anarchy' when we advocate and stand for organization? Is organization anarchy?" Delegate Elizabeth Gurley Flynn, speaking in favor of the change, declared: "The present preamble with its contradictions had been the cause of much discussion and confusion, and among the membership of the I.W.W. there were so many different versions as to the meaning of political action and few only are able to explain it. Political action has today no power in itself as thousands are disfranchised because they are out of employment and traveling through the country in search of work." Her remarks aroused a burst of applause from the "Overalls Brigade" whose members had just experienced the conditions Miss Flynn described.

Following the debate, the vote was called for. The report of the majority was defeated and the minority report was adopted by roll call vote of 35 to 32. The second paragraph of the new Preamble now read: "Between these two classes a struggle must go on until the workers of the world organize as a class, take possession of the earth and the machinery of production, and abolish the wage system." Two additional paragraphs were added at this time to the Preamble:

"Instead of the conservative motto, 'a fair day's wage for a fair day's work,' we must inscribe on our banner the revolutionary watchword, 'Abolition of the wage system.'

"It is the historic mission of the working class to do away with capitalism. The army of production must be organized, not only for the everyday struggle with capitalists, but also to carry on production when capitalism shall have been overthrown. By organizing industrially we are forming the structure of the new society within the shell of the old."

The I.W.W. was now under the control of the anarcho-syndicalists, headed by St. John and Trautmann, with the Western contingent as the backbone of their support. Despite this victory of the anti-political actionists, the closeness of the vote on the change in the Preamble revealed that those who opposed purely economic, direct action were still an important section of the I.W.W. Their influence, indeed, was sufficiently strong to compel the anarcho-syndicalists to join with them in adopting a resolution which was to be a signal to the world that the change in the Preamble did not mean that the I.W.W. was an anarchist organization, and did not favor "terrorism": "The I.W.W. refuses all alliances, direct or indirect, with existing political parties or anti-political sects, and disclaims responsibility for any individual opinion or act which may be at variance with the purposes herein expressed."[82]

RESULTS OF 1908 CONVENTION

St. John was elected general secretary-treasurer and the I.W.W. remained under his guiding hand until 1915. During these years the Western element took over control of the I.W.W. and made it an organization which reflected both the strength and the weaknesses of its composition and ideology. No sooner had the 1908 convention adjourned when the *Industrial Union Bulletin* predicted that the future of the organization was linked inextricably with the Western element. "The outstanding thing about the fourth convention," it observed, "is the spirit that actuated to an unusual degree those delegates who, lacking the means of transportation, had to cover hundreds of miles on foot, travel by freight and in boxcars in order to participate in the convention. . . . With such men in the ranks, the I.W.W. may confidently hope that success will crown their persistent efforts towards industrial emancipation." It acknowledged that there might be complaints from the East about the dominant influence of the West over the I.W.W. But it insisted that this was unjustified. "In proportion to population the West has by far purchased and distributed more I.W.W. literature, furnished more readers of the *Bulletin,* and contributed more to the financial support of the organization, than the entire section east of the Rocky Mountains." With a working class imbued with such "a revolutionary spirit," "class-consciousness," and devotion to the organization at its base, how could the I.W.W. not succeed in its mission?[83]

The second split in the I.W.W. was inevitably followed by the usual prediction that the organization was slated for immediate extinction. "We need no longer fear this crazy assortment of fanatics," Lennon wrote to Gompers in November 1908. "They have just about committed suicide at their recent gathering in Chicago. And when this so-called union is buried it will take along with it to its grave all the fanatical principles of 'industrialism' which it has so futilely sought to impress upon the American workers."[84] The viewpoint that the I.W.W. was a total failure and that, as a result, the idea of industrial unionism had suffered a tremendous setback, was also expressed by Charles H. Moyer. In an address to the 16th convention of the W.F. of M. late in 1908, President Moyer declared that "the I.W.W. has been landed high and dry on the rocks of destruction." He recalled the great enthusiasm with which the I.W.W. had been launched; the founders believing that its principle of industrial unionism would draw to it the support of the unorganized workers in the mass production industries as well as of existing industrial unions like the United Brewery Workers and the United Mine Workers. Consequently, the W.F. of M. had predicted that "industrial unionism was bound to win." But the friends of industrial unionism had been sorely disappointed, and so Moyer concluded: "After careful study, it occurs to me, and I believe that it is a well-established fact, that industrial unionism is by no means popular, and I feel safe in saying that it is not wanted by the working class of the United States.[85]

Lennon and Moyer were wrong on both accounts. The I.W.W. was far from dead. It had survived its most bitter cleavage to date. The structure of the union was intact. Although it now had perhaps only 3,700 members,[86] it could present a program on which substantial agreement had been secured. To be sure, the program virtually guaranteed the isolation of the I.W.W. from vast numbers of American workers who knew from experience that political action was a necessary weapon in the class struggle, and that, indeed, the existence of many unions, threatened by injunctions and other court decisions, could only be preserved by labor's effectiveness at the ballot box. Yet with all of its ideological weaknesses, its strategic mistakes and tactical errors, the I.W.W. continued in the forefront of the fight for industrial unionism. If most of the existing industrial unions refused to associate themselves with the I.W.W., there still were fertile fields for organizing. To these fields, the organizers of the I.W.W. now turned—to the steel and textile mills of the East, to the lumber camps of the Northwest and Southeast, and to the farm lands of the Pacific Coast and the great Midwest. The spectacular course of the I.W.W. in the next few years would, as we shall see, bring the principles of industrial unionism to the attention of hundreds of thousands of American workers, including even many of the A.F. of L.

CHAPTER 5

Composition and Principles

"In considering such a movement as the I.W.W.," declared the St. Louis *Republic* in 1912, "there is no need to pause over its history. . . . Nor is it necessary to consider the philosophy. It has none. It is mere brute ferocity. The tiger which springs on the traveler in the jungle has no philosophy—only a thirst for blood. He cannot be reasoned with—he must be overcome."[1] We have already seen that the I.W.W. had a history. We will now see that it also had a philosophy.

After the fourth convention in 1908, it was possible for the I.W.W. to begin organization again. The De Leon group had formed its own organization and the factional struggle that had torn the I.W.W. apart and held back organizational activities was laid to rest. This is not to say that doctrinal disputes had disappeared. For one thing, even in the relatively homogeneous I.W.W. that emerged from the schism of 1908, there was a continuing conflict as to whether the organization should be a functioning labor union, combining the struggle for higher wages and better working conditions with a program for revolutionary socialism, or a revolutionary cadre concentrating only on leading the working class to the revolution. The national headquarters stressed the first, while many of the more anarchical members emphasized the second, arguing that there was a contradiction between the goals of revolution and unionism, and that to concentrate on the latter would blind the workers to the final aim. Indeed, these members felt that the I.W.W. should abandon any pretense of being an economic organization and devote its energies exclusively to propaganda and agitation.[2]

In addition, hostility between eastern and western members often prevented unified action. "At every convention of our organization. . . ," the official I.W.W. journal conceded in 1911, "more or less rivalry or misunderstanding has been manifest between delegates from the East and West." Nevertheless, by 1909 the I.W.W., having defined itself as a revolutionary industrial union devoted to economic activity, was sufficiently united to move forward. Indeed, in the words of the official historian of the organization, the year 1909 can almost be regarded as "the launching of the I.W.W."[3]

COMPOSITION OF THE I.W.W.

Joining the I.W.W. was easy and the cost was the very minimum. The only requirements for membership were that candidates be "bona-fide workers in any one industry . . . or in several industries," and that they answer affirmatively two questions: "Do you agree to abide by the constitution and regulations of this organization?" and "Will you diligently study its principles and make yourself acquainted with its purposes?" Prospective members applied to the secretary of an I.W.W. union in their locality; if there was none, they wrote to the general secretary at Chicago headquarters and were enrolled by mail. Or, if there were several of them, they could charter their own local merely by sending a chapter application with the signature of at least 20 wage workers, none of whom needed to be I.W.W.'s, to the general secretary, along with a $10 charter fee. "Supplies, constitution and instruction will then be sent to you and you can proceed to organize the local."[4]

The founding convention of the I.W.W. set a constitutional limit of 50 cents a month on dues, and of $5 ranging down to $1.50 on initiation fees, the exact sum to be set by each industrial union. These limits were never exceeded in the period under study, and were often lowered. (When workers joined in large groups there was rarely an initiation fee.) Twenty-five cents a month dues and initiation fees of a dollar were fairly common, and even these were sometimes forgotten during an organizational drive.

These simple requirements were especially suited to meet the needs of specific groups of workers. One important group were the western migratory workers—the seasonal laborers of logging camps and lumber mills, mines and construction projects, orchards and agricultural fields, who, after 1908, were the majority of the I.W.W. members in the West and made up the core and backbone of the organization in that section. It was quite popular, even in Socialist circles, to deride the hobo as the "scum of the working class," but the I.W.W. made constant efforts to distinguish between the hoboes and the sedentary and derelict bums or non-working tramps. "The 'hobo' is the leaven of the revolutionary industrial union movement in the West," declared the *Industrial Union Bulletin* shortly after the 1908 convention, "and his absence in proportionate numbers from the East, accounts in large measure for the slowness of the Eastern workers to awaken from their lethargy." Later, the I.W.W. developed this theme even more fully. "Jesus Christ was a hobo," as were the most important figures throughout history. One writer declared in an article entitled "The Hobo's Vindication": "The miserable dirty hoboes are the brains of the nation. . . . The hobo camps have given to the world a Jack London, a Mark Twain, a Joaquin Miller, a Maxim Gorky."[5]

Not all hoboes, of course, were of this heroic mold. There were those who were inveterate drunkards and dope fiends, the "Skid-Row" type to be exact. But the main point, apart from all the romanticism, is that a dispossessed, homeless proletariat, the migratory worker, had been created throughout the West. It was a roaming army of several millions, who were not attached to any particular locality or to any special line of industry. These transients made possible the operation of the lumber, railroad construction, mining and agricultural industries of the West. Young, the typical age being under 25, wifeless, homeless, semi-skilled or unskilled, they moved about from job to job in empty boxcars or "side-door coaches," as the freight cars were called by the migratory workers. They followed seasonal occupations, in the main, harvesting wheat, logging, maintaining the grades for the great transcontinental railroads, or mining silver, lead, copper and tin in the Rocky Mountain mining region.[6]

Some of the migratory workers worked the entire year round. They usually worked in the lumber camps in the fall. Leaving the camps in the winter, they would head for the fruit groves of California, then Arizona and Texas. Spring would find them threading their way up through Kansas and Nebraska, Minnesota and the Dakotas where they took part in the planting and early harvesting. From there, they made the jump "over the hump" back into the logging camps of the Pacific Northwest.

The majority of the itinerant workers, however, did not work during the winter months. By the end of the fall or working season, they had accumulated as little as $30 in their "stakes," and with this in their pockets to see them through the cold months of idleness, they drifted into the cities—Portland, Spokane, San Francisco, Seattle, Chicago, and Minneapolis—wintering in their slums until the time came for them to hit the road again, following the jobs around the country.

These men had built and were building America's railroads and highways, had taken the timber out of the forests, plowed its lands, threshed its crops, husked its corn, and picked its apples. But their reward was to be treated as "scum" when employed, and as dangerous "parasites" when they lacked visible means of support. While they were doing their work, they were, as we shall see, forced to live under unspeakable unsanitary conditions in the jungles and labor camps, and to receive extremely low pay for sunup to sundown labor.

Samuel Gompers was correct when he said a few years before the first World War: "The lot of the migratory worker in the United States today is in some points worse than slavery."[7] But the A.F. of L. had made only a pass at organizing these workers and then abandoned them to the slave conditions. In 1911, Andrew Furuseth, president of the International Seamen's Union of America, submitted a plan to Gompers for the organization of the migratory workers. He urged that the first thing was "to gain their confidence and friendship," and conceded that the A.F. of L. was regarded by the migratory workers as indifferent to their needs. Nothing came of the proposal. The migrants were impossible to organize, the Federation concluded. They weren't stable. It was too expensive to keep track of them, etc., etc. On the surface, this appeared to be a realistic approach. The problem of organizing thousands of workers who were continually traveling, never remaining for long in one place, seemed insurmountable organizationally. Then again, although the majority of the migratory workers were native Americans, foreign-born workers made up an important part of the group, and employers mixed up several nationalities in order to make the task of organizers more difficult. As one I.W.W. organizer wrote in describing the problems involved in organizing the railroad section men in Oregon:

"Not only are there six different nationalities to deal with—Austrians, Italians, Greeks, Japanese, Chinese, and English-speaking workers—but the employers thoroughly understand the scientific distribution of these different nationalities to the different sections of the country which makes it nearly impossible for us to get to them. . . . It is necessary for six organizers, speaking six different languages to travel together, and cover a vast amount of territory in order to do the preparatory necessary work for the establishment of an industrial organization among the railroad workers."[8]

The A.F. of L. had declared that these conditions rendered it impossible to organize. But not the I.W.W. Its policy and its tactics were designed to overcome these obstacles. The refusal of the I.W.W. to differentiate between workers because of race, color, nationality or religion appealed to the migratory workers who, in their own travels on the boxcars, mingled freely, regardless of racial, nationality and religious differences. Low initiation fees and dues was ideal for a group of workers with meager incomes. Interchangeable membership cards permitted them to remain in the organization even when making frequent changes in jobs. The policy of "rank-and-file" rule appealed to them because of their hatred of centralized authority, so evident in the company towns and camps, and the rejection of political action appealed to them because they could not vote. The policy of organizing industrially and admitting all wage-earners, no matter what their occupation, had, of course, a great appeal to the less skilled, often unemployed, migratory workers. Moreover, wherever the migratory worker turned he found the I.W.W.—on the freight trains, in the jails, in the bunkhouses, in the jungles—its gospel spread by fervent converts who were workers themselves and followed the transients on and off the job.

Many of the active I.W.W.'s felt sufficiently at home with the workers of the industries towards which the migrants gravitated to be able to organize among any of them. Walter T. Nef was in rapid succession a "shovel man" on a Portland, Ore., construction job, a sawmill worker in Oregon, and organizer of lumber workers in the Duluth-Superior logging camps—all during the extent of one year, 1910. George Speed who was 50 years old when the I.W.W. was founded and had already had a long career in the labor and Socialist movements, worked and organized in West Coast sawmills, the Louisiana timber belt, and North Dakota wheat fields. John Pancner was a miner who participated in the I.W.W.'s first successful strike at Goldfield, Nev., in 1906, and thereafter for several years worked and organized in logging camps and sawmills in California, Oregon, and Washington. Thomas Whitehead worked on railroad construction jobs in British Columbia and in the Louisiana timber areas. E. F. Doree, one of the most experienced I.W.W. organizers, worked among harvest workers in Walla Walla, Wash., in 1910, among lumberjacks in northern California in 1911, making speeches in Italian, among the Louisiana timber workers in 1912, and the next year successfully organizing lumber workers of northern Michigan and northern Minnesota.[9]

Any I.W.W. member could become a "jawsmith" or organizer while pursuing the regular routine of a transitory worker. He supplied himself with membership cards, dues books and a notebook, and samples of I.W.W. literature, and carried the gospel with him on his job. The *Industrial Worker* and *Solidarity* carried information under "Job Notes" informing Wobblies where they could find work organizing migratory workers who needed to be organized. The job delegate recruited members, collected dues, kept records and established an I.W.W. headquarters wherever he happened to be working. He was, in short, "an official whose headquarters was where he hung his hat."[10]

This system spread the message of the I.W.W. insistently into towns, camps, and work gangs, bringing the organization directly to the migratory workers. The delegate, who was himself a worker, acted not only as an agent for the I.W.W. conducting business meetings in the jungle, but also as the spokesman in any grievances the men had. The job delegate could be fired by camp foremen, but as long as there were I.W.W. members in the area, new delegates could quickly take their places.

The traveling delegate-organizers of the I.W.W., supplied with membership cards and dues stamps, met the workers in the fields, in the jungles, and on freight cars and induced them to "line-up." They practiced "box-car recruiting" and made the "red card" or I.W.W. membership card a necessary ticket for all who traveled on the freight cars. Anti-union workers (called "scissorbills" by the I.W.W.) risked being thrown off the train.*

For migrants, I.W.W. affiliation served a number of purposes which were of the utmost importance. Fraudulent employment agencies who received money for jobs which were hundreds of miles away and which were often non-existent or not of the character described, bootleggers, boxcar robbers, gamblers, highjackers, and train crews which preyed upon migrants were reduced to a minimum by I.W.W. mutual protection associations. A paid-up dues card in the I.W.W. usually provided admission to the 'blind baggage" of freights carrying migrants from job to job, and even hostile brakemen learned to respect the I.W.W. cards. The I.W.W. served as a "bond of groping friendship" among the uprooted.

"The I.W.W.," William D. ["Big Bill"] Haywood correctly noted, "form in groups and establish what may be called community life in the jungles. When a crowd of members of this organization leave a train near the station, they go to the outskirts of the town or the bank of a stream if convenient. There a meeting is called, a Camp Committee is elected, the formation of which is to see the camp is kept clean and sanitary; a Job Committee is selected to rustle the town for work. Such pay as is received for work by any member of the group goes into a common fund. A treasurer is elected and an itemized account is kept of all receipts and expenses. These accounts are audited every night. A cook and assistants are appointed, who in addition to preparing the food, furnish the cans in which to cook it. Usually empty Standard Oil cans, vegetable cans, etc. are found and scoured and used for cooking utensils, plates and cups. A Spud and Gump Committee† forage around the farms for vegetables and other eatables, while the Buying Committee visit the town to purchase such supplies as are necessary and the Camp Treasury can afford. Every man is expected to do some work around the camp, though there are some of parasitic nature who accept service without giving service; these are called 'Jungle Buzzards.' But they are not tolerated for long by the I.W.W. Gamblers and 'Stick-ups' infest all harvest gangs, but in the I.W.W. camps the rule, No Gambling, is strictly observed."[11]

Most importantly, the I.W.W.'s militant philosophy gave outlet, meaning, and dignity to a group of workers who roamed rootless and poverty-stricken in a land of plenty, despised and exploited by society and unwanted by any other labor organization. The man who was considered a "bum" by most members of society was elevated by the I.W.W. into "the finest specimens of American manhood . . . the leaven of the revolu-

* The epithet "scissorbill" was also applied to any worker lacking class-consciousness or just plain common sense. In other words, a worker who cuts off his nose to spite his face, hence "scissorbill."

† Spud is hobo argot for potato and gump for hen or poultry in general.

tionary labor movement" around whom would be built a militant nucleus for revolutionary industrial unionism. In the I.W.W. the migratory worker was accepted, respected, and even glorified as "a real-proletarian" without whom "the farms would not be cultivated, the logs cut or the mines mined," and who would soon lead the rest of the working class toward the establishment of the inevitable Cooperative Commonwealth.

"The nomadic worker of the West embodies the very spirit of the I.W.W.," a writer proclaimed in *Solidarity*. "His cheerful cynicism, his frank and outspoken contempt for most of the conventions of bourgeois society . . . make him an admirable exemplar of the iconoclastic doctrines of revolutionary unionism. His anomalous position, half industrial slave, half vagabond adventurer leaves him infinitely less servile than his fellow worker in the East. Unlike the factory slave of the Atlantic seaboard and the central states he is most emphatically not 'afraid of his job.' No wife and family cumber him. The worker of the East, oppressed by the fear of want for wife and babies, dare not venture much." Even the migrant's mode of travel was a point in his favor. "He has to travel on the freight trains and there is absolutely no shame or crime in this," declared the *Industrial Worker*. "If he did not move this way, the wheat would not be harvested." Haywood went even further, stating flatly: "To understand the class struggle, you must ride on the top of the box-cars or underneath the box-cars."[12]

E. T. Booth, who worked as a harvest hand on the Pacific Coast, made this keen observation: "One found one's self working with men whose single hope of rehabilitation and human dignity lay in the revolutionary program of the I.W.W. Out of the heavy fatigue, the fetid torpor of the bunkhouse, at the end of the day's labor, the only influence that could stir the sullen hulks who lounged in the bunks was the zeal of the agitator tirelessly and astutely instructing the 'harvest stiff'* in the strategy of class warfare."[13] As the I.W.W. organizer talked, the cold and stench of the jungle, the hunger, the long hours of labor all fell into place. They were the results of a vicious system that thought in terms of profits not of human beings—the capitalist system. The migratory workers, like a hundred million others, were slaves, chained to this system. But now they could do something about it and end their needless misery. They knew their enemy, and they could fight him. Most important of all, they could fight not as downtrodden individuals, but as members of a militant organization which welcomed them and promised to improve their conditions and completely liberate them from slavery in the near future.

In short, the I.W.W. explained the hardships which were the lot of the migratory workers, provided a course of action to follow, and a

---

* In I.W.W. speech, "stiff" was commonly applied to all casual or migratory workers in the West and particularly to I.W.W. members. A "bindle stiff" was a western hobo who carried his blankets in a roll or a bindle.

promise of deliverance. Is it any wonder that these workers flocked into the I.W.W.? There was probably hardly a single migratory worker who did not become a member of the organization at one time or another during his career.[14]

Much the same reasons account for the attraction of the I.W.W. to the unskilled and semi-skilled immigrant workers in the East and Midwest —the "home guard," as the I.W.W. called the sedentary worker attached to home and a single job and with some sort of family responsibility. There were, of course, basic differences between the rebels of the West and members in the factories of the East; indeed, some felt that these differences produced two I.W.W.'s, one in the West and the other in the East. On the average, the representative western member of the I.W.W. was younger than the eastern member. He was likely to be unmarried, or at least, without binding family ties. The western members were mainly native Americans (although there were quite a few foreign-born members of the I.W.W. in the West), while the eastern members were mostly foreign-born, and even when the westerner was of foreign birth he was less likely to have preserved old country ties and characteristics. The westerners were mainly men, while women were an important element among the semiskilled and unskilled factory workers of the East.

But the similarities were greater than the differences. Like the migratory workers, the unskilled factory workers had turned to the A.F. of L. only to find the Federation was interested solely in the skilled craftsmen and had no desire to organize the unskilled, foreign-born workers in the mass production industries.* Like the migrants, immigrant workers found the I.W.W. a congenial organization. The policy of low initiation fees, small dues and "rank-and-file" rule appealed to these workers as much as it did to the transients. The I.W.W. opposition to political action appealed, too, to the foreign-born immigrant workers, many of whom were not yet naturalized. And, of course, like the migratory workers, the immigrant industrial workers whose foreign birth became a vehicle for ridicule in the commercial press where they were called "Hunks," "Bohunks," and "Dagoes," found dignity and status in the I.W.W.

While the A.F. of L. was clamoring for restrictive legislation to keep out European (especially southern and southeastern European) workers, the I.W.W. declared: "Meet the new arrival at the immigration dock; introduce him to his fellow workers in One Big Union of the working class, and help him fight for a higher standard of living against those masters who would quickly transform his energy and vitality into profits."

* For a discussion of the attitude of the A.F. of L. toward the foreign-born, unskilled, women and Negro workers, see Philip S. Foner, *History of the Labor Movement in the United States*, vol. III, *The Policies and Practices of the American Federation of Labor, 1900–1909*, New York, 1964, pp. 219–307.

All immigrant workers could be taken care of "by cutting down the hours of labor."

The I.W.W. took pride in its appeal to immigrant workers. An extensive foreign-language press was organized specifically to attract the foreign-born into the organization. I.W.W. organizers and soapboxers who could speak foreign languages were constantly sought to work in centers of immigrant workers. *Solidarity* and the *Industrial Worker* contained frequent articles about the outlook of the immigrant worker, suggesting ways in which he should and should not be approached by I.W.W. organizers and warning them never to regard the foreign-born worker as inferior to the American worker because he could not understand English.[15]

Most I.W.W. organizers took such advice to heart. The result was that the I.W.W. speedily won a reputation among the foreign-born as their spokesman and they came, often without being asked, to join. The following news item in the *Industrial Worker* of April 18, 1912, was duplicated many times: "Our hall was surprised yesterday morning when 200 discontented slaves, of seven different nationalities swarmed in quietly and arranged themselves for a meeting. When asked the purpose of their visit, they answered in chorus, 'We want to join the I.W.W.' Two secretaries were kept busy the rest of the day making out the red cards."

Although most often the different nationalities were organized in one local or branch as was the group just mentioned, where there was a large contingent of one nationality in an area or in an industry, separate branches, composed of members of that nationality, were organized. In addition, there were a few units of foreign propaganda leagues, particularly the Italian and Finnish. In chartering these foreign language locals or leagues, the I.W.W. appealed to immigrants by offering them the inducement of associating with the organization on the basis of their own cultural similarities. They did not, in short, need to feel that they were strangers in the union.

The commercial press conceded that the I.W.W. had great influence among the foreign-born workers, but attributed this entirely to the low state of intelligence of the immigrants rather than to the conditions that bred discontent and caused these workers to look for a champion. "This country has an obligation to these strangers who furnish so much of its labor force," piously editorialized one paper after describing the foreign-born as "like children." "It owes them the duty of protection against such an organization like the I.W.W. . . . They should not be permitted to impose their machinations on the most ignorant, the most helpless and the least able of our population." The I.W.W. agreed that the country did owe these workers "an obligation." It was its obligation to reward them for the wealth these workers produced so that they could enjoy the decencies of life rather than being forced to live in dire poverty. It was its obligation to protect these workers when they revolted against unbearable conditions, and not assist their exploiters to defeat their struggles and kill and imprison their leaders.[16]

In general, then, the I.W.W. after 1908 operated chiefly among the workers whom the A.F. of L. would not and did not reach—the migratory workers of the West and the unskilled industrial workers of the East—the most poorly paid and ill-treated. At a time when $800 per year was considered the minimum necessary to raise a family in a semblance of decency, approximately one-fourth of the adult fathers earned less than $400 per year and one-half earned less than $600 per year. To these members of the American working class, the promise of American life must have seemed dim indeed. It was to these workers that the I.W.W. held out a new promise. As one contemporary journalist correctly put it: "The I.W.W.'s deepest strength lies in the fact that it extends the red hand of fellowship to the lowliest of the workers, that it has made itself the special champion of those who are paid the least and work the hardest."[17]

LABOR SOLIDARITY

The basic creed of the I.W.W. demanded that all workingmen be considered equal and united in a common cause. There was only one qualification to become a member: "Are you a wage worker, exploited by a capitalist master? If so, then you are welcome, regardless of color, creed, nationality, sex or politics." In contrast to almost every other labor organization up to this time in American history, the I.W.W. made an active effort to organize the Chinese, Japanese, and Mexican workers, and never attacked these workers either officially or unofficially. When civic leaders of Redding, Calif., came to the I.W.W. to seek support in driving Chinese workers out of town, they were told bluntly: "If you want to raise the wages of the Chinese, we'll help, but we won't kick anybody off their job because of color." Likewise, when the Porters' Union in Spokane asked for cooperation "to eradicate the brown men from competition," the *Industrial Worker* informed the organization that if it "were but half as class conscious as the average Japanese worker, there would be better conditions for the porter than the wretched ones they are now forced to submit to." It concluded the lecture with the flat statement: "It must be understood that the I.W.W. will turn down any effort to discriminate against our Japanese fellow workers."[18]

The I.W.W. scoffed at the idea of a "yellow peril," especially criticizing the Socialists of the Pacific Coast for swallowing the "capitalist bait" that the Japanese and Chinese were an inferior people whose presence in America would drag down standards of living. "All workers can be organized regardless of race or color, as soon as their minds are cleared of the patiotic notion that there is any reason of being proud of having been born of a certain shade of skin or in an arbitrarily fenced off portion of the earth." There was a "yellow peril," but it did not come from Japanese and Chinese workers. "If the American workers need fear any 'yellow peril' it is from the yellow socialists." The *Industrial Worker* had only scorn for Socialist candidates in California who advocated Asian exclusion while continuing to wear their Socialist buttons showing clasped hands and inscribed, "Workers of the World, Unite." When Karl Marx penned this slogan, he did not mean "all workers except the Chinese and Japanese. He included the Negroes, the Hindus, and the Asiatics in the revolutionary call."[19]

It is impossible to determine the Asian membership of the I.W.W., but a considerable number of short news items in the Wobbly press specifically boasting of the inclusion of Japanese, Chinese, and Filipinos in I.W.W. locals,[20] testify to the fact that the I.W.W. practiced what it preached.

"The Negro has no chance in the old-line trade unions," an I.W.W. leaflet argued. "They do not want him. They admit him only under compulsion and treat him with contempt." There was only *one* labor organization in the United States "that admits the colored worker on a footing of absolute equality with the white—the Industrial Workers of the World. . . . In the I.W.W. the colored worker, man or woman, is on an equal footing with every other worker. He has the same voice in determining the policies of the organization, and his interests are protected as zealously as those of any other member."[21] This view was substantiated by Mary White Ovington, a wealthy white New Yorker who was one of the founders of the N.A.A.C.P., in her article, "The Status of the Negro in the United States," published in 1913. "There are two organizations in this country," she wrote, "that have shown they do care [about full rights for the Negro]. The first is the National Association for the Advancement of Colored People. . . . The second organization that attacks Negro segregation is the Industrial Workers of the World. . . . The I.W.W. has stood with the Negro."[22]

The Negro, the I.W.W. emphasized, was subject to discrimination, first, because of his color, and, second, because "for the most part the Negro still belongs in the category of the 'unskilled.' " This state of affairs could not be wiped out by appeals to sentiment alone. It could only be altered by the organization of the Negro in a union which educated its members to recognize all workers as equal regardless of color, and which organized the unskilled by the only method through which they could be organized—industrial unionism. Such a union was the I.W.W.[23]

All I.W.W. journals participated actively in this educational campaign, including *The Voice of the People,* the Southern organ of the I.W.W., published at New Orleans. In an article entitled, "Down With Race Prejudice," Phineas Eastman asked his "fellow workers of the South if they wish real good feeling to exist between the two races (and each is necessary to the other's success), to please stop calling the colored man 'Nigger'—the tone some use is an insult, much less the word. Call him Negro if you must refer to his race, but 'fellow worker' is the only form of salutation a rebel should use."[24]* Members of the I.W.W. were constantly reminded that the organization of the Negro was an "economic bread and butter" issue. "Leaving the Negro outside of your union makes him a potential, if not an actual scab, dangerous to the organized workers, to say nothing of his own interests as a worker." Race prejudice on the job could only have one result—"keeping the workers fighting each other, while the boss gets the benefit." The idea fostered by the capitalists that the white worker was "superior" was part of the same game. "Actually he is only 'superior' if he shows that he can produce more wealth for the boss, than his colored brother can." In an appeal to Southern white workers, the I.W.W. asked:

"If one of you were to fall in a river and could not swim, and a negro came along who could swim, would you drown rather than accept his offer of aid? Hardly!

"That is the I.W.W. position. Labor organized on race lines will drown. Only organized on *class* lines will it swim. . . .

"Don't let them sidetrack you from the main line which is, Shall we be freemen or slaves?"[25]

The I.W.W. and its leaders, including its Negro leader, Ben Fletcher, Philadelphia longshoreman, condemned all manifestations of Jim Crowism. It denounced the lynching of Negroes as "savagery," pointing out that it was usually resorted to when Negroes "are demanding more of their product."[26]

In a leaflet entitled "To Colored Workingmen and Women," the I.W.W. pointed out: "If you are a wage worker you are welcome in the I.W.W. halls, no matter what your color. By this you may see that the I.W.W. is not a white man's union, not a black man's union, not a red or yellow man's union, but a working man's union. All of the working

---

* When *Solidarity,* in its issue of Nov. 25, 1911, carried in a letter to the editor the word "nigger," it was sharply criticized for using "the opprobrious term on a par with 'sheeny,' 'mick,' 'guinea,' 'dago,' and other insulting terms used by arrogant and ignorant people—usually they are both." (Dec. 9, 1911.) Although *Solidarity* lamely tried to defend itself, it never again published the obnoxious word.

Sometimes the I.W.W. press capitalized "Negro," and at other times, printed the word without capitalizing it. I have reprinted it as it appeared in a particular article or editorial. The obnoxious word "nigger" is also reprinted as it appeared in the original.

class in one big union." The I.W.W. practiced what it preached, even in the deepest South where it raised the banner of "No Race, No Creed, No Color," and united Negro and white workers in a common struggle. In the heart of the South, as we shall see, the Brotherhood of Timber Workers, when it affiliated with the I.W.W., organized Negro workers into the same union as the white members. In 1910–11, the Industrial Workers' Union of South Africa, a branch of the I.W.W.,* conducted a vigorous campaign to convince the rank and file of the white workers "that their real enemy is not the colored laborer, and that it is only by combining and co-operating irrespective of color that the standard of life of the whites can be maintained and improved." The union led the strike of the trainwaymen of Johannesburg in which Negro and whites for the first time united in struggle. The *Voice of Labor,* the union's organ, asserted that while the strike was not successful, it had taught "the white and black workers of South Africa some much needed lessons."[27]

The Philadelphia longshoremen, with Ben Fletcher as their leader, constituting one of the largest and most effective I.W.W. units when it was first organized in 1913, was made up primarily but not entirely of Negroes. For years prior to 1913, organization on the docks of Philadelphia had been frustrated by the employers' policy of pitting Negroes and white against each other, threatening that if one group complained about conditions, their jobs would be given to the other. The I.W.W. entered the picture with the appeal that whether white and Negro liked each other or not, their only hope was to organize into one union. Within a few months the Marine Transport Workers Local 3 had been organized, the majority of its members Negroes, and struck for recognition on May 13, 1913. After a strike of two weeks, the dock workers won recognition of their union and the right to bargain collectively. The union's membership by the end of 1913 was close to 3,000 and strikes in 1915 and 1916 completed its control of the docks. In keeping with its belief in equality of Negro and white, the local had a rotating system of chairmen. One month a Negro was the chairman; the next month, a white member.[28]

No statistics are available which indicate Negro membership in the I.W.W. Sterling D. Spero and Abram L. Harris estimate that of the "one million membership cards" issued by the I.W.W. "during the active part

---

* The I.W.W. had branches in England, Australia, New Zealand, and South Africa, and "connections" with labor organizations in France, Italy, Spain, Russia, Scandinavia, Mexico, Argentina and other South American countries, and Canada. Outside of the United States, the I.W.W.'s greatest strength lay in Australia. In 1914 there were four locals: Adelaide, Sydney, Broken Hill, and Fort Pirie; early that year, the I.W.W. began publishing a weekly newspaper, *Direct Action,* which reached a circulation of 14,000. (Justice Ebert, *The I.W.W. in Theory and Practice,* Chicago, 1920, p. 33; E. W. Campbell, *History of the Australian Labor Movement,* Sydney, 1945, pp. 64–74.)

of its life" about "100,000 of these cards were issued to Negroes." This estimate is based, they note, on statements "made on the authority of Benjamin Fletcher, a Negro I.W.W. official." Actually, no I.W.W. publication ever made such a sweeping claim, and one student contends that the absence of claims by the I.W.W. of a substantial Negro membership suggests that not many Negroes were attracted to the Industrial Workers of the World.[29]*

Whatever the exact Negro membership, the I.W.W. stood squarely for the organization of the Negro workers on the basis of complete equality. The *Industrial Worker* summed up the I.W.W.'s attitude:

"In this country every tenth person is of acknowledged negro descent and a large percentage of these ten millions of people are wage workers. There may be for the whole society of America a negro problem but with the entrance of the Industrial Workers of the World into the industrial arena there was no further need for the labor problem to be complicated with a racial problem. The I.W.W. accepts the negro wage worker, asking of him the same initiation fees and dues as his white brother, and giving to him the same membership privileges as are the common property of all who join. The fight of the negro wage slave is the fight of the white wage slave; and the two must rise or fall together. Their economic interests are identical and an injury to one is an injury to the other. . . ."

To the I.W.W., then, there was "no race problem. There is only a class problem. . . . The economic interests of all workers, be they white, black, brown or yellow, are identical, and all are included in the program of the I.W.W. It has one program for the entire working class—'the abolition of the wage system.' "[30]

For the Negro facing discrimination, segregation, deprivation of civil and political rights and violence, the I.W.W. had no real program. The truth is that for the Negro people there was a "race problem," and it was no answer for them to be told that in "the abolition of the wage system" lay the Negro's salvation. Despite its advanced position against race prejudice and its opposition to segregation in the labor movement, the failure of the I.W.W. to concern itself with the Negro's demand and struggle for civil and political rights, restricted its appeal to the Negro masses.

The I.W.W. repeatedly pointed out that women were in industry to stay. "They cannot be driven back to the home. . . . They are part of the

* Recognizing that the vast majority of the Negro workers were still in the South, the eighth I.W.W. convention, September 1913, urged that "a permanent colored organizer should be employed in the South to organize the colored workers into One Big Union. . . . All locals should assist the general organization to carry out this program." (*International Socialist Review*, vol. XIV, Nov. 1913, p. 275.) There is no evidence that this proposal was ever carried out.

army of labor." There was only one thing to be done. "Organize them with the men, just as they work with the men." And organize them into the only type of unions to which women, most of whom were unskilled, could belong—industrial unions. The I.W.W. opposed "women's trade union leagues," arguing that they only increased the separation of men and women workers. It conceded that there were special problems in organizing women workers, but rejected the old craft-union cry that "women won't organize and strike." This was merely an excuse for doing nothing or a justification for barring women from the labor movement. The answer was "to encourage them wherever possible by granting them equal opportunities, duties and privileges, even to the holding of executive office."[31] Wobbly* papers paid special attention to any news of "the activity of girl workers," and reports of leading I.W.W. strikes, as we shall see, always pointed up the role played by the women either as strikers or supporters of the men on the picket lines. The *Industrial Worker* of August 19, 1916, proudly noted that one result of the activity of the Domestic Workers' Industrial Union of Denver, organized and led by Jane Street, "the plucky Denver housemaid," was that the men in the city were becoming imbued with the I.W.W. spirit and had organized a local of their own. "The new local, however, will have to go some to equal the fighting spirit permeating the Denver working women."

The exact number of women who became members of the I.W.W. during the pre-World War I period is impossible to determine accurately. But it is clear that the organization was more successful in attracting women in the East, especially the operatives in the textile factories, than it was in the West where so many of the members were men who tended to live in a predominantly male society in the lumber and construction camps and in the jungles. Joe Hill, the great Swedish-born Wobbly song writer, wrote in *Solidarity* of December 19, 1914, that in the West, the I.W.W. had "created a kind of one-legged, freakish animal of a union" because of its predominantly male membership. He recommended that the I.W.W.'s female organizers, like Elizabeth Gurley Flynn, be used "*exclusively* for building up of a strong organization among the female

* From 1905 to 1913, the Industrial Workers of the World were labeled by friend and foe, I.W.W. and its members "I.W.W.'s" The three terms most frequently used by members to describe themselves were "rebel" "Fellow Worker," and "slave." The term "Wobbly" circulated orally until August, 1913, when Herman D. Suhr, organizer of the hop pickers' strike on the Durst Brothers' farm at Wheatland, California, wired the I.W.W. headquarters at Sacramento: "Send all speakers and wobblies as quick as possible." The telegram appeared in *Solidarity* in its November 1, 1913, issue, but the attention it received when introduced in the court trial following the events at the Durst farm ranch, which we will discuss below, helped bring the word "Wobbly" to national attention. By 1914, the word "Wobbly was in current usage—the term "Wobs" being used interchangeably with "Wobblies." We will use it as a name for members of the I.W.W.

workers."[32] Although the I.W.W. press featured Hill's suggestion, little was done to put it into effect. However, the I.W.W. did realize its objective of giving those women it organized "equal opportunities, duties and privileges, even to the holding of executive office." Some of the top I.W.W. organizers were women, and Elizabeth Gurley Flynn could be considered "Miss I.W.W."

THE CLASS STRUGGLE

In an article in the *Industrial Worker* celebrating the centennial birthday of Karl Marx, a writer declared: "The I.W.W. . . . . clearly adheres to the bed-rock economic facts enunciated by Karl Marx . . . while its tactics and methods are born from the every-day experience of the toilers." While there was some disagreement among the Wobblies as to how much of Marx's doctrines to accept, all I.W.W. theorizers agreed with "the scientific teachings of Karl Marx" which explained "the history of all hitherto existing society was the history of the class struggle." The I.W.W. believed implicitly that the class struggle was inherent in the very nature of capitalist society. The economic laws of capitalism, the I.W.W. pointed out, operated the same in America as in the rest of the world, and American society, like all society, was divided into two classes—the exploiters and the exploited, the capitalists and the workers. (The middle class was dismissed as belonging basically to the capitalist class even though it might "profess a certain amount of sympathy with the working class when conditions are particularly unbearable.") The Wobblies emphasized that the class struggle in American society had intensified since the closing of the frontier and with it the lessening of opportunities for workers to move West.[33]

The I.W.W. accepted completely Marx's labor theory of value and doctrine of surplus value, and held that since all value was produced by labor, the capitalists who contributed nothing to industry except capital were pure and simple parasites. Their only function was to exploit the workers. Since the capitalists took almost everything and contributed no essential value, there could be no identity of interest between the two classes, and the workers must rid themselves of capitalist rule.

Every segment of life was viewed by the I.W.W. as reflecting the conflict of the two classes. Ads appeared in the *Industrial Worker* for "Big Class War Picnic." Obituaries of dead Wobblies spoke of them as "an indefatigable warrior in the class war," and usually closed: "Our duty is not to mourn, but to go on where Fellow Worker—left off, determined to show the ruling class that his work has not been in vain."[34]

In the eyes of the I.W.W. the capitalist class was the ruling class and the government was its tool. Existing laws and institutions were the creation of the owning class. The army, the police, and the militia were all allied with the capitalist class against the workers. So was the Church. Lawyers were "a lot of Parasites who fed out of the workers' money." The courts were merely the agencies of the capitalists, and many Wobbly defendants showed complete disdain for the courts by conducting a "silent defense," refusing to defend themselves. Any Wobbly sent to jail for his views or acts was considered a class-war prisoner.

"I glory in going to jail. It's for the cause," an I.W.W. member sent to prison for contempt of court in Sacramento was quoted as having told the judge. "It's an honor to be arrested on this kind of a charge," the judge was told by Leo Stark, a Jewish I.W.W. leader arrested in Duluth for violating a ban against free speech, "for Jesus himself was a persecuted Jew." The headline in the following day's Duluth *News Tribune* read: "A Jailed I.W.W. Calls It Honor." Class-conscious workers had to accept the fact that they would go to jail; indeed, as more workers went to jail, its terror would disappear. Hence workers, in most cases, should not pay fines. "To pay fines rather than go to jail, in case of labor troubles, unless in the most unusual and peculiar circumstances, is an act of downright scabbery on the revolutionary working class."[35]

The jail was to be used as an educational center. "In the city jail," went a report in the Seattle *Post-Intelligencer* of February 26, 1913, "all the I.W.W.'s are placed in one large cell. Regular service is in continual session. 'The Solidarity of Man,' the 'Russian Brotherhood,' the 'Capitalist Class' and the 'Workingman' are subjects of preachment and discussion. That all may be given a chance to be converted to their belief every opportunity is taken by the prisoners. When the city jailer opens the outer wooden door to admit more of the organization who have just arrived, the barred interior door is filled with faces of I.W.W.'s from top to bottom, shouting short sermons on what will happen when the organization comes to its own." Most Wobblies would have agreed with Jack London's comment: "Some of us have learned our Socialism at a jump— by going to jail. That's the way I got my Socialism. And I tell you these conditions are great educators for Socialism."[36]

Unfavorable court decisions against the Wobblies were taken more or less for granted. "After all, what can an I.W.W. expect in a capitalist court?" asked a Wobbly in *Solidarity* of July 17, 1915. "The only time we can expect anything favorable is when we are able to bring about economic pressure." However, the courtroom should be used to expose the capitalists and their agents, and, in speeches before the courts at the time of sentencing, the Wobblies did exactly that. The following excerpts from a speech by a Wobbly is typical:

"I have seen you, Judge—and others of your kind, send them [the workers] to prison because they dared to infringe upon the sacred rights of property. You have become blind and deaf to the rights of man to pursue life and happiness, and you have crushed these rights so that the sacred rights of property should be preserved. Then you tell me to respect the law. I don't. I did violate every one of your laws and still come before you and say: 'To hell with the courts,' because I believe that my right to live is far more sacred than the sacred right of property that you and your kind so ably defend."[37]

RELIGION, PATRIOTISM, AND MORALITY

The I.W.W. emphasized that its membership included workers of all religious faiths—"the followers of the carpenter of Nazareth—today He would be a member of the Building Constructors' Industrial Union,* . . . followers of Mahomet, and . . . followers of Confucius." It insisted, however, that its position was not affected by "the religious ideas of any of its members." The church was a tool of the exploiting class. Although Wobblies occasionally paid tribute to a clergyman who supported labor's cause, they generally viewed the majority of the "long-haired preachers" as betrayers of the workers' fight against the capitalists by inculcating a slavish acceptance of the *status quo*.

One of the chief I.W.W. criticisms of the A.F. of L. was that it was unduly influenced by the Catholic Church.† It denounced the fact that Catholic priests attended A.F. of L. conventions, some as fraternal delegates. The I.W.W., on the other hand, was fortunate in being free of domination by "both craft unionism and Catholicism. Each is equally opposed to the interests of the toilers, whose hope lies in an organization built upon a proletarian basis along the lines of industry."[38]

The Wobblies had a flag, a red one, and they urged the workers to "live and die . . . beneath the scarlet standard high." What could the flag of the United States mean to the workers when it was a country for the benefit of the capitalists? *Solidarity* declared that "the workers have no country except as they make one," and that "the intelligent worker knows no such thing as 'my country' and sheds his 'native land' every time he takes a wash." "Love of country?" asked the *Industrial Worker* speaking for the Wobblies. "They have no country. Love of flag? None floats for them. Love of birth place? No one loves the slums. Love of the spot where they were reared? Not when it is a mill and necessity cries ever 'move on.' Love of mother tongue? They know but the slave driver's jargon whose every word spells wearisome toil followed by enforced idleness." "The American flag," declared *Solidarity*, "has always accom-

---

*"Fellow Worker Christ" was used with frequency in the I.W.W. press, and the clergy were advised to "turn to history and be reminded that the 'hobo agitator of Nazareth' and his outcast and tramp followers were a menace to the Roman Empire and to its civilization, to its religion and its patriotism." (*Solidarity*, Aug. 14, 1915.)

† For a discussion of the role of the Catholic Church in the A.F. of L., *see* Foner, *op. cit.*, vol. III, pp. 211–16.

panied institutions of oppression against the workers." It had floated "over the industrial battlefields" of Homestead, Coeur d'Alene and Cripple Creek and other labor struggles, "and just as long as the Stars and Stripes are used for such purposes—as an emblem of oppression—just so long will red-blooded workers, socialists and others, refuse to accord it their respect." In an editorial entitled, "The Glorious Fourth," *Solidarity* urged: "Let us celebrate, not the battle of Bunker Hill, but the battle of Homestead, the first great labor war in the modern industrial era."[39]

A special Anti-Patriotic Issue of the *Industrial Worker* was published on March 28, 1912. It contained several articles devoted to the theme that patriotism was but one of several devices "whereby the employing class protect their stolen booty and enslave the workers for further exploitation." One article was devoted to the Boy Scout movement, a frequent target of the I.W.W. The growth of the movement was regarded as "fraught with danger to the revolutionists" since it filled the minds of "the children of the workers with capitalist rubbish."

The I.W.W.'s anti-patriotic fervor was heightened by a shameful incident in Seattle in the summer of 1913. On the night of July 18, a mob of soldiers and sailors from the Pacific reserve fleet raided the headquarters of the I.W.W. and the Socialist Party. With the Seattle police giving it "smiles of approval," the mob, aided by civilians, sacked both headquarters, smashed the windows and doors, piled the furniture in the streets, and burned it in a huge bonfire. "As it burned an American flag was waved," the Seattle *Post-Intelligencer* reported with pride. Admiral Reynolds' sole comment on the disgraceful riot was to express relief "that there had been no casualties."[40]

A migratory worker summed up the I.W.W. position on patriotism: "You ask me why the I.W.W. is not patriotic to the United States. If you were a bum without a blanket; if you had left your wife and kids when you went west for a job, and had never located them since; if you slept in a lousy, sour bunk-house, and ate food just as rotten as they could give you and get by with it; . . . if every person who represented law and order and the nation beat you up, railroaded you to jail, and the good Christian people cheered and told them to go to it, how the hell do you expect a man to be patriotic?"[41]

The I.W.W. also rejected conventional notions of morality and preached the need for a new "proletarian morality." Vincent St. John stated the theme bluntly: "The question of 'right' and 'wrong' does not concern us." This bare declaration evidently did not satisfy all members of the I.W.W., for the Wobbly press found it necessary to discuss St. John's meaning in great detail. Out of the discussion emerged the following concept. According to the I.W.W., a proletarian and bourgeois morality existed side by side. The former was natural, the latter artificial and existed solely for the purpose of keeping the proletariat in subjugation. Hitherto the false morality of the bourgeoisie had prevailed, but the I.W.W. called for a new morality. "New concepts of *Right* and *Wrong* must generate and permeate the workers. We must look on conduct and actions that advance the social and economic position of the working class as Right ethically, legally, religiously, socially and by every other measurement. That conduct and those actions which aid, helps to maintain and gives comfort to the capitalist class, we must consider *Wrong* by every standard." *Solidarity* wound up the discussion with the terse comment: "Whatever advances working class interests is always right and whatever retards working class interests is always wrong, and that is the end of it."

But how was the new "proletarian morality" to be established? Joseph J. Ettor gave the official answer: "But, if history teaches right, we know this much—right and wrong are relative terms—and it all resolves into a question of *Power*. Cold, unsentimental Power."[42]

THE ONE BIG UNION

The primary example of working-class power was the revolutionary industrial union. Local industrial unions were combined into national industrial unions and thence into industrial departments of related industries, which departments, taken together, composed the general organization—the One Big Union. In the eyes of many commentators, the One Big Union was synonymous with the I.W.W. This was certainly the case with many Wobblies who were fond of signing letters, "Yours for the O.B.U."

In 1905 when the I.W.W. was launched elaborate plans were laid for 13 industrial departments, but later revisions reduced the number to six. A form of geographic division was also present through the creation of district industrial councils made up of representatives from all Local industrial unions within a given area. These councils provided a direct link with the general organization and had the function of assuring "complete industrial solidarity among all the workers of each industry."[43]

In many areas of the country, however, the membership was not sufficiently large to permit the creation of locals formed on strictly industrial lines. Here "mixed locals," composed of members from different locals, were chartered. Originally the "mixed locals" were viewed as merely temporary bodies to retain membership until sufficient numbers of people could be recruited to form a local on a purely industrial basis, after which it would go out of existence. But in actual practice in the West, the "mixed local" tended to become more and more the standard form of organization. This is hardly surprising. The western Wobbly was usually a migrant whose connection with any particular industry was likely to be a transient one. (In a single year, his varied jobs might involve him in logging, construction, agriculture, and in mining.) Except in a few industries, such as mining and lumbering, it proved to be impossible to recruit sufficient members to justify the creation of industrial locals, thus tending to give permanence to the "mixed locals."[44]

The "mixed local" thus came to consist of a number of permanent members who lived in a town—known as "hall cats"—and groups of "foot-loose rebels" who drifted from job to job. The group was united not by links to any particular job, shop or industry but rather by their common interest in the I.W.W.

Somewhat akin to the "mixed locals" were the Propaganda Leagues. (These too, functioned mainly in the West.*) But whereas only wage workers could belong to the "mixed locals," membership in the Propaganda Leagues was open to anyone, including "non-wage workers"—housewives, the self-employed and small businessmen.† Members of other unions who worked where there were no I.W.W. unions could also belong, as could members of the Socialist Party. In short, the Propaganda Leagues were like auxiliaries to the I.W.W. and functioned solely for propaganda purposes: "soap boxing" for the principles of industrial unionism, vending I.W.W. papers and literature, and supporting strikes, I.W.W. or otherwise, which the members felt warranted their backing.[45]

Despite its loose and haphazard structure, especially as exemplified by the "mixed locals" and the Propaganda Leagues, the O.B.U., the revolutionary industrial union, in the eyes of the I.W.W., was, unlike craft unionism, "in conformity with that of capitalist production," and scientifically in accord with changes in production methods wrought by the industrial revolution. "The trust is the natural development of industrial progress," declared the *Industrial Worker*. So was its labor counterpart, the O.B.U. It was more than a form of labor organization embracing all workers, regardless of skill or tools, divided into separate departments. To the I.W.W. it embodied a philosophy of the present, a vision of the future. It was *revolutionary industrial unionism*, providing the means by which the unity of the workers would be solidified to the end of furthering and ending the class struggle.[46]

"DIRECT ACTION," STRIKE TACTICS, IMMEDIATE DEMANDS

The primary method of struggle in class warfare, in the eyes of the I.W.W., was "direct action." But the concept of "direct action" in the I.W.W. was often so broad as to confuse members, and letters to the Wobbly press complained "It's about time that the mouthpieces of the I.W.W. give a concise explanation of what the I.W.W. means by 'direct

---

* Brissenden lists eight Propaganda Leagues in existence in 1914, all but two in the West. (*op. cit.*, Appendix V, pp. 358–63.) There were a few others referred to in the I.W.W. press and not listed by Brissenden, but as a whole the number of Propaganda Leagues was not large.

† Because the Leagues were not labor unions, they had no voting representation at I.W.W. conventions, nor could their members vote for organization-wide officers.

action.'" The *Industrial Worker* offered the following simple statement as the best definition: "'Direct Action' is any effort made directly for the purpose of getting more of the goods from the boss." *Solidarity* went into greater detail, explaining that "direct action" contrasted with "'parliamentary action' either by begging capitalist lawmakers to put such laws on the statute books, or by electing their own representatives to legislative bodies." It then offered the following definition: "'Direct Action' means dealing directly with the boss through your labor union. The strike in its different forms, is the best known example of 'direct action.'"[47]

Although the I.W.W occasionally used the boycott,* the strike was considered the best example of labor's economic power. (Conversely strikebreaking, scabbing on union members during a strike, was considered the worst crime a worker could commit and was the main cause of expulsion from the I.W.W.)† The I.W.W. strike tactics are difficult to list in their entirety, for the Wobblies had a genius for improvising new tactics during the course of a struggle, thus continually setting new fashions in strike tactics. Indeed, apart from its free-speech fights, the I.W.W. became most famous for its strike tactics. The Wobblies rejected the idea that a strike should be a "passive siege" in which workers stayed in their homes or hung about street corners until, after a period of weeks or months, the strike was declared either lost or won. Instead, the I.W.W. introduced the idea of mass picketing, mass parades, and demonstrations. The theory was that unless each striker was given something to do, the workers could easily become demoralized. Through mass activity, however, "the strikers draw courage from one another, feel their common interest, and realize the necessity of solidarity."[48]

I.W.W. strike tactics were designed to educate the workers, through experience, to the realities of the class struggle. "We learn to fight by *fighting*," wrote Mary Marcy in a pamphlet published by the I.W.W. The *Industrial Worker,* however, gave the official position:

"The Industrial Workers of the World always has one fundamental aim in view when going on strike. Other aims and purposes may be at times—in fact generally are—the most widely advertised and better known. Decent camp conditions, shorter work days, larger wages, the release of class-war prisoners and other things may be put to the front as the main

---

* The I.W.W. sometimes advised members and sympathizers to boycott an entire community during strikes and free-speech fights. Boycotts against specific companies were very rare. One was projected during a strike against the Universal Motion Picture Film Co. in June 1914. The I.W.W. strike committee announced: "We are going to boycott every theatre owned by the Universal or showing Universal films in the United States." (*Solidarity,* June 27, 1914.)

† This did not apply only to I.W.W. strikes. Among men listed in the I.W.W. press as expelled for strikebreaking were those found guilty of crossing picket lines set up by non-I.W.W. unions. "The I.W.W. . . . does not stand for mutual scabbing or reprisals," the general secretary-treasurer explained. (*Industrial Worker,* Dec. 8, 1910.)

cause of the strike. But back of them all and vastly overshadowing them all in importance is the fundamental thing for which we strike: Raising the standard of consciousness and aggressiveness of the working class."[49]

In this sense, of course, no strike was lost no matter what the outcome!

"Strike when you like and wherever you like," was a key slogan of the I.W.W. But definitely not as long as you like. The strike, in the eyes of the I.W.W., was the main weapon of the working masses, but the superior economic power concentrated in the hands of the capitalist class made long fights impractical. The I.W.W. never had and usually did not believe in large treasuries. *Solidarity* claimed that the I.W.W. did not object to creating a "war chest" in strikes, but believed that many craft unions were wrong in stressing that "by a big treasury alone a union can wage a successful battle against their more powerfully organized and more financially resourceful employers." The key to victory lay in the solidarity of the workers and not in any "war chest." The *Industrial Worker* was more forthright: "Being a fighting organization we place but little faith in well-filled treasuries. They invariably lead the workers to rely upon the money rather than their own efforts, and demoralization results. The most conservative unions are always those with the largest treasuries."[50] Hence the I.W.W. usually paid no strike, out-of-work, sickness or death benefits—practices which were summarily rejected as "coffin unionism." James P. Thompson, a leading I.W.W. organizer, explained how the I.W.W. financed its strikes: "An appeal for funds is sent to all friends of labor. Lectures are organized in which the hat is passed around in aid of the strikers. A relief committee is appointed, for the I.W.W. does not pay cash strike benefits. Relief committees receive applications from destitute working men for food, clothing and shelter and investigate the cases. All unmarried strikers are served free meals at soup kitchens. Married strikers receive orders for food supplies."[51]*

Under these circumstances, long, drawn-out battles with the employers could not be readily supported. "We want a strike that is short and sweet," was a typical remark by an I.W.W. organizer. Or as an I.W.W. committee in California put it: "We want no long drawn out starvation strike. . . . If we should fail to win our demands in a few days, let us go back to the job and get wages while we strike on the job."[52]

The "strike on the job" would usually come when the formal strike seemed lost. Then the Wobblies returned to work, abruptly ending their formal strike. Announcing that they were "taking the strike to the job," they continued to harry the employers and to restrict production. They would follow foremen's orders to ludicrous, work-stoppage extremes or stand idle when minor decisions were required. Fired for these dilatory tactics, the Wobblies moved to other jobs and repeated their tactics.

---

* Reprinting this statement, the Toledo *Union Leader* called it " 'Soup House' Unionism," "an elaborate system of beggary." (Sept. 20, 1912.)

The I.W.W claimed many advantages for the "strike on the job." Authorities could no longer arrest strikers and pickets because every worker had ostensibly returned to work. The I.W.W. had no longer to think of ways of dealing with "scabs" because even the strikers "worked." The I.W.W. also rid itself of a financial responsibility because "much against their will the companies were forced to run the commissary department of the strike."[53]

Since there was obviously no community of interest between workers and employers, the I.W.W. stressed that it was necessary to struggle continually against the latter. "When you join the I.W.W.," *Solidarity* reminded the workers, "you are enlisting for a war. A bitter war." The war waged by the I.W.W. against the capitalists could result neither in victory nor defeat until the final triumph of the workers; nor could it be settled. If the workers' demands were accepted, work was resumed, but this was neither a triumph nor a settlement. It was only the closing of one more phase of the class struggle. I.W.W. members did not consider themselves bound by the employer's consent to their demands.[54] Most often, new demands were already under way before the strikers returned to their jobs.

At a time when many unions were fighting tenaciously for union recognition on the ground that without it the workers could not protect themselves adequately since employers would repudiate every concession made in a strike unless they were bound by a written agreement, the I.W.W. rejected the whole concept of a labor-management contract. "No contracts, no agreements, no compacts," Haywood declared. "These are unholy alliances, and must be damned as treason when entered into with the capitalist class." In 1912, an I.W.W. local in Great Falls, Mont., signed a contract with employers. This horrified the leaders of the I.W.W. and the charter of the local was immediately revoked by the G.E.B. By its action, the members were informed, the G.E.B. "saved the I.W.W. itself from dishonor, disgrace and so forth that would necessarily have occurred had this local remained in the I.W.W. with a contract with the employing class." The Philadelphia Marine Transport Workers Local 3 was pointed to as an example of an I.W.W. union which "maintained permanent organization without a contract by requiring all to wear monthly work buttons."[55]

In the eyes of the I.W.W., labor-management contracts, or "holy alliances," were typical of job or business unionism and revealed a lack of confidence in the ability of the rank and file to keep and maintain the union. In any case, the employers paid no attention to union contracts unless the union was strong enough to enforce them, "and when the Union is strong enough to force concessions it doesn't need to enter into time agreements." Such agreements gave the employer the time to prepare for a strike when they expired. "They keep the workers from taking ad-

vantage of business conditions that might offer a good chance for rein-
forcing their demands." The workers, in any event, were indispensable;
the plants could not operate without them, contract or no contract.
Moreover, contracts bred the feeling that once the strike was over, the
class struggle on the job was ended. But as St. John put it, in justifying
the stand against contracts: "No terms with an employer are final. All
peace so long as the wage system lasts is but an armed truce. At any
favorable opportunity the struggle for more control of industry is renewed."[56]

The protocol, a regularized system of airing grievances, was also condemned by the I.W.W. It allowed the employers and the leaders of the
union to "act together against the workers—the former are interested in
peace for profits' sake, the others for the sake of assuring a steady income
of dues without taking any of the risk involved in the class struggle."
The check-off, under which the employer deducted the union dues from
the workers' wages was also condemned. Where, asked the Wobblies,
under such an arrangement, was there any solidarity of the workers, any
dedication to the revolutionary cause? The Wobbly answer was that
there was none.[57]

"A labor organization to correctly represent the workers," declared an
I.W.W. pamphlet, "must have two things in view." First, it had to combine
the wage workers in such a way "that it can most successfully fight the
battles and protect the interests of the workers of today in their struggles
for fewer hours of toil, more wages and better conditions." Second, it had
to offer "a final solution of the labor problem—an emancipation from
strikes, injunctions, bull-pens, and scabbing against one another." Such
an organization, it made it clear, was the I.W.W. *Solidarity* explained
why in one sentence: "The I.W.W. is organizing for pork chops in the
present and for a new social system." Criticizing Wobblies who argued
that it was a waste of time and energy to fight for higher wages and
shorter hours and that everything should be geared to achieving "the
whole Co-operative Commonwealth at once," it cited Karl Marx to support its view that the struggle for such demands was a necessary step on
the path leading to the new society. With every strike for higher wages
and shorter hours, the workers were being drilled in the class struggle
and prepared "for the final abolition of the wage system and labor getting
the full product of its toil when capitalism shall have been overthrown."
To be sure, the I.W.W. had to make it clear that it fought for higher
wages and shorter hours "merely as a palliative but by no means as a cure."
But the experience of past labor organizations had proved that it was impossible to get the workers organized "by telling them about the industrial
republic we are going to have maybe 100 years from now. But get better
conditions now, and we will be able to get more radical dope into them."[58]

But some Wobblies charged that the I.W.W. was betraying the workers by calling upon them to fight for higher wages since (1) businessmen would immediately raise the price of goods to equal the rise in wages, so that the wage gains earned by some workers would come out of the pockets of other workers; and (2) a strike for higher wages distracted the working class from the real task, the overthrow of capitalism, and bred illusions among the workers that it was really impossible to improve their conditions under capitalism. Many of the replies to these critics based their answers on Marx's *Value, Price and Profit,* pointing out that he had already demolished the specific objections to the struggle for higher wages, and had admonished the workers not to abandon this struggle because "[by] cowardly giving way in their everyday conflict with capital, the workers would certainly disqualify themselves for the initiating of any larger movement." But a more direct answer was: "Higher wages is what we want now, and if the rise in wages didn't really mean anything to the working class, would the bosses kick so against it?"[59]

In 1911 the I.W.W. initiated a drive to line up the working class in a national demonstration for the eight-hour day to take place in a year, on May 1, 1912—May Day.* The Portland, Oregon, locals, in cooperation with the Socialist Party of the city, launched the campaign in January 1911, and asked the help of the Socialist press, the Socialist Party, all locals of the A.F. of L., "and all other organizations interested in the welfare of the working class." *Industrial Worker* endorsed the call, and began carrying as its top, banner headline on every issue the slogan: "Fight for the Eight Hour Day." By July 1911 Eight Hour Day Conferences and Eight Hour Leagues, under the sponsorship and leadership of the I.W.W., were formed in a number of cities, and Eight Hour stickers were printed and distributed which read:

"I
Won't Work
more
than 8 hours
After May 1st 1912
How About You
?"[60]

But at the sixth I.W.W. convention, held in Chicago in September 1911, James P. Thompson recommended that the designated date for the eight-hour strike be dropped, emphasizing "the futility of trying to carry this agitation to a successful culmination in such a short time." The con-

---

* May Day was celebrated annually by the I.W.W. Labor Day was for the "labor fakers" and other lackeys of capitalism. "It has no significance as a protest, carries with it no promise, and is not borne up by any ideals. Let us boycott it." (*Solidarity,* May 1, 1915.)

vention, heeding this advice, voted to "strike out the date of May 1, 1912, as the *Eight Hour Action Day*." Thompson recommended "a systematic course of action to be carried on 'for 8-hours' by stickers and otherwise and when the time is advantageous to set a date for its conquest."[61] While the I.W.W. did not again attempt to proclaim one particular day for the inauguration of shorter hours, it never dropped the issue from its demands.

THE GENERAL STRIKE AND THE NEW SOCIETY

I.W.W. strikes were fought to improve the economic welfare of the workers. Strike issues were higher wages, shorter hours, and better working conditions. But every one of these strikes was a school in which the workers trained themselves. "This training is most necessary to prepare the masses for the final 'catastrophe,' the general strike, which will complete the expropriation of the employers."[62]

The idea of a general strike did not, of course, originate with the I.W.W. It appeared in England as early as 1817, although William Benbow of Manchester is generally credited with originating the idea, in about 1832, and it became a feature of the Chartist movement. The idea was debated by the congresses of the First International and then faded away. It came to birth again in France in the 1880's as part of the system of syndicalism.[63] In the I.W.W. the general strike was first mentioned at the founding convention where it was advocated by Lucy E. Parsons, widow of Albert R. Parsons, one of the Haymarket martyrs, and the Industrial Workers' Club of Chicago. But the majority of the delegates were not prepared to endorse a general strike, and the proposals died for lack of support.[64] By 1910, and more especially in 1911, advocacy of the general strike began to appear quite regularly in the I.W.W. press.* It was urged (1) as a tactic in labor's guerrilla warfare with capitalism, especially to force favorable court decisions, and (2) as the means of achieving final emancipation.

I.W.W. publications and speakers seldom went into great detail in describing the various theoretical aspects of the general strike, especially as advanced and developed by European theoreticians. In a speech in 1911, Haywood, who was the author of the I.W.W. publication, *The General Strike,* confessed: "I must admit to you that I am not well posted on the

---

* As early as February 5, 1910, the *Industrial Worker* listed four types of strikes in the armory of the I.W.W. "We have the *partial* strike, the *passive* strike, the *irritant* strike, and the *general* strike—one continual series of skirmishes with the enemy." The passive strike was defined by *Solidarity* as one "in which the workers do not leave the shop, but temporarily suspend work pending the adjustment of some grievance." (July 2, 1910.) For all its talk of the general strike, it was unions affiliated with the A.F. of L. and not the I.W.W. which conducted the only general strike of this period. This was the general strike in Philadelphia in 1910 which will be discussed in the next volume.

theories advanced by Jaurès, Vandervelde, Kautsky and others who write and speak about the general strike. But I am not here to theorize, not here to talk in the abstract, but to get down to the concrete subject whether or not the general strike is an effective weapon for the working class."[65] Haywood then went on to develop the thesis that American experience alone proved that the general strike was an effective weapon.

The I.W.W.'s notion about the general strike was extremely simple. When a sufficient number of workers had been organized and trained, through strikes for immediate demands, it would be possible to achieve the seizure of industry in a single blow. Instead of walking out on strike, the workers would *stay on the job* and conduct a sitdown strike in all industry: "We fold our arms. The mills close. Industry is at a standstill. We then make our proposition to our former masters. It is this: We, the workers have labored long enough to support idlers. From now on, he who would not toil, neither shall he eat. We tear down to build up."[66]

But there were those who asked what would prevent the capitalists from using their state power and calling in the military to crush the workers. Charles E. Ruthenberg, Cleveland Socialist and later secretary of the Communist Party, put it concisely: "The trouble with the I.W.W. theorizing is that it overlooks entirely the fact that in the very process of organizing industrial unions and carrying on their strikes they run into opposition to the organized power of capitalism as embodied in the State. It is an illusion to think that the capitalists will fail to use their state power to check the development of these unions and defeat them in their strikes." But the I.W.W. dismissed such arguments with the contention that the workers, through their economic power alone, could paralyze the capitalists' state power. As for the use of the military to crush the general strike, the I.W.W. had a ready, if hardly convincing answer: "With the same power—industrial control—that the workers take over the industries they can cut off the supplies and transportation facilities of the army."[67]

Not all I.W.W. leaders believed in the general strike as the means for emancipation. (Vincent St. John, secretary-treasurer from 1908 to 1914, does not even mention it in his official *The I.W.W., Its History, Structure and Methods,* published in 1913.) Those who did believe in it were never very clear on what the workers would do after the strike. The *Industrial Worker* was at least frank when it conceded that it did not know: "To try to settle the question of '*just what we will do on the day after the general strike*' is like a man with black hair trying to foretell just when his hair will turn gray. Time alone will tell." Meanwhile, it urged Wobblies to educate themselves with technical and managerial knowledge so as to be prepared to operate industry after the general strike.[68]

What exactly the "new society" in the post-revolution world—variously called the Workers' Commonwealth, the Industrial Commonwealth, the

Cooperative Commonwealth, Industrial Democracy, Industrial Communism—would be like was also not made very clear. One Wobbly, in justifying the I.W.W. refusal to draw up detailed blueprints of the future, wrote: "Of course, we can't give a full and detailed plan of the whole structure; it must be sufficient to mark the tendency of production carried on by the unions. We dare go no further if we want to avoid landing in Utopia." *Solidarity* added that "the details must depend upon the future development of society."[69]

Within these limitations, I.W.W. writers did attempt to speculate on the structure of the new social order. From the time of the fourth convention (1908), the Preamble to the I.W.W.'s constitution had concluded with the statement: "By organizing industrially we are forming the structure of the new society within the shell of the old." Basing themselves on this principle, the Wobbly theoreticians emphasized that the foundation of the new society was already being laid by the I.W.W. "The industrial union furnishes a means of carrying on industry when capitalism is overthrown, and predicates the disappearance of the state. . . . Present political-geographical divisions will . . . die out under an industrially managed form of society." Thus the state would vanish. "Industrial divisions alone will remain."

In the new society, everyone would have to be a useful producer, or as one Wobbly put it more picturesquely "He who works not, neither shall he stick his feet under the table when the dinner bell ringeth." Each would be organized into an appropriate industrial union and all would be members of the Industrial Workers of the World. Representation would be by the method of voting for delegates from one's industrial union. In this way a functional democracy would be preserved:

"By means of the *Industrial Franchise*, which gives the vote to all useful workers in their productive capacity; by means of *Industrial Representation*, which gives us expert public servants from every line of human activity, and by means of the resulting *Industrial Administration, we propose to anchor all power for all times to come with the deep layers of the people who do the useful work with hand and brain,* so that it cannot possibly slip away from them and give rise to another system of class rule."[70]

All this added up to industrial democracy. "This government will have for its legislative halls the mills, the workshops and factories. Its legislators will be the men in the mills, the workshops and factories. Its legislative enactments will be those pertaining to the welfare of the workers." The entire structure would be managed by the workers who would also determine the amount of production and its distribution.[71]

While Wobblies differed among themselves as to the exact nature of the structure and operation of the new society, there was complete agreement as to the superiority of this society over capitalism:

"No more prostitutes. Girls will no longer sell their bodies when they can get for themselves the full product of their labor. Crime will disappear as the incentive for it is taken away. Poverty cannot exist where all are workers and none are shirkers. Children instead of working in the mills will be in the schools. Mothers will no longer dread the ordeal of motherhood from [sic] economic reasons. We will grow physically, intellectually and morally. A new race will result, a race that will live for the joy of living, a race that will look with horror upon the pages of history that will tell of our present day society."

There would be community dining rooms, theaters, shops, factories and services, art galleries and libraries, all owned and managed by industrial unions. "The work rooms will be superior to any ever conceived. Your work chairs will be morris chairs, so that when you become fatigued you may relax in comfort." In addition to improved working conditions, "the inventive genius of the human race can be enabled to blossom forth as never before in the history of mankind." Art and literature would also flourish, for talents would no longer be held in check by a master class. Greater leisure, too, would allow for a more widespread development of latent creative talents. The dread problems of sickness and old age would be eliminated.[72]

This vision of a new society suddenly brought within reach shared more of the charisimatic dreams of Edward Bellamy than the theories of Marx and Engels. In his novels *Looking Backward* and *Equality,* Bellamy also envisaged a new society owned and managed by "industrial armies" whose guilds were to run America. But both Marx and Engels emphasized again and again that to achieve communism the proletariat must take political power. Through the dictatorship of the proletariat, the transition would be achieved from capitalism "to the abolition of all classes and to a classless society."[73] This Marxian stress on the necessity of political action by the proletariat to gain control of the state apparatus and of the dictatorship of the proletariat for the achievement of communism was completely absent in the thinking of the I.W.W. The Wobblies, of course, rejected political action, had no conception of the dictatorship of the proletariat, and regarded industrial unions as the means of achieving the future classless society and the apparatus for operating it once achieved. To all who criticized the program as utopian, the I.W.W. had a ready answer: "These things are to be. No force can stop them. Armies will be of no avail. Capitalist governments may issue their mandates in vain. The power of the workers—industrially organized—is the only power on earth, worth considering. Once they realized that power, classes will disappear, and in their place will be he only useful members of society—the workers." It was all so very simple. But then, as Haywood put it: "Socialism is so plain, so clear, so simple that when a person becomes intellectual he doesn't understand Socialism."[74]

CONCEPT OF LEADERSHIP

The Manifesto calling the 1905 constituent meeting of the I.W.W. declared that in the new organization "All power should rest in a collective membership."[75] This doctrine was largely ignored in the early years of the I.W.W. But after the removal of Daniel De Leon, the theory that emerged was that leadership must not be based on any one or several individuals but must be a collective leadership; that the leadership must arise from the workers, and remain, at the same time, with the workers. A Kansas City Wobbly put it succinctly in defending himself in court on a street-speaking charge: "Every man in our organization has as much power and as much right as any other member. We have no . . . Samuel Gompers. . . . We follow no Moses out of the bullrushes." "It has been said," Haywood once wrote, "that every institution is but the lengthening shadow of a single man. This is not true when speaking of the Industrial Workers of the World."[76] To be sure, for many years the figure of "Big Bill" so dominated the public image of the I.W.W. that he was even called "Mr. I.W.W."* But Haywood always insisted: "We are all leaders."[77]

Basically, the I.W.W. slogan "We are all leaders" was designed to eliminate "the faultiness of constitutional provisions that invest the A.F. of L. officialdom with practically arbitrary power," and to insure that "union officials are regarded as servants rather than rulers of the organized workers." But as one student has correctly noted, it "led to a contempt for honest, courageous leadership, to confusion among the membership and to an individusalistic approach to the problems and tactics of the union."[78] Suspicion of any authority in the hands of leadership became a fixed characteristic of many Wobblies. Leaders of the I.W.W. had to expect regular attacks from within the ranks. Some of the examples of suspicion of leadership are so ridiculous as to be almost unbelievable. Fred Heslewood, editor of the *Industrial Worker,* came under attack because he owned his own home, and a secretary of the Spokane I.W.W. barely survived a recall vote because he wore a diamond ring, which he explained was left him by his mother as a keepsake and memento.[79]

One of the arguments for low fees and dues was that it would keep the I.W.W. officials from fattening their wallets. Another manifestation of suspicion of leadership was illustrated in the demand to set severe constitutional limits to officers' terms. Yearly elections of officers were provided for in the original constitution, but this was not enough to satisfy

---

* Some commentators believed that the title "Mr. I.W.W." belonged more properly to Vincent St. John on the ground that it was he who really led the movement when the I.W.W. reached the crest of its power and directed most of its operations. "The man who built the I.W.W. was . . . Vincent St. John," writes a former Wobbly in his memoirs. (Thomas J. Bogard, "My Memories of the I.W.W.," unpublished manuscript in possession of the author, p. 146.)

the anti-leadership elements. In 1911 a series of resolutions from several locals called for restrictions on the number of terms an officer could serve. One resolution, from Kansas City, demanding a two-term limit, was accompanied by the explanation that the I.W.W. advertised itself as having no leaders, yet "some of our officers [have become] professional Officials of the Revolution." This, according to the local, was dangerous because reelection of officers led to lazy members, dependent upon their officials instead of themselves.[80] Before 1919, when a one-year maximum term provision was finally adopted for the full organization, this demand did not get very far. But the whole controversy diverted energies needed for building the organization into endless squabbles over the limitations to be placed on leadership.

Yet the demand for a limitation on the term of officers was mild compared with the program of the decentralizers, the most vehement and noisiest of the anti-leadership element, a particularly influential force on the Pacific Coast, especially in California. Not only did they favor term limits to officers' tenure, but a number of them wanted to do away with *all* officers in the general administration; abolish the general executive board and the post of general organizer and replace them with a stenographer who would handle correspondence between locals. "What have they [G.E.B. members and the General Organizer] accomplished . . ., besides sign charters with rubber stamps, draw salary and mileage? Why have them?" Another demand was for abolition of the annual convention and substitution for it of the initiative and referendum. The convention was defined as "class government." "A working class union which elects representatives to such conventions, thereby vests its economic power in a political sovereign; therefore the L[ocal] U[nion] no longer has power, but has surrendered its power to its representatives. . . . Representative government . . . is in its structure Class Government." The position of the decentralizers was accurately summed up by John Pancner in opposing their demands: "No executive board, no headquarters, no dues, no cards, no secretaries, no convention, and no organization."[81]

Almost every issue of the *Industrial Worker* contained at least one article or resolution demanding decentralization of the national administration and greater autonomy for the Pacific Coast locals. In February 1911, a Pacific Coast conference was held at Portland to set up a regional organization for the purpose of gaining a greater degree of autonomy from the "tyranny of the General Executive Board." A Pacific Coast District Organization was established at the conference which planned to put three organizers and one secretary in the field working out of a western office.[82]

Nothing came of the "P.C.D.O.," as the regional organization was called in I.W.W. circles, but at the eighth national convention in 1913, the western delegates set up a clamor against bureaucratic control by the national organization. They proposed to abolish the general executive board; to cut down the financial support of the general office; to abolish the convention and substitute for it the initiative and referendum; to place agitators under the direct control of the rank and file; and to make the general officers mere clerical assistants. But the majority of the delegates rejected this anarchistic philosophy of organization. Except for securing a provision for initiative and referendum, the movement came to nothing. Nevertheless, the G.E.B. warned:

"We find a situation in the West that if continued means the complete disruption of the only industrial organization in the world. In time of strike they [the decentralizers] sit around the hall talking of what ought to be done or devising means to do away with the General Headquarters. It is impossible, however, to get them out on the picket line to fight the boss. They will talk of sabotage and direct action but leave it to the boss to use on the few who take up the fight. If this condition continues the I.W.W. will die of dry rot. . . ."[83]

The decentralization issue remained to haunt the I.W.W. well into the '20's. But in the years before the first World War, it was overshadowed by the organizational work conducted by the I.W.W. In these activities the Wobblies shelved their disagreements over leadership and presented a united front to the class enemy.*

---

* In the *Journal of Social History*, Spring, 1971 (p. 299), labor historian Joseph G. Rayback contends that the I.W.W. "was not conscious of nationality or race—unless the race was 'Asiatic.' It rejected Asians. That prejudice would lead me to conclude that the IWW would have rejected Negroes if any appreciable number of Negroes had worked in the textile centers of the East or in the fields, forests, and camps of the West." A more unjustified conclusion can hardly be imagined. The information in the pages above and in pages 232–57, 260, 272 alone should reveal how unjustified is Dr. Rayback's statement about Asian workers and his conclusion regarding the I.W.W.'s position on black workers.

Since this chapter was written, I have developed further the discussion of the I.W.W. and black workers. *See* my article, "The IWW and the Black Worker," *Journal of Negro History*, vol. LV, January, 1970.

CHAPTER 6

Ideology and Tactics

Judged in the light of reason, a union whose dues-paying membership in 1912 for the whole of the I.W.W., according to Vincent St. John, was only 25,000, could not be viewed as becoming the agency for the transformation of American society. But the Congressional Commission on Industrial Relations correctly observed that although the I.W.W.'s membership was small, "as a 'spirit and a vocabulary' [it] permeates to a large extent enormous masses of workers, particularly among the unskilled and migratory laborers." In its own eyes the I.W.W. represented the "militant minority" whose activity made the small organization a force out of all proportion to its actual membership. The "militant minority," it thought, was "the real driving force in the labor movement of every country," and in the United States, it would prove to be the force to mobilize the American workers both for short-term struggles and for the ultimate battle for a new social system. "We are the Revolution!" Haywood wrote in 1912, in an article entitled "The Fighting I.W.W."[1]*

EDUCATION

The duty of the "militant minority" was to promote class-consciousness and solidarity among the workers, fostering in them a revolutionary spirit. This could be accomplished in two ways: education in theory and education in class warfare. In this way, the workers would become conscious of their power, would learn the class nature of the capitalist state, gain greater insight into the nature of the class sruggle, and increase their solidarity. Such an education, the I.W.W. believed, was essential before

---

* The doctrine of the "militant minority" was a leading feature of European anarcho-syndicalism. Not all I.W.W. members favored the doctrine, believing that the idea of a revolutionary elite went counter to the principle of democratic trade unionism. However, Haywood and most of the other leaders of the I.W.W. endorsed the principle of the "militant minority." (*See* W. D. Haywood, *The General Strike*, Chicago, 1911, pp. 11-12.)

it could achieve its ultimate purpose—"complete surrender of industry to the organized workers"—and necessary, too, for the effective operation of the new society. "It will be the educated industrial unionists who will be at the posts when capitalism is abolished and the Industrial organization will be the administrating Government of the working class."[2]

The model I.W.W. member was one who understood that "one cannot be economically free unless he is intellectually free." This did not mean he was to be confused with "the intellectual who is generally in the employ of the capitalist class" or with those who "have always been long on theories and short on a knowledge of practical action." The workers had no need of assistance from such intellectuals. Only a worker could understand the workers and lead them, but to fulfill this role he had to be an educated worker.[3]

I.W.W. publications used the term "intellectuals" in two different ways. Intellectuals in general were regarded as servants of the capitalist class, and as such there was no room for them in the I.W.W. On the other hand, there was the working-class intellectual who studied to serve the interests of the working class, to lead the revolution and to rule the Cooperative Commonwealth.[4]

I.W.W. papers took delight in publishing reports of the amazement shown by college professors who heard Wobbly speakers deliver talks upon a wide variety of subjects and reveal a remarkable understanding of complex economic and social questions. Intellectuals—"so-called educators, professors and even scientists"—were depicted as being afraid to debate with I.W.W. speakers once they heard the Wobblies speak. "They ask: 'Where did that fellow come from? . . . and shake their heads when told that he is but one of the many taken from the ranks." Carleton Parker of the University of California testified to the general accuracy of the Wobbly speakers' use of statistics relating to the conditions of American workers: "Presumably they were better acquainted with American social statistics than the academic class." However, I.W.W. speakers were warned in the Wobbly press against speaking "over the head of the crowd. . . . The most successful speaker is without doubt the man who uses the knowledge of economics in connection with current events, conditions on the job, strikes and incidents of the everyday worker's life, also uses the plainest and simplest language and sometimes goes so far as to tell a funny story to emphasize his point."[5]

The I.W.W. organized Propaganda Leagues and Industrial Education Clubs for the purpose of education. It published hundreds of thousands of leaflets, many illustrated with simple but effective cartoons. It distributed pamphlets and "stickers." The latter, printed with gummed backs, were sold by the thousand (a dollar a thousand, usually) by national headquarters and by locals and branches for general distribution to members, and advertised in the Wobbly press with the slogan, "Stick

'Em Up Everywhere!" They were pasted on bunk houses, boxcars, employment offices, shovel handles, etc. Some carried brief messages such as "sit down and watch your pay go up." Others summed up the I.W.W. philosophy in a few short words such as:

> "Solidarity
> Takes the Whole Works
> Join the One Big Union."[6]

I.W.W. cartoons showed a worker striding up a path labeled "Solidarity" towards a sunrise labeled "Cooperative Commonwealth" or a fat-jowled man with a silk top hat labeled "Big Business" sitting on a pile of money labeled "Product of the workers' sweat and toil." I.W.W. newspapers featured a comic strip by Ernest Riebe of Minneapolis that depicted the stupidity of "Mr. Block," a square-headed worker who tenaciously clung to the conviction that he and his employer shared economic interests in spite of his regular disillusionments. A pamphlet entitled *Mr. Block,* consisting of 24 cartoons, was distributed by the I.W.W. It was described as "showing the different adventures of the average worker who has capitalist ideas. Just the thing to knock the scales off the eyes of the would-be-scabs."*

The I.W.W. staged hundreds of Sunday Educational meetings and open forums, held classes, toured speakers who addressed street-corner meetings and indoor mass meetings all over the country, opened union halls where workers could get their latest Wobbly literature, held "bull sessions" on such subjects as "Improved Machinery and Unemployment," "Direct Action," "Industrial Versus Craft Unionism," "The General Strike," etc. *Solidarity* of April 17, 1915, announced a lecture tour by Elizabeth Gurley Flynn in the Midwest which included talks on "Small Families a Proletarian Necessity"; "Violence and the Labor Movement"; "Solidarity, Labor's Road to Freedom." The lectures were to take place in union and public halls and the admission ranged from 10 to 25 cents.

On November 25, 1911, *Solidarity* reported that the I.W.W. published six newspapers in five different languages throughout the country. By the end of 1912, the number had increased to 13: English, French, Italian, Spanish, Portuguese, Russian, Polish, Slavic, Lithuanian, Hungarian, Swedish, Jewish, and Japanese. Most of these papers were short-lived, many never going beyond Volume 1, No. 1. The two principal and longest lasting weeklies were *Solidarity* and the *Industrial Worker*. *Solidarity,* whose first issue appeared on December 18, 1909, and the last on March 18, 1917, was published by the local unions of the I.W.W. at New Castle, Pa., and then by those in Cleveland and Chicago. It was

---

* The I.W.W., of course, never bothered to reveal how many of these "would-be-scabs" actually became scabs or why every worker with capitalist ideas was a "would-be-scab."

the "official" I.W.W. paper. The *Industrial Worker,* which began publication on March 18, 1909, and lasted until September 4, 1913—it started again in April, 1916, and is now the only English language paper of the I.W.W.—was not then an "official" I.W.W. paper.* Published weekly in Spokane and Seattle in the years before World War I, it was described as "A Red Hot Fearless Working Class Paper" which "Represents the Spirit of the West" and was the organ of the western I.W.W.

The logotype of both *Solidarity* and the *Industrial Worker,* as it was of most I.W.W. papers, contained a symbol of the northern hemisphere over which were three stars labeled "Emancipation," "Education," and "Organization." Above was the motto: "An Injury to One Is an Injury to All!"

Solidarity rarely published its circulation figures. It claimed that it had printed and sold 12,000 copies of its special Lawrence strike edition of March 2, 1912, but on August 7, 1915, stated that 75,000 copies had been sold of that issue. With such varying claims being fairly typical, it is hard even to guess at its circulation figures. The *Industrial Worker,* which published circulation figures, had a circulation in 1911 of between 3,000 to 5,000 an issue. Its special eight-page issue of July 25, 1912, in connection with the Ettor-Giovannitti trial, ran to 75,000 copies and led the editor to boast that the printing "breaks the world's record for a revolutionary wage worker's paper." By April, 1917, the *Industrial Worker* was printing a regular issue of 11,000 to 12,000 copies.[7]

I.W.W. pamphlets were on a high intellectual level. Their analyses of the histories and technological progress of the various industries were incisive and complete. Those dealing with evils within specific A.F. of L. unions were well-documented. One concluded:

"Why if horses were organized like the A.F. of L., we'd never get anywhere. One horse would be pulling forward with all his might, like a good labor leader, but one of the horses would be trying to go off to the side and another would be going backward. The fourth would probably jump right up in the driver's lap and help drive the other three. The Federation type of organization is vital to the bosses.

"Trade and craft unionism is doomed and will, through the inevitable laws of necessity, be supplanted by Industrial Unionism."[8]

The most widely circulated I.W.W. pamphlets were *Sabotage* (three different versions of the subject), *Direct Action,* William E. Trautmann's *Why Strikes Are Lost! How to Win!,* and *Tactics or Methods,* a copy of the last being "given to every member of the organization."[9] As their

* By "official organ" was meant a paper issued and regularly financed by the general executive board and whose editor and business manager was elected by the entire I.W.W. membership or hired by the G.E.B. The *Industrial Worker* simply announced that it was "Published by the G.E.B." However, it was financed by the general organization in December, 1910.

titles indicate, these pamphlets dealt primarily with tactics in the class struggle, and while they did not neglect theory entirely, they were essentially calls to action.

Thanks to the members of the I.W.W. who were migratory workers, I.W.W. literature was disseminated all over the West. "Thousands of books, pamphlets and papers are purchased by these workers, read and distributed by them wherever they go," an I.W.W. paper boasted.[10] As early as 1910, W. I. Fisher, an organizer, recommended that a library be set up in every Wobbly hall to be composed of "books, articles, and magazines on such subjects as improved machinery and methods of production, discoveries and application of science, general scientific knowledge, discussions on economics and public questions. . . . A working class movement based upon the knowledge of the workers' interest is invincible."[11] This advice was followed. Libraries were set up in many Wobbly halls. The typical hall, especially in the West, usually contained dog-eared copies of Marx, Darwin, Spencer, Voltaire, Tom Paine, Jack London, and a wide variety of government documents. The list of books recommended for the libraries in the halls reveals a wide interest in economic and social subjects. Indeed, the compiler of a list of books "from among which can be selected a good collection for any camp for the workers to read after working hours," apologized for some of the less serious selections, writing: "Several are fiction, but good nevertheless."[12] Jack London's *The Iron Heel* was an exception, and was always popular among the Wobblies.

"Entering a [Wobbly] hall in the evening," wrote one commentator, "one might see several shabbily dressed young men reading books taken from the shelves of the library in the room. Others crouched over a makeshift stove brewing a mulligan stew, its ambitious odor permeating the hall. While they tended their supper, they argued some point in economics or religion."[13]

Many fellow workers put public libraries to extensive use. Wobblies in the West often spent their winters of idleness in the public libraries, and, although often lacking in formal education, became acquainted in this way with the works of Marx and Engels, Herbert Spencer, Charles Darwin, Lewis Henry Morgan, Frederick Jackson Turner, and other writings in economics, philosophy, and science.[14]

I.W.W. SONGS: JOE HILL

To many Wobblies the best educational material published by the I.W.W. was *The Little Red Song Book*. "There are 38 songs in the I.W.W. song book," a Wobbly organizer wrote in 1912, "and out of that number 24 are educational, and I can truthfully say that every one of them is almost a lecture in itself." Some Wobblies even went so far as to recommend that the I.W.W. cease publishing pamphlets and other literature of an economic nature and concentrate solely on the *Song Book*. During 1911 and 1912 the I.W.W. press was filled with letters discussing the subject "Song vs. Education." Critics of the wide use of songs argued that an effective industrial union movement could not be built by "going out in the streets and telling a few funny stories and singing ragtime songs a la Salvation Army." This brought the reply that songs inspired the workers and made them go into action "while the intellectuals were left in our halls, chewing the volumes of Karl Marx." Joe Hill, the great Wobbly song-writer, argued that "if a person can put a few cold, common sense facts into a song and dress them (the facts) up in a cloak of humor to take the dryness out of them, he will succeed in reaching a great number of workers who are too unintelligent or too indifferent to read a pamphlet or an editorial on economic science."[15]

In May 1908, the *Industrial Union Bulletin* carried an article entitled, "The Value of Music in I.W.W. Meetings," written by James Wilson, Local No. 22, Spokane, Wash. "Here in Spokane," he wrote, "for the last two or three months at our agitational meetings, we have had a few songs by some of the fellow workers. It is really surprising how soon a crowd will form in the street to hear a song in the interest of the working class, familiar as they are with the maudlin sentimental music of the various religionists."[16] In 1909, four songs—"Hallelujah, I'm a Bum" and three parodies of the Salvation Army's gospel hymns, "When the Roll Is Called up Yonder," "Where the Silver Colorado Wends Its Way," and "Where Is My Wandering Boy Tonight?" were printed in a 10-cent leaflet which grew into the famous Wobblies' Bible, *The Little Red Song Book,* with the subhead on the cover, "To Fan the Flames of Discontent." Published once a year (and sometimes more frequently), it soon proved to be a tremendous aid to organizational work. Here, the workers were informed, were "Songs of the Miseries That Are. Songs of the Happiness To Be. Songs that strip capitalism bare; show the shams of civilization, mock at the master's morals, scorn the smug respectability of the satisfied class, and drown in one glad burst of passion the profit patriotism of the Plunderbund."[17] From 1909 to the present, the Wobbly song books have always printed, in addition to songs, poems, cartoons, and aphorisms, the I.W.W. Preamble.* Some of the poems in the I.W.W. songbooks were never written with the idea of their being sung, but were just written as poems.

Most of the Wobbly songs were set to popular song hits of the 1900–

---

* The latest edition of the I.W.W. song book is the twenty-ninth. It was issued in 1956 in commemoration of the 50th anniversary of the organization. A very full collection of the words and some of the music of the I.W.W. songs appears in *Rebel Voices: An I.W.W. Anthology,* edited, with introductions, by Joyce L. Kornbluh, Ann Arbor, Mich., 1964. The book also has an excellent section entitled, "Language of the Migratory Worker," pp. 405–08.

1915 period, or to familiar gospel and revival hymns. Often musically illiterate, Wobbly songwriters usually obtained their melodies orally. They had learned most of the hymns at street missions and from their contacts with the Salvation Army, the organization with which they often had to compete on street corners. Since the melodies of the hymns were frequently moving and melodic, the Wobbly song-maker, hunting for a melody to fit a set of lyrics, simply acquired the tune.

The I.W.W.'s most accomplished, most famous and most prolific songwriter was Joe Hill. Born in Sweden, October 7, 1879, and christened Joel Hägglund, he came to the United States in 1902 at the age of 23. For ten years he worked at many jobs, during which time he changed his name to Joseph Hillstrom and became popularly known as Joe Hill. Meanwhile, he wrote poems, songs, bits of verse, all kinds of things. In 1910, Joe Hill joined the I.W.W. local in San Pedro, Calif. A year later, while working as a dock-walloper in San Pedro, he wrote his first known song, "Casey Jones—the Union Scab," a parody of the original Casey Jones song which had appeared two years before. Written to assist the workers on strike on the South Pacific Line who were faced with defeat by the importation of scabs, the famous narrative ballad dealt with a scab who "got a wooden medal for being good and faithful on the S.P. line." It told of the I.W.W.'s sabotage of Casey Jones' engine, his trip to heaven where he even "went scabbing on the angels," his descent into hell, and the ignominious tasks assigned him there:

> *"Casey Jones," the Devil said, "oh fine;*
> *Casey Jones, get busy shoveling sulphur;*
> *That's what you get for scabbing on the S.P. line."*

The song was an immediate success. Printed on colored cards which were sold to help the strike fund, the song assisted in keeping the strike alive. Within a few months it was being sung by workers in many parts of the country as migratory laborers carried it across the land. "Casey Jones" is the classic American song on the scab, and it is as widely known today as in the period when it was written.

During the next three years, Joe Hill became one of the leading contributors to *The Little Red Song Book,* and by 1913 he was the most popular of the little band of poets and songwriters—Richard Brazier, Ralph Chaplin, Laura Payne Emerson, Covington Hall, James Connell (author of "The Red Flag," composed during the London dock strike of 1889), and Charles Ashleigh—whose works appeared in the pages of the song book. The "Preacher and the Slave," "Where the River Fraser Flows," "John Golden and the Lawrence Strike," "Mr. Block," "Scissorbill," "What We Want," "The Tramp," "There is Power in a Union," "The Rebel Girl" (inspired by Elizabeth Gurley Flynn and which

Joe Hill hoped "will help to line up the women workers in the OBU"), "Should I Ever Be a Soldier"—were some of the songs of Joe Hill which became famous as soon as they were published. As their titles reveal, Joe Hill's songs emerged out of actual conditions and struggles of the workers, were consciously written to be used as weapons in their struggles, and were sung on numerous picket lines during the heyday of the I.W.W. In her tribute to Joe Hill as a songwriter of the American labor movement, published in the May 22, 1915, issue of *Solidarity,* Elizabeth Gurley Flynn wrote: "Joe writes songs that sing, that lilt and laugh and sparkle, that kindle the fires of revolt in the most crushed spirit and quicken the desire for fuller life in the most humble slave. . . . He has crystallized the organization's spirit into imperishable forms, songs of the people—folk songs. . . ."

Elizabeth Gurley Flynn's article was written just after she had visited Joe Hill in prison at Salt Lake City where he was awaiting execution. He had been convicted of the slaying on January 10, 1914, of John G. Morrison, a Salt Lake City grocer. The conviction was based on the flimsiest of evidence—all circumstantial—after a trial conducted in an atmosphere of hatred for the I.W.W. organizer and troubadour. Joe Hill's lawyers summed up the situation aptly when they wrote in *Solidarity* of May 23, 1914: "The main thing the state has against Hill is that he is an I.W.W. and *therefore* sure to be guilty."

Although the campaign to defend Joe Hill started as an I.W.W. movement, it soon attracted wider support. Thousands of Americans and other thousands abroad were convinced that Joe Hill told the truth when he affirmed that he had nothing to do with the murder and that he was the victim of a frameup. So they joined in an international defense movement urging that the conviction be reversed or that Joe Hill be granted a new trial. At its 1915 convention, the A.F. of L. unanimously adopted a resolution which pointed out that "Joseph Hillstrom, a workingman of the State of Utah, and active in the cause of labor" had been sentenced to be shot; "the grounds for this conviction and sentence appear to be utterly inadequate . . . and that the rights of said Joseph Hillstrom did not have a fair and impartial trial." The resolution, in the name of the A.F. of L., urged the Governor of Utah "to exercise his prerogative of clemency in this case, and to stop the execution of the said Joe Hillstrom, and that he be given a new and fair trial."

By the spring and summer of 1915, the defense movement had grown to such proportions that President Woodrow Wilson twice asked Governor William Spry for "justice and . . . a thorough reconsideration of the case of Joseph Hillstrom." But the state authorities of Utah, fearing the rising militancy and organization of the workers for whom Joe Hill was an inspiring spokesman, decided that he had to die. On November 19, 1915, Joe Hill was executed, shot with four dum-dum bullets.

At Joe Hill's funeral procession in Chicago, 30,000 people marched, and a news reporter asked: "What kind of man is this whose death is celebrated with songs of revolt and who has at his bier more mourners than any prince or potentate?" Joe Hill's songs answer this question.* Several were written during his imprisonment, and these, like all of his other songs, show him as a class-conscious worker who concerned himself first and foremost with the problems confronting the American working class in its struggles against hunger and want.[18]

The greatest importance of the Wobbly song book was the vehicle for conveying the basic sentiments and program of the I.W.W. Nothing, for example, expressed the I.W.W. principle of solidarity better than the greatest song yet produced by American labor—"Solidarity Forever"— written to the tune of "John Brown's Body" by Ralph Chaplin, the artist, poet, workingman leader of the Chicago section of the I.W.W., and right-hand man to "Big Bill" Haywood.† Even today one hears the stirring words at union meetings and on picket lines:

> It is we who plowed the prairies, built the cities where
>   they stand;
> Dug the mines and built the workshops, endless miles of
>   railroad laid
> Now we stand outcast and starving, 'mid the wonders we have made.
> But the union makes us strong.
>
> Solidarity forever!
> Solidarity forever!
> Solidarity forever!
> For the union makes us strong.

The I.W.W. songwriters did their writing on their own time, during lunch hours, at night and often in jails. They paid for their own paper, ink and music sheets. They earned no royalties. Their sole reward was to help the struggle and the knowledge that their songs were being sung to advance it. And they were sung! The songs were heard everywhere—at mass meetings, in the jungles, on the picket lines, during the

---

* Joe Hill's letters written while he was in prison also answer this question. See Philip S. Foner, editor, The Letters of Joe Hill, New York, 1965. For a detailed study of the arrest, trial, imprisonment and execution of Joe Hill, as well as the great defense campaign in his behalf, see Philip S. Foner, The Case of Joe Hill, New York, 1965.

† "Solidarity Forever" was published for the first time in Solidarity, Jan. 9, 1915. It was originally known as "Wage Workers Come Join the Union." Ralph H. Chaplin was imprisoned in 1918, sentenced to a 20-years' term in Leavenworth under the Espionage Act. He emerged from prison a disillusioned man, regretting his earlier militant activities. This is reflected in his autobiography, Wobbly, published in 1948.

free-speech fights. They were sung in the jails.* Their steady, surging rhythms, their lilting melodies (taken usually from familiar hymns or songs already well known to many workers), and their inspiring words, repeated over and over again, generated a fervor that was almost religious in its intensity. Even the least articulate of workers could join in these group songs and respond to them fully.

By providing an outlet for the highly charged emotions during bitter struggles that might otherwise explode into individual acts of retaliation or anger, the songs lent firm support to the I.W.W.'s strategy of passive resistance. They gave the workers on the picket lines or at the corner meetings the collective courage to withstand the inevitable abuses heaped upon them by the police, the deputies, the militia, and the vigilantes. They welded individuals—some with doubts and terrors and weaknesses —into a dynamic and inexorable striking force.

Like many I.W.W. speakers and writers, Wobbly songwriters had a great gift for humor.† They could even poke fun at themselves and their movement. Using bitter satire, ridicule and exaggeration, humorous and ribald parodies, they exposed the exploitation of the workers, the evils of the loan sharks, the hypocrisy of many clergymen, the smugness of charity societies, and the viciousness of the police, jailers, deputy sheriffs, and vigilantes. And in their elegies written for fallen comrades, they poured out their deep feeling for those who had fought valiantly for the cause. As one contemporary journalist observed of the I.W.W. songs: "Crude though they may be in form, they nevertheless showed that the I.W.W. movement was developing the poetry of the proletariat. They expressed with vigor the new spirit of revolt and they spread economic ideas and social conceptions and inspirations that could not fail to reach and influence the feelings of large masses."[19]

So highly did the I.W.W. regard its songs that it viewed them as marking a real distinction between itself and the A.F. of L. "The A.F. of L., with its over two million members has no songs, no great poetry and prose," the *Industrial Worker* observer on May 27, 1916. "The I.W.W. has a vast wealth of both, rising out of the toil and anguish of the disinherited. Only those who feel strongly and greatly break into song. . . . Only

---

* The following item in the Duluth *News Tribune* of July 27, 1916, could be quoted almost word for word from scores of newspapers throughout the country: "As the accused men were taken to their cells last night, they were in a merry mood and singing I.W.W. melodies."

† Wobbly humor could make a small book by itself, for the I.W.W. has been one of the few revolutionary groups noted for its sense of humor. Here is one example that could go into such a book. It is a brief editorial squib on the death of J. P. Morgan, entitled "Out, Damned Spot!" It read: "A wireless dispatch from Heaven states that Soul Scrubbers Union No. 1 is on strike in resentment against the impossible task of removing the many foul spots on Morgan's soul." (*Industrial Worker*, May 15, 1913.)

great movements marking turning points in the history of humanity have produced great songs, appealing to the masses because they voice the inarticulate feelings and aspirations of the masses."

The I.W.W. songs were not written by "sideline" poets. They were written by men and women who understood the problems and hardships of the workers because they themselves were workers. They gave poetic and musical voice to thousands of other workers, and left behind one of the great heritages of the American labor movement.

SYNDICALISM, SABOTAGE, VIOLENCE

Probably no organization in America was so feared and hated by the "respectable elements" in society as the I.W.W. before and during the first World War, and the degree of fear and hatred which it enkindled in the employers amounted almost to insanity. "Against us," wrote the *Industrial Worker* on July 15, 1916, "were hurled the poison darts of ridicule, misstatement, abuse and slander." The initials "I.W.W." were derisively translated into "I Won't Work," "I Want Whiskey," "Irresponsible Wholesale Wreckers." The press made frequent use of these epithets, heaped vitriol on the Wobblies, lampooned them as the "I Won't Work Clan," and denounced them as "bums, saboteurs, revolutionaries, wandering Bedouins of crime." A.F. of L. leaders joined in the campaign of slander. John Keen, president of the Pacific District of the International Longshoremen's Association, sent a letter to 50 of his locals in 1912 in which he warned them against the "I.W.W., which to my mind stands for irresponsible wholesale wreckers."[20]

Many of the attacks on the I.W.W. were local in nature, applying only in certain specific situations and used to inflame a particular area or community against the organization. But two charges were repeated time and again from one end of the country to the other. The first of these emphasized the foreign origins of the I.W.W.'s ideas: "Its teachings and aims are derived from the Syndicalists and Anarchists of France and it holds the German Karl Marx as its idol and guide." The second charge accused the Wobblies of being dedicated primarily to the use of violence to gain their ends: "Violence is the only stock in trade of the I.W.W."[21] The two main accusations were frequently buttressed with quotations from I.W.W. publications which appeared to give them a certain basis in fact. But, in reality, they were distortions of the true ideas and motives of the organization.

Virtually every scholar who has dealt extensively with the I.W.W. has considered it as a form of syndicalism: that the Industrial Workers of the World constituted the American manifestation of a new kind of unionism, classified as syndicalism, which advocated the elimination of capitalism and the political state, and the substitution of an administration of things by unionized labor. As we have seen, French syndicalism did influence several of the men who played a leading role in shaping the early I.W.W. Yet there were important differences between the I.W.W. and the French syndicalists. A basic difference was in the attitude to dual unionism: The French revolutionists believed in working within the structure of the unions in the General Confederation of Labor or C.G.T.; the Wobblies, on the other hand, constituted themselves as a rival union to the A.F. of L., refusing to have anything to do with the unions affiliated with the Federation and rejecting the doctrine of "boring from within."

Tom Mann, English syndicalist leader, declared in 1912 that the I.W.W.'s antagonism to existing trade unions disqualified it as a syndicalist organization. William Z. Foster, who advocated the policy of "boring from within" as a member of the I.W.W. and when this doctrine was rejected, became the founder of the Syndicalist League of North America, called the I.W.W. "industrial socialism" as distinct from syndicalism, and agreed with Mann that the utilization of the existing unions was essential to syndicalism. Moreover, while the I.W.W., except in the case of the "mixed locals," organized only on industrial-union lines, French syndicalism incorporated craft unionism.[22]

It is clear, therefore, that there is no basis to the charge that the French syndicalist movement was the father of the I.W.W. and that after 1908 the Wobbies and the French syndicalists were closely interrelated. Nevertheless, it would be equally incorrect to ignore the intellectual kinship that did exist between the I.W.W. and the European, particularly the French syndicalists. For one thing, the official journals of the I.W.W. featured news of the French syndicalist movement, along with events of the syndicalist movement in other countries, and frequently headed these reports with the statement: "Le Syndicalisme in France is Industrialism in America. Its principles are substantially those of the I.W.W. in America." Industrial Unionism was often defined in the I.W.W. press as "syndicalism." Several of the I.W.W. leaders—especially St. John, Trautmann, and Haywood—repeatedly emphasized that it "is along the lines of the French syndicalists that the Industrial Workers of the World proposes to organize," and that "the I.W.W. represents in even more advanced forms and in tactics the principles as espoused by the syndicalists of France."[23]

These leaders certainly helped to permeate the I.W.W. with the syndicalist philosophy that the trade unions, in contrast to political organizations, would be the instrument by which the workers would take control of the means of production through the general strike. To be sure, most members of the I.W.W. were not attracted to the organization primarily because of the syndicalist philosophy. The appeal of the I.W.W. to its adherents lay basically in its readiness to do something about immediate injustices and in the solutions it offered to existing conditions in the American scene. Nevertheless, the members did learn of the doctrines of syndicalism once they were in the organization,* and, in the main, they accepted them.

The influence of French syndicalism on the I.W.W. increased noticeably after Haywood's European visit late in 1910 as a Socialist Party delegate to the Labor and Socialist Congress of the Second International at Copenhagen. In the course of his sojourn in Europe, he conferred with Tom Mann, and with leading French syndicalists of the C.G.T. It was after this visit that the pamphlet *Sabotage* by Émile Pouget, editor of the official organ of the French Confederation of Labor, was translated and distributed by the I.W.W. About the same time, the I.W.W. distributed among its members copies of Sorel's *Reflections on Violence.* In 1911 and 1912, the *Industrial Worker* and *Solidarity* carried numerous articles on French syndicalism and discussions by I.W.W. leaders and members on direct action, sabotage, and the general strike. Early in 1913, *Solidarity* carried, in several issues, an English translation of "French Syndicalism" by Leon Jouhaux, secretary of the C.G.T.[24]

One thing is definite: the basic nature of the I.W.W. was that of a syndicalist organization. This is true even though there were fundamental differences on major issues between the French syndicalists and the I.W.W. and even though the I.W.W. often went out of its way to make it clear that "Industrialism is not Syndicalism, though they have much in common," and that the I.W.W. form of organization was superior to and preferable to syndicalism.[25] Basically there was no difference on most fundamental issues between the syndicalists and the industrial unionists. Both agreed that capitalism must be destroyed and with it the political state must be overthrown; that these ends could only be accomplished by the working class itself; that these goals could not be obtained through political action but only as a result of the direct action of the workers; that society was to be reconstructed by the workers and economic exploitation thereby abolished, and that in the new society, the unions of the workers would own and manage all industries, regulate consumption, and administer the general social interests. There was to be no other form of government.[26] On only two counts did the I.W.W. differ significantly from their syndicalist brothers: in their promotion of industrial unions as opposed to craft unionism, and their refusal to work within the existing craft unions. But essentially, students of the I.W.W., like Paul F. Brissenden, John Graham Brooks, André Tridon, and David

* However, many Italian members of the I.W.W. had a fairly wide acquaintance with syndicalist ideas in Italy before they had emigrated to the United States. (Edwin Fenton, "Immigrants and Unions: A Case Study, Italians and American Labor, 1870–1920," unpublished Ph.D. thesis, Harvard University, 1937, pp. 183–85; *Solidarity,* April 29, 1911, Nov. 1, 1913.)

J. Saposs, were correct in referring to the Industrial Workers of the World as American syndicalists.

"Is the I.W.W. European?" *Solidarity* asked in 1912, and it answered: "The I.W.W., whatever it may have in common with European labor movements, is a distinct product of America and American conditions. . . . Whatever terms or phrases we may borrow from the French or other languages to denote our methods cut no figure; the methods conform to American conditions in relation to our aim."[27] To understand the I.W.W., then, it is necessary to realize that its revolutionary philosophy, rooted in American soil, was deepened by its contacts with syndicalist organizations throughout the world and particularly those of France. Those who shouted "foreign origin" naturally pointed to the influence of French syndicalism on the I.W.W. as proof. But actually it was proof only of the international solidarity of the working class.

One doctrine which the I.W.W. borrowed directly from the French syndicalists and which was to create the most difficulty for the organization was the advocacy of sabotage. The early I.W.W. denied that it believed in sabotage as a weapon in the class struggle. "It believes rather," declared the *Industrial Union Bulletin* on June 27, 1907, "in the efficacy of education and organization to bring it the power to take and hold all the essential means of life." This swiftly changed after the 1908 convention. By 1910 sabotage was included in lists of tactics to be used by Wobblies in the class war.* The value of sabotage was given impetus when news came to the United States of its effective use by the French railroad workers whose strike had been broken when the strikers were drafted in the army. A front-page article in the *Industrial Worker* announced: "Sabotage means in a general way, going on *strike without striking,* and has been proven by our Fellow Workers in France to be very effective." The Wobbly press urged American workers to emulate their brothers in France.[28]

In 1912 propaganda for sabotage began to appear regularly in the Wobbly press. It displayed in cartoons the familiar emblem of sabotage—the Sab-Cat—a black cat and a wooden shoe.† Beginning in January 1913 and continuing into April of that year, Walker C. Smith, then editor of the *Industrial Worker,* wrote a series of 13 editorials on sabotage in which he praised it as a method of carrying the class war right back to the capitalists and declared that it was beneficial because it removed the lethargy of the workers and incited them to battle.[29] In 1913, too, some

---

* The word appeared first in *Solidarity* of June 4, 1910, in a description of a strike of Chicago clothing workers.

† Most Wobblies incorrectly used the wooden shoe symbol as signifying the origin of the word "sabotage" in the act of a French workman in throwing his wooden shoe (*sabot*) into the machinery. The original meaning of the French word "sabotage" was to work clumsily, carelessly, slowly, or without thought or skill, as if by blows of a wooden shoe (a *coup de sabots*).

Los Angeles Wobbly factional locals began publishing *The Wooden Shoe,* using such boxed mottoes as: "A kick in time saves nine," "Kick your way out of wage slavery," "The foot in the wooden shoe will rock the world," "A kick on the job is worth ten at the ballot-box."

In 1912, while lodged in the Essex County jail in Massachusetts, awaiting trial in connection with the murder of a striker during the Lawrence strike, Arturo Giovannitti, one of the I.W.W. leaders of the strike, wrote an introduction to Émile Pouget's *Sabotage,* a work that he had translated from the French. The book was published by Charles H. Kerr Co. in 1913. Though not an official I.W.W. publication, it was hailed by the *Industrial Worker* as "the best thing yet issued on the subject" and widely circulated by the organization. About 1913, the I.W.W. issued two of its own works on the subject of sabotage: a pamphlet by Walker C. Smith (composed of the 13 editorials he wrote in the *Industrial Worker*) and another by Elizabeth Gurley Flynn. The latter particularly was widely distributed by the I.W.W. Publishing Bureau.[30]

Yet for all the material on sabotage issued by the I.W.W. press and Publishing Bureau, the organization itself was still reluctant to recommend it officially as a legitimate weapon in the class war. Indeed, while individual Wobblies endorsed sabotage earlier, it was not until 1914 that any official I.W.W. body did so. In September of that year, the ninth I.W.W. convention passed a motion "unanimously and without discussion" that "all speakers be instructed to recommend to the workers the necessity of curtailing production by means of 'slowing down' and sabotage. All rush work should be done in a wrong manner."[31] Thus the I.W.W. became the first and only labor group in American history to officially advocate sabotage.

The fact that the only type of sabotage specifically recommended by the convention was that "All rush work should be done in a wrong manner" indicates that, at least officially, the I.W.W. did not equate sabotage with destruction of property. Most of the time, the I.W.W. insisted that sabotage meant nothing more than the withdrawal of the workers' efficiency, nothing more criminal than "soldiering" on the job, and even when it was used to disable machinery, it was "intended not to destroy it or permanently render it defective, but only to temporarily disable it and put it out of running condition in order to make impossible the work of scabs and thus to secure the real stoppage of work during a strike." In any case, sabotage was directed against property and most emphatically not against people.[32]

At the same time that the I.W.W. was explaining that its advocacy of sabotage was not designed to destroy property and that it would, when used, only disable machinery temporarily, there would appear the following in the *Industrial Worker:* "Sabotage. Emery dust will cause bearings to heat, but sand, grounded up glass, brick dust or any other gutty substance is just as good. The best way to distribute emery dust is to put it in the oil can or the oil barrel or let the oiler or engineer put it in the bearings."[33] Would this destroy the machinery or merely temporarily disable it? The Wobbly press did not bother to answer.

The truth is it was exceedingly difficult to determine exactly what the I.W.W. meant by sabotage. Haywood did not clarify matters in his famous statement to a mass meeting in New York's Cooper Union in 1912: "I don't know of anything that will bring as much satisfaction to you, as much anguish to the boss as a little sabotage in the right place at the right time. Find out what it means. It won't hurt you, and it will cripple the boss."[34] But it was not easy to find out just "what it means" when I.W.W. publications declared that "Sabotage ranges all the way from 'passive resistance' at one extreme to violent destruction of property at the other," and then claimed that it meant no more than reducing efficiency on the job and merely "temporarily disabling" machinery and other forms of property.[35] This was further complicated by the fact that individual Wobblies openly advocated sabotage in such a fantastic manner that even Walker C. Smith, himself an advocate, had to announce in the *Industrial Worker:* "We quite agree with some of our critics that the soap box sabotage expounded by free lancers is a weird and wonderful thing. Certainly the I.W.W. cannot be held responsible for all the views of those who claim membership." As Fred Thompson notes: "Soapboxers found that talk of sabotage gave their audience a thrill."[36] The more lurid the form advocated the bigger the thrill.

While there were certainly differences within the I.W.W. over the precise meaning of sabotage, there was none on the justification of its use. Four main arguments were advanced. First, sabotage was justifiable because its purpose was to cut into capitalist profits, and hence was an attack on the evil system of capitalism itself. It was also justifiable because capitalists, too, were guilty of sabotage: Adulterated foods and clothing material; builders cheating on material specifications; manufacturers mixing tin and lead solutions into silks to make the product weigh more and look more valuable than it really was; railroads run into the ground to depreciate stock and capture ownership and control; faulty dams bursting and causing disastrous floods.* Thirdly, it was the only weapon a worker could use in expressing his resentment against inhuman exploitation. It was, in the words of *Solidarity*, "the blind

---

* To counteract forms of capitalist sabotage, the I.W.W. developed a form of sabotage by workers called "open mouth" sabotage. Waitresses and sales clerks were urged to inform restaurant patrons and merchandise customers what was *really* in the stew and how the cloth was actually manufactured and tailored. Since adulterated food and shoddy clothing were sold to the working class, it was perfectly justifiable to tell the customers the true facts. "Open mouth" sabotage was thus an act of solidarity. (*Industrial Worker,* Dec. 19, 1912, Jan. 23, April 24, 1913.)

vengeance of the under dog upon society. The ragged men who are harried wherever they go, who are criticized for roaming and who are driven out of a town by the law the moment they try to stop roaming— these men are like any under dogs. They bite back blindly, viciously, and the name of the bite is Sabotage."[37] Finally, it was justifiable as a most practicable form of striking. Workers who struck by walking off the job were at a heavy disadvantage in conflict with employers. Not only was pay lost during the strike, but jobs might also be lost to strikebreakers. Therefore, "striking on the job" by using sabotage was a means of redressing the economic imbalance between capitalist and worker.

It is easy to be carried away by slogans, songs and stories of sabotage, and it is extremely difficult to separate rhetoric from practice. Certainly, the Wobblies flaunted their slogans in the face of the world with sufficient bravado to make many people think that they did practice sabotage with great enthusiasm. The picture of the roughly-dressed, unkempt I.W.W. agitator, bomb in hand, dynamite in hip pockets, standing on a soapbox labeled "Sabotage" was common. So, too, were pictures of burning buildings, forest fires, railroad wrecks, broken machines, destroyed crops, and many other forms of wilful destruction of property and the endangering of human life—all bearing the caption, "I.W.W. Sabotage!"

But whether the I.W.W. actually committed sabotage is a question that has been disputed by historians and sociologists to this day and has never been satisfactorily answered.* One view is that the Wobblies talked big but did little. Although the I.W.W. in California was charged with hundreds of crimes involving sabotage, "not one single case of sabotage was proved in the courtroom."[38] During a trial in Washington, E. F. Blaine informed the court that, after extensive investigations into the possible use of sabotage by the I.W.W.: "We found no evidence on which we could found a charge."[39] One scholar, after an intensive study of the files of the *Industrial Worker*, points out that he could find only two writers who "specifically claimed to have practiced sabotage and their tales are scarcely lurid."[40] Another, who probed the question perhaps more than any other, concludes: *"Although there are contradictory opinions as to whether the I.W.W. practiced sabotage or not, it is interesting to note that no case of an I.W.W. saboteur caught practicing sabotage or convicted of its practice is available."*[41]

Most students of the I.W.W. agree that the organization's reputation for practicing sabotage was a creation of public hysteria.[42] Still it is true that this hysteria was encouraged by big-talking Wobblies who spoke so

---

* Actually, only one historian flatly states that the I.W.W. did practice sabotage. This is Louis Adamic, but his conclusion is largely based on conjecture and hearsay. (*Dynamite, The Story of Class Violence in America*, rev. ed., New York, 1935, chapter 32.)

casually about "the use of the wooden shoe" and adorned their publications with pictures of a hunched black cat showing its claws. To lessen the influence of this element, *Solidarity* occasionally pointed out that "Sabotage is not a principle of the I.W.W. . . . . It is a tactic the value of which will be determined by the workers who may use it." It also featured an article entitled, "Some Limitations on Sabotage," in which it pointed to the "danger of using sabotage en masse. It would destroy the entire machinery we want to take over. It also interferes with organizing since it makes the belief widespread that all that is needed is sabotage."[43] It could have added that the idea that a few broken saws, a few burnt threshing machines and a few slow-ups in logging camps would lead to a reconstruction of society was both romantic and fantastic!

Although sabotage was sanctioned by the I.W.W. it was usually accomplished with the caution to workers to "Avoid as far as possible the use of violence." Actually, although much has been said about the violence of the I.W.W., and although violence accompanied most of its strikes, the fact is that the organization hoped to gain its ends through methods other than violence. The general executive board officially opposed violence as a weapon in the class struggle, pointing out that the I.W.W. "does not now and never has believed in or advocated either destruction or violence as a means of accomplishing industrial reform; first, because no principle was ever settled by such methods; second, because industrial history has taught us that when strikers resort to violence and unlawful methods, all the resources of Government are immediately arrayed against them and they lose their cause; third, because such methods destroy the constructive impulse which it is the purpose of this organization to foster and develop in order that the workers may fit themselves to assume their places in the new society."[44]

But like sabotage, violence was the subject of endless discussion and debate in I.W.W. circles. This debate reached its height in the fall of 1913 and the spring and summer of 1914. During these months many statements by I.W.W. officials on the subject of violence appeared in the press, and a battle royal was on. Giovannitti, Adolph Lessig, St. John, and Gurley Flynn took the position that while the I.W.W. did not favor violence, it would resort to it if necessary to accomplish the social revolution. Haywood and Ettor opposed this stand, emphasizing that general strike for the overthrow of capitalism "is the only kind of force we are in favor of," and that this might even be accomplished peacefully. The I.W.W. press, in an effort to iron out these contradictions, simply stated that there was no "official" position on violence, and suggested that the discussion be brought to a close. "Now that the I.W.W. has heard both sides of the violence controversy, suppose it proceeds to organize the working class. More than one organization has died settling tactics."[45]

All who participated in the discussion agreed on one point: it was impossible to expect the class struggle to be free of violence, for the master class and its agents, as Marx had predicted, would always use force and violence to defeat the workers' struggles. The question was how to best meet the violence unleashed by the capitalist class. One school favored sole reliance on passive resistance. This meant that the Wobblies would not meet force with force but would go to jail if arrested without offering the slightest physical resistance. This would expose "the inner workings and purposes of the capitalist mind," and prove that it was the capitalists and their henchmen who were guilty of violence. At the same time, it would reveal "the fortitude, the courage, the inherent sense of order of the workers' mind." And it was bound to bring results. "As long as the workers keep their hands in their pockets," Joe Ettor proclaimed, "the capitalists cannot put theirs there. With passive resistance, with the workers absolutely refusing to move, laying absolutely silent, they are more powerful than all the weapons and instruments that the other side have for protection and attack."[46]

A number of newspapers pictured the I.W.W. as favoring only passive resistance as a weapon in the class struggle. ("One peculiarity of the Industrial Workers of the World," declared the Kansas City *Star* of October 24, 1911, "is that they believe in strikes, lockouts, boycotts and other means of obtaining their 'rights,' but only in the shape of passive resistance. Violence is denounced.") But this was far from the case. Many Wobblies made it clear that in opposing violence they meant only "unprovoked violence." Violence provoked by the capitalists had to be met by violence on the part of the working class. Vincent St. John made this clear in his testimony before the U.S. Commission on Industrial Relations: "I don't mean to say that we advocate violence; but we won't tell our members to allows themselves to be shot down and beaten up like cattle. Violence as a general rule is forced on us." Inevitably, then, incidents would arise in which the I.W.W. would be engaged in violent activities. "They are unavoidable in the class struggle." But it would be the opponents of the I.W.W. that fomented violence and was the violent element, not the I.W.W.[47] No one should join the I.W.W. unless he understood that the ruling class would resort to violence against the organization. "The only men who have any active place in the real labor movement of today," declared *Solidarity* on March 26, 1910, "are men with iron in their blood. Those who think that it is something of a picnic to go up with bare knuckles against the all powerful trusts and corporations of the present day had better go home and get a rubber ring."

The I.W.W. frequently, and, as we shall see, justifiably pointed out that employers and newspapers who accused the Wobblies of introducing violence as soon as they entered upon the scene of a working-class struggle, were actually fortunate to have the Wobblies present. Otherwise, the enraged workers would have wreaked a cruel vengeance upon their enemies. Under the leadership of the I.W.W., they had been welded into a disciplined army of strikers instead of an undisciplined mob. "If the I.W.W. had not been in control," declared a Wobbly leader during a strike, "the strikers would have gone on a rampage that would have meant the destruction of much life and property."[48] The I.W.W. often kept the strikers from taking reprisal against the hired gunmen and other agents of the employers. "I know of no movement in recent history," wrote Roger Baldwin in 1930, "which so withstood the temptation to violent reprisal as did the I.W.W."[49]

Although the I.W.W. confessed to borrowing from the anarchists "some useful tactics and vital principles," it made a special effort to distinguish itself from the anarchists, emphasizing repeatedly that the two had "entirely different organizations and concepts of solving the social problem." The I.W.W. did not, as did many, if not all, anarchists, advocate "propaganda of the deed," and recognized that bomb-throwing, killing of capitalists and public officials would not end the capitalist system.[50] In a signed editorial, B. H. Williams, editor of *Solidarity*, attacked the "gun" idea as a substitute for industrial organization. "It leads the slave to the notion that he can improve conditions or emancipate himself with a Springfield or a Mauser. I grant that such 'hardware' is handy to have around at times, and should not be overlooked; but the gun as a substitute for industrial organization is a fatal illusion. The 'gun' idea is equally fallacious with the 'ballot' idea."[51] Other distinctions emphasized were that "anarchism is individualism, but that the I.W.W. stands for economic Socialism, i.e., the collective ownership of the means of production and distribution by the working class"; that "anarchism denies the class struggle, while the I.W.W. teaches it"; that "anarchism is non-evolutionary while the I.W.W. follows the line of industrial development," and that "anarchism sees decentralization where none exists, while the I.W.W. recognizes the fact of centralization."[52]*

We may conclude then that while violence was not entirely excluded as an I.W.W. method, it was not regarded as the primary method, nor even the one that would most surely lead to success. Victory would be gained through the organization of labor power. "Mass action is far more

---

* Years later, however, Richard Brazier, a one-time member of the G.E.B., wrote: "There was a strong anarchist element among the I.W.W. that refused to accept majority rule and were strong for local autonomy." (Richard Brazier to T. J. Bogard, n.d., T. J. Bogard Collection, Washington State Historical Society, Tacoma, Wash.) However, I.W.W. publicists always insisted that this element did not represent the majority view in the I.W.W. One criticism of Paul F. Brissenden's book, *The I.W.W., A Study of American Syndicalism*, in I.W.W. circles, was that it placed too much emphasis upon anarchist and anarcho-syndicalist trends in the organization. "The use of these terms," a Wobbly reviewer wrote when Brissenden's book was first published, "are [sic] very misleading as they are bound to give the wrong impression to the reader of the Industrial Workers of the World." (Irving Freeman in *One Big Union Monthly*, vol. I, 1919, p. 473.)

up-to-date than personal or physical violence," declared Gurley Flynn. "Mass action means that the workers withdraw their labor power, and paralyze the wealth production of the city, cut off the means of life, the breath of life of the employers. Violence may mean just weakness on the part of those workers." The same mass action would achieve a nonviolent transition to the new society. "It will be a revolution, but it will be a bloodless revolution," Haywood prophesied.[53]

POLITICAL ACTION

In 1895, V. I. Lenin wrote: "The workers cannot wage the struggle for their emancipation without striving to influence the affairs of state, to influence the administration of the state, the passing of laws."[54] Had the I.W.W. recognized the truth of this statement, many of its most serious mistakes could have been avoided. But after 1908 the anti-political action viewpoint was dominant in the I.W.W. This was justified on the following grounds:

(1) The question of political action had been a chief bone of contention in the I.W.W. from its formation in 1905 to 1908, had paralyzed the organization, split locals apart and prevented effective propaganda and organizational work for the "One Big Union." Only by freeing itself from the incubus of political sectarianism was the I.W.W. able to extend its influence and only by remaining aloof from political activities and concentrating on direct action through industrial organization would the Wobblies be able to "unite the working class under the broad banner of the Industrial Workers of the World."[55]

(2) Even though the working class, according to I.W.W. spokesmen, made up 75 per cent of the country, revolutionary change through political institutions was impossible. Vast numbers of workers could not participate in political action even if they wished to do so. Political action was meaningless to non-voters. "The millions of women employed in the factories are denied the vote. The children employed will be deprived until they reach their majority. The millions of black men of the South have never been permitted freely to use their franchise. Though a great part of the country's work is done by foreigners, many are the limitations put upon them politically. They must be residents of the country for a period of five years. The lack of education is made a ban, the belief in certain ideas is a restriction and the sovereign born citizens are deprived of the right to vote by being compelled to move from place to place during periods of industrial depressions or are forced to violate their political conscience at the dictates of their employer who controls their job." Together with other restrictions such as the poll tax and residence requirements which, owing to their nomadic existence, many workers could not fulfill, a situation had arisen in America in which "the number

of voters unable to vote will soon exceed the number of those actually voting."[56] Under these conditions, a substantial section of the American working class had no reasons to look to political action for self-help.

However much it exposed the restrictions upon the right to vote as justifying its theory that political action was futile, the I.W.W. did not advocate that the workers devote themselves to altering this situation. It did not actively support the Negro struggle to achieve the right to vote, supposedly guaranteed by the Constitution, and while it did not formally oppose the woman suffrage movement, it regarded it as of no importance to working-class women who were reminded that the "vote will not free women" and were advised to "find their power at the point of production where they work." The woman suffrage movement, the I.W.W. charged, was dominated by "rich faddists," and working-class girls were being "made the tail of a suffrage kite in the hands of women of the very class driving the girls to lives of misery and shame."[57]*

(3) Labor legislation (I.W.W. publications and speakers always referred to it as "so-called labor legislation") was of no material benefit to the working class. For one thing, these laws were rarely if ever enforced, and, indeed, could only be enforced when the workers "enforced them through organized power." Then again, reliance on laws tended to develop the "waiting habit" on the part of the workers and to cause them "to 'look to the government' for relief, instead of organizing their forces on the job and learning to depend upon their own efforts for improved conditions." (This position was strikingly similar to the one adopted by Gompers and other A.F. of L. leaders toward political action.) Finally, all legislation to remedy evils within the capitalist system was simply devised and used by the capitalist class "to keep the workers from revolt." "Give to the worker the full product of his toil and his pension is assured," wrote Haywood in opposing old-age pension legislation. The same went for all social legislation proposed by liberal and progressive reformers. They were not only useless but dangerous since they created "myths" in the working class about the possibilities of solving their problems under capitalism. On one occasion, a member of the U.S. Commission on Industrial Relations suggested that the body might recommend the I.W.W. program to Congress in order to minimize industrial unrest. "It seems to me," Haywood replied, "a recommendation like that, coming from you gentlemen, would militate against the organization and have a tendency to dilute it and dilute its revolutionary strength."[58]

* Many Wobblies, however, admired the militant tactics and spirit of women suffragists in England who went to jail for their principles and refused an offer of pardon if it compromised their struggle. "They were just like the I.W.W. boys." (*Solidarity*, Dec. 2, 9, 1911.) In 1916, the *Industrial Worker* declared that American woman suffragists were using direct-action tactics in their fight for the ballot, and wondered why "if the women are to use direct action, they do not use it to get for themselves something of value." (July 15, 1916.)

(4) The class struggle would be solved only by the direct action of the workers, not by legislative reform or any other slow change. For a transformation had taken place in the United States in the course of which the industrial and financial monopolists had gained control of the nation. It was useless to hope to change this situation through trust-busting. The political governments at Washington and the state legislatures were useful as committees "employed to police the interests of the employing class," but they were, in reality, only secondary factors. The real power of the nation was economic, and only by controlling this power by gaining control of the industries through direct action could the workers as "citizens of industry" achieve control "over the affairs of their life and the conditions under which they labor." Their strength lay in industrial unions with which they could fight the capitalist enemy where they were strongest—on the economic field, at the point of production, on the job. One Wobbly summed it all up in the following question: "Shall we follow the road that science clearly indicates to us, to deal strictly with causes and effects—exploitation and economic conditions; or shall we bend our knees to the obtuse teachings of metaphysics and deal with a reflex of economic conditions—politics?"[59]

Most Wobblies adhered with great rigidity to their anti-political views. Yet several I.W.W. leaders, groups of individual members, and even whole locals did not, in actual practice, reject voting as useless and, in fact, participated in election campaigns. These Wobblies, along with many other American workers, *Solidarity* conceded, were "not convinced yet of the futility of political action." There was room for such members in the industrial union movement, it noted, for actually the I.W.W. was not anti-political action: "The 'ballot' or the 'political party' is a debatable question with a large part of the I.W.W. membership. For that reason the I.W.W. is an organization that takes a *Non*-political (party) rather than an *Anti*-political (party) attitude, thereby giving individual members the right to differ as widely as they find it necessary, on debatable questions. That distinction should be borne in mind always."[60]

Several I.W.W. theorists went even further, evidently realizing that more had to be said to win over the workers who were "not convinced yet of the futility of political action." Not only was the I.W.W. not "anti-political," but it was "the only real political factor in American society today." It simply had a new conception of political power; namely, "that political power rests on economic power; that if the working class would be a real political power it must first acquire economic power; that is, it must gain control of the shops, ships, railways, mines, mills, in a word, the capital of the country—through industrial organization." By joining the I.W.W., and organizing to control industry, the workers would be engaging in "real politics; all else is fake politics, wherewith to mislead the workers." St. John and Trautmann announced that while they

ordinarily opposed working-class political action, "in its accepted interpretation," they were adherents of "political action by an organized
working class." Speaking of the I.W.W.'s position, St. John declared:
"Inasmuch as every organization that in any way deals with the conditions of a class of people is, in the strict technical sense political, the
I.W.W. is the political machine of the working class."[61]

Even a Pacific Coast A.F. of L. official, bitterly opposed to the I.W.W.,
conceded that there was truth in St. John's statement. "While it denounces
politics and political action most vehemently, the I.W.W. is itself a quasi-
political organization. It differs from other political bodies in the means
more than the ends. It uses so-called direct action instead of the ballot-
box. Most of its big fights have been with the political authorities on
the political field."[62] This definition of political activity certainly did not
limit it to elections, and, in this sense, the Wobblies, through their un-
ceasing struggle for civil rights, engaged in many political campaigns.
Thus Haywood pointed out:

"The history of the I.W.W. has shown the significance of political
action. While there are some members who decry legislative and Congressional action and who refuse to cast a ballot for any political party,
yet the I.W.W. has fought more political battles for the working class
than any other labor organization or political party in America. They
have had one battle after another for free speech. They have fought
against vagrancy laws, against criminal syndicalism laws, and to establish
the right of workers to organize."[63]

Yet when all this had been said, the main fact still remains that by
rejecting political action as most workers understood it, the I.W.W.
isolated itself from the mainstream of America. It also isolated itself from
the real struggle for socialism. Lenin, writing in 1908, viewed the development of the independent political movement of labor in the United
States as of the utmost importance in the battle for socialism. "In America
and England this aggravation [of the struggle between the proletariat
and the bourgeoisie] manifests itself in the strengthening of the movement against the trusts, in the extraordinary growth of socialism and the
attention of the wealthy classes to it, *in the movements of workers'
organizations, sometimes purely economic, into the systematic and in-
dependent-proletarian, political struggle.*"[64]

In politics and, indeed, in every other field, the I.W.W. upheld the
principle that the individual member could act as he wished. "A workingman may be an anarchist or a socialist, a Catholic or a Protestant, a
republican or a democrat, but subscribing to the preamble of the I.W.W.
he is eligible for membership. And we are not responsible for his individual views and activities. . . . So long as the individual performs his
duties as a loyal member of the union, his personal affairs remain in-
violate."[65] One result of this approach was that the I.W.W., despite its

disclaimer of responsibility for the views and acts of members, was associated with as many philosophies and tactics as were preached and practiced by individual members. It was enough for the average newspaper to quote a Wobbly statement asserting that violence was inevitable in the class struggle and its use justified as a defense against the force and violence unleashed by the capitalists, to convince many people that the I.W.W. and the anarchists were one and the same. Joseph Ettor felt that it was necessary to put a halt to all discussions of violence and sabotage since many "wild-eyed statements" on these subjects by "irresponsible elements in the I.W.W." have helped "district attorneys all over the country to build up their cases and 'prove' before prejudiced jurors alleged 'violent' acts of dozens of our fellow-workers, putting them away in jail to rot."[66] This suggestion did not get very far, but the problem Ettor raised was to plague the I.W.W. throughout its history.

The ideology of the I.W.W., which has been presented and analyzed above, was subjected to scrutiny and criticism from within the organization itself and from more orthodox sections of the labor and Socialist movements. We shall deal with the criticisms when analyzing both the contributions and weaknesses of the I.W.W. But before doing this, let us investigate what happened when the Industrial Workers of the World brought its ideology to the cities, woods, and farms of the West and the South and the steel, textile, rubber, and auto towns of the East and Midwest—"to the submerged millions of unskilled wage slaves" to whom "the A.F. of L. extends no relief, offers no hope, gives no comfort." "To these," said Haywood, "the oppressed and downtrodden, the Industrial Workers of the World makes its appeal, fully realizing that within this mass of despised humanity there is a latent force, which if exerted by themselves, will arouse their consciousness, their love of liberty, will strengthen their bended backs, and lift their faces toward the sunlight of a new life of industrial freedom."[67]

CHAPTER 7

The Free-Speech Fights, 1909-1911

"Fellow workers and friends" was the usual salutation that opened the speech of an I.W.W. soapbox orator. In the years between 1909 and the first World War, these four words came to be associated with some of the most spectacular attempts to put the Bill of Rights into practice the country has ever seen—the free-speech fights of the I.W.W. The I.W.W. riveted national attention upon itself as Wobbly after Wobbly was yanked down from soapboxes by the police in scores of cities and marched off to jail, after uttering these four challenging words.

"The struggle for the use of the streets for free speech and the right to organize," was the usual I.W.W. description of a free-speech fight. It was essential for the I.W.W. that the right to speak on the streets be protected because this was the method the Wobblies relied upon to gather new recruits among the homeless, itinerant workers who poured into the western cities by the thousands every winter. "The street corner was their only hall," wrote an I.W.W. organizer, "and if denied the right to agitate there then they must be silent."[1] Here at the street-corner meetings they could distribute quantities of literature, newspapers, leaflets, and pamphlets, all carrying the message of industrial unionism to the unorganized. How important it was to the I.W.W. that this educational process continue was revealed in the *Industrial Worker*'s explanation for the free-speech fights: "We have little desire to enter into these scraps, neither will we stand idly by and see our only hope taken from us—the right to educate the working class. When we lose that we have lost all our hopes and ambitions, so take care what you are playing with when you try to throttle Freedom of Speech."[2] Street-speaking was important for still another reason. In a strike the worker's side was either completely suppressed or distorted by the commercial press. The most effective way the Wobblies could get their story to the public was by means of their open-air meetings. Being colorful speakers, the Wobblies usually attracted large audiences, and they not only aroused sympathy for the strikers, but, through the sale of literature and collections, helped build a much-needed strike fund.

By passing ordinances suppressing the I.W.W.'s right of free speech on the streets, the city officials, acting for the lumber, agricultural, mining interests, and other employers, were convinced that they could crush the organizing drives and destroy the movement. The issue for the I.W.W. was clear: The right to speak meant the right to organize, and the Wobblies rallied their strength across the continent to break down the attempt to stifle this right, convinced that in their battles to smash gag laws, they were upholding the constitutional rights of all people.

The practice of speaking in spite of official bans was not, of course, associated only with the Wobblies. It had long been followed by progressive groups, trade unions, and radical political parties before the I.W.W. Even specific aspects of the strategy followed by the I.W.W. had been used before their spectacular free-speech fights. In the fall of 1907, during the administration of Mayor W. H. Moore, Socialists in Seattle, led by Dr. Herman F. Titus, challenged a city ban against their speaking in the streets. One after another, they mounted the soapbox, were dragged down by the police and carted off to jail, denied bail, fined, and imprisoned. Police Chief Wappenstein threatened to throw all Socialists into jail "as regularly" as they spoke. But when Dr. Titus threatened from jail a mass invasion of free-speech fighters if Seattle did not stop arresting and imprisoning Socialists, the police backed down, permitted street meetings, and released the men and women in jail.[3]

In 1908, the Socialist Party, the Socialist Labor Party, and the I.W.W. jointly waged an effective free-speech fight in Los Angeles, deliberately violating a city ordinance forbidding street meetings without police permits for all organizations except religious groups. When a speaker was arrested for speaking without a permit, "his place was speedily filled upon the soap box." Speaker after speaker, men and women, Negro and white, mounted the soapbox, were arrested, and dragged off to jail. "The Jail Is Our Weapon," the free-speech fighters of Los Angeles announced late in June. "We are going to jail in numbers. That is the way the fight has been won wherever it has been really won."[4] Free-speech fighters so crowded the jail and clogged court calendars that the City Council was forced to repeal the objectionable ordinance. "Free Speech Is Won," was the headline in *Common Sense,* organ of the Socialist Party of Los Angeles and leader of the free-speech fight.[5] It had taken six months to achieve the victory.

PATTERN OF I.W.W. FIGHTS

Still, no labor organization, before the I.W.W., launched its major free-speech fights so dramatically or organized and publicized the battle for freedom of speech so effectively. The I.W.W. worked out a pattern of free-speech fighting which enabled it to make the most spectacular use of its scattered members and created the impression that ten men existed where there was only one. Vincent St. John explained it as follows: "Whenever any local union becomes involved in a free-speech fight, they notify the general office and that information is sent to all the local unions ... with the request that if they have any members that are foot-loose to send them along."[6] In response to these S.O.S.'s, Wobblies converged upon a town or city that prohibited street meetings. One after another, though denied the license, the Wobblies would mount the soap-box and begin: "Fellow workers and friends," ringing out their defiance of the police edicts. As soon as a Wobbly was hauled down by the police and marched off to jail, he would be replaced by another who would instantly mount the soapbox. He, too, would be hauled down to be replaced by another Wobbly. The "four-word speech" would continue all evening as the Wobblies kept being yanked off the soapbox. " 'Afraid of getting arrested? Hardly! We want to get arrested. We'll flood the jail, and the county farm and any other place they want to send us to.' That's what a member of the Industrial Workers of the World involved in the free-speech fight said yesterday to this reporter [for the Kansas City *Star*] at their headquarters."[7]

Thus the free-speech fighters invited arrest, cheerfully allowed them-selves to be marched off by the police, and crowded eagerly into the jails, bull pens, old schoolhouses, abandoned hospitals or any other available building called into use after the jails were filled, supremely confident that, as one of their songs put it:

> *There is one thing I can tell you,*
> *And it makes the bosses sore.*
> *As fast as they can pinch us,*
> *We can always get some more.*[8]

The pattern was clear: Speak; be arrested; crowd the jails; demand a separate trial—a trial by jury—for each and every Wobbly in jail; clog the administrative machinery of the courts, indeed the machinery of the entire municipal administration; become a burden on the taxpayers. Inside the jail, the free-speech fighters would sing rebel songs. "In jail we had one lively time. Rebel Red songs from the I.W.W. song books were sung almost continuously. . . . We spoke for the benefit of the police, loud enough for them to hear. We burned the stuff called food. Then we sang some more."[9] Working through an elected committee, the free-speech fighters in jail decided all questions of defense tactics. An outside committee publicized the struggle and rallied support for the imprisoned men. Usually no money was spent (or as Wobblies put it "wasted") on lawyers' fees. All funds received were used to take care of the men pouring into the community, to supply tobacco and, if possible, food to those in jail, and to get the widest publicity. By this pattern, the Wobblies hoped to win the support of liberal sympathizers outraged by the violation of a basic constitutional guarantee, and, in alliance with the progressive-minded citizens, to force the authorities to grant them the right to speak. And in most communities the I.W.W. did, by such tactics, win the right.

There were humorous aspects to the free-speech fights and many comical situations have been recorded by old-time I.W.W.'s that have become part of Wobbly lore.* And there were many stories that belong in the tradition of the bragging, fighting, "miracle men" tales of American folklore, joyous accounts, full of Wobbly humor.† But there was nothing humorous about the brutal methods used to smash the I.W.W.'s right of free speech. The police were often vicious right at the beginning of a free-speech fight, and as the battle continued—for days, weeks, and sometimes for months—their brutality increased. In addition, private individuals, organized as vigilante committees, worked hand-in-hand with the police, and together they committed unspeakable cruelties upon the Wobblies and their sympathizers. Almost every month, during the period of the epic free-speech fights, the I.W.W. papers carried stories and pictures of the victims of police and vigilante brutalities, of men murdered, maimed, beaten, and starved.

MISSOULA—1909

It was in a skirmish with the authorities of Missoula, Mont., in the summer of 1909 that the Wobblies first established their pattern of free-

---

* One story tells about the harvest hand who dropped off at Sioux City, Iowa, during a free-speech fight, and, finding no one in the corner, decided that the Wobblies were all in jail, and that he had better speak himself. Climbing onto the box, he began: "Fellow workers and friends." Nothing happened. The harvester paused, puzzled, and then started again: "Fellow workers and friends." Again nothing happened. Finally, in an aggrieved tone, the would-be free-speech fighter demanded: "Say, where's the cop?"

† One of the best examples is a running account of a 14-day, boxcar trek from San Francisco to Denver by a band of Wobblies on their way to a free-speech fight. They carried two signs: "On to Denver! Free Speech Fighters Denied the Right to Organize One Big Union" and "We are in your town and must eat." At every town they touched, they had a run-in with the police, but they finally approached the goal, still full of enthusiasm. Their account, written and mailed en route, closed: "We left Oakland, Cal., with twenty; arrived . . . seven miles south of Denver with ninety men, eighty of whom are members. . . . Our goal at last! Sixteen hundred and sixty-eight miles in fourteen days!" (Ed Nowlan, "From Frisco to Denver," *Industrial Worker*, April 17, 24, 1913.)

speech fighting.* Missoula was an industrial town of some importance, but more significant, it was a gateway to many lumber camps and mining towns, and migratory workers regularly moved in and out of the town. With the aim of organizing these transient workers, Vincent St. John sent Elizabeth Gurley Flynn and her husband, Jack Jones, to Missoula. They opened an I.W.W. hall in the basement of the leading theater, and began recruiting the migratory workers at street-corner meetings. The migrants responded eagerly to Gurley Flynn's vigorous attacks on the employment agencies who were fleecing the workers by collecting fees in advance and then sending them to non-existent jobs to be fired after their first wages, out of which they had had to pay a fee for the job. The employment agencies, in league with employers with whom they shared the fees, pressured the City Council to pass an ordinance making street-speaking illegal. The handful of I.W.W. leaders in town—five or six altogether, including Frank Little who was lynched by Vigilantes in Butte, Mont. eight years later—decided to defy the ordinance as unconstitutional. Within two days, four of the six had been arrested for trying to hold street-corner meetings and sentenced to 15 days in the county jail.

The two remaining I.W.W. leaders sent out a call from Missoula for assistance. On September 30, 1909, the *Industrial Worker* carried the first important I.W.W. notice for a free-speech fight, as well as an appeal to "every free born 'American' and every man who hates the tyrannical oppression of the police to go to Missoula and help the workers there to win out." A steady stream of Wobblies flocked into Missoula, "by freight cars—on top, inside and below." As soon as one speaker was arrested, another took his place. The jail was soon filled and the cellar under the firehouse was transformed into an additional jail. When the excrement from the horses leaked through, the I.W.W. prisoners "protested by song and speech, night and day." Since they were directly across the street from the city's main hotel, the guests complained of the continuous noise. Finally, all I.W.W.'s were taken back to the county jail.

Arrests continued and a number of Wobblies, including Jack Jones, were badly beaten in jail. Gurley Flynn and another woman were sent to jail. A new call went out. More Wobblies poured into town and went to jail. The cost of feeding the prisoners increased, and so did the complaints of the taxpayers. The I.W.W. deliberately held their meetings

* In 1945 an I.W.W. member referred to a struggle in Toronto in the summer of 1906 as "the first free speech fight of the I.W.W. . . . It was a small affair and its outcome is not known to the writer." (W.M. in *Industrial Worker,* June 30, 1945.) The reference was to the fact that the Toronto locals went into court when the police interfered with their street-corner meetings. "Against this denial of our *right,*" the Canadian industrial unionists announced, "we as revolutionary wage workers intend to fight." (*The Industrial Worker,* Aug. 1906.) There is no report of what happened in this fight. An examination of the files of the Toronto *Mail and Empire* for July and August, 1906, reveals no account of the event.

at a time when the men would be put into jail before supper, forcing the authorities to feed them. The police retaliated by releasing the prisoners before breakfast, but the men refused to leave the jail. "They had been arrested. They demanded a trial, and individual trials and jury trials at that."[10]

The speaking continued and crowds gathered to listen to the speakers. University professors supported the fight for free speech. Butte Miners Union No. 1, the biggest local in Montana, condemned the local officials for "an un-American and unjust action." Senator Robert M. La Follette, who spoke at a public forum in the theater above the I.W.W. hall, defended the free-speech fighters. By now, the townspeople, already worried by mounting costs, began to call for an end to the arrests and trials. The authorities finally gave up. All cases were dropped. The I.W.W. was allowed to resume its meetings. "We returned to our peaceful pursuit of agitating and organizing the I.W.W.," Gurley Flynn wrote."[11] C. O. Young, A.F. of L. organizer in Missoula, who had refused to permit the local A.F. of L. to support the free-speech fight, wrote disgustedly to Frank Morrison, A.F. of L. secretary-treasurer:

"The 'won't works' have tried the game here of filling the jails so full that the officials of the city would have to capitulate, and they have succeeded in forcing the local authorities to quit. Encouraged by their success at Missoula, they are publishing broadcast that they will do the same to any other city that denies them the privilege of using the streets for speaking."[12]

The battle for free speech in Missoula was nearing its successful end when the first major I.W.W. encounter with city authorities over this issue started in Spokane, Washington. Here the pattern begun in the preliminary skirmish was fully developed.

SPOKANE, 1909–10

"The I.W.W. storm center for the West just now appears to be Spokane, Wash.," the *Industrial Union Bulletin* of February 20, 1909, reported. Here in the largest western center of the migratory workers, the I.W.W. was conducting its most successful membership drive, and building the biggest local union in the organization. One reason for the success was the campaign it was leading to remedy the most pressing grievance of the "floaters" shipping out of Spokane—the fraudulent employment agencies, or as the Wobblies bitterly labeled them, the employment sharks. The sharks, in alliance with unscrupulous employers, fleeced the "floaters" of thousands of dollars by sending applicants to jobs that did not exist. Not only did the men lose the fee, paid in advance, but the railroad fare to and from the place where they had been sent, and, of course, the time spent. In cases where a job was landed, it usually turned out to last only long enough for the foreman to collect the fee which he split with the employment sharks. The vicious system provoked the grim joke that the sharks had discovered perpetual motion—"one man going to a job, one man on the job, and one man leaving the job." One Wobbly reported that a single firm employing only 100 men at a time hired and fired 5,000 men during the season.[13]

Late in 1908, I.W.W. speakers began to attack the system on streets in Spokane near the employment agencies, exposing their practices and citing evidence of hundreds of cases of workers who were fleeced by their trickery. The I.W.W. called for a boycott of the agencies and demanded that the employers hire through the union. The "Don't Buy Jobs" campaign of the I.W.W. so frightened the sharks that they formed the Associated Agencies of Spokane, and at its instigation, the City Council passed an ordinance in October 1908 prohibiting "the holding of public meetings on any of the streets, sidewalks or alleys within the fire limits" after January 1, 1909.[14] The ostensible reason for the ordinance was to prevent traffic congestion. The I.W.W. was informed that the Wobblies could hold their meetings in the public parks and vacant lots, but these were blocks away from the scene of the struggle against the sharks.

During the winter months the I.W.W. violated the ordinance, again holding meetings in front of the employment agencies. But the organization actually won commendation from the press for preventing indignant workers from violently venting their rage against the sharks. A report in the Spokane *Spokesman-Review* of January 18, 1909, described how two to three thousand workers were about to wreck the offices of the Red Cross Employment Agency "when James H. Walsh, organizer of the Industrial Workers of the World, mounting a chair in the street, stemmed the rising tide of riot and pacified the multitude. In the opinion of the police had it not been for the intervention of Walsh a riot would surely have followed. . . . Walsh discouraged violence and summoned all workers to the I.W.W. hall where he warned the crowd against any outbreak." This report is significant in view of the fact that when the recently-enacted ordinance was amended to exempt religious bodies, like the Salvation Army, from its application, the I.W.W. was refused exemption on the ground that it encouraged "violence and riots."[15] This rank discrimination touched off the free-speech fight.

On the evening of November 2, 1909, when James P. Thompson, local organizer for the I.W.W., took the platform at a street-corner meeting, a policeman yanked him down, arrested him on a disorderly conduct charge, and hauled him off to jail. Other Wobblies swarmed up to take his place on the stand. One hundred and fifty, including three women, were arrested and jailed for defying the ordinance from the soapbox. Late in the evening, the police raided the I.W.W. hall, arrested four I.W.W. leaders, closed the offices of the *Industrial Worker,* and proclaimed that they had eradicated the source of "violence and conspiracy" in the city.[16]

But the Wobbly tactics, worked out in the skirmish with the authorities of Missoula, were apparently unknown by the law-enforcement agents in Spokane. Before the arrested men had been fully locked in their cells, the following message was leaving Spokane for all parts of the Pacific Coast and as far east as Chicago: "Big free-speech fight in Spokane; come yourself if possible, and bring the boys with you!"[17] I.W.W. unionists answered by throwing down their shovels and pitchforks and axes and catching the next freight for Spokane. The evening of November 3 saw the I.W.W. tactics bearing fruit. The next morning's Portland *Oregonian,* which gave the battle complete coverage, told how a police officer had arrested the first "red-ribboned orator. . . . No sooner had the officer placed the first man under arrest than another took the stand. It was necessary to arrest nine of the offenders before the crowd quieted down. The prisoners were led to the city jail without giving resistance."[18] Thirty new arrivals talked their way into jail the second evening, and the press reported 1,000 men were on their way to Spokane in empty freight cars to join their I.W.W. brothers. By November 5, the city jail was filled to overflowing. "Still they come, and still they try to speak," the local press wailed.[19]

In an effort to halt the mounting conflict, delegates from the A.F. of L. and the Socialist Party petitioned the City Council to repeal the ordinance and permit unrestricted use of the streets. A hearing was held on the petition. An old soldier and the president of the Fidelity Bank testified in support of the ordinance, and their testimony "apparently outweighed that of the labor and Socialist witnesses because the Council did not repeal the ordinance." Later, the discriminatory part of the ordinance which permitted the Salvation Army to use the streets was abrogated by the State Superior Court. However, the Court upheld James Thompson's conviction in municipal court, thus giving the police the signal to proceed with the arrests and jailings.[20]

And proceed they did! The city jails overflowed, even though the crowding of the prisoners in the cells was characterized by one reporter as "monstrous." (Twenty-eight men were forced into a cell seven by eight feet in size.) On November 10, Mayor Pratt wired Governor M. E. Hay for state aid: "The police have so far been able to handle the proposition, but we have no room for prisoners." Governor Hay denounced the I.W.W. as composed of "illiterate hoboes" who were unfit for citizenship, and praised the authorities in Spokane as "clean, honorable, upright men." But he did not offer material aid to the city.[21]

The Spokane authorities put the overflow prisoners into the unused, unheated Franklin School building. Still the Wobblies poured into town on every freight, mounted the soapboxes, got arrested, and were hauled off to the city jails or the temporary cells in the school building. The Wobblies carried on the struggle even though imprisoned. Night and day they sang songs from *The Little Red Song Book*. "The singing and shouting service of the I.W.W.'s in jail continues at night; a veritable bedlam being created," the *Oregonian* reported.[22]

The police attempted to stop the flood of prisoners with brutality, bread-and-water rations, and atrocious jail conditions. William Z. Foster, who spent almost two months in jail with the free-speech fighters,* wrote that prisoners "were clubbed and packed into cells so closely they could not sit down. When they protested, the hose was turned on them, drenching them with icy water." Packed into small cells, prisoners were "sweated" by turning up the steam heat. Many fainted during this treatment, and only the pressure of closely-packed bodies kept them from falling to the floor. After the "sweating," the guards returned the prisoners to their cold cells.[23]

Food at the Franklin School was "one-third of a small baker's loaf twice a day." The prisoners went on a hunger strike, but the authorities refused to change the bread-and-water diet. Three times a week the police shuttled the prisoners from the school, eight at a time, over to the city jails for baths. One free-speech fighter, not a member of the I.W.W., recalled later what usually happened on the way:

"When we started back to the school house they marched us in the center of the street and on the sidewalks people had gathered with all kinds of tobacco, fruit, bread and everything in the line of eatables, but the police held them back and would not let them get near us so that the people began to throw tobacco, fruit and everything they had brought. Those who were lucky to get some of those things found themselves unlucky, for no sooner had they caught them when the police knocked them out of their hands. In one case one man had just caught an apple and had started to take a bite when the police struck at the apple and hit the poor fellow on the nose and broke it. This is only one instance of which there are many more."[24]

The Portland *Oregonian* sneered at the prisoners for protesting against the baths in the city jails, denouncing them as hoboes and tramps, and quoting Chief of Police Sullivan as saying that "he never saw such a filthy crowd of men." But it failed to report the reason for the prisoners' objections. Guards stripped the prisoners; pushed them under a scalding spray, then into an icy rinse, and then brought them back to their un-

---

* Foster came to Spokane to report the free-speech fight for *The Workingman's Paper* of Seattle (formerly *The Socialist*). He was picked out of "the thick of the crowd" while listening to the soapboxers and arrested. He was sentenced to 30 days in jail, $100 fine and costs, to be worked out on the rock pile. Foster described how he was "loaded with ball and chain (15-pound ball attached to ankle), and shackled by the leg to another man, and then marched to the rock pile, where I was told to work or freeze." (*The Workingman's Paper*, Jan. 1, 8, 15, 22, Feb. 12, 1910.)

heated, freezing quarters in the school. Three Wobblies died in the completely unheated Franklin School. Many prisoners developed pneumonia and other ailments. One month saw 334 prisoners in the hospital lists; another month, 681. William Z. Foster had his feet frozen while lying in jail. One of the prisoners, a veteran of the Civil War, declared that conditions in the School reminded him of Libby and Andersonville prisons.[25]

Still the Wobblies came. "Riding through blizzards on 'the rods,' 'on top' and on the 'front end' of every freight train, these traveling 'salesmen of an idea' poured into town to face pick handles and jails that awaited them at their journeys end."[26] On November 17, 1909, the Spokane *Spokesman-Review* carried the headline: "I.W.W. Man Hurt, Yearns for Jail. 'Martyr' Spurns Proffered Freedom and Begs to Suffer With 'the Boys.'" The morale of the prisoners did not slacken. Weak and sick from hunger and cold though they were, they had enough strength to adopt a resolution denouncing the imprisonment of "Fellow Workers Preston and Smith" who had been "railroaded to the Nevada State Penitentiary on a trumped-up charge of murder,"* and pledged themselves "when liberated to use every means in our power to secure their release."[27]

"The members of the I.W.W. confined in the city jail have organized themselves in a temporary organization, and hold regular meetings twice a week," William Z. Foster wrote to *The Workingman's Paper* of Seattle. ". . . Monday night is devoted to propaganda work, and that this is not without effect is evidenced by the large number of non-I.W.W. prisoners who have declared their intention of joining the organization on securing their release.† Wednesday night is business night, and it certainly is surprising the amount of business we have to transact. We have established 10:30 P.M. as the time when 'lights out' shall sound, have elected a secretary and a propaganda committee that has charge of the Sunday programs. . . . There are dozens of other rules and regulations that we have established."[28]

The free-speech prisoners served 30 days, and when "liberated," immediately attempted to speak again. Two youth of 18 years, arrested a second time, were offered a suspended sentence by Judge Mann if they would promise not to speak again and leave town. Both refused and were sentenced to another 30 days in jail and $100 fine, to be worked out on the rock pile.[29]

On November 16, the press reported the arrival on the scene of "Elizabeth Gurley Flynn [who] addressed a meeting in the Municipal Courtroom and after roasting the newspapers, police judges and city authorities, took up a collection of $25."[30] Since she was pregnant, the Wobblies decided that the "rebel girl" should not speak on the forbidden streets, but

---

* The incident referred to occurred during the Goldfield strike led by the I.W.W. in Nevada. *See above* pp. 93–98.
† Foster himself joined the I.W.W. after his release.

only in I.W.W. halls, clubs, and organizations willing to give her a hearing to raise defense funds. But the condition of "the beauteous, black-haired firebrand" did not concern the police. On November 31, the police arrested the second group of I.W.W. leaders, among them Gurley Flynn, and threw them in jail.[31] The Wobbly press flashed the news of the imprisonment of the "Joan of Arc of the I.W.W." in flaming headlines, and circulars were issued announcing that "Elizabeth Gurley Flynn, a girl organizer only 19 years old, soon to become a mother, was arrested, charged with criminal conspiracy, confined in jail with prostitutes and in-sulted by an officer of the law."* The Wobblies west of the Mississippi, now more aroused than ever, poured into Spokane in increased numbers. "Logging crews of pine camps deserted in a body to Spokane." In a special circular, the Spokane I.W.W. Free Speech Committee set March 1, 1910, as the day "to begin again new full scale invasions to fill Spokane jails and bull-pens. We will never surrender until we gain our constitutional right to speak on the streets of Spokane. The right to organize must be protected."[32]

It was becoming too much for the citizens of Spokane. With between 500 and 600 Wobblies in jail, all of whom announced that "we will serve 30 days on bread and water, and when we get out we will immediately be rearrested," with 1,200 arrests on the books, and with fresh delegations arriving from points as far as McKees Rocks, Penna., Canada, Mexico, and Skowhegan, Maine, it was obvious that the town was licked. Moreover, the I.W.W. had brought damage suits to the amount of $150,000 against the city and individual officials, and threatened to carry them to the Su-preme Court if necessary.[33]

On March 5, 1910, the city officials surrendered and made peace with the I.W.W. on the following terms: (1) Street speaking would be per-mitted; (2) all I.W.W. prisoners would be released; (3) the I.W.W. hall would reopen and remain undisturbed; (4) the *Industrial Worker* would be free to publish;† (5) all I.W.W. damage suits against the city would be dropped; (6) the I.W.W. would refrain from speaking on the streets until the prohibitive ordinance was officially repealed. The City Council unani-mously repealed the law on March 9, 1910. This great victory was made

---

* The reference was to Gurley Flynn's charge that an officer approached her in her cell and attempted to take improper liberties with her. (*See* Solidarity, Dec. 23, 1909.) Miss Flynn was not the only woman subjected to such treatment. Agnes Theela, a Spokane Socialist imprisoned for participating in the free-speech fight, wrote a description of attempts to rape her while in prison which, when published in *The Workingman's Paper,* almost shut it out of the mails. (*See* issue of July 2, 1910.)

† In all, eight successive editors of the *Industrial Worker* were jailed after getting out eight successive issues. Finally, the office of the paper was raided, and it was decided late in December 1909 to transfer the paper—masthead plates and all—to Seattle. It was returned to Spokane in May 1910.

complete shortly thereafter by the City Council's revocation of the licenses of 19 of the city's 31 employment agencies and the promise to repay some of the losses suffered by defrauded workers. Subsequently the Washington State Legislature passed a law forbidding employment agencies from charging fees. An effort was made to install a matron in the city jail to reform conditions publicized by Gurley Flynn, but although the City Council passed a resolution authorizing the appointment, the finance committee tabled it. However, two prison guards, especially denounced by the Wobblies for brutality, were discharged.[34]

On June 28, 1910, the Spokane *Inland Herald* carried this historic report: "For the first time in two years police-sanctioned street speaking occurred Saturday night. The free speech advocates could be heard for blocks, while nearly 1,500 gathered to listen to the contesting orators." "The free speech fight," a Wobbly wrote from Spokane, "has brought the I.W.W. so clearly before the working class of the Northwest that before another year has elapsed all of the workers in the lumber woods, the sawmills, shingle, sash and door factories will be organized."[35]

The Spokane free-speech fight was front-page news in every newspaper in the country. But one aspect of the epic battle was not reported in the commercial press or even in I.W.W. publications. The facts remained buried for years in the archives of the A.F. of L. During the free-speech fight, the I.W.W. issued a circular entitled "The Shame of Spokane," appealing for financial aid to help in carrying the struggle through to victory. The circular was sent to many A.F. of L. affiliates as well as to Socialist and progressive organizations. Moved by its detailed account of police brutalities, corroborated by reports in the press, and by admiration for the heroism of the free-speech fighters, Socialists held protest meetings in several cities, and a number of A.F. of L. affiliates contributed to the defense fund. Some unions wrote to Gompers and Morrison urging them to take a stand officially in favor of free speech and against police brutality in Spokane. "We feel that the rights of all organized labor is at stake in the battle now taking place in our city," the Spokane Central Council wrote. "Already decent people not associated with the I.W.W. are being deprived of their right of free speech if they attempt to criticize the authorities.* Certainly the American Federation of Labor cannot remain silent in the face of these facts." When more

---

* A mass meeting was called during the free-speech fight at the Masonic Temple by leaders of the Women's Equal Suffrage Club, the Women's Club, several respected clergymen, and a number of Socialists. It was announced as a gathering to protest the anti-speaking ordinance and police brutality against the I.W.W. At the last minute, the trustees of the Masonic Temple canceled use of their hall for the meeting. When a number of the planners of the meeting tried to gather in the streets to voice their protests, they were arrested and charged with disorderly conduct. (Portand *Oregonian*, Nov. 4, 5, 1909; Spokane *Spokesman-Review*, Nov. 6, 1909.)

letters of this nature came to A.F. of L. headquarters, Morrison designated C. O. Young, general organizer stationed at Missoula, to go to Spokane, ascertain the facts and report them to the A.F. of L. "so that we might be able to answer the numerous letters which reach us as to the purported treatment of said I.W.W. by Spokane authorities."[36]

It was a choice that guaranteed a whitewashing of the authorities, for Young had unsuccessfully tried in every possible way to prevent an I.W.W. victory for free speech in Missoula. In addition, he had only contempt for the migratory workers whom he referred to as "pauper cast offs." Young's report completely exonerated the Spokane authorities, and declared that the free-speech fight was due solely to the I.W.W.'s love for stirring up trouble. ("As you know, excitement is what our I.W.W. friends live upon.") He praised the Spokane employment agencies, police, courts, prison guards, and city officials, and critized liberals and reformers who tried to support the free-speech fighters. "The I.W.W. was encouraged by men and women who ought to have better sense, and do not realize that there should be no liberty or freedom of speech for those who destroy property. Yet those people, including some of our own fellows here, encouraged the free speechers by word and pen." Spokane was "a liberal city, with the best treatment for patriotic, truly American labor of any western city." But the I.W.W. deserved no such treatment, and Young urged Morrison to notify all A.F. of L. affiliates not to respond to the I.W.W. circular and refrain from sending funds to assist "an un-American organization carry on their unholy work of breaking the laws and defying the constituted authority of the various communities, and to help them to carry on their contemptible work and defeat the objects and aims of a great movement like the American Federation of Labor who love order and respect the laws and who go about reforms in a sane and rational way. . . . It is exceedingly strange that members of Federation and even officials of the Trades Union movement, will listen to those appeals emanating from a source so foul; from an organization whose every act is that of falsehood, whose every utterance is that of infamy, destructive of all that is good, with the only purpose to destroy."

"I trust that you will be satisfied with my efforts in this matter," Young wrote to Morrison. The A.F. of L. secretary-treasurer was more than "satisfied." "I am happy to receive your well-prepared report," he congratulated Young. "The facts contained therein are precisely what we need to convince some of our own people, who are not fully acquainted with what really happened in Spokane,* that they have been 'taken in'

---

* Morrison was especially happy that Young reported that "the police were not brutal, but, on the contrary, were cautioned and did deal gently with every one arrested," and that "the guards were maltreated by the 'won't-works' rather than the other way around. . . ." (C. O. Young to Frank Morrison, March 28, 1910; Frank Morrison to C. O. Young, April 2, 1910, *AFL Corr.*)

by the dual unionists. You need have no fear that the Executive Council will act in the matter. We do not propose to be stampeded into rash action by men who are blinded by sentimentality to the real dangers represented by the so-called Industrial Unionists."[37] It can certainly be argued that no action of the authorities in Spokane was more reprehensible than the part played by the secretary-treasurer of the A.F. of L. and the Federation's organizer in the Pacific Northwest.

FRESNO, 1910–11

The story of the free-speech fight in Spokane had barely disappeared from the newspapers when the front pages blared out the news of another major I.W.W. battle for free speech.* This occurred at Fresno, Calif.

Located in the heart of the San Joaquin Valley, the fruit belt of California, Fresno had long been the key concentration point for agricultural labor in the state. The city was also a center for construction workers who drifted into town in search of jobs. In November 1909, a small group of Wobblies set up headquarters of Local 66 at Fresno, began to hold street meetings and to distribute literature to the migratory workers. When these activities were halted by the police, Frank Little and a few other veterans of the Spokane fight came down from the Northwest to aid the local. Mexican laborers, imported to help construct a dam outside of Fresno, were organized, and the workers in the Santa Fe Railroad's electric power plant went out on strike under Local 66's leadership. Anxious to stop I.W.W. agitation, the employers began putting pressure on Chief of Police Shaw to ban the Wobblies from the streets of Fresno.[38]

Police Chief Shaw revoked the I.W.W. permit to speak in the streets; the Salvation Army, however, was permitted to continue. These repressive measures put a temporary halt to Local 66's growth. "If we had the streets so we could get to the workers we would build up a good fighting organization," Little informed the I.W.W. press, warning that a free-speech fight was brewing in Fresno.[39] The fight started on August 20 when Little was arrested while standing in the street.† He immediately

---

* There were a number of minor battles for free speech during this same period; indeed, the *Industrial Worker* commented on June 4, 1910: "There seems to be an epidemic of free speech fights on the part of the workers, due to the activity of the police in denying the workers the privilege of airing their views."

† Little was arrested several times during the fight, once for reading the Declaration of Independence from the soapbox, jailed, and when released, was again arrested for speaking from street corners. On November 26, he was arrested for having urged the police of Fresno to organize and strike for the eight-hour day. (The police worked ten hours per day.) "The idea of telling the police that they ought to go on strike!" declared Police Chief Shaw in explaining Little's arrest. (*Solidarity*, Dec. 17, 1910.)

wired headquarters in Chicago appealing for help. "F. E. Little sentenced before a perjured jury to 25 days in jail. A police conspiracy to get organizer Little out of town." These headlines in the *Industrial Worker* of September 10 put the members on notice that a real fight was imminent. The October 8 issue carried the news that the national organization officially supported the Fresno group in their fight for free speech, and called upon Wobblies "to go to Fresno and *break the law*. Break it, smash it into unrecognizable pulp." The I.W.W. journal did not hide the fact that those who went to Fresno would face brutal opposition. On October 26, it reprinted a threatening statement from the Fresno *Herald:* "For men to come here with the express purpose of creating trouble, a whipping post and a cat-o-nine tails well seasoned by being soaked in salt water is none too harsh a treatment for peace-breakers."[40]

But by the time this appeared, open warfare had started in Fresno. On October 16, in defiance of local ordinances, the Wobblies announced an open-air meeting. Nine speakers were arrested, as they arose in turn to address the crowd. The following night, five more were arrested. Here the struggle paused. Not enough men had yet arrived in Fresno to keep the meetings going, and the *Industrial Worker* announced on November 16 that the fight for free speech would be reopened as soon as 15 men were available to go to jail. Not only did this announcement bring 15 Wobblies into Fresno, but in less than a month, there were 50 men in jail for violating the ordinance against speaking on the streets, and more volunteers were on the way. "Industrial Workers Preach Discontent. Men Invite Arrest to Secure Sympathy," the San Francisco *Call's* headlines screamed.[41]

Early in the struggle, the I.W.W. had been forced by the owner to vacate its headquarters, and, unable to rent any other hall, the Wobblies hired a tent which they set up on a vacant lot belonging to a sympathizer. On December 9, a mob of over 1,000 vigilantes attacked and severely beat a number of I.W.W. men who sought to speak on the streets, then advanced on the I.W.W. tent headquarters, burned the camp and all the supplies, marched to the county jail and threatened to break into the jail and lynch the Wobbly prisoners. The mob had been encouraged by a statement by Police Chief Shaw that "if the citizens wished to act they might and he would not interfere." Shaw's statement followed the discovery that the city of Fresno had no ordinance prohibiting speaking on the streets, and that the actions of the police were accordingly entirely without authority. It was decided quickly that the city trustees would pass an ordinance requiring a permit to speak on the streets. Since meanwhile the police could not forbid the I.W.W. from speaking, Police Chief Shaw informed all would-be vigilantes that they could act to prevent street speaking without police interference.[42]

Vincent St. John immediately wired Mayor Powell of Fresno warning him that the acts of the mob would not deter the I.W.W. "Free speech will be established in Fresno if it takes twenty years." He also wired the Governor of California asking him what action he was preparing to take to halt the mob in the effort "to destroy constitutional rights of the members of this organization." The Governor was out of the state, but the Acting Governor refused to act.[43]

On December 22, the police, infuriated by the protests of the Wobblies in their cells over the manhandling of a drunk, placed all of the prisoners "on a bread and water diet and confined [them] in darkness." The Wobblies answered by going on a hunger strike. The next day they sang songs and held a street meeting, addressing the audience through the prison bars. The jailer turned the fire hose on the prisoners, but the Wobblies barricaded themselves behind "a fortress of their mattresses," and continued singing and shouting to the crowd. Firemen, armed with picks, battered down the fortress; the fire engine was called, and at close range, sprayed the men with the full force of the hose. The prisoners were left standing knee deep in water. The following morning the so-called "respectable elements" were pleased to read: "The officers believe the punishment inflicted last night (at the hands of a fire engine) has broken the spirit of the industrialists."

But the fight was far from over. About 150 Wobblies were in jail at this time, "crowded to more than the capacity of the prison." Another 50 were added over the next two months. Then the I.W.W. general office issued a new call for volunteers to participate in the campaign. In Portland, 150 men were mobilized to "bum" their way to Fresno. A week later, a group of 100 Wobblies and sympathizers left St. Louis. The St. Louis *Globe Democrat,* on February 26, 1911, carried the news that the group "left their quarters at 3 o'clock yesterday afternoon to march on Fresno, Calif., and take part in the free-speech fight there by the Industrial Workers. When the army reaches Kansas City the number will be enlarged to about 200. By picking up the unemployed along the route, the marchers expect to number more than a thousand when they reach Fresno. They say . . . the city of Fresno will be unable to provide for them should they be arrested, and this would cause the taxpayers to protest at the expense of feeding them." About the same time, the Denver *Post* reported that 5,000 men were "scheduled to start for Fresno. If they cannot beat their way on the railroad, the members of the army have announced their willingness to walk."[44]

Every day the newspapers carried reports of the progress of the invading armies of Wobblies en route to Fresno. Some, put off the freight trains, started walking. They were caught in snowstorms in the mountains. ". . . We walked," wrote one Wobbly who started out for Fresno from Seattle with 47 other volunteers, "over the Siskin mountains in four foot of snow and zero weather, down across the state line into California, then up again over the Shasta Mounts in four feet of snow again, then down through the Sacramento Valley when it was raining. . . . We held meetings every night all the way down advertising the Fresno fight, interviewing newspaper reporters."[45] The San Francisco *Call* shared the bewilderment of many newspapers when it commented on March 2, 1911, under the headline, "Hundred in Jail and More Seek Martyrdom": "It is one of those strange situations which crop up suddenly and are hard to understand. Some thousands of men, whose business is to work with their hands, tramping and stealing rides, suffering hardships and facing dangers—to get into jail. And to get into that particular jail in a town of which they never heard before, in which they have no direct interest."

Few of these invading Wobblies reached Fresno in time to participate in the fight.* But the threat of their arrival was largely responsible for bringing the fight to a close. This was particularly the effect created by the group of 150 I.W.W. men from Spokane. They walked through Washington and Oregon to the California line, crossing a mountain range high above the surrounding country which was entirely covered by snow. After weeks of marching the "army" reached Sacramento, California's capital and only a short distance from Fresno. In Sacramento they were received by a large force of I.W.W. members under Carl Browne, who had been first lieutenant to General Coxey on his famous march to Washington in 1894. Recruits poured in by the score and the augmented army prepared to leave for Fresno on February 20. The news of the intended departure of the "army" from Sacramento reached Fresno the same day. With the jails already filled, with the taxpayers lamenting the cost of the battle, the substantial citizens of Fresno met and decided that the fight must not be allowed to continue.[46]

On February 22, 1911 a committee was elected to act as mediators between the city officials and the Wobblies in prison. This group met with a committee elected by the men in jail to ascertain the I.W.W.'s terms of settlement. There were two conditions presented by the spokesmen for the prisoners: (1) The parole of all the prisoners under conviction and the release of all prisoners not yet convicted as a result of the free-speech fight; (2) the granting of a permit to the I.W.W. to use specific streets for meetings. If these conditions were met, the committee representing the men in jail would notify the general headquarters and all locals of the I.W.W. to stop sending men to Fresno and make every effort to stop the men already on the way to the city.

After the Wobblies had rejected a proposal that part of the settlement be an agreement in writing by the I.W.W. to leave the city, the citizens' committee left and reported the terms to a larger body (at which the

* Some of the I.W.W. marchers went on to lower California where they joined General Pryce's force of Socialist insurrectionists and fought in the Mexican Revolution. (For the role of the I.W.W. in this movement, *see* Lowell L. Blaisdell, *The Desert Revolution: Baja California, 1911,* Madison, Wis., 1962.)

mayor and city council were present), recommending the granting of the prisoners' terms. On March 2, the Fresno city officials rescinded the ban against street meetings. Three days later, the men in prison were released, and immediately issued a statement announcing that "Solidarity Won in Fresno," and that "at this writing, Sunday, March 5th, 1911, the Fresno Free Speech Fight has passed into history." A month later, Local 66, which had moved into a new hall, informed the I.W.W. press: "We are holding street meetings twice a week, which are well attended."[47]

It had taken the I.W.W. six months to gain the victory at Fresno. The cost to the organization was less than $1,000.[48] The publicity gained for the I.W.W. was enormous, for the story was featured in newspapers all over the country. Every American who cherished freedom of speech was now fully aware that a labor organization existed which was dedicated to defend that constitutional right.

CHAPTER 8

The Free-Speech Fights, 1912-1914

For several months after the Fresno victory, the I.W.W. in California had merely to threaten to use "Fresno tactics" to win the right of free speech. When Wobblies were arrested for speaking on the streets in San Jose and Marysville and arraigned before a police judge, they had only to threaten an I.W.W. invasion similar to the one that had taken place at Fresno. The defendants were quickly released, and the Wobblies held their street meetings unmolested.[1]

The same situation prevailed in Washington. In August 1911, the Tacoma commission announced that it planned to pass an ordinance forbidding speaking on the streets and that it was specifically aimed at the local members of the I.W.W. The Tacoma *Times* promptly warned the commission that if it went through with its plans, "there will be one delightful fight in this town. . . . It will cost the city a bunch of money to carry on such a fight—and it will lose in the end. Spokane lost a lot of money trying to stop free speech. So did Fresno, Cal." The Tacoma press notified the city authorities that the I.W.W. "will be backed by the 13 Socialist unions in the city," and quoted A. C. Cole, secretary of the Tacoma I.W.W., as threatening to bring 10,000 men into the city. The city commission abandoned the plan to adopt the proposed ordinance.[2]

The influence of I.W.W. free-speech victories spilled over into Canada. In the summer of 1911, the police in Victoria, B.C., revoked the right of the Wobblies and Socialists to hold meetings on street corners anywhere in the city and assigned them a part of one street in an isolated section of the community. Charging discrimination against their organization and the Socialist Party because the Salvation Army was not so restricted, the Wobblies announced their determination to speak on the forbidden street corners. On Sunday evening, July 21, a group of Wobblies, accompanied by several Socialists, mounted the box on one of the forbidden street corners. The speakers were promptly arrested and hauled into court on the charge of obstructing traffic. The following Tuesday, J. S. Biscay, I.W.W. organizer, arrived in Victoria. In an interview with the prosecuting attorney and the chief of police, Biscay charged that the ban against street-speaking originated with the Employers' Association which had just broken a building strike in Vancouver and was seeking to wipe out unionism in Canada. But nothing Biscay said made any impression until the very end of the interview. "In leaving I called his [the chief of police's] attention to Missoula, Spokane, and Fresno, where the authorities got wise as to what they were up against and gave in." The following morning Biscay was informed that the ban on street-speaking had been withdrawn. The men in prison were released and the previous right of the I.W.W. and the Socialists to speak anywhere in the city was restored.[3]

These I.W.W. successes so frightened the employers that they decided that new tactics were needed to prevent the Wobblies from moving on from victory to victory. The M. & M. (Merchants' and Manufacturers' Association) in various West Coast cities and towns organized a counter-free-speech movement to smash the I.W.W.'s right to free speech as the first step in their determined drive to destroy the I.W.W. itself. The M. & M. strategy was to organize small armies of vigilantes or deputies to invade the jails, drive the Wobblies out of town, and, by the most brutal terror keep them out. Harrison Gray Otis, whose Los Angeles *Times* was an official spokesman for the M. & M., summed up the brutal strategy: "During the visit of the Industrial Workers of the World they will be accorded a night and day guard of honor, composed of citizens armed with rifles. The Coroner will be in attendance at his office every day."[4]

ABERDEEN, 1911–12

The tactic of deputizing citizen police and deporting I.W.W. members was first unfolded in Aberdeen, Wash., chief center of Grays Harbor in Western Washington, heart of the lumber kingdom belonging to Frederick Weyerhaeuser. Anticipating an organizing drive by the I.W.W. among the lumber workers who came into Aberdeen, the City Council issued an ordinance in the summer of 1911 forbidding speaking and assembling on all the principal streets. This was later amended to permit all organizations except the I.W.W. to use the streets for corner meetings. The City Council frankly announced that the authorities "would not molest any organization but the 'I Won't Works' as these set the employees against their employers." Although the Socialist Party declared itself satisfied with the action of the City Council, since it had not been barred from use of the streets, Wobblies and liberals in Aberdeen demanded rescinding of the ban. They were supported by the national office of the I.W.W. Chicago headquarters warned the Mayor of Aberdeen in November 1911 that the I.W.W. would not accept the ordinance, and intended to force its repeal or "make the grass grow in the street."[5]

When this warning was ignored, the Wobblies began a major violation of the law. Police arrested five speakers on the evening of November 22, 1911, and marched them through the streets to jail. Late that same night, a mob of vigilantes, including many of the leading businessmen of the city, attempted to break into the jail and lynch the prisoners. They were held back by the police, but they let the Wobblies in jail know they would be back. The next day, the vigilantes organized themselves more efficiently. Five hundred of the city's "most prominent business and professional" men formed a battalion of special police. The Mayor deputized them immediately, and, armed with clubs, the deputized vigilantes took command of the city. When Wobblies and liberal sympathizers attempted to hold a mass protest meeting in the Empire Theatre, the deputies roped off the street and assisted the police in arresting all persons approaching the theatre. The Aberdeen *Daily World* proudly announced that "W. J. Patterson, president of the Hayes and Hayes bank, and Dudley G. Allen, secretary of the Chamber of Commerce, cooperated in making the first arrest in front of the theatre."[6]

In spite of the "armed terror," the Wobblies persisted in speaking on the streets. They were arrested and turned over to the citizen police to escort them to jail. The Portland *Oregonian* gleefully reported that few of the prisoners arrived in jail without broken heads and limbs. "The citizen police have been armed with wagon spokes and axe handles for use as clubs, and these weapons have proved most effective." The *Industrial Worker* condemned the conspiracy of "the gang of sluggers in Aberdeen to club our members to death." But it advised against meeting terror with terror: "We must be prepared to meet these new tactics and we must not meet them with axe handles because we have the queer faculty of knowing that there is no such thing as *equality before the law*." The Wobblies met the "new tactics" with the usual pattern of free-speech fighting. Wobbly after Wobbly spoke, was arrested, and went to jail. And the usual appeal went out to Wobblies all over the West: "On to Aberdeen. Free Speech fight on. . . . Help is needed at once. On to Aberdeen."[7]

In December the citizen deputies decided to end the practice of keeping the Wobblies in jail, "allowing them to feed off the taxpayers." They collected the prisoners at the jail, beat them viciously, escorted them out of town, and warned them not to return. "God bless you if you go, God help you if you return" were the usual parting words to the workers, some of whom had lived in Aberdeen for many years and left families behind who depended on their support. The armies of vigilantes patrolled the streets, ready to attack and deport any Wobblies on sight, and even broke into outlying jungles where Wobblies, preparing to invade Aberdeen, congregated, and drove them out of the region.[8]

The tactics of the citizen police aroused a storm of protest from the workers of the Grays Harbor area, in which the A.F. of L. Central Labor Council joined. On December 8, 1911, the Council unanimously passed a resolution which, while clearly indicating sharp disagreement with "the methods of organization and tactics" of the I.W.W., condemned the officials and citizens of Aberdeen for having "seen fit to wage war upon a working class organization, . . . breaking up their meetings, deporting them, confiscating their literature and in other violent and unlawful ways depriving them of their constitutional rights."[9] But the protest was ignored. In the face of the open threats of the citizen police to deport, with the aid of "wagon spokes and axehandles," any stranger to Aberdeen who looked like a Wobbly, the free-speech fighters kept pouring into the city. "Box-cars all the way from here to St. Paul," wrote the Aberdeen correspondent of the Seattle *Post-Intelligencer* on December 26, "have been placarded with notices, calling the workers to proceed against this city." He reported that news had reached Aberdeen that 250 Wobblies "have left St. Louis to aid the local members of the organization in their fight for free speech," and that 1,500 men had been deputized by the police ready to move "on the borders of the city, on the streets, and in the railroad yards to meet them."[10]

With the aid of new arrivals, I.W.W. headquarters, previously closed down in raids by the citizen police, were reopened, and the speaking at street corners resumed. "Not one sentence was finished by any of the speakers," the Portland *Oregonian* reported from Aberdeen on January 12. Fifteen men were arrested that night, driven blindfolded in automobiles beyond the city limits by the citizen police, beaten and warned never to return. But there were enough Wobblies on hand by now to put ten men on the street every night for two weeks. Speakers continued to be arrested, but the Mayor, at the suggestion of the "pick-handle brigade," began to negotiate with a committee of the I.W.W. elected by the men in jail. (It was conceded that a boycott of Aberdeen merchants by workers in the Grays Harbor area helped bring about the move to negotiate a settlement.) The negotiations resulted in "a clean-cut unqualified victory for the Industrial Workers of the World."[11] * On January 7, 1912, the City Council passed a new ordinance setting aside five of the most populated cross-streets in the city for street meetings. No permit would be required by any organization wishing to hold meetings on these corners. In addition, the City Council agreed to indemnify the I.W.W. local for damages to its headquarters during the fight. The local received $40 as indemnity.[12]

* Robert L. Tyler calls the Aberdeen free-speech fight a failure for the I.W.W., but his treatment of the battle ends with December 1911, the period of the temporary victory for the authorities and the citizen police. ("Rebels of the Woods: A Study of the I.W.W. in the Pacific Northwest," unpublished Ph.D. thesis, University of Oregon, 1953, p. 51.)

"Aberdeen, recently made famous as the city ruled by wagon spoke and axe handle, has again restored the right of free speech to its citizens," a New York paper reported. A huge victory street meeting was held on the evening of January 18, at which it was announced that a new campaign to organize the lumber workers would be launched. A month later, the I.W.W. local reported the formation of the Marine Workers' Industrial Union in Aberdeen, with 31 charter members, and noted gleefully: "This is a pretty pill for the pick-handle experts to swallow."[13]

SAN DIEGO, 1912

Brutal as was the struggle in Aberdeen, it seemed almost a tea party compared to what happened in the free-speech fight in San Diego, Calif., which began early in 1912 and continued for more than half a year. For 20 years the block on San Diego's E Street, between Fourth and Fifth, had been set aside for street meetings. "Soapbox Row," as the block came to be known, was frequently the scene of simultaneous meetings by single-taxers, Salvation Army preachers, Holy Roller evangelists, Socialists, and Wobblies. At times the block held several thousand listeners, but no incident of violence or riot had occurred in the two decades of street meetings.

Some police interference with I.W.W. speakers did occur in the summer and fall of 1910 when Local Union No. 13, I.W.W., of San Diego organized the Mexican workers employed at the San Diego Consolidated Gas and Electric Co., and led them in a successful strike for higher wages and shorter hours. Pressing forward after its victory, Local Union No. 13 held street meetings every night in both English and Spanish, with Laura Payne Emerson the chief English speaker. Then in November 1910, the police closed up the Germania Hall to prevent an I.W.W. meeting in commemoration of the hanging of the Haymarket victims in 1887. When the Wobblies took the meeting to "Soapbox Row" and continued their commemoration of the labor martyrs, the speakers were arrested, fingerprinted, photographed in jail, and then released. But this blatant interference with freedom of speech was sharply criticized by the San Diego *Sun,* a Scripps paper, which reminded Chief of Police Wilson that "the members of the I.W.W. . . . have as much right to live and speak, so long as they behave themselves, as . . . any other public speaker or public man." As a result of this and other protests, the harassments temporarily ceased. "Street meetings are held two or three times a week," Local Union No. 13 reported in May 1911.[14]

Then on December 8, 1911, without warning, the Grand Jury recommended that "Soapbox Row" be cleared and street-speaking be prohibited in the heart of the city. The Council passed an ordinance on January 8, creating a "restricted" district, 49 blocks in the center of town, in which street-corner meetings might not be held. The reason given was that the meetings blocked traffic. But the I.W.W. charged that the true reason was the determination of the M. & M. throughout California to suppress the Wobblies' efforts "to educate the floating and out-of-work population to a true understanding of the interests of labor as a whole," as well as their determination to organize the workers in San Diego who were neglected by the A.F. of L. Among these neglected workers were the mill and lumber and laundry workers and street-car conductors and motormen. This determination had infuriated John D. Spreckels, the millionaire sugar capitalist and owner of the streetcar franchise, and he and the M. & M. had applied pressure on the Council to pass the ordinance. Certainly San Diego had plenty of room for her traffic, and no one believed that this little town in Southern California would suffer a transportation crisis if street meetings continued.[15]

On the day the ordinance was supposed to go into effect, a great meeting of the I.W.W. and the Socialists was held in the center of the restricted district. But the police made no effort to break up the meeting, and, as a result of a technicality, the ordinance was held up for a month. During this month, the California Free Speech League, composed of members of the I.W.W., the A.F. of L. trade unions, the Socialist Party, and some church organizations,* was organized. On February 8, 1912, the day on which the ordinance went into effect, 38 men and three women (Laura Payne Emerson, a leading figure in Local No. 13 among them) were arrested for violating the ban against speaking on the streets. During the next few days more street speakers were arrested, and on February 12, Local No. 13 informed I.W.W. headquarters of what was happening, and affirmed: "Will fight to a finish." The word spread in the hobo jungles that

> *Out there in San Diego*
> *Where the western breakers beat,*
> *They're jailing men and women*
> *For speaking on the street.*[16]

Wobblies began pouring into San Diego. On February 13, Superintendent of Police John C. Sehon issued orders for a general roundup of all vagrants. That same evening the police arrested seven men as they rose to speak to an audience of a thousand people. Still more Wobblies poured into town, coming by foot and rail; the San Francisco *Call*

---

* Unlike ordinances in other cities banning street-speaking, that in San Diego made no exception for religious utterances. All street-speaking was banned in the so-called "congested district." As a consequence, a number of religious leaders of the community, including evangelists, took part in the San Diego fight. Lulu Whitman, an old-time evangelist, became a member of the executive committee of the Free Speech League. Frank Ellison, a Negro preacher, was also active in the fight. (San Diego *Sun*, March 2, 1912; San Francisco *Bulletin*, March 16, 1912.)

reported that the men "drew lots to determine which ten of their number would go to jail," and on February 10, it announced that five to ten thousand Wobblies were heading for San Diego. Within the next few days, the police filled the four jails with 280 men and women. Still they came, and the I.W.W. assured the authorities of San Diego that the fight would be fought to a finish "if it takes 20,000 members and twenty years to do so."[17]

The response of the authorities was to step up the drive against free speech. The original ordinance had simply banned street-speaking in the "congested district." Legally, therefore, the police could not interfere with assemblies outside of the district. Consequently, another ordinance —a "move-on" ordinance such as had been used to halt picketing in many communities—was enacted, which gave the police arbitrary authority to order any group or individual to move on anywhere in San Diego. This ordinance took effect on March 28, and was used for extending and intensifying police terrorism. On March 29, the San Diego *Sun* reported: "Police clubs were freely used last night when Sehon's men began the enforcement of the new 'move-on' ordinance and blood flowed as a result."

With the exception of the San Diego *Sun,* the Scripps daily which, however, supported the arrests, and the San Diego *Herald,* a liberal weekly, newspapers in the city were maniacal in their fury against the free-speech fighters. The San Diego *Tribune* shrieked on March 4, 1912: "Hanging is none too good for them and they would be much better dead; for they are absolutely useless in the human economy; they are waste material of creation and should be drained off in the sewer of oblivion there to rot in cold obstruction like any other excrement." It called for the shooting of the men in jail. "This method of dealing with the evil that has fastened itself on San Diego would end the trouble in half an hour." Other newspapers, echoing the *Tribune,* spoke of "an unwritten law" to which the citizens might appeal to put down "anarchy and disloyalty," and asserted that they had the right to choose their "own weapons" in applying this law. Beatings, deportations, and other tactics of terror should be invoked if necessary, declared the San Diego *Union,* "and this is what these agitators (all of them) may expect from now on, that the outside world may know that they have been to San Diego." "If this action be lawlessness, make the most of it," the *Union* challenged.[18] *

Early in the fight the police and the vigilantes started to apply the tactics advocated by the leading newspapers of San Diego. The police did not merely arrest the free-speech advocates; they beat them en route

* A citizen of San Diego described the *Union* as "an old-line, stand-pat newspaper, rotten to the core and owned and run in the interests of John D. Spreckels, who owns the street-car franchise. . . ." (Wm. Templeton to Amos Pinchot, April 27, 1912, Amos Pinchot Papers, Library of Congress.)

to prison; shoved them into a jail built to accommodate not more than 60 inmates but which already had over 150 prisoners in it; finger-printed and photographed them for the rogues' gallery; provided the prisoners with meager food twice a day and frequently kept their prisoners in a state of diarrhea. One San Diegan who investigated conditions in the jail was quoted by the *Sun* as stating that "the dogs in the city pound are treated much better than these men." *Free Speech,* the publication of the Free Speech League, carried a description of conditions from one of the prisoners which closed: "As an additional piece of small cruelty, men who are near sighted and have glasses in the office, are refused their glasses, thereby withholding even the consolation of reading."[19]

Michael Hoey, a member of the I.W.W., aged about 65, a veteran of three free-speech fights, was arrested and jailed by the police. In the jail, three officers set upon him and kicked him repeatedly in the groin. Seriously injured and insensible, he was thrown into the overcrowded cell and lay on the cement floor for several days. He was then visited by a prison physician who let him remain in jail. After 40 days in jail, he was removed to the hospital where he died seven days later. The coroner's jury rendered a verdict that death was caused by tuberculosis of the lung and valvular disease of the heart. Not a word was said about the rupture caused by the police beating nor that an old man had been unable to obtain proper medical treatment while in jail.[20]

Protests against police brutality mounted. On February 26, the Free Speech League, in conjunction with the A.F. of L. Central Labor Council, staged a protest parade that extended for two miles, with the men marching five abreast. On March 10, the I.W.W. held a protest meeting in front of the city jail for the purpose of demanding better treatment for the free-speech prisoners. An audience of 5,000 people gathered to voice their protest, and were given a first-hand demonstration of police brutality. The police called in the fire department to disperse the crowd by spraying it with a three-inch stream of water. An eyewitness reported to the Oakland *World:*

"For a full hour hundreds packed themselves in a solid mass around Mrs. [Laura Payne] Emerson as she stood upon the speaker's stand. Bending themselves to the terrific torrent that poured upon them they held their ground until swept from their feet by the irresistible flood. An old grey-haired woman was knocked down by the direct force of the stream from the hose. . . . A mother was deluged with a babe in her arms. . . . An awestruck American patriot wrapped himself in the flag to test its efficiency against police outrage, but he was knocked down and jailed and fined $30.00 for insulting the national emblem."[21]

The vigilantes began to work hand in hand with the police soon after the first arrests. Prisoners were turned over to squads of vigilantes at midnight, night after night, rushed in autos to the county line, or 20 miles into the desert. They were then set upon and beaten with clubs, threatened with death if they ever returned, and left in the desert. Some of the men walked back again to San Diego, and swore to affidavits which were printed in the weekly San Diego *Herald,* a courageous pro-free-speech paper.[22] On the evening of April 5, 1912, Abram R. Sauer, editor of the paper which dared to print the affidavits, was kidnapped in front of his home by six vigilantes, bound, and run out of town. A rope was placed around his neck, and he was told never to return. Sauer did return to edit his paper, and in a telling article, exposed the make-up of the vigilantes: "The personnel of the vigilantes represents not only the bankers and merchants but has as its workers leading Church members and bartenders. Chamber of Commerce and the Real Estate Board are well represented. The press and the public utility corporations, as well as members of the grand jury, are known to belong." Shortly after this article appeared, 30 vigilantes went to the office where the *Herald* was printed and destroyed the forms of the forthcoming edition. They told the printer that if any other issue of the paper was printed on his press, they would destroy his plant. The *Herald* continued to appear, however, but it was printed outside of San Diego, and smuggled into the city.[23]

On April 3, Fred H. Moore and Marcus W. Robbins, attorneys for the I.W.W., wired Governor Hiram W. Johnson from San Diego advising him that vigilantes, sworn in as deputy sheriffs and armed with Win-chester rifles, had been sent north "to intercept peaceful and unarmed members of the Industrial Workers of the World who have committed no offense and are guilty of no crime." Since the sheriff's office had re-fused to act, they demanded that the Governor exercise his "executive power to prevent breach of public peace and possible loss of life."[24] But the Governor did nothing, and, unhindered by the authorities, the vigilantes met the freight cars at the San Onofre county line, where there was a large camp of their colleagues armed to the teeth, ordered the Wobblies off the cars, beat them unmercifully, and finally forced them to run a gauntlet of 106 men armed with clubs, whips, and guns, and put them on trains going north. At the San Onofre camp occurred the notorious flag-kissing incident. Charles Hanson described this shameful event in his unpublished, "My Experience During the San Diego Free Speech Fight":

"The first thing on the program was to kiss the flag. 'You son of a B——, Come on Kiss it, G— damn you.' As he said it I was hit with a wagon spoke all over, when you had kissed the flag you were told to run the gauntlet. 50 men being on each side and each man being armed with a gun and a club and some had long whips. When I started to run the gauntlet the men were ready for action, they were in high spirits from booze. I got about 30 feet when I was suddenly struck across the knee. I felt the wagon spoke sink in splitting my knee. I reeled over. As

I was lying there I saw other fellow workers running the gauntlet. Some were bleeding freely from cracked heads, others were knocked down to be made to get up to run again. Some tried to break the line only to be beaten back. It was the most cowardly and inhuman cracking of heads I ever witnessed."[25]

As the brutality of police and vigilantes increased, the Free Speech League circulated an appeal "To Organized Labor and All Lovers of Liberty" throughout the nation, calling for a torrent of protests to descend upon the authorities of San Diego and for financial aid to defend the free-speech fighters.[26] * This appeal, coming on top of the events in "Barbarous San Diego," brought results. The central body of the A.F. of L. in Los Angeles held a huge protest meeting.† Various trade union bodies in San Francisco protested the police brutalities. Petitions and telegrams from organizations throughout the state and nation poured in on Governor Hiram Johnson requesting him to investigate the frightful reports. On April 15, the Governor sent Colonel Harris Weinstock to San Diego "to investigate charges of cruelty in all matters pertaining to the recent disturbances in the City of San Diego, California." Commissioner Weinstock held open hearings from April 18 to 20, in the Grand Jury room of the San Diego Court House, at which he heard testimony from many free-speech witnesses and some city and county officials. (Most of the officials received the Commissioner coldly and were reluctant to testify in open hearing.) In addition, he conducted his own extensive investigation of the free-speech battle. Then he submitted a long and closely documented report to the Governor which was officially published by the state of California in 1912.

Although he was critical of many of the I.W.W.'s general principles and specific practices, and particularly attacked its free-speech tactics, Weinstock vigorously condemned San Diego's police and other officials, its press, and its leading citizens who comprised the bulk of the vigilantes:

"Your commissioner has visited Russia and while there has heard many horrible tales of high-handed proceedings and outrageous treatment of innocent people at the hands of despotic and tyrannic Russian authorities.

"Your commissioner is frank to confess that when he became satisfied

---

* The call was also circulated abroad. *The Syndicalist* of London announced that it would "remit a small amount," and urged its readers to "follow suit" and show their solidarity with the free-speech fighters in San Diego. (May 1912.)
† One of the speakers at the meeting was Joe Hill, the I.W.W. songwriter. A victim of the vigilantes, he had been severely beaten in the San Diego free-speech fight. "He explained," one reporter wrote, "that he had just come from the hospitality of the M. & M. in San Diego, that owing to that hospitality he was physically unable to make any lengthy speech. He looked as though he had just risen from a sick bed." (*Industrial Worker,* April 11, 1912.)

of the truth of the stories, as related by these unfortunate men [victims of police and vigilante brutality in San Diego], it was hard for him to believe that he still was not sojourning in Russia, conducting his investigation there, instead of in this alleged 'land of the free and home of the brave.' Surely, these American men, who as the overwhelming evidence shows, in large numbers assaulted with weapons in a most cowardly and brutal manner their helpless and defenseless fellows, were certainly far from 'brave' and their victims far from 'free.' "

Commissioner Weinstock showed that the Merchants' Association, the Chamber of Commerce and other local commercial bodies, and the leading daily newspapers encouraged and approved the brutalities of the police and vigilantes, and "pledged to them their support and assistance." He expressed horror at the idea that those who represented "much of the intelligence, the wealth, the conservatism, the enterprise, and also the good citizenship of the community" should have organized the vigilante groups, participated in their criminal activities, and encouraged others to do the same. These, he concluded, were the real criminals, the real fomentors of violence and not the I.W.W. Indeed, after carefully examining a wide collection of I.W.W. literature, Weinstock concluded that "the charge of anarchism against the I.W.W. (which was advanced to justify depriving the organization of the right of street speaking) falls."

At the same time that Commissioner Weinstock was conducting his official investigation, the A.F. of L. San Francisco Labor Council sent a committee to San Diego to investigate. The committee talked to Chief of Police Wilson who wailed to them: "These people do not belong to any country, no flag, no laws, no Supreme Being. I do not know what to do. I cannot punish them. Listen to them singing. They are singing all the time, and yelling and hollering, and telling the jailors to quit work and join the union. They are worse than animals." J. M. Porter, realty operator and leader of the vigilantes, said bluntly: "We don't care about Weinstock or Governor Johnson. Only troops can stop us."[27]

In its report, the Labor Council Committee corroborated most of what Commissioner Weinstock reported, although unlike the latter, it pointed out that the A.F. of L. unions were involved in the free-speech fight as well as the I.W.W.* The committee took pains to point out that though

---

* The California Free Speech League criticized Weinstock's report for leaving the impression that only the I.W.W. was involved in the San Diego free-speech fight. Weinstock then conceded that this was an omission that should be rectified, and informed the press that the Socialists and A.F. of L. in San Diego had supported the I.W.W. and acted with them as a unit, "and, in my opinion, rightly so, on the theory that if the I.W.W. could be robbed of free speech today by the Chief of Police of a city, tomorrow the same Chief of Police could rob the socialists and the trade unionists or any other body of citizens, of their right of free speech." (San Francisco *Call*, May 21, 28, 1912.)

it deplored and disapproved "some of the methods and tactics" of the I.W.W. and considered the free-speech fights open to question as a method of struggle, the I.W.W. and their sympathizers were part of the American working class and "their acts are part of the workers' struggle for better conditions and brighter lives." The committee concluded that the reports of police and vigilante brutality were completely accurate, and that the justification for its use completely unfounded. For what were "the 'anarchists' really doing? Beyond singing a few songs in the crowded jail and asking to have the vermin suppressed and the vile food improved . . . they made no trouble. Outside the jail *not a single act of violence or even of wantonness* has been committed! Not a blow has been struck; not a weapon used; not a threat of any kind made by an I.W.W. or other sympathizer with the Free Speech movement. Such patience under the most infamous and galling inhumanity and injustice speaks well for the discipline maintained by the leaders of such men."[28]

Despite repeated appeals to Governor Johnson to follow up Weinstock's report with an indictment of the vigilantes, no such action was taken. To be sure, following the investigations and the publication of the reports, the brutality of police and vigilantes declined somewhat. But it was only a temporary respite. On May 4, Joseph Mikolasek (the name is variously spelled), Hungarian member of a Los Angeles I.W.W. local and one of the first volunteers to go to San Diego, was approached by two policemen while he was standing in front of the I.W.W. headquarters, and shot in the leg by one of them. In self-defense he reached for an axe and defended himself. Mikolasek received four more bullets in his body and died 19 hours later. A general round-up of men suspected of being Wobblies followed directly after the brutal murder.[29] *

On May 15, Ben Reitman, manager and consort of Emma Goldman, the anarchist propagandist and free-speech fighter, arrived in Los Angeles from San Diego in a pitiable condition. Emma Goldman had come to San Diego with Reitman the previous evening. They were met by a howling mob of vigilantes at the railroad station, many of them "upper class women who hooted and yelled: 'Give us that anarchist; we will strip her naked; we will tear out her guts.' " Emma was scheduled to lecture in the city on Ibsen's *An Enemy of the People,* and George Edwards, a courageous believer in free speech offered her the recital hall of the Conservatory of Music of which he was the head. But the Mayor, in a private conference at her hotel, appealed to her not to go out and face the mob milling around the building. When she returned to her

---

* The I.W.W. attempted to hold a funeral demonstration in San Diego and have Mikolasek buried in the city. But the authorities refused permission, and the body was shipped to Los Angeles where a huge public demonstration was held in honor of the martyred free-speech fighter. (*Industrial Worker,* May 23, 1912; *The Agitator,* June 15, 1912.)

room at the hotel, she found Ben Reitman gone. In the middle of the night she was rushed off to board a train to Los Angeles, with the vigilantes again at the station waiting to attack her. The train sped away before the mob could board it.[30]

Meanwhile, Reitman had been taken from the hotel by vigilantes, operating under police protection, thrown into a waiting automobile and tortured. One of the men urinated on him while the others held him down. He was taken some 20 miles out of San Diego. There the armed vigilantes tarred, and, in the absence of feathers, sagebrushed him. Then, Reitman reported, "with tar taken from a can [they] traced I.W.W. on my back and a doctor burned the letters in with a lighted cigar. . . . Then I was made to run the gauntlet of fourteen of these ruffians, who told me that they were not working men, but doctors, lawyers, real-estate men. They tortured me and humiliated me in the most unspeakable manner. One of them was to put my cane in my rectum." At the end of the painful ceremony, he was forced to kiss the flag and sing "The Star Spangled Banner." When he finished, he was allowed to drag himself away in his underclothes and vest. He was permitted these garments "because the Christian gentlemen thought that I might meet some ladies and shock them."[31]

Protest meetings followed the publication of Reitman's story, and Mrs. Fremont Older, speaking to a packed audience at San Francisco's Dreamland Park, said: "When the vigilantes of San Diego burned I.W.W. into the back of a man, they burned I.W.W. into the hearts and soul and blood of every worker in the United States."[32]

Weinstock's report to Governor Johnson had concluded with a recommendation that the Governor direct the state attorney general to intervene in the free-speech fight. On May 25, Attorney General U.S. Webb arrived in San Diego. After a conference with "both sides" (the Socialists and A.F. of L. leaders on the one hand, and the official authorities on the other, with I.W.W. spokesmen being ignored), Webb declared that if the local authorities could not handle the situation *within the law,* the state would step in with all the resources required. Aside from this implied threat to call out the militia if overt vigilante outrages were not stopped, the attorney general's office repeatedly threatened to institute criminal prosecution of vigilante leaders. The consequence was that vigilante outrages did stop—but free speech was not restored on San Diego's streets.[33]

The California Free Speech League appealed to all Americans to support the fight in San Diego, "this outlying province of Russia," to the finish. The fight continued during the summer and early fall of 1912, in the midst of a smallpox epidemic that hit the city, with new replacements arriving each week. At various times there were between 500 and

1,000 Wobblies in San Diego.* The original strength of the I.W.W. when the campaign started was not more than 50 men![34]

Alarmed and infuriated by the failure of the local authorities and vigilantes to end the battle and realizing that the state government, after Commissioner Weinstock's report, would do nothing to crush the free-speech fight, a citizens' committee of 500, sponsored by millionaire John D. Spreckels, sent a representative early in September to Washington to confer personally with President Taft and urge that "the Government should use all its power to crush out the methods of this [I.W.W.] organization." The President was warned that some 10,000 Wobblies were mobilizing in a "conspiracy to overthrow the United States Government" and create a new government in the Southern California region. The U.S. Attorney at Los Angeles supported the San Diego citizens' committee request and urged a federal indictment against the I.W.W. for conspiring to overthrow the government of the United States.[35]

The drive to get the federal government to smash the free-speech fight failed. President Taft was convinced that the threat "of some 10,000 men to introduce a new form of government, or non-government" was genuine, and concluded that it was decidedly "our business to go and show the strong hand of the United States in a marked way so they shall understand that we are on the job." But a careful examination by the Department of Justice failed to reveal sufficient evidence to indict the I.W.W. leaders for conspiracy to overthrow the government of the United States, or to prevent the execution of any of its laws by force. Nor could federal troops be dispatched to preserve the state of California against domestic violence under Section 4, Article V of the Constitution except on the request of the Governor or the legislature. There was, the Department of Justice informed the President, simply no way to "show the strong hand of the United States," as Taft had demanded.[36]

During the long span of the San Diego free-speech fight at least a dozen men capitulated while in jail and accepted release on probation.[37] All this proved was that not all the participants in the free-speech fight were heroes. It also highlighted the heroism of the others who stood valiantly by their principles in the face of some of the worst brutality against prisoners in American history.

Gradually the free-speech fighters in San Diego were released from jail. Some, however, were tried, fined, and sentenced to prison terms. E. E. Kirk and Harry McKee, Socialist lawyers, were sentenced to six and three months in jail and $300 fine for each. Their sentence was upheld by the higher courts, and Governor Johnson refused to pardon them. In reply to an appeal for their pardon, the Governor, elected by

* On August 8, 1912, the *Industrial Worker* estimated that 5,000 Wobblies had arrived in San Diego since the beginning of the free-speech fight, but a study of the local press makes it clear that this figure was highly inflated.

the progressive movement, wrote that "the anarchy of the I.W.W. and their brutality are worse than the anarchy of the vigilantes."[38] Weinstock's report evidently had had little effect on the Governor.

McKee summed up the results of the San Diego free-speech fight when he told the court just before he was sentenced: "We are not defeated. . . . We are triumphant no matter what sentence your honor may inflict." As Carey McWilliams points out in his account of the great battle: "The Wobbly campaign was finally successful and the right of free speech was vindicated."[39] But the "finally" was a long time in coming. A dispatch from "San Diego (Russia)" in the *Industrial Worker* of November 28, 1912, reported that it was "impossible to hold propaganda meetings here or do very effective work. Not only are the streets denied us but halls as well. " In May 1913, Emma Goldman and Ben Reitman returned to San Diego to deliver a scheduled lecture. As the pair stepped off the train, they were immediately arrested and jailed. A gang of vigilantes threatened to break into the jail and lynch the pair who had dared to return in face of past atrocities, and they were barely able to get out of the city under police escort.[40]

Still the battle continued. In January 1914, the I.W.W. pledged that "the fight in San Diego shall be carried to a finish for absolute and unrestricted free speech with no compromise." The Open Forum, formed in 1912 by a small group of decent elements in San Diego, grew in membership and gave support to the I.W.W. campaign. By the summer of 1914, the right of the I.W.W. to hold street meetings was established. Although the ordinance still remained on the statute books, the police no longer interfered when Wobblies spoke at street corners in the forbidden district. In 1915 Emma Goldman returned to San Diego and finally delivered her lecture on *An Enemy of the People*. San Diego had been restored to civilization, and as George Edwards, one of the leading members of the Open Forum noted, "out of the fire [of the free-speech fight] has come the intellectual salvation not only of the martyrs, but of all the inhabitants of the city."[41]

With the exception of the Lawrence strike which occurred at the same time, the San Diego free-speech fight received more publicity in the newspapers of the nation than any struggle yet associated with the I.W.W. *Organized Labor,* official journal of the Building Trades Council of San Francisco, noting that "the fight in San Diego has made the I.W.W. famous," conceded that it had also aroused widespread respect among all workers for the heroism of the Wobblies.[42]

Like all the other free-speech fights, San Diego revealed clearly that it was the law-enforcement officers and the businessmen-dominated vigilantes, and not the I.W.W., which preached and practiced force and violence in the class struggle. And the violence visited upon the members of the I.W.W. and their allies solidified the working class on the Pacific

Coast. The many resolutions of sympathy sent from all types of labor organizations, including affiliates of the A.F. of L., to the free-speech fighters was proof of this solidarity.

But among the top leaders of the A.F. of L. these evidences of working-class solidarity aroused no cheers. On the contrary, they were infuriated by reports that the San Francisco Labor Council had rallied to the defense of the free-speech fighters and had called for support of their struggle. T. V. O'Connor, president of the International Longshoremen's Union and a member of the A.F. of L. Executive Council, furiously rejected a suggestion from the Western Division of the I.L.U. that the International respond immediately to the Labor Council's appeal: "We cannot afford to associate with, or to harbor men, who act in a disrespectful manner toward or insult our country's flag. . . . The I.W.W.'s have shown that they have no respect for the flag, for the home or for Christianity, and these are just what we intend to protect and uphold."[43] When Frank Morrison received the San Francisco Labor Council's pamphlet, containing the report of its committee which investigated conditions in San Diego, he replied coldly to Paul Scharrenberg, one of the two men who had investigated the situation for the Council: "I am not impressed by the charges directed against the authorities of San 'Diego relative to the so-called brutality against the insane men who defy all law and logic. We heard similar charges against the authorities of Spokane two years ago, and they were proved false by the general organizer, C. O. Young who investigated the charges thoroughly at my request. May I call your attention to the enclosed editorial which appeared in the *Call* in your city which we recently received."[44]

The enclosed editorial from the San Francisco *Call* appeared in that paper on May 31, 1912. It read in part: "The I.W.W. are disloyal to this government, foes alike of labor, of capital, of organized society. They should not be permitted to preach or teach or practice their hateful doctrines anywhere in the United States." The *Call* happened to be owned by John D. Spreckels, who also owned the San Diego *Union,* official organ of the vigilantes. Spreckels, of course, was the major force behind not only the suppression of free speech in San Diego, but also the open-shop drive in that city. Thus the national officialdom of the A.F. of L. placed itself side by side with the worst enemies of organized labor in the United States!

OTHER FREE SPEECH FIGHTS, 1912–13

At the same time that the free-speech fight was being waged in San Diego, similar, if not equally sensational, battles were being conducted by the I.W.W. in Vancouver, B.C., San Francisco and Oakland, Calif. Two of these battles resulted in victories for the principles of free speech.

For several years it had been the custom in Vancouver to allow all labor, political, and religious organizations the free use of the streets and open places of the city for the purpose of holding meetings. During this period not a single incident arose which created the slightest disturbance. But in January 1912, Vancouver changed its policy. Thousands of workers in the city were unemployed, many of them construction workers lured to the city with the promise of jobs on the Canadian Pacific Railroad, only to find their places already filled. With the I.W.W. and the Socialist Party charging that the employers wanted a large pool of unemployed workers to drive down wages, and, along with the A.F. of L. Vancouver Trades and Labor Council, demanding government aid for the unemployed, the city decided to stave off agitation by preventing street meetings. On January 21, 1912, a meeting of unemployed workers, presided over by I.W.W., Socialist, and A.F. of L. leaders, was broken up by the police who let it be known that no more outdoor meetings would be allowed in the city. (The Salvation Army was exempted from this ban.) The I.W.W. and the Socialist Party immediately announced a meeting to be held on the Powell Street football grounds—a public park —the following Sunday, January 28, and the Vancouver Trades and Labor Council announced its support so as to prove "that freedom of speech in the British Empire is guaranteed by higher authority than any city administration."[45]

A large crowd of workers, employed and unemployed, with their families, gathered on the Powell Street grounds for the free-speech meeting. During the speech of R. F. Pettipiece, head of the Trades and Labor Council's delegation to Victoria, capital of the provincial government, to secure some aid for the unemployed, Deputy Chief of Police Mulhern ordered the meeting dispersed. When Pettipiece replied that the gathering was orderly, Mulhern gave a signal, and a long line of policemen advanced upon the peaceable crowd swinging clubs. Defenseless men, women, and children were knocked senseless and bleeding to the ground. Those who escaped from the police on foot were hotly pursued by mounted men, armed with heavy whips. Pettipiece and 20 others, I.W.W., Socialist, and A.F. of L. members, were jailed. Except for some of the I.W.W. members who insisted on remaining in jail as a protest, the men were released on bail.[46]

"Bloody Sunday" in "Vile, Vicious Vancouver," as the city was now called, brought a wave of protest from all parts of Canada and sections of the United States. The British Columbia *Federationist,* organ of the Vancouver Trades and Labor Council, denounced "Cossack Rule," charged the police with "violence, brutality, riot and ruffianism," and asked if the employers and city officials believed that the solution for "the conditions of unemployment is to beat up unemployed and empty stomached men on the streets." From Chicago, Vincent St. John announced that a free-speech fight was in full swing, and urged all Wobblies to "keep traveling to Vancouver until the city gets enough and is willing to say so."[47]

"All organizations—the I.W.W., the Socialist Party, and the A.F. of L. —have joined forces and are prepared to fight to a finish," a dispatch from Vancouver reported.[48] Sunday, February 4, and Sunday, February 11, saw huge demonstrations for freedom of speech in Stanley Park with all the workers and their allies present wearing cards bearing the words: "Shall British Freedom of Speech and Assemblage be Denied? I Say *No!*" When the first meeting was quickly broken up by the police, with more workers injured and arrested, the free-speech fighters introduced a new feature in the struggle. On Sunday, February 11, they hired several boats and I.W.W., Socialist, and A.F. of L. speakers addressed the crowd on shore while standing on the vessels.* The speeches continued until a police patrol boat attacked the free speechers' vessels and armed policemen swarmed aboard and arrested the speakers.

The following day the free-speech fighters announced that on Sunday, February 18, they would charter a balloon and address the crowd in Stanley Park from the air. By now the authorities had had enough, and the press reported that future meetings would not be molested. A huge meeting was held in Stanley Park on February 18, but no police showed up. The free-speech fight had been won! All street meetings after February 18 were conducted without interference by the police.[49]

In San Francisco, during February and March 1912, I.W.W. speakers were unceremoniously pulled from the platforms by the police, beaten and arrested. The threat of "another earthquake in the form of an I.W.W. invasion unless they allow our membership the right to speak upon the street" brought an end to police interference with street meetings.[50] When in January 1912, the police of Oakland refused the I.W.W. the right to speak on the streets and broke up their meetings, a free-speech battle started which continued for several months. I.W.W. and Socialist Party speakers were arrested indiscriminately and brutally manhandled in jail. In June 1912, the Socialist Party, which officially tendered the I.W.W. "any support in this conflict demanded of us as members of the working class," initiated an election to recall Mayor Frank E. Mott. The recall petition accused the Mayor of violating the right of free speech and maintaining the third degree at the city jail and a chain gang of prisoners. Sufficient signatures were obtained to schedule the election. (No thanks were due to the I.W.W. for this achievement; the Wobblies

---

* The I.W.W. in Vancouver proposed the idea of hiring the boats, and the Wobblies may have got the inspiration for the plan from an item which appeared in the *Industrial Worker* of July 20, 1911: "Women have set the pace in New York State. A number of suffragettes have leased a boat and will go up the Erie canal and stop at each town, advocating their principles on suffrage. Good idea for us I.W.W.'s."

boycotted the recall drive on the ground that it was a useless expenditure of energy which could be better used in direct-action tactics.) As the day of election approached, 75 of the most prominent businessmen of Oakland issued a statement justifying the restriction on the right of the I.W.W. to speak on the streets, and, in an hysterical outburst, called upon the people of Oakland to "decide at this election whether they stand for the stars and stripes or the red flag of anarchy; . . . whether they stand for those who wish to proclaim openly on the streets that the women of Oakland are no better than inmates of the dive and the brothel, or whether they stand for those who resent these statements and deny the accusations." Every "God fearing, home loving, patriotic man and woman" was urged by the press "to go to the polls today and vote for Oakland; for their homes; for their flag." Factory whistles were blown in the city every hour to remind the people to go to the polls to "uphold civic decency and to defend their homes." Sufficient voters were swept off their feet by the hysteria to continue Mott in office.[51]

The year 1913 found the I.W.W. engaged in free-speech fights in points as far separated as Cleveland, Denver, Detroit, Peoria, Philadelphia, Hilo, Hawaii, Juneau, Alaska, Minot, N.D., Omaha, Neb. All but the one in Peoria, Ill. were victorious. The Minot free-speech fight was the bloodiest of these battles, with city officials and vigilantes violating every constitutional right of the men involved in the struggle,[52] and the one in Denver was the longest. The Denver free-speech fight actually began on December 26, 1912, when three I.W.W. speakers were arrested and thrown into jail. The customary call was sent out for volunteers, and within the next few weeks, over 40 Wobblies were arrested for speaking to crowds in the streets. Although the I.W.W. in Denver expressed disappointment at the "apathy of the rebels throughout the country in not responding more readily to the call," the Wobblies kept up the fight by returning to jail as soon as they were released.[53]

Then in March, the battle began in earnest. Early in the month, Frank Little and a group of California Wobblies, most of them veteran free-speech fighters, left from Taft, Calif., to take part in the Denver battle. They traveled the freight cars through Bakersfield, Fresno, Stockton, San Francisco, and Sacramento, gaining recruits on the way. By the time they reached Denver, several hundred free-speech fighters were ready to do battle with the police.[54]

Scores of Wobblies were arrested early in April, and on April 12, 75 men entering the city were arrested and thrown into the "bull pen" when they told the judge that they had come to Denver to speak on the streets. Fed only on bread and water, the prisoners decided to go on a hunger strike. They informed the authorities that if they were kept in jail for the duration of the 61 days of their sentence, the city would have the additional expense of burying them since "61 days is ample time for all of us to starve." The authorities held a hurried council and decided to release the prisoners. The men promptly took up positions at various street corners, were rearrested, and again released when they announced their determination to renew their hunger strike.[55]

On April 28, the fight ended. The Denver authorities agreed to permit the I.W.W. freedom to speak in the streets unmolested. "Since the settlement of the free-speech fight," Local 26 of Denver wrote to headquarters in June 1913, "extensive agitation has been carried on with splendid results."[56]

KANSAS CITY—1914

Free speech fights occurred in 1914 in Kansas City, Des Moines, Iowa, Aberdeen, S.D., and Victoria, B.C. All of these battles were won.[57] Frank Little was a leading figure in the outstanding free-speech fight of the year, that in Kansas City, Mo. Actually, Little had also been a leader of the earlier free-speech fight in Kansas City which began on October 6, 1911, when he was arrested for speaking on the streets, and ended on November 2, after the Wobblies threatened a mass invasion, with the granting to the I.W.W. of the right to speak on any corner in the city.[58] For three years, the Wobblies continued to speak unmolested, but in the fall of 1913, the businessmen began putting pressure on the city officials to stop street agitation, and when 1914 opened, the police were ready to act. Early in January, five men were arrested and jailed for holding street meetings. Inside of a week, the number in jail had grown to 50, including Little, who had headed for Kansas City with a contingent of free-speech fighters as soon as he heard of the initial arrests. Vincent St. John immediately appealed from Chicago: "If you are foot loose make for Kansas City at once. . . . Wire the local that you are coming."[59]

This appeal brought some additional free-speech fighters which, of course, produced additional arrests. But the Kansas City local indicated late in February that new "jail recruits" were needed "in order further to test the attitude of the police." But even this appeal failed to produce an invasion of the city. Eighty-three men were in jail by the first of March. They represented mainly the original group of Wobblies who had begun the fight, and the small number of reinforcements. They tried to make up for their lack of numbers by moving in and out of jail, addressing street meetings as soon as they were released from prison in order to be arrested again.[60]

To frustrate these tactics, the police and a reserve corps of citizen police began deporting the I.W.W.'s as soon as they were released from jail. In addition, any man in jail, found guilty of the slightest disturbance, such as singing or shouting at night, was punished by being condemned to the "hole." Prisoners sent to the dungeon were forced to stay in unheated cells, sleep on concrete floors, and received for food a two-and-a-half-inch slice of bread, three times a day, with water. The Wobblies in jail answered the police cruelty by going on a hunger strike. The Kansas City *Journal* headlined the action as "I.W.W. Pulls Off New Stunt," and predicted that the authorities would permit the "hobo leaders" to starve to death before seeing them victorious. But the "new stunt" did produce results. Deportations ceased; the authorities, for the first time, consented to meet a committee of the men in jail.[61]

Negotiations continued until the first week of March. On March 4, the Kansas City authorities agreed to permit the I.W.W. to hold street meetings without police interference. The men in jail, however, refused to call off the battle officially until the promise had been thoroughly tested. For several nights I.W.W. speakers addressed crowds at various street corners and no one was arrested. On March 8, the jail committee announced that the fight was over, and wired all I.W.W. journals: "After three months of battle with K.C. authorities the right of free speech is established. . . . Men in jail are released in groups for fear we may resort to a grand display. Direct Action again gets the goods."[62]

DECLINE AND ACHIEVEMENTS OF FREE SPEECH FIGHTS

The struggle in Kansas City was the last of the great free-speech fights* until the early months of 1915 when, as we shall see below, a battle for free-speech erupted in Sioux City, Iowa. Already in the Kansas City fight it was clear that recruiting an invading army of free-speech fighters was becoming more and more difficult. The rebels were being kept too busy with organizing activities, strike struggles and unemployed demonstrations, and simply could not respond to appeals as they had in the past.[63] Some I.W.W. leaders had long protested against the free-speech fights, declaring that they led to "fighting the bull instead of the boss." In December 1911, John Pancner, one of the best I.W.W. organizers, urged that the free-speech demonstrations be dropped because they were destructive to the organization; defense money for those jailed took funds better spent on constructive organization on the job, and the jailings, beatings, and bread-and-water diets were ruining the cream of the move-

---

* It is impossible to determine the exact number of battles for the right to speak in public places in which the I.W.W. was engaged. The national headquarters did not even know, for when the U.S. Commission on Industrial Relations requested information about free-speech fights, *Solidarity* called upon the locals to furnish it with the requested data. (Sept. 19, 1914.) The response was a series of letters describing the writers' experiences. These were forwarded to the Commission on Industrial Relations and are in the National Archives. Brissenden lists 26 free-speech fights, 20 of which occurred between 1909 and 1913 alone, and all but one of which took place between 1909 and 1916. (*op. cit.*, p. 367.) His list ends with the bloody battle at Everett, Wash., November 1916, which will be discussed below.

ment. Free speech should be employed on the job: "Organize the wage slave, not the bourgeois, the street moocher and the saloon soak."[64] Others felt that the entire strategy of passive resistance used in the free-speech fights, with special care being taken by the Wobblies that no act of violence be committed by the free-speech fighters, put the membership at a terrible disadvantage. "The free-speech fighters are restricted by these tactics to the *very weakest weapon* in the arsenal of Industrial Unionism —passive resistance," *Solidarity* complained as early as 1910.[65*]

Still another objection to the free-speech fights was that while they attracted widespread attention and even aroused sympathy among many who otherwise were hostile to the doctrines and activities of the I.W.W., they interfered with the effective conduct of strikes. Wobbly organizers objected that strikes were lost because they were allowed "to degenerate into a free-speech fight," and charged that this was precisely what the employers wanted. Free-speech fights, it was further charged, did not result in any organizational growth in the community affected. For one thing, agitation or "soap boxing" were viewed by these critics as a limited means of reaching the mass of the workers, the majority of whom did not congregate at street corners.[66] Then again, invading free-speech fighters scattered as soon as they were released from jail, and some of the most competent organizers, like Frank Little, went on to participate in other free-speech battles. "Having won the free-speech fight," the Wobblies were reminded, "the work of the Fresno I.W.W. has just begun. It is now up to them to do what they started out to do when they first came here—to organize the unskilled workers."[67] But by the time this advice was published, many of the Fresno free-speech fighters were off to another battle. The following account in the Spokane *Spokesman-Review* early in 1912, describing the aftermath of a free-speech victory in a Washington community, was all too frequently repeated:

"Having been granted the privilege of speaking in the streets . . . and having no more 'worlds to conquer' in this section, 100 members of the Industrial Workers of the World are preparing to shift the scene of their activities to San Francisco, where public-speaking rights have been denied members of their order.

"The leaders of the contingent, many of whom came here from St. Louis, declare that they do not care to speak where the privilege has been extended, but prefer to promote their campaign in those localities where the right is denied or curtailed."[68]

---

* No effective substitute for passive resistance was, however, developed. In the midst of the San Diego battle, the Wobbly press declared that "new methods" were needed to resist "police and vigilante thugs," and that the free-speech fighters should begin "*to actively protect themselves from these thugs,*" but when Walker C. Smith recommended that "ammunition" be shipped to the free-speech fighters in San Diego, the *Industrial Worker* denounced the suggestion. It recommended an ounce of sabotage. (April 25, 1912.)

The criticism of the free-speech fights we have mentioned do not in the slightest detract from the heroism of the fighters nor of the contributions they made. These battles publicized the I.W.W. and made the people of the United States aware of the existence of a national organization dedicated to preserve a basic principle of American democracy—freedom of speech—at a time when no other national organization existed to uphold this principle.* There were, to be sure, Wobblies who put this principle this way: "Free speech—say anything you want to, but keep your mouth shut." Fortunately for the American workers, this was mere irony; the free-speech fighters usually brought about the repeal of the undemocratic ordinances and opened the gates to the entrance of unionism in many communities heretofore completely closed to such so-called "un-American" principles.

The free-speech fights, of course, demonstrated how little regard the business interests had for the Constitution, and how ready they were to resort to force and violence to keep unorganized workers from hearing the message of unionism. The vigilantes, historians Perlman and Taft correctly point out, are "properly to be classed with the fascist formations in Italy and Germany."[69] Moreover, the "respectable elements" were often the most vicious. A shocked citizen of Minot, N.D., recorded the following conversation with Judge Davis, a leading light in the community and a magistrate in the city courts:

" 'Judge, Can't you do something to prevent the beating down of innocent men?' I asked.

" 'Prevent Hell. We'll drive the G--D--- Sons of B-----s into the river and drown them. We'll starve them. We'll kill every damned man of them or drive them together with the Socialists from the city,' he thundered back."

A similar appeal to an official of the Second National Bank of Minot brought this reply: "There ain't no use in treating those fellows with kindness. The only thing to do is to club them down. Beat them up. Drive them out of the city."[70]

The free-speech fights exposed the inequality of "justice" meted out to those who upheld constitutional liberties and to those guilty of destroying them. As the *Industrial Worker* aptly put it: "A demonstration of working men in the interests of the constitutional right of freedom of speech is judged a 'riot' by the courts; but violence and terrorism on the part of the capitalists and their tools is 'law and order.' "[71]

* In 1911 Theodore Schroeder founded the Free Speech League, but this organization was little more than an outlet for Schroeder's lectures and writings and did little work in the free-speech fights. The first national organization, apart from the I.W.W., that did important work for free speech was the National Civil Liberties Bureau, forerunner of the American Civil Liberties Union, founded around 1917. (Donald Johnson, *The Challenge to American Freedoms: World War I and the Rise of the American Civil Liberties Union*, Lexington, Ky., 1963, pp. 194-95.)

The free-speech fights may have contributed little to building an organization, but they did build within the movement a spirit of unity in action. They were also significant in cementing a bond of solidarity among I.W.W., Socialist Party, and A.F. of L. members. In several communities, as we have seen, these three groups worked together in conducting the free-speech fight, and in most others, where the Wobblies carried the brunt of the battle, they received support from local S.P. and A.F. of L. officials. But, of course, as we have also seen, the free-speech fights exposed the cowardly role of the national leadership of the A.F. of L. During the entire period of the free-speech fights, there was *not a single* reference in the *American Federationist* to these battles!

The I.W.W. free-speech fights are part of the great American tradition. Writing in *Pearson's Magazine* on the subject of "Free Speech in the United States," Courtenay Lemon paid a glowing tribute to the I.W.W., praising it for taking "the lead in the fight for free speech":

"Whether they agree or disagree with its methods and aims, all lovers of liberty everywhere owe a debt to this organization for its defense of free speech. Absolutely irreconcilable, absolutely fearless, and unsuppressibly persistent, it has kept alight the fires of freedom, like some outcast vestal of human liberty. That the defense of traditional rights to which this government is supposed to be dedicated should devolve upon an organization so often denounced as 'unpatriotic' and 'un-American,' is but the usual, the unfailing irony of history."[72]

CHAPTER 9

Organizing the Lumber and Construction Workers

The impression, created by newspaper accounts, that the I.W.W. was exclusively a free-speech organization was far from the truth. While the organization was conducting a vigorous fight for free speech, filling the jails of Spokane, Fresno, San Diego and many other cities, Wobblies were active in the lumber and construction camps, organizing the workers and mobilizing them to strike against low wages, long hours, and uncivilized working conditions.

CONDITIONS IN LUMBER INDUSTRY

In dealing with the lumber industry, the I.W.W. quickly learned that there were two fairly distinct, though interrelated, groups of workers employed by the timber companies: the mill workers and the lumberjacks. The sawmill worker lived in or near towns—Seattle, Portland, Spokane, Aberdeen, Hoquiam, Everett, Centralia, Marshfield, Eureka, and other towns and cities of the Northwest and California where major mills were located. He was usually married, with children, and lived in the town where he worked. Life for the millman was stable as long as the mill remained in operation. His work was regulated; he worked indoors, and when his day was done, he would return home. His wages were higher than the lumberjack's, but the work, though certainly not harder than in the woods, was monotonous, with speed being the principal prerequisite.

The lumberjack lived in camps, which, as timber-cutting increased, were located farther and farther from the cities and towns. The logger usually got to a city only once or twice during the year and then only for a four- or five-day spree which sent him back to the camp a poor man or forced him to travel by "side-door coach" to different areas where jobs might be available. In either case, it might be another six months before he returned again to the town. During the better part of the year, the logger lived in a hastily constructed camp in the woods, located 20 or 30 miles from the nearest town, isolated except for a logging road. Women and children were seldom, if ever, present. Generally speaking, the logger was an immigrant from northern and eastern Europe, a single man, unhindered by the concerns of family life and, unlike the mill worker, able and willing at any moment to quit work and move on to a new job or no job at all.

The conditions under which the logger worked were notoriously bad. The men lived in bunkhouses which averaged 100 feet in length and 20 in width. Each building housed 50 to 100 men. The men's bunks were not arranged horizontally along the walls, but were instead placed side by side, with the occupant's head facing the center aisle. As this arrangement resembled a stable, the men were forced to climb into their bed feet first; the bunks were referred to as "stalls." Each man had approximately three square feet of breathing space. The beds had neither mattresses nor straw, but consisted of several planks nailed together. Blankets, sheets, and pillow cases were rarely supplied by the lumber companies; the men ordinarily carried their own blankets. Lice infested every camp, the companies seldom bothering to exterminate them. When the living quarters were cleaned, it was the men themselves who did the work. "Camps dirty, badly drained, poorly ventilated, crowded, unsanitary and generally vermin ridden, with no facilities for bathing or for washing clothes," was a contemporary description. Another contemporary described the typical camps as "relics of barbarism—more like cattle pens than the habitations of civilized men in the Twentieth Century." One former logger recalled: "When I worked in the woods we were packed into bunkhouses like sardines. You had to be an acrobat to get into your bunk. There were no bathing facilities in the camps and the camps were so lousy, the louses were lousy. . . . Can you imagine, men were actually carrying their whole households on their backs while they were looking for jobs."[1]

Each bunkhouse contained two stoves, placed at either end of the building. During the winter, when the temperatures commonly dropped to below zero, this arrangement became unbearable. Those lumberjacks sleeping near the stove suffered from the tremendous heat, while those in the middle of the bunkhouse shivered with cold.

Loggers worked in all kinds of weather and oftentimes returned to camp in soaked clothes. Over half the camps as late as 1917 had no facilities for bathing or for drying clothes,[2] and the men ate supper sitting in wet clothes. The food was abominable. The standard meals were either beans or pancakes for breakfast, "Mulligan stew" for lunch, and a combination of both for supper. Each man was charged from 90 cents to

$1.25 per day for his board, the amount being deducted from his wages. Meals were prepared in the camp's cookshack. In many cases, when a professional cook was unavailable, the company simply designated any man available regardless of experience. Needless to say, few cooks, professional or amateur, could do much with the food provided by the company. A logger recalls: "I saw quarters of condemned beef being served to lumbermen. I remember watching one cook making stew. He had his face turned away from the pot in order to keep from smelling the rotten meat. That was in 1912."[3] The cookshack was as unsanitary as the bunkhouse; food decomposed in the heat and flies landed anywhere.

The lumberjack's daily schedule was rigorous. The men usually arose at 4:00 A.M. to the foreman's call: "Roll out or roll up!" (get out of bed or roll up your blanket and leave camp). After dressing by the light of a kerosene lamp, the men ate breakfast in the dining room adjacent to the cookshack. By five o'clock they had started the long walk to the cutting area, sometimes a distance of several miles. After working for ten hours, they walked back to camp, arriving there after dark. Thus though the working day was supposed to last ten hours, in reality it often stretched to twelve.

For his labor, a lumberjack received from $2.25 to $4.50 a day. Out of his wages he had to pay a hospital fee of $1 to $1.50 per month. The fee was to cover expenses for hospitalization and other medical care for the loggers. The type of work, hazardous at all times, gave the lumber industry a death rate second only to that in the mines and "higher than that of the First World War." On the face of it, the small medical fee providing insurance against injury, should have met with favorable reaction from the lumberjacks. Actually, it was a chief grievance of the workers. The failure of the companies to provide adequate medical facilities, either in camps or hospitals, made the fee a token payment for services never rendered. Numerous examples could be cited of men crippled permanently because of the failure of company doctors and hospitals to provide adequate attention. Often doctors were not doctors at all, but men hired by the companies to play the role.[4]

In order to obtain work, a prospective logger literally had to buy his job. Some men were able to find work in the various camps by themselves, but in most cases the lumberjack secured a job through a local employment agency. These agencies were either independent business organizations or controlled by the timber firms. Invariably a man ended up at an employment agency where he paid from $1.00 to $5.00 to the agent, who gave him a slip of paper entitling him to a job; without such credentials a lumber worker was commonly refused work by the camp foreman. The employment shark worked with the foreman, giving the latter a "kickback" for every man he hired. This was called the "three-gang system," whereby there was always "one gang coming, one working, and the third going back to town to buy more jobs from the employment shark." The system resulted in increased commissions to employment sharks who split the profits with the cooperating foremen. The men having spent their money, were left in a strange area, broke, with no chance of redress against the shark. A bitter complaint of the lumberjack was that he never had any job security. He could be fired without reason, or, after having walked to the camp from the agency, be refused a job even though he had purchased a work slip.

Situated in thinly settled forest regions, the men lived in "a peculiar mixture of capitalism and feudalism, civilization and barbarism . . . ruled by a foreman who [had] the power of a petty czar." "A 'get-the-hell-out-of-here' philosophy was to too great an extent in vogue when any of the men complained about the conditions."[5]

The following terse comment by the British Columbia *Federationist,* though it referred to Canada, could just as well be applied to the United States: "If there ever was a class of workmen who needed organization that class is the lumberjacks engaged in the timber industry."[6]

The life of the sawmill operator, though better than that of his brother in the logging camps, was far from good. The workers and their families in the mill towns lived in houses rather than barracks, but ofttimes these, too, were inferior in quality. Built of wood, frequently covered with tar paper, the homes were arranged in blocks, accessible by roads which turned into quagmires in the spring. Working conditions in the mills were little better than in the woods. Although a mill worker received higher wages for his effort, and physical exertion was less strenuous than in the woods, boredom was at a maximum because of the repetitious nature of his job. For ten hours each day a man stood beside a whirling, razor-sharp saw with instantaneous death his constant companion because the timber firms failed to supply safety devices on their machinery. Accident rates were exceedingly high and newspapers carried weekly reports of deaths and maimings "down at the mill." For this $1 per month hospitalization fee, the mill worker received inadequate care. Factory doctors and nurses were unknown and frequently mill towns were unable to support a hospital. Small wonder that even a spokesman for the lumber industry wrote: "Shingle-weaving is not a trade; it is a battle."[7]

By the time the I.W.W. was organized in 1905, working conditions in the lumber industry were worse than they had ever been. The shift of the industry from the comparatively small and easy-to-fell trees of the Great Lakes to the giant firs of Washington and Oregon and the redwoods of California (and to a lesser extent to the pine areas of Louisiana, Alabama, Mississippi, and Texas) brought with it many new methods in logging. Huge corporations, dominated by absentee owners, new inventions which speeded up the work and displaced many workers by making their traditional skills obsolete, new methods of logging which "established a sort of mobile factory in the woods, a maze of cables, engines, pumps, saws, rails, locomotive cars, trucks, power plants, and chains,"[8] all produced fabulous profits for the employers. But the workers in the logging camps and mill towns shared little of this prosperity. Their wages had hardly risen, and their living conditions had deteriorated. In 1905 woodsmen were putting in ten to twelve hours time a day and millmen ten hours. Prior to 1904, no charge for board was made in the logging camps when the men were inactive on account of sickness or bad weather. But in that year the workers were forced to pay for board while inactive. This, of course, effectively reduced wages.[9]

The lumber industry was thus an ideal field for the I.W.W. Conditions were bad; the lumberjack was hardly considered civilized and was generally called a "timber beast," a brute interested only in "booze, bawds and battle." The feeble attempts of the A.F. of L.* had amply demonstrated that the lumber industry was not suited for craft organization since there was a preponderance of unskilled, or at best, semiskilled workers, and even had it been possible to allot each man to a particular craft, the result would have been an impossible litter of separate unions. As the I.W.W. pointed out: "One set of men fell the trees. Others cut them up into logs. One man acts as hook tender; others set the chokers. A fireman keeps up steam in the boiler, and the engineer runs the donkey. Some load the logs on cars and the railroad crew haul them out of the woods. Some act as riggers, and some as cooks and flunkeys."[10] The industry, in short, included many different trades, each of which, if organized separately, would have had only one or possibly two or three members in each camp.

---

* In 1890 the International Shingle Weavers' Union of America entered the field, and affiliated itself with the A.F. of L. But the 1893 strike against wage cuts was lost, and the union was destroyed in the developing depression. Years later, the union was reorganized, and in January 1903, the International Shingle Weavers' Union of America, A.F. of L., took its place again in the lumber industry with 1,300 members. But it represented only the skilled workers in the industry, an ever-decreasing percentage of the total working force. Attempts at organizing the loggers and sawmill workers were made by the Western and American Labor Union during this period, and largely as a response to this challenge, the A.F. of L. in 1905 authorized the formation of the International Brotherhood of Woodsmen and Sawmill Workers. But the A.F. of L. was not really interested in organizing the workers, and the union, emphasizing that it wished to avoid strikes, stressed benefit features and cooperative societies. This "coffin society," as it was called by the timber workers, soon lost the woodsmen and sawmill workers it had recruited during the spring of 1905. By 1906, all the locals on the West Coast had fallen apart. (Vernon H. Jensen, *Lumber and Labor*, New York, 1945, pp. 117–19; *Industrial Union Bulletin*, June 15, 1907.)

I.W.W. IN LUMBER, 1905–12

The I.W.W. made its appearance in the lumber industry during 1905 and 1906, but the conflicts within the organization prevented it from devoting the required attention to this field. It was not until the militant sawmill strike in Portland in March 1907 that the organization really came to the attention of the lumber workers. The unity of mill workers and lumberjacks in this strike, in the face of A.F. of L. scabbing, was so unprecedented a development that it gave heart to thousands of discouraged forest workers. I.W.W. lumber locals were established in Seattle and in the California Redwoods. Despite these gains, the depression of 1907–08 kept I.W.W. activity down to a minimum. But by late 1909 the Wobblies were fully active again in the Northwest, and, following the Spokane free-speech fight, the I.W.W. undertook a new agitation among the lumber workers, confident that this great victory would produce immediate results. In February 1910, the I.W.W. announced that delegates were being placed in logging camps, lumber and shingle mills "as fast as possible," and urged all lumberjacks and mill workers to "get in touch with them."[11]

During the next year, I.W.W. publications carried reports of the work of these "job delegates." Not all of these reports were encouraging. Too many of the delegates simply told off the boss about conditions in the camp, quit work, and went on to another camp. There they found conditions just as bad, again told off that boss, and went on to another job. Instead of organizing the workers, they sent reports to the *Industrial Worker* notifying the lumberjacks: "Bum job, stay away." Fred Heslewood, a veteran organizer, advised Wobbly lumberjacks that instead of quitting, "When conditions . . . are so intolerable . . . call a meeting in one end of the bunkhouse of all I.W.W. men and as many more as are in favor of effecting the particular cure you wish. . . . March to the boss; and let Mr. Boss know that if such and such is not granted right away that you will all go down the line. That will be found effective, where one quitting at a time will amount to nothing."[12]

A number of Wobblies took this advice to heart. "I was fired from six camps in one week," a logger wrote from Oaks Point, Wash., "because I talked I.W.W. to the men. But I am going to give them all the hell I can."[13] Reports of organizational progress among California lumber workers began to occupy space in the I.W.W. press. In July 1911, a year after John Pancner began his organizational work in Eureka, the secretary of Lumber Workers Industrial Union No. 431 was able to report that more than 500 loggers attended the I.W.W. meeting. Thirty-five new members were signed up and the secretary attributed the success of the drive to the excellent camp-delegate system and the agitation for an eight-hour day which was being led by the Wobblies. He confidently predicted that the entire redwood industry would be organized by the end of 1911.[14]

Nevertheless, the year ended with these optimistic predictions far from realized. Lumber Workers Industrial Union No. 432 of Seattle, the largest local made up only of lumber workers, had grown from 68 members to over 600 in nine months. But even though its system of organizing directly in the camps was the envy of the other lumber locals, it was far from satisfied either with its own progress or that of the I.W.W. as a whole in the lumber industry. In October 1911, it recommended that a convention of all lumber locals be held to adopt more efficient methods of organizing the industry. The *Industrial Worker* endorsed this recommendation in a "Loggers and Lumber Workers' Special" issue.[15]

On February 12, 1912, the I.W.W. locals in the lumber industry met in Seattle, and formed the National Industrial Union of Forest and Lumber Workers. It was to include all rangers, foresters, game wardens, wood-choppers, lumber workers, saw-and-shingle mill workers, and collectors of sap, herbs, leaves, cork, and bark. Plans to gather and hold these workers in a powerful forestry and lumbering union were outlined. They called for placing two "live delegates" in each camp and sawmill who would visit every worker personally and try to get him to join the union; regular publication of conditions in the camp and mill; monthly discussions in the camps on such subjects as economics, tactics, methods, and history of the labor movement; entertainments, such as smokers, boxing matches, picnics and dances, where loggers and mill workers could meet socially; regular visits by the organized loggers to the towns where they should join the organized sawmill workers in displaying their union buttons, and a campaign to line up all town workers—cooks, waiters, dishwashers, chambermaids, porters, bartenders, butchers, bakers, clerks, laundry girls, laborers, teamsters, etc.—behind the lumberjacks and mill workers so that when they went on strike they would have the town workers behind them. The combined power of the lumber workers and the town workers "would make it impossible for the gigantic lumber trust to break the strike by physical violence of mob or military." "Come on you loggers and millworkers," the new union appealed, "get wise to your conditions and make them better by getting into One Big Union."[16]

GRAYS HARBOR AND COOS BAY

One month after the industrial union was organized, the first strike of lumber workers erupted in Grays Harbor in Western Washington, beginning in the mills of Hoquiam and spreading to Raymond and Aberdeen. With Aberdeen as its capital, Grays Harbor was the chief center of the huge lumber barony of Frederick Weyerhaeuser, the German immigrant who became "the most powerful single lumberman in the history of American forests." Although he had a reputation of being a man of social vision, who had built a huge fortune by hard work, Weyerhaeuser had acquired a large part of his huge timber holdings in the states of Oregon and Washington by devious methods of fraud, graft, coercion, and outright theft, most of it at the expense of the American people.[17] Weyerhaeuser's labor policy was summarized by one of his lieutenants in the Grays Harbor mills: "Don't have too great a percentage of one nationality. For their own sake and your own, mix them up and obliterate clannishness and selfish social prejudices. Keep out the disturbers; they are dear at any price."[18] Into Grays Harbor, the emigrant bureaus sent Greeks, Slavs, Croatians, and the mill owners, agents of Weyerhaeuser, the absentee feudal baron, were confident that this policy of keeping a wide assortment of different nationalities would keep unionism out of the mills. Their confidence was bolstered by the knowledge that the local A.F. of L. unions showed no interest in organizing these foreign-born, unskilled workers.

But in the summer of 1911, the Wobblies entered the area, carrying their offices in their pockets, speaking on the street corners in the evenings, distributing leaflets to the mill workers and selling song sheets. The great free-speech fight soon followed in Aberdeen, and though that ended in a victory for the I.W.W. in mid-January 1912, it was but the prologue to the big battle for improvement in the conditions of the lumber workers. On March 14, 1912, the unorganized Greek, Austrian, and Finnish mill workers, in Hoquiam, unable any longer to tolerate working conditions, walked out spontaneously. The I.W.W. quickly stepped into the situation. The majority of the workers in the walkout were Greeks, and, for some time, the newspapers in Washington and Oregon referred to it as the "I.W.W.-Greek strike."[19]

On the second day of the strike, a list of demands was agreed upon at a mass meeting of the strikers in Hoquiam, chaired by Dr. Herman F. Titus who had come from Seattle to aid in the struggle. Workers had been paid $2 and $2.50 for a ten-hour day. Now they demanded an eight-hour work day and raises of 25 and 50 cents per day, bringing the minimum wage scale up to $2.25. Although the list of demands was formally presented on the following day to the mill owners, there were no prolonged negotiations and, as the strike spread, the men generally quit without even asking for an increase in wages. "This," the Portland *Oregonian* reported, "is in furtherance of the ideas advanced by the I.W.W. agitators that a demand for higher wages is not necessary when a man draws only $2 a day. They say that such wages imply a demand for an increase, and that a request for an advance is superfluous."[20]

Plants all over the Grays Harbor area were called out by roving I.W.W. pickets while other pickets blockaded mills and railroads. Day after day the mills were pulled out of activity in threes and fours, and by March 28, the walkout which had started in Hoquiam had resulted in a general tie-up of the Grays Harbor lumber industry. Most of the major mills in the area were closed up tight, and though there had been many arrests and some fighting, the I.W.W. refrained from using violence in closing the plants. The strike at this point was successful, and the workers' ranks were strong.

At first, the mill owners had done little to fight the strike. Since the market at the time was poor, they saw no reason to hurry reopening of the plants. But as the strike spread and the A.F. of L. skilled mechanics in the mills walked out in sympathy, they became alarmed. The alarm increased when A.F. of L. longshoremen in Aberdeen and Hoquiam also went out on strike in sympathy with the mill workers, leaving boats loaded with lumber idle. (In Snohomish County, loggers struck in sympathy with the millmen of Grays Harbor.[21]) On March 29, a new phase of the strike started as the employers set out to smash the walkout by violence. The citizen police, which had been a notorious feature of the Aberdeen free-speech fight, was revived. Years later, a lumberman and shipbuilder of Grays Harbor told an interviewer: "Guided by a simple physical reaction . . . we organized a vigilante committee . . . A Citizens Committee I think we called it . . . to put down the strike by intimidation and force. I was elected leader of the committee. We got hundreds of heavy clubs of the weight and size of pick-handles, armed our vigilantes with them, and that night raided all the I.W.W. headquarters, rounded up as many of the men as we could find and escorted them out of town. . . . Then began a programme of systematic deportations."[22] The report in the Seattle *Post-Intelligencer* of March 31, 1912, fills in the details:

"Today [March 30] was moving day in Raymond and if the census were taken tomorrow Raymond's population would be shy some 155 names, unless all signs fail. Hereafter Raymond is to be strictly an American city. The exodus began this afternoon when fifty Finlanders boarded a boat and steamed down the bay. They were followed shortly afterward by twice that number of Greeks, who elected to travel by rail and went in another direction.

"The reason for the hurried departure is no mystery. Beginning at 10:30 this morning, 200 special police began a weeding-out process and the strikers who refused to go to work were loaded into a boxcar and later in the afternoon were loaded into a launch and shipped to Nahcotta.

"The posse went out to the Greek settlement and announced that all who did not report for work by 1 o'clock this afternoon would be sent out of town. At 1:30 o'clock special police went to the Greek quarters and all who had refused to report for work were herded down to the railroad track and held in boxcars until the departure of the afternoon train, when they were loaded into the passenger cars. The number sent out will run up to nearly 150. . . .

"Efforts will be made to get in American labor from the larger cities. . . . Men have been sent to the larger cities to pick up good American laborers, preferably married men."

The following day, the *Post-Intelligencer* reported: "One hundred of the Greeks who were shipped out of Raymond Saturday returned to this city on the afternoon train yesterday. They got off the train, turned right around and went right back, with two hundred angry citizens prodding them along." The Greek consul at Tacoma, Wash., angered by the treatment accorded his countrymen, came to investigate the situation. He found that there was not a single case of violence sustained against the I.W.W. even though the authorities tried to prove the strikers guilty of lawlessness.[23]

The deportations were followed by a month of violent acts against the I.W.W., carried out over the protest of decent citizens, including Mayor Ferguson of Hoquiam, by "shot-gun brigades" of businessmen in each of the struck towns. Halls were raided by the special police; individual members jailed (100 daily in Aberdeen alone), beaten, and deported in box-cars. A group of masked men seized Joseph Biscay and W. A. Thorn, two of the leaders of the strike, in their hotel room in Aberdeen, led them struggling through the downtown streets to a waiting automobile, and outside the city limits, the vigilantes beat them and sent them on their way. Although the sheriff and the city attorney admitted that the action was a violation of the law, they made no effort to prosecute the case. The regular police not only did not interfere but encouraged the vigilantes. Aberdeen's Chief of Police told Arthur Jensen, a Scripps reporter, that he would "bust the strike or bust their god damned heads."[24]

Fifteen hundred men, women and children, wearing badges reading, "Against the Shotgun Brigade," paraded in Aberdeen for the I.W.W. on March 31. The authorities greeted the paraders by having fire hoses turned upon them. Several of the women paraders were arrested, and one, Manti Niemi, a mother of seven children, had her infant of two months brought to her in jail so that she could feed the child.[25]

The arrests, deportations, and the mass violence of the employers took their toll. By April 9, most of the mills of Grays Harbor were running close to capacity "with a strictly American crew." Fighting still continued, however, with the wives of the strikers taking an active part. On April 10 the Seattle *Post-Intelligencer* reported from Aberdeen: "At noon twenty-five women pickets at Slade's mill . . . laid hold of men returning to work in the mill and refused to desist when warned. The mill hose was turned on the women and they were drenched. Several of the women had babies in carriages with them. . . . The women later marched in a body to the city hall and demanded protection for themselves. Tonight the women

pickets at Slade's mill were again in the front rank, the men standing behind them." Two days later, it reported: "Women sympathizers of the
strikers went to the woods today and cut five 'hundred switches, which
they declared they would lay on the backs of men who go to work in
the sawmills tomorrow. Every morning women have appeared at the mills
with baby buggies, and every morning the mill hose has been turned on
them."

The I.W.W. did not officially call off the strike until May 7. Although
the strikers' wage demands were partially met, hours of work remained
the same. But the I.W.W. had been thrown out of Grays Harbor, and
foreign workers had either been deported or forced into what was almost
slavery—being faced with an ultimatum to work or be deported.[26] One
final aspect of the strike is of interest. Several A.F. of L. officials in the
Pacific Northwest were openly critical of the actions of the members in
the mills and the longshoremen who had supported the strike. The *Labor
World* of Spokane, official journal of the A.F. of L. Central Labor Council, angrily called such critics "pretty scabby trash": "Whatever may be
said of some of the foolish things that the I.W.W. is frequently guilty of,
they at least seem to have the courage in this case to put up a good fight
for decent working conditions in the Grays Harbor district that some
other working men seem too cowardly to tackle."[27]

The I.W.W. was more successful in the spring of 1912 on Puget Sound
in Washington. Here about 5,000 loggers and sawmill workers, under the
leadership of the National Industrial Union of Forest and Lumber
Workers, went on strike for better conditions. They demanded that
springs, mattresses, and good, clean blankets be furnished by the lumber
companies. The companies yielded after two weeks, and in the camps of
Puget Sound the men slept under clean blankets on clean mattresses with
springs, and instead of the usual 10 to 40 men in each room there were
now only two men to a room. The I.W.W. boasted that "the first thing
that strikes a lumber worker in looking at the employment boards in
Seattle is the fact that there are many signs stating 'No Blankets
Needed.' "[28] The idea of a lumber worker who was not a "blanket stiff"
was so revolutionary that the I.W.W. made a special point of its victory on
Puget Sound, and assured workers in every lumber camp that they had
only to join the N.I.U. of F. and L.W. and "the blanket carrying can be
done away with in your camp."[29]

But the employers of Grays Harbor had developed a method of operation against the organizing efforts of the I.W.W. in the lumber industry
which was to make additional victories difficult to achieve. In the Coos
Bay region of Oregon (which included Mansfield, North Bend, Bandon,
Coquille, and Myrtle Point), the loggers organized in Local No. 435 of
the Forest and Lumber Workers walked off the job in May 1913, in protest against a lockout of I.W.W. members in the lumber camps. At the

same time, they formulated demands for higher wages, shorter hours and better living conditions in the camps. The battle continued through November, marked by beatings, arrests, raids on the I.W.W halls, and deportations of strikers by armed vigilantes, businessmen of the communities, and agents of the lumber barons. W. J. Edgworth and Wesley Everett, I.W.W. organizers, and Dr. B. K. Leech, a physician friendly to the strikers, were rounded up by 600 vigilantes, dragged through the streets of Mansfield, beaten, periodically forced to kneel and kiss an American flag, and deported from town in a small boat. "The Vigilantes, all of them prominent 'patriots,'" wrote a reporter, "marched to the building where the I.W.W. had been holding its organization meetings, and notified the proprietor that he had better refuse the I.W.W. the right to gather there or he and all members of the union would be treated to a similar experience as that visited upon Edgworth, Everett and Leech."[30]

So shocking was the vigilante terrorism in the Coos Bay area that Oswald West, Governor of Oregon, was forced to order the attorney general to look into the matter. The report, though extremely critical of the I.W.W. and especially of appeals for sabotage, conceded that the strike was a legitimate effort of the loggers to remedy intolerable conditions in the camps, and that the mob violence against the I.W.W. was due solely to the fact that the organization was the only one that dared to do something about improving these conditions. After receiving the report, Governor West commented: "The alleged practices of the I.W.W. and their damnable methods of crippling and destroying the property of an employer are no worse than mob violence, for, while the former may result in the driving of spikes into saw logs and the destruction of a mill, the latter is equivalent to driving spikes into the law of the land and the destruction of established government." (The Governor failed to draw a distinction between the "alleged practices" of the I.W.W. and the proven "mob violence" against the strikers.) This statement condemning mob violence, published late in November 1913, came too late to be of much assistance to the strikers. The vigilantes had, by this time, driven many of the strikers out of the area, and forced the others back to their jobs.[31]

WEAKNESS OF I.W.W. IN LUMBER

About the same time that the violent battle was raging in the Coos Bay area, the N.U. of F. and L.W. began a campaign for a general strike of lumber workers in the Northwest and California. The demands were for an eight-hour day; a minimum wage of $3.00 per day in the lumber camps and a minimum wage of $2.50 in all mills and lumber yards; time and a half for overtime and Sunday work; clean, sanitary bunkhouses without top bunks and with springs, mattresses, and bedding furnished free of charge; clean towels and soap furnished free of charge in all camps;

all camps to be supplied with bathrooms and dry rooms; safety precautions in the mills, and abolition of paid employment offices.[32] The general strike began on June 5, 1913, and it soon became apparent that either it was inadequately prepared or else the lumber workers did not believe it was possible to achieve these demands at this stage. In any event, there was little evidence of any strike activity, and, on July 3, the I.W.W. called off the general strike. However, even opponents of the I.W.W. conceded that "camp conditions were much bettered, even though they failed to get the eight-hour day."[33]

By the summer of 1913 it was apparent that the National Union of Forest and Lumber Workers was getting nowhere in its efforts to organize the industry. It reported only 640 members to the I.W.W. national convention in September 1913, with only local units in the Northwest remaining to carry on activity.[34] During 1914 the union remained in this condition, and the year was devoted primarily to stock-taking. Most of the discussion revolved around methods of organization. Up to this period the main method of organization had been to set up I.W.W. headquarters in the towns where the lumberjacks congregated between jobs. The theory had been that the men, listening to Wobbly street-corner speakers in the towns, would join the I.W.W. Sleeping in the Wobbly halls and going to meetings where they were plied with literature, they would then carry the message of the "One Big Union" back with them to their jobs in the woods, making the I.W.W. a dominant force there.

But the theory did not work out in practice. For one thing, Wobbly leaders soon found that many of the newly recruited members forgot all about the "One Big Union" when they left the town for the woods. Moreover, during strikes of the mill workers, as in the case of the strike in the Grays Harbor area in the spring of 1912, the town locals could not sufficiently influence the lumberjacks to join the strike. Unable to function in the camps, the town locals simply could not include the loggers in their plans for the strike, and, even when they were able to do so, they found the loggers cool to appeals from men who were not themselves lumberjacks and who carried on the management of the strike from towns remote from the camps.[35]

It was clear, then, that the whole idea of recruiting workers and obtaining job control miles away from the job violated all principles of effective organization. As J. S. Biscay, a veteran I.W.W. organizer among the lumber workers, put it: "In general, the lumberjack sees no economic advantage in joining a lumber local in Seattle while he must toil along the Columbia River all winter. He sees little economic control from the distant city and his toilsome nightmare of a job is right under his nose along with his misery. In his eyes the town local is simply a very loosely decentralized fraternity of lumberjacks with a hall to sit in while in town for a week or so. Being absent he has practically nothing to say about the business of the local which should be his."[36] The answer to this problem, which emerged after several experiments, was the "job-delegate" system.* This plan of organization provided for having a delegate in each camp, who was a logger himself, to sign up members, and with a permanent branch in or near the camp and a secretary in charge. The men, once introduced to the I.W.W. on the job and often seeing the "job delegate" take up their grievances with the boss on the spot, tended either to join the Wobblies in the camps or to migrate to the friendly I.W.W. hall when they arrived in town. And when they returned to the camps, they no longer lost contact with the organization, for the permanent branch was there and the delegate and the secretary were present to act as spokesmen on any grievances the men had, and, in case of a worker meeting with an accident, to see that he received immediate and proper medical attention.[37]

CONDITIONS OF CONSTRUCTION WORKERS

The "job delegate" system of organization was first introduced by the I.W.W. among the railroad-construction workers. This is not surprising. For the most part, this type of work, like lumber, was temporary, and it employed a large number of migratory workers who also lived in camps. The wages were low, the work hard, and the living conditions no better than those in the lumber camps. All along the Canadian Northern Railway the places provided for the workers to live in were termed "bunkhouses only by courtesy." The men lived in shacks without floors or windows, the only ventilation being provided by the doors. Tier after tier of bunks were crowded into these unventilated shacks, and scarcely sufficient space was left between them to permit a man to crawl into bed. An investigating committee reported in 1912: "Owing to overcrowding and lack of ventilation, the air became so foul nights that it was not an uncommon occurrence for the men to arise in the morning too sick to work."[38] In some of the camps, the construction workers were forced to rustle through the woods to get grass and leaves to lay on. And in all, the food was poor. "Grub unfit for a dog—everything rotten and the embalmed meat has been doctored to such an extent that even the flies won't go near it," was a typical description.[39]

Other conditions in these camps which aroused the resentment of the

* The "job delegate" system was preceded by the "camp delegate" system. The delegate, instead of operating in town, would go out to the camp, collect dues, distribute literature there, and generally bring the organization to the men. He would keep in touch with the local in town by correspondence, informing the secretary at least once a month regarding conditions in the camp. But even this system proved to be faulty, for the local was still unable to function effectively on a job while it was located at a distance from the camp. (*Industrial Worker*, Feb. 1, 1912.)

workers was the fact that water was available only from a creek some distance from the camp; that only seven or eight dishpans were supplied for washing purposes for all the men, and the long hours of work, most often 12 hours a day. A complaint in all construction camps was the indifference of the contractors to the safety of the workers. The work by its nature was extremely dangerous even under the most careful administration, but the workers charged that contractors, in their greed, failed to provide enough timber to prevent rock falls. "It was common," wrote a reporter who made a study of the conditions in the camps, "to hear a crippled worker, when speaking of the accident that had robbed him of an arm or leg, remark bitterly that men were cheaper to the contractor than timber, and that it cost him less if the worker lost a limb than it would be to provide timber that would have prevented the fall of rock that had caused the accident."[40]

THE CANADIAN NORTHERN STRIKE

The *Industrial Worker* of August 17, 1911, carried a call from a group of construction workers building the Canadian Northern Railway in British Columbia for an I.W.W. organizer to help them form a union. In response, J. S. Biscay was sent from Vancouver and, by the end of August, recruiting drives in Lytton, Spences Bridge, Ashcraft, and other camps as far as Kamloops had produced Local No. 327 with 900 members. In September, along 100 miles of construction, the men began strikes for higher pay. The contractors appealed to the authorities to send in troops to force the men to work, but the request was rejected. On September 22, while visiting a camp near Savons, Biscay was kidnapped, then arrested on the charge of having a gun in his possession and of being "a dangerous character and a menace to public safety." He was locked up in the provincial jail at Kamloops. Announcing that it would not stand by idly "and see our fellow worker railroaded to jail for the crime of organizing the working class," Local No. 327 threatened a mass exodus of workers from the construction camps all along the Canadian Northern if Biscay was not released. The threat produced results. After a speedy trial, Biscay was found not guilty of being a "dangerous character." By November 1911, when he returned to organizing work, Local No. 327 had grown to a membership of 3,000.[41]

It was at this time that Local No. 327 introduced the "job delegate" system. Lytton was the central point of the construction work on the Canadian Northern, the two others being Yale and Savona. These three were the principal stopping-off points for workers on the way to many camps. The local set up branches at Yale and Savona, each with secretaries. Four to six organizers were kept on the road mainly to collect dues, instruct the membership in the camps, and take up their grievances. So powerful did the local become through the "job delegate" system that in December 1911 it won a raise of 50 cents a day without a strike. Camp conditions were improved. By February 1912, the membership had swelled to nearly 8,000. As the workers moved from one point on the line to another, they only changed branches. The local remained a unit.[42]

Despite some improvements, conditions still remained extremely poor, particularly the unsanitary nature of the construction camps along the Canadian Northern. A petition with 5,000 signers was forwarded to the H alth Department in Vancouver in February 1912, requesting an investigation of violations of the Provincial Health Act governing camps. A government inspector investigated, spelled out numerous violations of the law, and called for immediate action to prevent an outburst from the workers. But the government failed to act.[43]

In March the unrest became marked in all the camps. On March 27, the men in Nelson Benson's Camp No. 4, unable to stand the unbearable conditions any longer, walked out in a body. On their way to Lytton they were joined by the crews of the camps they passed. Upon reaching Lytton, a meeting was held in the headquarters of Local No. 327, a strike call issued, and delegates appointed to carry it along the entire line. Camp after camp walked out, and in three days close to 400 miles of the line were tied up completely. Out of 8,000 construction workers, of all nationalities, fewer than 50 remained at work. The strikers demanded: (1) That the Provincial Health Act be strictly enforced in all camps; (2) a nine-hour day with a minimum wage of $3; for tunnelmen eight hours at $3; (3) meals to be charged at the rate of 25 cents each; (4) cooks, teamsters, and muckers to be paid $3, and (5) blacksmiths to be paid $4 for nine hours of outdoor work and eight hours of inside work.[44]

The strike extended over 400 miles of territory, but actually the I.W.W. established a "thousand-mile picket line" as Wobblies picketed the employment offices in Vancouver, Seattle, Tacoma, Minneapolis, and San Francisco. The pickets kept many from departing for the camps, and I.W.W. missionaries who joined those who shipped out induced others to quit en route.[45]

The strike was fought ferociously by the railroad officials and contractors. Constables were rushed in, in the hope that incidents of violence could be used to arrest and imprison the strikers. But the strike committee appointed its own constables to maintain order. Committees were elected to supervise every aspect of the strike. Commissaries, sleeping quarters, and details of housing and feeding over 7,000 men were attended to. A system of communication between the various strike camps was established, with scouts moving back and forth to report any attempt to import scabs. Strict discipline was maintained. Strikers were forbidden to take more than two drinks a day and no bottled liquor was permitted. A strikers' constable stood guard at each saloon to enforce the rule, and a court set up by the strikers punished any infraction of the strike committee's rule on drinking with such sentences as: "Go out and cut ten big armfuls of firewood"; "Carry ten coaloil cans full of water for the camp cooks"; "Help the cooks for one day." When it was discovered that even then some strikers were sneaking out of the saloon's backway, a boycott was ordered against the establishments and all strikers were ordered to stay away. The saloons now were picketed as well as the camps. "Before the strike," wrote a visitor to the scene, "the saloons had been taking $300 a day; $1,200 on holidays. After the strike began, the saloons complained to me that they could not sell a single drink."[46] To occupy the spare time of the strikers when they were not picketing camps, the strike committee established lectures on "working class matters, not only from the viewpoint of the immediate strike, but also as to the future."[47]

All visitors, including reporters for the Canadian press, marveled at the order maintained and the sense of solidarity of the strikers in the camps. The camp at Yale was even called "a miniature socialist republic." While the *Industrial Worker* did not go this far, it insisted that the strikers at Yale "are laying a broad and deep foundation for a system of society managed industrially by those who do the world's work." The strike as a whole was "proof that the workers are becoming capable of managing their own affairs and thereby are demonstrating their fitness to manage industry when power is gained to take and hold the industries." A Canadian labor paper saw in the strike a warning to foreign capitalists to stay away from Canada. "As an example of working-class solidarity, it would be hard to find another to compare with the present strike of unskilled workers. To see Canadians, Americans, Italians, Austrians, Swedes, Norwegians, French, and old countrymen—one huge 'melting pot' into which creed, color, flag, religion, language and all other differences have been flung—is a hint for king Capital to look out for some other country more healthy for him to exploit labor than this."[48]

Unable to make arrests on the charge of creating violence, the authorities arrested the strikers for "unlawful assemblage," and vagrancy. Hundreds of strikers filled the jails of British Columbia, but with the cost of maintaining them in jail mounting, the arrests ceased. Instead, strikers were forcibly deported. The men were ordered at the point of guns to return to work or leave the region of the construction camps. Martial law was in operation even without a formal declaration. Still the strike remained unbroken. Picket lines were still maintained at every point where the contractors attempted to obtain scabs, including all the large cities of the Pacific Northwest. "The tie-up is as complete now as it was after the walkout," a Canadian paper reported late in June, "and the strikers are standing firm."[49]

In August, the strike merged with a similar walkout on the construction of the Grand Trunk Pacific in British Columbia and Alberta. Here 3,000 men quit work demanding $3.25 to $3.50 for a nine-hour day; time and a half for all overtime and Sundays; board not to exceed $1.00 a day; better food and strict enforcement of the sanitary laws governing camps; hospital fees to be turned over to the I.W.W. which would equip and maintain all hospitals, and the right of organizers and delegates to have access to the camps at all times.[50]

Both strikes were supported by the labor movement of western Canada, including most of the A.F. of L. unions. Indeed, without their aid it would have been difficult for the I.W.W. to have carried on the struggle on the Canadian Northern. After the third month, the British Columbia *Federationist* served as the regular weekly strike bulletin. "The strike," the *Federationist* noted, "has resulted in drawing the various labor organizations closer together and creating a spirit of harmony and solidarity among them." "The spirit of the rank and file of the A.F. of L. towards the strike," declared E. N. Gilbert, secretary of the Strike Committee, "has been commendable and shows that not only is the rank and file with us but also the officials of the A.F. of L. I am sure the strikers appreciate it."[51] But C. O. Young, the A.F. of L. organizer in the area, did not appreciate it. Young, who, it will be recalled, had played such a despicable role in the free-speech fights, was furious. He complained to Frank Morrison that the labor leaders in Vancouver "have lent the I.W.W. aid and advised the unions to assist these out-laws. The unions, strange to say, have neglected their own suffering members on strike, to aid a band of lawless brigands."[52]

The strike on the Canadian Northern lasted until the fall of 1912 when it was ended with some minor improvements for the workers. (The strike on the Grand Trunk Pacific was called off in January 1913 when the Dominion Government promised to enforce the sanitary laws.[53]) But the militancy of the construction workers, their labor solidarity, their method of organization, exemplified in the "job delegate" system, and their strike strategy, were to furnish an important chapter in the history of the Canadian labor movement.

I.W.W. ACCOMPLISHMENTS

Since almost every migratory worker at one time or another spent part of his time on some railroad-construction job, it was to be expected that the "job delegate" system should be eventually carried over into lumbering with some modifications. But it was not introduced by the I.W.W. on an extensive scale until 1915 when it was used to launch a new national organizing drive among the workers in the grain fields. From there, it was carried over into the woods, with results that were to astound the entire nation. The seeds that produced the great harvest after 1916 in the organization of the lumber industry in the Pacific Northwest had been planted years before. For over a decade the Wobblies had moved among the homeless men of the logging camps, preaching their message of "One Big Union" in bunkhouses and in towns where the loggers gathered. Time and again they were driven out of the towns by vigilantes, and the strikes they led were broken by terrorist tactics. But they had introduced the loggers to the I.W.W. and many of them joined the organization at one time or another during these years.

Poor plans and tactics of organization failed to keep them as loyal members who paid their dues regularly, and by 1915 the National Union of Forest and Lumber Workers, which recruited the loggers, consisted of only a few scattered locals.* Then, as we shall see, in 1917 the years of earnest proselytizing among the exploited lumber workers returned dividends. The propaganda and agitation among the lumber workers over the years had created a considerable body of Wobbly sympathizers. *Solidarity* was not boasting without cause when it observed on April 13, 1912: "If there is one section of the country where I.W.W. propaganda has been practically universal and has left an indelible impression on the brains of the slaves, that section is among the entire Pacific Coast from Vancouver to San Diego. For seven years the I.W.W. agitators have moved up and down, in and out, through mining and lumber camps, along water fronts, on street corners, carrying and leaving the message and literature of the One Big Union."

This was the foundation which the I.W.W. used to build a powerful union based on a new method of organization in the lumber industry of the Pacific Northwest, the influence of which spread rapidly to California and helped to create a strong organization in the lumber industry of that state. Wobbly activity among the lumber workers in the Northwest and California finally produced results.

* The National Union of Forest and Lumber Workers went out of existence in 1915, and between that time and 1917 most Wobblies in the lumber industry belonged to the Agricultural Workers' Organization.

CHAPTER 10

The Southern Lumber Drive

Although the story of the I.W.W. in the lumber industry is mainly associated with the loggers and mill workers of the Pacific Northwest and California, one of its most interesting and inspiring chapters relates to the lumber industry of the South. There were important differences between the labor force in Southern and Western lumbering. One was that the former was not composed of migratory workers but rather of men who lived the year round in the area.[1] Another was that the labor force in the Southern lumber industry was made up of both white and Negro workers; indeed, in 1910, over half of the labor force of 262,000 workers was composed of Negroes. In the main, the Negroes were unskilled workers in the lowest-paid jobs, and had little opportunity to rise to higher-paid jobs. They did most of the heavy manual work in the sawmills, on railroads, in the turpentine camps, at skidways, and in the swamps. In 1910, of 7,958 Negroes in the sawmills and planing mills of Texas, 7,216 were laborers; there was not a single Negro sawyer. St. Louis *Lumberman* justified this situation on the ground that "there is a limit to the amount of wages that can be paid with safety to colored laborers around sawmills and wood camps. Too much pay breeds discontent and idleness among them."[2] To the Negro lumber worker, notes a student of the Mississippi lumber industry, "emancipation from slavery had not brought the fruits of freedom. He simply had exchanged his lot for a different system of economic bondage."[3]

CONDITIONS IN SOUTHERN LUMBER INDUSTRY

The magnificent forests of Florida, Alabama, Louisiana, Mississippi, East Texas, and South Georgia were literally stolen by the lumber companies from the public domain; many of the forests were supposed to be school lands set aside for the benefit of education by the U.S. Government. Instead, they were handed over to the lumber kings for prices ranging from 12.5 cents to 75 cents an acre, and this, too, at a time when public schools in these states were closing for lack of funds. Having grabbed these forests—one company owned 87,000 acres in a single tract in Western Louisiana and Eastern Texas—the companies proceeded to operate them as feudal domains, filling the towns with gunmen whom the authorities had commissioned as deputy sheriffs, and jailing anyone who questioned their rule.

The jails also provided the companies with a cheap supply of labor. Men were seized on the railroads for "beating their way" and sentenced to 90 days in jail. Then these unfortunate workers were forced to toil for the period of their sentence in the turpentine camps. Negro and white laborers were frequently arrested, fined, and imprisoned for no offense at all, or simply for being out of a job, and forced to work out their sentence in the lumber camps. Often an employer would arrange to pay the fine on condition that the debt was worked out.[4] In 1904 the Supreme Court upheld laws enacted at the close of the century eliminating peonage, but in the isolated camps in the Southern woods these laws and the Supreme Court decision cut little ice. To be sure, individuals found guilty of establishing peonage could be prosecuted and convicted, but few workers in Southern lumbering, particularly Negro workers, dared to protest to the authorities, knowing that the company-dominated local courts would never convict the guilty parties. Furthermore, although federal laws outlawed peonage, state laws permitted ample leeway for upholding peonage and other kinds of involuntary servitude. "The timber and lumber workers," read a complaint in 1912, "in many places are being practically held as peons within barbed wire enclosures; where there is no law except the will of the Lumber Trust's imported thugs and gunmen."[5]

Wages in Southern lumbering were from 15 to 25 per cent below the national average for the industry, and the Southern work week was approximately two hours longer than that which prevailed in the Northwest. For wages as low as $1.25 a day or average weekly wages of from $7 to $9, men were forced to labor ten to 12 hours a day. With few exceptions, wages were paid monthly, and usually either entirely, or in large part, in scrip or time checks. "Scrip" was simply some substitute for legal money—paper chit, cardboard coin, metal tag, etc.—which ordinarily bore the name of the issuing company, a valuation and the statement "good for merchandise only." If spent in the company store, it passed at face value; but it could be converted to cash only at a customary discount of five to 30 per cent. (Since prices in the company stores ranged from one-third to 50 per cent above prices in surrounding communities, the face value of the wages used for merchandise was always considerably reduced.)

The time check bore the condition that it was to be cashed at some future specified date. If the bearer, for whatever reason, cashed it prior to the specified date, he was generally forced to take a discount of from five to ten per cent. "Given the irregular and infrequent paydays, which were then virtually universal in the southern lumbering industry, these forms of payment amounted to extortion, pure and simple. For no man, however prudent, could manage to get from payday to payday without coming in need of legal currency—which is to say, without being forced by the system to take some portion of his earnings at a sizable discount." Some workers, to obtain legal currency, were forced to borrow from the employer at usurious rates of interest. In other words, these workers were actually paying interest on their wages being withheld from them.[6]

The great majority of the lumber workers lived and died in communities owned and operated by the mill companies. They were charged outrageous rents for primitive huts heated with open fires. They were forced to pay a compulsory medical-insurance fee, usually $1.00 to $1.50 a month, for doctors in whose selection they had no voice and who knew little or nothing of medicine. They were forced to pay from 75 cents to $1 per month for "accident insurance," which was bought by the lumber companies at from 50 to 60 cents per month per man. The casualty companies were paid either on the basis of the average number of workers employed during the month or on a certain percentage of the payroll, while the lumber companies collected 75 cents to $1 a month from every man who went to work, no matter if he worked a month, a week or a day, thereby reaping a huge profit on the insurance.[7]

A comprehensive study of conditions in the lumber industry in Louisiana by the State Bureau of Statistics of Labor pointed out: "We found . . . every labor law on the statutes being violated." Following a similar study in Texas, the Commission on Industrial Relations found "that in such communities, political liberty does not exist and its forms are hollow mockery. . . . Free speech, free assembly, and a free press may be denied as they have been denied time and again, and the employer's agent may be placed in public office to do his bidding." The lumber communities, George Creel wrote in 1915, "are as far removed from freedom and democracy as though time had rolled back to the days of Ivanhoe."[8]

FORMATION OF BROTHERHOOD OF TIMBER WORKERS

The spirit of resentment among Southern lumber workers had produced a series of strikes starting in the late 1880's, under the leadership of the Knights of Labor, and continuing sporadically thereafter in local walkouts, with the first notable attempt at organization occurring in 1902. All of them were unsuccessful, and the unions that were formed during these years soon ceased to function.[9] The first widespread revolt of the lumber workers occurred in the autumn of 1907. On top of the poor wages and and hours, "gouging" in company stores, payment in scrip, excessive insurance and hospital fees, inadequate housing and sanitation, and irregularity of paydays, the lumber companies, taking advantage of the panic of 1907, issued orders to cut wages 20 per cent or more, and lengthened the hours of work. Against these orders, all the lumber workers in Western Louisiana and Eastern Texas rose en masse, and in a spontaneous general strike closed hundreds of mills. Promises of wage increases when economic conditions improved were made to the strikers, and most of them went back to work immediately. Workers from the mills around De Ridder, La., held out for several weeks, but neither they nor the original group that returned, gained anything. Not only were the promises not kept, but the oppression grew even worse.[10]

Although the workers had failed to organize a union in 1907, the strike and the imminent threat of unionization led to the formation of the Southern Lumber Operators' Association. Organized specifically to combat unionism, the Association began immediately to introduce methods to prevent organization. Knowing that cash was necessary to finance a union extending over several states, the members of the Association intensified their efforts to keep actual money from their workers by refusing to exchange coin for commissary checks at any discount.[11] At the same time, they reinforced their long-standing practice of fostering racial antagonism between Negro and white lumber workers. In secret correspondence, the companies who belonged to the Association boasted to each other that race hatred was helping them prevent the formation of a union of lumber workers. One journalist wrote: "The Lumber Trust carefully studies methods for intensifying race antagonism and then sits back to watch it work. Black men or white men, a few lives more or less, are of no consequence to the masters of the swamp lands if their snuffing-out turns a profit to the companies."[12]

So effective were these anti-union methods that by 1910 the Southern Lumber Operators' Association practically ceased to function. But it was soon to be revived. In the face of obstacles which seemed impossible to overcome, the Southern lumber workers finally did organize a union—the Brotherhood of Timber Workers.

After a visit to the lumber district of the Pacific Northwest, Arthur L. Emerson returned to his work as a lumberjack in the Texas-Louisiana timber regions convinced that the only way the lumber workers in Dixieland could lift their wages and conditions to the level of those in the Northwest (which were none too high) was through organization. He enlisted the support of Jay Smith and together they carried the message of unionism to the Southern lumber workers.[13] They met with an immediate response from the workers in the De Ridder area of Louisiana where, it will be remembered, the unsuccessful strike of 1907 had lasted longer than anywhere else. About 90 lumber workers, most of them sympathetic to the I.W.W. (a number were Wobblies) and to the Socialist views of Eugene V. Debs, were the first to join the new movement. On December 3, 1910, Emerson and Smith formed the first local at Carson, La., a lumber camp about six miles south of De Ridder. The organization of locals continued throughout the winter of 1910–11, with the drive supported by *The Rebel*, a Socialist paper published in Halletsville, Tex., and *The Toiler*, published in Leesville, La., by "Uncle" Pat O'Neill, a veteran of the United Mine Workers. At first it had been decided to organize only the woodsmen, but Emerson noted: "We soon saw that the mills would also have to be organized."[14]

Emerson, Smith, and a few others traveled in the guise of book agents, insurance solicitors, evangelists, even card sharps, to avoid company gunmen, going from camp to camp, mill to mill, bringing the message of unionism to the lumber workers.[15] By June 1911, enough locals had been organized to warrant a general convention for the adoption of a formal constitution. It was decided that the future headquarters of the organization should be Alexandria, La., and the convention was held there. At the convention, the Brotherhood of Timber Workers (or B. of T.W. as it was popularly called) was set up as a national union with Emerson as president, Smith as general secretary, and Pat Guillory as treasurer. The constitution provided for a two-level organization: the local units, composed of 25 or more members; and the central body, composed of delegates elected from the locals. (Later, as the Brotherhood grew, district councils were informally established in many areas.) When the "Grand Lodge," as the central organization was called, was not in convention, an executive committee of permanent salaried officers acted in its name. The initiation fee was $1; dues were 50 cents monthly. Membership was open to "all persons, regardless of vocation, who may be in sympathy with the labor movement, and who comply with the constitution, rules, and by-laws of the organization, except only, officers and employers in the above industries [timber and lumber] and those whose livelihood was obtained by questionable means."

Since Negroes comprised so large a portion of the labor force, the leaders of the Brotherhood knew that no union could be effective in the yellow pine region unless it opened its doors to Negroes as well as whites. The basic concept of the organization required that membership be open to Negroes, but the Southern tradition of segregation was retained by providing for "colored lodges," which were forbidden to retain their initiation fees and dues but were required to deliver all such funds for safe-keeping to the nearest white local.

Just as the leaders of the Brotherhood were anxious to avoid being charged with upsetting the Jim-Crow pattern of Southern life, they were determined to avoid the charge of being too radical. The constitution emphasized only limited objectives, went out of its way to recognize the "rights" of the employer, and rejected the use of violence "in whatever guise it may assume." How far the union bent backwards to assure the employers that it was not radical is evident in the statement: "Our appeal shall be to reason and enlightened humanity. . . . At all times, and in all things, we shall be glad to meet and counsel with those who employ us, and by acts of reason, justice, and persuasion, try to convince them of the righteousness of our cause. We demand: Recognition, Equal Rights, a Living Wage, A Just Consideration of Abuses, Exact and Equal Justice to those who work with their hands, and who contribute so much to the comforts of mankind, and who get so little in return."[16]

The conservative tone and contents of the constitution did not appease the employers. Shortly after the Alexandria convention, the Southern Lumber Operators' Association charged the Brotherhood with being an offshoot of the I.W.W. and represented it as a violent, revolutionary organization.[17]

THE 1911 LOCKOUT

The B. of T.W. spread rapidly over Texas, Louisiana, and Arkansas, recruiting Negro and white lumberjacks, mill workers, tenant and small farmers who worked in the lumber industry for parts of the year, and town craftsmen. From its headquarters in Alexandria, the union cautioned its members and all workers to refrain at this stage from starting strikes and to avoid disturbances which could be used by the lumber companies as a pretext to smash the organization. "Go on with your work and be content with present conditions."[18] The Brotherhood had good reason to be cautious at this stage. The union's rapid growth had alarmed the employers. In the summer of 1911, individual mill owners began to take action against the organization, requiring all workers to sign a card declaring that they would not join the union. This caused several strikes and a number of mills shut down, discharged every Brotherhood member, and kept closed down for weeks.[19]

But the operators did not rely upon individual action alone to combat the growing union. The Southern Lumber Operators' Association was speedily reactivated and a secret meeting of its membership was called for July 19 at New Orleans. The meeting was attended by some 150 lumbermen from Texas, Arkansas, and Louisiana. The president of the Association at this time was C. R. Johnson of St. Louis, but the meeting was controlled by John H. Kirby, the largest lumber operator in Texas, who actually directed the activities of the organization. A one-time president of the National Association of Manufacturers, Kirby was determined to smash the Brotherhood of Timber Workers.

The leading speech at the session was delivered by Kirby. He began by announcing that "whenever any efforts are discovered to organize unions the mills will be closed down and will remain so until the union is killed."

He went on to attack the Brotherhood as an organization which proposed to affiliate with the "Industrial Workers of the World, of Chicago, a socialistic organization, composed largely of foreign-born citizens and whose teachings reject the Constitution of this republic and deny to any citizen the right to own property." Then the former head of the N.A.M. and a prime leader of the open-shop drive* who had frequently condemned the A.F. of L., launched into a tirade against the I.W.W. on the ground that it "seeks to destroy the American Federation of Labor and will put the latter out of business if it can." In contrast to the I.W.W., the A.F. of L. was "based on the right of property and respect thereof," and it rejected the "immoral and criminal philosophy" of the Wobblies. Since it was evident that the lumber workers were determined to organize, the question was how to channel this desire into the proper avenue, how, in short, to work out arrangements with the proper organizations of labor:

"Organization of our workers cannot be prevented. It has already gone too far, and we may as well put up with it. But we are not going to stand for the tactics outlined by the Industrial Workers of the World. We will deal with organizations and leaders who will guarantee the owners a fair and just return of profits for legitimate investments, be it in capital or our ability to develop the vast lumber resources of the South."

With this in mind, Kirby had already contacted Ralph M. Easley, secretary of the National Civic Federation, "and he gave me the assurance that the American Federation of Labor is the organization that will serve our purposes and he referred me to Mr. Samuel Gompers who would be more than willing to give us advice and suggestions to meet the situation." Gompers agreed to help the lumber companies in their plight, but insisted that the matter not be discussed through correspondence. Kirby then arranged to meet Gompers in Chicago prior to the New Orleans secret session. He told the delegates at New Orleans that Gompers had made the following suggestions "how to meet best the embarrassing situation which we are in." First, the timber workers had to be convinced that the only unions that would be tolerated would be those affiliated with the A.F. of L. Second, all members of the Brotherhod of Timber Workers were to be kept out of the mills, and to achieve this the mills would be shut down. The locked-out workers would return on the employers' terms.

Arrangements were worked out between Kirby and Gompers for the Southern Lumber Operators' Association to drive its workers out of the B. of T.W., and, after that union was destroyed, to extend recognition to the A.F. of L. which would send its representatives into the lumber camps and mills to recruit the skilled, white craftsmen.[20] On August 1, 1911, St. Louis *Lumberman,* organ of the operators, confirmed the willingness of the employers to make a deal with the A.F. of L. "They have no ob-

* For Kirby's role as a leader of the open-shop drive, see Foner, *op. cit.,* vol. III, pp. 34, 36, 37, 57, 69, 258, 333, 349.

jection to unions as such, provided their aims and purposes are reasonable and fair. But they are utterly opposed to labor associations of the character and of the lack of sanity with which they are now confronted, and rather than submit to their demands wholesale shut-downs of plants will be ordered."

Publication of Kirby's speech in the New Orleans *Times-Democrat* produced a storm of protesting letters to Gompers from A.F. of L. members. Typical is a letter from a group of Southern trade unionists:

"We, the undersigned, members of A.F. of L. unionists in Shreveport, Louisana, have read with feelings of astonishment a report of your meeting with John H. Kirby of the Southern Lumber Operators Association and a notorious open-shop employer, in which you were quoted as being ready to join hands with this Association, whose reputation for opposition to unionism is known to all union men in the South, for the purpose of assisting the companies in destroying the right of their workers to organize. We cannot possibly believe that the leader of the American Federation of Labor would descend to such depths, and we urge that you immediately issue a statement unequivocally denouncing Mr. Kirby as a liar."[21]

Not only did Gompers issue no such statement; he did not even bother to reply to this and similar letters protesting the deal announced by Kirby.

Meanwhile, the companies were carrying out plans for a lockout. Announcing to the press that "the lumber manufacturers are all determined that this apparently anarchistic organization [B. of T.W.] must not get any further, both for the good of the lumber industry and for the good of the employes themselves," the Association ordered the immediate shutdown of eleven mills in the De Ridder area. By this action, 3,000 men were locked out. During the next few months over 300 other mills in Texas, Arkansas, and Louisiana were closed down, and union men were locked out of, or blacklisted from, every mill within the Association's sphere of influence.[22]

Early in the lockout, the Brotherhood countered with a series of demands which included: (1) A minimum of $2.00 per day, the work day not to exceed ten hours in duration; (2) a two-weeks pay-day, in United States, and not commissary, currency; (3) the right of free trade, the workers not to be forced to buy from company stores; (4) a discontinuance of the practice of discounting wages; (5) reasonable rents; (6) a revision of insurance, hospital and doctor fees, the men to have the right to elect their doctors, to see the insurance policy and to have representatives on a committee that was to control these funds; (7) a general improvement in the sanitary and living conditions of the lumber towns and camps; (8) the disarming and discharge of all gunmen; (9) the right of free speech, press and assembly.[23]

Denouncing these demands as "revolutionary" and advanced by "a movement run wild,"[24] the lumber kings answered the union with their brutal campaign of blacklisting. Despite the existence of anti-blacklist laws in the Southern states, the Association kept a "labor clearing house" through which the operators exchanged information concerning objectionable employees. Association members were required to keep a list of their employees at the central office, supplementing it daily by reports on men discharged and new men employed. A principal question on each report was, "Have you any reason to believe that he sympathizes with or is a member of the order of Timber Workers of the World?" A letter sent by the Executive Committee of the Association to the Little River Lumber Co. of Manistee, La., showed the way in which the blacklisting method was used: "We will undoubtedly at some future time re-employ large numbers of our former employees whom we have discharged and reported as being affiliated with the Brotherhood of Timber Workers. This will be only done upon their evidencing in some satisfactory way that they have renounced their allegiance to the Brotherhood of Timber Workers."[25]

There were two ways in which the locked-out workers could furnish "satisfactory" evidence. One was by individually signing the familiar "yellow-dog" contract or iron-clad oath in which they promised not to belong to the Brotherhood as long as they remained in the company's employ. The other was for groups of workers to sign resolutions condemning the B. of T.W. and pledging their loyalty to the operator. Usually these resolutions were circulated at meetings at which the employees heard anti-union speakers, many supplied by the Good Citizens' Protective Leagues which were organized in Eastern Texas and Western Louisiana to break up local meetings of the Brotherhood and to intimidate its speakers and organizers. A typical resolution circulated at these meetings read: "Resolved: That we, the undersigned employees of the Pickering Land and Timber Company of Cravens, Louisiana, are opposed to the organization known as the Brotherhood of Timber Workers and hereby pledge our support to the said company in stamping out the movement of the said organization at this place in order that the plant may continue in operation."[26] The fact that the company had deliberately shut down the plant was, of course, ignored.

During the summer and fall of 1911 between 5,000 and 7,000 of the most active members of the Brotherhood, white and Negro, were blacklisted.[27] Those members who were farmers and had some small source of income to fall back on when discharged from the mills, could still survive. But for those blacklisted workers who had no other source of income, it was indeed a tragedy. In the Southern timber region, outside of farming and lumbering, there were few, if any, sources of employment open to the unemployed worker who had incurred the hostility of the operators. Nevertheless, the vast majority of the lumber workers refused to sign the "yellow-dog" contract. One worker expressed the common attitude: "Only a low-life lickskillet would do such a thing. . . . I would live on wild plants that grow in the hills before I would sign."[28]

Meeting again in secret session in New Orleans on October 31, the Southern Lumber Operators' Association appointed a committee to devise plans for the reopening of the mills. Kirby told the delegates that the war against the Brotherhood was progressing satisfactorily, and that "the mills seemed to be in better shape, as far as their labor was concerned." But he conceded that the union was still alive, though considerably weakened, and that with respect to completely destroying the Brotherhood, the lockout had been far from a total success. The strategy worked out was to reopen the plants, invite Negro members of the Brotherhood to go back to work at higher wages, and recruit Negro scabs from all parts of Louisiana and Texas to keep the mills operating.[29] The first part of this strategy failed completely; no Negro members of the Brotherhood went back to work. To meet the second weapon of the Association, the Brotherhood widely circulated an appeal to Negroes throughout Louisiana and Texas which read:

"If you allow yourselves to be made tools of by these men who are sent out to hunt you up and hold out flattering promises of good wages and good treatment, you are doing the very thing that our organization proposes to prevent and forever put a stop to. The Brotherhood of Timber Workers is the only one that has ever been organized in the South that takes the negro and protects him and his family along with the white wage worker and his family on an industrial basis. Thousands of your race have taken advantage of the opportunities afforded by our order and have nobly and loyally performed their part in the great struggle of the wage worker for the right to organize and correct the abuses now fastened upon us by the companies. They seem to fully realize that we must all pull together and that each must perform his duty honorably if we expect to win the fight and take our proper place among the organized powers of the world. Are you one of this number of good, loyal negroes who are willing to stand by their own class, or are you one of those fellows who have no thought of the future welfare of your race as well as yourself and family? If you go in and take the jobs that have been wrongfully taken away from honest, hard-working white and colored men, you will not only assist these mill men to keep up their systems of low wages and abuses unmentionable, but you will also assist them in whipping the many thousands of white men and men of your own color and race. . . . Let us plead with you to get in and help us in this great fight for you and yours. If you can not do this, in the name of all that is high and holy do not be misled and made tools of against the best interests of your own class and your own color."[30]

The appeal was effective. When the mills reopened in the winter of 1912—the lockout was officially ended by February—it was not with scab labor. While the union did not win its demands, slightly higher wages were gained by many workers, and the ten-hour day was instituted in a number of mills. To be sure, the Brotherhood locals were not recognized, but the union still existed as a force after the infamous war to exterminate it. By May 1912, the Brotherhood had a membership of between 20,000 to 25,000 workers, about half of whom were Negroes. (Of these about 5,000 were paid-up members and probably 15,000 to 20,000 lumber workers and working farmers who were in arrears in dues, but who still claimed membership.) In the spring of 1912, E. F. Presely was elected mayor of De Ridder on the Socialist-B. of T.W. ticket.[31]

B. OF T.W. JOINS I.W.W.

The experience in the battle against the lockout had imbued the Brotherhood with an increased spirit of militancy and class consciousness. In the pamphlet, *An Appeal to Timber and Lumber Workers,* written by Jay Smith, secretary of the Brotherhood and published in April 1912 by the union, there was not a hint of the conciliatory position set forth in the organization's constitution. The pamphlet opened on a militant note proclaiming the union's purpose to be "the organization of all wage workers employed in and around the timber and lumber industry, into *One Big Union,* regardless of creed, color, or nationality. It is, too, our purpose to give sympathy and every assistance in our power to all those who labor in other trade and industry, expecting them to do likewise by us, to the end that all workers may be bound together in one solid, compact army, whose motto shall be, 'An injury to one is an injury to all,' having for its final aim the overthrow of slavery and the emancipation of the race."

After repudiating the principle of craft unionism on the ground "that it divides the workers on the job which is just what the bosses want," the pamphlet tackled the "negro question," which it defined in these terms: "As far as the 'negro question' goes, it means simply this: Either the whites organize with the negroes, or the bosses will organize the negroes against the whites, in which last case it is hardly up to the whites to damn the 'niggers.' " Southern workers ought to realize that while there were two colors among the workers in the South there was actually only one class. It was "the main object of this organization . . . to teach that the only hope of the workers is through industrial organization; that while the colors in question are two, the class in question is only one; that the first thing for a real workingman to do is to learn by a little study that he belongs to the working class, line up with the

Brotherhood of Timber Workers or the Industrial Workers of the World, and make a start for industrial freedom."

In reprinting sections of the pamphlet, the *Industrial Worker* noted correctly: "For years the South has been in a backward state of development and has to confront a tremendous race prejudice in the form of the 'negro question.' This pamphlet, when the conditions of the South are taken into consideration, is one that requires a lot of courage to issue, and its widespread distribution will do much to clarify the labor atmosphere of the South."[32]

At the September 1911 I.W.W. convention, three fraternal delegates were present from the Brotherhood of Timber Workers, and during the union's battle against the lockout, the I.W.W. had rendered it whatever support it could, mainly by publicizing its struggle in the Wobbly press. Affiliation with the I.W.W. was raised as soon as the lockout was over. The Brotherhood realized that it needed the prestige and support of a stronger organization, and that the I.W.W. was the only effective union in the lumber industry. Moreover, it was the only significant union in the entire labor movement that would welcome a Southern organization which cut across craft and racial lines. When the proposed affiliation was agreed to by the leaders of the B. of T.W. and the I.W.W., the latter organization sent Bill Haywood and Covington Hall to the Brotherhood's second annual convention at Alexandria, May 6–9, 1912, to present the case for affiliation to the delegates.

Arriving at the convention, Haywood expressed surprise that no Negroes were present. He was informed that the Negro workers were meeting separately in another hall because it was against the law in Louisiana for whites and Negroes to meet together. Haywood brushed this explanation aside, declaring:

"You work in the same mills together. Sometimes a black man and a white man chop down the same tree together. You are meeting in convention now to discuss the conditions under which you labor. This can't be done intelligently by passing resolutions here and then sending them out to another room for the black man to act upon. Why not be sensible about this and call the Negroes into this convention? If it is against the law, this is one time when the law should be broken."

Haywood's advice was followed, and the Negroes were called into the session. The mixed gathering adopted the proposal of affiliation with the I.W.W. by a vote of 71½ to 26½ and elected Negro and white delegates to the September convention of the I.W.W. in Chicago where the merger was to be formally effected.

Haywood also addressed a mass meeting at the Alexandria Opera House under the Brotherhood's sponsorship. Here, too, there was no segregation, and for the first time in the city's history, Negro and white sat together in all parts of the hall at a public meeting.* "There was no interference by the management or the police," Haywood reported, "and the meeting had a tremendous effect on the workers who discovered that they could mingle in meetings as they mingled at work." *Solidarity* featured the news from Alexandria under the heading: "Rebels of the New South No Longer Fighting to Uphold Slavery but to Abolish It." The *Industrial Worker* carried the news under the heading: "Miracle of the New South."

In July, the convention's vote to affiliate with the I.W.W. was overwhelmingly confirmed by the Brotherhood's rank and file membership in a general referendum. At the September convention of the I.W.W., the merger was consummated and the Brotherhood of Timber Workers became the Southern District of the National Industrial Union of Forest and Lumber Workers. (However, the union still continued to be referred to as the Brotherhood.) *Solidarity's* correspondent, covering the convention, wrote from Chicago:

"Proof that we have surmounted all barriers of race and color is here in the presence of delegates of many nationalities as well as that of two colored delegates, B. H. Fletcher from Philadelphia and D. R. Gordon of the B.T.W. Both of the latter are taking active part in the convention and show a clear understanding of the great idea of the One Big Union of the whole working class."[33]

THE GRABOW AFFAIR

The decision to affiliate with the I.W.W. gave new spirit to the Southern lumber workers. On May 13, 1912, just four days after the adjournment of the second annual convention, the Brotherhood presented a few of the mills in the De Ridder area with its old list of demands. The demands were summarily rejected, and the union members went out on strike at the mills concerned. The Southern Lumber Operators' Association hit back by calling a general lockout throughout the industry. The *Lumber Trade Journal,* organ of the operators, declared that the lockout would remain in force until the union was destroyed. "That the lumber-

* Not even the Socialist Party in Louisiana allowed Negroes and whites to meet together. Indeed, with the exception of one local, that in Lutcher, which was composed only of Negroes, every S.P. local in Louisiana was "composed exclusively of white members." (William C. Seyler, "The Rise and Decline of the Socialist Party in the United States," unpublished Ph.D. thesis, Duke University, 1952, pp. 99–100. *See also* Grady McWhiney, "Louisiana Socialists in the Early Twentieth Century: A Study in Rustic Radicalism," *Journal of Southern History,* vol. XXX, Aug. 1954, p. 332.)
Not only were Negroes allowed to join the Brotherhood, but women were also given the right to hold membership and to vote which was also "a very radical move" in the Deep South. (Covington Hall, "Labor Struggles in the Deep South," unpublished manuscript, Howard-Tilton Library, Tulane University, pp. 136–38.)

men of the South will not treat with these agitators goes without saying.
. . . The only policy which the lumbermen can pursue is that followed
in the past . . . to fight the question to a finish. . . : The mills will never
agree to recognize the union." The fact that the union had allowed
Negro and white members to meet and consult together in complete
violation of the "traditions of the South" was cited as a sufficient reason
for the employers to seek its destruction.[34]

The Association resumed its former policy of blacklisting all union
members. Men applying for employment were forced to sign "yellow-
dog" contracts, and all members of the Association were required to send
"reports of men now on your payroll and opposite their names please
state whether or not they were former members of the union." The
Association recruited an army of gunmen and deputies and rushed them
into the lumbering districts; notices were posted around camps reading:
"Private Property. All Unionists, Socialists, Peddlers and Solicitors, Keep
Out Under Penalty of the Law."[35]

By the first week in June, the mills began reopening with scab labor. To
counter this move, the B. of T.W. leaders called general meetings, usually
on weekends, of union members and sympathizers. When the men had
gathered, they would then march to various mills employing non-union
labor and there deliver speeches and distribute literature outlining the
position of the Brotherhood and pointing out the benefits to be derived
from organization of all lumber workers into "One Big Union." The
operators struck back by breaking up the Brotherhood's meetings. Mobs,
led by mill managers and deputy sheriffs, attacked the union gatherings
and forced members and sympathizers to leave the area.[36]

The climax of terrorism was reached on Sunday, July 7, at Grabow, La.
A. L. Emerson and a group of union members and sympathizers were
conducting a speaking tour of a number of closely connected camps.
Learning that company thugs had gathered at Bon Ami, La., they by-
passed this area and headed for the mill, operated by the Galloway
Lumber Co., at Grabow, where a non-union crew had been employed for
the past month. It was around six o'clock in the evening when the crowd
arrived at Grabow. They assembled before the mill, and Emerson began
to address the crowd from the bed of a wagon parked near the gallery of
the company office. Suddenly three shots were fired into the crowd in
rapid succession. With the first shots, the union crowd dispersed and
sought cover in the nearby timber. Those of the union men who were
armed exchanged shots with the company guards who were firing from
concealment in the company office, from a planing mill and an empty
boxcar. When the firing was over, three men were dead and more than
40 wounded, one of whom died a few days later. Two of the dead, Uriah
(Roy) Martin and Decatur Hall, were union members; the third was a

company guard. The man who died later was Phillip Fazeral, an Italian laborer and member of the Brotherhood. Of the forty-odd wounded, all but two or three were union men.

Emerson and 64 other unionists were arrested. Galloway and four of the company men were also arrested. On July 23, the grand jury returned true bills of indictment (one bill for each of the three men killed outright at Grabow) for murder against Emerson and the 64 union men. At the same time, the jury absolved the company men involved.[37]

The trial was not scheduled to begin before October. From the end of July to the close of the trial in November, there were over 60 union men in jail at Lake Charles. This parish prison, never meant to accommodate anything near that number of prisoners, was unbearably overcrowded. In response to protests from the families of the prisoners, the president of the State Board of Health, Dr. Oscar Dowling, examined the Lake Charles prison. He found 60 men in one 42-by-30-foot room, and reported that the poor ventilation and defective sewer connections in the room constituted a serious hazard to the health of the prisoners. As a result of the investigation, the number of men held in the room was reduced to 25; the others were removed to the basement of the new courthouse building which was then under construction. But this change was only a slight improvement. In a statement denouncing "Barbarous Louisiana," the B. of T.W. Defense Committee called upon all workers to "Protest! Deluge the Governor of Louisiana and the President of the United States with letters and telegrams denouncing this iniquitous prison, ye men and women of labor, ye lovers of freedom and justice everywhere."[38]

The Defense Committee's main function was to win sympathy and financial support for the arrested members of the Brotherhood. In addition to the expense of securing counsel, the committee was faced with the burden of providing support for the prisoners' families for several months. Circulars headed "Shall Emerson Die?" and appealing for funds were distributed throughout the entire country and published in the I.W.W. and Socialist press. One of the most important, and certainly the most widely discussed of the Defense Committee's appeals was addressed "To all Negro Workers, and especially to the Negro Forest and Lumber Workers of the South." Pointing out that the moment the B. of T.W. started to revolt against peonage, the lumber kings raised the cries of " 'white supremacy' and 'social equality' coupled with that other cry, 'They are organizing negroes against the whites!" the appeal noted:

"For a generation, under the influence of these specious cries, they have kept us fighting against each other—us to secure the 'white supremacy' of a tramp and *you* the 'social equality' of a vagrant. Our fathers 'fell for it,' but we, their children, have come to the conclusion that . . . the 'white supremacy' that means starvation wages and child slavery for us and the 'social equality' that means the same to you, though they may mean the 'high life' and 'Christian civilization' to the lumber kings and landlords, will have to go. As far as we, the workers of the South, are concerned, the only 'supremacy' and 'equality' they have ever granted us is the supremacy of misery and the equality of rags. This supremacy and this equality we, the Brotherhood of Timber Workers, mean to stand no longer than we have an organization big and strong enough to enforce our demands, chief among which is 'A man's life for all the workers in the mills and forests of the South.' Because the negro workers comprise one-half or more of the labor employed in the Southern lumber industry, this battle cry of ours . . . has been considered a menace and therefore a crime in the eyes of the Southern oligarchy, for they, as well as we, are fully alive to the fact that we can never raise our standard of living and better our conditions as long as they can keep us split, whether on race, craft or religious or national lines. . . . Emerson and his associates are in prison because they fought for the unity of all workers. Will you remain silent, turn no hand to help them in this, their hour of great danger?"[39]

The Defense Committee's appeals for contributions to the defense and relief funds received a general response from labor (including A.F. of L. and Railroad Brotherhood locals) and Socialist organizations, and from Negroes and Socialist farmers in Eastern Texas and Western Louisiana. Years later, Covington Hall, who headed the defense activities, recalled: "Never before or since have I seen the solidarity of labor that was lined up for the defense in the 'Grabow Trial.' I would die happy if I could only witness the same solidarity of workers from one end of this continent to the other."[40]

The trial opened in Lake Charles on October 7, 1912. The Brotherhood declared October 7 a "union holiday," and urged "no member . . . or sympathizers with it . . . to go to his toil in the mills or in the logging camps," but, instead, to come to Lake Charles and "show the authorities that organized labor is against legalized murder." "No one," the union warned, "shall upon that day allow himself to be intoxicated or enter into heated argument that may cause trouble. All weapons must be kept at home. No guns or rifles will be tolerated." Hundreds of union members poured into Lake Charles. In keeping with the Brotherhood's instructions, they conducted a peaceable demonstration.[41]

The prosecution filed a motion to sever the trial of a selected nine defendants from that of the remaining 49. The motion was granted by the court. The chances of convicting the nine were much greater than that of 58 men *en bloc,* and since the nine selected were the most militant members of the union, their conviction would achieve what the Southern Lumber Operators' Association was after. As finally selected, the jury was composed of seven farmers, a bill collector, a manager of a bottle works, a well-driller, a machinist, and a tram motorman. (No union man nor anyone who admitted to reading a labor or Socialist paper was allowed to serve on the jury.)[42] "Judge" E. G. Hunter, leading counsel for the defense, noted that the prosecution was not being conducted by the State of Louisiana, but rather by the Southern Lumber Operators' Association. "The State of Louisiana is nothing but a spectator in the trial. The real force is the Southern Lumbermen's Association's fight to break the union." He noted, too, that the bulk of the evidence-gathering and investigation was not conducted by investigative agencies of the state, but rather by a "small army" of operatives of the Burns International Detective Agency. Hunter accused the detectives of having tampered with veniremen, endeavoring to find out where the sympathies of these prospective jurors lay, and informing attorneys for the prosecution so that those favorable to the defense could be peremptorily challenged. These detectives, he made it clear, were being paid by the employers' association.[43]

The prosecution, headed by Congressman A. P. Pujo—it was common knowledge that his fee was being paid by the operators' association and not by the state—tried to prove (1) that the union men, in unprovoked aggression at Grabow, had forced the company men to return their fire in self-defense; and (2) that this armed aggression was the outcome of a conspiracy previously planned by the defendants. But 22 witnesses for the defense swore that the first shot came from the office of the Galloway Lumber Co., and seven of them swore that John Galloway, owner of the mill, himself fired the first shot. The prosecution was unable to shake their testimony on a single point.

The state witnesses, James Ross and Shirley Buxton, testified completely in favor of the defense. Buxton swore that the first shot came from the office of the lumber company and that nearly all the gunmen were drunk when the unionists had arrived at Grabow. The defense proved that the guards were drunk and were waiting to shoot union men; A. T. Vincent, a guard who was killed, was proved to have been very drunk at the time of the shooting and had been heard to say several times that afternoon that he "would like to kill him a union son of a bitch." No wonder the New Orleans *Times-Democrat* reported that some of the state's witnesses "plainly disappointed the State."[44]

Pujo tried to overcome the weaknesses in the state's case by proving that the Brotherhood was a revolutionary organization bent on destroying Southern institutions. He offered as an exhibit the circular addressed "To all Negro Workers, and especially the Negro Forest and Lumber Workers of the South." The defense objected and Judge Overton ruled the circular could not be submitted since it was not proved that one of the defendants on trial had written and distributed it.[45] But Pujo returned to the theme in his final statement to the jury in which he called the trial the most important issue to have confronted Louisiana since the days of Reconstruction. "It is a question of whether we shall have social justice and civilization in Louisiana or anarchy. I do not wish to accuse these defendants of being anarchists, but the things these men advocated prior to and leading up to the tragedy of Grabow will, if persisted in, lead to anarchy and bloodshed and the destruction of civilization and law and order. It is for you, the jury, to decide whether the red hand of anarchy shall reach up and pull down the temples of justice and thwart the authority of constituted government."[46]

In less than an hour after retiring, the jury, having taken but one ballot, returned a verdict of not guilty. Acquittal of these nine defendants meant that a conviction of the 49 yet untried was impossible. District Attorney Moore moved that the court declare the charges against these 49 *nolle prosequi*. The court so ordered and the men were released.[47]

THE MERRYVILLE STRIKE

A few hours after his release from prison, Emerson addressed a victory meeting at Union Hall in Lake Charles. "It was evident from the first that this charge was trumped up by agents of the lumbermen," he told the assembled workers. "They thought by this move they could ruin us of funds. Of course it was successful in that respect. It has cost us an immense sum to maintain the families of the men in jail, and the lawyers, and fight the case."[48] Emerson's point was well taken. Nevertheless, the outcome of the frameup was a major defeat for the Southern Lumber Operators' Association. Even though they had deprived the union of its militant core for months, the operators had failed to destroy the Brotherhood. An appeal was published in the *Industrial Worker* urging "all lumberjack agitators" in the Northwest who were footloose to head "for the Southern timber belt and . . . go to work in the camps to take up the work laid down by the many brave rebels who are in jail." A number of top organizers in the Northwest lumber camps, led by George Speed, moved into Louisiana in August 1912. They visited the men in jail, and then began organizing in Louisiana and Texas, setting up new locals and strengthening the existing ones. Paying tribute to the assistance from their union brothers from the Northwest, the Brotherhood announced: "New applications began to pour in . . . following the visit of organizers from the Northwest lumber camps, and the massacre of Grabow, far from shattering the Brotherhood, as the Association hoped, has but produced a greater solidarity of labor."[49]

There was some hope among the lumber workers that the verdict in the trial would bring peace in the area and that "the terror for the time being will come to an end." But the Association was not one to take its defeat lightly. On the day following the release of the union men, news reports indicated that many of the large mills were already increasing their contingents of armed guards and erecting enclosures about their plants and employees' living quarters. Others were discharging union men and evicting them from company houses. "We paid every man in full and demanded our houses," the head of one mill said frankly. "We are not in sympathy with the Brotherhood of Timber Workers and have no employment for them."[50]

The most vicious attack took place at the American Lumber Co. at Merryville, La. The company employed around 1,300 men, all of them members of the Brotherhood, making Merryville a center of union activity rivaled only by De Ridder. But shortly after the Grabow trial, the company was taken over by the Santa Fe Railway, and one of its first acts was to fire 15 of its union employees who had participated, either as defendants or as witnesses, in the Grabow trial. The Brotherhood immediately appealed to Governor Luther E. Hall of Louisiana to order the American Lumber Co. and the Santa Fe Railroad "to show cause why they should not be punished for contempt" since the men were being "penalized for obeying the court's order." But the Governor ignored the appeal, and the Brotherhood in a circular headed, "Louisiana—A Rival to Despotic Russia," declared bitterly: "The state of Louisiana only indicts and arrests working men and working farmers. Even now it is silent when lumber companies are discharging men practically for obeying the summons of the court to appear as witnesses in the Grabow trial. Yet we are told to 'respect the law,' which, in Louisiana, has degenerated into nothing but the whim of a sawmill manager or a landlord's overseer."

Failing to get relief from the Governor, the Brotherhood petitioned President William Howard Taft to ask of Congress the authority to intervene in Louisiana on the ground that a republican form of government no longer existed in that state. As grounds for the petition, the Brotherhood cited the fact that a "clearing-house for labor" had been established and that "no man today can secure employment in the southern lumber industry unless he takes an anti-union oath and signs an employment application blank, releasing everyone, except himself, from legal liability; it has, through this 'clearing-house,' blacklisted and hounded from state to state more than 1,000 men, thereby causing them, their friends and families untold suffering; it holds thousands of other workers, especially the colored people, under conditions that are nothing short of peonage." The petition went on to cite the fencing in of whole towns, the importation of "an army of gunmen of the lowest type" who were commissioned as deputy sheriffs and who freely attacked union members and sympathizers. It also cited the massacre at Grabow and the trial that followed, and the firing of workers who participated in any way in the trial. But the petition was ignored by President Taft.[51] *

On November 11, nine days after the close of the Grabow trial, 1,300 union men, whites, Indians, and Negroes, went on strike at the American Lumber Co. This was to be the biggest strike in the Brotherhood's history. Unfortunately, it came at a time when, as a result of the Grabow trial, the union's resources were exhausted. Indeed, the leaders of the Brotherhood were convinced that the operators' association, or more specifically, John H. Kirby, had precipitated the strike in order to draw the union into a major conflict which it would find it exceedingly difficult to sustain. They had tried to avoid the strike by appealing to the Governor, but when he refused to intervene, the union men at the American Lumber Co., enraged at the reprisal against their brothers, felt that there was no alternative but to walk out.[52]

Soon after the strike began, the company erected enclosures about the workers' shacks and the mills and began shipping in non-union crews, especially Negroes, from other parts of Louisiana and Texas—men who knew nothing of what had taken place in the mill. The Negro quarters were surrounded with a high barbed-wire fence which was charged with electricity to keep the strikers from talking to the scabs. But the strikers did get to them nevertheless. The railroad track was lined with pickets four miles on each side of the town, and as the trains carrying the scabs slowed down to enter Merryville, leaflets were thrown through the windows or on the platforms, pointing out the cause of the strike, and appealing "to you colored wage workers of Louisiana and Texas to do your duty by the lumberjacks of Merryville, white, Indian and Negro members of Local 218, Brotherhood of Timber Workers, and stay away from the mills."[53]

The appeal brought results. Many Negroes refused to enter the mill, and quite a few joined the strikers, living with the families of Negro strikers. Foreign-born workers and Mexicans who were brought in as scabs also showed their solidarity with the strikers. As the Brotherhood pointed out in a statement that was widely published:

"It is a glorious sight to see, the miracle that has happened here in Dixie. This coming true of the 'impossible'—this union of workers regardless of color, creed or nationality. To hear the Americans saying 'You can starve us, but you cannot whip us'; the Negroes crying, 'You can fence us in, but you cannot make us scab'; the Italians singing the

---

* A similar petition was sent by the Brotherhood to President Woodrow Wilson in May 1913, charging "that a republican form of government no longer exists in the State of Louisiana" and demanding "that you exercise the authority vested in you by the constitution to restore the same." (New York *Call*, May 29, 1913.) Again nothing resulted.

Marseillaise and the Mexicans shouting vivas for the Brotherhood. Never did the Santa Fe Railroad, the Southern Lumber Operators' Association and the American Lumber Company expect to see such complete and defiant solidarity."[54]

In answer to the question: "Peons or Men. Which Shall We Be?" the Negro and white strikers raised the battle cry of the lumberjacks of Dixie: "Don't be a Peon! Be a Man!" "The Southern Lumber Operators' Association started this fight," they asserted as the fifth week of the strike opened, "and we are going to carry it on till we get a man's life in every mill in Dixie." The unity of the Negro and white workers was so firm that one of the I.W.W. organizers in the area cited it as a lesson for the entire working class which "may feel proud of the solidarity displayed by these fighting timbermen and their wives and daughters. . . . For be it known, that the many colored men belonging to Local 218, are standing pat with their white fellow slaves; and also be it known that the writer has realized for years that all the colored workers needed was for the white workers 'to meet them half way,' and they will always respond, eager and anxious to fight to better their conditions." He pointed out that even though not one of the 15 blacklisted workers had been a Negro, "our colored fellow-workers showed their solidarity by walking out with their white comrades," and no amount of terror could induce them to scab.* "They were arrested and jailed on different absurd charges, such as 'unlawfully meeting in the same hall with white men,' but they laughingly lined up and marched to the town bastile, singing the rebel songs they had learned at the daily mass meetings in the Union Hall, and despite threats, after their release, they appeared in greater number the next day to hear the speakers, and sing more songs to fan the flames of discontent."[55]

Solidarity between strikers and farmers was also a feature of the struggle. When one worker told a meeting that even though he had nine children, he was willing to strike "if the Union can guarantee food for my children," the following dramatic episode occurred:

"When he made his plea for food for his family every farmer in the audience rose and confirmed the pledge of the one Negro present, who said, 'We farmers and workers will have to stick together in the Union and win this fight, or all of us, white and colored, are going back to slavery. I have so many pigs in my pen, so many head of cattle in the woods, so many chickens in the yard, and so many bushels of corn and sweet potatoes, and so many gallons of syrup in my barn, and I pledge myself that so long as I have a pound of meat or a peck of corn, no man, white or colored, who goes out in this strike will starve, nor will his

* Negroes used as strikebreakers in this strike were brought in from outside of Merryville, and few knew what a union was. They were kept under "constant surveillance of 'nigger-killing' deputy sheriffs." (McWhiney, *op. cit.,* p. 335.)

children; and I believe all the white farmers here are ready to pledge the same.'"

"They did to a man," notes Covington Hall in his account of the incident.[56]

Failing to break the strike by the usual methods—evictions, importing of scabs (most of whom refused to work when they learned the true state of affairs), attempted bribery of union leaders to induce them to quit the union, and threats of injunction—the company recruited a gang of "strong-arm men." A characteristic "public-spirited" committee, named the "Good Citizens' League," was formed by all the principal businessmen who followed the company's policy. The "strong-arm men" were taken into the League, and were also made deputy sheriffs.

The company, in conjunction with the "Good Citizens' League" and the city authorities, now launched its attack on the union. The deputies rambled around the town, molested Negro strikers, and ransacked their homes. On January 9, Robert Allen, a Negro striker, who had been one of the most faithful pickets, was arrested at a union meeting and taken away to jail. No warrant was served nor any reason given for the arrest. That same evening, Allen was placed in an automobile and deported from Merryville. The following night several other strikers received the same treatment.[57]

The arrests and deportations reached a climax on Sunday, February 16, when mob violence broke loose against the strikers. Five organizers were kidnapped, terribly beaten and deported on that day. One, F. W. Oliver, a Negro, was shot, after being called "a g-d- son of a union nigger." The mob of 300, composed of businessmen, gunmen, and employees of the company had decided to make an "example" of Oliver so as to intimidate all Negro strikers. On February 18, a mob of gunmen and Citizen Leaguers proceeded to the union headquarters, raided the office, seized all books and papers, and carried them into the offices of the American Lumber Co. That same day, the mob deported the acting secretary of the union, tore down the tent in which the strikers' soup kitchen was run, and wrecked it, driving the women who were in attendance from it at the point of guns. On February 19, all remaining union men in Merryville were deported under penalty of death if they returned. Union signs were torn off from shops and houses. Citizens were searched without a warrant, and anyone found with a union leaflet or circular on him was arrested. The town of Merryville was now completely in the hands of the mob as company gunmen, many deputized as sheriffs, armed with rifles, marched through the streets, terrorizing every family.[58]

Into De Ridder, 20 miles away, there hobbled during these days of terror hundreds of union members, bruised and sore from rifle beatings and the long hike. Although threatened with hanging if they returned, a number did hike back to Merryville to man the picket line. But the main job of picketing was carried on by the wives and daughters of the deported strikers. Meanwhile, the union tried to get Governor Hall to do something to halt the reign of terror, pointing out that under the civil rights bill, the town was liable for expulsion of even strangers without due process of law. But he refused to act. The Governor had sent the state militia into Merryville early in the strike at the request of the agents of the company. The troops had been removed after it was discovered that the strikers were quiet and orderly, and replaced by deputy sheriffs, many of whom were on the payroll of the American Lumber Co. and the Santa Fe. The Governor refused to do anything to protect the rights of the organized workers.[59]

The back of the strike had been broken by the four-day wave of mob violence, but officially, it dragged on for four months, as it was not called off by the union until May 1913. Most of the Negro and white strikers were refused reemployment and blacklisted throughout the entire Southern lumber industry.[60]

DECLINE OF B. OF T.W.

On May 19, 1913, the Brotherhood of Timber Workers (now renamed the Southern District of the National Industrial Union of Forest and Lumber Workers, I.W.W.), met with the Western District in convention at Alexandria, La. It announced bravely that it had launched an official journal, *The Lumberjack*, "a red-hot, fearless exponent of revolutionary unionism dealing particularly with the lumber industry," published at Alexandria, La.[61] But the weekly survived less than a year. The truth is that the defeat of the Merryville strike was the beginning of the Brotherhood's decline and the union was in the throes of disintegration. The years of blacklisting, jailings, and mob violence had taken their toll. The union lost its leader, A. L. Emerson, who left the Brotherhood after he received a severe beating in May 1913 at Singer, La. by a group of Santa Fe guards.[62] His position of command was assumed by Jay Smith who continued as head of the organization for the rest of its active existence. On November 6, he published a revised version of the old list of union demands. Most significant of these demands were: (1) An eight-hour day; (2) a minimum wage of $2.50 a day; (3) abolition of the discount system; (4) pay of time and half for overtime and Sunday work; (5) access to camps for union delegates and organizers; (6) a union-administered hospital insurance system and the right of the men to select their own doctors. Smith cautioned all locals against undertaking a strike action on their own initiative to secure these demands. He urged a waiting policy until the entire union would be strong enough to call a general strike of timber workers, and appealed: "Unite, colored and white, for the purpose of making an industrial change."[63]

But in little more than a month Local 275 went on strike and this led to the last organized conflict between the members of the Brotherhood and the lumber operators. Local 275 in the fall·of 1913 had organized the workers in the mill of the Sweet Home Lumber Co. at Sweet Home Front, a small lumber camp a few miles north of Ball, La. After it had completely unionized the company and presented it with the union's list of demands, the employers took steps to break the union and to replace all members of the Brotherhood with non-union workers. The local called the entire crew, about 100 men, out on strike. In the latter part of March 1914, four members of Local 275 were arrested, and jailed at Colfax on the charge of having shot a strikebreaker at Sweet Home Front with intent to kill. The trial, which lasted about a week, ended in the acquittal of all four defendants. The strike itself lasted until the middle of August when the men were forced to capitulate.[64]

Although it continued to exist if only on paper until some time in 1916, the Brotherhood was effectively destroyed by the spring of 1914. By this time, the operators had adopted a number of the union's demands in order to keep the workers from organizing: Abolition of payment in scrip, forced use of company stores and monthly payment in wages, small wage increases and shorter hours.[65]

Spero and Harris view the efforts of the Brotherhood to organize Negro and white workers together as a major cause for its decline since it antagonized public opinion in the South and intensified employer opposition to the union. Another student regards the decision to affiliate with the I.W.W. as a major factor in the union's decline since "it gave the lumber operators a convenient means to misguide public opinion and to evoke that popular hysteria which the name 'I.W.W.' generally produced in the minds of substantial citizens."[66] But these arguments ignore the fact that even before the Brotherhood took so advanced a position on Negro and white unity and before it affiliated with the I.W.W., it was being attacked by the operators as a revolutionary, anarchistic organization. The truth is that the lumber kings wanted no unionism in the industry and had the power, together with the state apparatus which they controlled, to prevent it. "From the standpoint of the laboring man," Bill Haywood declared in July 1912, in a speech in Louisiana, "the lumber trust is more autocratic and vicious in its mandatory rule than any other employer of labor."[67]

To be sure, the Southern Lumber Operators' Association, when it was frightened by the rapid growth of the Brotherhood, indicated a willingness to make a deal with the A.F. of L. But having destroyed the Brotherhood, the Association saw no need to welcome the A.F. of L. Of course, the A.F. of L. actually showed no real interest in replacing the Brotherhood as spokesman for the Negro and white loggers and sawmill workers in the South. But in 1919, when progressive forces were making solid headway in the A.F. of L. and achieving important gains in organizing the mass production industries, the Federation did attempt to carry on organizing work among the Southern timber workers. The A.F. of L. unions met the same bitter opposition, brutal oppression, blacklisting and discrimination that had characterized the existence of the Brotherhood of Timber Workers.[68]

The Brotherhood of Timber Workers left behind a noble tradition of militant struggle and labor solidarity, uniting Negro and white workers as never before in a Southern industry. This tradition, together with the improvements in conditions its struggles wrung from one of the most vicious and oppressive sections of the American capitalist class, remained long after the union disappeared.

CHAPTER II

Migratory Farm Workers:
The Wheatland Affair

SHOULD SMALL FARMERS BE ORGANIZED?

In the initial number of *The Lumberjack* (January 1, 1913), the militant though short-lived organ of the Southern lumber workers, a leading article stressed the need for the I.W.W. to launch an active campaign to organize the Southern tenant farmers who, it predicted, would prove to be "our best fighting material." The article, reprinted in the *Industrial Worker*, provoked wide discussion in I.W.W. circles as to whether or not farmers, small farmers and tenant farmers, should be allowed to join the organization. The editor of the *Industrial Worker,* noting that he had received "an increasing number of letters from farmers . . . who bemoan their inability to join us," suggested that the I.W.W. should begin to think of organizing the small farmers and tenant farmers.[1]

The editorial swamped the office with mail—so much so in fact that the editor claimed he could print only a few of the letters. Some came from farmers, several of whom insisted that the I.W.W. ought to accept all those who were exploited, and that the family farmer, forced to buy and sell in a "trustified" market represented "about the worst exploited class in the whole country." A number of Wobblies agreed that the I.W.W. should attempt to arrive at a working arrangement with some farmers, perhaps the small farmer, at the very least the tenant farmer. Others suggested that the small and tenant farmers ought to organize a union of their own and become attached to the I.W.W. as a sort of fraternal organization, along the lines of the I.W.W. Propaganda Leagues.

But the majority sentiment expressed was opposed to any association between the I.W.W. and farmers. The economic interests of farmers, large, small, and tenant, most Wobblies argued, were not identical with farm laborers, hence to admit them into the I.W.W. would blur the class nature of the organization. Indeed, the I.W.W. might become like the Socialist Party which had lost its revolutionary fervor because it "accepts everyone to membership on a profession of faith, regardless of their economic interests" and aimed a good deal of its propaganda at farmers on the erroneous theory that they were among the most revolutionary forces in America. One letter noted: "The tenant farmer is a producer. . . . Anyone who adds use-value to a commodity is a producer. . . . The I.W.W. is not a producers' union—it is a *wage-workers'* union. . . . If the tenant farmers are revolutionary, carrying an I.W.W. card will not make them more so. . . . Better a few revolutionary tenant farmers without cards than thousands of 'hopeful' capitalist-minded, dues-paying members." One small California group of agricultural workers, while admitting that the small farmers were exploited by the capitalist system, nevertheless opposed membership for them. "Small farmers may treat their slaves in a more familiar or democratic manner than the big employer but any man who has worked on both bonanza farms and for petty farmers not much better off than himself, knows he is better off on the big farm."[2]

The official position of the I.W.W., as it emerged from the discussion, was to organize the farm laborers, many of whom were nomadic workers, line them up against the farmowners for higher wages and better conditions, and build powerful industrial unions of agricultural laborers which would not only function effectively in harvest times, but would "educate and train the farm laborers for their subsequent operation and control of the agricultural industry." Under no circumstance should farmers be allowed to affiliate directly or indirectly with the I.W.W.[3] In due time, the combined operation of monopoly capitalism and of the industrial union of agricultural workers "will tend rapidly to make the small farm-owner's position untenable." "His eligibility to membership in the I.W.W. will not then be open to question."[4]

EARLY EFFORTS TO ORGANIZE AGRICULTURAL WORKERS

While the theoretical discussion was being waged in the I.W.W. press, Wobblies were recruiting agricultural laborers in the main labor markets in California, the Northwest, and the Dakotas. And few workers in the country were in greater need of organization. A study of California labor camps described the average accommodations provided for farm laborers in these terms: "Ranch after ranch was devoid of accommodations given horses. When a Mexican asked for shelter he was told that he had the sky for a roof; when he asked for water he was referred to the ditches to drink from and in which to bathe. He slept on the warm side of a levee, huddled like a dog, often without blankets. If he boarded himself, he cooked in the open, he always drank from ditches, and the water in these ditches is liquid mud." Further comment is not needed, but a few resulting facts may be stated. Communicable diseases were rife in the camps. Dysentery, diarrhea, and typhoid were common.[5]

Sporadic efforts to unionize the migratory workers had been made by the A.F. of L. before the I.W.W. actively entered upon the scene, but little was accomplished. The only real attempt by the A.F. of L. to organize the agricultural laborers took place in California in 1911, and then it "was designed to favor white workers at the expense of the Orientals." The A.F. of L. organizers in Fresno, where the drive took place, openly appealed to the employers that by recognizing the United Laborers of America, they could eliminate the Japanese employed in harvesting grapes and replace them with white workers who "eat American food and spend their money here." But the attempt failed, and the unionizing drive was soon abandoned.[6] As Stuart Jamieson notes in his study, *Labor Unionism in American Agriculture:*

"The organizing drive of the A.F. of L. came to little. . . . The migratory and casual workers were difficult to hold for any length of time in an organization that appealed primarily to a minority of skilled workers. Casual farm laborers whose work was seasonal and poorly paid, could not afford regular union dues even when set by the A.F. of L. at an especially low level, and the dues which could be collected from the workers were not sufficient to maintain the staff of organizers needed to keep a union functioning effectively."[7]

"The harvest is ripe," the I.W.W. press appealed in 1910. "Let us all work with a determination to bring every farm laborer into the fold of the I.W.W." During the next year, the Wobbly press reported organizing activity in Minnesota, Colorado, the Dakotas, Washington, and California, and claims were even advanced of I.W.W. success in getting a wage rate of $3.00 per 12-hour day for groups of wheat harvesters. But in 1912 the number of agricultural workers in the ranks of the I.W.W. was so insignificant that they were not even included in a breakdown of the membership's occupations made by Vincent St. John, general secretary.[8]

The truth is that the organizing tactics of the I.W.W. in agriculture during this period were no more successful than those used by the A.F. of L. Writing from Tulare, Calif., in the midst of an alfalfa harvest, a Wobbly organizer urged greater effort among the migrant farm workers, predicting that "we could practically own California" in five years if the proper organizing methods were employed. Unfortunately, the fellow workers moved about the country too much to be able to conduct continuous organizing drives. Moreover, the strategy of waiting for the agricultural laborer to blow into town during the off season and then recruiting him into the I.W.W. proved to be no more effective in terms of a lasting membership than it did with the lumber workers. While the

I.W.W. claimed thousands of members in California agriculture during 1912, the Wobbly press conceded that many of them had been recruited in lumber camps and railroad construction gangs, where they worked before the harvest season; that a large number moved in and out of the organization and were not formal members in the sense of paying dues to any local organizations, and that it was difficult, under these circumstances, to organize an effective drive to improve working conditions in the agricultural fields.[9]

In order to improve the organizing work among the farm migrants, the Spokane local initiated the "delegate system." These camp delegates were to be given full organizers' responsibilities in handling initiation blanks, dues books and dues stamps, and were to be held responsible to their local unions for the care of this material as well as for all literature furnished them for sale. The delegate system was not immediately successful among the workers in the grain fields, although, as we shall see below, it brought in thousands of new members in 1915–16. But it did result, by the end of 1912, in producing more effective results in California agriculture. Delegates were sent from San Francisco, Oakland, Fresno, and Bakersfield, where the I.W.W. had strong locals, into the fields to organize workers "on the job" and lead them in "job-action strikes." These "job delegates" would speedily become the spokesmen for the farm laborers, and present their grievances to the ranch foremen. Behind them stood a group of militant workers, already members of the I.W.W., and ready for strike action if steps were not taken to remedy the grievance. Once the strike started, a majority of the workers on the ranch would join the walkout and become members of the I.W.W.[10]

THE WHEATLAND STRIKE

The free-speech fights had considerably enhanced the prestige of the I.W.W. among the agricultural workers. Then on August 3, 1913, on the ranch of the Durst Brothers at Wheatland near Marysville, Calif., an event occurred which was to make the I.W.W. the undisputed spokesman for the agricultural workers of the entire Pacific Coast. More than any other event, the so-called "Wheatland Hop-Fields Riot," the largest agricultural strike in California up to this time, brought to public attention the brutal exploitation of these migratory workers and the "intolerable conditions under which these people worked at the time."[11]

As was the usual custom of all large-scale ranchers, Durst Brothers, millionaire hop-growers, advertised in newspapers throughout California, southern Oregon, and Nevada to secure labor for the harvest season of 1913. Although they later admitted that they could provide employment for only about 1,500 workers, and that living arrangements were inadequate for even that number, in order to depress wages they had sent out advertisements offering to employ at least 3,000 pickers. The advertisements invited all who wished to enjoy a picnic and pick hops to assemble at the Durst camp.

About 2,800 workers, men, women and children—Syrians, Mexicans, Hawaiians, Japanese, Lithuanians, Italians, Greeks, Poles, Hindus, Cubans, and Puerto Ricans—speaking among them 27 different languages, answered the colorful advertisements and poured into the Durst camp by every conceivable means of transportation. They found immediately that although Durst advertised that they would receive the "going wage" of $1 per hundred pounds, this was not the case at all. For one thing, the Dursts required cleaner picking than most ranchers, making it harder for the workers to get credit for a hundred pounds. For another, they kept ten cents out of each dollar per hundred pounds to be paid at the end of the harvest. This sum was forfeited if the workers left before the end of the season. Due to the Dursts' method of withholding pay and their requirement for especially clean picking, workers on the ranch would rarely earn more than $1.50 per day for 12 or more hours as compared with $3.00 on other hop ranches.

The Dursts knew what they were doing when they withheld part of the wages until the harvest was over. Conditions in the camp were so abominable that few workers could be expected to complete the season, thus forfeiting a large sum of money to the rancher. The workers paid 75 cents a week for tents rented from Durst. But there were no blankets provided even for the 1,000 women and children, and the workers, sleeping on straw piled on the floors, huddled together for warmth. Many slept in the fields. Food was so sparse and poor in quality that most of the workers were soon suffering from hunger. There were nine toilets for 2,800 people, and they were used indiscriminately by men, women and children so that by the end of the second day, they were covered by filth. There were no toilets in the fields and the workers were forced to use the vines for their toilets. Within three days, the fields, too, were in a filthy condition. No provision was made to take care of the garbage, and the toilets were used as garbage receptacles.

Despite the fact that the temperature rose as high as 122° in the hop fields, no water was available to the pickers. To get a drink, a worker had to walk a mile or a mile and a quarter. And this was piecework! Durst sold acetic acid lemonade to the workers at five cents a glass. In this terrible heat, with drinking water almost inaccessible, the Dursts had eliminated certain practices which heretofore had made the work much easier for the women and children. As one hop-picker explained to a reporter for the Sacramento *Bee:* "A German foreman recently introduced in the fields by Durst conceived the idea of economizing by doing away with the 'high pole men,' the fellows who detach the hop vines from the highest wires for the women and children. Under the new system the women and children have to reach the hops, no matter how high the growth; must carry filled sacks weighing 80 to 100 pounds to the scales, and then load them on the wagon, no matter how high. Heretofore the 'high pole men' operated two to each row and the weighing of the hops and the loading into the wagons was part of their duty."

Three days after the 2,800 workers had arrived, a dangerous epidemic ran through the camp. Many workers were ill with typhoid as well as dysentery.[12]

In this situation, crying for correction, a small group of Wobblies began to take action. There were no more than 100 I.W.W. "card men" among the entire labor force at the Durst ranch, many of them veterans of the Spokane, Fresno, and San Diego free-speech fights. About 30 of these organized a local, and these men, led by Richard Ford, better known as "Blackie" Ford, and Herman D. Suhr, began to urge the workers to take some action to better their conditions. A mass protest meeting was called on Saturday evening, August 2, followed by another one, Sunday morning. Ford and Suhr and a few other Wobblies were elected as a committee to present ten demands to the ranch-owners. These called for an improvement of conditions, including, in particular, drinking water to be furnished in the fields twice a day; reinstatement of the "high pole men"; improved sanitary conditions in the camps, especially separate toilets for men and for women, and a flat rate of $1.25 per hundred of hops picked. The meeting would await the report of the delegation, and if nothing concrete emerged from the conference with the Dursts, there would be a strike.

Ralph Durst promised vaguely to improve camp conditions, but refused the committee's demands to raise wages and to reinstate the "high pole men," claiming that past experience had "proved it unnecessary." When he was given an hour to reconsider his refusal to yield on the question of wages, Durst fired the leaders of the committee, and ordered them to call for their pay and vacate the premises. When the committee replied that unless there was immediate action to improve conditions and adjust wages to the "going scale," there would be a strike, Durst hit Ford, its spokesman, with a heavy glove, and called in the local constable. The latter, gun in hand, ordered Ford off the ranch. A little later, the constable tried to arrest Ford, but when he failed to produce a warrant, the pickers blocked his efforts.

That afternoon, Ford reported to a mass meeting, and urged the hop-pickers to strike if their demands were not met and "knock the blocks off the scissorbills." Taking a sick baby from its mother's arms, he held the infant before the eyes of the 1,500 workers, and cried out: "It's for the life of the kids we're doing this." The meeting up to this point, as the county sheriff later testified, was entirely peaceful; indeed, the hop-pickers, men, women, and children, gathered on and about a dance platform, were singing Wobbly songs between listening to the speakers.

Meanwhile, Durst had telephoned the authorities for help, informing them that the I.W.W. leaders "were causing much feeling by the anarchistic speeches they were making." Two cars, loaded with armed men, led by the constable, the sheriff and the district attorney, arrived from Marysville at the meeting just as the crowd was singing the famous Wobbly song, "Mr. Block." As the sheriff and his deputies went forward to arrest Ford, who was on the platform, the crowd closed in to prevent the arrest. One deputy sheriff, George Voss, fired a shot in the air, and others began threatening to shoot the workers, women as well as men. A general mêlée ensued, during which District Attorney E. T. Manwell, Deputy Sheriff Eugene Reardon, and two unidentified hop-pickers—one Puerto Rican and the other English—were killed. Many hop-pickers were injured. Even the Marysville *Appeal,* the local newspaper, conceded the next day that it was difficult to tell exactly what had actually occurred, for although a number of people saw the shooting, "their stories varied considerably." A reporter for the Sacramento *Union* wrote from Wheatland on August 4: "The firing of a revolver in the air by Sheriff George Voss, when he sought to add emphasis to his command, together with the sudden breaking of a railing throwing a mass of striking hop-pickers upon the sheriff and his posse, cost the four lives that were blotted out on the Durst hop ranch here yesterday afternoon—a tragedy that might have easily been averted and which probably would, had not these circumstances occurred together. This version of the fatal riot . . . is given not only in the statements of several witnesses of both sides, but also by a signed statement given out today by Ralph H. Durst, one of the owners of the Durst ranch, an eye witness."[13]

Following the shooting, the sheriff's posse fled and left the ranch in control of another posse of armed citizens until the state militia arrived the next morning from Sacramento. Actually, only a few of the people on the ranch waited for the militia to arrive. The majority, terrified, had fled in all directions as soon as they could get away. Jack London, who met many of the fleeing hop-pickers in Sonoma County, wrote that they reminded him "of nothing so much as the refugees after the earthquake. When I did get one of them to tell about the affair they all spoke of it as an accident, a spontaneous, unpremeditated explosion."[14]

Eight of the hop-pickers who remained in Wheatland were immediately arrested, and a state-wide manhunt of the others who had dispersed began immediately, the local authorities employing Burns detectives to aid them. Echoing Ralph H. Durst's statement that Wheatland's "Bloody Sunday" was "entirely due to the I.W.W. element," the local press called for the arrest for murder of every Wobbly member who had been on the Durst ranch. It was not necessary to prove their guilt. They were guilty by their very nature. "These venomous human snakes," raged the Marysville *Democrat* on August 4, "always urged armed resistance to constituted authority. . . . These human animals are more dangerous and deadly than the wild animals of the jungles."[15]

Yet two days later, the only time during the entire Wheatland affair, the Marysville *Democrat* put its finger on just who and what was responsible for the tragedy. The lead article in the paper opened: "As the situation begins to clear up it becomes more evident that the real cause of the trouble lies with the hop-growers." I.W.W. agitators, to be sure, had stirred up the hop-pickers, but had the Durst Brothers evinced the slightest interest in the welfare of the men, women and children on their ranch, the "great majority of the pickers" would have had no reason to listen to the Wobbly leaders. It was clear, however, that the workers could "not make a living," that twice as many workers had been induced by the Dursts to come to their ranch as could be supplied with work, that the "hop-pickers could not make any money at the price paid," that there was no water provided even though "people who pick hops all day—and the day means from twelve to fourteen hours—get very dry and need lots of water and they want it fresh too," and that conditions in the field were generally "bad." It was clear, too, that the Dursts felt that "so long as there were so many people on the grounds that these people needed work badly and would be glad to stay at any price and so they did not trouble themselves to pay heed to demands for better conditions. This is something that should be looked after by the state authorities as the conditions prevailing in the fields would soon become unhealthy and be a menace to the public."[16]

THE ROUND-UP

The logical conclusion from all this, of course, was that the Durst Brothers should have been indicted both for murder and for having created a public menace. But, despite the evidence it had presented, the *Democrat* held that "the real cause of the trouble" was the I.W.W. And the coroner's jury, meeting in Marysville on August 7, blamed the I.W.W. for the death of District Attorney Manwell on the ground that he had been shot by a gun "in the hand or hands of rioters incited to murderous anger by I.W.W. leaders and agitators. We therefore strongly recommend that the Yuba County officers do all in their power to capture one Blackie Ford and all other guilty parties." "The jury," announced the Marysville *Democrat*, "based its verdict largely on the testimony of Ralph Durst."[17]

California and neighboring states were plastered with notices that "Blackie" or "Shorty" Ford and H. D. Suhr were "wanted by the Sheriff's office at Marysville, Calif., on charge of murder committed at

Wheatland, Calif., on the 3rd day of August, 1913." At the same time arrests of hop-pickers who had been at Wheatland were carried out. Deputy sheriffs and Burns detectives were given free license to handle prisoners as they saw fit, and many were severely beaten, tortured, and held incommunicado for weeks. Alfred Nelson, arrested and charged with complicity in the Wheatland riot, even though he had been two blocks away from the shooting, was dragged about the state from one county to another, sweated, starved, beaten up, and repeatedly threatened with death by a deputy sheriff and a Burns detective unless he confessed to his share in the crime. At Martinez, Nelson was taken from the jail to a room in a hotel and there the sheriff and private detective beat him with their revolvers and a rubber hose and threatened to shoot him unless he confessed. He refused and was returned to jail more dead than alive. Martinez's District Attorney, A. B. McKenzie, after investigating the incident on Nelson's appeal, called it "one of the biggest outrages that has ever been perpetrated in this State. This man has been dragged from county to county, from one jail to another and then taken out and beaten up."* Nelson was a native of Sweden, and the Swedish consulate at San Francisco, shocked by his story, lodged a protest with the authorities.[18]

Edward Glaser, a 15-year-old boy and a hop-picker on the Durst ranch, was seized by a Burns detective who tried to force him to say that he saw Suhr with a revolver on the day of the riot. When Glaser refused, he was arrested, taken from jail to jail, beaten, placed on a bread-and-water diet, and kept in prison for weeks without examination, with his whereabouts kept secret from his family. When his uncle asked to see the boy, he was refused permission, and only succeeded in securing his release by petitioning for a writ of *habeas corpus*. Chief Justice Beatty, in a scathing comment on the way the boy was treated, declared:

"The thing that strikes me is, it is very irregular practice under our law, in view of the provisions of the Penal Code, to hold a man under a criminal charge for a month without examination, and in the meantime refuse permission to those who wanted to see him in jail. He had been held there for weeks, and the law requires an examination to be held immediately when a man is under arrest. . . . I know something of the ways of detectives in regard to prisoners in the variety of cases that come before this Court, and I know they set a defiance in detaining people without authority and keeping them secluded, and in the meantime subjecting them to the third degree."[19]

---

* McKenzie was so infuriated that he charged the private detective with assault under color of his authority as an officer. The Burns detective was convicted following a jury trial, and given one year in jail and a fine of $1,000. The jury was out less than 20 minutes. (Natchez *Standard*, Nov. 21, 1913, in "Scrapbooks of Clippings on the Wheatland Hop Field Riots, Wheatland, California, 1913–1915," University of California Library, Berkeley. Hereinafter cited as *WS*.)

Neils Nelson, arrested in the round-up, was tortured so frequently to extort a confession that he committed suicide by hanging himself in his cell in Yuba County jail.* Another arrested hop-picker attempted suicide, and still another was committed to the insane asylum.[20]

Herman Suhr was arrested in Arizona, brought to California, secretly spirited from one jail to another to evade his attorney, and kept without adequate food and without sleep under constant torture for an entire week. On the point of collapse, he "confessed" to shooting two members of the sheriff's posse. When he was able to get two hours of sleep, he repudiated the "confession."[21]

ARREST AND TRIAL OF FORD AND SUHR

Finally, out of the men arrested, the two leading I.W.W. organizers on the Durst ranch—Ford and Suhr—and two others—Walter Bagan and William Beck—were charged with being accessories to the murder. All four were to be tried at the same time in the Marysville court house. Austin Lewis, the Socialist lawyer, and R. M. Royce, attorneys for the defendants, immediately asked for a change of venue, charging that a fair and impartial trial could not take place in Marysville: first, because of the bitter prejudice against the I.W.W.; second, because Judge E. P. McDaniel was a personal friend of the slain district attorney, as was the new D.A., Edward B. Stanwood, and third, because the son of the late district attorney was associated with the prosecution. The request was denied. Governor Johnson likewise rejected a plea to appoint another judge at the trial.[22]

On September 25, 1913, delegates to the ninth annual convention of the I.W.W. in Chicago heard of the arrest of Ford and Suhr on murder charges. They immediately voted to hold a meeting to raise a defense fund for the two Wobbly leaders and the other prisoners in Marysville and to "arouse the working class of the country" to rally to their support. In California, the Wheatland Hop Pickers' Defense League was organized, soon to be assisted by the International Workers' Defense League. The two organizations raised funds to help the defense—by February 14, 1914, $5,573.68 had been collected—and sponsored meetings to arouse support for the men in prison, especially among trade unions and Socialist locals. Resolutions of protest were adopted by the San Francisco Labor Council, the Oakland Building Trades Council, the California State Federation of Labor, and a number of labor organizations and Socialist groups in Los Angeles and other cities of California.[23] "Over 100,000 working men have protested," announced the Sacramento *Star*

---

* The I.W.W. denied that Nelson had committed suicide, and charged that he had been beaten to death. (Sacramento *Bee*, Dec. 1, 1913, WS.)

as early as November 11, 1913* A month later, the San Francisco *Chronicle* noted in surprise that the case was "assuming international importance" as protests were pouring in from trade unions in Canada. It added: "Hundreds of letters have been received by the Yuba County officials from labor unions throughout the United States that are interesting themselves in the approaching trial."[24]

The Marysville press was amazed at the protests pouring into the community. (As Austin Lewis correctly noted: "The fact that this 'hobo' has a mind or a soul is surprising to these big farmers. The fact that he has friends is astounding."[25]) "All over the labor world in this continent," wailed the Marysville *Appeal*, "the imprisoned suspects are held as martyrs to the cause of labor." It warned A.F. of L. unions to refrain from further protests lest the public get "the wrong idea" and confuse them with the I.W.W.[26] When the First Congregational Church of Oakland, whose members were "the most prominent leaders in the business circles," denounced the "inhuman and unfair treatment of the men involved in the hopfield riots," and called upon Governor Johnson to investigate, even the Marysville *Democrat* was impressed. "This is the first time in the history of the state," it declared in awe, "that a large and representative congregation has taken up a fight on behalf of organized labor."[27] Although the Marysville Women's Club coldly rejected a plea from the International Workers' Defense League to investigate charges of brutality against the prisoners and the unbearable conditions in the hop fields that were responsible for the Wheatland riot, and to ask the state authorities to use their powers "to see that justice is accorded" to the prisoners, many other women's clubs in California responded favorably to this plea.[28]

"As quietly as though it had been an ordinary civil case, instead of a murder trial attracting nationwide attention among the various classes of people, the trial commenced in the superior court before Judge E. P. McDaniel," announced the Marysville *Democrat* on January 12, 1914. For weeks the Marysville papers had predicted an I.W.W. invasion to kidnap the prisoners as soon as they entered the courtroom, and had advised citizens to arm themselves against the invaders. Hence the emphasis on the quietness of the opening day of the trial. Actually, a Wobbly "invasion" of Marysville did occur, but it was so quiet and dignified that it aroused respect and admiration for the I.W.W. even from quarters heretofore bitterly hostile to the organization.[29]

---

* That same issue of the *Star* carried a detailed exposé of the brutal methods used "to punish penniless workers charged with murder in connection with the recent Wheatland riots." The article caused the Sacramento *Bee,* a more important and influential paper, to assign its crack reporter, C. K. McClathy, Jr. to investigate the matter. His findings, published in the *Bee,* helped arouse support for the prisoners. (Sacramento *Bee,* Jan. 14, 1914, WS.)

On the eve of the trial, 60 I.W.W. members and a handful of sympathizers arrived in the neighborhood of Marysville. When asked why they came, "plodding through storms; on freight trains; singly and in groups; giving up jobs, unmindful of personal advantage," the answer was: "So the hop-pickers on trial here, industrial comrades, shall know that they are not without friends." They pooled their dimes and dollars, and hired an old house on the outskirts of Marysville, the "defense camp" as it was called. They bound themselves not to drink, and fed and took care of themselves. They spent their evenings washing and mending, playing cards, chess, solitaire, reading books borrowed from the Marysville public library, discussing theory and singing Wobbly songs. Every morning at 10, however, and every afternoon at 2, after removing from their coat lapels and jacket fronts the green buttons inscribed, "Justice for the Hoppickers," they marched into court and sat quietly throughout the proceedings. Whenever Austin Lewis needed a witness for the defense, he would hand a slip of paper to one of the I.W.W. men in the courtroom. The latter would then turn it over to a Wobbly outside the courtroom who would board a freight train to search for the desired witness.[30]

The I.W.W. "jungle" in Marysville became almost as well known as the trial itself. Reporters, social workers, clubwomen, and writers attending the trial, made it a practice to visit the "defense camp," and they were invariably impressed by what they saw in contrast to what they had believed or been led to believe about the Wobblies. "Good citizens of Marysville had warned me not to pass this house at night; it harbored dangerous men, ruffians, they said," explained one reporter. Instead, he found young men from the mines, the woods, factories, even from colleges—"clean-cut boys with eager faces and level glances"—sitting, in the light of candles, about a long table of planks, supported by sawbucks, discussing "some tenet in their creed of solidarity and economic justice for the world's toilers," and singing songs which "drifted across to the county jail where the hop-pickers on trial for murder are confined." And on not one breath could he smell "the taint of liquor." "We cannot fight the booze and fight the laboring man's battle," he was informed. "We do not drink. You haven't noticed any of us in the saloons up town. Not one Marysville saloon will be enriched by a nickel from our pockets."[31]

The trial itself was featured by repeated appeals by the Judge and prosecution to stir up feeling against the defendants solely on the ground of membership in the I.W.W. Judge McDaniel referred scornfully to the term "Wobblies," used by Suhr in his telegram for help in the Wheatland strike. "We have a right," he told the jury, "to mistrust any body of people that speaks a language not understood by civilized folks." District Attorney Stanwood produced in court "an ominous looking little red book," and from it read the words of "Mr. Block"—the song the hop-pickers were singing, under Ford's direction, just before the riot. It was introduced as evidence by the prosecution "to show the hatred entertained by the defendant toward anything and everybody above his own standard." "But it was not the song itself that was so suggestive," noted the Marysville *Appeal,* "as it was the flaming red covers of the book wherein it was contained. . . . On the front page in bold type there was a key to the contents of the book, which read: 'Industrial Workers of the World —Songs to Fan the Flames of Discontent.' " The purpose of the prosecution was clear: "It was in keeping with the plan of the state to prove the anarchistic creed and hatred of government of the defendants."[32]

The testimony of the witnesses for the prosecution laid stress on the fact that Ford and Suhr were "agitators." Not even the most hostile witnesses testified that he had seen "Blackie" Ford with a gun. Indeed, the prosecution admitted that he probably had not done the shooting, but that by stirring up the hop-pickers he had "filled the magazines of wrath." Although Suhr's "confession" was not introduced—a fact which proved that it had been obtained by "third-degree methods"[33]—three deputies testified that Suhr had confided to them that he had taken a gun from the hands of an old man while fleeing from the mêlée and had fired twice. This Suhr denied, and the deputies did not claim to have seen Suhr actually shoot the slain men.

Those who had actually seen the shooting—the hop-pickers themselves —testified that the unidentified Puerto Rican had shot Manwell and Reardon with the revolver he had seized from the latter. In his speech to the jury, Austin Lewis, concluding the case for the defense, emphasized: "None of the defendants took part in the shooting. None was seen with a gun in his hands. None advised or abetted violence. Nothing in the evidence points to conspiracy—much less proves it." But, as Inez Haynes Gillmore pointed out in *Harper's Weekly:* "Marysville wanted to teach the I.W.W. to stay away from Yuba County." On January 31, 1914, the jury acquitted Bagan and Beck, two of the four men on trial, and convicted Ford and Suhr of second-degree murder. The theory behind the conviction was that they were guilty of conspiracy to murder Manwell by leading the strike which resulted in the shooting and by urging the workers not to permit the officers to arrest them. Judge McDaniel sentenced Ford and Suhr to life imprisonment in Folsom penitentiary. Bail was denied pending appeal.[34]

A storm of protest swept California and large parts of the nation. Letters and telegrams poured in upon the officials of Yuba County from all sections of the United States, condemning the verdict and the sentence and calling for a new trial. Three weeks after the end of the trial, the Marysville *Appeal* expressed alarm over the fact that "the wrong impression is going out all over the country" that Ford and Suhr were victims of a frameup engineered by the wealthy hop ranchers. The *Appeal* was indignant over "the manner in which organized labor is contributing to the defense fund of the Wheatland hop-field murderers."[35]

Meanwhile, a special committee of the California Commission of Immigration and Housing, headed by Dr. Carleton Parker of the University of California, had been investigating the causes of the strike on the Durst ranch and its tragic aftermath. In his report to Governor Johnson, made public in February 1914, Dr. Parker laid bare the miserable living and sanitary conditions on the Durst ranch, and while he refused to pass judgment on whether Ford and Suhr were guilty, he did point out: "The question of what persons were guilty of the murder seems, in comparison with the deeper social and economic responsibility, of insignificant importance. The posse was, I am convinced, over-nervous and unfortunately over-rigorous." Dr. Parker did not approve of the I.W.W. nor its ideology and tactics—he believed that the "new" methods used by the Wobblies in labor struggles posed a "danger for organized society"—but he felt that the I.W.W. was expressing the legitimate grievances of the migratory workers and was, in the absence of any other interested labor group, not only their recognized spokesman but would continue to grow among these and other unorganized workers if their conditions were not improved. The I.W.W. leaders, Dr. Parker wrote, "have volunteered the beginning of a cure; it is to clean up the housing and wage problem of the seasonal worker."[36]*

The findings of the California Commission on Immigration and Housing were supplemented and given even wider publicity by the investigations made by the U.S. Commission on Industrial Relations. Hearings were held in San Francisco late in August 1914 concerning the Wheatland affair. The evidence taken fully exposed the conditions on the Durst ranch and bore out all the previous charges that suspects arrested in connection with the case were brutally mistreated by private detective agencies in full cooperation with the county authorities.[37] The state and federal investigations aroused new support for the Ford and Suhr defense campaign. But the I.W.W., while welcoming the investigations, reminded the migratory workers that "scientific reports, like sympathetic resolutions, do not fight working-class battles or settle working-class battles or settle working-class wrongs." "Direct action" on the job was the only real way to redress the grievances of the hop workers and free Ford and Suhr.[38]

---

* In a minority report, Paul Scharrenberg of the California State Federation of Labor, who was secretary of the State Commission, took exception to the idea that the I.W.W. had introduced anything "new" to the labor movement, that it was growing in influence, and that it had anything constructive to offer the workers. "I.W.W.ism," he concluded, "is possible only among unorganized workers," a statement with which most I.W.W. leaders would agree, although they would have added that due to the indifference of the A.F. of L., the "unorganized workers" remained unorganized. (Sacramento *Bee,* May 30, 1914, *WS.*)

THE 1914 STRIKE

Immediately after the Marysville trial, the I.W.W. launched a mass campaign, under the direction of Mortimer Downing, its ace publicity man, to protest the "judicial crime" and to demand the release of Ford and Suhr. It was conducted on two levels: (1) Appeal to the higher courts of California and for support in the form of letters and telegrams to Governor Johnson demanding a new trial; (2) general strike action. In the spring of 1914, the I.W.W. press carried the following notice, headed "Hop-Pickers, Attention!":

"Our Demands for Season 1914:

"1. Ford and Suhr to be given a new trial at once and dismissed, or no crops will be picked.

"2. Minimum of $1.25 per hundred pounds. 3. Free tents. 4. Free drinking water in the fields. 5. High pole men. 6. Men to help women and children lift heavy sacks into wagons. 7. One toilet for every fifty men, women and children. 8. Women's toilets to be on opposite side of camps from men's toilets. 9. Abolition of bonus graft.

"Hop-pickers are requested to boycott every field that does not grant all these demands before picking commences.—HOP PICKERS GENERAL STRIKE COMMITTEE."[39]

The A.F. of L. councils in Sacramento, San Diego, and Fresno endorsed the strike call.* August 1, 1914, was set as the day for the general strike for the release of the jailed Wobbly leaders and the redress of grievances of the pickers. Leaflets were distributed through the agricultural region of California appealing: "Do-Not-Pick-Any-Hops And Ford and Suhr Will Be Free. Don't Scab on Men in Jail. Let the Hops Rot." On each leaflet was a picture of the wooden shoe! Hundreds of thousands of stickers carrying similar messages were plastered on trees and fences.[40]

All over California the hop-growers were alarmed over the impending strike, and Yuba County, especially Wheatland, was the center of considerable agitation. The Marysville press called upon the state to protect the hop-growers of the county, and urged the citizens to organize vigilance committees and apply "that stripe of justice which, in the early days of California, cleared the atmosphere through the punctuation of the landscape with dangling bodies suspended from brave oaks or gallant syca-

---

* An interesting aspect of the A.F. of L. support was the decision of the Japanese hop-pickers to withdraw from the campaign, in which they had been active from the start, on the ground "that if they were to cooperate openly, the whites would lose what support they had from the A.F. of L. because of the anti-Oriental sentiment of that organization." Instead, the Japanese workers published advertisements in the Japanese-language papers calling upon their countrymen to stay away from the hop fields until Ford and Suhr were released. (Stuart Jamieson, *Labor Unionism in American Agriculture*, Washington, D.C., 1945, p. 62; *Solidarity*, July 24, 1915.)

mores." The *Appeal* warned the I.W.W. to call off the strike "or take a chance with an outraged and law-abiding public whose feeling is such that it isn't friendly to these nefarious outlaws who live by begging, stealing and pillaging."[41]

The warnings and threats had no effect on the I.W.W. Nor did the news that the ranchers were organizing private armies of gunmen. At every railroad station in the hop section, small bands of I.W.W. members, equipped with bundles of leaflets, were gathered, ready to begin picketing the ranches. On August 1, three big ranches in the Wheatland area were closed down by continuous picket lines. One of the first was the Durst ranch. During the next ten days, the strike spread over the state. On August 10, 75 I.W.W. members left Sacramento for the Durst hop fields at Wheatland to join the picket line. "We have the word of the Transport Loaders of England," they informed reporters, "that they will not unload hops sent to Liverpool from California. But the hops will never get that far. If they ever leave the Durst ranch they will not reach New York by freight trains."[42]

By the end of September, the Hop Pickers Defense Committee estimated that "owing to the action of the I.W.W. the hop crop is 24,000 bales short," and that partly due to the general strike and partly to the boycott put on the hop fields by the I.W.W., "it is a very conservative estimate to state that the hop crop was damaged $500,000. The total hop crop is valued at $5,000,000; so any workers who want to figure can see what a tremendous fine has been leveled upon the hop barons." Although many California newspapers challenged this estimate, they conceded that the strike had brought the Ford and Suhr case to a wide public and had added to the disclosures of the abominable conditions of the migratory workers.[43]

But the strike failed to bring about the freedom of Ford and Suhr. On September 10, 1914, the Appellate Court denied the defendants a new trial, and two months later, the State Supreme Court denied their petition for a rehearing of the cases. So far as the state of California was concerned, the last chance of freeing Ford and Suhr through appeals to the courts was closed. But shortly after the Supreme Court's denial of a new trial, the Marysville *Democrat* reported angrily that "some misguided labor unions, whose members know nothing of the real facts but are actuated solely by misplaced sympathy, have started a petition asking Governor Johnson to pardon these arch conspirators."[44] Meanwhile, the Hop Pickers Defense Committee was gathering new evidence to present to Governor Johnson revealing how Ford and Suhr had been railroaded to prison. The Committee was able to secure statements from most of the jurymen that they had been unduly influenced by the hysteria that swept Marysville during the trial.[45] In February 1915, an application for pardon, covering 78 printed pages, was presented to Governor Johnson. It was backed by "labor unions in most of the large cities of the state," all the central bodies of the A.F. of L. in the San Francisco Bay District and the A.F. of L. Council of Alameda County.[46]

On March 5, 1915, the hearing for a pardon took place before Governor Johnson. Among the speakers were representatives of the A.F. of L. unions, the I.W.W., society and club women, professional men, city, county, and state officials, and migratory workers. Supervisor Andrew J. Gallegher told the Governor: "The only charge that could justly have been lodged against Ford and Suhr was that of being agitators." Paul Scharrenberg, secretary of the California State Federation of Labor, endorsed Gallegher's statement, and said: "Labor, without clique or faction, believes that Ford and Suhr were unjustly convicted and as a unit demands their release." Anita Whitney, social worker and suffragist, speaking for the California Y.W.C.A. and other women's clubs, told the Governor: "A nation is valued by the ability of the people to organize. That is what Ford and Suhr were doing at the time of their arrest—trying to organize their own people for their own protection and interests. They should not be made to pay the penalty for the introduction of an armed force for which they were not responsible."

At the conclusion of the hearing, Governor Johnson announced that he would study the record of the trial "with extreme care," and if he found the men innocent they would be freed; if guilty, "they will remain where they are."[47] The A.F. of L. unions throughout California suspended activities in behalf of the imprisoned men until the Governor handed down his decision. Not so, however, the I.W.W. The Wobblies had little confidence that Ford and Suhr's release could be achieved by relying on Johnson's "impartial" study of the record; they were convinced that so far as I.W.W. members were concerned, thte Governor, hating the organization as he did, was anything but "impartial." "Direct action" on the job was worth more than appeals to Governor Johnson.[48]

THE 1915 CAMPAIGN

In the summer of 1915, while Johnson was considering the pardon appeal, the I.W.W. initiated a new "direct action" campaign. But, unlike 1914, this did not involve a picket line of the hop fields. As Charles L. Lambert, I.W.W. organizer in Sacramento, explained to Ford, the picket line was "far too expensive to keep up, too dangerous on account of the gunmen [hired by the ranchers] and too unwieldy to handle." Instead, the Wobblies would "depend on their own individual action to make every kick count."[49] The 1915 campaign for Ford and Suhr took the form of a boycott against California hop fields, canneries and their products, publicized through hundreds of thousands of stickers distributed in California, the Eastern states, and as far away as Great Britain, Australia, and New Zealand. These stickers, printed in red ink, announced that the boycott was on and would continue until Ford and Suhr were free; called upon hay hands to demand $2 or more and board for 10 hours or less, and urged:

"Don't Forget Ford and Suhr ⌐ the Job. As long as Ford and Suhr Are in Prison. Don't Stick Copper Nails or Tacks in Fruit Trees or Grape Vines. It Hurts Them."

This admonition was distributed only in the State of California. The I.W.W. explained that "being solicitous of the welfare of our masters' property," it was simply trying to prevent "hotheads" from resorting to sabotage to free Ford and Suhr. But it did not expect its warning to be heeded by all. "There are still among the working class those to whom one can tell nothing."[50]

During the summer of 1915, California newspapers were filled with reports of fires in the hop fields—all, according to the papers, set by the Wobblies. ("Trail of Fire Follows Ford and Suhr," read the headline in the San Francisco *Examiner* of September 2.) On June 10, 1915, Lambert wrote to Bill Haywood from Sacramento: "The wheat fields are on fire about fifty miles from here, damage so far is about $250,000." Officially, however, the I.W.W. either labeled the fires "mysterious" or pointed out that "numerous 'fires' occur in all parts of the country at all times—apparently only those taking place in California are being recorded in the newspapers and laid at the door of the I.W.W." But there is no doubt that in fighting the California farmers and fruit-growers, the I.W.W. was using direct action. As Lambert explained: "The fact that we spread stickers all over the country and raise our voices on the street corners in protest will not help matters much, it will take action on the job and vigorous action at that to get these boys out." Yet he conceded that while many Wobblies were ready to plaster the state with stickers, and start strikes, they were not so eager to resort to sabotage. "The whole trouble is that there are not enough men willing to make the cat effective to any extent."[51]

For all the reports of sabotage in the press, there was no concrete evidence of I.W.W. responsibility for any act of destruction. In 1915, the California Commission on Immigration and Housing charged that the I.W.W. was preaching all kinds of lawlessness such as "arson, sabotage, and assassination." But after two years of intense investigation, the Commission had been unable to unearth an indictable offense under California law. During the Chicago trial of 165 leaders and members of the I.W.W. in 1917–18, Horace Thorwalder, the sheriff of Fresno County, Calif., was called to the witness stand. He told of many fires in his county following the trial of Ford and Suhr, but when asked if the members of the I.W.W. set the fires, he replied: "I never said they did. I don't know who did it." The most sensational evidence in the trial were the letters of

C. L. Lambert as secretary of the Ford and Suhr Defense Committee. Lambert's boast, in a letter to St. John, that the reduced hop crop in California was the result of I.W.W. sabotage, was cited by the prosecution as proof that the I.W.W. had both preached and practiced violence and sabotage. In his testimony at the trials, Lambert commented on his letters as follows: "With regard to the suggestion by my counsel that it was just a bluff, with regarding to driving copper nails in trees, and things of that kind, I will say that there has been no case produced here, and there was nothing of it done. I will say that it was just bluff."[52] This testimony is in keeping with Lambert's revelation in the *Industrial Worker* of May 1, 1917, that only "threats of sabotage" had been employed up to that time to free Ford and Suhr.

On September 11, 1915, after seven months of study of the case, Governor Johnson handed down his decision in the pardon appeal. He described the conviction of Ford and Suhr in such a way as to indicate that they were innocent: "By a forced construction of the law of conspiracy of an industrial revolt, those who had committed no wrong themselves were convicted of a heinous offense." He went on to admit that "a survey of the entire case, while not authorizing a pardon, would justify a mitigation of the sentences imposed." Then in a bitter attack upon the I.W.W. campaign to free the two men, he declared: "But so long as in behalf of these men the threats of injury and sabotage continue . . . so long as incendiarism is attempted, I will neither listen to appeals for clemency on behalf of Ford and Suhr, nor in any fashion consider the shortening of their terms of imprisonment." He concluded by advising the A.F. of L. unions in California to dissociate themselves from the defense campaign, warning them that they were only creating publicity for the I.W.W.[53]

The Alameda Building Trades, in its protest to Johnson, one of many sent by labor bodies in California, accused the Governor of a major inconsistency: "You admit that Ford and Suhr could not have had any part in the alleged campaign of violence, and yet they are to be punished as long as 'threats of injury and sabotage continue.'" Tom Mooney, secretary-treasurer of the International Workers' Defense League, warned the A.F. of L. unions not to fall for Johnson's attempt to win their favor, and urged them to unite with the I.W.W. in continuing the campaign to free the imprisoned men. "The workers must act, and they will act until Ford and Suhr walk out free men vindicated to the labor world as their champion in the greatest cause in history."[54]

Mooney's concluding words sent a chill through the California ranch bosses. While they hailed Johnson's refusal to pardon Ford and Suhr, they were far from satisfied in view of the threat of a renewal of the "direct action" campaign to free the prisoners. Durst and his associates had created their own police force of private gunmen and detectives as a protection against the I.W.W. at a cost of over $10,000 a year for individual growers. By the end of 1915, they were complaining that they were still unable to do business effectively, "with such a menace as the I.W.W. hovering over our heads day and night," and that it was "not going to be an easy matter to rid the Coast of these operators." Through the Farmers' Protective League, they appealed to the U.S. government to eliminate the I.W.W. by federal prosecution. The appeal was endorsed by the governors of California, Oregon, Washington, and Utah who, led by Governor Johnson, charged an "interstate conspiracy" by the Wobblies to create "abnormal disorder and incendiarism," and urged the Wilson administration to investigate the I.W.W. immediately for possible federal prosecution.[55]

President Wilson, prodded by his Secretary of the Interior, Franklin K. Lane, authorized the inquiry. The Department of Justice dispatched a special agent to uncover the interstate conspiracy and prosecute the I.W.W. leaders. The federals sought information from the California Commission on Immigration and Housing only to be told by Simon J. Lubin, its chairman: "We are not in a position, we regret to say, to point out to you definitely any violations of federal law." The special agent's own investigation corroborated this statement, for he was unable to discover any violations of the nation's criminal laws. The agent placed the I.W.W. membership in California and Washington at 4,000, "chiefly panhandlers, without homes, mostly foreigners, the discontented and unemployed, who are not anxious to work." (He thus revealed his ignorance of the influence exerted by the I.W.W. among the migratory workers.) Its speakers abused the "existing government," but never talked " 'dynamiting' only 'sabotage.' " The fires in California were "caused by individual members and are not believed to be instigated by the home office. . . . The large number of tramps frequenting California in winter gives good material for speakers to work on."[56]

Following this report, the Justice Department concluded that "it will not be possible to develop violations of the Federal criminal laws by these people, unless by the use of the mails."* Anticipating this finding,

* The reference was to threatening letters sent to Governor Johnson warning that "if you don't turn these men free by Nov. 1st, then after that date you can look for trouble." Some of these letters are unprintable, but since they were anonymous and usually signed "Yours, I.W.W.," it was impossible to track down the senders. (A number of these letters are in the Department of Justice File, 150139/47, NA.) Hatred of Governor Johnson was so intense among I.W.W. members that a private state investigator, who worked inside the I.W.W., reported, after a discussion with three California Wobbly leaders, one of whom was Charles L. Lambert: "The men seemed to be more bitter towards the Governor than any of the private interests of the State." (E. Clemens Horst Investigation. Report of Thomas McGowan covering period from October 30th to November 4th, (1915), Hiram W. Johnsᵣ Papers, University of California, Berkeley.)

Lubin had proposed "that our national laws should be modified."[57] After the United States entered the World War, Lubin's suggestion was adopted and the Espionage and Selective Service laws gave the Department of Justice the power to prosecute and outlaw the I.W.W. which it did not yet possess in 1915![58]

By 1917 the I.W.W. estimated that the convictions of Ford and Suhr had cost the California farmers $10 million a year while the authorities themselves set the total figure at $15 to $20 million since 1914.[59] Meanwhile, Ford and Suhr remained in Folson prison. On April 29, 1916, the *Industrial Worker* published a letter from Ford which contained this advice: "It is better to be locked up for life than to be a miserable Mr. Block, indifferent to your class, but willing, so damned willing to receive the benefits of the struggles of the others. So I say, you workingmen and women, get together now, in *One Big Union,* for better pay, shorter hours, better surroundings."

WHAT THE WHEATLAND AFFAIR ACCOMPLISHED

It was not until 1925 and 1926 that Ford and Suhr were finally released from prison.* While the agitation of the I.W.W. to secure their immediate release was not successful, it had the effect, along with the general publicity given the Wheatland affair, of producing legislation to improve living and housing conditions for migratory workers. In the report of the Commission on Immigration and Housing, which had investigated the Wheatland riot and its aftermath, Dr. Carleton Parker wrote: "The employers must be shown that it is essential that living conditions among their employees be improved not only in the fulfillment of their obligations to society in general, but also to protect and promote their own welfare." Of course, the ranchers, as we have seen, were convinced that their own welfare would be best promoted by their private gunmen and by federal action outlawing the I.W.W. But despite their opposition, legislation was passed to improve conditions for the migratory workers. In appealing to these workers to keep up the campaign to free Ford and Suhr, the Wheatland Defense Committee asked in April 1916: "Have you noticed how much better are the conditions in the hop fields and other agricultural jobs since that eventful Sunday in August 1913? Did you ever stop to think that Ford and Suhr because of their efforts to organize the slaves on Durst's hop fields, are paying their

---

* Ford applied for a parole which was granted on September 11, 1925. But as he left Folsom Prison, he was rearrested for the murder of Deputy Sheriff Eugene Riordan during the Wheatland affair. He was tried in January 1926 and acquitted. Suhr was released on parole on October 26, 1926. (*See Industrial Worker,* Nov. 28, Dec. 19, 1925, Jan. 2, 16, 23, 30, 1926; *Industrial Pioneer,* March, 1926; *The Story of the Ford Case,* American Civil Liberties Union pamphlet, December 1925.)

liberty for the benefits you are now receiving?" Among these benefits, the Committee cited that water was being brought to workers in the fields free of charge and that the State Commission had the police power to force the cleaning up of camps, not only in the hop fields but on construction jobs as well.[60]

Another result of the Wheatland affair was an increase in I.W.W. prestige and membership due to its championing of the most oppressed section of the California working class and the publicity it received during the trial and the struggle to free Ford and Suhr. President Wilson's Federal Commission on Western Labor reported that in March 1914, the I.W.W. in California had 40 locals, five full-time paid organizers, and several hundred part-time organizers ("soapboxers") who supported themselves through the sale of literature. The membership in the state was estimated at 5,000. "Unheard of eight years ago in this State," complained a California labor paper in August 1914, "the number of individuals now professing the lawless doctrines of this lawless association has increased sufficiently to prompt the hop-growers to ask protection from county authorities."[61] Respect for the I.W.W. had grown among A.F. of L. members as a result of the struggle to improve "the unspeakable conditions of migratory workers." Paul Brissenden in his report to the Department of Labor, August 1914, wrote: "The I.W.W. doctrine does not now meet with the indifference among the conservative working men that it did but a few years ago. Said one member: 'Three years ago I had a hard time to get those scissor-bill working stiffs to even listen to the I.W.W. dope. Now it's easy. They come around and ask for it." The "dope" was influencing the A.F. of L. in California. "Though, compared with the A.F. of L.," John D. Barry noted in the San Francisco *Bulletin,* "[the I.W.W.] seems almost insignificant, it is exerting a powerful influence on the older and larger organization. Already its ideas have quickened the A.F. of L. and started it into greater activity."[62]

Due to the industrial depression of 1913–15, which hit the West Coast especially hard and put 75 per cent of I.W.W. members in this region out of work,[63] the gain in the organization's membership did not prove to be permanent. But several things of permanent value did emerge from the Wheatland affair. For one thing, it brought into the forefront the entire problem of migratory labor, and opened in this respect, as Dr. Carleton Parker noted, "a new and momentous labor epoch." Then again, it made the I.W.W. the militant spokesman for the agricultural workers. George Speed, testifying before the Commission on Industrial Relations in 1915, pointed out correctly that "the sentiment of the great number of migratory workers is strongly with the I.W.W."[64] Whatever sentiment existed among these workers for organization during the next decade was to be expressed through the I.W.W.

Before turning to a study of the I.W.W. in the eastern industrial sections of the country, let us summarize what the organization accomplished in the Pacific Northwest, the South, and California during the period 1909 to 1915. It developed and tested its tactics in organizing the workers in the lumber, construction, and agricultural industries, the vast majority of whom were migratory; it discarded those tactics which proved ineffective, and began, towards the end of this period, to develop new and more effective methods which were to bear fruit in the next period. While the results of these years of activity did not loom large in terms of the size, strength, and permanency of the unions established in these industries, they left an imprint which could not be erased. The free-speech fights and strikes associated with the I.W.W.'s drive to better the living conditions of these exploited workers, neglected by the A.F. of L., and the solidarity established during these struggles among men and women of different races, religions, and nationalities did produce some improvements in living conditions and laid the foundation for still others to come later. Surveying the work of the I.W.W. among the Western migratory workers in the period from 1909 to 1915, a writer in *Sunset Magazine* for February 1917 concluded:

"Dismal unsanitary bunkhouses, poor food, unscreened eating houses swarming with flies, bunks enlivened by vermin, grafting foremen and the total lack of opportunity for wholesome recreation were the principal factors which caused men to listen respectfully to I.W.W. orators. In the Western states the menace of the I.W.W. caused farsighted employers to look at their laborers with different eyes, to provide better living conditions. These farsighted employers cleaned and spruced their camps, provided better food, established reading rooms and camp Y.M.C.A. branches, not as charity, but because it paid. And the stubborn, bull-headed employers still befogged by ancient habits of thought were forced by law to make their camps sanitary."

Reprinting this statement, the *Industrial Worker* noted that there were still many improvements to be made in the conditions of these workers. But it added that "if that were the sum total of our several years' work, the organization would still justify its existence."[65]

CHAPTER 12

Organizing the "Home Guard" in Steel

The leading article in the first issue of *Solidarity*, December 18, 1909, opened with the sentence: "The event of prime significance in the industrial history of America during the past year was the McKees Rocks strike." Since this was the year that saw "The Uprising of the 20,000," the general strike of the shirtwaist makers of New York,* the statement was dismissed in some circles as an example of boasting by the I.W.W. which had played an important role at McKees Rocks. But without in the least detracting from the significance of the other great struggle of 1909, the strike against the Pressed Steel Car Co., a U.S. Steel subsidiary, merits the place assigned to it in *Solidarity*. It was the first important demonstration of the fallacy of the widespread dual theory that immigrant workers were too downtrodden to resist oppression and too lacking in ability, experience, and unity to organize effectively along industrial lines.

The McKees Rocks strike was important in still another sense. It marked the first victory against the Steel Trust since the disastrous defeat of 1901. In 1904, 1905, 1906, 1907, and 1908, U.S. Steel had delivered blow after blow against the organized steel workers, reducing the membership of the Amalgamated Association of Iron and Steel Workers from 60,000 in 1901, when the Trust was organized, to 8,000 in 1908, when it shut down the last union plant of the National Tube Co. to starve the strikers out, and transferred the work to its non-union plants. By the beginning of 1909, it appeared that J. P. Morgan had kept his word when he had promised four years before to drive unionism out of every plant in the gigantic Steel Trust. The figures spoke for themselves: 118,000 workers and 8,000 union men in these plants, the latter primarily the skilled workmen.[1]

* This strike will be discussed in Vol. V, *History of the Labor Movement in the United States*.

THE MCKEES ROCKS STRIKE

Then in July 1909, a strike broke out among the unorganized workers at the Pressed Steel Car Co. in McKees Rocks, Pa., located six miles below Pittsburgh, which reversed the tragic trend.

The company fabricated railway and steel railway cars on an assembly line basis, employing mainly foreign-born workers. A deliberate policy of splitting up the working force into various nationality and language groups was followed with the expectation that this would prevent the workers from acting in a unified manner. In 1909, there were 16 different nationalities among the 5,000 workers employed at the plants—Americans, Germans, Hungarians, Ruthenians, Slovaks, Croatians, Poles, Turks, Lithuanians, Russians, Greeks, Italians, Armenians, Roumanians, Bulgarians, and Swiss. Of these the largest nationality group were the Hungarians—the "Hunkies" as they were derisively called—who were regarded by both the corporation owners and the leaders of the craft unions as "the least intelligent, the least independent, the least-Americanized workers, and the most content to be driven like slaves."[2] The Americans were the skilled workers—riveters and axle-turners—and a very small percentage of the workers in the plants. Most of the others were semi-skilled and unskilled, and could be trained on the job within a few days after being hired.

The company heaped abuse after abuse upon the workers, operating on the theory that a working force, composed largely of recent arrivals in the country who were without money or friends and were unable to speak the language of the country or of many of the other workers in the plants, was in a helpless condition.

(1) The men were forced to work in pools. According to this system, men with specific ratings, such as riveters, heaters, or helpers, were lumped into gangs, and their earnings made dependent upon the gross output of the gang. There were 52 pools, ranging from 10 men to 150 each. There was no fixed wage, but at the end of the completion of a car, the company announced the sum that had been set aside for each gang. If, due to the foreman's error or to a mistake of a gang mate, the car was not completed, the whole gang went unpaid. Moreover, 25 to 40 cents per hour to pay the wages of the foreman was taken out of the pool formed for the workmen's wages. Since the company refused to post the rates, the men had no idea of what money was due them at the end of each week.[3] *

Under the gang system, skilled workmen labored from 1 A.M. to 1:30

---

* This was a special hardship for the immigrants. "The foreigners," a Pittsburgh paper pointed out, "labor under men speaking a strange tongue. The 'pooling' and intricate pay system of the strangers are beyond the comprehension of the foreign-born toilers." (Pittsburgh *Leader,* July 15, 1909.)

P.M., six days a week at a rate of less than $1 a day. Affidavits submitted by the workers in the form of pay checks showed earnings for unskilled men of $1 for 3 days' work, $15 for 14 days, and for riveters, $14.50 for 10½ days.[4]

(2) A track or belt system used in the construction of the cars was continually being speeded up. The gang system, of course, drove the workers to the very limit of their endurance, since the fastest worker set the pace for the entire gang.

(3) A vicious system of extortion existed in the plants. Workers had to pay superintendents and foremen to get a job, and then had to pay to keep the job. The fee ranged from $5 to $50 for a job at the plant. Even then there was no certainty of holding the job. Many workers were discharged after a few weeks, and others hired to obtain the entrance fee. Those who were fired could get their jobs back by paying the fee. Thus men were constantly being hired, fired, and rehired simply to extort payments from them. (It was estimated that company officials extorted $10,000 a month from the workers in graft fees.) Evidence existed also of wives and daughters of the workers being forced to submit to the company's agents in the knowledge that unless they did so their relatives would be discharged.[5]

(4) A horrifying disregard of the life and limb of the workers resulted in a tremendously high rate of fatal accidents. One of the plants was known as the "Slaughter House" because so many men were killed there, and another as the "Last Chance," for it was said that "if a man ever worked in this mill he has no chance on earth outside." According to Joseph Armstrong, formerly coroner of Pittsburgh, who had investigated conditions at the plant during his tenure in office, the Pressed Steel Car Co. killed an average of one man a day at its works because of the speed-up system and the failure to protect machinery.[6]

(5) Although the Pennsylvania state law prohibited company stores, the company got around this by forcing the workers to trade at stores it owned through agents. Those who purchased goods elsewhere were discharged. Prices at the company stores were much higher than at privately owned stores in the community.

(6) Under the name of the Fidelity Land Co., the Pressed Steel Car Co. owned 200 double houses for the rental of which it charged exorbitant rents—$12 a month for four rooms with no water or toilet facilities in them. This was deducted from the workers' pay. A Pittsburgh reporter described the shacks:

"I spent several hours in the dwelling places—for they cannot be called homes—of these workingmen yesterday [July 14, 1909]. They are all alike, both without and within. . . . Children and parents live in dingy two-story frame houses which, jammed close together in the long rows which line the yellow clay of the street, cause one to think of abandoned pest houses in a region which has been swept by virulent disease. These houses have four stalls, described by the company officials as rooms. They rent for $12 a month. Workingmen are not forced to live in them, but for some inexplicable reason those who dwell elsewhere do not remain long in the employ of the company."[7]

President Frank N. Hoffstot of the Pressed Steel Car Co. dismissed the notion that $12 for a four-room shack without facilities was exorbitant: "As every family has a number of roomers, the rent does not amount to much." He did not add that, as established by affidavits of the workers, the company forced the occupants of its houses to pay a percentage of the rent received from boarders.[8]

The Pittsburgh *Leader* angrily denounced "the Pressed Steel Car works as the most outrageous of all the industrial plants in the United States. And it is not on record that the most industrially degraded sections of degraded Europe has its like." Reverend Father A. F. Toner, pastor of St. Mary's Roman Catholic Church at McKees Rocks, made an on-the-spot investigation of the plants prior to the outbreak of the strike. In a public statement, he corroborated the *Leader*'s indictment of the company:

"Men are persecuted, robbed and slaughtered, and their wives are abused in a manner worse than death—all to obtain or retain positions that barely keep starvation from the door. It is a pit of infamy where men are driven lower than the degradation of slaves and compelled to sacrifice their wives and daughters to the villainous foremen and little bosses to be allowed to work. It is a disgrace to a civilized country. A man is given less consideration than a dog, and dead bodies are simply kicked aside while the men are literally driven to their death."[9]

To all this President Hoffstot had but one reply: "If a man is dissatisfied, it is his privilege to quit."[10]

The strike at the Pressed Steel Car works thus grew out of long-standing grievances. But it was precipitated by the refusal of the company to restore wage-cuts made during the Panic of 1907. Although the workers had been assured that the reductions would only be temporary, the wages, instead of being restored to pre-Panic levels, were cut still further, and beginning early in 1909 reductions were made almost weekly. Workers who earned $3, $4 and $5 a day in 1907 were actually taking home 50 cents, 75 cents and $1 a day in 1909—or an average of 12 cents an hour—for the same work. When reminded that the company had assured the workers that the reductions after 1907 were only to be temporary, President Hoffstot remarked coldly: "We buy labor in the cheapest market."[11] The "cheapest market," of course, was Castle Garden, where the immigrants landed from Europe.

On Saturday, July 10, 1909, the men were paid as usual. On Monday, there were many complaints by the workers to timekeepers and foremen that they had no way of telling from their pay envelopes what they had actually earned. Many also complained that the long-promised restoration of wages had once again failed to materialize. But 40 riveters at the "Last Chance" plant did more than complain. They refused to work unless they were told their rate of pay and guaranteed the rescinding of the wage-cuts. When they returned on Tuesday, July 13, they were discharged. The same day, 60 men in the erection department were out with the same demands. Men from the shearing and pressing departments followed them. Now 600 men were on strike. In a petition to the company, they presented their demand for the abolition of the pooling system and a return to the 1907 rate. But the management refused an audience to the committee presenting the petition. Word of the company's action spread rapidly to the various departments. On July 14, all the men in the plant, except 500 in the wooden works and a small group of union electricians, stopped work. Five thousand men were out. "Without organization, without knowing how many would strike, without funds, they quit," wrote a reporter.[12]

Although taken by surprise, the company swung immediately into action to break the strike. A call was sent to the local police for assistance and then to Pittsburgh and Cleveland for strikebreakers. The local chief of police hurried to the yards and attempted to arrest a striker, hoping this would frighten the rest of the men. He was set upon by 50 strikers, severely beaten, and driven off. The battle now shifted to the banks of the Ohio River. Learning that the steamer, *Steel Queen,* owned by the company, was attempting to land strikebreakers in the mills by way of the water gates leading from the river, 300 strikers, armed with rifles, rushed to the river bank. As the steamer attempted to land the strikebreakers, the strikers let loose a round of shots. The strikebreakers and the boat crew, armed in advance, returned the fire. After 100 shots were exchanged, without causing any casualty, the *Steel Queen* turned and made for the opposite shore where the scabs were disembarked. The strikers had won "The Battle of the Ohio."[13] Seventeen years before, less only one week, the steel strikers at Homestead had repulsed a similar attempt to land the hated Pinkertons from barges in the famous "Battle of the Monongahela."

What followed on July 15 also brought back memories of Homestead where the Carnegie Iron and Steel Co. had had the help of the local police force, armed deputies, and National Guardsmen to break the strike. By the morning of July 15, 300 deputy sheriffs, armed with rifles, and aided by 200 state constables, including 62 mounted troopers—the hated "Cossacks"—surrounded the plant at McKees Rocks. Rioting started when 50 mounted constables tried to evict families of the strikers from the company houses. (Since the workers had no leases on their dwellings, they could be evicted at any time by the company.) The wives of the strikers, threatening to burn the company houses, fought back, and shouted to their husbands: "Kill the Cossacks! Crush them! Stamp them out! If you are afraid, go home to the children and leave the work to us!" The mounted troops charged the strikers and their wives, riding them down. The workers replied with rocks and missiles whereupon the troopers fired volleys into the crowd, first of blank cartridges and then of real bullets. Nearly 100 strikers and sympathizers were injured. Twenty-five strikers were arrested and charged with inciting a riot. But the evictions were stopped! As one reporter wrote: "The strikers have announced that any attempt to oust their families from their houses in the company row will be fought to a finish and more violence is sure to follow if this is attempted."[14]

Meeting that same evening at historic Indian Mound, a mile from the works, on a ridge of ground overlooking the Ohio River, the strikers elected a committee of ten, representing as many nationalities, to present the workers' grievances to the company officials in Pittsburgh and offer arbitration. The committee came to Pittsburgh on July 16 with signed credentials proving that they were *bona fide* representatives of all the strikers. But President Hoffstot refused even to see them. "There is no strike," he declared. The plant would continue to operate. The strikers then had their photographs taken, 5,000 strong, to prove there was a strike. But this meant nothing to the company. Hoffstot announced that the management not only would not negotiate with the strikers, but that they would never be allowed to work again for the company. "They're dead to us. There are more than enough idle men in Pittsburgh to fill every vacancy."[15]

This arrogant refusal to arbitrate caused the Pittsburgh *Leader* to ask: "Who is this Hoffstot who assumes the power of a Czar?* Does he not know that he is in America, and not in Russia?"[16] The immediate effect of Hoffstot's arrogance was to drive the strikers to organize the struggle more effectively. At first, the American and foreign-born workers operated separately, each through a committee. But when it became clear that the company was girding for a long battle, it was decided to amalgamate both groups. A committee known as the "Big Six," composed of representatives of the American and foreign-born strikers, was elected, headed by C. A. Wise, an American-born worker in the axle department. The "Big Six" was empowered to meet with management for negotiations, when it was ready to sit down with the committee, arrange mass meet-

* Several months later, the newspaper was in a better position to answer the question as to who Hoffstot was. The President of the Pressed Steel Car Co. was indicted for bribery in the Pittsburgh graft cases and was arrested as a fugitive from justice. (New York *Call,* April 8, 21, 1910.)

ings, run the commissary, and preserve order. Since most of the members of the committee were inexperienced in strike strategy, the group sought help from the Socialist Party in Pittsburgh which assigned a party lawyer to help the group obtain a settlement of the strike.[17]

The unity of the skilled and unskilled, American and foreign-born workers thus far was indeed remarkable. Before the strike, the American workers had never mingled with the "Hunkies." But as C. A. Wise put it, after the strike started: "They have got the whole of us to fight now. We are trying to be men among men." To prove this point, 50 union electricians of the Westinghouse Electric Co. doing erecting work at the Pressed Steel Car plant, left their jobs on July 16 in sympathy with the strikers.[18]

Nevertheless, there was an important difference in the attitudes as to how the strike should be conducted between the skilled American and the unskilled, foreign-born workers. Some of the skilled workers, such as the repair men and electricians, were not affected by the pooling system. Yet they had a higher degree of representation on the "Big Six" than those who worked under this system. (C. A. Wise, chairman of the "Big Six" worked in a department which was not affected by the pool.) None of the skilled workers lived in the company shacks, and few of them were required to pay graft to obtain and hold their jobs. Furthermore, the Americans had less to fear from the "Cossacks" than did the foreign-born workers who were held in contempt by the constabulary and were always the special targets in attacks upon the strikers.

For all these reasons, the skilled, American workers and their spokesmen were more eager to seek a compromise settlement early in the strike which would omit many of the most pressing grievances of the foreign-born strikers. They urged the men "to be patient," favored placing stress on appeals to civic bodies to intervene with management in behalf of the strikers, and made no plans for a prolonged struggle.[19]

A group of the foreign-born strikers, however, had had experience in revolutionary and labor struggles in Europe. They realized early in the strike that only a vigorous, militant strategy would achieve victory. This group elected a committee among themselves which became known as the "Unknown Committee," composed of men who had had strike and revolutionary experience in Russia, England, France, Austria, Poland, Germany, Italy, etc.* This committee quietly took charge of the strike, planned the tactics of the battle, and put into operation methods of strike

---

* According to one contemporary reporter, many of the Hungarians on the committee had participated in the great railway strike in Hungary; the Russians had taken part in the "Bloody Sunday" massacre at St. Petersburg; the Swiss had participated in the railroad strike in Switzerland; the Italians in the resistance movement of Italy, and the Germans had been members of the "Metallarbeiter Verein" (Metal Workers' Industrial Union) of Germany. (Louis Duchez, "Victory at McKees Rock," *International Socialist Review,* Vol. X, Oct. 1909, pp. 295–96.)

strategy which, though used often in Europe, were new to the American labor movement and were to influence the conduct of strikes among the foreign-born workers for many years to come. Among the McKees Rocks strikers, the committee was known as the "Kerntruppen," a term derived from the military system of Germany where it referred to "a choice group of fearless and trained men who may be trusted on any occasion."[20]

Although the I.W.W. did not openly enter the strike until mid-August, it was to that organization that the "Unknown Committee," three of whose members were Wobblies when the strike started,* turned early in the struggle for advice and direction. After discussions with I.W.W. leaders in New Castle, Pa., where, as we shall see, the I.W.W. Union No. 208 was playing an active role in the strike of the tin workers against the American Sheet & Tin Plate Co., the "Unknown Committee" established a 24-hour picket system, a signal and watch system to notify the strikers of any attempts to introduce strikebreakers, and committees of pickets to stop every street car entering the town and every ferry boat entering the area, compel the passengers to account for themselves, and take off anyone who might be a strikebreaker. It also organized speakers for each of the 16 nationalities among the strikers to address mass meetings, arranged by nationality, at which emphasis was placed upon the importance of uniting all workers along industrial lines which would eliminate craft, language, and nationality barriers. Thus early in the struggle, due to the work of the "Unknown Committee," the McKees Rocks strikers displayed an intelligence, discipline, and solidarity which amazed veteran reporters who had come to the city expecting to find a confused rabble.[21]

It was certainly not a confused rabble which issued a moving statement of grievances on July 18, in which they presented evidence of pay checks of 90 cents for 45 hours work and others disclosing payments ranging from a low of 2 cents to a high of 10 cents an hour. "Is it possible to live on such wages in a decent manner and provide for a family?" the statement asked, and concluded: "We shall fight to a finish, as it is our right. . . . We beg all the workingmen and citizens to help us in our victory. Help the workers in this struggle, for this is a fight not only for ourselves, but also to save our wives and children from starvation."[22]

The appeal brought an immediate response. The District Council of the Carpenters and Joiners in Pittsburgh announced its support of the strikers, stating: "We sympathize with these poor men and their wives and children, whose condition is worse than that of the African slave." On July 24, 20 wagon-loads of bread and meat, supplied by trade unionists and sympathetic merchants of Pittsburgh, arrived at the strikers' commissary which was now supplying more than 3,000 families with food.[23]

* Louis Duchez lists these men as Ignatz Klavier, Polish; Henigly, Hungarian; and Max Foraker, German. (Duchez, *op. cit.*, p. 295.)

Evidently this growing public support frightened the local authorities, for on July 26, the sheriff prohibited bringing in strikebreakers. Mass picketing continued, however, and the plants remained closed. On July 27, C. A. Wise, speaking for the "Big Six" Committee, announced that by the 30th, the strike would be settled on the basis of the pre-Panic of 1907 scale of wages. For the next three days, the press carried reports under the headlines: "Strikers Optimistic"; "McKees Rocks Workers Feel Sure That Company Will Yield"; "Pressed Steel Car Company Must Give In."[24] But the "Unknown Committee" was under no such illusions. It knew that the company was sending agents to New York and Cleveland to recruit scabs; that the sheriff would yield to company pressure and permit them to be brought into the plants; that the constabulary were still beating up strikers, and that a plan was being hatched to evict all the company's tenants. The optimistic reports of the chairman of the "Big Six" indicated simply that there were elements among the strikers, a group of skilled workers in particular, that favored compromise and surrender.[25]

Events justified the "Unknown Committee's" evaluation of the situation. On August 6, the company denied all reports that it would institute a new wage policy, and secured a writ to evict 47 company tenants. The following day, battles broke out again between the constabulary and the strikers as the former attempted to evict the workers and their families. The next day, another battle was fought to prevent the constabulary from escorting strikebreakers into the plants. On August 11, Steve Howat, a striker, was killed by the constabulary as he tried to halt the scabs. Five thousand were in the funeral procession, with other thousands along the line, and representatives of 16 nationalities paid their respects to the victim of the "Cossacks."[26]

From this point on, the "Unknown Committee" completely replaced the "Big Six" and took over total leadership of the strike. The Committee let the constables know that for "every man you kill of us, we will kill one of you."[27] The soldiers and the police became more careful. On August 15, the strikers prevented another steamer, *P. M. Pfeil,* from landing scabs with a volley of rifle shots from the shore. That same day, the strikers, at a mass meeting, called by the "Unknown Committee," resolved that they would not return to work until the pooling system was abolished and all of their other grievances settled.[28]

On August 15, the I.W.W. openly entered the strike. Huge posters appeared in McKees Rocks on that day, printed in five languages, advertising that W. E. Trautmann, I.W.W. general organizer, would address a mass meeting on Indian Mound on August 17. Eight thousand attended the meeting, most of them strikers and trade unionists from Pittsburgh. Trautmann who came to McKees Rocks with B. H. Williams and Charles McKeever, I.W.W. organizers at New Castle who had been advising the

"Unknown Committee," addressed the meeting in English and German while others translated his address into Polish, Hungarian, Croatian and Roumanian. He called the strike "one of the most important in labor history," and predicted success if it was organized properly. After his speech, the audience was divided into different nationalities, and speakers in the language of each group addressed them on the need to organize into an industrial union.[29]

On August 20, at another mass meeting, the Car Builders' Industrial Union, I.W.W., was organized. Three thousand strikers immediately signed up, and issued a manifesto in which they announced that they would never again "return to work unorganized and unprotected. Inspired by the great principles of class solidarity, they have organized industrially, all of one plant or industry into one powerful union, irrespective of craft, sex, creed, color or nationality."[30]

Up to this time, the McKees Rocks strike had not aroused too much interest outside of Pennsylvania. Then, during the week of August 22, the picture changed, and the labor and Socialist press throughout the country carried headlines like: "Bloody Sunday at McKees Rocks! Worse Than in Russia."[31] On Sunday, August 22, a squad of strikers had boarded a street car entering the strike zone in search of scabs. Harry Exler, a deputy sheriff notorious for strikebreaking, was ordered to leave the car. He denounced the strikers in vile language, pulled a gun and fired at the strikers. In the battle that followed, Exler was killed. A company of state troopers rushed in, and fired at the retreating strikers. In the battle between the strikers and their wives against the "Cossacks," 11 lives were lost: eight strikers and sympathizers, two scabs and one mounted trooper. Forty strikers were wounded and many were arrested, including the wounded, who were dragged off to jail with the blood streaming from their wounds. Others were "manacled to the troopers' horses and dragged through the streets." On the following day, the troopers stormed through "Hunkeyville," the name of the community where most of the company houses were located, and attacked men and women in the shacks, driving them out of their homes. All strike meetings were raided and strikers dispersed.[32]

The two-day holocaust produced an outburst of indignation from the labor and Socialist press. St. Louis *Labor* cried out furiously: "When future historians compare the present labor wars of America with those of Russia, they will conclude that in the murderous treatment of the working class, Uncle Sam and his capitalist plutocracy were far ahead of the Muscovite rulers in Northeastern Europe and Siberia." Even the conservative press was angered by the company announcement that it was not concerned with what measures were used against the strikers since they were no longer its employees. The only discordant note in the outcries of protest was struck by Frank Morrison, A.F. of L. secretary-treasurer, and, in the absence of Gompers in Europe, the leading spokes-man for the Federation. He blamed the trouble at McKees Rocks on the introduction of "ignorant foreign labor, aliens who do not speak our language and understand our institutions," and he went to great pains to let it be known that the strikers were in no way connected with the A.F. of L. which should, therefore, not be held responsible for the violence that featured the strike. Morrison did not add that the A.F. of L. had never concerned itself with the needs and problems of the workers at the Pressed Steel Car Co.[33]

Meanwhile, the strikers had regrouped their ranks and determined to hold meetings despite the troopers' threat to disperse all gatherings. A mass meeting was scheduled at Indian Mound on August 25, and Eugene V. Debs, the Socialist leader, was invited to be the principal speaker. Debs accepted immediately, and then in a public statement announced that he had been threatened with "bodily harm" if he came to McKees Rocks. "I will be there to make an address if I am alive. No Pennsylvania troopers will prevent me from addressing those men." Debs came to McKees Rocks on schedule. He saw the streets dotted with families trudging along with baby buggies in which were the children, bedding and other household furnishings. These refugees were the strikers who had been evicted from the company houses.[34]

Later that day, 10,000 strikers and sympathizers heard Debs speak at Indian Mound. The Socialist leader called the strike "the greatest labor fight in all my history in the labor movement," and predicted that it would not only end in victory for the workers, but serve as "a harbinger of a new spirit among the unorganized, foreign-born workers in the mass-production industries who can see here in McKees Rocks the road on which they must travel—the road of industrial unionism." Referring to Morrison's effort to disassociate the A.F. of L. from the violence of the strikers, he declared that the violence had not been caused by the workers but by the corporations and their minions who were "hired to assassinate workmen."[35]

Debs' prediction of victory for the strikers was justified by the facts. The company was not making the slightest headway in breaking the solidarity of the strikers. The evicted families were as determined to continue the struggle as those who still lived at home; indeed, the children of all the strikers agreed not to attend school until victory. So effective was the picket patrol of the street cars that the Pittsburgh Street Railway Co. suspended service through the strike area. The president explained that "for some time we have been unable to protect our pas-sengers." He could have added that "for some time" transportation workers had refused to haul strikebreakers on the street railway because of sympathy for the strikers.[36]

Strikebreakers were being brought into the plants, but many kept deserting with stories of "peonage" in the mills. Since many of these men were Hungarians who had been recruited at Castle Garden and brought to McKees Rocks without any knowledge of the strike, their stories of being forcibly detained in the plant aroused the interest of the Austro-Hungary vice-consul in Washington. He asked the United States government to investigate, and a federal investigator was sent to McKees Rocks.

Actually, Austro-Hungary representatives had made a study of the strikers' grievances early in the struggle, and had asked the United States Department of Commerce and Labor to investigate. But their request had been ignored. Now, however, the cry of "peonage" was so loud that the complaint of the Austro-Hungary vice-consul could not be buried. The New York *Call* remarked bitterly on August 26, 1909: "The intervention of the Austro-Hungarian representatives to this country in defense of the alien laborers at McKees Rocks—an intervention made necessary by the inactivity and torpor of our government—is calculated to mantle the cheek of every American with the blush of shame."

The effect of the government's investigation was succinctly reflected in headlines in *The New York Times*. On August 26, 1909, before the investigation opened, its headline read: "No Peonage Proof Found at McKees Rocks." On August 28, the headlines were: "Steel Car Plant Called a Prison," and "Strikebreakers Testify They Were Held in Stockade Against Their Will." The investigation, the *Times* concluded, had established that "many of the strikebreakers have been shipped direct to McKees Rocks from immigrant vessels without realizing that they were to assume the part of strikebreakers and without understanding how they were to be paid or what perils they wound encounter." Once inside the stockade, the men had been fed with rotten food, resulting in ptomaine poisoning; they had been refused their wages, and they had been forced to remain in the plants against their will.[37]

The exposure of conditions at the Pressed Steel Car plant horrified even conservative newsaper champions of the corporation. Public sympathy for the strikers mounted daily, and when the Pittsburgh *Leader* printed blank petitions requesting Governor Edward S. Stuart to intervene and mediate the dispute, thousands of citizens in McKees Rocks and Pittsburgh rushed to sign. The *Leader* also raised a fund to help feed the hungry strikers and their families, and by September 1, close to $9,000 had been collected. An additional fund was raised by the New York *Volkszeitung* in response to an appeal from Car Builders' Industrial Union at McKees Rocks to help "more than 5,000 men and the 16,000 women and children, depending upon them, who are starving because they have become aware of the fact that they are human beings and will not allow themselves to be treated worse than cattle."[38]

By the beginning of September there were definite signs that a victory for the strikers was in the offing. One was the fact, openly admitted by newspapers friendly to the company, that the attempt to operate the works with strikebreakers had failed. One of the dramatic episodes in this connection took place on August 28 when 60 strikers, mobilized by the "Unknown Committee," volunteered to hire out to work in the plant in order to persuade the scabs to leave. They succeeded in bringing out 300 scabs, leaving, as the New York *Sun* pointed out in describing the daring feat, "less than 100 workmen within the stockade."[39]

Directly after this stirring victory for the strikers, the company received two major setbacks. For over two weeks, the "Unknown Committee" had been attempting to convince the trainmen of the Pittsburgh, Fort Wayne & Chicago and the Pittsburgh & Lake Erie railroads, members of the Brotherhood of Trainmen, to refuse to haul scabs into the plant. Since these were the only railroads running into McKees Rocks, this action would effectively cut off the supply of scabs. But the history of the Brotherhood promised little hope that this action would be forthcoming; indeed, the union's officials often rejected appeals from other Railway Brotherhoods on strike asking the Trainmen not to work with scabs.[40] It was certainly sensational news, then, when on September 1, a committee representing the Brotherhood of Railway Trainmen visited McKees Rocks and informed the strikers that the trainmen on both roads had voted unanimously not to haul any more strikebreakers for the Pressed Steel Car Co. When the crews of the two company steamers learned of the decision of the trainmen, they also sent a committee to the strikers informing them that they, too, would no longer haul scabs for the company.[41] On top of this came reports that trade unions, the labor press and Socialist deputies in Austria-Hungary were warning prospective immigrants to the United States about the strike at McKees Rocks and urging them to stay away from the area.[42]*

The management was now defeated all along the line, and it acknowledged its defeat by entering into negotiations. A settlement was reached on September 7 which incorporated nearly all of the strikers' demands. The pool system was abolished; there was to be an immediate five per cent increase in wages which was to be followed by an additional ten per cent within 60 days; pay slips were to be made returnable daily; all strikebreakers were to be discharged and all the strikers rehired, including the 600 strikers who had first laid down their tools, and the members of the strike committees; a Saturday half-holiday and abolition of Sunday work except where absolutely necessary; institution of precautions to

---

* In his report to the Fifth Convention of the I.W.W., November 1910, Trautmann praised this outstanding example of international labor solidarity and declared that it had played a vital role in the victory of the strikers. The accounts in the Austrian, Serbian and Bulgarian labor press, he emphasized, "practically stopped immigration," and seriously hampered the company in obtaining strikebreakers. (*Solidarity*, Nov. 19, 1910.)

prevent accidents inside the mills; abolition of graft among the company's agents, with any foreman caught grafting on the men to be discharged; families were to be restored to their homes; rentals at houses owned by the company were to be readjusted as well as prices at the company stores, and the practice of forcing workers to deal at these stores was to be abolished.

At a mass meeting at Indian Mound on the following day, the 5,000 strikers voted to accept the settlement. Thus, on September 8, after 45 days during which over 13 men had been killed and more than 500 injured, the McKees Rocks strike ended officially in a victory for the workers, and the men joyously returned to work. But first they secured two American flags and marched 5,000 strong, with their leaders, through the principal streets of McKees Rocks and "Hunkeytown." They sang victory songs, "almost everything from the 'Marseillaise' to 'Hail, Hail, the Gang's All Here.'" Then they marched to the car plant to resume work.[43]

The strikers had left their jobs unorganized; they returned six and one-half weeks later, members of an industrial union, the Car Builders' Industrial Union, a branch of the I.W.W. In a statement to the workers of America in their hour of triumph, the strikers urged them to "disseminate and spread the message of industrial solidarity among those who will draw their object lessons from the McKees Rocks strike." As for themselves: "With the impulse given us in this struggle, we, the workers in McKees Rocks, will do our share in the sacred duty to bring about the awakening of the hundreds of thousands suffering under such abominable bondage and exploitation."[44]

The McKees Rocks strike was the major instance before the coming of the C.I.O. where unskilled steelworkers won a victory. It was one of the bloodiest battles waged in American labor history and one of the most inspiring examples of working-class solidarity ever witnessed in this country. It was a strike against the most powerful corporation in the United States, U.S. Steel, having behind it the government of Pennsylvania with its powerful, strikebreaking mounted constabulary. It was a strike which saw 5,000 unorganized men of 16 nationalities welded into a solid front which did not waver at any stage of the strike—not a single striker scabbed[45]—and achieved a magnificent victory.

The significance of the strike was immediately apparent and it grew with the passing years. It proved that the foreign-born workers were not, as so many A.F. of L. leaders repeatedly insisted in excusing their failure to organize them, an "ignorant, debased mass of humanity, content to work under conditions no decent human beings would tolerate." It proved that they were militant strikers, so militant, in fact, that even members of the state militia, experienced in breaking strikes, conceded that they had never seen anything to match the determination of the foreign-born strikers of McKees Rocks to achieve victory.[46] It proved that among these workers, especially among the Hungarians, Germans, Russians, Italians and Slavs, were many who had been active in the labor and revolutionary movements of Europe and had much to contribute to the American labor movement. It proved that the revolts of the exploited workers in the mass-production industries need not be blind uprisings, but could be conducted along the most efficient and effective lines by the workers themselves, led by men trained in the class struggle in Europe.

By recognizing these truths early in the strike, by drawing the experienced, militant elements from the ranks of the strikers, and helping them to lead the struggle, by organizing the workers into an industrial union which united skilled and unskilled, American and foreign-born, and bringing them through a magnificent struggle to victory, the I.W.W. played a crucial role at McKees Rocks.* Its prestige soared, and it was further enhanced by Frank Morrison's frantic efforts to disassociate the A.F. of L. from the strike. It was obvious now to the unorganized workers in the basic industries that while the A.F. of L. was not concerned with their needs, the I.W.W. was ready to help them organize, and to offer advice and direction in their struggles.

THE HAMMOND STRIKE

"Make no mistake," the New York *Call* predicted on October 9, 1909, "the spirit of McKees Rocks will grow." W. E. Trautmann carried "the spirit of McKees Rocks" to East Hammond, Ind., early in 1910 and organized Car Builders Union No. 301, I.W.W., among the workers employed at the Standard Steel Car Co., another subsidiary of U.S. Steel, which also operated plants at Butler and New Castle, Pa. Conditions were ripe for the growth of the union. As in McKees Rocks, the workers were mainly foreign-born emigrants from 20 different lands, and here, too, the workers were forced to pay graft to the foremen to obtain and hold their jobs. Wages had been reduced by 40 to 60 per cent since the industrial depression of 1907 so that many of the workers were earning as little as 11 cents an hour. A particular grievance was management's policy of charging rent for the company houses which had not been occupied for many months during the depression, and deducting this from the workers' pay.[47]

On January 14, 1910, a grievance committee representing the I.W.W. union asked the general manager for a conference. They were literally kicked out of the office, and were bluntly told that "if the Hunkeys don't

---

* Perlman and Taft maintain that the role of the I.W.W. was a "subordinate one," but this, as we have seen, is a vast underestimation. (Selig Perlman and Philip Taft, *History of Labor in the United States, 1896–1932*, New York, 1935, p. 265.)

like it here, they can get out." The riveters and heaters quit work as soon as the committee returned with its report, and immediately the I.W.W. raised the slogan, "Make it an industrial-union strike." Circulars, printed in five languages, appealed to all workers to make it "a fight of all for all." The Lake County *Times,* the leading local newspaper, blamed the movement on "the agitators who have come to Hammond from McKees Rocks, Pa.," but was forced to admit regretfully "that the circulars were printed by a local establishment."[48]

On the morning of January 16, the workers of all departments quit, with the exception of the A.F. of L. electricians and machinists who had separate contracts with the management. "But forcible persuasion prompted the machinists and electricians to quit also," the I.W.W. reported. On January 17, the plant was completely shut down and 1,500 strikers were picketing to make sure that no scabs got through.[49]

Refusing to negotiate, the company rushed to operate with strikebreakers. When the police attempted to escort the scabs into the plant, the strikers and their wives fought back and stopped the first invasion. The company retaliated by ordering the strikers and their families evicted from the company houses, and when the workers resisted, many were clubbed and arrested. But those still on picket duty saw to it that the strikebreakers did not get through. "The plant is practically tied up," the Lake County *Times* wailed on January 19. The following day it announced gloomily: "The plant will remain closed for an indefinite period." And it was all due to the fact that "the foreigners, hundreds of them, are as sheep led to the slaughter, in the hands of the strike leaders imported from McKees Rocks."[50]

"All agitators of the I.W.W. and the Socialists ought to be tarred and feathered and run out of town on a rail," the same paper cried. Then peace would be restored to Hammond. The strikers reminded the paper that it was "because of unbearable working conditions that we are on strike. Thousands are facing the hardships of a cruel winter rather than endure any longer the adversities of unscrupulous employers and their agents."[51] They appealed to Harry Slough, State Labor Commissioner, to investigate the conditions under which they were forced to work. Slough came to East Hammond, and conceded that the strikers' grievances were justified. But he refused to lift a finger for them unless they first repudiated the I.W.W. He assured them he would get the company to sign an agreement if they joined the A.F. of L. instead, and declared that the Federation was ready to represent them. He appealed especially to American workers to leave the I.W.W. which he charged with seeking "the overthrow of the government."[52]

At a mass meeting on January 23, the strikers—American and foreign-born—unanimously rejected Slough's proposal on the ground that they could only defend their interests through an industrial union which united all workers irrespective of craft or nationality. Slough angrily left the city, declaring that he could do nothing for the strikers because of their "anarchist tendencies," and that "the movement at the Standard plant is more of a socialistic movement than a strike." That same evening Car Builders' Industrial Union No. 301, I.W.W., issued an appeal "To All Workers of America and Friends" explaining why the strikers had rejected Slough's proposal, and calling for aid in their struggle:

"All workers are out—and the American workers can not and will not be separated from their fellow men—as hard as the company is trying to accomplish this feat, even using government officials to aid them in this sinister endeavor. *United We Stand, Divided We Fall* is our motto.

"Thousands are involved in this struggle, all of different nationalities cemented together against one powerful enemy. Hand in hand, all together as were our brothers at McKees Rocks—and, with your aid, we, too, shall triumph over this union crusher offspring of the Steel Trust."[53]

On January 24, the wives of the strikers organized an anti-scab battalion. The following day, the battalion helped the strikers fight the police to a standstill and prevented the strikebreakers from getting into the plant. "Women Get Into Standard Steel Car Strike Trouble and Commit Mayhem," shrieked the headline in the Lake County *Times*. A reporter for the Indianapolis *Star* wrote:

"Armed with brooms, clubs, stove pokers, rolling pins and other kitchen utensils, hundreds of women from the foreign settlement surrounding the Standard Steel Works today joined the ranks of their striking husbands as pickets and brought about the worst clash that the authorities have yet encountered since the strike began. The women stood with the husbands against the weight of the policemen who tried to open a way to the gate for the workmen going to work. . . .

"A number of the special police were targets for the broomhandles and irons, one of them being severely injured with a long poker that an amazon had measured across his back.

"The women held a mass meeting this afternoon and promised to do picket duty again tomorrow morning."

The Lake County *Times* contained a further detail: "A woman, whom officer Borchet was attempting to subdue, bit him on the arm and had it not been for the heavy coat he wore she would have injured him severely. Emil Helwig, a special officer, deputized to serve during the strike, was struck over the back with a broomstick by a woman and when he tried to subdue her she bit his wrist and the flesh is badly lacerated." One woman was shot by the police and 12 were arrested. But the same evening the company sent the Mayor and a spokesman for the Hammond Businessmen's Association to the union headquarters to ascertain the terms of settlement.[54]

Negotiations between the strikers' committee and Standard Steel's legal representative resulted in an agreement on January 29 under which all strikers were to be rehired without discrimination; wages would be increased ten per cent immediately and another ten per cent within 60 days; no rents would be charged in the future for company houses when not occupied by the workers and all back-rents due for the period of non-occupancy would be canceled; all forms of bribery would be abolished and those found guilty of extorting fees from the workers would be discharged; the workers' grievance committees would be recognized as would any organization selected by the workers to represent them.[55] The terms of the settlement had just been joyously ratified by the strikers when word came that the company had repudiated the agreement accepted by its representative. The strikers' committee hastened to the plant where H. B. Douglas, general manager, informed them that the company would not accept the ten per cent immediate wage increase and under no circumstances would recognize committees of the workers or a union of their own choosing. "You can come as individuals as you want to," Douglas declared, "but I cannot and will not recognize the workers as a body." When the committee refused to accept the modifications in the settlement, Douglas vowed to break the strike with scabs, the militia, and, if necessary, federal troops.[56]

After leaving Douglas, the committee called a mass meeting of the strikers who were addressed in English, Hungarian, Croatian, Lithuanian, German, Italian, Russian, and other languages. Whatever the language used, the theme was the same—no backing down. The 1,500 strikers shouted their agreement, and a proposal was made and carried that each striker swear an oath before a crucifix not to go back to work until the fight was finished. John Herman, secretary of Car Builders Union, No. 301, administered the oath. A reporter described the ceremony:

"The scene, picturesque and pathetic, could not be reproduced by the most modern stage. The lights of the hall were extinguished. A candle stuck into a bottle was placed on the platform. One by one the 1,500 men, representing twenty separate nationalities, came and kissed the ivory image on the cross, kneeling before it. They swore that they would not scab or go back to work until the company grants the terms it had acceded to when its representative met with a committee of the strikers."[57]

The next day, February 1, the pickets resumed their posts. Two days later, the company capitulated, and the original settlement, with one modification, was agreed to by both Douglas and the strikers' committee. Grievance committees would be recognized, but the company refused to recognize the workers' union. However, in all matters relating to wages and other conditions, a committee of three workers' representatives would meet with a committee of three representing management. If the committees failed to agree, the six would select a seventh man to arbitrate and his decision would be final.

Although this was a retreat from the original settlement, the strikers agreed with their committee that it was not a fatal weakness since the three men on the workers' committee would always be union representatives, thus opening the door to full union recognition. Since a number of I.W.W. leaders did not regard the question of union recognition as important, they did not view the absence of it from the settlement as a weakness. "Get the union that will get you the goods and you'll have the recognition," a spokesman for this viewpoint pointed out. The modified settlement was accepted by a vote of the strikers. On February 4, the 1,500 strikers returned to work, and the labor press heralded the news, "Strike at Hammond Car Shops Won."[58]

In an editorial entitled "Lessons of the Strike," the Lake County *Times* concluded: "The public should make it so hot for intruding agitators whose only interest in a strike is the $3 a day they receive from assessments on the strikers, that they will not dare to put in an appearance again."[59] The real lesson, however, was the same as at McKees Rocks—working class solidarity and militancy and effective organization could triumph over a powerful corporation. The lesson was brought home even more sharply because of the defeat of a strike at the Standard Steel Car Company's plant at Butler, Pa., in July 1909. Here there was no union formed among the strikers, and the American workers deserted the foreign-born and returned without any improvement in conditions. The result was that the company was able to smash the strike with the aid of the State Constabulary.[60] But at Hammond, as at McKees Rocks, the I.W.W. built a solid front among the strikers and not a single worker, American or foreign-born, scabbed during the struggle.

THE STRUGGLE AT NEW CASTLE

Meanwhile, at New Castle, Pa., an unusual example of labor solidarity was being exhibited. On June 1, 1909, the American Sheet & Tin Plate Co. announced that it would not renew its contracts with the Amalgamated Association of Iron, Steel and Tin Workers, that all its plants would henceforth be operated as open shops, and that the scale of wages would be reduced by about three per cent. Since the mills of the company in Pennsylvania, Ohio, and Indiana were the only union plants in the United States Steel Corp., the union prepared for a showdown to maintain what was left of unionism in the steel trust. One of its steps was to sign an agreement with the independent manufacturers under which these companies would be allowed to operate in the event of a strike if they signed the scale for 1909–10.

The company and the central office of U.S. Steel in New York refused to even discuss the issue with the union, and on June 30, a strike order was issued. The International Protective Association of Tin Workers to which the finishers in the company's tin mills belonged, voted to join the strike. On July 1, 8,000 sheet and mill workers at all plants of American Sheet and Steel Co., except the one in Cambridge, Ohio, struck.[61]

In preparing for the strike, the steel union issued an appeal to the unorganized in the plants to join the walkout. In all 11 plants, the unorganized responded and the mills were tied up. But in ten of the strike areas, the unorganized, unskilled workers did not have any place to go. The Amalgamated Association had no intention of recruiting them as members, nor did the International Association of Tin Plate Workers. Consequently, the majority of the strikers in these mills were left to drift for themselves with the result that many soon drifted back to work.[62] At New Castle, however, every one of the 3,000 workers employed at the company's mill came out on strike, and, with the exception of about 30 men, remained out for over six months.

The difference between New Castle and the other strike areas was that in New Castle a vigorous I.W.W. local existed even before the outbreak of the strike, that it established cordial relations with the other unions in the mills, and worked closely with them. The 3,000 strikers were members of three separate unions: the National Protective Association of Tin Workers (independent), which organized only the finishers, the Amalgamated Association (A.F. of L.), which organized only the other skilled workers, and Local Union No. 28 (I.W.W.) which organized all unskilled workers kept out of the other two unions. The majority of the workers employed by the company were thus members of the I.W.W. However, the I.W.W. relief station in New Castle was open to all strikers, regardless of which union they belonged to, and, in the absence of strike relief from their own union, the members of the Amalgamated Association and their families depended completely on the I.W.W. relief station for food and clothing.[63]

Six weeks after the strike started, the press reported from New Castle that "all three organizations are working harmoniously together," a fact which was heralded as the "most remarkable news in the American labor scene of the last decade."[64] And when the Amalgamated Association, through President P. J. McCardle, pledged that the union would not enter into separate negotiations with the company and would "maintain a faithful alliance with the Tin Workers Association and the I.W.W. until a conclusion has been reached and an agreement signed with all three organizations," the press commented that "labor history is being made at New Castle."[65] The New York *Call* urged that steps be taken immediately to establish the same type of unity at the other struck mills of the American Sheet & Tin Plate Co., and that this be followed throughout the entire iron and steel industry. Already the open-shop declaration of the Steel Trust in its sheet and tin mills "has produced an effect, the very reverse of which the Trust has anticipated," and if the common front created by "the Tin Workers' Protective Association, the Amalgamated Association, and the I.W.W." were to be pursued elsewhere, the result would be "a complete amalgamation of all the organizations of the iron and steel industry into one powerful organization that shall be capable of meeting the Steel Trust in something like an established fact." In an interview at New Castle, late in the strike, Eugene W. Paginew, president of the American Sheet & Tin Plate Co., conceded the truth of the *Call*'s observation. He acknowledged that "the workmen here have shown more strength and solidarity than the United States Steel Corporation officials in New York have been given to believe they could show," and that if the same unity were established at the other strike centers, the company would be in real trouble.[66]

Unfortunately, the Amalgamated Association did nothing at the other centers to organize the unskilled workers and keep them in the battle. By September, the strike was broken at all mills except the one in New Castle where, in the face of a suit for $200,000 brought by the company against union men, in addition to one of the most sweeping injunctions issued up to this time in American labor struggles and daily arrests of the strikers and their wives when they tried to keep the scabs out of the mill, the struggle dragged on through the winter of 1909–10. As it continued against almost insuperable obstacles, the bitterness of the strikers towards the Amalgamated Association mounted. Resentment against the Amalgamated's leadership for failing to organize the unskilled at the other plants of the company, for not paying strike benefits to its striking members, and for not calling out the independent union mills in support of the workers of the trust-owned mills, was expressed at mass meetings of the strikers. The strikers felt that the independent mills were not truly independent; that they had only signed with the Amalgamated Association to help the Steel Trust break the union and that they would institute the open shop once the strike was lost.* There was only one way to meet this strategy, they argued: "Every union mill man should come out and stay out until the strike was settled."[67]

Despite the solidarity and militancy of the New Castle tin-mill strikers, the battle against American Sheet & Tin Plate appeared by mid-October to be heading for the same outcome as had every previous steel struggle since 1901. But this time something new emerged from the struggle. Coming as it did at the same time as the McKees Rocks strike, the tinworkers' strike provided a contrast between the antiquated methods of the Amalgamated Association's craft unionism and the modern methods of the I.W.W.'s industrial unionism. And the efforts of the strikers at New Castle to adjust the old to the new served to emphasize this dif-

---

* This was an accurate prediction. Once the strike was broken, the independent tin mills broke their contract with the Amalgamated Association and operated as open shops. (New York *Call*, April 15, 1910; *Solidarity*, April 16, 1910.)

ference by pointing up the weakness of the A.A.'s conduct of the strike in other mills. "The lesson of the two strikes—the one at the Pressed Steel Car Company and the other at the American Sheet and Tin Plate Company—is the necessity for one union, an industrial union in the iron and steel industry," declared the official organ of the Wheeling (Pa.) Trades Assembly.[68] This lesson was being taken to heart by the workers in the industry. A reporter for the New York *Call* wrote in mid-October 1909 that even though it appeared that the tin-mill strike was lost, "the spirit of solidarity and organization is growing stronger every day. It is remarkable to note the amount of interest that is being taken in unionism and industrial organization during the last few months in the Pittsburgh district." It had all begun with the victory at McKees Rocks. "Just now remarkable interest is being taken in the I.W.W. . . . The tin-mill workers, also, are taking a deep interest in the I.W.W. In New Castle, the I.W.W., the leaders of which are all Socialist party members, is growing steadily. Already there are more affiliations for membership in the new organization than there are members in both the Amalgamated and Protective Associations."[69]

The accuracy of this report was reflected in the correspondence of the Amalgamated Association's leaders. On October 15, 1909, President McCardle wrote to Frank Morrison:

"There is no question but that more and more of the foreign-born workers in the industry are becoming impressed by the vision held out by the Industrial Unionists, and the victory at McKees Rocks has given them a strong talking point so much so, in fact, that even our members are beginning to pay attention to what they say. While it was necessary for us to cooperate with them at New Castle, we certainly do not look forward to the prospect of their growing influence among the iron, steel and tin workers. I am sure that you share our concern, but it will avail us nothing if we merely bewail these unfortunate developments. We must take steps to prove to the workers that the A.F. of L. is capable of winning the strike against the American Sheet and Tin Plate Company and move on to organize all the non-union mills in the industry, and I cannot sufficiently stress the need for immediate action. The time is past when words alone will solve anything, if indeed they ever did."[70]

A.F. of L. organizers in the steel districts corroborated McCardle's report on the growing influence of the I.W.W. Emmett Flood, an A.F. of L. organizer who had been working with the Amalgamated Association during the steel strike, wrote to Morrison on October 20 that the unorganized men who had joined the battle only to find themselves excluded from the union, were extremely bitter and turning towards the I.W.W. for an answer to their problems. "We must do something speedily in this strike to turn the tide in favor of the Amalgamated Association or the dual unionists will make considerable headway, especially among the

Slavs. The I.W.W.'ers are making much of the victory at McKees Rocks, and we must act to overcome its effects."[71]

The A.F. of L. could no longer remain indifferent to the struggle in the steel industry, and at a conference in Pittsburgh, December 13, 40 national and international unions recommended that "an earnest effort be made to organize all employes in the iron, steel and tin plate industry and subsidiary and co-related industries." But the A.F. of L.'s campaign to organize steel, geared as it was to craft unionism, ended without any concrete results by the second week in February 1910. The strike against American Sheet and Tin Plate Co. dragged on until August 23, 1910, when it ended in miserable failure. Even earlier, a strike against the Bethlehem Steel Co., the largest independent producer and long an open-shop citadel, ended in failure. Nothing was left of the craft organization set up by the A.F. of L. during the strike.[72]*

RESULTS OF ORGANIZING DRIVE IN STEEL

By the late spring of 1910, the I.W.W. was the only functioning labor organization in the steel industry. The Federation's campaign which had opened with the promise that the steel workers would be organized, had closed with the last vestige of A.F. of L. unionism in the steel industry eliminated. In McKees Rocks, however, the I.W.W. Car Builders Industrial Union was still an active, functioning union, a fact attested to by a petition of the businessmen to the Burgess of the city, April 20, 1910, which complained of the continued activities of the "Industrial Workers of the World, which is composed principally of foreign-speaking employes of the Pressed Steel Car Co." These "professional agitators" were continually urging workers of McKees Rocks to organize and strike for improvements.[73]

The I.W.W. had to conduct a continuous struggle against repeated efforts of Pressed Steel Car Co. to rob the workers of the fruits of victory.[74] For it soon became obvious that the future of the union at McKees Rocks was a precarious one as long as the entire steel industry remained unorganized. It was only a matter of time before the giant Steel Trust would concentrate its entire power on eliminating an organization whose

---

* During the Bethlehem strike, a group of the Hungarian and Polish strikers sent a telegram to Joseph Ettor inviting him to come to the strike area and bring along men who could speak to the strikers in Hungarian and Polish. (None of the A.F. of L. organizers could speak these languages.) Ettor came to Bethlehem with Joseph Schmidt, another I.W.W. organizer, and the two, knowing both languages, did what they could to assist the strike. However, the A.F. of L. leaders in the area accused Ettor and Schmidt of "inciting the strikers to violence," and forced them to leave. (John Fairley to Frank Morrison, March 1, 2, 1910; Jacob Tazelaar to Frank Morrison, March 2, 4, 1910, *AFL Corr.; Solidarity*, Feb. 26, March 4, 1910.)

existence in one of its subsidiaries would continue to stimulate the steel workers elsewhere. "We fear," the I.W.W. acknowledged, "that the powerful forces arrayed against us are likely to drive us out of the field already conquered for the labor movement."[75]

Partly to meet this problem, the I.W.W. launched a campaign in July 1910 to organize a national industrial union of all workers in the iron and steel mills of America which would seek to achieve a general eight-hour day for all workers in the industry; a minimum wage scale of $2.50 a day for all unskilled workers; abolition of all piece and pool work; a half day's rest on Saturdays, and abolition of all Sunday work. It was an ambitious project, and in its first call announcing the campaign the I.W.W. conceded that "the organization which has taken up the enormous work of organizing and educating these down-trodden workers is of limited resources."[76] The I.W.W. soon learned, however, that lack of finances was not the only obstacle to the success of the campaign. The drive was seriously hampered from the beginning by the hostility of the local officials in the non-union steel towns, and in most communities I.W.W. speakers could not even rent halls for meetings. Again, the I.W.W. found that it was not easy to quickly overcome the "anti-Hunky" prejudice among the skilled American craftsmen. It was all very well for the I.W.W., in "An Appeal to the Native," to urge the American workers to "center your attention on your master. He brought the 'Hunky' here. . . . By uniting with the foreigner you can compel the master to grant each and all of you better conditions." But the I.W.W. organizers were compelled to admit that the years of anti-foreigner propaganda of the companies could not be entirely overcome with leaflets alone. It would take actual struggle to teach the American workers the necessity of solidarity.[77]

By October 1909, the I.W.W. was forced to concede that "due to the sad experience of the past," the steel workers had grown "completely pessimistic," and had concluded that it was impossible to make headway against the mighty power of the United States Steel Corp. with its firm control over local and state governments in the steel districts. Not even the story of the victory at McKees Rocks could overcome the demoralizing effects of the great defeats suffered in the strikes at American Sheet & Steel and Bethlehem Steel.[78]

All of these factors resulted in the failure of the I.W.W.'s campaign to organize the steel workers.* As the I.W.W. had feared, the McKees

* Another factor was that the I.W.W. was devoting most of its energy and funds in the free-speech fights and organizational work among the lumber and agricultural workers of the West. The Wobblies had, as yet, little to spare for the campaign in steel and for the organization of other industries in the East. This tendency to be engrossed in the struggles in the West was reflected in "A Call From the West to Fellow Workers of the East" which urged: "Come out West.

Rocks union became the main target of attack by the Steel Trust. In the face of repeated attacks by the company and the police, assisted by the full power of United States Steel, the vigorous solidarity among the victorious steel workers weakened. The English-speaking workers were split away from the foreign-born workers. Disillusionment set in and a year after the strike, the Car Builders' Industrial Union at McKees Rocks was little more than a paper organization.[79]*

The experience gained by the I.W.W. in the steel industry in 1909 and 1910 was soon to make itself evident in a different industry. In 1912, the Citizens' Association of Lawrence, Mass., distributed a circular letter giving a history of the textile strike in that city "for the purpose of warning other municipalities against the methods of the labor agitators who were behind the strike movement." The circular letter included the following paragraph:

"That the strike leaders' methods in conducting the Lawrence strike were not new or experimental is shown by the history of the strikes against the Pressed Steel Car Company at McKees Rocks, Pa. A study of the conduct of the strikes at McKees Rocks, Pa. in 1909 and 1910 reveals the similarity in the methods of the I.W.W. leaders there and in Lawrence during the recent strike."[80]

Come by the hundreds of thousands. Start moving from Maine to California. . . . Let us finish them in the West, and then we will all move East." (*Solidarity,* Oct. 7, 1911, March 16, 1912.)

* Car Builders Union No. 301 of Hammond succumbed about the same time.

CHAPTER 13

The Lawrence Strike

STATUS OF I.W.W. IN EAST, 1911

By the spring of 1911, the I.W.W. in the East was in a state of quiescence. The organizing drive in steel had netted few permanent results, and even though the I.W.W. had more locals in Pennsylvania than in any other state in the Union, the majority were inactive.[1]

Late in 1910, the I.W.W. seemed about to make a startling breakthrough in the shoe industry. The field was ripe for militant organization. The vast majority of the shoe workers, most of them unskilled, and a large percentage Italians, were unorganized. In September 1910, Joseph Ettor came to New York from McKees Rocks and spoke in English and Italian at a big meeting of shoe workers. (Several I.W.W. organizers, including Gurley Flynn, joined Ettor.) Soon 150 men were organized in Local 168, I.W.W. In mid-November, the local had grown to 450 members and was supporting strikers in two Brooklyn factories where the workers had come out in sympathy with several Italians who had been fired for union activity.[2] Inspired by these strikes, the workers of the Wickert & Gardiner Co., organized by the A.F. of L.'s Boot and Shoe Workers Union, asked the union to negotiate a raise in their wages. The union replied that the contract ran until April 1911 and contained the usual clause outlawing strikes. Infuriated, the workers, most of whom were Italians, struck anyway and joined the I.W.W. The Boot and Shoe Workers fined each of them $10, suspended them from the union, and began to fill their places with shoemakers from Boston and Philadelphia and unskilled laborers hired from an Italian labor contractor in New York City.[3]

Under the leadership of the I.W.W., the strikers fought back against scabs, police and private detectives. The strike spread to nearby factories until about 3,000 men and women were out by the end of December. The I.W.W. began mass picketing around each of the strike-bound plants, and launched a defense fund to sustain several thousand strikers. The fund received contributions from a number of A.F. of L. unions, especially

Socialist-led Italian unions, and from Italian anarchists and syndicalists. But the money raised hardly met the needs of the strikers. Then in February 1911, Frank Buccafori, a shoe worker in a plant which was not on strike, shot and killed his foreman in self-defense after the latter attacked him with a shoe last. The Wobblies spent much of their energy in his defense.[4]* In the midst of this crisis, the Central Labor Union of Brooklyn ordered A.F. of L. unions to cease sending contributions to the I.W.W. defense fund, warning them that if the Wobblies were successful in their "war of extermination" against the Boot and Shoe Workers, "they will naturally have ambitions to attack another trade, which may be your own."[5] As the strike dragged on, and as the Boot and Shoe Workers, with police assistance, continued to supply strikebreakers, the strikers, many of them on the picket line for the first time, became discouraged. On March 4, 1911, *Solidarity* conceded that the "strikers, poverty-stricken and on the verge of starvation, are being driven back to work." The strike was called off near the end of the month, and the strikers returned without gaining any concessions. In the following months, the I.W.W. local dissolved.[6]

On March 18, 1911, when the Brooklyn shoe strike was reaching its unfortunate end, *Solidarity* lamented that the I.W.W. in the East was asleep, urged all Wobblies to "wake up," and pointed to an industrial city in which effective organizing work could be done. The city was Lawrence, Mass. "Here," declared *Solidarity*, "is the opportunity for the Industrial Workers to make themselves known." Inside of a year this prophecy was to be fulfilled.

CONDITIONS IN LAWRENCE MILLS

Situated in the Merrimack River Valley, about 30 miles north of Boston, Lawrence had the reputation in 1912 of being "the worsted center of the world." The American Woolen Co., Morgan-controlled, the most powerful textile corporation in America, had three of its largest woolen mills in Lawrence: The Washington, employing about 6,500 hands; the Wood, with 5,200 operatives, and the Ayer, with 2,000 hands. The only independent woolen mill was the George E. Kunhardt, employing about 950. There were four large cotton mills in Lawrence: The Arlington, employing about 6,500 workers; the Pacific, the largest producer of cotton-print goods in the world, with 5,200 employees; the Everett, employing 2,000 operatives, and the Atlantic, giving employment to 1,300 hands. There were also two small cotton mills employing together 1,100 people, and a large textile dyeing establishment, owned by the U.S. Worsted Co., employing 600 workers. All told, the 12 mills in Lawrence, when operating at maximum capacity, furnished employment to approximately 32,000 men, women and children.[7]

* Buccafori was sentenced to ten years in Sing Sing. (*Solidarity*, April 1, 8, 1911.)

The mill owners reaped huge profits. Dudley Holman, secretary to Governor Foss of Massachusetts, proved this statistically by disclosing that in 1902 when its capital stock was valued at $49,501,000, the American Woolen Co. paid out $1,400,000 in dividends, while in 1911, when the capital stock was valued at $60,000,000, it paid dividends of $2,800,000. Thus in the course of ten years, dividends increased 100 per cent while the capital invested rose less than 20 per cent. In 1911, the American Woolen Co.'s dividend was seven per cent; that of Pacific Mills, 12 per cent, and that of the Arlington Mill, eight per cent.[8]

The character of the working population in Lawrence's textile mills had undergone a sharp change in the nearly seven decades between the founding of the city in 1845 and the great strike of 1912. Until the 1880's, the native Americans, English, Irish, Scotch, and French-Canadians were the dominant elements in the textile factories, and many of them were skilled workers. With the technological advances of the 1880's, the skilled personnel were rapidly displaced, and, after 1890, the Italians, Greeks, Portuguese, Russians, Poles, Lithuanians, Syrians and Armenians took their places. By 1912, the Italians, Poles, Russians, Syrians, and Lithuanians had definitely replaced the native Americans and Western Europeans as the predominant groups in the textile mills of Lawrence. Within a one-mile radius of the mill district, there lived 25 different nationalities, speaking a half hundred different languages. The largest ethnic group in the city was Italian.[9]

To induce the new immigrants to work in Lawrence, the American Woolen Co. had posted placards in the towns throughout Southern Europe which pictured the textile workers holding bags of gold, displaying bankbooks with substantial bank accounts and standing outside handsome homes which they were said to own.[10] What was the real state of affairs these foreign-born workers found awaiting them in Lawrence? They can be summed up succinctly: Inadequate wages, difficult working conditions, sub-human housing facilities, and a community unsympathetic, when not hostile, to their needs.

The U.S. Bureau of Labor Statistics made a study of the payroll reports from four woolen and three cotton mills in Lawrence for the week ending nearest to November 25, 1911, about seven weeks before the strike. It covered a total of 21,922 workers (excluding overseers and clerks)—or about two-thirds of the total number in the mills on the eve of the strike. The average rate per hour of 16,578 operatives, skilled and unskilled, in the four woolen and worsted mills was 16 cents, and the average amount earned for the week under study was $8.75. The average hourly rate of 5,344 employees, skilled and unskilled, in the cotton mills was 15.8 cents, and the average weekly earnings were $8.78. These wages included premiums or bonuses! But 59.8 per cent of the operatives in the woolen mills earned less than 15 cents an hour, and 14 per cent of those in the cotton mills less than 12 cents. Almost one-third—33.2 per cent —of both woolen and cotton operatives received less than $7.00 per week.[11] The average weekly wages revealed by this study were based on earnings during a week when the mills were running full time. But none of the mills worked full time throughout the year. Although the Bureau declared that it could not ascertain the amount of unemployment, it conceded that there was a serious curtailment of earnings due to lost time, and concluded that the $8.75 and $8.78 average wages for the week under study were far too high for an annual average.[12]

The Lawrence textile industry was a "family industry." But this pleasant-sounding phrase had a deadly meaning for the workers. To keep the family alive, the husbands, wives, and children worked in the mills. On the eve of the strike in 1912, one-half of all children in Lawrence between 14 and 18 were employed in the mills; 44.6 per cent of the textile workers were females, and 11.5 per cent were boys and girls under 18. If the earnings of the wives were pitifully small, those of the children were even less. Testimony before a Congressional Committee revealed that the youngsters, boys and girls, 14 to 16 years of age, earned seven and five dollars or less per week when the mills were running full time![13]

Confronted with such frightening statistics, the mill owners claimed that competition from other New England states and the South forced wages down. But they did not mention that this did not keep profits from soaring, and that they were expanding their operations in Lawrence rather than reducing them because of this competition. Actually, profits had gone up, while wages had gone down in the face of rising living costs. Congressman Victor Berger, Socialist, Wisc., revealed that in 1890, when the industry showed a profit of $164,598,665, labor received 22 per cent of the gross profit. In 1905, when profits had increased to $212,690,048, wages accounted for only 19.5 per cent of the total profits.[14]

According to the U.S. Bureau of Labor, the average work week in the mills of Lawrence was 56 hours. But 21.6 per cent worked more than 56 hours, and none of the workers were paid a rate higher for overtime than the regular scale.[15] While the demand for a shorter work week was not an important issue in the strike—a fact which is hardly surprising since with hourly rates as low as they were, the workers needed a lengthened week not a shorter one to earn enough to stay alive—one of the strikers' demands was for double pay for all overtime.

Chief among the grievances of the Lawrence workers was the premium or bonus system which was introduced by William M. Wood, president of the American Woolen Co., and was used extensively in the mills. Essentially a speed-up plan, designed to obtain the highest possible production from each employee, it provided, in the case of the better-paid occupations such as the weavers, loom-fixers, warp dressers, assistant overseers, slashers, and menders, for a bonus to the worker whose output exceeded some fixed standard. In the other occupations the bonus was paid for regular attendance. Any employee who had not missed more than one day during a four-week period received a premium.

While all the workers were adversely affected by the speed-up, the weavers especially suffered because of the cunning operation of the plan. The loom-fixer's bonus was dependent upon the earnings of the weavers whose looms he tended, and that of the assistant overseer was based upon the earnings of all the loom-fixers under his direction. Consequently the weavers were "driven" to the limit of their endurance to raise the loom-fixers' premiums and so increase the pay envelopes of the assistant overseers. Weavers who did not produce an overseer's pay envelope that met with the latter's satisfaction did not remain in the weaving room for long; nor did a loom-fixer who did not consistently prod the weavers, whose looms he attended, to hasten their pace. The bonus arrangement for regular attendance had its own ingenious device for intensifying the exploitation of the workers. A worker could produce extra cloth for three weeks, and then fall sick during the fourth and last week of the bonus period. He would, of course, lose the premium. It is not difficult to imagine the terrible nervous strain undergone by the worker toward the close of the premium period as he feared that illness might cause his loss of the bonus. Nor was this his only worry. If his machine broke down, a not-uncommon occurrence, his record of regular production would be marred and the premium for the entire four-week period would go by the board.[16]

In its study of the Lawrence mills, the U.S. Bureau of Labor showed that premium money formed an important share of the total average weekly earnings, For the four-week period ending November 1911, two worsted mills had 1,241 weavers on their payrolls. Eighty-six per cent —1,099 weavers—received a premium. These men earned $64,579.27 for the month; $8,367.71 or eight per cent was premium money.[17] In general, the premium system encouraged weavers and other craftsmen to drive themselves mercilessly for the few extra dollars which meant so much to the family.

The cunning of the employers to increase their profits at the expense of the workers was also reflected in the system of fining and grading. In 1891, the Massachusetts legislature had seemingly stopped the vicious practice under which the textile workers had long been fined for any imperfect cloth manufactured, by making it illegal for employers to deduct, directly or indirectly, from wages for such imperfections. The manufacturers then devised a clever scheme called "grading," to get around the law. Two sets of wages were paid—one for producing the very finest cloth, the other for goods of inferior grades. A striker, testifying before the Committee on Rules, pointed out that with the machines operating at a rapid speed and constantly being "speeded up," the cloth was frequently damaged and consequently graded as "inferior." Thus through no fault of their own, the workers saw a good part of their output graded as "inferior," resulting in a reduction of their wages.

Various other complaints were voiced by workers appearing as witnesses at the Congressional hearings. Water supplied by the mills was usually so warm, due to the presence of numerous steampipes in the weaving rooms, that the workers were forced, in order to quench their thirst, to buy cold drinking water at a weekly charge of ten cents. The mills held back a week's wages on all new workers, thus imposing a heavy burden on them during the first two weeks of employment. Workers, especially children, were "docked" one hour's pay for coming five or ten minutes late, and if the lateness was repeated three times, they were fired. And all witnesses expressed severe indignation at the tyrannical attitude of the foremen in their dealings with the workers. The overseers insisted that the women workers sleep with them as a condition of holding on to their jobs, swore at the men, women and children alike, constantly cursed at the foreign-born workers, calling them "ignorant Dagoes and Hunkies," and treating them as if they were "dumb cattle."[18]

We have already seen enough of the conditions in the Lawrence mills to understand how inevitable it was that a mass uprising of the workers should occur. But even this is only part of the story. What sort of life did the earnings of the mill workers permit?

Nearly all the textile workers lived in a slum area so congested that two tenements were erected on the same lot—one in front, the other on the rear of the lot. A dark alley between the front houses provided the only entrance for the rear buildings. The rooms in these wooden firetraps were gloomy and dingy. Toilet facilities were totally inadequate and plumbing defective. One or two toilets, placed in the dark tenement halls, for a four-story tenement, was not unusual. In his report for the year 1912, the Lawrence Inspector of Buildings wrote: "Conditions in the congested districts of the city are drawing close to the danger line in the manner of building construction for tenement purposes. The tendency of some property owners to use every inch of available space has in some quarters developed conditions that are not alone a menace to health, but to life itself." "Each year," he complained, "I have recommended that the City Council take up the matter of revising the Building Ordinances."[19] But each year the proposal was buried by a Council dominated by property owners loath to increase taxes,* and convinced that these conditions were good enough for "Hunkeys, Poles and Wops."

* The mill owners, living in Boston or in New York, paid no personal taxes to the city and the mills paid only a moderate property tax. The shopkeepers and property owners of Lawrence frowned on higher expenditures for services for the foreign-born since this would increase their tax burden.

Rents were so high that most families had to take in boarders and lodgers to meet the payment. They ranged from $2.75 per week for four-room flats to $4.50 for five, and $5.00 for six-room flats. Little wonder that the Health Department found that four or five persons lived in a room. The U.S. Bureau of Labor discovered that the Italians in Lawrence paid more per room than did their countrymen in the crowded sections of Chicago, Cleveland, Buffalo, Milwaukee, and other large cities.[20]

The cost of food, clothing and fuel was equally excessive. Testimony before the Congressional Committee revealed that the price of meat was so high, even of stew-beef (a cheap grade which sold at ten to 14 cents a pound and for which there was a great demand by the foreign workers) that its presence on the table was more or less regarded as an occasion for a holiday. Meat usually appeared only at Sunday dinner; for the rest of the week the diet consisted of black bread, coffee, molasses or lard. Milk, selling at seven cents a quart, was out of reach of most workers' families who depended entirely on condensed or evaporated milk. "Often," one witness reported, "the children went hungry; there were days when only bread and water kept them alive." There being no place for the storage of coal in the crowded tenements, coal and wood had to be purchased in small quantities. This naturally increased the cost tremendously. For a 20-pound bag of coal the common price was ten to 13 cents, that is, from $10 to $13 per ton, an increase of from 40 to 80 per cent over the price of coal if purchased by the ton.[21]

As for clothing, the comment of one student of conditions in Lawrence aptly sums up the situation: "Ironically enough, in the greatest woolen center in the country the producers of suits could not afford the price of $15.00 which was prohibitive to them, nor could the women who made the cotton dresses pay $3.00 for them. Cotton shirts sold at exorbitant prices ranging from $2.00 to $5.00. As for overcoats, they were out of the question, and to the spectator, it appeared that most of the workers of Lawrence wore sweaters beneath the coats of their suits."[22]

Public charitable institutions failed, from lack of funds and indifference to the needs of the workers to supplement inadequate wages. Rev. Clark Carter, Director of Public Health and Charity, who defended child labor as a beneficent influence in the community, declared that the standard of living of the factory workers was all that should be expected.[23]

Lawrence had two dubious honors. One was that it was a leading contender for being the most congested city in the nation, with 33,700 people, one-third of the population, dwelling on less than one-thirteenth of the city's area—the slum area. The other was that the infant mortality death rate in Lawrence was one of the highest of the industrial cities of the nation. Of the 1,524 deaths in Lawrence in 1910, 711 or 46.6 per cent were of children less than six years. Indeed, in that year, the total deaths in Lawrence was exceeded, according to the U.S. Census office, by only six cities out of 40 selected.[24]*

Unquestionably, the foul tenements, poor diet, and lack of warm clothing were important factors in the high number of deaths. Overcrowded housing—in 1912, the Director of Public Safety found only four rooms without beds in them on a whole block of tenements—and an inadequate diet probably accounted for the high tuberculosis rate. In 1912, the Department of Health estimated that 800 people in the city had tuberculosis. The Lawrence Survey, conducted in 1911, fixed the number of deaths due to this disease at 150 yearly.[25]

Here, then, were the conditions which led to the great upheaval of the Lawrence textile workers. (These conditions, one might add, were no better in other New England textile centers.) In explaining why they finally revolted, the strikers stated:

"For years the employers have forced conditions upon us that gradually and surely broke up our homes. They have taken away our wives from the homes, our children have been driven from the playground, stolen out of schools and driven into the mills, where they were strapped to the machines, not only to force the fathers to compete, but that their young lives may be coined into dollars for a parasite class, that their very nerves, their laughter and joy denied, may be woven into cloth. . . .

"We hold that as useful members of society, and as producers we have the right to lead decent and honorable lives; that we are to have homes and not shacks; that we ought to have clean food and not adulterated food at high prices; that we ought to have clothes suited to the weather."[26]

UNIONIZATION BEFORE 1912

In January 1912, before the strike started, the total union membership among the 30,000 mill workers was less than 2,500. Most of them were distributed among ten weak craft locals, each representing an individual skilled trade, and all ten speaking only for the better-paid English-speaking workers—loom-fixers, mule-spinners, warp preparers, wool sorters, cotton and woolen yarn workers, engineers and machinists. Only two unions were affiliated with national organizations: The Mule-spinners' Union, with 200 members, affiliated with the United Textile Workers of America, A.F. of L., and Local 20 of the National Industrial Union of Textile Workers, affiliated with the I.W.W., and composed largely of low-paid

* Of the six, three—Lowell, Fall River, and New Bedford—were also textile centers.

unskilled workers, especially French, Belgians, Italians, and some English-speaking. The rest were independent unions.[27]

The A.F. of L.'s United Textile Workers gave no thought to organizing the vast majority of workers in the mills, the unskilled, foreign-speaking element. A Massachusetts state official quoted the officers of the U.T.W. as saying that, after 1905, it was a waste of effort and money to attempt to organize Lawrence. "The settlement in Lawrence of some 15,000 immigrants during the period 1905 to 1910 added to the population of that city an unassimilated and un-American element so large and so varied in its racial composition as to make it well nigh impossible to disseminate among these people the advantages of unionism."[28] But Local 20, I.W.W., was convinced that these workers could be organized, and that it was only a matter of time before a major upheaval would occur in Lawrence. And in August 1911, a strike did break out among cotton weavers in the Atlantic Mill when management ordered that the workers tend 12 looms at 49 cents per cut instead of seven looms at 79 cents per cut. The speed-up brought the weavers only 35 cents more a week for the increased additional work; in addition, management announced that 40 per cent of the weavers would be discharged. When the management refused to negotiate new wage and work rates, the weavers walked out and joined the I.W.W. They remained on strike for the following four months, a constant reminder to the rest of the city's workers that revolt was possible and that the I.W.W. would assist their cause. Although the strikers were assisted by Elizabeth Gurley Flynn, fresh from leading a victorious strike of women in the textile mills at Minersville, Pa., they were unsuccessful.[29] Nevertheless, during the strike, English, Polish, and Italian branches joined the French and Belgians in the I.W.W. The atmosphere in Lawrence was becoming so charged with the rising tide of workers' resentment that in October 1911, William Yates, national secretary of the National Industrial Union of Textile Workers, wrote to James P. Thompson, general organizer of the I.W.W., urging him to come to Lawrence since "the time is favorable for the spread of our principles and methods." Thompson went to the mill city, and instructed Local 20 to watch the situation carefully, and, if a strike broke out, to immediately send for Joseph J. Ettor, the eastern organizer for the I.W.W.[30]

Although the Wobblies had only a few hundred dues-paying members in Lawrence by January 1912, the workers of the city had at last found a union which spoke for the unskilled foreign-born. This nucleus of an organization helped lay the foundation for the tremendous revolt on January 12, 1912.

OUTBREAK OF THE GREAT STRIKE

The spark that set off the explosion was the cut in wages for all workers following the passage of the 54-hour law for women and for children under 18 years of age.* The law, adopted in 1911 by the state legislature as a result of pressure from organized labor in Massachusetts and over the opposition of the corporations, was to go into effect on January 1, 1912. In 1910, after an act had been passed prohibiting all women and children under 18 years of age from working more than 56 hours a week after January 1, 1910, the Lawrence mills, to forestall an outburst from the workers, had so adjusted the rates that the earnings for the 56-hour week remained the same as for the 58-hour week.[31] But in 1912, the manufacturers, having smashed several organizing attempts and broken a number of smaller strikes, were confident that the workers were incapable of protesting effectively. Hence they refused to pay for the shorter week the wages paid for the 56-hour week.[32] On January 1, 1912, in accordance with the requirements of the new law, the mills posted schedules cutting the weekly work hours to 54 for all workers, men, women, and children, in all departments. However, no notices were posted concerning any change in wage rates. To ascertain the companies' intentions, a committee of the Loom-fixers' Union conferred on January 4 with the mill agents. They reported back that the agents stated definitely that this time, unlike 1910, there would be no increase in hourly rates to compensate for the new shorter week. The loom-fixers then voted to strike unless such a raise was granted.[33]

On January 3, the I.W.W. Local 20 met to discuss the effects of the new law. The members agreed that the silence concerning the new hourly rates meant a wage-cut. A committee of the I.W.W. local was appointed to visit the mills of the American Woolen Co. and learn definitely whether or not rates would be changed. The company's agents refused to give the committee a definite reply. Instead, they were told to communicate with President Wood at the Boston office. A special delivery letter was immediately dispatched, but no reply was ever received. However, Local 20 did not simply sit and wait for a reply. On Wednesday morning, January 10, under the auspices of the Italian branch, a mass meeting was held. About 1,000 Italian workers filled the hall, and by unanimous vote, they decided to call all the Italian workers out on strike on Friday evening, January 12, immediately after they were paid for the week, if their envelopes showed reductions.[34] On Thursday, January 11, 1,750 weavers left their looms in the Everett Cotton Mill. They were joined by 100 spinners of the Arlington Mills, and the nearly 2,000 workers, in a noisy demonstration, vowed to stay out as long as necessary to keep their wages from being reduced.[35]

* "While the new law did not apply to the working hours of men," the organ of the textile industry explained, "the manufacturers saw at once that it would not be economy to manage their force on dissimilar periods of labor, and applied the time to all, reducing the pay according to the previous basis of hour work." (*Textile American*, Feb. 1912, p. 13.)

The protest meetings, local walkouts, and threats of broader strikes were not taken seriously by the mill agents. They went ahead with preparations to announce the wage-cut on payday, January 12, but took no steps to meet any outburst this might produce. The idea that the workers, separated into numerous crafts and 25 nationalities and speaking at least 45 different languages, could stage a general strike was to them a sheer impossibility.[36] The looms had been going for about two hours when the pay envelopes were passed out by the various foremen. When the Italian workers in the Washington Mills opened their envelopes, they found that their weekly earnings had been reduced by an amount equivalent to two hours work, or, as the workers put it, by "four loaves of bread." The wages of these Italian workers, among the lowest in the mill, were already at the starvation point. Suddenly all the years of suffering from lack of food, miserable housing, inadequate clothing, and poor health came to a head. Their hatred of the bosses who grew wealthier as they grew poorer broke out in an outburst of rage against the machines, symbol of the bosses' oppression. From room to room the Italian workers ran, stopping the motors, cutting the belts, tearing the cloth, breaking the electric lights, and dragging the other operatives from the looms. Knives were brandished before workers who refused to walk out, and bobbins, shuttles, and anything else that came at hand, were thrown at other employees who hesitated. Within 30 minutes, work at the mill came to a standstill.

At 11:30 A.M. January 12, 1912, the Battle of Lawrence, one of the epic struggles between labor and capital in American history, was on!

With Washington Mill silenced, the unorganized strikers, waving American and Italian flags and shouting, "Better to starve fighting than to starve working"—soon to become the battle-cry of the general strike— rushed out of the plant and headed for the Wood Mill as the first of several mills they planned to visit to draw out the workers and shut down the operation. At the Wood Mill, the engineer was threatened with death unless he stopped the machines. He shut off all power. The rooms were invaded; motors were smashed; looms were disabled. All the 5,000 employees walked out; some who hesitated were quickly brought to their senses by the invading army of strikers.

The flying squadron, composed of strikers from the Washington and Wood Mills, next stormed the Ayer Mill. They broke through the large iron gate and shut off the power. Then, breaking through the inside doors, they sent bolts of cloth crashing to the floor. All the 2,000 workers inside the mill stopped work. The augmented flying squadron swept to the Duck Mills. Here the police, in response to a riot call, were waiting for the strikers. The strikers attempted to storm the gates, but were driven back by the police under the command of Acting Chief of Police, John J. Sullivan.

Repulsed at the Duck Mills, the crowd of strikers surged over to the

Pacific Mill and then to the Prospect Mill where their attempts to enter were again checked by the police. The strikers then decided to abandon attempts at other mills. In the mass assaults on the five mills, the strikers had destroyed and damaged machinery and other equipment. Some workers had been slightly injured and six Italians arrested for inciting to riot.[37]

By Saturday night, January 13, the strikers estimated that 20,000 textile workers had left their machines. By Monday night, January 15, Lawrence was an armed camp; police and militia guarded the mills through the night.

ORGANIZATION OF THE STRIKE

While the strikers were still assaulting the mills in the late morning and early afternoon of January 12, the Italian branch of Local 20 quickly ran off leaflets calling for a mass meeting that very afternoon. When the strikers left the grounds of the Prospect Mill, they did not go to their homes. Instead, they immediately congregated at the mass meeting. It became immediately clear in the discussion that without organization and leadership, the strike was doomed to failure. Therefore, the strikers enthusiastically greeted the suggestion that Joseph J. ("Smiling Joe") Ettor be summoned to organize and lead the strike. A telegram was sent to Ettor in New York to come immediately to Lawrence. The next morning he arrived in the mill city, accompanied by his friend Arturo Giovannitti, editor of *Il Proletario* and secretary of the Italian Socialist Federation.[38*]

The summons to Ettor was to assume increasing significance as the strike progressed. A spokesman for the mill owners wrote that if Ettor had not reached Lawrence at the outset of the strike, it might have collapsed in a few days from lack of support and leadership. Ettor, he noted, "swayed the undisciplined mob as completely as any general ever controlled his disciplined troops. . . . Immediately upon his arrival he began to organize these thousands of heterogeneous, heretofore unsympathetic, and jealous nationalities into a militant body of class-conscious workers." By the time he arrived in Lawrence, Ettor, though only 27 years of age, had had the unique experience of doing organizing work among the Western miners and migratory workers and the foreign-born workers in the Eastern steel mills and shoe factories. He had absorbed the militant tactics of the I.W.W. in the West and helped introduce them to the East. He had seen how the foreign-born workers at McKees Rocks had produced from their ranks men of revolutionary experience and had introduced tactics in the strike which were drawn from European struggles.

* Giovannitti did not join the I.W.W. until the time of the Lawrence strike. Although Ettor was not a member of the Italian Socialist Federation, he worked closely with the organization.

He was thus able to bring to Lawrence the best of a number of well-tested strike tactics drawn from the West, from the battle at McKees Rocks and from the European labor and revolutionary movements. This, together with the contributions of William D. Haywood, who replaced Ettor after the latter's arrest, produced at Lawrence a new type of labor struggle. Lincoln Steffens characterized it as follows: "This is an I.W.W. strike. It's a western strike in the East; a strike conducted in New England by western miners, who have brought here the methods and the spirit employed by them in Colorado, Idaho, and Nevada, improved, if you please, or corrected by their experience there and by radical philosophies from abroad."[39]

Joe Ettor arrived in Lawrence on Saturday, January 13. With his arrival, the first stage of the strike came to an end. The spontaneous outburst quickly gave way to a methodical strike organization rarely paralleled in the annals of the American labor movement. To unite the different nationalities into one harmonious group, Ettor decided to give each nationality equal representation in all phases of the management of the strike. A general strike committee of 56 members was set up. The 14 largest nationality groups were each allowed to elect four members. (Later, another nationality was given representation thus increasing the membership to 60.) Of the principal nationalities taking part in the strike, only the Germans were not represented on the committee.* The strike committee was the executive board of the strikers, charged with complete authority to conduct the strike, and subject only to the popular mandate of the strikers themselves. All mills on strike and their component parts, all crafts and phases of work, were represented. The committee spoke for all workers. This remarkable organization was started on January 13, the day of Ettor's arrival. Ettor was elected chairman of the committee the following day.[40]

The principle of national equality was also carried out in the sub-committees elected: Relief, finance, publicity, investigation, and organization. The sub-committees consisted of one representative from each nationality. Thus every nationality group had its own organization in the management of the strike, and complete unity was obtained for this working-class machine through the general strike committee. Ettor left nothing to chance. He realized the need of replacing any of the 60 key men who might be unable, either through illness or imprisonment, to continue on the committee. Hence, each member had an alternate trained

* Although some of the Germans, mainly the Socialists, left work early in the strike, the majority did not join the walkout until halfway through the struggle. Donald B. Cole asserts that "the Irish had no representative on the strike committee." (*Immigrant City: Lawrence, Massachusetts, 1845–1921*, Chapel Hill, 1963, p. 184.) He overlooks Ed Reilly, an Irish textile worker, who was an active member of the strike committee. (Mary Heaton Vorse, *A Footnote to Folly*, New York, 1935, p. 9.)

to step into his place at a moment's notice. Precautions were also taken to prevent company agents worming their way into the committee. Ettor asserted that numerous Pinkerton detectives, disguised as strikers, were all known to the committee and were constantly under surveillance.[41]

Every morning the general strike committee met. The roll would be called by nationality groups and the representative of each would rise and report for his people, who held frequent meetings among themselves in halls scattered over the city. Since a good many of the representatives could not speak English, it was necessary to use interpreters to translate the speech. This was done by a corps of trusted interpreters who were constantly available for duty.

A completely democratic system was used for the conduct of the strike. Each nationality group was entitled to one vote on the strike committee, and could, by popular referendum, instruct its representative how to vote. Supreme power to decide all important questions resided in the mass or general meeting of all the strikers—men, women, and children. The mass meetings served two other purposes: To acquaint the strikers with the latest developments, and to give them renewed courage to continue with the struggle. Few bulletins and no newspapers were issued by the strike committee—probably because of the many languages in which they had to be printed and the high rate of illiteracy among the strikers—but the daily mass meetings supplied the personal relationship between leaders and workers which the printed word could not have achieved. Most of the daily meetings were for particular nationality groups. On Saturday and Sunday, monster mass meetings of all the strikers would be held to ratify measures the strike committee had adopted. These were colorful affairs, with speeches and native music and songs of the different nationalities. All, however, joined in singing "The Internationale," the favorite song of the strikers.

The general strike committee was not a committee of the I.W.W. Few of the members had been associated with the I.W.W. when the strike began, and several of them never joined the organization. It had been organized to win the strike and not to represent the I.W.W. However, all members of the committee acknowledged the leadership of the I.W.W., and looked for advice on every issue to the Wobbly leaders who served as "advisory" members on both the general strike committee and the various sub-committees. Besides Ettor and Haywood, the chief I.W.W. leaders who aided in directing the strike were William Yates, possessor of great executive ability; William E. Trautmann, the I.W.W. leader of the McKees Rocks and other strikes; and James P. Thompson, Gildo Mazzerella, and Elizabeth Gurley Flynn, three of the best I.W.W. organizers. All of them strove to develop leaders from among the rank and file of the strikers in order to have the leadership vested, so far as possible, in the workers themselves. And from the strikers came remarkable examples of leadership and administrative ability, like John Adamson, a skilled textile operative and head of Lawrence Local 20 of the I.W.W., Samuel Lipson, a Jewish weaver, and Anne Welzenbach, an American-born, skilled worker.[42]

The I.W.W., through its leaders, organized the strikers into an efficient, fighting machine, a remarkable army of struggle, gave them direction, and planned with the committees every move in the strike. It is not surprising, then, that the strikers turned enthusiastically to join the I.W.W. No recruiting drive was necessary. They rushed to join the only union that had ever welcomed and helped these exploited foreign-born workers to gain a better livelihood. Entire nationality groups would vote at mass meetings to join Local 20. Seven thousand had joined by the end of February, and before the strike was over, more than 10,000 Lawrence textile workers were members of the I.W.W. More than 90 per cent of these new members were Italians, Poles, Lithuanians, Syrians, French, Belgians, and Portuguese. Most of them had been in the United States less than three years, and nearly all were "unorganizable" immigrants from Southern and Eastern Europe.[43]

The Lawrence strike was one of the most widely reported labor struggles in American history up to this time. No reporter, no matter how he distorted the news by constantly picturing the strikers as perpetrators of all kinds of violent deeds, could help but admire the powerful organization set up by Ettor so quickly (and continued by Haywood after the former's arrest), and the precision with which it operated. The truth is that at no time previously in American labor history were so many diverse nationality and language groups so effectively united in a strike. "Never before," commented the New York *Sun* in mid-February, "has a strike of such magnitude succeeded in uniting in one unflinching, unyielding, determined and united army so large and diverse a number of human beings." The Lawrence *Evening Tribune,* hardly a friend of the strikers, grudgingly conceded early in March that "from the day of its formation there was never any hint of friction among the different representatives on the strike committee."[44]

The mill owners were ready, early in the strike, to remove the original grievance that had sparked the mass uprising by continuing the same amount of pay as the workers had formerly received for 56 hours.[45] But once the battle was put on an organized basis, this was replaced by a full set of demands, and it was to achieve them that the strike was fought. On January 14, the strikers drew up their demands at a mass meeting, the usual procedure of the I.W.W., which always insisted that demands emerge from the body of the strikers rather than from their representatives. There were four demands. The strikers asked for (1) A 15-per cent increase in wages; (2) the adoption of the 54-hour week; (3) abolition of the premium and bonus systems and double pay for overtime, and (4) no discrimination against the strikers for strike activities. These demands could hardly be called extravagant in view of the widespread grievances of the workers. They clearly were not designed, as the mill owners and the press friendly to them charged, to further syndicalism or to promote a revolution.[46]

The strikers remained steadfast behind these demands. At the suggestion of the general strike committee, those strikers who could write English or some other language sent hundreds of letters to the mill agents asserting that until their demands were granted they would not return to work. "The mills," reported the Lawrence *Evening Tribune* late in February, "are actually being bombarded with these letters."[47]

Once the general strike committee was perfected and the demands clearly formulated, the strike spread like wildfire through all the textile mills. About 33,000 textile workers were on the payrolls of the mills on January 12, the day the strike started. On that day, about 15,000 workers walked out. Eight days later, on January 20, the local press reported that 22,000 workers were out. Thus the strike reached its greatest strength one week after the start, for at no time did the total of workers on strike (and those thrown out of work) exceed 23,000. These, with their dependents, comprised about 60 per cent of the city's population.[48] At the time of the settlement of the strike, March 14, there were still about 20,000 workers out. This was a remarkable manifestation of the determination of the strikers not to go back to work until they won their demands. During the nine long weeks of the bitter struggle, some of the mills were shut down completely, while others maintained a skeleton force to ship out the cloth that had been woven just before the strike occurred. But the official journal of the manufacturers conceded that not a single mill produced new material.[49]

The tactics introduced early in the strike kept the mills closed. These tactics drew the admiration of workers and labor leaders throughout the nation because of their effectiveness, and were to influence strike strategy of American labor for years to come.

MASS PICKETING

On Monday morning, January 15, pickets turned out *en masse* before each of the mills. This began a daily practice that continued until the end of the strike. Never before had there been picketing on the scale employed in Lawrence. Indeed, it was the picket line that made the Lawrence strike a milestone in the history of American labor struggles. Every striker took his place on the picket lines, including those who, at first, joined the walkout through fear of reprisal as a result of the mills closing down.[50]

At the outbreak of the strike, it appears that the city administration had agreed to grant the strikers the privilege of "peaceful picketing." This was construed to mean the use of vocal persuasion by the strikers to keep scabs out of the mills. But when groups of strikers massed before the various mills, they were dispersed by the police and militia.[51] To get around the prohibition against gathering in front of the mills, the strike committee developed an ingenious strategy. This was the famous moving picket line. Day after day, long lines of pickets moved in an endless chain around the mill district to discourage strikebreakers. Each picket wore a white ribbon or card that said, "Don't be a Scab." The chain, kept moving 24 hours a day during the entire strike, was extremely effective. No one could get through the lines without being accosted. What is more, it was not contrary to the law. The strikers did not mass in front of the mills.[52]

When reporters, writing from Lawrence, referred in awe to "mass picketing," they meant precisely that. It was not unusual to find 20,000 strikers on the picket line. And that number could still be found on the line a few days before the strike ended, moving always "in a dense mass along Essex Street and Broadway," in endless file around and around the streets near the mills, singing their songs and sending chills down the spines of potential scabs with their ceaseless cry of "Boo! Boo! Boo!" When the police tried to stop them from halting potential scabs, the pickets refused. They would fall to the sidewalk daring the police to arrest them.[53]

The picket lines gave a clear impression of the organized power of the workers. So, too, did the frequent parades of the strikers. Few strikes in the United States have witnessed the number of parades the people of Lawrence saw during these nine weeks. Every few days a parade would be held, with from 3,000 to 10,000 people marching to the music of bands and drum corps, singing "The Internationale," "The Marseillaise," "Solidarity Forever," and other radical and Wobbly songs. ("This movement in Lawrence," wrote Ray Stannard Baker, "was strangely a singing movement.") Many of the paraders wore I.W.W. buttons. As the thousands of paraders marched through the streets, it is not difficult to see why the Citizens' Association felt that a revolution had come to Lawrence. Indeed, one of the militia officers who was on strike duty wrote an article entitled, "The Lawrence Revolution," in which he noted that strikers had taken over the government of the city.[54]

Late in January, all parades and mass meetings held on city property were forbidden by the militia. But the ingenuity of the strike committee was again revealed. The strikers were instructed to conduct sidewalk parades. Groups of 20, 30, or 50 would lock arms on the sidewalk, take up its entire width, and walk along, sweeping everyone off the sidewalks or against the walls of the buildings. When the police, with great difficulty, broke up the sidewalk parades, the strikers resorted to a new strategy. This was to pass in and out of stores, not to buy anything, but to go in crowds into the principal places of business, walk around and out again. Captain Sullivan, acting chief of police, testified that "they had our shopkeepers in a state of terror. It was a question whether or not they would shut up their shops."[55]

The McKees Rocks and Hammond strikes, as we have seen, had already demonstrated that the foreign-born women were the most militant fighters in these struggles. The Lawrence strike fully corroborated this fact. In all the picketing and parades, the women strikers themselves or wives of strikers, played a vital role. They trod the frozen streets besides the men, and often occupied the front ranks in demonstrations and parades, expectant mothers and women with babes in their arms marching with the others, and like the other mill girls, carrying signs which read: "We Want Bread and Roses Too." "The women pickets were very active today and very few scabs entered the mills," was a fairly typical report from Lawrence. Most reporters agreed that they proved themselves to be fiercer and more courageous than the men. While Haywood did not go this far in his tribute to them, he acknowledged that "the women were as active as the men, and fought as well." In fact, more women than men appear to have been arrested for intimidating scabs while picketing. Even when they had enough money with them, they refused to pay the fine, choosing rather to go to jail. This was particularly true of the Italian, Polish, Russian, and Lithuanian women.[56]

The campaign against the scabs was conducted on other fronts besides the picket lines. Ettor's plan was to "make life miserable for the scabs and they will finally have to line up with us." The strikers executed this plan to perfection. For every group of scabs in a mill, no matter how small, a special meeting would be held. The strikers at the meeting would be advised to obtain the names and addresses of the scabs. Once these were secured, the scabs would be visited at their homes, the errors of their ways pointed out, and appeal made to them to quit work. If they refused, stronger measures were employed. Their names would be published and sent back to their native lands. A large group of strikers would serenade the homes of the scabs all night, marching up and down, shouting "Scab."[57]

During Haywood's leadership of the strike after Ettor's arrest and imprisonment, the process of making "life miserable" for the scabs was continued, but in a more subtle manner. This work was effectively carried on by the two nationality groups which were in the forefront of all phases of the strikework, the Italians and the Poles, and they applied techniques which were drawn from varied ones in their native lands. Red paint was splashed on the houses of the strikebreakers; pictures of the black hand and the word "scab" were painted on the houses; threatening letters were sent to their homes; their homes were visited while they were at work and the wife was advised to keep the "traitor" at home or he "would be found with his throat cut the next morning." The Lawrence Citizens' Association conceded that these techniques not only produced the desired results, but were so cleverly executed that it was impossible for the authorities to pin the blame upon any specific strikers.[58]

But all the efficiency and militancy of the strikers would have gone for nought had the mill owners been able to starve them back to work. The propaganda of the mill owners pictured the textile workers as preferring to live in squalor in order to save a good part of their ample earnings, amass some capital, and return to their native lands. One spokesman even triumphantly pointed to the fact that about $21,000,000 were deposited in the Lawrence Savings Banks, presumably by the workers.[59] The banks in Lawrence, however, offered evidence which proved that the poorly-paid textile workers possessed no savings upon which they could draw during the course of the struggle.

Since it was apparent by the first week that the strike would be a long fight, it was clear to the strike leaders that it was of paramount importance that some provision for relief be made. Unlike many A.F. of L. unions which could depend on strike funds accumulated from dues and assessments, the I.W.W., its National Industrial Union of Textile Workers, and Local 20 neither believed in nor had a war chest to finance the textile workers. Instead, the strikers immediately organized a general relief committee, composed of the heads of 18 lesser relief committees, each one dealing with one nationality or craft group, and appeals were circulated for aid throughout the United States. In a leaflet headed, "Help Your Fellow Workers Who Need Bread and Your Support," the Textile Workers' Strike Committee appealed: "We workers, who have done our utmost share to clothe the world are asking the world of labor and all those who sympathize with the cause of the workers for bread."[60] "Big Bill" Haywood, Elizabeth Gurley Flynn, Arturo Giovannitti, and other I.W.W. spokesmen helped raise funds for the strikers. Haywood, who originally came to Lawrence to help finance the strike, personally brought the strikers' appeal to workers and other sympathizers, addressing meetings in New York City and other large urban centers, especially the mill towns of New England. Haywood was very successful as a fund raiser and publicity agent for the strike, and, in this capacity, made some of his most valuable contributions to the struggle.[61]

During the weeks following January 15, money from outside Lawrence began to flow into the city. The largest contributors were trade unions, Socialist organizations, and Polish, Portuguese, Italian, French, and Belgian national societies; private individuals contributed the least. The New York *Call,* organ of the Socialist Party, leaped to the aid of the strikers with editorial support and began a campaign to raise money. About $75,000, apart from clothing, was collected during the nine weeks of the strike.[62]

Fifteen relief stations were opened, each catering to a particular nationality group or groups. No money was given, but groceries, drugs, medical services, shoes, and clothing were always available. Five soup kitchens fed some 2,300 people daily. While there were occasional headlines in the press such as "Starving Strikers Raid Food Wagons in Lawrence, Mass.," the fact is that with few exceptions, the strikers and their dependents did not suffer from dire hunger or need during the course of the strike. The work of the relief committee in keeping the strikers adequately fed and clothed played an important role in the final triumph of the strikers. In its analysis of the strike, the U.S. Bureau of Labor wrote: "The fact that an organization for furnishing relief to all strikers was immediately established, and successfully operated throughout the strike was undoubtedly the all-important factor in enabling the strikers to enforce their demands to the extent that they did."[63]

REMOVAL OF THE CHILDREN

No move of the strikers was more sensational or more effectively exposed the callousness (and stupidity) of the Lawrence authorities than did the removal of the strikers' children from the city. Since the beginning of the strike, the Italians had considered sending their children to the homes of Italian Socialist Federation members in other cities. Both French and Italian unions had used this tactic many times in strikes in Europe, but it had rarely been employed in the United States.* Early in February, the strike committee, under Haywood's leadership, decided to send the children of the strikers to stay with friends and relatives outside of the strike-bound city for the duration of the struggle. There were two reasons for the decision. One was to keep the children from seeing the horrors of class warfare. The other was to lessen the burden of relief by having fewer mouths to feed.[64]

Socialist Party locals in New York and other cities immediately organized committees of women to receive the children and care for them. The New York *Call,* describing the plan as "a novelty in the history of the labor movement in this country," issued a special appeal on February 7: "Take the Children." The response was tremendous, and the Socialists, including the Italian Socialist Federation, made plans for a giant demonstration in New York in which the children would play a major role. "Send us Your Children," went out the cry from New York to Lawrence.[65]

On February 10, the first contingent of children, 119 strong, embarked

* In December 1910, during the strike of coal miners in the Irwin fields of Pennsylvania, Local No. 11, I.W.W., of Philadelphia recommended "that all working-class organizations aid in the care of the striking miners, by taking as many of the children as possible into their homes during the strike." (*Solidarity,* Dec. 23, 1910.)

by train for New York. On February 17, 126 additional children joined the exodus, 91 to New York and 35 to Barre, Vt. Margaret Sanger, then a nurse and later a well-known crusader for birth control, was one of those in charge of the exodus from Lawrence, and her account is moving: "They were pale, emaciated, dejected children. I have seen the children of workers of other industries. I have worked in the slums of New York, but I have never found children who were so uniformly ill-nourished, ill-fed and ill-clothed. There was not a stitch of wool on their bodies." One labor paper put it ironically: "Though from the 'Wool City,' they had no woolen clothing."[66]

The pitiful, emaciated condition of the children as they paraded up New York's Fifth Avenue marked Lawrence as a city of starvation wages and aroused great resentment against the mill owners. With the assistance of Gurley Flynn, who was in charge of the exodus, arrangements had been carefully made for the children's care. Through the cooperation of the Socialist Party, the children were placed mainly in the homes of Socialist working men who had been investigated before being permitted to care for any of the children. No child had been taken unless the parent consented. Nevertheless, the anti-labor press, led by Hearst's Boston *American,* attacked the action of the strikers as an inhuman practice, and a threat against the sanctity of the home. The *American* quoted leading women of Boston's fashionable circle who denounced the strike leaders, and predicted that the children "would become in time veritable breeders of anarchy." "It must be stopped," the *American* shrieked editorially. The mill owners determined to put a stop to further departures.[67]

On February 22, seven children, scheduled to leave for Bridgeport, Conn., and accompanied to the station by their parents, were arrested, taken to the police station in a patrol wagon, and informed that if they were in need, the city would care for them. That same day, Police Captain Sullivan issued the following statement: "There will be no more children leaving Lawrence until we are satisfied that the police cannot stop their going. . . . I will not hesitate to use all the forces of power and authority I possess or may summon to my aid."[68]

A delegation of 200 children was scheduled to leave on February 24 for Philadelphia under the care of Gurley Flynn. At the appointed time, however, only 40 appeared, accompanied by their parents; the other parents had become frightened, expecting trouble from the police. They were right. Thirty policemen, under Captain Sullivan, ordered the mothers not to place the children on the train. When they started to take the children to the train, the police stood at the door of the station with drawn clubs and did not permit them to leave. Many of the mothers, including some who were pregnant, and children were pushed, beaten, choked, and clubbed. Fifteen children and eight adults were arrested, thrust into patrol wagons and taken to the police station.[69]

As the nation's press headlined the news of the police brutality, a wave of protests swept the nation and carried over to Europe. "It is the greatest outrage that I know of," protested Ernest Bohm, financial secretary of the New York Central Federated Union. William Dean Howells, leading American man of letters, declared angrily: "It is an outrage. . . . I cannot think of any more outrageous thing that could have been done at Lawrence than for the police to prevent these innocent sufferers in the strike from being taken away from the scene of industrial strife, to places where they could be properly cared for while their parents fought the battle for better working and living conditions." A convention of Illinois miners denounced the Lawrence authorities and called upon the American people to "rise up in their might and put an end to these Russianized methods."[70]

Petitions poured into Congress demanding an investigation of the Lawrence strike. On February 26, both Houses of Congress were afire with speeches on the strike. Declaring that it seemed "incredible that children should be practically imprisoned and starved with their parents in order to bring about the capitulation of workingmen and working women fighting for better conditions," Socialist Congressman Victor Berger urged quick action on a resolution he had previously introduced to investigate the strike. The House Committee on Rules held hearings to determine whether there was a need for an official investigation. The Senate went further and, over the objection of Senator Henry Cabot Lodge of Massachusetts that the action would constitute interference with the affairs of the state, ordered an investigation of the strike by the U.S. Commissioner of Labor.[71]

Needless to say, the further exodus of the children was not interfered with by the Lawrence police. Everywhere these children were greeted as heroes. In New York City, the Italian Socialist Federation and the Socialist Party met them with a brass band and marched them to a hall where they were fêted at a banquet. The Committee provided medical and dental care, placed children suffering from malnutrition on special diets, and publicized information about their health.[72] All told about 250 children remained in New York City, Barre, and Philadelphia until March 31, two weeks after the strike ended, when they were returned to Lawrence to be met by a thousand strikers from nearby Lowell, a battery of brass bands, and a parade of former strikers marshaled in nationality groups.[73]

The "children's affair" helped to change public opinion from hostility to sympathy towards the strikers. Up to the exodus of the children, the citizen who picked up his daily newspaper in Boston, New York, Philadelphia or San Francisco received only the impression that a war was being waged in Lawrence against law and order by the I.W.W., and that violence and disorder on the part of the strikers was so great as to approach insurrection. The systematic misrepresentation by the press of the conduct of the strikers continued. But the pictures of the near-starvation state of the Lawrence children and the accounts of the brutality of the authorities brought the real facts of the strike to the attention of the American people, and their sympathy was now definitely with the strikers.

CHAPTER 14

Victory at Lawrence and After

Few strikes in American labor history had to combat as many and as varied forces designed to defeat the struggle of the workers as were arrayed against the Lawrence strikers. As Haywood put it in a speech at a mass meeting of the strikers on February 9: "We are opposed by the courts, police, detectives that now spy among you, pulpit, press, soldiers, and legislature—all are arrayed against us."[1]

FORCES AGAINST THE STRIKERS

The brutality and provocative tactics of the police were noted by numerous investigators. *The New York Times* reported that they "served to infuriate rather than subdue the strikers."[2] U.S. Senator Poindexter, after a personal investigation, issued a statement to the United Press in which he accused the police of helping the mill owners to fight the strikers. He was horrified at the brutality of the authorities. "It's like a chapter in the story of Russia's brutal treatment of the Jews. I never expected to hear of such things in the United States. The State of Massachusetts, in Lawrence, is Russia." The Toledo *Union Leader* drew the same analogy. Reprinting a press dispatch quoting Lawrence policemen "who swung heavy clubs against the defenseless ranks of textile workers" as crying out: "Hit the women on the hips and arms. We don't want to break any woman's head," it commented: "With what mad zeal would we protest against such an order by Russian Cossacks living so far away that 'distance lends an enchantment to the view.'" The Lawrence police "could give points on fiendish cruelty to Russian Cossacks."[3]

The truth is that it was considered a crime by the police to be a striker in Lawrence. Anyone walking along the street was liable to be arrested on a charge of intimidation or disturbing the peace. To call a man a "scab" was a misdemeanor against the public peace. For such and lesser "crimes," strikers were arrested, given no opportunity to consult counsel, and kept in jail for several weeks. Before the Police Court of Lawrence there came 355 cases in which strikers were involved. But there were hundreds of others arrested, held in jail for a time and then released without a hearing. These cases were not recorded.[4] Most of them were heard by Judge Mahoney, a man who openly admitted to reporters his bias against the strikers. He meted out the severest sentences possible under the law. At all times, he justified the action of the police, no matter what the testimony revealed, imposed heavy bail and rendered decisions in quick time. In one single day, Judge Mahoney sentenced 34 strikers, arrested for rioting, to one year each in jail. Only five to ten minutes' consideration was given each case. Pending appeal, the 34 men sentenced in this summary fashion were held in $800 bail each. The Massachusetts Superior Court later showed its attitude toward the type of justice dealt out by the local court in Lawrence by reducing most of these severe sentences to fines of $15 or $20."[5]

"Because we dared to rebel," the strike committee declared, "militiamen have been sent to drive us back to work, and already the bayonets of the hired Hessians have welled in the blood of our fellow workers."[6] Arriving at the scene at the very outset of the strike, the number of soldiers in the city reached a peak early in February when there were 22 companies of infantry and two troops of cavalry, about 2,500 men in all. (Almost all were of English, Yankee, Scotch, or Irish ancestry). The troops, under the command of Colonel Sweetser, proceeded to establish a military rule which approached martial law. Taking complete charge of the mill district, the soldiers mounted guard over the mills and bridges. Some of the mills had the iron fences surrounding their property charged with electricity. Powerful flashlights were set up to sweep over the mill yards at night. Barricades of cotton bales were erected. Behind them, sharp-shooters were stationed with orders to shoot to kill if the strikers succeeded in breaking through the gates. Thus the troops were placed at the service of the mill owners to be used as strikebreakers; indeed, Owen R. Lovejoy of the National Conference of Charities and Correction, who interviewed the militiamen, reported that "many frankly professed keen interest in breaking the strike."[7]

On January 29, the strikers staged one of the biggest and most spirited demonstrations of the strike. The mill owners had announced that they would make determined efforts that day to open the mills. For about two and one half hours, from 5:30 A.M. to 8 A.M., Monday morning, the strikers, 15,000 strong, in the words of one reporter, "had full control of the streets of this city." All who even appeared to be headed for the mills were prevented from going on. The police were helpless before the over-whelming number of the strikers.[8] That night the City Council met and voted to place the entire policing of the city in the hands of Colonel Sweetser, announcing that the soldiers had been instructed to "shoot to kill." The very next day, Colonel Sweetser declared that the militia would take over the entire city, and that "lawlessness will be repressed by whatever measures will be found necessary." It was a virtual declaration of martial law, notwithstanding the fact the legislature had not authorized such a declaration.[9]

With additional troops, the commander had his men patrolling all the streets of the city. Every corner had a sentry, every street his patrol. The strikers were warned that the soldiers had orders to shoot. Parades and meetings were prohibited. Three or more persons on the street would be considered a crowd and hence subject to arrest. All citizens were advised to keep off the streets unless on business.* Lawrence was an armed camp with the militia controlling the entire city, and it remained that way until February 23 when the troops withdrew to their original position, the mill area, and the job of policing the city was returned to the police department.

On January 30 a tragedy occurred which was clearly due to the free hand given to the troops. John Ramy, an 18-year-old Syrian lad, a member of the strikers' drum and bugle corps, was trying to escape from a squad of soldiers who were advancing with fixed bayonets. He was not armed, unless a musical instrument is considered a deadly weapon. Yet he was bayoneted to death by a soldier. The civil authorities were legally required to investigate the case, but they did nothing. The military inquiry was cursory, exonerating the soldier who was responsible for the bayoneting, but his name was not revealed. The investigation failed to explain how or when the boy was stabbed. However, the autopsy revealed that the boy had been killed by a bayonet thrust into his back as he fled down the street.[10]

The militia was now confident that in the face of bayoneted rifles and tear gas, the strikers were sufficiently awed to enable the mills to open. Lieutenant Pratt, a member of Colonel Sweetser's staff, boasted: "The strikers and their sympathizers were plainly cowed by the show of arms. The glistening bayonets which had inflicted many wounds the day before seemed to particularly impress the crowds." But Haywood told the strikers that he had never seen "a strike defeated by the soldiers," and the strikers kept the scabs out.[11]

Haywood, who spoke from vast experience in the bitter class struggles of the Western Federation of Miners, commented late in February: "The police and militia here [in Lawrence] are the worst I have ever encountered, having no regard for sex or age. They are the most hardened set of criminals that ever wore uniforms."[12] But even this did not satisfy the mill owners. Hundreds of private detectives were brought in to supplement the work of the police and militia, most of them supplied by the

* The militia molested so many citizens, who were not strikers that the city government was inundated by protests. (Lawrence *Sun*, Feb. 6, 14, 15, 16, 20, 1912.)

Burns, Pinkerton, and Drummond detective agencies. Some of them were regular licensed officers, but most were thugs, hired out by the agencies as strikebreakers.[13]

With the city flooded with police, militia and private detectives, a bloodbath could easily have occurred. That it did not was due entirely to the efforts of the strike leaders and the discipline of the strikers. During this supposedly very violent strike, in which some 23,000 workers were out in the streets for nine weeks, acts of destruction and violence were few, and only two people were killed—both strikers. The I.W.W. doctrine preached at Lawrence was not violence but rather solidarity. Ettor and Haywood warned the strikers to keep cool and avoid riots. Both the police and the militia, the strikers were told, wanted them to provoke trouble so that they could beat or shoot the strikers and then break up the strike. Again and again the strikers were warned to keep away from the soldiers, and Ettor himself would go out on the picket line to see that the workers did not get into trouble with them.[14] Haywood advised the strikers not to give the armed forces or police an opportunity to "get them." The strikers followed the strict orders of their leaders not to riot. In late February, the Lawrence *Evening Tribune* conceded that the strikers had convinced the people of Lawrence that they were conducting a peaceful battle. "The public as a whole realize that the strikers are peacefully inclined although determined in their manner."[15]

In spite of this, the mill owners were able to obtain the aid of the business leaders of the community and of a good many of the religious leaders in their drive to smash the strike.

In the early stage of the strike, many citizens of Lawrence, convinced that the strikers were entitled to earn more money, favored their cause, and a few contributed to the relief fund.[16] To change this attitude, toward the end of February, representatives of the Merchants' Association, the Board of Trade, and the Real Estate Owners' Association met to form the Citizens' Association of Lawrence. This Association, composed of leading businessmen, merchants, professional men, and politicians—the social and economic leaders of the community—succeeded in recruiting about 5,000 citizens to join the organization.[17]

The Association immediately launched a vicious campaign against the I.W.W. and its leaders. It charged that the I.W.W. had incited the strike and that its representatives, "a gang of outside agitators," had seized the city and kept it in a state of terror for the duration of the strike. The aim of the I.W.W. was the revolutionary overthrow of society, and the organization had convinced the poor, ignorant strikers "that all property in the city belonged to them, including the mills, and that it was going to be divided among them just as soon as the I.W.W. won the strike." This statement was preposterous; the strike leaders had never made such a statement. Upholding and praising the work of the police and militia, the Association stated that only through their efforts was whole-sale slaughter avoided. The charge of police brutality was denied. If any-thing, the authorities were to be criticized for restraining them, for if the police had been given a free hand, they would easily have ended "the reign of terror."[18]

In the name of patriotism, the Citizens' Association flooded the news-paper offices of the nation with publicity releases which related "the truth about the strike" in contrast to the "series of misrepresentations and exaggerations" of the out-of-town newspapers, especially those served by the United Press which it accused of working "hand-in-glove" with the I.W.W. press bureau. The papers were asked to print the stories so that other American cities might be spared the menace of anarchism. The notices usually ended with the slogan, "For Lawrence—Here She Stands: For God and Country! The Stars and Stripes Forever. The Red Flag Never."[19]

Many priests and ministers of all denominations in Lawrence and in Boston joined the Citizens' Association in denouncing the leadership of the strike, although practically all members of the clergy agreed that wages were too low and that working and living conditions of the strikers were in need of considerable improvement. At the church masses, many of the Polish, Italian, Syrian, and Lithuanian priests attacked the strike as an "anarchistic, industrial revolution," the violence of which found disfavor in the eyes of God. Many warned against the dangers of socialism and even encouraged their parishioners to return to work.[20] Father James T. O'Reilly of St. Mary's Roman Catholic Church, the most influential clergyman in Lawrence, was absent from the city until mid-February. When he returned, he immediately organized a campaign against the I.W.W. and "socialism." His statement to the press was widely quoted:

"I wish to state most emphatically that the question in Lawrence today is not whether the operatives shall have more pay or whether the manufacturers shall yield to their demands. That state has been passed. It is now a war against society—the abolition of the wage system—the destruction of the present social order."[21]

There were Syrian and Italian priests, however, who, although they did not endorse the principles of the I.W.W., were closer to the problems of the poorer unskilled workers, and supported the strikers. Father Mariano Milanese of the Holy Rosary (Italian) Parish, whose church was directly opposite the Everett Mill, endorsed the strike and the cause of the strikers. He was influential in the formation of a relief committee for the strikers and their families. Father Vasile Nahas, Pastor of St. Joseph's (Syrian) Church, not only favored the demands of the strikers, but urged all workers to keep away from the mills until these demands were won: "The mill-workers have been poorly paid for the hard work they have had to do; and I believe they deserve higher wages. I hope they will win the strike. . . . The five or six dollars a week they have been getting at the mills is too little for them to live properly."[22]

But these champions of the strikers among the clergy were in the minority. Throughout the strike, the workers had to overcome the efforts of many priests and ministers to break their ranks through propaganda against the "I.W.W. objective of establishing socialism in Lawrence," and had to overcome, as well, repeated back-to-work movements sponsored by the clergy.[23]

Another widely known strikebreaking tactic that employers in past labor struggles had used was the "frame-up" for the purpose of either arousing public opinion against the strikers or getting rid of the leaders. The Lawrence mill magnates were guilty of both offenses.

On January 19, the Lawrence *Sun* printed a rumor that dynamite had been smuggled into Lawrence by the strikers. The following day screaming headlines announced that the State Police had discovered three caches of dynamite: One of them was at the base of a tree in the cemetery; another was in the tailor's shop of Ferris Mared, a Syrian who had led his countrymen in several parades and was a friend of the strikers; the third in a shoe-repair shop owned by an Italian named Urbano De Prato, and located next to the printing shop where Antonio Colombo, an Italian Socialist Federation member, turned out leaflets for the strikers. Eight people were arrested. The authorities stated that the dynamite had been taken by two Italians from New York City to be used to blow up the bridges leading to the mills and the mills themselves. Ettor promptly charged that bosses had probably "planted" the dynamite sticks.[24]

The frame-up was simply too crude. From the beginning, it was impossible to make out a case against those arrested. On January 20, Captain Proctor of the State Police issued a statement absolving the strikers from any connection with the case. Then on January 29, John J. Breen, a member of a prominent Lawrence family and a school committeeman and former alderman, was arrested on charges of importing the dynamite and planting it on the strikers. A few days later, all complaints against those previously arrested were dropped. In June, long after the strike was ended, Breen was tried, found guilty of conspiracy to injure the cause of the Lawrence strikers by illegally storing dynamite, and fined $500, a petty sum considering the penalties levied against some of the strikers for far lesser offenses.[25]

The case might have been closed then and there had not some of the Boston newspapers demanded that the authorities delve further into the plot in order to discover who was behind Breen. They, together with the I.W.W., insisted that Breen was merely a tool employed by others more powerful.[26] Late in August, the Suffolk County Grand Jury started an investigation into the alleged conspiracy perpetrated by a number of the mill officials to plant dynamite during the strike. On the same day that Ernest W. Pitman, a wealthy Andover contractor, was summoned to appear before the Grand Jury to relate what he knew of the case, he committed suicide. Pitman, who had built the Wood Mill, was a close friend of both William M. Wood, president of the American Woolen Co., and John J. Breen. Pitman, however, had disclosed what he knew about the affair to District Attorney Pelletier before he was summoned to the Grand Jury. Pitman confessed that he, Breen, Dennis J. Collins, a friend of Breen's, and Fred E. Atteaux, Lawrence dye manufacturer and an associate of William M. Wood, were responsible for the planting of the dynamite. Pitman obtained the dynamite and gave it to Breen. Breen and Collins took it to Lawrence. Breen was paid for his work by Atteaux who in return received money from Wood. Breen informed his friend Inspector Rooney that a stranger in Boston had told him where the dynamite was to be found.[27]

Dennis Collins was indicted on two counts of carrying dynamite. But the real sensation was still to come. On September 3, William M. Wood, president of American Woolen and Frederick E. Atteaux, were charged with six counts of conspiracy in the affair and released under $500 bail. In 1913, Collins, Atteaux, and Wood came up for trial. Collins turned state's evidence and admitted that Breen had hired him to transport the dynamite. But District Attorney Pelletier failed to link Wood with the case, and the result was a hung jury. None of the three men were brought to trial again, but the American people believed that the president of the American Woolen Co. was guilty of engineering the entire plot to break the strike.[28]

ARREST OF ETTOR AND GIOVANNITTI

The leading attempt to break the strike was the arrest and detention of Ettor and Giovannitti on the charge of murder. By the removal of these leaders, the employers hoped to bring the leaderless strike to a quick end.

Ettor knew that the successful conduct of the strike made him a marked man among the mill agents and the authorities. Others, too, sensed the impending arrest of the strike leader as he strengthened the ranks of the strikers. Bill Haywood, in a letter to Ettor, wrote: "They want you, Joe, and will get you if they can. Get your committee in shape so that every detail of work will go on without interruption, even if you are arrested." Ettor did precisely that. He asked Haywood to come to Lawrence to help manage the strike, so that if he were arrested, "Big Bill" could immediately assume control. He took great pains, too, to teach the inexperienced strike committee the strategy of industrial warfare by analyzing with them every move of the mill managers and their allies, and the counter-attacks to be launched.[29]

Ettor proved to be a good prophet. In the beginning of the "dynamite plot," the police had rifled his brief case, hoping to involve him directly in the plot, but to no avail. But Ettor was not to remain free for long. On January 29, the general strike committee organized several parades. When the police and militia tried to halt a parade of about 1,000 strikers, shots were exchanged and a bystander, Annie LoPezzo, was killed. The strikers claimed that a policeman, Oscar Benoit, had fired the fatal shot; the police and militia accused a striker, Joseph Caruso. Although neither Ettor nor Giovannitti had participated in the parade, they were arrested the next day, charged with being accessories before the fact to the murder by inciting the "riot" which led to the fatal shooting. Caruso was also arrested, and when Angelo Rocco, the local Italian leader, visited the three men in jail, he, too, was thrown behind bars, charged with rioting and delivering inflammatory speeches.[30]

Although Rocco was later released, Ettor, Giovannitti, and Caruso were held without bail. On February 9, Ettor and Giovannitti were arraigned before Police Judge Mahoney. The hearing lasted eight days, and, since the Grand Jury was not sitting, it took the form of a thorough trial of the facts. The state charged the defendants with spreading propaganda of violence, claiming that their incendiary speeches incited a person, unknown as yet, to shoot at the police. The bullet went wide of its mark and killed the Italian woman. The prisoners, it was brought out, were not present at the scene of the crime. The defense reiterated that Policeman Benoit had fired the fatal shot, and produced witnesses who stated that they had seen him fire the shot that had killed Annie LoPezzo. The star witnesses for the state against Ettor and Giovannitti were two detectives employed by the Callahan Detective Agency to watch the strike leaders. Detective Buccardo testified that on January 29 he had heard Giovannitti speak to the strikers in Italian and had told them to prowl around during the night and go looking for blood. On cross-examination, the detectives admitted that they were employed to obtain evidence against the strikers, and that they had destroyed their notes of the speeches in order to prevent them from falling into the hands of defense lawyers. Their knowledge of Italian was very scanty and Buccardo had only a vague notion of the exact language used by Giovannitti. The state contended that violence had been counseled by Ettor throughout the strike and that rioting could not have broken out on its own accord. The defense countered by showing that rioting had occurred spontaneously on the first day of the strike, which was before the I.W.W. appeared on the scene.

On February 21, Judge Mahoney found probable cause of guilt against

Ettor and Giovannitti and held them without bail for the Grand Jury. In his findings, Judge Mahoney wrote: "The Government does not claim that the defendants were present in the unlawful assembly, participating in the violence and breach of the peace when the fatal shot was fired, but contends that having encouraged, advised and counseled the unlawful violence and riot, they are responsible as accessories before the fact for the homicide resulting."[31]

The workers of America, regardless of their affiliation, liberal intellectuals, public figures, and many others were convinced that the accused were being railroaded to the electric chair on a flimsy "trumped-up" charge of murder. They rallied to the I.W.W. slogan, "Ettor and Giovannitti Shall Not Die." Professor William T. Taussig of Harvard University, one of America's most distinguished economists, expressed the attitude of the liberal-thinking people of the nation. "The indications are that Ettor was arrested not because of a determination to enforce the criminal law but in order to put him out of action."[32]

But even in this the mill owners were not successful. While defense committees, organized in every large city of the nation to collect funds and obtain publicity for the release of the prisoners, carried on a vigorous attack on the Lawrence "frame-up," the strike continued. Ettor's foresight had not been in vain. Without any hesitancy or wavering, the strike committee continued to function smoothly. From jail, Ettor issued a statement explaining that he had been arrested because the mill owners believed him to be the "backbone of the strike" which would collapse if he were removed. He advised William Yates to carry on until Bill Haywood and Trautmann arrived in Lawrence. "Meanwhile, fellow workers, be of good cheer and remember that the watchword is 'no arbitration, no compromise.' "[33]

Bill Haywood and Elizabeth Gurley Flynn inherited the mantle of Ettor and Giovannitti for the remainder of the strike. Gurley Flynn was a tireless worker. "For Elizabeth that winter of the strike there was ceaseless work," writes Mary Heaton Vorse. "Speaking, sitting with the strike committee, going to visit the prisoners in jail, organizing their defense, and endlessly raising money. Speaking, speaking, speaking, taking trains only to run back to the town that was ramparted by prison-like mills before which soldiers with fixed bayonets paced all day long. She was the spirit of that strike."[34]

Haywood was the astute general of the strike. His popularity with the Lawrence strikers was evident even before he took charge. When he first arrived in the city on January 24, he was given the greatest demonstration ever accorded a visitor. Fifteen thousand strikers, accompanied by three bands and two drum corps, turned out to greet the hero of so many struggles in the West. Before long, the mill owners realized that in jailing Ettor they had succeeded in replacing him with another heroic leader, and one who, in some respects, was even more fitted to carry on the struggle to victory. Ettor, younger and more fiery, was especially effective in the early stage of the strike, when the big problem was to create order out of chaos. But he lacked Haywood's experience in carrying through patiently from day to day. Haywood, the battle-scarred veteran of numerous strikes, acted with greater deliberation. He led the strike for about six weeks while Ettor led it for only three. To Haywood remained the more difficult task of keeping the ranks of the strikers intact in the face of daily attacks by the mill owners and their henchmen, and leading them to triumph. So well did he perform this task that his fellow Wobblies looked upon the Lawrence strike as revealing "William D. Haywood at his best in the role of strike strategist."[35]

STRIKEBREAKING ROLE OF A.F. OF L.

The employers, local and state authorities, police, police court, militia, private detectives, citizens' associations, religious leaders, and the press were enough adversaries for any strike to handle. But the Lawrence strikers found themselves fighting the A.F. of L. as well. During the first week of the strike, John Golden, president of the United Textile Workers of America, came to Lawrence at the request of the city officials "to assist in quelling the strike." Golden stated that he believed the workers were justified in striking against unbearable conditions, but he castigated as outrageous the manner in which the strike was being conducted, and refused to have any relations with the strike leaders.[36] He went immediately to the Lawrence Central Labor Union to organize a campaign to split the strikers from their leaders and to keep the skilled workers from joining the strike. Golden received the cooperation of the leaders of the Central Labor Union. Asked by a reporter if he was cooperating with the I.W.W. in the strike, G. W. Ramsden, vice-president of the Council replied, "No." There was "nothing to cooperate with," he explained, because the A.F. of L. "does not recognize the I.W.W. as an organization." "Is it not a fact that 22,000 men and women are out on strike and are organized?" the reporter asked. "I suppose they are," Ramsden answered. "But what of it?"[37]

Despite the efforts of the A.F. of L. leaders, the I.W.W. did succeed in the early stage of the strike in winning over groups of the skilled workers to the cause of the strikers. Golden and the leaders of the Central Labor Union worked feverishly to prevent this early cooperation between the skilled and unskilled workers from proceeding further. In the main, they were successful. The skilled craftsmen, organized in the A.F. of L. unions, were forced to leave the mills because the factories were not operating or because they were afraid to challenge the strikers' mass picket lines. Each of the craft unions, eight in all, began independent negotiations with the managers of the mills. The craft unions called for individual increases for each skilled trade in the different mills. (The increases demanded varied from four to 20 per cent, depending upon the specific craft and mill.) The craft unions were to go out on strike if these demands were not granted within a specified time.

The ultimatum was delivered on February 6 and the Central Labor Union waited two weeks for a reply from the mill owners, but none came. Instead, on the day the ultimatum expired, the mills announced a flat five per cent increase effective March 4. At first, Golden and the Central Labor Union refused to accept this concession and threatened to call a strike of all the crafts. But on the same day that the increased wages were to go into effect, the skilled crafts voted to return to work. On March 5, the A.F. of L. crafts, members of the United Textile Workers, went back into the mills.[38]

Thus the craft unions, supported by the A.F. of L. leaders, had won a slight increase in wages without joining the fight of their unskilled brothers and sisters, precisely because of the battle waged by these workers under the leadership of the I.W.W. Robert R. Brooks points out in his study of the United Textile Workers that without the militancy of the strikers and the effective leadership of the I.W.W., "it is doubtful whether the U.T.W. could have won even the slight concessions for which they claimed the credit."[39] The A.F. of L. had once again followed its custom of improving the lot of a small group of skilled workers regardless of the interest of the majority in the mills.

The A.F. of L. engaged in other strikebreaking activities. Golden appeared to testify before the Rules Committee of the House of Representatives, condemned the strike—"This is a revolution, not a strike"— the manner in which it was led by the "anarchistic" I.W.W., and denounced the sending of the strikers' children from Lawrence, the chief motive being, he charged, "to keep up the agitation and further the propaganda of the I.W.W." When he tried to excuse the brutality of the Lawrence police, Congressman Victor Berger called his remarks "contemptible."[40] Early in February, Golden organized the joint relief committee composed of representatives of the U.T.W., the C.L.U., and the Boston Women's Trade Union League. A relief station was opened, and the strikers urged to come to it. But when they appeared, only workers who pledged to go back to work received aid; any worker who insisted on continuing to strike was turned down.[41]

Mary O'Sullivan, an old-line A.F. of L. organizer who was present at Lawrence, bitterly condemned Golden's actions and the entire role of the A.F. of L. in the strike. "The American Federation of Labor alone refused to cooperate [with the strikers]. As a consequence, the strikers came to look upon the Federation as a force almost as dangerous to their success as the force of the employers themselves."[42] To the strikers, the role of the A.F. of L. fully substantiated the I.W.W. charge that the leaders of the Federation were misleaders and traitors to the working class.

VICTORY

Early in the strike, the Massachusetts Board of Arbitration asked Ettor to submit the conflict to arbitration. Ettor was unalterably opposed to arbitration, believing that outside arbitrators were always in sympathy, if not actually allied, with the employers. His position was adopted by the general strike committee.[43] However, Ettor and the committee were ready to accept the Board's services as mediators between the companies and the strikers. But the mill agents refused to meet a committee of the strikers as a group, arguing that a diversity of products and conditions in the several mills made collective negotiations impracticable. The Board then tried to arrange for separate conferences with the different mills, but the strikers rejected this approach. They were willing to meet any employers authorized to act for all the mills, but they would not allow the mill owners to split up the strikers by having each mill treat separately with its own employees. The strike could easily be broken if separate groups withdrew after negotiating a settlement solely for themselves. The remaining strikers would lack the power and solidarity to continue fighting. The activities of the Board of Arbitration thus came to nothing.[44]

The next step was taken by Governor Foss of Massachusetts. On January 25, the day following the end of the Board's activities, he sent a special message to the State Legislature, asking for a sweeping investigation of the strike to disclose the conditions in the textile industry. When the legislature turned down his request, Governor Foss urged the mill owners and strikers to declare a 30-day armistice during which the workers were to return to the looms while an attempt would be made to settle the strike. This appeal was turned down unconditionally by both sides. Thereupon, Governor Foss requested the legislature to appoint a special joint committee on conciliation. Such a committee, composed of three Senators and five Representatives, was selected on February 7. Calvin Coolidge, then a State Senator, was appointed chairman. The committee went to Lawrence and tried to bring the opposing parties together. But again, the refusal of the mill owners to agree to act as a unit left matters as they were.[45]

Nothing really important developed until the police prevented the strikers' children from leaving the city on February 24. The nation-wide protest against the police brutality at the railroad station had swift repercussions. As we have seen, the federal government stepped into the scene and the U.S. Bureau of Labor ordered its agents to proceed immediately to Lawrence and make a complete investigation of the strike. Close on the heels of this action, the House Committee on Rules opened hearings on resolutions calling for a Congressional investigation of both the Lawrence strike and the textile industry. These investigations, following upon the adverse publicity the textile companies were receiving, had an important effect on the mill owners. They particularly feared that the Congressional investigation would act as the spearhead for a drive against the notorious tariff on woolens. Determined to keep their beloved tariff, the mill owners began to think seriously of settling the strike.[46]

Another factor which contributed to the settlement of the strike was mentioned by Dudley M. Holman, secretary to Governor Foss, in a letter to Julius Gerber, New York Socialist leader, March 2, 1912: "The Governor notified the mill-owners the early part of this week that he was disappointed in their attitude in failing to attempt to make a settlement, and that he should withdraw the troops almost immediately because he did not propose to have the military forces of Massachusetts used for the purpose of tiring out or starving out the strikers; and the result was at once evident, for yesterday morning's papers contained notices from the mill-owners of an increase in wages to be granted by them at Lawrence."[47] Why it took the Governor so many weeks to decide that "the military forces of Massachusetts" should not be used "for the purpose of tiring out or starving out the strikers," his secretary did not bother to explain.

On February 29, American Woolen Co. authorized the Joint Committee of the legislature to act for it in arranging a meeting with the strikers' representatives. The general strike committee, after much discussion, decided to abandon its earlier stand against negotiations with individual mills. For one thing, while the strikers' ranks were completely intact, the strike was under pressure because the craft unions had accepted the employers' terms and were beginning to send their members through the picket lines. Moreover, a settlement with American Woolen Co., the largest mill owner in Lawrence, would practically guarantee that the other mills would be forced to settle on the same terms. The general strike committee, therefore, appointed a subcommittee of ten, all of whom had worked in the company's mills. Negotiations were held in Boston between the subcommittee and representatives of American Woolen Co.

After several meetings, the subcommittee finally accepted raises of at least five per cent for every worker, time and a quarter for overtime, an agreement not to discriminate against strikers in hiring, and an agreement to pay premiums every two weeks instead of each month.[48] The strikers gained a substantial victory though they did not achieve their demands completely. They had demanded a 15 per cent wage increase and obtained increases varying from 5 to 22 per cent. The lowest paid workers, moreover, received more than a 15 per cent increase.* Their demand for a 100 per cent increase for overtime work was cut down to 25 per cent. The premium system was not abolished. In all, however, the settlement was a sweeping victory for the workers.

On March 13, the general strike committee accepted the report of its subcommittee. Another committee was appointed to negotiate with the other mills on similar terms. The next day, at a mass meeting of 15,000 strikers, the agreement was accepted. The strike against the four mills of American Woolen Co. was called off. The strikers voted to return to work on the following Monday, March 18. Then Haywood told the workers: "I want to say that this is the first time in the history of the American labor movement that a strike has been conducted as this one has. You, the strikers of Lawrence, have won the most signal victory of any organized body of working men in the world. You have demonstrated that there is a common interest in the working class that can bring all its members together." Haywood then led the whole audience in singing the "Internationale" in as many languages as were represented on the general strike committee.[49]

Before Monday, March 18, the strike committee had signed similar agreements with the Atlantic, Kunhardt, and Pemberton Mills, and the strike at these mills was called off. On March 24, the strike was officially declared off and the general strike committee disbanded. The following day, the last company of militia left Lawrence.[50]

Those workers in mills that had not signed agreements with the strikers in time received the same wages and other benefits won by the operatives in mills that had signed agreements. The Pacific, Arlington, Duck, Everett, and Brightwood Mills were forced to take this step in order to forestall future strikes and to obtain sufficient hands to carry on operations.[51]

The outcome of the Lawrence strike was more than a local victory. The struggle was the forerunner of a wave of industrial conflicts that swept over Massachusetts and left its mark as well in other sections of New England. In 1912, all Massachusetts was ablaze with strikes. The textile industry was the one most affected (28.3 per cent of all strikes and 66.6 per cent of all strikers were in that industry).[52] Besides the Lawrence strike, important textile struggles took place at Lowell, New Bedford, and Fall River. Other strikes were prevented when the alarmed textile industry decided voluntarily to grant wage increases and other concessions. Soon after American Woolen Co. announced increases for the Lawrence strikers, the New England mills began to post increased wages for their

* Those formerly receiving nine cents or less per hour received an increase of two cents an hour or 22 per cent while those receiving 12 to 20 cents received an increase of one cent an hour or five to eight per cent. These wages were for a 54-hour week.

workers. By April 1, about 275,000 textile workers of New England had received wage increases as an indirect result of the Lawrence strike. In Manchester, England, the *Textile Manufacturer* commented in awe: "The increase in wages in the cotton and woolen mills in the five New England States that came into effect at the end of March was one of the most remarkable episodes in the history of the textile industries in the United States."[53] On April 3, 1912, the Detroit *News* reported: "As a result of the [Lawrence] strike it is estimated that 438,000 textile workers, all over the country, will receive between $12,000,000 and $15,000,000 a year additional wages, employers having volunteered raises to forestall strikes and unionization."

ETTOR-GIOVANNITTI DEFENSE CAMPAIGN

Meanwhile in Lawrence, the end of the great strike did not ring down the curtain for the textile workers. Haywood had closed the tremendous mass meeting that ratified the settlement with American Woolen Co. with these words: "Do not parade today. . . . Wait till Ettor and Giovannitti are out of jail. Then we will have a parade."[54] As soon as the strike ended, the 23,000 strikers threw themselves into defense activities for their imprisoned leaders. They were joined by hundreds of thousands of workers, organized and unorganized, Socialists (including the entire membership of the Italian Socialist Federation), and thousands of sympathizers throughout the country.

The case was an international issue. On June 17, 1912, a huge protest meeting was held in Berlin and resolutions of protest in the name of the Free Union of German Syndicates were addressed to President Taft and Governor Foss. The Socialists of Sweden not only sent protests but urged the International Trade Union Secretariat to order a world-wide boycott of American goods, and to request "the organizations of transportation workers in all countries of the world to refuse, from a certain date, to have anything to do with vessels and goods arriving from or departing for America, until Ettor and Giovannitti are liberated." Meanwhile, they urged "all Swedish workers from this day until the liberation of Ettor and Giovannitti, to completely boycott all American goods of all kinds." The Bologna (Italy) trade unions sent fraternal greetings to the imprisoned labor leaders, and the Social Union made Giovannitti a candidate for the national legislature from a constituency in Modena. All major cities in Italy had branches of the Ettor-Giovannitti Defense Committee; Italian Socialists, led by Giovannitti's brother, Aristide, even considered a general strike.[55] On September 14, 1912, *Il Proletario* published letters from labor leaders in eight nations expressing solidarity with the imprisoned men and demanding their release. The September 1912 issue of *The Syndicalist,* published in London, emphasized that the case revealed a conspiracy of American capitalists to establish a precedent "which will make it dangerous for any speaker to point out the evils of the infamous system under which we live."

Defense committees were organized in every large city of the United States to collect funds and obtain publicity for the release of the prisoners. In all about $60,000 was raised for the defense.[56] For the first time on a national scale, members of the I.W.W., the A.F. of L., and the Socialist Party fought shoulder to shoulder in a major campaign. Many trade unionists regarded the case as a trial not only of Ettor and Giovannitti but of the entire labor movement. For the case involved an extremely important principle for the labor unions—the question of indirect responsibility of strike leaders. If these leaders were to be held responsible for the disorder and violence that occurred during a strike, then the very right to strike was endangered, for a strike could be broken by arresting the leaders.[57]

Although protest meetings were held in hundreds of towns all over the country, especially in those where an Italian colony had settled, Lawrence continued to be the center of the defense battle. The I.W.W. refused to regard the textile strike as terminated until the prisoners were released, and in this determination, the Wobblies were supported by the great mass of the strikers.[58] The defense efforts of the Lawrence workers took the form of direct mass action. On May 1 (May Day), 5,000 textile workers, now regular members of the I.W.W., marched past the jail where Ettor and Giovannitti were lodged. Singing the "Internationale," they shouted for the release of the prisoners. A banner carried at the head of the procession read, "If Ettor and Giovannitti Are To Die, Twenty Million Working Men Will Know The Reason Why." As the trial approached at the end of September,* the textile workers were spurred to more vigorous action. On September 14, despite a heavy rain, a protest meeting attracted several thousand people who heard 14 speakers denounce the persecution of the imprisoned labor leaders in a wide variety of tongues. On the following day, thousands of workers from all over Massachusetts, including a large delegation from Lawrence, gathered on the Boston Common where 25 speakers took up the Ettor and Giovannitti case.

On September 27, the second Lawrence strike was called. Despite the opposition from their cells by Ettor and Giovannitti, about 10,000 textile workers, led by the Italians, walked out of the mills as a protest against the imprisonment of their former leaders. It grew in volume until by September 30, at the beginning of the trial, a 24-hour general strike began.

---

* In April, the Essex County Grand Jury returned true bills against Ettor and Giovannitti, and indicted Joseph Caruso as a principal in the murder of Annie LoPezzo. The State claimed that Caruso aided the actual murderer, a man named Scuito, who was never captured.

Twelve thousand workers were idle that day, closing the Wood, Ayer, Everett, Arlington, and Lower Pacific Mills. One writer in an article entitled, "The Second Battle of Lawrence," described this "as the first mass protest strike we have had in this country, thereby marking a new era in American labor history."[59]

The trial began on September 30 in the Superior Court of Essex County, sitting at Salem. That day the I.W.W. called for sympathy strikes throughout the nation, and announced that it would lead a national general strike if Ettor and Giovannitti were not acquitted.[60] The accused men were represented by a battery of attorneys led by W. Scott Peters, a former district attorney; the state forces were led by District Attorney Attwill. It was not until 600 jurymen had been examined that a jury was completed. Four carpenters, one sailmaker, one hair-dresser, one leather dealer, one stock fitter, one Morocco dresser, one grocer, one truck driver, and one lamp worker made up the jury. The trial lasted 58 days, and covered much the same ground as the examination before the Lawrence Police Court. The state, quoting speeches made by the defendants, tried to prove that they had incited the strikers to violence and riot. The witnesses for the defense swore that these men had never given such advice, but, on the contrary, had counseled peaceful methods of procedure. Essentially, however, the trial was an attempt to try the I.W.W. as a revolutionary, anarchistic organization pledged to overthrow the American government by force and violence. It was not Ettor and Giovannitti who were being tried, but rather the principles and methods of the I.W.W.

The great strength of the defense, apart from the fact that there was no real evidence on which to convict the I.W.W. leaders,[*] lay in the testimony of Ettor and Giovannitti. Attwill told the jury that the defendants, whom he termed "labor buzzards" and "social vultures," were not interested in bettering the lives of the working class but rather in exploiting it for their own advancement. "They came of their own volition," he charged, "seeking the lust of power, the lust of notoriety, if not the lust of money." Ettor replied, pleading with the jury that if he and Giovannitti were to be sentenced to death, the verdict should find them guilty of their real offense—their beliefs—and not for the crime charged:

"What are my social views? I may be wrong but I contend that all the wealth in this country is the product of labor and that it belongs to labor. My views are the same as Giovannitti's. We will give all that there is in us that the workers may organize and in due time emancipate themselves, that the mills and workshops may become their property and for their benefit. If we are set at liberty these shall still be our views. If you be-

---

[*] None of the state's witnesses understood Italian and they were unable to determine whether the defendants had or had not incited their audience to violence. (Boston *Evening Transcript*, Nov. 2, 1912.)

lieve that we should not go out, and that view will place the responsibility full upon us, I ask you one favor, that Ettor and Giovannitti because of their ideas became murderers, and that in your verdict you will say plainly, we shall die for it. . . . I neither offer apology nor ask a favor. I ask for justice."[61]

Giovannitti made an impassioned speech in English to the jury, which according to contemporary reports, drew tears from the most jaded reporters. He declared that, indeed, he preferred to live, but conscience and loyalty to his comrades and cause were holier than life. The poetical quality* of the concluding words captivated the audience: "And if it be that these hearts of ours must be stilled on the same death chair and by the same current of fire that has destroyed the life of the wife murderer and the patricide and the parricide, then I say that tomorrow we shall pass into a greater judgment, that tomorrow we shall go from your presence into a presence where history shall give its last word to us."[62]

On November 25, the jury returned a verdict of not guilty for the defendants. (Caruso was also acquitted.) As the decision was read, pandemonium burst forth in the courtroom. Men cheered and shouted; others wept. Ettor and Giovannitti embraced each other. Even the conservative Boston *Evening Transcript* declared that "the verdict, rendered by a jury regarded as very competent and fair, was an entirely just one."[63]

THE SIGNIFICANCE OF THE LAWRENCE STRIKE

With the acquittal of Ettor and Giovannitti, close to a year of titanic class struggle ended in Lawrence. In the face of all possible obstacles placed in their way, a conglomerate mass of over 20,000 workers who spoke 45 different dialects had given the labor movement an amazing demonstration of solidarity and fortitude. The idea so widely promulgated by the A.F. of L. that foreign-born workers were unorganizable and could not be welded into an effective fighting machine was completely disproved by the miracle of Lawrence. The Lawrence strikers were the forgotten refuse of a labor movement interested in organizing the skilled craft minority. Ignored and disdained by the A.F. of L., these neglected, downtrodden masses—foreign-born, unskilled, half of them women—had proved to the entire labor movement that they were capable of maintaining the discipline, spirit, unity, and faithfulness to unionism, essential to victory. They proved, too, that theirs was the true Americanism. As William Allen White, the distinguished Kansas journalist, wrote from

---

* Giovannitti's reputation as a poet grew enormously during his prison experience. Two poems written in the Lawrence jail, "The Cage" and "The Walker," received widespread praise from publications usually hostile to the I.W.W. and were reprinted in leading magazines such as the *Atlantic, Outlook, Survey, Current Literature.* A volume of Giovannitti's prison poems, *Arrows in the Gate,* was published, with an introduction by Helen Keller.

Lawrence: "The strikers are foreigners, but many of them at their mass meetings, in their homes and in their gatherings upon the streets, reflected to me at least a better Americanism, a clearer vision of what America stands for than did many of those who sneered at them."[64]

The miracle of Lawrence, all observers agreed, was the vibrant spirit that welded the strikers together, despite clashing religions, varied tongues, and differing customs, in unbreakable unity. And it was the leadership of the I.W.W., it was freely conceded, that did more than anything else to forge that spirit. Had it not been for the appearance of the I.W.W. leaders, with their know-how for conducting strikes and their oratorical skill, the amorphous mass of workers might have trickled back to work or they might have gotten completely out of hand and moved in all directions, dissipating their strength and committing acts of violence. The Wobblies brought the skill and technique necessary to conduct a large-scale strike. Although the I.W.W. leaders stressed the democratic management of the strike by the strikers themselves, their advice was also accepted by the strike committee and by the mass meetings of the strikers. It was they who planned the major moves and saw to their execution. Above all, the eloquent speeches of Ettor, Haywood, and Gurley Flynn gave the strikers confidence in themselves and animated them with determination to carry on until victory was won. Under this type of leadership, the unorganized, foreign-born, unskilled workers revealed the full potential of mass action.[65]

Lawrence, together with the free-speech fights, "really introduced the Industrial Workers of the World to the American public."[66] Thousands of columns of publicity in all the leading newspapers and magazines during the course of the strike served to acquaint the American people with the aims and ideals of the I.W.W. One might not like the I.W.W., but one could no longer ignore it.

Although the Lawrence strike did not bring the revolution close to America, as some Wobblies and Socialists predicted it would, and as many conservatives feared it had, it did enhance the reputation of the I.W.W. as the spokesman for America's impoverished, unorganized workers. (Conversely, the reputation of the A.F. of L., and especially its affiliate, the United Textile Workers, suffered in the eyes of many workers as a result of its role in the strike.) But events in Lawrence soon gave the I.W.W. another and much less attractive reputation—that of being unable to hold its membership gains after a strike victory.

Immediately after the strike there were over 10,000 members in the I.W.W. in Lawrence. Local 20 was reorganized into 14 language branches and a number of shop committees.[67] In the three months after March 15, Local 20 led and supported 17 shop strikes, most of them caused by discrimination against I.W.W. members, dissatisfaction with the way in which the strike settlement was carried out, the presence of former scabs in the mills, or opposition to assigned work loads. These struggles kept the workers active, united, and loyal to the union. But above else, the defense campaign for Ettor and Giovannitti maintained the strength of Local 20. On September 4, the I.W.W. claimed 16,000 members in Lawrence, 10,000 in good standing.[68]

This was the high point. On September 30 an event occurred in Lawrence which marked the beginning of the I.W.W.'s decline in the city. As we have seen, a general strike to coincide with the opening of the Ettor and Giovannitti trial occurred on that day. The City Council, having learned a lesson from the incidents involving the children's exodus, issued a permit, but laid down the following conditions: The American flag was to be carried; no red flags and no bands were permitted, and the paraders were to keep in order. But about 10 A.M. several thousand Italians arrived in the city from nearby towns. They brought a band, 50 red flags, and a large sign which read, "No God, No Master." Through the streets they went, the sign conspicuously displayed and the American flag conspicuous by its absence, until a cordon of police tried to arrest Carlo Tresca, the anarchist leader of the parade and the major speaker of the day. In the riot which followed, Tresca escaped from the police, two of whom were stabbed.[69]

The event was seized upon by the press throughout the country for a mammoth offensive against the Wobblies. In Lawrence, it gave the foes of the I.W.W. the handle they had been looking for. The Roman Catholic clergy, led by Father James T. O'Reilly, began an all-out drive to convince the foreign-born workers that the September 30 parade proved that the I.W.W. was opposed to all religion. The Citizens' Association of Lawrence called upon all citizens to unite against the "atheistical, anarchistical" organization that stood for "No God and No Country." There is no question that these campaigns had an effect among many foreigners who had been the backbone of the I.W.W. and had already been alarmed by the events of September 30.[70]

On October 14, Flag Day, about 32,000 people participated in a well-prepared parade in Lawrence, including most of the school children, each of whom carried a small American flag. The adult paraders marched through the city carrying banners inscribed with "God and Country." While the parade was taking place, Local 20 held a picnic which, according to the I.W.W., attracted some 4,000 workers. It was clear to many observers that the I.W.W. was losing influence.[71] This became clearer when Ettor and Giovannitti were welcomed back to Lawrence by a small if enthusiastic crowd. Possibly if Ettor and other I.W.W. leaders had remained in Lawrence, the process of disintegration might have been halted, and Local 20 might have rebuilt its former strength. But as one member of Local 20 wrote later: "When the strike and the Ettor and Giovannitti struggle was over, every one of the organizers packed his suitcase and left. No doubt the organizers had work to do elsewhere;* but the fact stands out, that the work of agitation during the strike was not followed by the more important work of organization."[72]

In the next few months, the strength of Local 20 was further depleted. The mill owners, aware of the local's weakened condition, began an active opposition to the union, discharging the most militant members and even forcing them to leave the city.[73] Internal conflict over syndicalism versus political action caused some branches to withdraw. Charges that some of the funds collected for the relief of strikers and their families during the strike had been misused, led to further withdrawals. Many members, including the Italians who were most devoted to the union, stopped paying dues to an organization which failed to improve their working conditions.[74]

By the summer of 1913, the I.W.W. in Lawrence was again a small organization with about 700 members. Similar declines in I.W.W. membership occurred in Lowell, New Bedford, Fall River, and other New England textile centers.[75] The aftermath of the great Lawrence strike proved the I.W.W. to be as weak in building up a stable organization and maintaining a permanent hold over its members after a struggle as it had been strong in leading the workers to victory. But the over-all effect of the Lawrence strike was not diminished by its aftermath. For one thing, as Donald B. Cole notes, as a result of the strike, "Lawrence was never again the anti-union city it had once been."[76] For another, the influence of the strike seeped into wide areas of the A.F. of L., despite efforts of the national leadership to discredit the struggle. Although Mary E. McDowell, director of Chicago's University Settlement and a pioneer organizer among the huge packinghouse companies, was extremely hostile to the I.W.W., she was wise enough to realize that the A.F. of L. had much to learn from Lawrence, and she conducted an intensive campaign, shortly after the strike ended, to convince A.F. of L.

---

* Ettor went on to help organize the hotel workers of New York City and lead them in their strike. During the strike, he attracted nation-wide attention by reminding the strikers that if they had to go back to work "under unsatisfactory conditions," they should go back with minds made up "that it is the unsafest thing in the world for the capitalist to eat food prepared by members of your union." An outcry immediately arose that Ettor had asked the workers "to poison the food of the capitalists." When Arthur Brisbane, the Hearst editor, was asked if Ettor should not be jailed for his remarks, he is said to have replied: "I am in favor of jailing Ettor for his remarks at that meeting, but not until you jail the manufacturers who are poisoning the food of the nation." (New York *Herald*, Jan. 11, 1913; *Solidarity*, May 17, 1913.)

Elizabeth Gurley Flynn, who also was active in the hotel workers' strike, describes it as the most "hectic strike" she ever participated in. She mentions one unusual tactic widely used in the strike: "Well-dressed sympathizers, as diners, would go into the places not yet on strike and at an agreed moment blow a whistle, which was a signal for all the cooks and waiters to go out." (*I Speak My Own Piece*, New York, 1955, pp. 140–42; interview with Elizabeth Gurley Flynn, Feb. 19, 1964.)

leaders all over the country to apply the lessons of the struggle. To Homer D. Call, secretary-treasurer of the Amalgamated Meat Cutters and Butcher Workmen, Miss McDowell wrote:

"I was East and have talked with several thoughtful & observant men & women who have been in Lawrence & have investigated the conditions before & during & after the strike. I am greatly impressed with what they told me. These people said to me that Haywood had a *method* of organizing the foreigners in a great industry where there was little skill and much specialization that was most wise and successful, and would have to be applied to such industries and Packing and Steel. . . . We dare not ignore the one fact that they [the I.W.W.] have a *method* that will have to be used by the A.F. of L. or harm will come to the unions."

Miss McDowell urged Call to make an effort to persuade Gompers and other A.F. of L. leaders to begin organizing the mass-production industries, using the I.W.W.'s "method," employing militant organizers who spoke the languages of the foreign-born workers. "Mr. Gompers must not be afraid of even *socialists* if they are intelligent trade unionists and see the danger of letting the I.W.W. get ahead." To another A.F. of L. leader, Miss McDowell wrote: "It will be a great waste of time & energy, if the A.F. of L. misses the point that has been so terribly emphasized at Lawrence, Mass. . . . In such industries as those of the steel, meat, textile & harvesters, etc., Industrial Unionism of a constructive type is surely the need of this moment. The A.F. of L. will lose out unless it wakes up and adds to the I.W.W.'s clever method, that of permanent and constructive organization."[77]

Miss McDowell did not get very far in her crusade to convince the A.F. of L. of the need to learn the lesson of Lawrence,[78] but she was fundamentally correct when she emphasized that the crying need of the American labor movement was a combination of the I.W.W.'s "method" of organizing and "permanent and constructive organization."

CHAPTER 15

The Paterson Strike

The year 1913 opened with another I.W.W. victory in the textile industry—this time at Little Falls, N.Y., a major center for knit goods and
underwear. On January 2, 1,500 mill workers, native Americans, Italians,
Poles and Hungarians—70 per cent of them women—ended their 12-week
strike with a wage increase. They had walked out of the Phoenix and
Gilbert Knitting Mills on October 10, 1912, in protest against a reduction
in wages ranging from 75 cents to $2 per week, following the application
of a state law reducing hours for women workers from 60 to 54 per week.
With average weekly wages of $8 to $9 for men, $5 for women, and
$3.75 for children, the wage cut spelled starvation for many of the
strikers.[1]

Soon after the strike started, the mill workers rallied behind the I.W.W.
whose organizers, led by Benjamin J. Legere, Phillipo Bocchino, and
Matilda Rabinowitz, came to Little Falls in response to an appeal for
assistance. Daily parades of the strikers past the mills started. A moving
chain of pickets, mainly women and girls wearing red sweaters, circled
'round and 'round the mills. In spite of some of the worst police brutality
in a strike of this period and mass arrests, the picketing continued. But
gradually all forms of activity were suppressed. No picketing, no parad-
ing, no open-air meetings were allowed, and it was dangerous for even a
small group of strikers to gather at any one spot on the streets. On
October 15, Dr. George R. Lunn, the Socialist Mayor of Schenectady, was
arrested while addressing the strikers. On October 30, all I.W.W. organizers, speakers, and committeemen were arrested and jailed.[2]*

The strikers maintained their ranks unbroken, supported by liberals,
Socialists, and trade unionists throughout the East. The strike was ended

---

* Fourteen of those arrested remain in the Herkimer jail awaiting trial which
did not take place until March and May 1913. (New York *Call*, March 1, 20, 21,
1913.) Legere and Bocchino were convicted of assault and were not released from
jail until July 1914.

on terms arranged by state mediators with wage increases ranging from 5 to 18 per cent. "The terms on which the strikers agreed to go back to work are a substantial increase over what was paid previously," noted the Utica *Press*. On January 6, 1913, the victorious strikers returned to work. "Another victory scored for the One Big Union," I.W.W. organizers wired from Little Falls.[3]

Meeting in convention a week later, the National Industrial Union of Textile Workers pointed to the victories at Lawrence, Lowell, New Bedford, Little Falls, and other textile centers as proof that the ideology and tactics of the I.W.W. represented the only hope for the textile workers of America.[4] Then came Paterson, and after this bitter struggle was ended, the bright hopes of the I.W.W. in the textile industry lay shattered.

CONDITIONS IN PATERSON SILK INDUSTRY

In 1912, there were about 200 mills making broad ribbons in New Jersey, about 35 silk throwing mills, and about 25 dye houses. Ninety per cent of these establishments were in Paterson and its surrounding area. About 25,000 of Paterson's 73,000 workers were employed in the silk industry, with 17,000 directly engaged in the weaving of broad silk and ribbon. Most of these workers were Italian and Jewish immigrants whose jobs were either unskilled or semi-skilled. However, many other nationalities were also represented in the silk industry—Germans, English, Irish, Dutch, Scotch, Swiss, Austrians, French, Belgian, Canadian, Hungarian. Like the Lawrence textile production, Paterson's silk production was a polyglot industry.[5]

In 1911, the latest period for which compiled data relating to earnings of the silk workers prior to the strikes of 1912–13 are available, the dyehouse employees worked an average of 297 days, 55.5 hours per week, and earned an average per employee, skilled and unskilled, of $563.62. During the same year, the employees of the broad silk and ribbon mills, working 290.5 days, 55 hours per week, showed average earnings for all classes of labor, skilled and unskilled, of $498.00. In general, the average silk worker, with the exception of the dyer, was on the job ten hours a day, at a wage which gave him a yearly income of $580—the lowest paid by any of the 25 top New Jersey industries.[6]

Not only were the wages inadequate and the hours long, but the conditions under which the average worker had to labor were almost unbearable. Many of the mills were firetraps. Sanitary conditions were abominable. Some factories were entirely unheated in winter and the weavers had to work in overcoats. Workers in the dye plants worked in steam-filled rooms all day where they were "unable to see the person they were working with." Dampness, bad air, poor sanitation, and fatigue after long hours of constant standing and stooping caused a high percentage of illnesses and deaths among the silk workers.[7]

Although the textile industries of New Jersey had a long and turbulent history of struggles by the workers to better their conditions, in 1912 the overwhelming majority of the operatives were almost totally unorganized. At the outbreak of the strike in 1912, the A.F. of L. membership in Paterson was limited to several locals of loom-fixers, twisters, and weavers, most of them employed in the Doherty Co.'s mills. Asked by a U.S. Senate Commission why the A.F. of L. had kept aloof from the great mass of textile workers, the secretary of the loom-fixers' local answered that the majority of the weavers were foreign-born or of recent foreign extraction, and had a labor philosophy which clashed radically with that of the Federation. He complained that "these people want instant action—join today, and strike tomorrow," and that this attitude could not be fitted into the policy of the A.F. of L.[8]

THE 1912 STRIKE

The first strike in Paterson occurred in 1828 when some cotton weavers went out for a reduction of the work day from 11 hours to nine. From 1828 to 1910, there were many strikes in the Paterson silk mills—in 1906 alone, the I.W.W. conducted 24 strikes; of these, two resulted in victories for the workers—but none attracted more than local attention.[9] Then in September 1911, a strike broke out in Henry Doherty Mill, and the spark was struck that two years later was to burst into open flames.

In 1909, Henry Doherty visited the mills in Massachusetts, Rhode Island, and Pennsylvania where he saw weavers running three- and four-power looms. He decided to introduce the system in Paterson, went to the A.F. of L.'s United Textile Workers, and entered into a contract with the union. In consideration of his permitting the U.T.W. to organize the skilled crafts in his mill, the union would furnish Doherty with weavers who would run four looms in place of the customary two which workers had heretofore operated.[10]

Everything went along smoothly at first. The four-loom system was installed in the Doherty Silk Co. for one class of weavers in 1910. But when in September 1911, the system was extended to other classes, the weavers struck. They charged that the four-loom system meant the loss of jobs for many workers, and sheer exhaustion with no increase of pay for those who remained employed. The strikers were members of the U.T.W. Silk Weavers' Local 607, and the U.T.W. officials submitted the dispute to arbitration; meanwhile, the strikers were to return to work. On November 10, disgusted by the failure of the arbitrator to reach a decision, the Doherty workers struck again, and when they were suspended by the

U.T.W. for striking in violation of their contract, they looked about for a new union to join.[11]

Since 1910, agents of Daniel De Leon's Detroit faction of the I.W.W. had been quietly at work in Paterson under the leadership of Rudolph Katz, head of the S.L.P. in that city; it was to the Detroit I.W.W. that the weavers of the Doherty mill now turned. Under its leadership, an attempt was made to extend the strike at the Doherty mill to other parts of the industry and to demand other improvements in conditions beside the removal of the four-loom system. On February 20, 1912, a mass meeting of weavers from various mills was held, shop committees elected, and a new wage schedule drawn up. (The prices demanded in the new minimum wage were from nine to 11 cents a yard, depending on the scale of goods, instead of seven to nine cents a yard.) This scale was embodied in a contract, that was to be submitted to the manufacturers, which also contained demands against introduction of the four-loom system and for recognition of Local 25, Detroit I.W.W., including the right to maintain shop committees. On February 25, various committees of weavers, members of Local 25, handed about 70 firms the new wage schedule and other demands. Seventeen of the smaller firms, caught with large orders on hand, accepted the proposed schedule. The bulk of the manufacturers refused to sign a contract with Local 25, whereupon the weavers walked out of the mills in orderly fashion. In the mills where the manufacturers signed, the weavers continued to work, but by February 27 the strike had spread until 5,000 weavers—fully one-third of the 15,000 weavers employed in Paterson's silk mills—had stopped.[12]

In keeping with the philosophy of the Detroit I.W.W., the strike was conducted in a quiet, orderly fashion. No effort was made to keep scabs from entering the struck mills. " 'Peaceful means' is the slogan," a newspaper reported from Paterson. "All forms of disorder and even peaceful picketing are barred. The strike-leaders notified the strikers that if any of them took the law into their own hands the union would not help them out of trouble with the police."[13]

But a number of strikers were becoming increasingly dissatisfied with Katz's tactics and contrasted them scornfully with the militant tactics used by the I.W.W. in Lawrence at the very same time. With its top leaders massed at Lawrence, the I.W.W. had heretofore played no important role in the struggle at Paterson. But when a group of Italians in Paterson sent a message to the I.W.W. for organizers, James Thompson, Edmondo Rossoni, and Bill Haywood were all dispatched to the scene.[14]

On March 22, 4,000 strikers returned to the mills when the manufacturers for whom they worked agreed to raise wages but rejected recognition of the Detroit I.W.W. and its shop committees. However, these gains were short-lived. As soon as the strike was settled and the pressure removed, and with the slow season on, the manufacturers repudiated their contracts. They gave as their reason the interference of the shop committees with the orderly conduct of their business. On April 4, the weavers and other operatives in these mills again went on strike. Influenced by the successful strike at Lawrence, the strikers this time conducted a more militant struggle, as far as they were able to do so under the leadership of the Detroit I.W.W. Pickets, displaying cards reading, "Don't Be a Scab!" in their hatbands, went from mill to mill. Despite the absence of any violence, a number of strikers were arrested for picketing and charged with "loitering" and "blocking traffic." One day, 50 pickets were arrested *en masse,* and Recorder James F. Carroll fined each of them $20, with the alternative of going to jail for 20 days. Not having the money, most of them went to jail. Rudolph Katz was himself sentenced to six months in jail on the charge of "disorderly conduct." He was later released after serving almost two and one-half months of his sentence.[15]

On May 1, agreements were reached in most of the shops covering wages, hours, and the number of looms to be run by each weaver. But a few groups of strikers could not come to terms with their individual mills and still remained on strike. The last phase of the strike was over by the latter part of May.[16]

By the fall of 1912, it became clear that nothing had been won in the two strikes. The manufacturers once again repudiated their agreements to raise wages and reduce hours. Scabs, hired during the strikes, were still on the job, and in Henry Doherty Mill, the weavers were running three and even four looms.[17] The Detroit I.W.W. blamed the failure of the strike to achieve any of its goals on the discord spread by the "wild talk" about militant tactics by the spokesmen of "The Bummery," particularly Haywood. The same talk had convinced the employers that they were faced with a revolution rather than with legitimate demands for redress of grievances; hence their haste in repudiating their agreements. The I.W.W. leaders rejected these charges, and maintained that the strike had been lost because of the inept management of the Detroit I.W.W.[18] With the two factions of the I.W.W. at each other's throats, it was difficult for many workers to determine the accuracy of the charges hurled back and forth. But one thing was clear: The successful strike at Lawrence convinced many silk workers that the strike in Paterson had been lost because of the refusal of the Detroit I.W.W. to encourage militant tactics. They were still fully dissatisfied with their conditions, and they now knew that a strong union alone could prevent the manufacturers from installing the four-loom system. They were ready to fight again, this time under the leadership of the men and women who had won fame at Lawrence.[19]

THE 1913 STRIKE

Late in January 1913, the lull that followed the 1912 strike in Paterson came to an abrupt end, and soon the city was locked in a struggle that was to equal the gigantic Lawrence strike itself both in extent and intensity. The struggle began as a walkout in Henry Doherty Silk Co. and the issue was once again the multiple-loom system. On January 27, 800 men and women, the entire working force of the mill, quit work because the four members of a committee which had carried the workers' protest against resumption of the three- and four-loom system had been fired. The members of the committee informed the Paterson *Press* that Doherty "thought that we were a disturbing element in the mill, and that by getting rid of us he could continue with his plan to adopt the four-loom. . . . The entire working force, however, left with us."[20]

The walkout did not take place at the instigation of or under the leadership of the I.W.W. (The event was not even mentioned in *Solidarity*.) But as soon as the Doherty weavers struck, Local 152, I.W.W., which had been in existence since 1907 and was led by Adolph Lessig and Ewald Koettgen, called a meeting of its 100 members, and decided to launch a campaign to win the allegiance of the strikers and involve the workers in the other mills in the struggle. With pamphlets, meetings, pickets, and sympathy, the I.W.W. local threw its forces behind the strikers. "Do away with the four-loom system in Paterson," the I.W.W. appealed. The slogan was music to the silk weavers' ears; they joined Local 152 and entrusted control of the strike to the I.W.W.[21]

On February 24, 1913, at a mass meeting in Turn Hall, Local 152 issued a call for an industry-wide strike to begin the following morning, and announced that Bill Haywood was on his way to Paterson to take charge of the strike. "Fellow Workers," Local 152's Executive Committee announced in a leaflet notifying the silk workers of the call for a general strike, "Close down the mills and dye houses of Paterson. Stand together. Act now. Organize in one big union and fight for a chance to live as human beings should live. All together now and victory will be ours."[22]

On February 25, some 4,000 workers, primarily broad-silk weavers, left work, and, led by I.W.W. organizers, paraded through the streets of Paterson. The emptying of the mills went on from day to day. On March 3, the ribbon weavers and the dye-house workers joined the ranks of the strikers, and the tie-up of the silk industry was complete. Upwards of 25,000 silk workers were out in what Haywood called "the closest approach to a general strike that has yet taken place in American industry."[23]* Local 152, with a membership of about 1,000, the only official

* The 1913 strike was not confined to Paterson, although its most dramatic incidents occurred in that city. From March until May over 4,000 workers in the mills of Hudson and Bergen counties were on strike, and several of them were

members of the I.W.W. involved in the struggle, now led a strike of over 25,000 workers.[24]

The ready response to the I.W.W. strike call can be easily understood. The silk workers were tired of years of A.F. of L. indifference to their needs, and it only required a militant appeal for action to crystallize the latent discontent. As John H. Steiger pointed out in *The Memoirs of a Silk Striker,* published in 1914: "The American Federation of Labor had no standing in Paterson. The workers had lost confidence in the more conservative organization because of previous experiences under its leadership, and there were no other sane advisers to whom they felt they could turn with any degree of certainty that their interests would be properly safeguarded [except the I.W.W.]."[25] Even the Paterson newspapers, viciously hostile to the strikers, termed "ridiculous" a statement of the Silk Association of America that "90 per cent of the operatives now on strike were forced to leave their looms and dye-tubs by intimidation."[26]

Originally the I.W.W. had advised the strikers not to go back to work until they had abolished the four-loom system. Early in March, the I.W.W. and the strikers supplemented this demand to include I.W.W. recognition, an eight-hour day, and a minimum wage of $12 a week. The manufacturers categorically rejected all the demands. "New Jersey workers" they replied, "must permit the three or four looms on plain, simple fabrics or they must be made elsewhere." Recognition of the I.W.W. was completely out of the question: "The manufacturers cannot treat with the I.W.W. These people say that they will not be bound by any agreement and will continue to strike again and again until they own the mills. It would be foolhardy to treat with an organization of that kind." Wages and hours were satisfactory as they stood. Samuel McCollom, president of the Paterson Manufacturers' Association, supplemented this statement with the remark that "we'd rather go to the wall at once than yield everything we own to them [the I.W.W.] by degrees."[27]

The I.W.W. theory that leadership must spring from the mass was put into practice at Paterson. A general strike committee, estimated as "in the neighborhood of about 250 or 300," with Haywood as chairman, was in charge of conducting the struggle. An executive board, composed of 15 to 20 strikers, met every night with the I.W.W. leaders, Bill Haywood, Gurley Flynn, Patrick Quinlan, Adolph Lessig, and Carlo Tresca, who acted in an advisory capacity. The general strike committee was divided into subcommittees on ways and means, publicity, information, strike relief and other necessary functions.[28]

Day after day the strikers manned the picket lines, massing each morning before those mills which attempted to keep running. Although the

successful. Increases in wages were won by silk strikers in West New York, Quinmet, and Carlstadt. (*Report of the Bureau of Statistics of Labor and Industry of New Jersey for 1913,* Camden, N.J., 1914, pp. 33-34.)

mill owners complained that the pickets used violence, most reporters agreed that there was a total absence of violence by the strikers. Indeed, the I.W.W. organizers took pride in the order with which the strike was carried out. "We advised them all during the strike to keep their hands in their pockets and do nothing," the I.W.W. boasted.[29] That this advice was followed was acknowledged by a number of contemporary observers who pointed out that if the I.W.W. leaders had wanted violence they could have had it. Rabbi Louis Mannheimer, one of Paterson's leading citizens, declared: "I hold no brief for the I.W.W. I abhor a number of the teachings and principles. But I cannot refrain from paying tribute to the leadership of William Haywood, Elizabeth Gurley Flynn, Patrick Quinlan, Adolph Lessig and Carlo Tresca. For 13 weeks they have held in check and directed an army of 25,000 men and women. Had they been preaching anarchism and violence there would have been anarchism and violence. . . . A police force of 150 could hardly have coped with an army of 25,000 people if that army intended to make war." On May 4, when the strike had been on for almost ten weeks, Mayor Andrew McBride acknowledged publicly: "Except in certain sporadic cases, I must say that the great body of working men have been orderly and peaceful."[30] This did not, as we shall see, keep the Mayor from backing his police chief to the hilt in arresting and jailing these working men!

Such violence as occurred was not caused by the strikers. On April 17, scabs were being escorted from the Weidmann dye house by police and private detectives. (The strikers claimed that the latter were hired gunmen imported from New York by the company.) When the strikers started hooting at the scabs, the detectives fired on the unarmed workers, wounding several. One onlooker, Modestino Valentino, standing on the porch of his home watching the proceedings, was killed by a bullet. Although not a striker, nor a member of the I.W.W., Valentino's funeral was marked by a great demonstration. Twenty thousand strikers filed silently past his open coffin, each dropping on it a red carnation.[31]

As in Lawrence, the I.W.W. leaders held mass outdoor rallies to keep the strikers' ranks unbroken. But unlike Lawrence these took place outside the city. At the outbreak of the struggle, Mayor McBride made it illegal to hold outdoor meetings in Paterson. This constituted a real problem for the conduct of the strike. But not for long. William Breckman, the Socialist Mayor of the neighboring suburb of Haledon, invited the strikers to meet in that town whenever they desired. As Haledon was outside the jurisdiction of the Paterson police, these open-air meetings could not be prevented by Mayor McBride. Nevertheless, Mayor Breckman announced that he would call out the Haledon police if it were necessary to meet any attack upon open-air mass meetings by "the blue-coated Cossacks of Paterson."[32]

Regular Sunday meetings in Haledon became a feature of the strike, the first one being held on March 3. The strikers marched each week, as many as 10,000 strong, to Haledon to sing songs of solidarity and to hear Haywood, Tresca, and Gurley Flynn urge them to hold their ranks firm and extend the scope of the strike. The closing words of each meeting were, "Tomorrow, Monday, we start another week of this strike."[33] In an article entitled, "Sunday at Haledon," a reporter described the mass meetings as "one of the most dramatic spectacles and greatest manifestations of solidarity ever exhibited in the United States":

"The feeling of comradeship between all the workers was beautiful to see; all nationalities stood side by side in perfect order and listened to the counsel of the leaders. Here and there some one would be translating the speech as it went along for the benefit of those who could not understand it. . . .

"To hear that immense throng of men and women sing their songs was indeed a thrilling moment. What other organization, political or otherwise, had spirituality enough to dare to mingle music with its deliberations as it did? What cultured and educated audience ever entered so completely, body and soul, into an art work as did these simple workers into their music?"[34]

"To speak at these meetings is worth a lifetime of agitation," Haywood wrote.[35]

PATERSON'S DESPOTISM

Throughout the strike, the civil liberties of the strikers, their leaders and sympathizers were flagrantly violated. On the first day, Paterson's Police Chief John ("Bums") Bimson entered a meeting of the strikers in one of the large halls of the city and notified the workers that "out-of-town agitators" would not be allowed to address meetings. He also read the riot act to the assembled strikers, warning them that they were not "to group about the mills, or parade through the streets, for that is in direct violation of the law." (Under a New Jersey law placed on the statute books following a Paterson strike in 1904, practically anything uttered from a strike platform might be construed as "inciting to riot" or "preaching anarchy.") A committee of four shop chairmen, representing the I.W.W., immediately protested to Mayor McBride, but nothing came of the protest. This is hardly surprising since the Mayor himself forbade the owner of Turn Hall to lease it to the strikers if "outside agitators" were to speak.[36]

On the first day of the general strike, too, three I.W.W. leaders, Gurley Flynn, Tresca, and Quinlan, were arrested and accused of inciting to riot. All three were released on $1,000 bail. The next day, Wilson Killingbeck, a prominent Socialist, was arrested by the police while addressing a meeting of strikers in Turn Hall, and charged with "inciting to riot."

Killingbeck was reading from the Constitution of the United States when arrested, and when this was pointed out to the Mayor, he took the position that this made no difference. "Protecting the city, the industries and its people against reckless agitators who have no interest in the city except insofar as it affords them an opportunity to preach revolution, does not constitute a violation of any constitutional right."[37]

Alexander Scott, editor of the Passaic *Weekly Issue,* a Socialist journal, severely condemned the police for acting "like a bunch of drunken Cossacks. . . . This strike of the mill workers of Paterson is a matter between them and the manufacturers. Let the Paterson police keep their hands off." On February 28, Scott's place of publication was raided by the police and all copies of the paper found there were confiscated. Four men, engaged in distributing copies of the *Weekly Issue* and editor Scott were arrested on charges of criminal libel and "preaching hostility to the government," and released on bail.[38]

Rarely was there a strike in American labor history in which mass arrests of the strikers took place on a scale similar to Paterson. Recorder James F. Carroll was kept busy day after day during the strike, sending strikers to jail for unlawful assemblage; on one occasion he sent 164 to jail. One jury found 41 strikers guilty of unlawful assembly because they were doing picket duty around the Harding Mill. Judge Klienert sentenced 31 strikers to three months in county jail at hard labor, and then suspended sentence during good behavior. He admonished the strikers that if they did not like the laws they were at liberty to leave the country. All of the strikers thus addressed went right back to the picket line and most of them ended up in jail. Seventeen-year-old Hannah Silverman, a young striker, was sent to the county jail three times during the strike and was on the picket line the following morning each time she was released. Haywood called her "the greatest little I.W.W. woman in America."[39]

All together during the strike 4,800 strikers were arrested and 1,300 sent to jail. The vast majority were the foreign-born strikers, of whom the Italians were the most militant. Over and over again they were arrested for continuing on the picket line. But the police were unable to keep the pickets from the factories.[40]

The city authorities, acting for the mill owners, also moved against the strikers through their leaders. On Sunday, March 30, the strike leaders determined to hold an outdoor meeting in Paterson. Several thousand men gathered to hear an address by Haywood, when the latter was informed that Chief Bimson had forbidden the meeting, and that if he tried to speak he would be arrested. When Haywood informed the crowd of this order, there was a great shout of "On to Haledon," and the two-mile walk to the little Socialist municipality began. The crowd was perfectly orderly, but when the procession was within half a block of the city limits, a patrol wagon thundered through the mass of the people to where the organizers were walking in front, and Haywood and Lessig were placed under arrest. At the Recorder's Court the two strike leaders were charged with obstructing traffic and unlawful assemblage. Later, they were found guilty of unlawful assemblage and sentenced to six months at hard labor. A writ of *certiorari* was obtained, and on April 5, Supreme Court Justice Minturn ordered the release of the men on the ground that they had been illegally arrested and that it was clear that "at the time of their arrest they had no intention of exciting alarm." The two strike leaders were officially released, but the authorities had succeeded in limiting their work for the strikers.[41]

The four strike leaders—Gurley Flynn, Lessig, Tresca, and Quinlan— who had been arrested for "unlawful assemblage" and "inciting to riot" at a meeting of the strikers on the first day of the strike, were brought to trial in May. Quinlan was found guilty after a second trial in the middle of May and sentenced in July to from two to seven years at hard labor in the state prison at Trenton. Miss Flynn was released when the jury was unable to reach a verdict; she was tried again in 1915 and acquitted. The charges against Lessig and Tresca were dropped.[42] On June 6, 1913, Alexander Scott, who had been arrested at the beginning of the strike for "preaching hostility to the government" through the columns of the *Weekly Issue,* was found guilty and sentenced to a term of one to 15 years in the state prison at Trenton and ordered to pay a fine of $250.[43]

The wholesale sentencing of the strikers, their leaders and sympathizers to jail, and, in general, the wilful violation of fundamental democratic rights by city officials, aroused indignation throughout the country. "Do the rights of free speech and of free press no longer hold in Paterson?" asked the New York *Tribune.* Even the conservative *Outlook* conceded that the strikers' complaints against Paterson's officials were justified. "The county jail has been crowded with strikers sent there on charges of inciting to riot, unlawful assemblage, etc. In many cases the only offense of these prisoners has seemed to be their presence on the picket line or on the platform at strike meetings." Amos Pinchot, leader of the Progressive Party and liberal-minded lawyer, voiced the opinion of many Americans when he wrote that "a very vital principle of American life is at stake [in the Paterson strike]. A mayor, a police board, a chief of police and a recorder have become partisans in an industrial dispute, and are now using the police, the courts, and other machinery of city and county government, including the jury system for the purpose of crushing the silk-workers' strike. The vital question is whether or not the officials of the city of Paterson and the county of Passaic have become partisans in this dispute, and used their offices, the courts and machinery of government to fight the silk workers and break the strike."[44]

Actually, the "vital question" had already been answered. From the beginning of the strike, city officials and the police were the close allies of the mill owners. So, too, were the newspapers of Paterson with, of course, the sole exception of the *Weekly Issue*. The daily press did not hesitate to urge any measure that might break the strike—from tar and feathers to forcible deportation of the organizers. "Get Haywood," the Paterson *Press* shrieked. "Never mind the manner; don't hesitate at the method; don't bother about the means. Get Haywood!" It urged the citizens of Paterson to form a vigilance committee and run the Wobblies out of town.[45] Needless to add, the editor of the Paterson *Press* was not indicted and sentenced to prison like Alexander Scott, even though the *Press* editorials, unlike Scott's, were open calls for violation of law and order. What was especially vicious about the *Press*'s call for vigilante terror is that throughout the strike it acknowledged that the strikers, under the leadership of the I.W.W., were conducting themselves in the most extraordinarily peaceful manner. On July 7, 1913, it editorialized:

"The strike has had one remarkable feature that the Paterson people will not forget. It is that although many thousand workers stayed away from the mills for five months, not only was there practically no violence but the rank and file of the strikers behaved themselves during a trying time in a manner that entitled them to admiration. The *Press* believes that this phase of the great strike stands without a parallel in this or any other country."

But this did not prevent the *Press* from calling for violence against the men and women whose leadership was mainly responsible for such conduct on the part of the strikers.

On March 13, the Paterson *Press* launched a campaign to convince the strikers that it was their patriotic duty to desert the I.W.W. and return to work "under the American Flag and in the American Way." The mill owners immediately popularized the idea and set aside March 19, as "flag day" on which the city was to be decorated with American flags "as a protest against the 'foreign' and 'anarchistic' methods of the I.W.W." On March 19, the mill owners bedecked the city with flags and banners urging the workers to return to their jobs under the slogan: "We live under the flag; we fight for this flag; and we will work under this flag." The next day, the strikers thrust back. Each strikers wore an American flag on his chest and underneath it the message: "We wove the flag; we dyed the flag; we live under the flag; but we won't scab under the flag!"[46]

ROLE OF THE A.F. OF L.

By the first week of April, the strike was having a disastrous effect on Paterson's economy. A mass meeting of all classes of Patersonians, under the auspices of the Mayor and the Board of Aldermen, was held on April 10 to see if some way of settling the strike could not be found. Representatives of the strikers and mill owners were invited to a conference with the Board of Aldermen on April 14 for the purpose of effecting a settlement. The mill owners refused to attend, but the strike committee cooperated, and its representatives informed the Aldermen that the strikers would settle if they received a "uniform wage schedule in every mill in the city," an eight-hour work day, and abolition of the three- and four-loom system. They denied that they were dominated by the I.W.W. and pointed out that they would not insist that the employers recognize the organization. Encouraged, the Aldermen urged the mill owners to meet with the strikers' committee and an an aldermanic committee on April 17, emphasizing that recognition of the I.W.W. was no longer an issue. But their appeal fell on deaf ears. The mill owners stubbornly refused to confer with the strike committee, "knowing, as we do, that they are completely dominated by the I.W.W.," and insisted that they would meet with any workers, "who are independent of the I.W.W.," and discuss any grievances with them. However, the manufacturers let it be known that they were prepared to listen to the strikers' demands if they were presented by a conservative labor body which they could trust.[47]

The manufacturers' statement was an open bid for the A.F. of L. to try to take over the leadership of the strike. Thus far the United Textile Workers had not played an active role in the struggle, but it had refused to call out the loom-fixers, winders, warpers, and twisters who were members of the union, and wherever possible had allowed them to work side by side with the scabs. But when the manufacturers indicated a willingness to discuss a settlement if a conservative labor body represented the strikers, O. B. White, secretary-treasurer of the A.F. of L.'s United Trades and Labor Council, promptly accepted the bid, and announced that the leadership of the United Textile Workers would be on the scene to enroll the strikers as members. Then the strike could be ended, for the mill owners knew that the A.F. of L. union "will play fair with the manufacturers. It will not try to take possession of the mills."[48]

To get the attention of the workers, the Central Labor body announced that a meeting would be held on April 21 at the Armory at which John Golden and Sarah Conboy, representing the United Textile Workers, and I.W.W. leaders would speak. Although they knew that Golden and Conboy had tried to break the Lawrence strike the year before, the strikers were still interested in attending a meeting at which the I.W.W. leaders could challenge the A.F. of L. position, and they themselves could question the U.T.W. leaders. Fifteen thousand workers packed the Armory.

The strikers listened silently as Golden urged them to appoint a committee to work in conjunction with the A.F. of L. to end the strike, and assured them that the manufacturers would meet with them once they had taken this step. They listened silently as Steve McDonald of the

Scranton Labor Union said that "any man who declares that there is no God, no church, can't help you," and urged them to drop "your red-flag leaders." But they refused to remain silent when it was announced that the I.W.W. leaders would not be permitted to speak and that no questions would be permitted. Pandemonium broke loose in spite of the strong guard of police, firemen, and even state militia that surrounded the audience. The strikers started to file out of the hall, making a good deal of derisive noise. The A.F. of L. speakers could not make themselves heard above the din. In desperation, Sarah Conboy thought to quiet the crowd by wrapping around herself the large American flag which covered the speakers' table, whereupon the strikers cried out: "Three cheers for the stars and stripes—hurrah!"—and continued the cheer until Chief Bimson ordered the hall cleared. Then the A.F. of L. leaders resumed their speaking—but this time their only audience was the police and a handful of reporters.

Thus ended the invasion of Paterson by the A.F. of L. When asked in June about permitting the A.F. of L. to organize in Paterson, the president of the Broad-Silk Manufacturers (which represented 60 per cent of the silk industry in Paterson) replied: "No form of labor organization among the silk employees would be tolerated in Paterson." With the A.F. of L. repudiated by the strikers, the manufacturers could wash their hands of their former invitation to the U.T.W. to organize their workers.[49]

Late in April, Rabbi Leo Mannheimer, stressing that if the strike "continues very much longer, [it] will bring ruin to a large number of commercial enterprises and will seriously affect the prosperity of our city," pleaded with U.S. Secretary of Labor William B. Wilson to conduct an investigation of the "entire controversy and all conditions in the silk industry," and attempt to mediate the dispute. Although the employers had refused to meet with anyone to settle the strike, he was confident that if the federal government entered the picture, the struggle could be brought to an end. Secretary Wilson rejected the proposal on the ground that the Department of Labor was not authorized to enter the controversy and had no funds for this purpose even if it had wanted to do so.[50] Thus ended the final hope of settling the strike through mediation.

THE PATERSON PAGEANT

On May 30, the New York *Call* announced: "The strikers are as determined to fight to the end as they were the first week of the strike." For 14 long weeks the 25,000 silk workers had been out on strike. They had withstood every weapon the employers and their agents had brought to bear against them. Police had clubbed and assaulted their pickets, intimidated hall proprietors from renting them meeting places, confiscated friendly Socialist papers, and denied them the rights of free public assembly. The courts had fined and sentenced hundreds of them to jail on trivial charges. The press had misrepresented and maligned them, and had even advocated the formation of vigilance committees to break the strike by violence. The A.F. of L. had tried to stampede them back to work. But all this had failed.

Unfortunately, at this point in their struggle, the economic position of the workers and their families was desperate. They had had no savings to fall back on when the strike started. While funds had come in to the strike relief committee from Socialists and Italian societies, such as the local lodges of the Sons of Italy, from benefit performances, dances, cake sales, and contributions by silk workers in districts not affected by the strike, the amounts raised had never been large. For most of the strike, one not very filling meal a day was what the men and women on the picket line lived on[51] Now at the end of the 14th week of the strike, the treasury was empty, and unless it was replenished the position of the strikers would become hopeless To obtain money for the strike relief fund, and, at the same time, give the real story of the strike which had been so distorted by the newspapers, it was decided to hold a dramatic pageant in New York's Madison Square Garden. It would be called the "Pageant of the Paterson Strike," and all the parts would be played by the strikers themselves.

The idea for the pageant came from John Reed, a graduate of Harvard, class of 1910. Though he rose swiftly in the journalistic world of New York City and craved the limelight of success, the big money, and the easy life, he had come in contact with men of Socialist ideas on the *Masses*. After he had heard Bill Haywood talk about the struggle at Mabel Dodge's salon in her house on Fifth Avenue, he went to observe the Paterson strike at first hand. He was arrested in April 18, in Paterson and jailed for four days merely for watching the strike.[52] ("He is the first magazine writer," commented the New York *Call,* "to take the educational course which Paterson is gratuitously supplying to all comers.")[53] Upon his release, Reed quite his job with the *American Magazine* and went back to Paterson again and again, addressing the strikers, and leading them in singing. But it was with the preparation of the pageant, once his idea was accepted by the strike committee, that he especially busied himself. He enlisted an army of talent in New York to help in the preparations, but the script was written in Paterson with the strikers, aided by Reed, evolving the details of each scene. At the outset the pageant was a modest venture. The first public report announced that 200 strikers had been selected to march the 23 miles to Madison Square Garden and recreate the strike for a New York audience. On June 4, three days before the performance, the New York *Call* announced that 1,000 strikers would present "America's First Labor Play." The actual cast consisted of 1,029 striking workers from Paterson.[54]

Before a standing-room-only crowd of over 15,000, and against Bobby Jones' set of a silk mill, the entire action of the strike was presented in the form of a tableau. The six episodes showed the walkout, the picketing and brutality of the police, the funeral of Modestino Valentino, a mass meeting at Haledon, the departure of the strikers' children, and a typical strike meeting in Turn Hall at which Gurley Flynn, Carlo Tresca, and Bill Haywood addressed the crowd.[55] As the pageant unfolded, the audience was deeply stirred. One witness to the historic event wrote: "Here and there, from the balcony, the boxes, and the great main floor, the sound of sobbing that was drowned in singing, proved that the audience had 'got' Paterson."[56]

The New York police department was prepared for rioting and violence, and Sheriff Julius Harburger, in advance of the performance, characterized it as containing "sedition, treasonable utterances, un-American doctrines, advocating sabotage, fulmination of paranoical ebullitions, inflammatory, hysterical unsound doctrines." Seated in a box near the stage, Harburger told reporters: "Just let anybody say one word of disrespect to the flag and I will stop the show so quickly it will take their breath away."[57] But the Pageant was played through without any outbursts from the sheriff or the police.

Press reaction to the Pageant varied. *The New York Times* denounced the performance as a "show with the design of stimulating mad passions against law and order and promulgating a gospel of discontent." But the New York *Call* hailed the Pageant for having "showed the self-directing ability of the workers, and it manifests their great spirit of solidarity." *The Independent* declared that "no stage in the country had ever seen a more real dramatic expression of American life."[58] Insofar as bringing the strike and the I.W.W. before the public, the Pageant was a success. But as a fund-raising device it was a failure. The large attendance was no true index of the gate receipts. At the last moment the seats priced at a dollar or two dollars were still vacant so the large crowd for whom no cheap seats remained were admitted at 25 cents each. Actually, there were not enough guards and ushers to handle the overflow crowds, and thousands entered the Garden free. Workers constituted the major part of the audience.[59]

The strikers' vision of a swollen relief fund from the Pageant soon proved to be an illusion. On the night of the Pageant, Haywood announced a $6,000 profit. After the calculation of expenses, the Pageant showed not a huge profit, as had been expected, but a deficit of $1,996. (John Reed explained that it was impossible to make a profit from a single performance when it cost $600 to build a stage, $750 for scenery, and $1,000 for rental of the Garden, beside the cost of transporting the huge cast to New York.) Rumors that the deficit was due to the fact that the organizers were dishonest, probably spread by the manufacturers in an effort to create dissension among the strikers, ran through Paterson.[60] Although the I.W.W. denounced these rumors, citing evidence to prove that no one involved made any money on the Pageant, the damage had been done. The failure of the Pageant from a financial standpoint at a moment when the strikers had been led to expect thousands of dollars marked the beginning of the end of the strike. Early in the following year, Elizabeth Gurley Flynn asserted that "the Pageant marked the climax of the Paterson strike," and was a fundamental reason for its failure.[61] When the Pageant failed to replenish the strike treasury, it became impossible to maintain the morale of the strikers. Less hardy workers began drifting back to their jobs.

DEFEAT OF STRIKERS

Late in June, with nerves strained and the treasury almost empty, the general strike committee made a last bid for victory. Circulars labeled "Starvation Stalks Through Paterson" were distributed in neighboring cities urging all workers "to aid us in our need. We will hold the picket line; we will fill the jails if need be. But *you* must help us fight starvation. Help us and we will win."[62] A determined effort was simultaneously made to keep the picket line moving around the mills. But both efforts were unsuccessful. Little came in to the treasury, and the manufacturers, realizing that the ranks of the strikers were beginning to weaken, began to apply extra pressure on the authorities. The arrests of pickets were stepped up, and the I.W.W. began to find it more and more difficult to replace the pickets who were put in jail.[63] A group of prominent liberal New Yorkers addressed a petition to President Wilson asking for a Congressional investigation of the widespread violation of civil liberties in Paterson, pointing out that hundreds of strikers were being "fined and imprisoned for no other offense than walking the streets in a peaceful manner." Nothing came of this petition.[64]

By this time, strike meetings began to hear talk about sabotage "if they had to go back."* It was clear that the end of the strike was in sight. On June 27, for the first time, strike headquarters conceded that while a proposal for shop by shop settlement of the strike was voted down by

---

* Frederick Sumner Boyd, an English intellectual, a Socialist and I.W.W. member from New York, was arrested, convicted, and sent to jail "for advocating sabotage to a crowd of strikers." (Paterson *Press,* July 6, Aug. 20, 1913.) Although there was opposition to this approach among the strikers, the I.W.W. defended him on the grounds of free speech and the fact that he had not actually violated any law.

the strikers, a large number had favored the idea. On July 7, however, the employers offered to deal with the workers by shops, and more and more shops began to desert the strike and return to work. Actually, from the first of July on the strike was in the process of disintegration, although a few rear-guard actions were still fought. By July 17, several plants were running almost in full swing. The collapse came with vengeance on July 18; the general strike committee was repudiated when it still held out against shop by shop settlements and was forced to give its approval to this method of settling the strike.[65] Broken into 300 separate groups, the strikers were forced to give up their demands and return, hoping to get some concessions from the employers. But the majority returned to work under the same conditions which they had left four months before. The manufacturers boasted: "The main point upon which the silk manufacturers can congratulate themselves is that the operatives are returning to work under the same conditions as existed before the strike, no concessions having been granted."[66]

Not all the strikers returned to work. Rather than surrender, at least 2,500 workers, including many Italians, left the city. Moreover, many mills refused to dismiss the scabs taken on during the strike which meant no employment for the workers they had replaced. Two thousand workers were put on a "blacklist" by the mill owners with little hope of gaining employment.[67]

The strike was officially ended on August 1. (Haywood, however, insisted that it was "just beginning" since the workers meant "to fight them [the bosses] with sabotage."[68]) On August 3, the children of the strikers who had been living with sympathizers in New York and other cities were sent back to their parents. With this, the curtain rang down on the Paterson strike. A year later, a post-mortem was held when the Commission on Industrial Relations heard testimony for three days in Paterson on the causes of the strike, the conduct of the police and other authorities, and the role of the I.W.W. in the struggle. While the hearings were valuable in exposing once again the abominable conditions in the silk mills, in reminding Americans of how the civil liberties of the strikers had been destroyed, and in revealing once again the heroism of the strikers, it had no effect on the determination of the employers to keep unionism out of the plants. The upshot of the investigation was reflected in the Paterson *Press*'s joyful report of an interview with Chairman Frank P. Walsh who told the *Press* reporter: "You have indeed a city to be proud of and I congratulate you."[69] It was an opinion few workers in Paterson shared.

It was useless for the I.W.W. to argue that "the strike has not been lost."[70] The plain truth is that the strikers, starved into submission, had been defeated in spite of their remarkable display of courage and solidarity for 22 weeks. In the vast majority of cases, the strikers had to go back to work unconditionally, so that so far as material results were concerned the strike was a failure. Some workers did receive wage increases, but the 55-hour week was retained by all the Paterson mills and the three-and four-loom system continued in operation.[71]

As the strike drew to a close, the foes of the I.W.W. opened fire on the Wobblies. They charged that the strike leaders had committed one blunder after another, dooming the strikers to defeat. By endorsing mass picketing, the argument ran, they invited arrest, gave the police an excuse to jail hundreds of strikers, and involved the strike committee in expensive, time-consuming legal battles. By stubbornly refusing to settle with individual manufacturers, they aligned the entire industry against the strike and promoted the solidarity of capital while rupturing the ranks of the strikers. Unlike Lawrence, there were many Paterson employers and they were without organization. A wise leadership, the critics of the I.W.W. charged, would have tried to get them pulling against each other by negotiating settlements with some, thereby weakening the enemy and increasing the strikers' strength. But the I.W.W. refused to permit such tactics, and the consequence was that the employers united and starved the workers back to their jobs. The insistence of the Wobblies upon diverting the strikers' activities into the Pageant and the prolonging of the strike long after it was clear that victory was impossible—these were among the other tactical errors charged against the I.W.W. In addition, there were charges of misappropriation of funds by the strike leaders.[72]

Some of these criticisms were justified, but the critics overlooked the fact that the same tactics used by the I.W.W. at Paterson had worked at Lawrence. At Paterson, they proved wanting. Elizabeth Gurley Flynn explained shortly after the strike what she regarded to be the major difference between Lawrence and Paterson. "In Paterson there was . . . no trustification, no company that had the balance of power upon whom we could concentrate our attack. In Lawrence, we had the American Woolen Company. Once having forced the American Woolen Company to settle, it was an easy matter to gather in the threads of the other mills."[73] There was another difference between Lawrence and Paterson. In Lawrence the I.W.W. stopped the only source of income for the mill owners. But the Paterson silk manufacturers also owned plants in Pennsylvania and the I.W.W. was never able to stop production in these mills. Even though they were slowed by the strike, they continued to produce moderate amounts of cheap silk.[74] Probably the strikers could have forced the smaller Paterson firms who had no branches in Pennsylvania to settle, but since the Wobblies opposed individual shop settlements, this opportunity was allowed to go by the board.

Whether the strikers could have forced the individual mill owners to sign separate settlements is open to question. In the hearings of the U.S.

Commission on Industrial Relations, which investigated the causes of the Paterson strike, all the mill owners asserted that they never would have signed an agreement with the I.W.W. The New Jersey Bureau of Statistics of Labor and Industries also claimed that the 300 mill owners would never have yielded as long as the strikers were led by the I.W.W. because they regarded the organization as "an evil influence and positive menace which must not be yielded to." Naturally, the enemies of the I.W.W. seized upon such statements as proof of their argument that the mere presence of the I.W.W. in the strike guaranteed its failure.[75]

The I.W.W. officially explained the defeat of the strikers on one cause alone: "Hunger. Nothing else. Five months' Hunger."[76]* While this was an oversimplification, there was much truth in it. The owners could see at any time the pitiful condition of the strikers and intensify their pressure to smash the strike. But there was another basic course for the defeat of the strikers: the brutal suppression of their democratic rights.

In 1914, Patrick F. Gill and Redmond S. Brennan made a thorough investigation of the Paterson strike for the Commission on Industrial Relations. They found that "the police organization coupled with the police magistrates' court, became tools of oppression," and "acted in the capacity of despots." They found, too, that "the police authority of the State was, in effect, turned over to the mill-owners." They also found that "private detectives, to the number of about sixty, were brought into the city, clothed with the authority of the police and of the sheriff, and employed, not strictly as an adjunct to the state authority, but as a private army of the mill-owners." They noted that the mill owners had not resorted to injunctions to break the strike, and explained: "[They] fully, speedily, and completely accomplished the same purpose by using the grand juries, the police magistrates and police, and by arresting the strikers, principally on charges of disorderly conduct and unlawful assemblage. Injunction proceedings, with the summary actions on charges of contempt, were not needed in Paterson in view of the manner in which the county prosecutor, the police and the police magistrate acted during the trouble." They found

---

* The I.W.W. was critical of the Socialist Party for not coming to the assistance of the strikers more effectively with funds and supplies for the relief fund. There was some justification for this criticism even though the New York *Call* gave the strike wider coverage than did any other newspaper and rallied full support for the Pageant. In general, the New York Socialists were never solidly behind the I.W.W. in the strike, and tried to play down the role of the Wobblies until the struggle was over, when they blamed them as being solely responsible for the defeat. When the strikers were asked to appear in the May Day parade in New York, it was done with the expressed warning that no I.W.W. insignias be displayed, and that no I.W.W. speak. (*Solidarity*, Aug. 9, 1913; Patrick L. Quinlan, "The Paterson Strike and After," *The New Review*, Jan. 1914, p. 33; John H. Steiger, *The Memoirs of a Silk Striker*, Paterson, 1914, p. 35.)

that violence had occurred during the strike, but they placed the responsibility for it clearly where it belonged:

"All violence that engaged the attention of your investigators was found on the part of the police officials and the inferior courts, who trespassed every natural right and constitutional guarantee of the citizens. Such physical violence as occurred during the silk-workers' strike was inconsequential."

Gill and Brennan concluded that the basic reason for the loss of the strike was the complete violation of the fundamental rights of the strikers, and that so great was the destruction of civil liberties in Paterson during the struggle that no organization could have achieved victory![77]

There have been few labor battles in American history that have equaled the Paterson strike in the grim determination and courage of the strikers in the face of the use of every kind of terrorism to drive them back to work. Nor have there been many labor struggles in which the leaders of the workers proved themselves, as did the I.W.W. leaders at Paterson, such sincere, idealistic union organizers, ready to share the strikers' privations, ready to face the police clubs and jails. In a statement issued by a group of progressive women headed by Leonora O'Reilly, organizer of women workers, woman suffragist and Socialist, Elizabeth Gurley Flynn was hailed for her courage in the strike: "Elizabeth Gurley Flynn is fighting woman's battle, fighting it loyally and fighting it well. She fights for justice and for equality."[78] Bill Haywood fought so furiously for the same cause in the strike that he suffered a complete breakdown as a result of the strain. "He is dead broke, and has to depend on the good will of some of the New York Fellow Workers for his bed and board," *Solidarity* reported on October 25, 1913, appealing for contributions to help "Big Bill" pay his doctor bills.

For 22 weeks, the ranks of the strikers—composed of so many different ethnic groups—were practically unbroken, and in the end, it was mainly hunger that forced them to return to their looms. The tragedy was that they returned with almost nothing to show for their five months of heroism and hardship.

The I.W.W. suffered a setback in Paterson from which it never completely recovered. Its prestige in the East, at a high point following the victory at Lawrence, underwent a tremendous decline, and talk of I.W.W. infallibility in strikes ceased.[79] The Paterson strike put the finishing touch to the I.W.W. textile unions. Never again were I.W.W. organizers able to rally a significant number of textile workers to their banner, and never again was the I.W.W. able to organize a major strike in a textile center. Their locals melted away, leaving the scattered remnants of the United Textile Workers in charge of the field. (In Paterson the Brotherhood of Silk Workers, in reality a company union, was organized to pick up those workers still ready to join a union.[80]) For the rest of the decade, the textile workers, except for the skilled craftsmen, abstained almost entirely from union activity.[81]

The defeat of the Paterson strikers helped destroy the I.W.W. in the East. Never after 1913 did the immigrants in the East, who had been the backbone of so many I.W.W. strikes, follow the Wobblies in a major struggle.

CHAPTER 16

Akron and Detroit: Rubber and Auto

In August 1912, flushed with the victory at Lawrence, I.W.W. organizers addressed a mass meeting of rubber workers in Akron, Ohio. "If you are not satisfied with your conditions," Elizabeth Gurley Flynn told the rubber workers, "the I.W.W. will lead the war. . . . What was done in Lawrence textile mills may be done in Akron rubber shops."[1] In an editorial headed, "This is not Lawrence, Mass.," the Akron *Press* warned the I.W.W. not to compare "this peaceful and law-abiding city of the Western Reserve," with its thousands of native American workers, with the "alien" city in Massachusetts, "where there are about 37 varieties of languages and as many workers." It went on to remind the Wobblies that "there are in Akron thousands of workingmen who are paying for Akron homes with wages paid by Akron industries. . . . These people are not interested in having a strike that will paralyze Akron industry and destroy the source of the city's continued prosperity."[2]

A few months after this smug editorial appeared, 20,000 rubber workers in the Akron plants, all but 1,500 native Americans, were out on strike under the leadership of the I.W.W.!

CONDITIONS IN THE RUBBER INDUSTRY

In 1913, Akron, the "Rubber Capital" of the world, was also one of the worst open-shop towns in the country; the rubber industry was completely open-shop. In 1903, the A.F. of L.'s Amalgamated Rubber Workers' Union of North America set up a local union in Akron and began an organizational drive. But the union was destroyed through the activity of spies sent into the organization by the rubber companies. The books containing the membership list was stolen from the secretary's room, and those workers whose names were on it were discharged and blacklisted. One of the blacklisted men even brought suit against the Diamond Rubber Co. for having placed his name on a blacklist because of his membership in the union. By 1904, every vestige of unionism among the rubber workers in Akron had been destroyed. In 1906, having lost several strikes, especially one in Trenton, N.J., in 1904, the Amalgamated was suspended from the A.F. of L. for failure to pay the per capita tax, and shortly thereafter completely disintegrated.[3] *

Although organization of the rubber workers disappeared, the companies in Akron were taking no chances. An Employers' Association was organized, with the rubber companies as its mainstay, to combat unionism the moment it would raise its head. Meanwhile, the industry expanded as the growing automobile industry brought an ever increasing demand for rubber tires. With the introduction of new machinery and job specialization, the demand for unskilled labor mounted. The rubber industry recruited thousands of unskilled workers from other parts of Ohio, West Virginia, and Pennsylvania, and from European countries. Advertisements inserted by the companies promised these workers steady work and high wages in Akron's rubber factories. The companies assured themselves of an over-supply of workers through the advertisements, and by keeping a steady waiting line at the door of the factories, they succeeded in keeping wages down and intimidating the workers in the mills from protesting.[4]

But the conditions the workers found made an eventual outburst inevitable. The speed-up system prevailed throughout the industry. A Taylor-trained man with a stop watch selected the speediest workers in a department for a test, and, thereafter, wages for the whole department were determined by the production of the fastest worker.[5] Men and women, working mostly at piece work, were pitted against each other, and driven at a high rate of speed. To earn a living the rubber worker had to keep going at full capacity—men ten and 11 hours in the daytime and 13 hours at night, and women nine hours a day. Both groups worked six days a week. Wages for men workers by the day ranged from 17½ to 25 cents per hour; for women workers from $5 to $12 per week. Most workers were paid at piecework rates and these were being continually lowered while the work was speeded up.[6] A tiremaker told one reporter: "Under the conditions as they now are, it is impossible to make out unless you work at such speed that an ordinary man cannot stand it long. It is simply beyond human endurance to work with such speed day after day, which we are obliged to do in order to earn a living wage."[7]

The profits of the companies, however, soared. The principal rubber firms in Akron—B. F. Goodrich, Diamond, Firestone, Swineheart, Miller, Buckeye, and Goodyear—netted millions in profits annually. On January 1, 1913, B. F. Goodrich Co. declared a huge dividend. A few weeks before it had reduced piecework prices 20 per cent.[8]

* Thirty years passed before the A.F. of L. chartered another national union covering the workers in the rubber industry.

THE 1913 STRIKE

In the summer of 1912, at the request of some of the rubber workers, the I.W.W. organizers came to Akron. Secret recruiting of members into Local No. 470, I.W.W., followed, and between 15 and 50 signed up.[9] Working closely with the local Socialist Party, the Wobblies made headway among the rubber workers, but before the I.W.W. could mobilize enough workers to launch a strike, a spontaneous outburst erupted. The revolt started on February 10, 1913, when the Firestone Tire Co. announced a reduction of about 35 per cent in the piecework price paid to the finishers in the automobile tire department to go into effect that same day. One hundred and fifty tire builders walked out, arranged for a strike meeting that same afternoon, and accepted the offer of the I.W.W. to lead the strike. That same day over 600 Firestone tire builders walked out, practically tying up the tire-making departments of the company, and they were followed by men in the other departments. The following morning men from the Goodyear and Goodrich factories joined the strike, and on the third day of the walkout, 4,000 were reported to have left the factories, one-half of whom were said to have signed up with the I.W.W.[10]

"Situation here is alarming," Mayor Frank W. Rockwell of Akron wired Governor Cox of Ohio on February 14, requesting the use of the National Guard. "Serious results apprehended. Strike of rubber workers has been on three days, and growing in intensity." Governor Cox rejected the request.[11] The strike did grow in intensity. On February 15, Secretary Yeager of the strike committee claimed that 12,000 workers were out. That same day a mass meeting was held at the strike headquarters— Reindeer Hall, a building shared jointly by the I.W.W. and the Socialist Party local—and a committee of 100 was elected by the strikers to draft demands to be submitted to the companies. Picketing of the factories began, and girls on strike both picketed and paraded the streets of Akron with tin pans, taking up collections for the strike fund along the way. The Akron *Press* interviewed Annie Fetjko, an 18-year-old striker, employed by Goodrich, who explained why she joined the picket line:

"My average two weeks' pay is $8 or $9. I can't save anything and I haven't seen papa or mama or the little brothers and sisters since I came here. They only live in Pennsylvania, too, but I can't save enough to go and see them. The last day I worked I made 75 cents, and lots of days I made less. . . . Friday, Charlie, one of the pickets, talked to me at noon. I decided I couldn't be much worse off so I laid down my tools and four other girls in that department followed me out."[12]

The number of strikers with little red ribbons on their coats, signifying they had joined the I.W.W., grew rapidly. By the end of the first week of the strike, the strikers requested additional assistance from the I.W.W.

George Speed, Arturo Giovannitti, and W. E. Trautmann arrived in Akron to lead the strike, and Big Bill Haywood left the West to do his part. As the strike moved into its ninth day, between 15,000 and 20,000 were reported to be out of the factories, 1,000 of whom were women. Of the strikers, all but 1,500 (mainly Hungarians and Germans) were native Americans. While this did not prevent the Akron *Beacon Journal* from referring to the strikers throughout the struggle as a "mob of foreigners," the Cleveland *Socialist* did note that "in this strike differing from the other great strikes of the past few years, the majority are Americans." The I.W.W. broadcast this news all over the country, hailing it as "an encouraging feature which indicates that the American is beginning to line up in the great class war." It heralded the fact that 6,000 strikers had already joined the I.W.W.[13]

At the opening of the second week of the strike, the strike committee issued an appeal for nation-wide support, stressing that "our present strike will determine whether we shall have a voice in the making of conditions under which we are compelled to live."[14] Response to this appeal came from Socialists all over Ohio, especially Cleveland, and from A.F. of L. unions in Akron.[15] At first, the Central Labor Union of Akron also indicated its willingness to assist the strikers in every possible way to win victory, "since in a life and death struggle such as this strike is bound to become, it is the duty of the members of the working class to forget labels and show a solid front against the exploiters of labor."[16] But this expression of solidarity with strikers led by the I.W.W. was too much for the national A.F. of L. leaders to swallow. At Gompers' instruction, Carl Wyatt, A.F. of L. national organizer, came down from Pittsburgh to persuade the Central Labor Union to change its position and attempt to take over leadership of the strike. After a conference with the C.L.U., Wyatt announced: "Akron rubber workers will be afforded the opportunity of deciding whether they prefer to have the assistance of an organization of 2,000,000 members, which has the funds on hand to finance a strike, such as is now on in this city, or to rely on the help of a body which has to make a public appeal for funds every time it takes a hand in a strike." He warned all A.F. of L. members in Akron to think twice before contributing to the strike fund, reminding them "that this is an I.W.W. movement."[17]

This obvious effort to split the strikers' ranks and thus serve the interests of the employers failed. Where was the A.F. of L. during all the years of increasing exploitation in the factories, the strikers asked. The I.W.W. had been appealed to and responded, and only when the workers had rallied under the Wobbly leadership did the A.F. of L. show any interest in the plight of the rubber workers.[18] Wyatt replied lamely to this accusation, asserting that the Federation had planned to send organizers to Akron "for the specific purpose of organizing the rubber workers several weeks previous to the present strike." Unfortunately, because of "the enormous amount of work devolving upon its organizers in the textile and iron and steel industries, they were unable to reach the city of Akron to take up and prosecute the work of organizing the rubber workers of this city." Although this explanation convinced none of the strikers, who were aware that A.F. of L. activity in the textile industry consisted of working with the employers to defeat the strikes led by the I.W.W., the Federation did succeed in organizing an A.F. of L. union of Akron rubber workers. In contrast to the I.W.W. strikers who wore red ribbons, its members would be required to wear red, white and blue ribbons.[19]

Ten days after the strike began, the committee of 100 finally presented its demands. In brief, they provided for: (1) Reinstatement of all employees to their former positions—the employees not to be considered "new" employees; (2) an eight-hour day and a six-day week; (3) a minimum starting rate for both male and female employees of not less than 22½ cents an hour; (4) time-and-a-half for overtime. These demands were followed by a long list of rates ranging from 25 to 60 cents per hour for various classes of workers.[20] *

The companies rejected the strikers' demands, and announced they would not even meet with a committee to discuss them. They would deal with the workers only as individuals, "but as a body, never," and, under no circumstances, would they "submit to any arrangement with a union." As for the strikers' grievances, they were non-existent, and the workers would have been perfectly happy to continue working under existing conditions "had it not been for the meddlesome interference of outsiders." The strike itself, the companies charged, was started by a few "outside agitators" who by "intimidation" were able to coerce the workers to leave the plants. It was being run by "outside agitators," and the companies would never deal with these men. "That is our position now; it will be our position next year; and ten years from now," declared Frank A. Sieberling, president of Goodrich Tire & Rubber Co., who had hurried back from a Pacific cruise to deal with the situation.[21]

The fact that, as the strikers pointed out, many of the members of the Committee of 100 had lived in Akron for several years, some even "for the greater part of their lives," cut no ice. To the companies they were still "outside agitators."[22]

* The long delay in presenting the demands was due mainly to the complicated problem of drawing up a new wage schedule for so many different departments. Three committeemen from each department of each rubber factory met daily in order to arrive at a just wage schedule. Unfortunately, the time it took the strikers to formulate their demands gave the employers the opportunity to depict the strike as "without justification." The I.W.W. blamed the workers' lack of experience in strikes for this delay, and later conceded that it was a factor leading to the defeat of the strike. (Akron *Beacon Journal*, Feb. 21, 1913; *Solidarity*, April 26, 1916.)

In an effort to break the unified front of the companies, the strike committee offered to meet with manufacturers "individually or collectively, it not being the desire to prolong the contest." But the employers indicated a willingness to deal only with each employee separately as an individual.[23] They maintained this attitude throughout the strike. Once during the strike, the heads of the Firestone and Goodyear plants declared that they were not opposed to unionization, that they had always been willing and were now willing to meet with their employees for the purpose of considering grievances. Immediately shop committees, selected by the strikers, visited the companies asking employers to enter into negotiations with them on grievances. Invariably each member of the committee was asked whether he was an employee of the company. Since all the committee members were on strike, they were told that they were not now employees and thus could not meet the qualification set for a meeting to consider grievances. By means of this subterfuge, the companies got around their previous statement.[24] So brazen was the stand taken by these companies that the Central Labor Union even considered calling upon its affiliated unions to go out in sympathy with the strikers. But it quickly changed its stand, and contented itself with announcing that it would establish a committee which would seek a conference with manufacturers in an effort to settle the strike. Nothing came of this plan.[25]

In a statement issued by the Executive Committee, the strikers indicated their insistence on obtaining some degree of collective bargaining, the acceptance of their union and committees for collective action. In language that was to be incorporated later into national law, the Committee stated: *"The right of workers to organize in labor organizations of their own choice should not be infringed upon."*[26]

The employers ignored this declaration, and the Akron press fully supported them in their refusal to meet with the strikers' committees. What was the use, the press emphasized, in discussing grievances with members of an organization that refused to sign a written agreement, and would go on strike again the moment this dispute was settled? Considerable publicity was given to W. E. Trautmann's advice to the strikers against signing a time contract. "He urged the men," the press announced in bold-face type, "to sign no agreement, but to remain free to strike at any time they should see fit."[27]

During the first weeks of the strike, the workers, obeying instructions of the I.W.W. leaders to keep the struggle orderly, were so peaceful that even the hostile press praised their behavior. Indeed, the Akron *Beacon Journal* acknowledged on February 17 that "throughout Akron there is only praise for the very orderly way in which the strikers have behaved up to date." When the State Board of Arbitration, which was investigating the strike in an effort to settle the controversy, asked the strike leaders to temporarily suspend parades and other demonstrations, the request was granted. One of the board members stated that he found the strikers "a good-natured crowd, not intent on violence."[28]

Even when the companies attempted to keep the plants running with scabs who ate and slept in the factories, the strikers did not use force to keep food from being brought in. "Bakers," reported the Akron *Beacon Journal* on February 18, "who delivered food at the [Goodyear] plant this morning were jeered at by the strikers, although no violence was attempted." The Cleveland *Socialist* expressed the hope that such conduct of the strikers, under the leadership of the Wobblies, would go a long way toward reversing the popular conception spread by "the capitalist newspapers and some Socialist papers . . . [that] the I.W.W. preaches violence and destruction. . . . In Akron, they are teaching the reverse. Their message to the striking rubber workers is that in solidarity, mass action, and in peaceable demonstrations lies their strength. This is the I.W.W. in action and these are quite different tactics than the phrasemongers are trying to make the workers believe the I.W.W. uses. These tactics have won the confidence of the rubber workers and are making an incoherent mass an effective disciplined organization."[29]

By the third week, with the strikers' ranks unbroken and the police and special deputies unable to provoke them into acts of violence, the companies launched a back-to-work movement to break the strike. This consisted of the following strategy: (1) The companies and their agents issued statements condemning the strike as "un-American." It was not a struggle "between employer and employe. It is a conflict between the stars and stripes and the red flag of anarchy"; (2) the companies issued statements that the men were rushing back to work, and they assured those who wanted to return that they would be protected on and off the job; (3) a Citizens' Welfare League (C.W.L.) was formed, composed of business and professional men linked to the rubber companies, which announced that it would protect the "person and property [of] every person who desires work." The A.F. of L. aided the back-to-work movement by issuing a leaflet announcing its willingness to support the C.W.L. "in the direction of co-operation with the organization towards bringing about peace in the present labor trouble."[30]

Despite pressure from the C.W.L. and the newspapers and the treachery of the A.F. of L., few strikers returned to work. The companies now decided that it was time to break the strike by force, and the police and deputies launched an offensive against the strikers. On February 25, French Midney, editor of the Youngstown *Socialist,* was arrested for addressing pickets, and was sentenced to jail when he refused to pay a fine. The strikers protested this "miscarriage of justice," but announced that the rubber companies would not succeed, through such incidents, to anger them "to disorder." Carl Wyatt, A.F. of L. organizer, urged the police not to be concerned by the strikers' protests. Midney's arrest, he charged, was part of a deliberate I.W.W. plan to "get leaders in jail to win sympathy for them on the plea that they are being persecuted."[31]

REIGN OF TERROR SMASHES STRIKE

Despite these provocations, the strikers still heeded the advice of the I.W.W. leaders not to take any action which would give the police an opportunity to assault them. Addressing a meeting of strikers on March 5, Bill Haywood declared: "I say to you, let there be no violence here of a physical kind. Let there be no destruction of property."[32] The police, however, were out to smash the strike no matter how peaceful the strikers remained. At noon on Saturday, March 8, about 350 strikers gathered near the Goodrich plant and began "chain picketing." The police ordered them to stop and then, without warning, as the Akron *Beacon Journal* reported, "the police charged them, and succeeded in driving them to Cedar Street, about two blocks distant where the strikers made a stand. . . . Steadily the clubs of the officers rose and fell as the excited mob was slowly battered back. As the strikers were unarmed they could not long endure the severe punishment. Some of them seized bricks and stones and threw them. Mostly they fought with fists."[33]

Scores of strikers were arrested and jailed. On March 11, the strikers were again "clubbed into submission by the police," and again scores were jailed. "The jail is filled with striking members of the I.W.W.," a reporter wrote, "who keep up their courage and that of their fellow-workers by making the jails resound with revolutionary songs."[34]

Evidently police clubs and arrests were not enough to break the courage of the strikers. On March 11, Sheriff Ferguson issued an order which virtually placed the city under martial law, and asked for "good citizens" to assist him in breaking the strike. That same day, Mayor Rockwell called upon the chief of police to prevent further mass picketing. The strike had passed the stage, he declared, where it could be tolerated. Instead of being a strike for better wages and working conditions, "it is an effort under the leadership principally of men and women who are not residents of Akron, and who have no interest except their financial gains inveigled out of the pockets of the striking workmen to cripple or ruin the industry."[35]

Although the strikers protested to Governor Cox that the city officials had "arbitrarily abridged all civic rights of the residents of Akron who happen to be participants in the strike," the Governor did nothing to halt the mounting reign of terror.[36] Thus encouraged, vigilantes swung into action. Active strikers were informed that they were "undesirable citizens," and that unless they left town on their own, they would be driven out. The Citizens' Volunteer Police Association, composed of hundreds of prominent business and professional men sworn in as deputies, was formed. (Most of the members were also members of the Citizens' Welfare League.) The strikers wired Governor Cox and asked for protection against a "Mob of the Rich," but once again their protest was ignored. A similar protest against imported gunmen from Pittsburgh went unheeded.[37]

Wherever and whenever the strikers gathered, the Citizens' Police Association broke up the gathering, often inflicting physical violence with their clubs. Still on March 15, the picket lines were reported to be intact and the rubber factories free of scabs.[38] But from this point on, it became virtually impossible for the strikers to function. The vigilante organization with its flying squadrons in automobiles, "armed with clubs and axe-handles and sworn in as special policemen," broke up the ranks of the strikers. This vicious technique of strikebreaking was praised by the *India Rubber World,* trade journal of the rubber industry, as "a model on how to defeat a union organizing drive."[39]

On March 12, Bill Haywood got off the train at Akron to be met by 200 vigilantes armed with clubs and pick handles. A reporter present described the ensuing conversation:

" 'Mr. Haywood the Citizens' Welfare League has decided that we do not want you to speak here and we are here to give you a ticket to wherever you want to go.'

" 'Have you a warrant for me?' was Haywood's question.

" 'No.'

" 'Then get out of my road.' And Haywood stalked through the lines of the 'yellows'* who fell back out of the way."[40]

Haywood's defiance of the vigilantes infuriated the mob, and the citizen deputies determined to drive him out of town. Rather than risk being "tarred and feathered," Haywood left Akron on March 22. The strike by now was all but crushed, although it was not officially terminated until March 31 at a mass meeting. In a special telegram to I.W.W. papers, the strike committee wired: "The strike in Akron is called off. The men have gone back into the factories for the purpose of perfecting their organization."[41] How "perfect" the organization, was illustrated at the convention of the I.W.W. held in Chicago, September 1913. The voting strength of the rubber local indicated a membership of approximately 150.[42]

"Your acts," Frank Dawson, publicity man for the strike, wrote in a bitter letter to Mayor Rockwell, condemning him for the "Reign of Terror" in Akron, "have been the cause of seventeen thousand people going back to a living hell, compared to which Dante's Inferno is but a flicker. In which as was stated during the probe, 'No man can work at the speed required without being dead in 5 years.' " The "probe" was

---

* Sheriff Ferguson decorated his deputies with yellow ribbons.

an investigation during the strike of its causes by a committee of three state Senators headed by William Green (later president of the A.F. of L.). In testimony before the Green Investigating Committee (as the state body was called), strikers told of the inhuman Taylor speed-up system in the plants, and even the employers, in their testimony, boasted that as a result of the speed-up system, "we got 40 per cent more production with the same number of men."[43]

In its report on the strike, submitted two weeks after the official termination of the struggle, the Green Committee acknowledged that most of the strikers' grievances were justified. It condemned the "speeding-up system" as "fraught with danger" and recommended its abolition; described the complaint against long hours of work as "justifiable," and found that the workers' "fear of discharge," if they submitted grievances to the companies, was universal in the rubber factories. But after justifying the strike, the Committee exonerated the employers for their refusal to deal with the workers because the I.W.W.'s doctrines were "immoral and destructive," and its belief in sabotage justified management in not being willing to meet with committees representing the strikers. That the I.W.W. had actually advised the strikers against violence or destruction of property and that it was the agents of the employers who preached and practiced violence during the strike was not mentioned in the Committee's report. (There was only one sentence in the entire report which dealt with this subject, and it did not even mention police brutality, arrests of the strikers, and the role of the vigilantes. It read: "Many additional police and deputy sheriffs were sworn in, while the peace and tranquillity of Akron was greatly disturbed."*) It was enough for the Committee that the I.W.W. believed in sabotage for it to excuse the employers for refusing to settle with the strikers. But it went further: "The leaders of the organization of the I.W.W. instead of helping the striking employees of the rubber factories of Akron did them much injury and are largely responsible for their failure to secure a redress for any wrongs which may have existed and the adjustment of any grievance about which they complained."[44]

Throughout the country the enemies of the I.W.W. joyfully reprinted this sentence from the Committee's report, and called upon workers to keep it in mind when asked in the future to assist a strike led by "this band of traitors who upon the least pretense flood the country with appeals for aid." A.F. of L. spokesmen, ignoring the strikebreaking role played by the Federation's organizers during the strike, insisted that the struggle was lost because of the I.W.W. opposition to building up an

---

* Since Senator William Green had been elected by a constituency composed mainly of members of the United Mine Workers, of which he was an official, there was great criticism among the miners of his failure to condemn police and vigilante terror against the strikers. (Akron *Beacon Journal*, May 13, 1913.)

effective strike fund. "The Wonder Workers failed because they couldn't support the strikers. The beauty of low dues and no treasury was here shown."[45]

EFFECT OF DEFEAT

The I.W.W. drew one comfort from the defeat. "Akron is a strike of Americans whose ideals about constitutional rights, American freedom and other bourgeois abstractions have been rudely and crudely shattered by the crush of the club and zipp of the bullets." Shorn of these illusions, the rubber workers were in a better position to fight effectively in the future.[46] Unfortunately for the I.W.W. the strikers had also been shorn of respect for the power and effectiveness of the I.W.W.* Actually, the defeat of the rubber workers spelled the doom of all unionism in the Akron plants until the 1930's. This was the second major setback suffered by the rubber workers in their attempts to organize the industry, and two decades were to pass before they were ready to risk another struggle with the powerful corporations.[47]

The lesson the I.W.W. drew from the Akron strike was that "a series of short, sharp conflicts with the master class, which requires little financial aid, will prove more effective in dealing with the powerful forces of organized capital than long drawn-out 'endurance tests.' "[48] A few months after the Akron strike ended, the I.W.W. attempted to apply this principle in the Detroit automobile industry.

STATUS OF UNIONISM IN AUTO INDUSTRY

In the early days of the automobile industry, when shops were small and production slow, the skilled workers predominated, mostly recruited from the old steamboat-engine business of the Great Lakes and the carriage and vehicle factories of the Middle West. But the steady mechanization of the industry reduced the skilled workers to a small fraction of the total number in the industry. The majority of the auto workers became mere machine operators with a job that could be picked up in a few hours. Unskilled workers poured into Detroit from failing Michigan copper mines, from logging camps, from farms in Canada and the West and South of the United States, and from Poland, Austria-Hungary, the Balkans, and Italy.

In no other industry was the process of production more subdivided and specialized and speed-up more prevalent. Pace setters under the direction

* Revelations by the enemies of the I.W.W., and even admitted by the I.W.W. itself, that leading officials of Local 470 during the strike were paid detectives working as spies for the rubber companies, did not increase the workers' respect for the Wobblies. (New York *Call*, June 16, 1913; *Solidarity*, Dec. 13, 1913, Jan. 24, 31, 1914.)

of "speed kings," as they were called by the workers, with stop watches in hand, timed the men on every operation. A standard was thus obtained by which every job was to be done. If a worker failed to meet the standard, he was discharged.[49]

The majority of the craft unions in Detroit were dying; the metal trades crafts such as the machinists, drop-forgers, metal-polishers, and molders, were actually passing out of existence. Most of the men in the automobile industry were unorganized. The only unions were the tool-makers and the metal-polishers. In 1910, the Carriage and Wagon Workers, whose membership had declined from 5,500 in 1902 to 1,100, petitioned the A.F. of L. to grant it jurisdiction over all workers in the automobile industry, contending that the industry could only be organized by industrial unionism. The union was allowed to make a trial and a few craft unions were willing to cooperate, and agreed to allow the workers in their crafts to choose between craft and industrial representation. The union's title was changed to Carriage, Wagon and Automobile Workers.[50] But it could accomplish little in the face of bitter opposition by the auto manufacturers. Organized as part of the Employers' Association of Detroit, known as the "Union Wreckers' Association," the manufacturers discharged and blacklisted any workers who showed interest in unionism. The Detroit police were willing partners of the employers in curbing unionism.[51]

This was the situation when the I.W.W. entered the picture. In the spring of 1911, the I.W.W. received an appeal from a group of auto workers urging it to send an organizer to the auto capital of the world.* In answer to this appeal, W. E. Trautmann began organizing in and about the city in the summer of 1911. He held noon-hour meetings in front of the automobile plants, preaching the eight-hour day and the "One Big Union." Trautmann spent three months in Detroit, and one result of his stay was the formation of Auto Workers' Industrial Union Local 16, I.W.W.[52]

After Trautmann left, Local 16 tried to recruit new members through circulating literature and holding street-corner meetings. Although the local reported in May 1912 that it was "growing stronger in influence," it later conceded that this was wishful thinking, and that members, discouraged by the union's slow progress and the power of the Employers' Association, had left the organization, convinced that "the auto workers can't be organized."[53]

Yet, even a spokesman for the employers conceded that an uprising of the workers would occur in the auto industry if conditions were not im-

---

* The I.W.W. had conducted an organizing campaign in Detroit in 1909 and 1910, but by 1911 most of the locals set up in these drives were disbanded. None were among the auto workers. (Henry Fagin, "The Industrial Workers of the World in Detroit and Michigan From the Period of Beginnings Through the World War," unpublished M.A. thesis, Wayne University, 1937, p. 88.)

proved. Early in 1912, John L. Whirl, secretary of the Automotive Division of the Detroit Employers' Association, sent a memorandum to the auto manufacturers in which he warned: "There ... is at this time more restlessness, more aggression among the workmen of Detroit and elsewhere than there has been for several years past. .... There is a lot of inflammable matter scattered about the plants and it is up to you ... whether or not a spark ignites it, or it is cleared away before damage results."[54]

But the auto manufacturers were confident that the A.F. of L. unions were too supine and the workers too fearful of being discharged and blacklisted to cause them any difficulty. They refused to heed the warning. Indeed, at the beginning of 1913, the Ford Motor Co., which had been operating on the nine-hour day since 1905, reinstituted the ten-hour day.[55]

For a while the employers' confidence seemed justified. The Detroit situation remained calm. Then in March 1913 Matilda Rabinowitz (the "little Russian beauty"), Jack Walsh, and other I.W.W. organizers came to Detroit to give Local 16 a helping hand. They decided to bring the union's message directly to the auto workers at the plant gates, as they came out of doors at lunch time. The organizing campaign would be concentrated at the Ford plant at Highland Park where the speed-up had reached a point that a worker almost did not have time "to catch his breath," and where the monotony of going through the same set of semi-automatic motions on the moving beltlines, ten hours a day, was causing increasing resentment among the workers. Denouncing "Henry Ford, the Speed-up King," the I.W.W. organizers carried the message of organization and the eight-hour day to the very doorsteps of Ford Motor Co.[56]

The Ford Co. called upon the police for assistance, and response was immediate. "Russian Girl Leads Clash With Police," was the headline in the Detroit *Press* of April 30, 1913. Miss Rabinowitz and a group of Wobblies were arrested by the police and carted off to the police court as soon as they mounted the soapboxes and "attempted to address a crowd of more than 3,000 employes of the Ford plant." They were fined $5 each by a Highland Park judge on charges of obstructing traffic. Undaunted by the fine, Miss Rabinowitz said: "I am going to speak to the motor car workers of Detroit if I rot in jail for it."[57] And after they were released, the Wobblies returned to the Ford plant and addressed the employees from a nearby vacant lot. "As soon as the Ford employees were dismissed for lunch," reported the *Free Press* on May 3, "the I.W.W. gang started its work, distributing inflammatory literature."

THE STUDEBAKER STRIKE

When the Ford Co. summarily withdrew the workers' outdoor lunch privileges, the Wobblies transferred their organizing drive to the Studebaker plant, meanwhile calling upon the Ford workers to attend meetings at Local 16's headquarters. A militant corps of I.W.W. members was set up in the Studebakers plant, and literature was distributed denouncing the company's labor policies. All told, Local 16 had grown within a month from a handful of members to over 200.[58]

The Studebaker workers had the same grievance of excessive speed-up and long hours. Moreover, the company had replaced weekly wages with a twice-a-month pay day, and to top it off, it posted notices to the effect that if a pay day fell on a Sunday or a holiday, the workers would be paid a day later and not a day before as previously. A committee was elected by the workers to confer with the company and demand a weekly pay day. When Dale Schlosser, one of the committee members, was discharged for circulating a petition demanding weekly pay days, the workers in his department demanded his reinstatement. This demand was rejected. Under the leadership of the I.W.W. a mass meeting was held on June 14, to discuss the next step. Another committee was elected which called on General Manager I. M. Gunn the following day, and was told that the company would let them know by the end of the week as to its decision. The workers demanded an immediate answer, and on June 17, the men employed in Studebaker Plant No. 3, near Delray, walked out in a body and were addressed by I.W.W. speakers in a vacant lot adjacent to the plant.

After the meeting the workers formed in line and marched seven miles to Plant No. 1 of Studebaker, arriving there at noon and "adding about 2,000 more" to their ranks. On June 17, the strikers were joined by almost the entire force of Plant No. 5, making a total of 6,000 men on strike. The metal-polishers and iron-molders remained at work, but sent a committee to confer with the men on strike, and informed them they would demand a hearing for the strike committee or they would walk out in a body. But the A.F. of L. tool-makers refused even to discuss joint action with the strikers.[59]

This was the first important strike in the history of the Detroit automobile industry.* At one stroke, the Studebaker workers had shattered the myth created by the Detroit *Free Press* that "labor conditions in the city at the present time approach the ideal . . . and the relations between employers and employes are cordial and pleasant."[60] On July 18, the *Free Press* sadly admitted that its estimate of the labor scene in Detroit was inaccurate. But it was all due to the Wobblies. "Detroit has become actively

---

* What was probably the first strike in the automobile industry occurred in the summer and fall of 1906 and winter of 1907 at the Pope Motor Car Co. of Toledo, then the largest manufacturer of automobiles in the world. The strike, led by the A.F. of L.'s International Union of Machinists, was to halt a union-breaking drive by management in cooperation with the open shop Metal Trades' Association. The strike ended in a victory for the union and for the right of labor in Toledo to organize. (Donald G. Dahna, "The Pope-Toledo Strike of 1907," *Northwest Ohio Quarterly,* vol. XXXV, Summer, 1963, pp. 106–21; Autumn, 1963, pp. 172–81.)

infected with the propaganda of the Industrial Workers of the World, better known as the I.W.W." The paper called upon the auto workers to kick the I.W.W. organizers out of the city before these "industrial vultures" destroyed Detroit's "prosperity and good name. In some cities the workers have thrown the I.W.W. out, bag and baggage. The example they have set is a good one."

The workers of Detroit rejected this vigilante-type advice, but the police decided to do the job instead. At first, the police stood by while the strikers addressed workers at the Studebaker plants who were having their lunch period. On one side of the street were the strikers and on the other were the men from the plant. A man with an American flag walked up and down the street trying to gain recruits for the strikers who were described in the Detroit *Times* as a "motley army, consisting of dapper American youths, frowsy-looking foreigners, husky young workers in working clothes, and a scattering of men with gray hair and moustaches." When a striker who was exhorting the men at the plant to join the walkout "reached more heated portions of his remarks, he was ordered to stop speaking by the police."[61] But on July 19, the police did more than issue orders. The headlines in the Detroit *Free Press* the following morning told the story: "AUTO STRIKERS IN CLASH WITH POLICE. Detroit Policemen Charge Crowd Assembled at Packard Plant. I.W.W. Organizer Feels Force of Officers' Club."

A meeting had been held on July 19 at Plant No. 1, after which the Studebaker strikers marched in a body down the boulevard to the Packard plant to get the Packard workers to join the strike. They marched peacefully around the plant and started to go around a second time when the police, both on foot and horseback, charged the marchers with their clubs. Jack Walsh, the Wobbly leader, was severely beaten. Several strikers and David Fishman, 23-year-old I.W.W. organizer, were arrested and jailed on the charge of being "malicious persons."[62]

A committee of strikers led by Jack Walsh conferred with Police Commissioner Gillespie and protested against the attack on the peaceful picketers. In a perfect illustration of double-talk, the Commissioner said: "I have nothing against your organization, but I do not believe in your methods. Any differences you may have with the automobile companies must be settled lawfully or the police will interfere." When the committee protested that the strikers had been acting lawfully, Gillespie agreed to permit ordinary picketing, but prohibited all parades or mass picketing.[63]

On July 20, a meeting was held in the Arbeiter Hall where the workers were addressed by "the girl strike leader," Matilda Rabinowitz, and other I.W.W. organizers. A set of demands to be presented to the Studebaker Co. was drawn up and unanimously adopted. The strikers demanded a weekly pay day, eight hours' work with ten hours' pay, improved sanitary conditions, and no discrimination to be shown against the strikers after the settlement. Leaflets carrying these demands were distributed throughout the city to persuade the workers in other plants to join the Studebaker men in the strike.[64]

All this was done despite the fact that the strikers knew that their walk-out had to be of short duration, for the slack season in the auto industry lasted from May to September and there were hundreds of unemployed men lined up at the Employers' Association employment office seeking jobs. On June 23, one week after the strike started, the men voted to return to work. Their "one week rebellion" had failed to achieve its official demands. But three days after the walk-out, Studebaker posted notices that a weekly "draw-pay" had been instituted under which any worker might draw up to 70 per cent of his first week's salary, the balance to be paid one week later. Although the Detroit *Free Press* exaggerated when it predicted that the "draw-pay" system "will do away with the objection to the bi-weekly pay," it did influence the strikers' decision to return.[65]

The *Free Press* knew that the threat of future uprisings remained, and it urged the A.F. of L. to "step in" before the I.W.W. would succeed in gaining "sufficient strength to affect the industry." It conceded that the aims of the I.W.W. in the auto industry appealed to the workers, especially to the foreign-born in the plants, but its methods made the organization totally unacceptable. Its appeal to the foreign-born could be attributed to their ignorance of the American labor movement. "To the immigrant fresh from Europe, the title 'Industrial Workers of the World' has as respectable a sound as the title 'American Federation of Labor.' The newcomer does not know that the first is an avowedly destructive organization, and that the latter is a legitimate labor organization, and he is very likely to be led by the side that shouts the loudest and makes the biggest promise." Nevertheless, it warned the A.F. of L. to do something, lest the I.W.W. "take hold in the auto industry."[66]

Taking heart from this advice, the Carriage, Wagon and Automobile Workers began organizing the auto plants, basing its drive on the pact entered into with a number of the craft unions under which the automobile workers would be allowed to choose between craft and industrial representation. But the moment the crafts discovered that the skilled workers in whom they were interested preferred to join the C.W.A.W., the crafts repudiated the pact and reasserted their autonomous rights. At the 1913 A.F. of L. convention, the Blacksmiths, Upholsters, Machinists, Metal Polishers, Molders, Pattern Makers, Sheet Metal Workers, Carpenters, and Painters, demanded that the Federation order the C.W.A.W. to cease organizing their men and release all those it had already organized. The convention acceded to this request and the order was issued to the one A.F. of L. union that was trying to organize the auto industry in the only manner in which it could be organized—through industrial union-ism. The nine craft unions, acting through the A.F. of L.'s Metal Trades Department, set out to prove that they could do the job themselves. Their campaign to organize the automobile industry lasted from January to June 1914 and was a complete failure. Explaining that the "dull season" and unemployment in Detroit had retarded the drive, the Metal Trades Department confidently predicted that by a second effort "we shall organize the automobile industry beyond doubt." But the "second effort" was never made. Indeed, "not until 1926 did the A.F. of L. as a whole, seriously discuss the organization of automobile workers."[67]

RESULTS OF I.W.W. DRIVE

Meanwhile, the I.W.W. organizers remained in Detroit. They were arrested for speaking, but they continued to reach the auto workers with handbills. By the winter of 1914, despite the widespread unemployment, it was common knowledge that a strike at Ford, where conditions were growing worse by the week, was in the offing. "Then," writes Keith Sward, "James Couzens, Ford's business manager, came to the rescue. Confronted by a spontaneous labor insurrection from within and by the threat of union organization from without, Couzens late in 1913 conceived the Five-Dollar Day. He announced it to the world on January 5, 1914."[68] An eight-hour day and five-dollar minimum wage for all employees!

The I.W.W. quickly claimed credit for the five-dollar, eight-hour day, and for once many commentators agreed that for all of Ford's claim that he was motivated solely by humanitarianism and social justice, it was primarily caused by his desire to ward off a challenge from the Wobblies. Joseph Galamb, an Hungarian engineer who joined Ford's staff in 1905, recalled later: "Mr. Ford said he would lick the I.W.W. by paying the men $5 a day."[69]

But this was all the comfort the I.W.W. could derive from its organ-izing drive in the automobile industry. After the Studebaker strike, Miss Rabinowitz wrote confidently that the men had "returned to work, more determined than ever to fight for bread and freedom, and intent on organizing the entire automobile industry." She was convinced that "the I.W.W. has become firmly imbedded in the hearts and minds of those who even for one week fought under its banners," and that this would be reflected in future organizing campaigns.[70] But this proved to be without foundation. To be sure, the I.W.W.'s efforts to continue organ-izing were seriously blocked by police interference with its speakers and by the undercover agents and labor spies hired by the companies. In fact, in the summer of 1915, the latter problem had become so severe that Local 16 had to assure the auto workers that "We will not hold any meetings until we get a large body of men organized. Your names and addresses will be kept out of the record books of the union, only the number of each dues book being put therein."[71] But its assurance that with these precautions the auto workers were "perfectly safe" in joining the I.W.W. did not carry much weight. Too many workers had been discharged for joining even the conservative A.F. of L. unions to be convinced that it was safe to join a union that was condemned in the Detroit press as being "un-American to the core."[72]

Yet the I.W.W. organizing drive in the automobile industry was not without its real significance. It had done much to bring in a shorter work day, and as Allan Nevins points out: "It had indicated the existence of considerable underlying unrest, and done something in preparing a psychology favorable to the eventual rise of industrial unionism among the unskilled workers in the new mass industries."[73] Perhaps that was what Frank Bohn, the I.W.W. organizer, had in mind when he told a meeting of the Studebaker strikers that "the strike was not for a few days or weeks, but maybe twenty or thirty years."[74]

CHAPTER 17

The Socialist Party and the I.W.W., 1909-1914

"There are few men in the I.W.W. but what have at some time or other been connected with the Socialist party, either in Canada or the United States," noted the *Industrial Worker* on July 20, 1911. Three years later, there were few men in the I.W.W. who still maintained any connection with the Socialist Party. They had either been expelled from the party or quit in disgust.

What brought about the change?

In the first years of the I.W.W., the forces in the Socialist Party opposed to the new industrial union had taken some steps to discipline members of the party who were also active in the I.W.W. In the fall of 1906, Trautmann and A. S. Edwards—both very active I.W.W.'ers and S.P. members—were expelled from the Socialist Party by the Cook County Central Committee because "the action of these two men . . . showed them to be hostile to the principles of political action upon which the Socialist Party rests."[1] But this policy soon ceased, mainly because very few S.P. leaders expected the I.W.W. to exist for long. When the second split in the I.W.W. occurred at the 1908 convention, most leaders of the Socialist Party, especially those of the Right-wing who had been bitterly hostile to the industrial union organization from its inception, were certain that this was the last they had heard from it. Yet in less than three years, the I.W.W. was still very much alive and a conflict over its "direct action" tactics was tearing the Socialist Party apart.

This clash, of course, was part of a more general split within the party over its attitude toward the trade unions and reform which had started before the I.W.W. was born and had been building up for years.* During this period the Right and Center elements of the party had con-

---

* For a discussion of this conflict within the Socialist Party in the period 1900–1905, *see* P. Foner, *History of the Labor Movement in the United States,* vol. III, New York, 1964, pp. 367–92.

trolled the national organization and had insisted upon limiting its activities to electioneering, had abandoned all pretense of combatting the conservative policies of the A.F. of L., and had generally played down a revolutionary program for fear of antagonizing potential voters for Socialist candidates who, once elected, would secure reform legislation which would "increase the socialist content of the national political and economic life." Opposed to them was the Left-wing which wanted the party to advance the principles of revolutionary socialism, and lead in developing mass struggles, particularly in the field of industrial unionism. Many of the adherents of the Left-wing position were also members of the I.W.W. or friendly to it so that, in a sense, the clash within the Socialist Party began to assume the form of a conflict over the I.W.W.

Meanwhile, however, a good many rank and file members of the party, and even whole locals, even when they disagreed with the principles and tactics of the I.W.W., were supporting it in its free-speech fights and strike activities. To be sure, this cooperation was not without its own conflict. The S.P. locals and members often complained that the I.W.W. failed to give them credit for their contributions while the Wobblies just as often complained, "that the Socialist Party and press deliberately tried to cover themselves with the laurels that were earned by the working stiffs that did the fighting and suffering."[2] Nevertheless, as we have seen, the I.W.W. and S.P. branches cooperated effectively and fairly harmoniously in many communities in these struggles during the years when the relations between the two national organizations were becoming more and more hostile.

RELATIONS IN 1910–11

This conflict did not begin in earnest until 1911. At the Socialist Party's national convention in May 1910, the attitude of the party toward labor organizations consumed virtually no time. A minority report from the Resolutions Committee sought to commit the party to the principle of industrial unionism as opposed to craft unionism. It was rejected by a vote of 54 to 29, and the delegates adopted the majority report which reiterated the traditional attitude of the party: "That the party has neither the right nor the desire to interfere in any controversies which may exist within the labor-union movement over the questions of form of organization or methods of action in the industrial struggle, but trusts to the labor organizations themselves to solve these questions and to evolve in the direction of ever closer solidarity and even more effective action on the industrial field."[3]

The Socialist Party was growing so rapidly in influence and prestige in 1910 that the leadership did not regard the I.W.W. as a threat. In the spring, the Social Democratic Party of Milwaukee carried this 12th largest city in the United States by the largest plurality that any political party had ever carried it. In the fall, the Socialists won the major offices in Milwaukee County and elected the first Socialist Congressman, Victor L. Berger, to sit in the U.S. House of Representatives. Socialist leaders hailed Berger's election as "the beginning of a new and more hopeful era in the history of American socialism," and predicted that even "the new impossibilists in the I.W.W." would now see that their scorn for political action was unjustified. But the I.W.W. was not impressed by the S.P.'s rising vote and electoral victories. The *Industrial Worker* noted that "the first thing Milwaukee did after the great triumph was to say that 'We are not [going] to do anything revolutionary.' "[4]

Although he did not look with favor on the I.W.W.'s hostility to political action, Eugene V. Debs shared some of the Wobblies' skepticism about the value of the electoral victories scored by the Socialist Party. In a private letter to William English Walling, December 7, 1909, Debs complained that "the Socialist Party has already catered far too much to the American Federation of Labor, and there is no doubt that a halt will have to be called." He concluded that "the revolutionary character of our party and our movement must be preserved in all its integrity at all cost, for if that be compromised, it had better cease to exist." Publicly, Debs expressed his concern in an article entitled "Danger Ahead" in the *International Socialist Review* of January 1911. Debs wrote: "Of greater importance than increasing the vote of the Socialist Party is the economic organization of the working class. To the extent, and only to the extent, that the workers are organized and disciplined in their respective industries can the Socialist movement advance and the Socialist Party hold what is registered by the ballot."[5] To the disgust of the constructionist Socialists, represented by the Right and Center elements, Debs' firm stand for revolutionary principles was hailed by the I.W.W. as justifying its call for placing prime emphasis on the industrial organization of the workers. The Right-wing elements were alarmed because Debs' article was cited by the supporters of the I.W.W. at the convention of the Italian Socialist Federation in Utica, N.Y., April 1911, where the adherents of syndicalism and revolutionary socialism scored an overwhelming victory. The convention endorsed the I.W.W., and *Solidarity* reported joyfully that all members of the new executive committee of the Federation, except one, were I.W.W. members. Arturo Giovannitti informed the National Executive Committee of the Socialist Party that the I.S.F. still considered itself Socialist despite its I.W.W. affiliation. The N.E.C. showed what it thought of this development by accepting the affiliation of a rival Italian Socialist Federation, formed after the Utica convention.[6]

The I.W.W. gained further popularity in Socialist Party circles as the

International Socialist Review devoted increasing space to articles disapproving of "the political tactics and reformist policies of the S.P. leadership," and approving of "the new type of unionism, revolutionary as Marx himself," represented by the I.W.W. In March 1911, *Solidarity* announced that it had arranged with the *International Socialist Review* to make the I.W.W. weekly and the Socialist monthly available to subscribers at a special rate of $1, a saving of 85 cents to those who subscribed to each separately. "Big Bill" Haywood, just back from a European visit during which he attended the 1910 Labor and Socialist Congress of the Second International at Copenhagen as a S.P. delegate and afterwards conferred with European syndicalists, went on a speaking tour under the dual sponsorship of the I.W.W. and the *International Socialist Review*.[7]

Haywood's popularity as a labor organizer and a strike leader combined to make him a powerful figure in the Socialist Party. During his imprisonment in Idaho, the Colorado Socialist Party had nominated him as its candidate for Governor. Following his acquittal, he had toured the country "to convey the message of the class struggle," and the Socialist press reported that "Haywood is being greeted by audiences that pack every meeting place, and . . . the people are deeply interested in the narratives relating to the Western miners." His tour following his return from Europe in 1910 had similar effects in Socialist circles. "Bill Haywood speeches are stirring up the Socialist Party," *Solidarity* announced proudly. But the constructionist Socialists were so "stirred up" that they decided to put a halt to Haywood's tour. The Executive Board of the California Socialist Party, dominated by the Right-wing, informed the *International Socialist Review,* which was set to sponsor Haywood's engagements throughout the state, that it could not allow him to address the California locals "because of his pronounced opposition to political action and his advocacy of direct action in lieu thereof. . . . The impossibility of anyone being a consistent I.W.W. and at the same time a true Socialist is apparent."[8]

By the summer of 1911, Haywood had come to symbolize the developing conflict between the Socialist Party and the I.W.W. as well as the broader conflict between the reform and revolutionary Socialists. Haywood made no bones about his opposition to the tactics pursued by the dominant leadership of the party. He had made this crystal clear in a pamphlet he had published (in collaboration with Frank Bohn) early in 1911 entitled *Industrial Socialism*. The foreword set forth immediately the authors' belief that "industrial unionism . . . is the most essential feature in the study of Socialism." Although it did not mention the I.W.W., it was clear to all readers that it was the "One Big Union" and not the craft-dominated A.F. of L. which should be supported by all Socialists. Political action was not disregarded, but its major, though not only, function was to prevent the capitalists from using the state power to smash the attempts of the workers, through the industrial unions and the general strike, to take over the control of industry.[9]

HAYWOOD VS. HILLQUIT

In November 1911, Haywood was nominated to the National Executive Committee of the Socialist Party. In accepting the nomination, Haywood let loose a blast against the hypocritical stand taken by the party on the issue of organized labor:

"As a candidate I do not wish to be elected under a misapprehension. The Socialist Party in conventions has proclaimed a neutral position as regards the labor movement. It is well known that this neutrality is not observed. There are members vigorous in their effort to co-operate with the decadent craft unions. The Socialist Party being a working class organization, it is my belief that our purpose will never be fully achieved until we carry to the working class the message of industrial unionism which means that the productive workers shall be organized as the capitalists have assembled them in the industries. Therefore the work directed by the National Committee and its executive committee should include the education of the working class to the end of industrial as well as political solidarity."[10]

Morris Hillquit led the attack on Haywood's candidacy. In a letter to the New York *Call* of November 20, 1911, Hillquit quoted a paragraph from *Industrial Socialism* in which Haywood stated in the fight against capital, the worker "retains absolutely no respect for the property 'rights' of the profit takers. He will use any weapon which will win this fight. He knows that the present laws of property are made by and for the capitalists. Therefore he does not hesitate to break them." Hillquit charged that this was "good anarchist doctrine," was "diametrically opposed to the accepted policies of Socialism," and that wherever this policy had been adopted, whether it was called "terrorism," "propaganda of the deed," "direct action," "sabotage," or "anarchism," the result had been "to demoralize and destroy the movement by attracting to it professional criminals, infesting it with spies, leading the workers to needless and senseless slaughter, and ultimately engendering a spirit of disgust and reaction." Hillquit urged that Haywood's position "should be disavowed in our party press, promptly and emphatically."

After reading this attack, Haywood shot back with a letter to the *Call* in which he announced that he stood by every word he had written in *Industrial Socialism*. He accused Hillquit of deliberately confusing "direct action" and "sabotage" with "anarchism," and asked him if he had at any time publicly criticized or disavowed Victor Berger's "Bullets or Ballots" article "in which Comrade Berger urged every Socialist and union man in the United States to arm himself with a modern improved rifle."* Hillquit had failed "'promptly and emphatically [to] disavow this doctrine,'" because "on the question of trade unionism he and Berger are hand in glove." There was common agreement, Haywood wrote, that the ballot was important and effective, but by itself it was no protection for the working class. The key to the whole conflict in the Socialist movement revolved about the attitude toward industrial unionism, hence Haywood flung out a challenge: "On this question of industrial organization I am willing to meet Comrade Hillquit in debate at time and place convenient."[11]

In spite of Hillquit's attack, the leader of the I.W.W. was decisively elected to the National Executive Committee. (Haywood polled 2,000 votes more than Hillquit.) W. J. Ghent gloomily characterized the outcome of the vote as a "grave misfortune." He compared its effects on retarding the Socialist movement with that caused by the formation of the I.W.W. in 1905, from which the party, he claimed, did not recover until 1910. "The general acceptance of his [Haywood's] policies would disintegrate and disrupt the Socialist party."[12]

Haywood's challenge to debate Hillquit was accepted. The debate was to be on the topic: "What Shall the Attitude of the Socialist Party Be Toward the Economic Organization of the Workers?" It was recognized that the debate represented the clear emergence of the real internal schism in the Socialist Party which could conceivably rip the organization apart, for both Haywood and Hillquit were now members of the National Executive Committee. *Solidarity,* with keen foresight, predicted that the debate was "the prelude to the factional struggle for supremacy in the next national convention of the Socialist Party" to be held in May 1912. It expected Haywood would lose out to "the forces of opportunism and A.F. of L.'sm" which dominated the Socialist Party, but felt that his fight would contribute to the spread of industrial unionism, "and so we rejoice to see him make it."[13]

Cooper Union was packed on January 12, 1912, as the two leaders of the Socialist Party met. (Admission was by paid-up membership cards only.) The debate centered about the correct attitude toward labor organization, and behind every argument stood the question: Should the Socialist Party support the I.W.W. or the A.F. of L? Haywood made it clear at the outset of his presentation that only through supporting the

* Haywood was referring to an article by Berger in the *Social-Democratic Herald* of July 31, 1909, in which the Milwaukee Socialist predicted that "the safety and hope of the country will finally be in one direction only,—that of a violent and bloody revolution," and suggested that "in order to be prepared for all emergencies, Socialists and working men should make it their duty to have rifles and necessary rounds of ammunition at their homes, and be prepared to back up their ballots if necessary." Berger soon regretted this article, and frequently tried to explain it away by pointing to many statements in which he took a diametrically opposite position.

I.W.W. could the Socialist Party achieve its goal. "An organization that sets forth the class struggle is the kind of an organization that the Socialist Party should at all times indorse and work for." Such an organization already existed: the I.W.W. Haywood charged that the A.F. of L. was too reactionary to reform; it was not a "labor organization," had "nothing in common with the principles of the Socialist Party," and "should not be recognized by the Socialist Party." He concluded by charging that Hillquit did not understand the meaning of the term "industrial union-ism" because he viewed it as "simply an enlarged kind of craft unionism. I will say to Comrade Hillquit that industrial unionism comprehends all that Socialism comprehends, and that industrial unionism is Socialism with its working clothes on."

Hillquit replied that the issue of industrial unionism was not really an issue. He recognized that industrial unionism was unquestionably superior to craft organization. The real issue was: Should the Socialist Party interfere with the internal organization of unions, and insist that it would support only those which conformed to the industrial pattern? Hillquit said "No"; "it is not within the province of the Socialist Party to make special propaganda for the industrial form of labor." He con-ceded that the A.F. of L. leaders were reactionary, but insisted that the Socialists were making big inroads into the Federation, and that the increase in the Socialist vote nationally came to no small extent from the support it was gaining from the A.F. of L. rank and file. It would be a serious mistake for the party to aid the I.W.W. "a purely anarchistic organization. . . . Who in the American Federation of Labor cares for the I.W.W.? What do the organized workers or the unorganized workers know about the I.W.W.? Nothing!" He closed with a prediction: "I assure you that within five years and no longer the American Federation of Labor and its rank and file will be socialistic."[14]

After the debate was over, Hubert Harrison, a Negro member of the party, approached Haywood and reminded him that "while Douglas had won the debate, Lincoln had carried the country." Haywood took this to mean that although "Hillquit had won the debate, the workers of the nation were with me."[15] The debate itself, however, was soon forgotten with the publication in the February 1912 issue of the *International Socialist Review* of the full text of Haywood's speech at Cooper Union, December 21, 1911, a few days after his election to the National Execu-tive Committee, in which he set forth most frankly his attitude towards political action, "direct action," violence, and sabotage. Even on the basis of garbled reports which had appeared in the New York *Call* and other New York papers, the Right and Center Socialists in New York decided that Haywood had read himself out of the Socialist Party.[16] No wonder copies of the February 1912 issue of the *International Socialist Review* were gobbled up.

HAYWOOD'S COOPER UNION SPEECH

"Socialism, the Hope of the Working Class," the stenographic report of Haywood's Cooper Union speech, opened with his statement that he would discuss the class struggle in terms so simple that even a lawyer would be able to understand it. He then recounted the long and bloody struggles of the Western Federation of Miners. He told how, despite many election promises and victories, the miners had won the eight-hour day only after a long and bitter strike. And only when the eight-hour day had been won through economic action, had it proved to be "court-decision proof." The experience of the miners had shown how important was "direct action." "I believe in direct action," Haywood announced. "You are certain of it, and it isn't nearly so expensive." At the same time, the experience of the miners had shown how important was the control of the police and militia. When the Socialists had won political office, they would use the powers of government to protect strikers. "That's about as far as I can go on political action. But that's a long way."

After boldly announcing that he was "not a law-abiding citizen," and that "no Socialist *can* be a law-abiding citizen," Haywood described his visit to various European countries in 1910 and his discussions with the European syndicalists. Then came a statement that was to have wide repercussions in the Socialist Party:

"I am not going to take time tonight to describe to you the conditions in France, though I would like to do so, because I again want to justify direct action and sabotage. You have plenty of it over there. (*Applause.*) I don't know of anything that can be applied that will bring as much satisfaction to you, as much anguish to the boss as a little sabotage in the right place at the right time. Find out what it means. It won't hurt you, and it will cripple the boss."

Haywood concluded his speech with the bold affirmation that "it is our purpose to overthrow the capitalist system by forcible means if necessary. And I urge you workers tonight to determine upon this program."[17]

With the publication of the full text of Haywood's speech, the worst fears of the reformist Socialists were confirmed. In an editorial meaningfully entitled, "The New Utopianism," the New York *Call* denounced Haywood as a man who had never learned how to think, a pseudo "intellectual worker" who was a "soft-handed, soft-sitting non-productive member of society." He had not the slightest "grasp of Socialist theory," a fact which alone disqualified him "as a teacher." He misunderstood the class struggle, basing "all his concepts on a personal experience," in the Western minefields, struggles which were not typical of American industrial society. "Comrade Haywood's speech showed wonderfully picturesque ability, flashing insight into certain important questions—and a lack of constructive understanding of Socialist principles."[18]

But the most effective criticism of Haywood's recommended tactics came from Eugene V. Debs in his article, "Sound Socialist Tactics" in the same issue of the *International Socialist Review*. Debs wrote that he was unalterably opposed "to sabotage and to 'direct action'. . . . These and similar measures are reactionary, not revolutionary, and they invariably have a demoralizing effect upon the following of those who practice them. If I believed in the doctrine of violence and destruction as party policy; if I regarded the class struggle as guerrilla warfare, I would join the anarchists and practice as well as preach such tactics."

Debs went on to explain that "the physical forcist is the victim of his own boomerang," that the blow he struck invariably reacted upon himself and his followers. But his chief opposition "to any tactics which involve stealth, intrigue, and necessitate acts of individual violence for their execution" was based on the firm belief that "the American workers are law-abiding, and no amount of sneering and derision will alter that fact. Direct action will never appeal to any considerable number of them while they have the ballot and the right of industrial and political organization." He was convinced that the I.W.W. would never amount to anything in the American labor scene as long as it pursued tactics that antagonized the workers of the country:

"Its tactics alone have prevented the growth of the Industrial Workers of the World. Its principles of industrial unionism are sound, but its tactics are not. Sabotage repels the American worker. He is ready for the industrial union, but he is oposed to the 'propaganda of the deed,' and as long as the I.W.W. adheres to its present tactics and ignores political action, or treats it with contempt by advising the workers to 'strike at the ballot-box with an ax,' they will regard it as an anarchist organization, it will never be more than a small fraction of the labor movement."

Debs concluded with the recommendation that the Socialist Party, at its 1912 national convention, place itself on record "against sabotage and every other form of violence and destructiveness suggested by what is known as 'direct action.' "[19]

The I.W.W. press had ignored most of the attacks on Haywood's defense of "direct action" tactics in the Socialist papers. But it did not ignore Debs' article, particularly his statement that "its tactics alone have prevented the growth of the Industrial Workers of the World." *Solidarity* denied this, and accused Debs of having lied about the I.W.W.'s policies. For one thing, the I.W.W. did not believe in dynamite and violent destruction of property. As for sabotage, this was "not a principle of the I.W.W., and Comrade Debs knows it. It is a tactic the value of which will be determined by the workers who may use it rather than the academicians who study it from afar." Debs was reminded that his old union, the American Railway Union, "not only used 'direct action' and 'sabotage,' but preached therewith the 'propaganda of the deed'." Did not the members of the A.R.U. burn cars during the great Pullman strike led by Debs?[20]

The *Industrial Worker* charged that Debs "belongs to the past," and did not understand "the new generation" of American workers. "He looks upon things of today with the eyes of the past." He simply failed to understand that the workers were "rapidly losing all respect for property rights and will use, in the future, any means to gain their ends, despite the efforts of agents—either provocateur or circumventeur."[21]

EFFECT OF LAWRENCE STRIKE

While the debate over tactics was growing more bitter,* an event occurred which pushed aside, for the time being, the sharpening conflict between the Socialist Party and the I.W.W. During his debate with Haywood, Hillquit, it will be recalled, had said: "What do the organized workers or the unorganized workers know about the I.W.W.? Nothing." As he was speaking, the textile workers at Lawrence were beginning the strike that was to make the I.W.W. known to every worker, organized and unorganized, in the United States, and would soon arouse increased respect for I.W.W. tactics in the ranks of the Socialist Party. As the strike developed, the conflict over tactics temporarily faded into the background, replaced by close cooperation between the Socialist Party and the I.W.W.

Early in the strike, Haywood notified the Socialist Party that the struggle in Lawrence gave it a real opportunity "to show that it is behind the workers." On the day the strikers ratified the settlement, Haywood declared publicly that the Socialist Party had fulfilled this obligation, and urged the strikers to forward messages of appreciation to the party "for their splendid service." These messages were deserved. Early in the strike, the National Executive Committee of the Socialist Party adopted Haywood's plan—he was then a member of the Committee—to furnish "every possible assistance" to the strikers. The plan was carried out. The party and its locals and leading Socialists made notable contributions to the Lawrence victory. To be sure, Elizabeth Gurley Flynn attacked Emil Seidel, Socialist Mayor of Milwaukee, for not helping her in her appeal for the strikers when she came to the city in behalf of the Lawrence Strike Committee. On the other hand, Haywood remarked that Victor Berger, Socialist Congressman from Milwaukee, "worked day and night on the strike situation, and, while he is a member of the American Federation of Labor, his castigation of Golden and Gompers was quite as strong as any delivered by any member of the I.W.W."[22] The New York

---

* This entire debate, it should be noted, took place during the McNamara Case which had increased the fears of reformist Socialists over any advocacy of violence by members of the Socialist Party. The case will be discussed at length in the next volume.

Call, which itself played a distinguished role in aiding the strikers, felt that the Socialist Party had a special duty to assist the struggle since its organization in Massachusetts, by ignoring their needs in the past, had been partly responsible for "the degradation that had overtaken the mill workers, the oppression and the starvation they faced from day to day."

The *Call,* of course, exaggerated when it stated that "behind the Industrial Workers of the World, who conducted the fight,* was the Socialist Party, giving cohesion to their efforts, direction to their attacks, enthusiasm to their members, hope to all—and also practically financing the battle." It was this assistance, it claimed, that gave the strike "form and coherence." There is no doubt that the Socialist Party was largely instrumental in directing public attention to the strike. As a result, funds were obtained from an aroused public and the wide support of American labor gained for the strikers' cause. The Socialist Party also conducted a national campaign to finance the strike. The huge relief fund collected by the strike committee was in large measure the work of the Socialists. The party also was a leading agency in the removal of the strikers' children. Together with the I.W.W., the party branches in Philadelphia and New York made all arrangements for entraining the children and feeding and housing them on their arrival in these cities. Invaluable assistance was again rendered by the party in the Ettor and Giovannitti case. So industriously did the party work in their defense that Haywood declared that without its aid, the defense campaign would have been paralyzed.[23]

Some Socialists saw in the bold and aggressive tactics pursued by the I.W.W. at Lawrence the foreshadowing of a successful proletarian revolt through "direct action" and the general strike, and even predicted the disappearance of the Socialist movement as a political process. But Rev. Ronald D. Sawyer, Socialist leader in Massachusetts, felt that the "great lesson for political socialism" emerging out of the Lawrence victory was "the immense valuable aid that it may receive from this new fighting unionism." The strike itself had both increased membership of the Socialist Party because Haywood was known to be a leading Socialist and had achieved a unity in the party that would have seemed impossible before this struggle erupted:

"Berger may have sympathy for the A.F. of L., and Haywood in the heat of battle may shout, 'I will not vote again,' but the forces of the situation force them to strike hands and show to the world the splendid example of working class solidarity which brought the masters to their knees. Every revolutionary socialist welcomes with a shout of approval the advent of the I.W.W. into labor unionism, and I believe revolutionary

---

* At least the *Call* mentioned the I.W.W. as the organization which "conducted the fight." Some Right-wing Socialist papers barely mentioned the I.W.W. in their coverage of the strike.

political socialism will find itself working hand in hand with this revolutionary labor unionism."

Sawyer suggested that the forthcoming Socialist national convention cement still further the unity between revolutionary political socialism and revolutionary labor unionism. His appeal, originally published in the New York *Call,* was reprinted by *Solidarity* which endorsed his plea for unity in the name of the I.W.W.[24]

But the constructive Socialists were convinced that if they did not act now against the Left-wing, pro-I.W.W. Socialists, whose prestige had been so decidedly raised by the Lawrence victory, the trend away from evolutionary political tactics would grow to the point where it would dominate the party. On the eve of the Socialist convention, a campaign was begun to minimize the significance of the Lawrence victory and to intimate that whatever had been gained had really been won by the Socialist Party. W. J. Ghent, editor of Victor Berger's Washington paper, *The National Socialist,* and a leading ideologist of the Right-wing, argued that the strike was not won on the picket lines but in the House of Representatives. Without Victor Berger's help and the Congressional action that flowed from it, the strikers would have been defeated. Haywood and "direct action" had nothing to do with the triumph at Lawrence. Haywood had contributed as much to the victory, Ghent concluded, as "Dr. Cook or the nebular hypothesis."[25]

It was clear that every effort would be made by the constructive Socialists to remove Haywood from the National Executive Committee. Indeed, even during the Lawrence strike, Local Yuma, Ariz., had called for a national referendum on the removal of Haywood. This proposal was seconded at a meeting on March 9 of the New York Central Committee by the vote of 14 to 11. However, after the Lawrence victory, the New York Central Committee withdrew its endorsement of the referendum to recall Haywood, and the Yuma motion died for lack of a second.[26] But it remained dead for only a short time. The move to eliminate Haywood from the Socialist Party leadership was soon to be revived. The leaders of the Right and Center actually wanted much more than this—"to discipline some of our more impatient elements who now and then grow weary of the long, hard, tedious struggle and want to take some short cut by way of *Direct Action*," meaning the expulsion from the party of anyone who favored the tactics of the I.W.W. Two weeks before the Socialist convention opened in Indianapolis, *Solidarity* predicted that the party leadership would try "to get rid" of all members who were friendly to the I.W.W. by "calling them anarchists."[27] The composition of the convention made it highly likely that this prediction would come true. Of the 293 delegates, there were 32 newspaper men, 21 lecturers, 29 lawyers, 12 mayors, 160 doctors, dentists, ministers, employers, etc. Only 30 could be called semi-skilled or unskilled workers. "Clearly," writes Ira Kipnis, "the unskilled workers who had joined the Left-wing after 1909 were not at the convention in force."[28]

1912 SOCIALIST PARTY CONVENTION

The issue of the I.W.W. and its tactics arose a month before the 1912 convention opened in May 1912, when Haywood called upon the National Executive Committee to give the utmost moral and financial aid to the heroic free-speech fighters in San Diego. Over Haywood's protest that the need was urgent, Victor Berger amended the motion to request an investigation by the California state committee. The amendment was carried, and it took three weeks before the National Executive Committee concluded that the free-speech fight was a legitimate struggle. Over John Spargo's protest that the free-speech fighters were "a vicious element with criminal faces," the Committee recommended to the party's national convention, scheduled to open on May 12, that the California party be sent $250 to use in San Diego.[29]

The delaying tactics of the Right-wing were resumed at the national convention. The Left-wing moved that telegrams of support be sent to the groups engaged in the San Diego struggle and protests to Governor Johnson and President Taft. The Right-wing amended the motion to instruct the Executive Committee to investigate the situation and report its recommendations to the convention. Even though the Left-wing pointed out that the Committee had already investigated the free-speech fight, the Executive Committee brought in a report suggesting that telegrams be sent to all groups engaged in the San Diego struggle, with the exception of the I.W.W. The Left-wing delegates immediately protested that this was like performing *Hamlet* without Hamlet, since the Industrial Workers were leading the struggle. Nor were they placated by the reply of the Right-wing that the I.W.W. was to be implicitly recognized because the telegram was to be sent to the Free Speech League on which the I.W.W. was represented. It was high time, they argued, that the party explicitly recognized the existence of the organization that was heroically leading the historic free-speech fights. A majority of the delegates agreed, and a telegram of support was sent to each of the three groups represented in the Free Speech League. The convention also wired Governor Johnson, demanding "immediate assistance to the citizens of San Diego, to the end that their rights may be preserved and order restored," and urging release of the Weinstock Report.* These telegrams and the contribution of $250 to the California party to use in San Diego represented the extent of assistance rendered the free-speech fight by the

---

* Although Weinstock conducted his inquiry in mid-April, his report, as of the time of the convention action (May 15), had not been released. It was finally released three days later on May 18.

National Convention of the Socialist Party. It was little indeed, even though it did represent a minor victory for the Left.[30]

The Right-wing countered this minor victory for the friends of the I.W.W. by having the convention addressed by a foreign visitor who was a bitter foe of everything the I.W.W. stood for: Karl Legien, secretary of the German General Federation of Labor Unions and Right-wing leader of the German Social-Democratic Party. When Legien arrived in New York on April 16, to begin a trade union lecture tour arranged by Samuel Gompers and the Socialist Party,* he told a delegation of trade unionists and Socialists that "strikes are very good for employers, as then they can get a chance to raise the prices, but until the workers control their legislative bodies they cannot gain much through strikes."† This then was the honored guest who addressed the Socialist convention, and proudly told the delegates how the German Socialist Party had expelled all members of unions with "syndicalist tendencies."[31]

Following this, the convention temporarily enjoyed a "harmony festival." It began when the committee on "Labor Organizations and Their Relation to the Party" presented a single resolution, agreed to by the Right and Left. The resolution opened by pointing out that political and economic organization were equally "necessary in the struggle for working class emancipation." It praised the "amalgamation of related trades into federations and industrial unions," and hailed the fact that increasingly unions were repudiating the "demoralizing politics represented by the National Civic Federation." It held that only those engaged in the struggle in the various trades and industries could "solve the problems of forms of organization," and then reaffirmed the Socialist Party's neutrality on "questions of form of organization or technical methods of action in the industrial struggle, but trusts to the labor organizations themselves to solve these questions." But it also called on unions to undertake the "task of organizing the unorganized, especially the immigrants who stand in greatest need of organized protection," and it urged all labor organizations who had already not done so, "to throw their doors open to the workers of their respective trades and industries, abolishing all onerous conditions of membership and artificial restrictions." Finally, it was the duty of the Party to give moral and material support to the unions in all of their struggles, and of all Socialists to join and participate in the unions in which they were eligible for membership.[32]

The resolution, of course, was a compromise, but one which the Left

---

* Gompers arranged for the tour across the United States and the Socialist Party for the return trip.

† Even the New York *Call* found this difficult to swallow while *Solidarity* furiously denounced the Socialist Party for sponsoring an apologist for the employers in speeches before American workers. "The working class is sick of 'personifications' who are used as stalking horses for capitalism in the name of socialism." (New York *Call*, April 17, 1912; *Solidarity*, April 20, 1912.)

could regard as a victory. It made concessions to the industrial unionists, and even praised industrial unionism without, however, specifically endorsing it or even telling how to get it. It pointed up the problem of organizing the unorganized, especially the immigrants and the unskilled laborers, which the I.W.W. had done the most to try to solve and the A.F. of L. had neglected. It declared that the Socialists should support the struggles of any group of workers, which the New York *Call* asserted was practically an official recognition of the existence of the I.W.W., and even *Solidarity* felt that the resolution's position on industrial unionism was a step forward for the party.[33] I.W.W. delegates at the convention were much less restrained in their estimate. One wrote from Indianapolis: "The I.W.W. . . . has done great work in lining up the forces for industrial unionism, and it was this tremendous force that brought this body to a definite stand on the industrial field. There was some gloom at the beginning; things looked kind of dark, but the great force and spirit of the I.W.W. finally cleared up the horizon and let the sun of solidarity shine forth in its full glory."[34] Haywood evidently shared this evaluation, for he told the delegates that when the resolution was adopted (and he hoped it would be adopted unanimously),

"I feel that I can go to the working class, to the eight million women and children, to the four million black men, to the disfranchised white men, to the white man who is disfranchised by industrial depression, the men who have no votes, and I can carry to them the message of Socialism. I can urge them, and do it from the Socialist platform, to organize the only power that is left to them, their industrial power. That is what you have placed at my disposition, or will, when you adopt this motion. To my mind this is the greatest step that has ever been taken by the Socialist party of America. . . . I feel that I can shake hands with every delegate in this convention and say that we are a united working class."

Haywood's moving speech was greeted by a prolonged roar of applause. The resolution was adopted unanimously "amid a new outburst of applause, songs and cheers."[35]

The "harmony festival" continued as the delegates overwhelmingly endorsed the party platform with its emphasis on the class struggle: "Society is divided into warring groups and classes, based upon material interests. Fundamentally, this is a conflict between the two main classes, one of which, the capitalist class, owns the means of production, and the other, the working class, must use the means of production on terms dictated by the owners." Impressed by the revolutionary tone of the preamble, the Left-wing delegates did not seriously object to anything in the platform except a plank suggested by Berger calling for tariff reduction.[36]

"Now, Thursday, the fifth day of the convention," wrote an overjoyed Wobbly delegate, "you cannot find a delegate here who is opposed to the I.W.W." He was naive. The very next day the issue that had divided the party from its inception and had become intensified since Haywood's election to the National Executive Committee, emerged. Victor Berger told the delegates: "You will have a split yet, and I am ready to split right now."[37] The "harmony festival" had ended.

To the Right-wing leaders, the applause and cheers hailing the passage of the trade union resolution and signifying the spirit of harmony that prevailed at the convention was a bitter pill to swallow. And swallow it they would not. They quickly moved to remedy what they regarded to be a most unsatisfactory situation, one which, in the words of Berger's *Social-Democratic Herald,* only demonstrated "how the direct actionists have spread their position in our movement."[38] Immediately after the adoption of the trade union resolution and the platform, Berger, Hillquit, Job Harriman and John Spargo "summoned their cohorts into action." At the caucus of Right-wing leaders it was decided to present a constitutional amendment "designed to eliminate Haywood and the Left."[39]

When the Constitutional Committee presented Article II, Section 6, an amendment was introduced, framed by Berger and Ghent, which read: "Any member of the party who opposes political action or advocates crime, sabotage, or other methods of violence as a weapon of the working class to aid in its emancipation, shall be expelled from membership in the party." Moreover, political action which had hitherto been without specific definition, was now defined as "participation in elections for public office and practical legislation and administrative work along the lines of the Socialist party platform." Hillquit announced that the Committee on Constitution "unanimously accepts the amendment."[40] With the cry of the Right-wingers, "The syndicalists must go," rising from the floor, a heated debate ensued. The I.W.W. was the target of those who defended the section against violence, sabotage, and crime. Berger stated the case against the I.W.W. in a vitriolic speech:

"There is no bridge between Socialism and Anarchism. . . . Those of you who stand against the bomb, the dagger and every other form of violence—will know how to vote on this amendment without any further parley. . . .

"Comrades, the trouble with our party is that we have men in our councils . . . who use our political organization—Our Socialist party—as a cloak for what they call direct action; for I.W.W.-ism, sabotage and syndicalism. It is anarchism by a new name. . . .

"Every true Socialist will agree with me when I say that those who believe that we should substitute 'Hallelujah, I'm a Bum' for the Marseillaise, and for the 'International' should start a 'Bum Organization' of their own.* (Loud laughter and great cheering.)"[41]

* Haywood noted later that if Berger had ever seen a song book of the I.W.W., he would know that the "Marseillaise" and the "International" were included along with "Hallelujah, I'm a Bum." (*Bill Haywood's Book,* p. 258.)

The Left-wing protested vigorously against the amendment. The question of violence was a false issue. "You would think," shrewdly observed Delegate Bessember, a member of the A.F. of L.'s Retail Clerks Protective Association, "that every bit of violence ever committed in the United States in working-class struggles have been done by the I.W.W. . . . We should throw out the entire thing." The real question, the Left-wing insisted, was whether the party should go forward or backward. Delegate J. O. Bentall of Illinois put his finger on the real purpose of the proposed amendment:

"There is an element in the Socialist party today that is progressive and wants to go forward, wants to move and go ahead, so that we may gain something and there is another element that stands conservative, reactionary, monkeying with the old, out-worn machinery. There is the division and you can talk for ten months, and that is the only kind of thing and not Sabotage, or violence or anything of the kind."

But the Right-wing was deaf to all appeals to meet the real issue squarely, and, on a roll-call vote, a motion to strike out the amendment to Article II, Section 6 was defeated, 191 to 90. It was then approved by voice vote.[42]

Immediately following this momentous decision, the convention moved to the nomination of presidential candidates. Although the party's two powerful figures—Berger and Hillquit—opposed Debs, doubting his reliability despite his opposition to sabotage and "direct action," he carried an absolute majority. Emil Seidel, a leader of the extreme Right-wing, was selected as Debs' running mate, and party harmony, at least on the surface, seemed restored. With the action taken against the I.W.W., the party could begin the presidential campaign fully "respectable."

The Right-wing delegates left Indianapolis jubilant. Ghent wrote that the new clause against crime, sabotage and violence "expresses in set terms the historic attitude of the party." The fact that the commercial press hailed the vote on the clause as evidence that the party had "sat down on the I.W.W." and as a victory for all Americans "without regard to party," was pointed to by the Right-wing leaders as justification for the convention's action.[43] The I.W.W. press reacted calmly to the action taken at Indianapolis. It had published reports of the harmony that existed prior to the report of the Constitutional Committee, but had predicted that this would not last, and that steps would be taken to expel the I.W.W. "The diverse elements that still compose the Socialist Party—some of them non-working class—cannot all, hereafter any more than heretofore, be expected to support the I.W.W. Such professional or middle-class elements will construe any I.W.W. criticism of their conduct as an 'unwarranted attack upon the S.P.'" When the amendment to Article II, Section 6 was adopted, *Solidarity* seemed almost happy: "The 'repudiation of sabotage' by the Socialist Party convention is a good thing.

Thousands of socialists who never heard of the word will now want to know what it means, where it originated and what role it has played in the labor movement. Those asinine politicians have saved us a lot of extra work, for which we may well thank them." *Solidarity* even hoped that the proposed referendum on the new constitution, Article II, Section 6 would be adopted and all members of the I.W.W. expelled from the party:

"The editor of *Solidarity* would like to see them fired, all right. We have been long convinced that many good workers were wasting time and energy trying to work in conjunction with middle class and professional elements who have never been in contact with the class struggle and know not the mind of the working class except for temporary purposes of exploiting suckers. . . . Cut out the bickering with politicians, who cannot be harmonized, and get busy with the slaves who, at every moment, are insisting more strongly upon the industrial organization of their class."[44]

RECALL OF HAYWOOD

With only 11 per cent of the membership participating in the referendum on the new constitution, Article II, Section 6 was adopted, 13,215 in favor, and 4,196 against. Berger hailed the vote, and called for speedy action so that the party could rid itself of the anarchists and syndicalists, "and the sooner . . . the better."[45] The action did not occur, however, until the late fall of 1912. The key target, as was to be expected, was Bill Haywood, and the operation began in earnest after the I.W.W. leader's speech in Harlem Casino, New York City on December 1, at a meeting called by Branch 7, Local New York of the Socialist Party to celebrate the "Not Guilty" verdict in the Ettor-Giovannitti case. Two days after the meeting, the New York *Call* started the ball rolling by publishing a number of disconnected sentences from the speech under the heading, "Haywood Causes Surprise." The "surprise" had been created, the *Call* announced, by the fact that in his speech Haywood had "made recommendations which were repudiated by the last national Socialist party convention," by reiterating "his belief in direct action," and his scorn for political action. For the benefit of those who had not attended the meeting, the *Call* reproduced the following extracts from Haywood's speech:

" 'Well, direct action is the shortest way home. It is the surest way, particularly for women and children, the black men and especially for the disfranchised American workingman.' . . .

" 'And I believe in sabotage, that much misunderstood word.'

" 'There is no revolutionary action that can be too strong if we will only throw the capitalistic class back.' . . .

" 'The I.W.W. is a fighting, militant organization that takes up the conflict with the savage hirelings of the fiercest of the capitalist class.'

" 'At present we are hampered with too many jails. The jails all over the country are filled with many of the working class this very day. But they are not filled with political Socialists, but are filled by the men and women Socialists of the Industrial Workers of the World.' "[46]

This report served as the basis for the concrete action that was taken to remove Haywood from the National Executive Committee. Although it did not reveal that Haywood had said anything about political action and voting, the *Call,* the New York *Forward,* the *New Yorker Volkszeitung* and other Right-wing Socialist papers charged that Haywood had boasted that he had never advocated political action. They continued to insist that this was his position even though a few days after the Harlem Casino meeting, Haywood told another rally that "I do believe in political action, because it gives us control of the policeman's club."[47]

A move to recall Haywood from the National Executive Committee was initiated by the New York and New Jersey State Committees, both of which defeated motions requesting an explanation from Haywood before voting. On December 28, 1912, the National headquarters of the Socialist Party mailed a notice from Chicago to all party members charging Haywood with having stated in public meetings in New York City that he "never advocated the use of the ballot by the workers, and instead advised them to use direct action and sabotage, a violation of Article II, Section 6, of the National Constitution." It was, therefore, resolved by the State Committee representing the Socialist Party of the State of New York "that W. D. Haywood is unworthy to remain any longer a member of the National Executive Committee, that the committee therefore initiates a motion for his recall from the National Executive Committee as provided by the National Constitution." Party members were asked to vote "yes" or "no" on the motion and to file their ballots with their local or branch secretaries not later than February 12, 1913.[48] Haywood, as his supporters charged, was thus to be removed from his post on the basis of an amendment which provided for expulsion from the Socialist Party and nothing else. He was to be removed, too, on the basis of a speech for which there was not even an official transcript. Local Schenectady pointed out, moreover, that the referendum ballot was "improper in form and decidedly unfair," because Haywood was given no opportunity to reply to the "unsupported charges," and secondly, because the preamble assumed that Haywood was guilty as charged and then asked the party membership whether or not he should be recalled. The Local asked the national officials "to withdraw the ballot" and substitute one that was not "so obviously unfair."

Thirty-seven prominent members of the Socialist Party, including Walter Lippmann, William English Walling, Margaret M. Sanger, Max

Eastman, J. G. Phelps Stokes, Rose Strunsky, Timothy Walsh, Osmond K. Fraenkel, Louis B. Boudin, and Hubert Harrison, Negro Socialist leader in Harlem, signed a "Resolution of Protest," calling the action against Haywood to be "unwise and unwarranted, and to tend to create dissent and ill-will within the ranks of the Socialist Party." It noted further "that we know Comrade Haywood to believe in political action, and to have been of great service to our party in helping to solve the difficult problems that confront the working class upon the industrial field. We also believe that instead of exaggerating inevitable differences of opinion, instead of reviving DeLeonistic tactics of personal incrimination, heresy-hunting and disruption, we should make use of the special talents of every member within our ranks, and in this way secure loyal service and cooperation. We believe in a united working class."[49]

These protests, along with others, were ignored. W. J. Ghent voiced the sentiments of the S.P. officialdom when he wrote: "Either Haywood or the Socialist Party will have to go." With about 25 per cent of the membership participating in the balloting, Haywood was recalled from the National Executive Committee by a vote of 22,000 to 11,000.[50]

The commercial press hailed the outcome of the referendum, and praised the party for repudiating "I.W.W.-ism and its offsprings, anarchism, sabotage and violence." "The I.W.W., while somewhat socialistic in its ideas and aims, is distinct from the Socialist Party in this country, which does not countenance violence or unlawful methods of any sort."[51] Debs supported the recall as "inevitable," although he noted that he would "not have put section 6 in the Constitution." Since it was there, it should be obeyed, "and Haywood deliberately violated it." The I.W.W. press took the vote calmly. The *Industrial Worker* even saw an advantage in the outcome for the Wobblies, since it "has caused ten persons to become interested in industrial organization, direct action and sabotage, where before there was but one. It is 'heads we win, tails they lose' in our toss-up with the reactionists."[52]

A determined effort was made to "Recall the Recall" and reelect Haywood to the National Executive Committee. But it failed. So, too, did a campaign to repeal Article II, Section 6, despite an appeal by Walter Lippmann, a young Socialist and secretary to George R. Lunn, Socialist Mayor of Schenectady, to the Socialist Party to give up its campaign against the I.W.W., which, "with all its faults," was making a notable contribution to the American working class, and whose "follies," Lippmann felt, should be dealt with by "rejuvenation" and not by "excommunication."[53]

Writing in *The Syndicalist*, the British journal, in its issue of March–April 1913, William Z. Foster expressed the view that "the recall was effected for the deliberate purpose of splitting the party and thus forcing the radicals out of it," and he concluded that "the S.P. is facing one of the greatest crises in its career." It was a thoughtful estimate. Haywood resigned from the Socialist Party, and, in the ensuing months, others who believed in his views or were disgusted by the way in which the recall referendum had been conducted followed. On August 16, 1913, *Solidarity* reported that "thousands friendly to the I.W.W. have left the Socialist Party." Two months later, it reported the expulsion of other thousands. "Misconduct on the question of direct action is punished by ostracism, very often with suspension. The greater offense of whispering sabotage (not against the ballot box, but against the product controlled by the capitalist class) means banishment from the Socialist Party."[54]

By the summer of 1913, relations between the party and the I.W.W. were so bitter that any hope of reconciliation was out of the question. The Right-wing Socialist press, which since the 1912 national convention had increasingly devoted space to a general assault on the I.W.W., its ideology and activities, reached its nadir a year later. Long-time Socialist enemies of the I.W.W. seized upon the setbacks suffered by the Wobblies beginning with the loss of the Paterson strike, to launch a vitriolic campaign of denunciation against the industrial union organization. They charged the Wobblies with having misled hundreds of thousands of workers; with having misappropriated or stolen strike funds, particularly those of the Lawrence strikers,* and the funds for the defense of Ettor, Giovannitti and other victims of I.W.W. struggles; with having mismanaged strikes "to the extent of amounting to a crime," and with having organized far fewer unskilled workers than the A.F. of L. They labeled the free-speech fights as nothing but a plot "by shiftless 'blanket stiffs' with a premeditated object to live and fatten on defense funds," and characterized all I.W.W. strikes as "schemes of I.W.W. leaders, ambitious for office and for publicity." The I.W.W. was described as an organization of self-seeking leaders who were "in the game for profit and not for love of humanity," with a handful of members "pretending to act in the name of the working class of America." In short, it was "the arch foe of all unionism, the infamous trafficker in and seller-out of the working class."[55]

All this and much more filled columns in the New York *Call,* the Milwaukee *Leader,* the Washington *National Socialist,* the New York *Jewish Forward,* the *New Yorker Volkszeitung* and many other Socialist

* On May 30, 1913, the New York *Call* gleefully published a report of a Lawrence manufacturers' investigating committee which stated, without offering any proof, that "when the Lawrence textile workers were starving," Haywood was "habitually consuming porterhouse steaks, mushrooms and hothouse strawberries with his associates, Ettor, Giovannitti, and Trautmann." Trautmann, incidentally, filled columns of the *Call* with charges of misappropriation of funds during the Lawrence strike and the Ettor-Giovannitti defense campaign. (June 23, July 12, 1913.) He was answered by Ettor. (*Solidarity,* Nov. 1, 1913.)

papers following the defeat at Paterson. So vicious were these attacks on the I.W.W. that readers were moved to complain. "At least the I.W.W.'s are working men and entitled to a square deal from Socialist publications," one wrote to the New York *Call*. Another pointed out:

"Under tremendous difficulties the I.W.W. is doing noble work. The services which it had already rendered to the working class are of inestimable value. It has carried the banner of revolt to the unorganized, underpaid, overworked masses. Certainly, the leaders of the I.W.W. have their foibles. Their theories are crude, but they will learn.

"Should the I.W.W. pass away tomorrow, we shall yet say that it was a great boon to the working class. For be it remembered—the economic condition of the working class is determined far more by the 50 cents fourteen-hour-day-worker than by the $5-seven-hour day worker."[56]

But the campaign of vilification against the I.W.W. and the ouster of those who believed in its principles continued. In 1914, 3,000 supporters of the I.W.W. were expelled or withdrew from the Finnish Socialist Federation. That same year, the *Appeal to Reason* published *Who's Who in Socialist America for 1914* which was euphemistically described as "the Men and Women who have made Socialism the greatest Power in the Nation." Not a single member of the I.W.W. was listed![57]

The conduct of the European Socialist parties, especially the German party, at the time of the outbreak of the first World War in August 1914, fully convinced the I.W.W. that it had nothing to lose and much to gain by the severance of its connections with the Socialist Party in the United States. American Socialists, argued the I.W.W., had never tired of pointing to Germany with much pride. Germany had constantly served the party in America as a Socialist ideal, on account of its many deputies in the Reichstag and its large vote. "Time and again, when I.W.W. agitators pointed out the futility of 'pure and simple political Socialism' as a revolutionary force, we were told to look to Germany 'where one million dues paying Socialists and three million Socialist votes menace the rule of the Kaiser, and stand in the way of all war plans of European monarchs and capitalists.'" But what happened when the chips were down? The Socialist Party of Germany had more than 100 representatives in the German Parliament when the war broke out. But only one of these Socialists had the courage to protest against the war—Karl Liebknecht. And what about the Socialists of France and other European countries? They, too, had betrayed the workers of the world by supporting the war* In short, the events leading up to and into the outbreak of the European war had "laid low the pretenses of the political socialist movement," and the fact

---

* The I.W.W. excepted the Social Democrats in the Russian Duma who had refused to vote for military appropriations and opposed the war. "The country that contains such stalwart revolutionary elements is not to be feared, but welcomed." (*Solidarity*, Oct. 10, 1914.)

that the I.W.W. in the United States was regarded as an enemy by such a movement only proved that it was on the right track.[58]

RESULTS OF ADOPTION OF ARTICLE II, SECTION 6

Shortly after the 1912 Socialist Party convention, W. J. Ghent predicted: "Clause 6, Article II, in the constitution is its [the I.W.W.'s] death warrant." The I.W.W. cited this several months later as it set out to demonstrate that the constitutional amendment was really the "death warrant" for the Socialist Party. "Some time has elapsed since the inauguration of the famous section of the Indinapolis convention of the S.P. and the seed is beginning to bear fruit. . . . The recent loss in membership in the Socialist Party is stupendous."[59] Ira Kipnis, in his study, *The American Socialist Movement, 1897-1912,* substantiates this viewpoint. He points out that after Haywood was recalled, "the decline in membership was precipitous. . . . Thousands of Left-wing Socialists followed his [Haywood's] lead" in refusing to renew their membership. Before the May 1912 convention, the party membership had reached 150,000. By June 1913, the membership had declined to 78,000. Equally, if not more important, many non-syndicalist radicals from the Midwest and Southwest who followed Debs began to have doubts about the party.[60]

The stand taken by the Right-wing Socialists at the 1912 convention was to have disastrous consequences for the entire radical movement in the United States. Fred Merrick, editor of the Left-wing Socialist, pro-I.W.W. Pittsburgh paper, *Justice,* who was expelled from the party for having violated the anti-sabotage clause, forecast this as early as April 1913. "The Socialist Party," he wrote bitterly, "is the first institution in America to make the advocacy of sabotage a crime. It beats the capitalist government and the Catholic Church all hollow. A person can still advocate sabotage and keep outside the jail and inside the Roman Church. But you have got to be mighty careful who you train with and what you think, if you want to hold a red card in the yellow S.P." Merrick predicted that the government would soon take a leaf from the Socialist Party and apply the same rule to imprison radicals.[61] This is precisely what happened. Haywood pointed out that the adoption of Article II, Section 6 gave the federal government the go-ahead signal during the first World War for the enactment of criminal syndicalist laws under which "hundreds of men and women have been sent to the penitentiary though not one of them had committed any offense except that of holding an opinion or being a member of the Industrial Workers of the World. . . . The men who have been prosecuted can thank the traitors of the Socialist Party."[62] William Preston, Jr., in his authoritative study of Federal suppression of radicals, agrees with Haywood:

"The Socialists were the first group to create an index of permissible belief and action within the framework of discontent. The Socialist anti-sabotage clause was the ideological forerunner of the criminal syndicalism laws and the deportation statutes aimed at dissident members of the community. It was not surprising, moreover, that the more conservative and moderate elements of society should rush in where the Socialists had not feared to tread."[63]

CHAPTER 18

The Debate over "Boring-from-Within"

Although the major issues in the conflict between the I.W.W. and the Socialist Party revolved about direct versus political action, and especially sabotage, many Socialists had criticized the I.W.W. for "dual unionism" since its birth. Socialist theorists regularly predicted that this policy, along with the I.W.W.'s opposition to political action and reliance on "direct action," would prevent the organization from growing and stabilizing itself. Unless this policy was reversed and replaced by the policy of "boring-from-within," the I.W.W. would pass into oblivion like the Socialist Trade and Labor Alliance. A number of these critics acknowledged the sincerity of the I.W.W. and admired the courage and militancy of those associated with the organization who adhered to their convictions in the face of imprisonment, terror, and death. But they criticized the I.W.W. for withdrawing the revolutionary blood from the old trade unions at a time when it was most needed, contending that the abandonment of the old unions by the militants amounted to a complete surrender to the conservative labor bureaucracy, and that this was a mortal blow to all revolutionary sentiments of organized labor in the United States.

The Wobblies had always heaped scorn on these arguments, and, as relations between the Socialist Party and the I.W.W. became increasingly bitter, this was reflected in the bitterness with which the case for "boring-from-within" was greeted in I.W.W. circles. In 1910, the I.W.W. dismissed the Socialist call for the Wobblies to use their energy "inside the A.F. of L. to gradually transform said organization into an industrial organization" with the statement that the A.F. of L. "is not a labor organization," and that even if its leadership "is succeeded by 'Socialists' of the S.P. type the A.F. of L. would be almost as yellow as it is today. The S.P. proves this itself, as it is becoming more reactionary every year."[1] In December 1910, Haywood thought he had clinched the argument against "boring-from-within" by quoting Eugene V. Debs as having told him: " 'Bill, there is no other thing than this: there is nothing but industrial unionism. To work in the ranks of the A.F. of L. and try to reorganize that movement is the same as to try to revolutionize the English trade unions. It is impossible."[2]

In reality, the debate over this issue was just beginning. For the Socialists outside the I.W.W. were not the only ones to criticize the policy of "dual unionism." In 1911, a group inside the I.W.W., led by William Z. Foster, also raised the issue.

ROLE OF WILLIAM Z. FOSTER

Foster, it will be remembered, had participated in the Spokane free-speech fight in 1909, and as a result served almost two months in jail. While imprisoned, he joined the I.W.W. He wrote later that "it was chiefly disgust with the petty-bourgeois leadership and policies of the S.P. that made me join the I.W.W. . . . It was an easy step for me to conclude from the paralyzing reformism of the S.P. that political action in general was fruitless and that the way to working-class emancipation was through militant trade-union action, culminating in the general strike."[3] Now a convinced syndicalist, Foster decided to visit France "to study French syndicalism at first hand." As he wrote on board the German steamer that was taking him to Cherbourg: "I don't profess to know a great deal about direct action but at present writing, I am on my way to a country where I should learn a little, namely, France."[4]

Foster stayed in France six months, learned the French language, carried on lengthy discussions with the leaders of the General Confederation of Labor (C.G.T.), and read the writings of the French syndicalist theorists. From France he went to Germany where he also stayed six months studying the labor movement. In August 1911, Vincent St. John instructed him to go to Budapest, Hungary, to represent the I.W.W. at the Socialist-dominated national Trade Union Secretariat. There he challenged the credentials of James Duncan, vice-president of the A.F. of L., on the grounds that the Federation "was not a revolutionary organization and that Duncan was a member of the National Civic Federation," a fact which alone should disqualify him from representing the American working class. Foster demanded the seating of the I.W.W. which he described as "a revolutionary group of 30,000 members." He received the vote of the French C.G.T., but the I.W.W. was almost unanimously rejected and Duncan seated.[5]

In September 1911, after receiving a cable from St. John requesting that he attend the forthcoming I.W.W. convention, Foster returned to the United States. P. Monatte, editor of *La Vie Ouvrière*, the semi-monthly syndicalist review published in Paris, informed the I.W.W. that Foster's stay in France had enabled him "to penetrate more and more the spirit of the French movement and to get a clear grasp of its different aspects."[6]

One aspect of French syndicalism which had deeply impressed Foster was the tactic of "boring-from-within," the policy of militant workers penetrating conservative unions rather than withdrawing from them and "trying to construct new, ideal, industrial unions on the outside." This policy was based in the C.G.T. upon the theory of the militant minority, according to which the most revolutionary elements among the masses organized themselves into definite groups, *noyaux,* within the broad trade unions. Through this organized militant minority, Foster discovered, the revolutionary syndicalists gained control of the French trade unions.[7]

It took some time for Foster to become convinced that this policy was correct and should be applied in the United States. In a letter from France, published in *Solidarity* of November 19, 1910, one of many he sent to the I.W.W. press from Europe, Foster wrote of the A.F. of L.: "The various unions composing it are reactionary and the cliques controlling them are doing their best to keep them so. Time after time these cliques have frustrated the attempts of progressive members of the rank and file to make the organizations more in accord with modern conditions. So strongly are the cliques intrenched that in all likelihood their organizations must perish, incapable of evolution." The contention that the A.F. of L. could never evolve into an industrial union was standard I.W.W. ideology, and was hammered home to the membership again and again by Wobbly leaders.[8]

What caused Foster to change his mind was not only that the French syndicalists convinced him that they, too, had once held the same opinion about the conservative trade unions in their own country only to be proven wrong once they began to apply the "boring-from-within" policy, but also that the British syndicalists had had the same experience. Tom Mann, the fiery orator and superb organizer, a man who has been called "an entire movement in himself," had been deeply influenced by the ideas of the I.W.W. as they were outlined to him by the Irish radical, James Connolly, who had emigrated to the United States. Mann at first agreed with Connolly that the A.F. of L. was nothing but a "usurper on the throne of labor," and that the I.W.W. held out the only hope for the American workers. Mann returned to England in 1908 after a long sojourn in Australia, determined to work for the principles of the I.W.W. in his native land. But first he went to France to study the French syndicalist movement. Like Foster, he became convinced that "boring-from-within," as practiced by the syndicalists of France, was correct, and he returned to England determined that the British syndicalists should join the existing trade unions and prove to the members that they could "make these organizations what they desired them to be."

To pursue the policy of "permeation" (as the British called "boring-from-within"), Mann and his followers, against the bitter opposition of the British division of the I.W.W., formed the Industrial Syndicalist

Education League. The League conducted such effective propaganda that it was responsible for the establishment of a number of "Amalgamation Committees" in different industries—especially building, engineering, and transport—to campaign for the formation of industrial unions out of existing craft societies. Mann started preaching his gospel of syndicalism in May 1910, and by the spring of 1911, he and his followers had begun to transform the conservative trade unions in England into militant organizations, with their rank and file imbued with a fighting spirit.[9]

In the summer of 1911, a great wave of industrial unrest broke out in Great Britain and flowed over into Ireland. Two gigantic national strikes of the transit workers and the railway men in Britain heralded the dawn of a new day for labor. The first of these began with the seamen's and firemens' strike which broke out in Hull in the middle of June 1911 and which, by the end of the month, had crippled every port in Britain. This was only the beginning of a sympathetic strike movement in the waterside trades. Dockers, coal-fillers and carters were soon out in sympathy with the seamen and firemen, demanding also an improvement in their own wages and conditions. In Dublin, the dockers refused to unload ships from striking ports in Britain. The strike ended in a tremendous victory for the waterside trades in Britain.

The second great national strike was the great railway strike called in August 1911. This, too, ended in a victory for the strikers. These victories, moreover, were won in the face of government opposition and brutality on the part of the police and troops. Winston Churchill, Home Secretary, threatened to dispatch 25,000 troops to the docks of London to break the strike by doing the dockers' work. Both strikes revealed that a new spirit had emerged in British labor, a spirit greatly influenced by the work of Tom Mann and his followers. Mann himself led the great general transport strike in Liverpool, embracing dockers, seamen, carters, tramwaymen and railwaymen, a total of 70,000 being on strike. All told, more men went on strike in England in 1911 than in any previous year.[10]

Leon Jouhaux, Secretary of the French C.G.T., convinced Foster that what the French syndicalists had achieved and what Tom Mann and the British syndicalists were accomplishing, could be duplicated in the United States. He urged Foster "to tell the I.W.W. when you return to America to get into the labor movement."[11]

FOSTER URGES I.W.W. TO ADOPT "BORING-FROM-WITHIN"

Foster had kept silent on the issue of "boring-from-within" in his dispatches to the I.W.W. press from Europe, but he decided to heed Jouhaux's advice, follow in Mann's footsteps, and, upon his return to the United States, try to win "the I.W.W. for a policy of working within the conservative unions." At the I.W.W. convention in September 1911, the main point of discussion revolved about the efforts of the decentralizing faction from the West to amend the Constitution so as to abolish the General Executive Board or to strip it of all authority to exercise power in the organization. Both proposals were defeated. Behind the scenes, Foster, meanwhile, was informing the 31 delegates of his experiences in Europe, emphasizing his conviction that the I.W.W. should seriously discuss the need for reversing its policy on "boring-from-within." He won the support of about five delegates, including J. W. Johnstone of British Columbia and Earl C. Ford of Seattle, but was ridiculed by St. John, Ettor, Thompson, Trautmann, and other I.W.W. leaders. To Foster's message from Jouhaux urging the I.W.W. "to get into the labor movement," their reply was that "the I.W.W. is not only *in* the labor movement of the United States; but that the I.W.W. is itself *the vital and essential part of the American labor movement,* and is destined ere long to become the whole thing."[12]

Convinced that his proposal, if put in the form of a resolution at the convention, would be overwhelmingly defeated, Foster decided to bring the issue directly to the I.W.W. membership. Having been nominated for editor of the *Industrial Worker,* he raised as his platform the "boring-from-within" policy, and called for wide discussion of the issue in the I.W.W. press. He opened the discussion with a letter to the *Industrial Worker* and *Solidarity* entitled, "As To My Candidacy." After noting that he had been nominated as editor of the *Industrial Worker,* Foster said that he felt the members should know that his observations while in Europe had given him ideas conflicting with certain aspects of I.W.W. policy. He then declared bluntly:

"The question: 'Why don't the I.W.W. grow?' is being asked on every hand as well within our ranks as without. And justly, too, as only the blindest enthusiast is satisfied with the progress, or rather lack of progress, of the organization up to date. In spite of truly heroic efforts of our organizers and members in general and 'that the working class is rotten ripe for industrial unionism,' the I.W.W. remains small in membership and weak in influence. It is indeed time to examine the situation and discover what is wrong."

The reason for this failure, Foster insisted, came from blindly following the "dogma" of the founders of the I.W.W. that it was necessary to build a new labor organization because the existing craft unions were incapable of developing into revolutionary unions. He, too, had accepted this "dogma" without question "like the vast majority of the I.W.W. membership," until he visited Europe. In contrast with this failure of "dual unionism," Foster pointed to the tactics of the French C.G.T. which "literally made a raid on the labor movement, captured it and revolutionized it and in so doing developed the new working-class theory of Syndicalism. . . . By propagating their doctrine in the old unions and forcing them to become revolutionary, they have made their labor movement the most feared in the world." In Spain and Italy, where the radicals were copying French tactics, the syndicalist movement was also growing rapidly in power and influence. "But it is in England that we have the most striking example of the comparative effectiveness of the two varieties of tactics. For several years the English I.W.W., with its dual organization theory, carried on a practically barren agitation. About a year ago Tom Mann, Guy Bowman and a few other revolutionists, using the 'boring from within' tactics, commenced, in the face of strong I.W.W. opposition, to work in the old trades unions, which Debs had called impossible.* Some of the fruits of their labor were seen in the recent series of great strikes in England." The article concluded:

"I am satisfied from my observation that the only way for the I.W.W. to have the workers adopt and practice the principles of revolutionary unionism—which I take is its mission—is to give up its attempt to create a new labor movement, turn itself into a propaganda league, get into the organized labor movement, and by building up better fighting machines within the old unions than those possessed by our reactionary enemies, revolutionize these unions even as our French Syndicalist fellow workers have so successfully done with theirs."[13]

Basically, of course, Foster's advice to the I.W.W. was that it cease functioning both as a labor union and a revolutionary group. He had raised a point that was to plague the I.W.W. for many years to come.

The *Industrial Worker* and *Solidarity* opened their columns to the discussion, and for the next two months letters argued the pros and cons of the proposal that the I.W.W. abandon its efforts to build a new labor movement, convert itself into a propaganda league and begin "boring-from-within." Either because there were few who supported the proposal, or, as Foster later charged, because the editors of the I.W.W. press suppressed them, there were a mere handful of letters endorsing Foster's plan. One correspondent from Seattle told how an A.F. of L. Plasterers' Union had been built into a militant organization which exerted progressive influence in the Central Federated Trades Union, only to be reduced to a nonentity when the leaders abandoned the union and joined the I.W.W. Another correspondent, J. W. Johnstone, who had supported Foster at the convention, argued that the "strongest weapon" the leaders of the existing trade unions used against the I.W.W. was that it "is trying to destroy their organization." He was convinced that "good results will be accomplished if the I.W.W. follows Foster's plan."[14]

---

* Foster was referring to the fact that Debs had told Haywood that it was "impossible" to revolutionize the English trade unions.

The anti-Foster letters, the bulk of the correspondence, though repetitious, raised the following major arguments against the proposal:

(1) The A.F. of L. was not a labor organization, but "a job trust and nothing else." Why waste time trying to capture a corpse? The I.W.W. was not trying to create a dual organization to the A.F. of L.; it was simply trying to organize the workers of America into a *real* labor organization," for it alone had the program which could meet the needs of "the unorganized and hitherto despised millions of workers. Our policy of low initiation fees, low dues, universal transfer card system, no age, sex or color limitations, no apprenticeship laws and no closed books, together with our constructive propaganda, looking toward the building of a new society within the shell of the old, will soon penetrate and permeate this mass and the consequent action of the aroused workers will bring about the change in society for which we are striving."

(2) The situation in the United States was quite different from that in France where industry was on a much smaller scale than that of America. In France, the skilled workers, the majority of the workers, could be reached by a revolutionary element who were eligible to join the existing unions, and could exert a powerful influence inside these organizations. But the majority of the workers in the United States were the unskilled and were not eligible for membership in the craft unions. Even the majority of the I.W.W. members were the unskilled and would be prevented from joining the craft unions to "bore-from-within." What, then, would happen to the unorganized if the I.W.W. followed Foster's advice? They would remain unorganized. "Craft unionism has no room for the great majority of the unskilled. And we would have no room for them if we join the A.F. of L." Instead of boring into the ten per cent of the working class organized in the A.F. of L., "let us bore into the 90 per cent unorganized and we will be better off, besides fulfilling our duties."

(3) "Our growth is small, but normal and steady, and for this reason it is safe and healthy." The influence of the I.W.W. upon the working class, especially among the unorganized, was considerably greater than Foster claimed. It was better to "grow slowly with the right tactics than to create a fake industrial union by using the wrong methods."

(4) Active members of the I.W.W. had had sufficient experience with "boring-from-within," and the only result they had achieved was that of being "kicked out." If they now decided to follow Foster's advice, what guarantee did they have that they would not be once more "kicked out" of the A.F. of L.? "The A.F. of L. does not want us; if they did, they would not have kicked us out in the first place."

(5) The best way to "bore-from-within" was to "bore-from-without." Already there were many A.F. of L. members who carried I.W.W. cards, and they were the ones to do the job of "boring-from-within," applying

the principles they learned from membership in the I.W.W. But if the I.W.W. were to disappear, they would find it impossible to continue their efforts to continue their effective work inside the A.F. of L. In short, "why not bore within the A.F. of L. and build the I.W.W.?"[15]

The letter of J. S. Biscay entitled, "Building from Without," was judged by the editors of the I.W.W. press the "best reply" to Foster. In it, Biscay emphasized that to adopt the "boring-from-within" tactic "would mean the disbanding of the I.W.W., and hardly cause a ripple in the crafts." He pointed out that the few Wobblies who would be eligible for craft-union membership would be overwhelmed in that movement, while the "rest of the rank and file of the I.W.W. being the floating element to a large extent, can't even get into the crafts to 'bore.' "

"Had this been done from the start, there might have been some success, but not at this stage of the game. To change our ideas at this time would only spell defeat. The I.W.W. would pass out of being as an organization and it would remain then for others to start all over, with the disadvantage of defeat against our principles. By building from without, we will demonstrate to the crafts that we are right. Then the men who stand for progress will do their own boring from within—and far better than any of us could do it. I know of many such examples already in practice. So let us all buckle down to active work and not talk about what we are going to do, but *do it*. Action is all that counts."[16]

"Discussion Closed," wrote *Solidarity* on December 16, 1911, as it called a halt to the publication of new letters on Foster's proposal. Everything that had to be said on the subject had already been said, and it was obvious that "there is comparatively little support of Foster's proposition in the I.W.W." The discussion would prove valuable if it taught I.W.W. members to use "more tact and common sense" in dealing with craft unionists. But there was not the slightest chance that the proposal to turn the I.W.W. into a propaganda league to "bore-from-within" the A.F. of L. would be given serious consideration by the membership. Indeed, it was to be hoped "that Fellow Worker Foster himself will abandon the idea when he becomes better acquainted with the American situation."

FOSTER ON "REVOLUTIONARY TACTICS"

Fellow Worker Foster, however, objected to the closing of the discussion, insisting that he had not been given an opportunity to state his position fully.[17] When the I.W.W. press refused to reopen the discussion, Foster submitted his articles to *The Agitator,* a bi-monthly anarchist paper published by Jay Fox in the state of Washington. In six articles in *The Agitator* (April–July 1912) under the heading "Revolutionary Tactics," Foster developed his answer to the question "Why Doesn't the I.W.W. Grow?" and pointed the way for it to accomplish the mission of organizing the American working class.

He emphasized that a basic error had been made by the founders of the I.W.W. when they duplicated in the economic field what had been done in the political field. In the political field, there was no party that even pretended to represent the working class. So the growth of the Socialist Party was easy. But in the economic field, the A.F. of L., the Railroad Brotherhoods, and unaffiliated labor organizations, while in no sense revolutionary, were still made up of workers and largely represented their ideas and their efforts to defend themselves from the inroads of capitalism. It was these organizations that the I.W.W. had to contend with when it entered the economic field to organize the workers. Naturally, it met with resentment and opposition from the old unions who regarded the I.W.W. as an interloper attempting to divide their ranks, to split them up and to cause bitterness and strife when their experience had shown them that only through close unity could they ever hope to succeed. As a consequence of this bitter feeling of rivalry, the existing unions refused and still refuse to listen to the I.W.W.'s essential message —the need for industrial unionism. Yet to teach this message was the revolutionary duty of the I.W.W., and for this purpose, it had been hailed everywhere by the revolutionary element in the working class when it was founded. But this message failed to reach the ears of the American workers because the I.W.W. presented itself as a labor organization besides being a propagandist organization. The proof of this failure was shown by the fact that after six years of effort, the I.W.W. was numerically smaller than when it was started.

The I.W.W., then, had a double program, and it was in this double program that Foster saw the cause of its failure to reach the mass of the organized workers with its message. The logical question then was: Why the need for a dual program? In England and France, Foster pointed out, the syndicalists did not combine the two functions of labor organization and propaganda league. They carried their propaganda into the old unions; rejuvenated, inspired and fired them with revolutionary spirit; published papers and pamphlets to educate them; routed the politicians and fakers, and made the unions of England and France by far the most potent factors in the labor world. Why could not the I.W.W. do for the American labor movement what the syndicalists did and were doing for the English and French?

But first the I.W.W. had to rid itself of the "absurd and egotistic" claim "to be the whole labor movement," that all other unions were "interlopers and must disappear as rivals." This Foster described as "I.W.W. patriotism," the theory "that all non-I.W.W. unions cannot evolve and that the I.W.W. is the only possible bona fide labor organization." As a prime example of "I.W.W. patriotism," Foster cited its changed attitude towards the Western Federation of Miners. When the W.F. of M. was affiliated with the I.W.W., it had been hailed as "a progressive labor union and part of the structure of the future society which the I.W.W. has the exclusive contract to build." But when it withdrew from the I.W.W., it was no longer regarded as a progressive union. "To us the W.F. of M. is no longer even a labor union, much less a progressive one. It has had its sub-contract to build the mining department of the future society revoked. It has lost jurisdiction over even its own members and like all other non-I.W.W. unions is a target for our condemnation and dual organization tactics. Many of us would rejoice to see it wiped out of existence."* Yet nothing had basically changed in the W.F. of M. "Its membership and form have remained the same and to an unsophisticated observer, it is as much a labor union as ever. But to us I.W.W. patriots consideration of form or membership don't necessarily enter into the determination of whether or not an organization is a labor union. The determining factor is whether or not it is affiliated with the I.W.W. Those organizations affiliated are labor unions, the unaffiliated ones are not."

The truth, Foster emphasized, was that the I.W.W. no longer had even a monopoly on industrial unionism, for many Socialists who were not I.W.W. members and even non-Socialist groups in the A.F. of L. now saw the urgent necessity of industrial unionism. Nor could the I.W.W. pass a blanket judgment against all A.F. of L. unions. Some unions in the A.F. of L. were "decadent, scabby, yellow unions and apparently doomed to extinction." Others were unions of a much higher type and susceptible to progress, and for the I.W.W. to assert that none of these could become

---

* That Foster was not exaggerating when he wrote that many I.W.W. members would "rejoice" to see the W.F. of M. "wiped out of existence," is illustrated in the bitter fight waged precisely at the time he was writing by I.W.W. followers in the miners' union, along with other elements, to displace its leadership. While it is true that this leadership, particularly President Moyer, had become less militant, a chief objection to it by the followers of the I.W.W. was the efforts being made, particularly by Moyer, to affiliate the W.F. of M. with the A.F. of L. In any event, the unprincipled attacks upon the W.F. of M. leadership, charging it with having abandoned the principles of industrial unionism—a definite distortion of the facts— weakened the union, and, in Butte, where the struggle was most intense, led to the destruction of a strong local. (*See* Vernon H. Jensen, *Heritage of Conflict: Labor Relations in the NonFerrous Metals Industry Up to 1930*, Ithaca, New York, 1950, pp. 314-53.) Jensen, however, overlooks the fact, which William Z. Foster later conceded, that while the I.W.W. had played a role in the upheaval in Butte, it was basically a revolt against corrupt elements in the W.F. of M. leadership who were collaborating with the mine owners against the union membership. (*See* Paul F. Brissenden, "The Butte Miners and the Rustling Card," *American Economic Review*, vol. X, Dec. 1920, pp. 755-75 and *Rebel Voices, op. cit.*, pp. 291-92.)

revolutionary unless they affiliated with the I.W.W. was ridiculous. The British and French had shown that even the conservative unions could be gradually revolutionized; that the form of organization made little difference if the membership had a revolutionary spirit. Why should not the I.W.W. seek to imbue the American unions, regardless of their form and organization, with this spirit? But what had been the actual results of I.W.W. dual unionism up to now? It had actually disorganized "the potentially powerful militant minorities in all American unions," instilling them with the idea that the sooner these unions went out of existence, the better, and that to speed this process, they should either leave the unions or cease to try to improve them. "The double result of this is to absolutely disorganize the militant minorities and to leave the old unions in the undisputed possession of the conservatives and fakers."

Foster set out to prove that the I.W.W. could not possibly succeed in its present line of action. He showed, citing various examples, that the A.F. of L. would not permit a rival organization to grow; that it felt justified in crushing such an organization whenever it began to attain strength, by scabbing on it and using other means well known to the craft unions. He did not approve of such tactics, but noted that "dual unionism" always invited them. Foster rejected the I.W.W. argument that its members who were also members of A.F. of L. unions enabled it to conduct effective work "boring-from-within" the Federation. These members were handicapped by the label of "dual unionism," and were rendered impotent.

Foster outlined how the I.W.W. could continue as an integral organization for purely propaganda purposes. Recommending the plan of organization of the British syndicalists as best fitted for American conditions, he proposed that the national headquarters of the I.W.W. be retained and maintained by a dues-paying membership; that a national paper (or papers) be published which would not specialize in any particular industry, but would occupy itself with the entire labor movement, and that a national corps of organizers be established to spread propaganda among the workers in the unions, especially during strikes, when workers readily accepted revolutionary ideas, "pointing out the fallacy and futility of craft unionism and the advantage of industrial unionism, etc., and generally educating and stimulating the workers to revolutionary action." This national corps of organizers, acting in conjunction with the organized militant minorities in the unions involved, would "force labor fakers to give up many of their demoralizing practices."

But what of the unskilled? Since they were neglected by the A.F. of L., would not the transformation of the I.W.W. into a propaganda league deprive these workers of their chief hope of being organized? Foster denied this. More unskilled workers would be organized under his plan. The militants among them would, with the aid, if necessary, of the national propaganda organization's funds, literature, and organizers, set up unions of the unskilled. These unions would decide for themselves whether to remain independent or affiliate with the A.F. of L., and the chances were that, through the cooperation of the militants working inside the Federation, the final outcome would be that they would become part of the A.F. of L. In any event, the efforts to organize the unskilled by the propaganda league would not have "to face the strong opposition of the A.F. of L. they do now."

By entering the old unions, and working in conjunction with the radical element already there, the membership of the I.W.W. would form a powerful militant minority that would revolutionize these organizations. Not only, Foster concluded, was this the *best* way to propagate the principles of industrial unionism, but it was the *only* way the I.W.W. would ever become a potent force in the labor world. He closed with these words:

"Every day we delay makes our task the more difficult, for while we are patriotically quarantining ourselves from the labor movement, the Socialists are busy 'boring from within' and taking charge of it. Their well organized machines will be immeasurably harder for us to vanquish than the present decrepit ones. And capture the conservative labor movement we must sooner or later if we are going to have a rebel movement in the United States. As it will never voluntarily come to us, nor is it showing any signs of breaking up. The sooner we throw aside our present idiotic tactics and adopt sane ones the better it will be for us and the labor movement in general."[18]

Foster probably knew as he was writing that his articles would have little effect upon the I.W.W. membership. For his articles appeared during and immediately after the Lawrence strike when the I.W.W. had reached the "crest of power," had gained many new members, especially in the textile industry, when the entire membership was convinced, as were many progressive and liberal Americans, that the organization was the "wave of the future," and when to talk of its mistakes seemed entirely out of place. Foster acknowledged this problem in his very first article, for he insisted that his argument that the workers had failed to respond to the I.W.W.'s dual program of being a labor organization and a propaganda league was "true in spite of the I.W.W.'s recent large increase of membership in the textile industry . . . as a result of the great Lawrence strike. But this by no means signifies that the new membership is a permanent one. We have time and again in the past had large groups of workers organized, only to have them desert the organization as the W.F. of M., or disintegrate, as the McKees Rocks organization, in response to influences still at work in the I.W.W."[19]

When this prediction, as we have seen, proved to be true, Foster's articles gained a new audience.* They were publicized, too, by a new organization—the Syndicalist League of North America.

FORMATION OF SYNDICALIST LEAGUE OF NORTH AMERICA

"Is another split threatening in the I.W.W.?" asked the Cleveland *Citizen* of December 30, 1911, as it reported the debate over William Z. Foster's proposal to concentrate the total energy of the I.W.W. on "boring-from-within" the A.F. of L. and other existing unions. It was an accurate forecast, but at the time this was published and for several months thereafter, Foster and his supporters were still involved in a campaign to win over the I.W.W. to the policy of "boring-from-within." An I.W.W. "Syndicalist Militant Minority League" was established for this purpose in January 1912, with Chicago as its headquarters and Foster as its secretary. The purpose was to send to various I.W.W. locals lecturers who would address the members, after the regular business meeting was adjourned, on the merits of "boring-from-within." A.F. of L. members would also be invited to attend the lectures.[20] On February 15, 1912, *The Agitator* announced that Foster was setting out on a tour of the West Coast from Chicago, "intending to discuss the matter at (I.W.W.) locals en route." It expressed the hope that "he will be given an attentive hearing."

Riding the freight cars in the bitter winter, Foster carried his message to I.W.W. locals and succeeded in forming a number of local Syndicalist Leagues within that organization. But in the midst of the tour came the news that the I.W.W. was forging ahead at Lawrence and winning thousands of new recruits as a result of the magnificent strike it was leading in the textile center. I.W.W. locals, confident that the organization's policy was correct and bearing fruit, refused to permit Foster to use their facilities for his lectures. Convinced that nothing could be gained by pursuing agitation against dual unionism within the I.W.W., several of the newly formed Syndicalist Leagues, led by No. 1 in Nelson, British Columbia (the first league to have been organized), split off from the I.W.W., and urged its members to join the A.F. of L. and work inside the Federation. Foster himself paid his "last dues to the I.W.W. in February 1912," and, in Chicago, joined the A.F. of L. union of his craft, the Brotherhood of Railway Carmen.[21]

---

* Foster's articles were made available by *The Agitator* as a package selling for 25 cents. Included in the package was a follow-up article entitled, "Theory and Practice," which appeared in *The Syndicalist* (the new name of *The Agitator*) on July 1, 1913. In this article, Foster pointed out that the I.W.W. was being forced by reality to adopt many of the practices of A.F. of L. unions such as signing contracts (as it had done in the New York barbers' strike) and keeping workers out on long strikes, a practice which it had previously condemned but which it was forced to follow in Lawrence and Paterson. He suggested that the I.W.W. take one additional step and "join forces with the A.F. of L."

While working as a car inspector, 12 hours a day, seven days a week, Foster was urging I.W.W. members all over the country, through correspondence, to form Syndicalist Leagues and join the A.F. of L. unions. By July 1912, Leagues (composed of former I.W.W. members who, like Foster, were joining A.F. of L. unions, and working-class members of the rapidly declining Anarchist movement) were in existence in Kansas City, St. Louis, Omaha, Chicago, Minneapolis, Nelson and Vancouver, B.C., San Francisco, Los Angeles, Seattle, Tacoma, Denver, and a number of other Midwestern and Western cities. "With Syndicalist Leagues in all parts of the country," optimistically predicted the St. Louis group, "we believe it would require only a short time to put the A.F. of L. on a revolutionary basis and having done that our emancipation would be at hand."[22]

In August 1912, at the request of the various leagues, Foster issued "A Call to Direct Actionists," announcing that a national organization of syndicalists was about to be organized, and urging all workers "interested in the fight on the forces that are making the American labor movement the laughing stock of the world's labor movement and a calamity to the American working class" to contact him in Chicago. These "forces," of course, were the adherents of "the absurd theory that nothing can be done in the old unions." This theory, Foster noted, had already been proven fallacious in France and England where the syndicalists were revitalizing the trade union movement from within, and a movement to duplicate their achievements "is being formed in the United States. It is being organized on the famed principle of the 'militant minority' that is, the rebels in all the unions are to be organized to concertedly exert their might in these unions against the fakers and conservatives now controlling them." Already propaganda leagues to achieve this end had been organized in various cities, and as soon as the national organization was formed, the American labor movement could take the first, and long-needed, steps to achieve the status of the labor movement in England and France.[23]

Foster's call was published in a number of radical and trade union papers. (The I.W.W. press refused to publish it, confining itself to the comment that steps were being taken to form "a new 'order,' a sort of half-brother to the vomiting S.L.P.") The national organization came into being in September 1912 without the benefit of a national convention, it being agreed that the new movement was still too weak to afford such a gathering. Instead, in agreement with the already existing leagues, the Chicago Syndicalist League acted as the national conference. It drew up a constitution, selected an executive board, and elected Foster as national secretary of the Syndicalist League of North America. This action was subject to ratification by the existing leagues. "Thus was born the first definite organization in the United States," Foster notes, "for boring-from-within the trade unions by revolutionaries."* The founders of the new organization were almost all former members of the I.W.W.[24]

The S.L. of N.A. constitution, based largely upon the program adopted previously by the Chicago League, provided for the chartering of local leagues in the various industrial centers. Members of the leagues were empowered to subdivide themselves into craft or industrial groups of militants, according to the structure of their respective unions. The leagues, in keeping with the S.L. of N.A.'s belief in decentralization, were completely autonomous. Each league could determine its own qualifications for membership. The various leagues collected their own funds, published their own journals and literature, and adopted and carried through their local policies. The national office received no per capita tax, relying solely upon the sale of its journal, pamphlets, collections, etc. for revenue. Foster received no salary, working as national secretary when he had completed his 12-hour, seven-day-a-week stint as a car inspector.[25]

The S.L. of N.A. announced its birth in a statement in September 1912, informing the American workers that it was an "educational organization." It planned to establish branches everywhere, publish and distribute literature, and furnish speakers for unions and other organizations. It invited the cooperation of every union man and woman "interested in the advancement of their cause," and urged all non-unionists to attend its meetings and read its literature, "and learn why they shud [sic] become unionists." The S.L. of N.A. was not a political party or a labor union. "It will not organize unions except that it will assist workers wishing to organize and be a recruiting ground for all unions." Those seeking further information were urged to communicate with William Z. Foster in Chicago.[26]

Foster informed the "English rebels," through the medium of *The Syndicalist* of January 1913, that there had been "organized in the United States a national Syndicalist propaganda organisation," and explained the reasons that had led to its formation, summarizing much of what he had already written on the weaknesses of the I.W.W.† He went

---

* Foster did not believe that the Socialist movement fulfilled this function. For one thing, the Left-wing of the S.P. "was saturated with I.W.W. dual unionism." For another, the Right-wing, while advocating "boring-from-within" the A.F. of L., did not conduct a militant enough struggle against the policies of the existing bureaucracy. (*The Syndicalist,* Jan. 15, 1913.)

† Foster, however, conceded that there was still room for the I.W.W. in such industries as textiles, steel, etc. Here the workers "were a gang of wretched slaves working on a common level of starvation," and the A.F. of L. unions offered these workers "no protection and had no prestige." Hence these workers were " 'rotten ripe' for the I.W.W. type of Unionism." (*The Syndicalist,* January, 1913, copy in British Museum.) This was quite a concession on Foster's part. The curious thing is that the I.W.W. press did not pick up this statement and use it against the advocates of "boring-from-within."

on to assure the British syndicalists that "the S.L. of N.A. is not an anti-I.W.W. organization; nor is it pro-A.F. of L. . . . . They consider the interests of the working class to be paramount to those of any of the ambitious, general organisations. Consequently, they intend to enter wholeheartedly into all struggles of the workers regardless of what organisations may be conducting them." Nevertheless, he made it clear that its main objective would be to mobilize the militant elements in the labor movement to work inside the trade unions affiliated with the A.F. of L. and the Railroad Brotherhoods. Hence we will consider the activities of the Syndicalist League of North America in the next volume which is devoted to the organizations on which the S.L. of N.A. concentrated. Here, however, it is worth discussing its role in sponsoring, along with other organizations, Tom Mann's lecture tour of the United States in the summer and fall of 1913. For this represented the last effort to convert the I.W.W. to the principle of "boring-from-within."

MANN URGES I.W.W. TO "BORE-FROM-WITHIN"

Tom Mann was already known to the American trade union and Socialist movements because of his leadership of the great strikes of miners, dockers, and railroad workers in Great Britain and his imprisonment for daring to read to a working-class audience the "Open Letter to British Soldiers" (usually known as the "Don't Shoot" Manifesto) which appealed to soldiers not to fire on strikers.[27] Mann came to the United States on a lecture tour arranged originally by the Pittsburgh Workers Defense League, an organization sponsored by *Justice,* a Left-wing Socialist paper published in that city which was friendly to the I.W.W. and fully in support of its doctrines of "direct action" and sabotage. But the paper was unable to organize a nation-wide tour, and Mann spoke under the sponsorship of different organizations: I.W.W. locals, A.F. of L. unions and central labor bodies, Socialist Party branches, even the Italian Paterson Relief Fund. But many of his most important meetings were organized by the recently formed Syndicalist League of North America and its branches. "One friend in particular gave much assistance in arranging meetings," Mann wrote later. "This was W. Z. Foster."[28]

Mann toured the United States for five months, addressing meetings in 70 cities from the Atlantic to the Pacific. The Socialist Party grew increasingly cool to him as he expounded his syndicalist belief that political action on the part of the working class was a waste of time. The I.W.W., of course, was delighted, and at first hailed Mann's tour. "As a spur to further activity on militant lines, Tom Mann is a tonic for lagging rebels," Ed Rowan, I.W.W. leader in Salt Lake City wrote enthusiastically, after Mann's speech in that city.[29] But the I.W.W. grew cool, too, as Mann began to place increasing emphasis in his speeches on the necessity for the revolutionary forces in the United States to join the existing unions and "bore-from-within" the A.F. of L. Even Mann's original sponsors, who shared the I.W.W.'s attitude toward "boring-from-within," were critical of their distinguished guest. When Mann spoke in Pittsburgh, he expressed his belief, based on personal observations during his tour, that there was an immediate possibility for the development of the A.F. of L. in the West into industrial unions. "I do not believe," he added, "the old time trade unions will disappear. I believe they will broaden until they express industrial organization sentiment." *Justice* remarked coldly: "It is a tribute to the demand for Free Speech by the Workers Defense League that Mann was cordially encouraged to express his opinion even though it differed from the viewpoint of those who promote these meetings. Members of the Workers Defense League practically see no hope for industrial organization through the existing craft unions of Pittsburgh. . . . Undoubtedly, Mann's experience with the trade unions of England, where there is far less fakiry [*sic*] than in America, evidently encourages him in this viewpoint."[30]

Mann made effective use of his visit to Pittsburgh to buttress his argument that the need of the hour for American labor was to join together—A.F. of L. and I.W.W.—in a united effort to organize the unorganized. In "A Plea for Solidarity," published in the *International Socialist Review* at the conclusion of his tour, he cited his "deep disappointment" at discovering that in the "vitally important industrial center" of Pittsburgh, with its 250,000 steel workers, engineers and every variety of machinists, "not three per cent are organized," and his shock on learning that the steel workers still worked 12 hours a day, seven days a week. "A.F. of L. men criticize the I.W.W. and vice versa, and neither are showing any capacity to organize the workers." Mann praised the I.W.W. for its work among the hitherto neglected migratory workers. But, pointing to the 14,000 I.W.W. members reported in good standing in September 1913, he asked: "If this is the net organized result after so much energy, does not the case call for inquiry as to whether the present lines are the right ones?" He was convinced, as a result of his tour, that "if the fine energy exhibited by the I.W.W. were put into the A.F. of L. or into the existing trade-union movement . . . the results would be fiftyfold greater than they now are." He went on to "urge the advisability, not of dropping the I.W.W., but certainly of dropping all dual organizations and serving as a feeder and purifier of the big movement. Line up with the rest."[31]

I.W.W. REJECTS MANN'S APPEAL

Although regretting its advice to Wobblies early in Mann's tour to make every effort "to bring out big crowds to his meetings since he is the ablest exponent of revolutionary unionism now on the platform,"[32] and chafing under his criticism of the radical elements for not working inside the existing unions, the I.W.W. press had refrained from attacking his position. (I.W.W. papers, however, never reported the contents of Mann's speeches except for quoting his attacks upon political action.) But with the publication of "A Plea for Solidarity," the I.W.W. decided to reply. Haywood, titling his reply, "An Appeal for Industrial Solidarity," denied Mann's contention that the membership of the I.W.W. was an indication of its failure to reach the great mass of the American workers. He insisted that the One Big Union idea had "thoroughly permeated and inspired the working class of America." He dismissed Mann's argument that if the I.W.W.'s energy "were put into the A.F. of L.," the results would be 50 times greater with the comment: "It might as well be said that if the fine energy exhibited by the I.W.W. were put into the Catholic Church, that the results would be the establishment of the control of industry." Haywood proceeded to show that it was virtually impossible for the "millions of unskilled wage slaves," to become members of the A.F. of L. because of "insurmountable barriers" such as "exorbitant fees," "a vicious system of apprenticeship," "discrimination against women, and the absolute refusal of some unions to accept colored persons as members." Only the I.W.W. held out the hope that these workers would be organized.

Ettor endorsed Haywood's attack on Mann, and added the point that the I.W.W. did not want to save the A.F. of L. "We aim at destroying it."[33]

Asked by the syndicalists in Europe if his trip through the United States had enabled him to answer the question "whether the I.W.W. has succeeded or failed," Mann replied in an article in *La Vie Ouvrière,* the French syndicalist journal:

"There is no doubt that the propaganda voiced by the I.W.W. has done much to educate the mass of unorganized, unskilled workers, particularly those workers who change jobs frequently, because of seasonal demands, as well as that floating group known as 'migratory workers.' In fact it is quite probable that if the I.W.W. had not taken this special interest in this class of workers, recent improvements in their working conditions would not have taken place.

"But, while I admire the fighting spirit of the militant I.W.W., I find it impossible to praise their capacity for organization.

"In a country of almost 100,000,000 inhabitants, after 8 years of continuous effort to organize, not to have succeeded in building up a group of at least 100,000 organized workers cannot be considered very encouraging. In some of the cities where the I.W.W. carried out the most effective struggles, we find, in a number, an embryonic form of union, in others—nothing."

Mann acknowledged that there was no single explanation for the failure of the I.W.W. to achieve this minimum goal, but he was more than ever convinced, as a result of his trip, that the chief reason was its refusal to abandon the principle of "dual unionism":

"As the situation appears to me after many varied and deep conversations and discussions with working men of all conditions, I say very emphatically that the I.W.W. should work in harmony with the American Federation of Labor. There is not the least necessity for having two organizations. The field of action is wide enough for all to be able to cooperate in the struggle for better economic conditions.

"The American Federation of Labor is not on the wane, it is developing; its concepts are not shrinking, they are enlarging. The American Federation of Labor is no more reactionary than it has been in the past, it is less reactionary. The greatest danger to which it is subject at present is the firm hold the politicians have on it. Their influence grows in the unions as well as in the Federation, and this because the devoted, spirited, militant men who make up the I.W.W. refuse to work in the inside of the unions, so that they leave a free field to the politicians, and make their task relatively easy. . . . I say that it is a great pity and that this could lead to a disaster that the admirable, militant ardor of the industrialists, at present banded together in the I.W.W., does not operate inside the American Federation of Labor. To continue using the I.W.W. in opposition to the A.F. of L. is for me to go counter to all that I have learned from bitter experience.

"I am convinced that if these militant workers adopt the tactic that I propose, the working class will respond admirably to the call, that the field of action of the workers would broaden considerably, and that organizing would pick up at a greater speed than has been felt up to the present."[34]

The reaction of the I.W.W. to Mann's impressions of the organization and his final advice to it was summed up in *Solidarity:* "To Mann the salvation of the American Federation of Labor from the grasp of the politicians is more important than the organization of millions of exploited wage slaves. . . . Something wrong here? Oh, no. Only that Mann has to keep his job in the English safe and sane trade unions."[35] Nothing that had happened in the great offensive of the British trade unions since 1911 had made the slightest impression upon the I.W.W. leadership.

It is clear that nothing that could be said by the advocates of "boring-from-within" would have any influence in I.W.W. circles. "So much animosity is aroused in the average I.W.W. man at the mention of the A.F. of L.," a contemporary journal correctly observed, "that he cannot see the simplest proposition in logic."[36] During and immediately after

Lawrence, the I.W.W., as Elizabeth Gurley Flynn later acknowledged, was "'dizzy with success' and had no time for sober estimates or criticisms."[37] After the defeats at Paterson, Akron, and Detroit, the leadership of the I.W.W. still refused to acknowledge that there was anything fundamentally wrong in the organization's policies. There was no room in this type of thinking for the program advocated by the adherents of "boring-from-within."

CHAPTER 19

The I.W.W. and the Unemployed, 1913-1915

On April 20, 1913, a Midwest correspondent warned Secretary of Labor William B. Wilson that there was danger of an impending economic crisis, and urged that his department take steps at once to prepare to deal with "the problem of unemployment." Secretary Wilson acknowledged the letter, but assured the writer that there was no need to be worried about the state of the nation's economy.[1] A few weeks later, there were signs that the correspondent's fears were justified. Beginning in May 1913, pig-iron production in the United States declined. On November 7, E. D. Brought, secretary of the Switchmen's Union of North America, wrote to Secretary Wilson from Chicago: "As a progressive labor organization we view with alarm the present tendencies of certain corporations throughout the country; more especially so with regard to the United States Steel Corporation. This corporation is gradually closing down its mills, different departments at a time, throwing thousands out of employment, all in the face of repeated statements by Mr. Gary [president of U.S. Steel] that there has (*sic*) been no men laid off."[2] By the time this was written, business failures were increasing, and by the end of 1913–14, an economic crisis was in full swing. It was to increase in intensity after August 1914, when the war broke out in Europe, severely disrupting American industry and causing food prices in the United States to skyrocket. The economic crisis reached its worst stage in the winter months of 1914–15.

Unemployment began to be felt keenly by the winter of 1913–14 as industry throughout the country laid off workers. Early in December 1913, B. C. Forbes, Wall Street correspondent for the Hearst newspapers, wrote: "The United States, very unfortunately, will be strewn with unemployed this winter. At least 250,000 have already been discharged by railroad, industrial and mercantile companies. And retrenchment has only begun."[3] By January 1914, charitable societies were taxed to the limit to meet the demands of applicants desiring their help. "A thousand hungry men and boys lined the Bowery in the cold early morning yesterday from the Bowery Mission to Houston street," the New York *Call* reported on January 12, 1914. "The line was ever increasing and hundreds were turned away when a bell, rung from the kitchen of the mission, announced that the supply of rolls and coffee had vanished. The great majority of the 'down and outs' were not old men, but comparatively young fellows. At least, 80 per cent of the men were below the age of 35."

Practically nothing was done by the state and local governments to relieve the suffering and distress of the unemployed. Nor did the A.F. of L. appear to be concerned with this problem. Indeed, Gompers seemed to have been unaware that large-scale unemployment existed in the winter of 1913–14 even though the percentage of idleness among representative unions in New York, due to lack of work, had leaped from 17.5 per cent in January 1913 to 31 per cent in January 1914, and the percentage of unemployed among the organized workers in Massachusetts had increased in the same period from 11.3 to 16.6 per cent.[4]

I.W.W. ORGANIZES UNEMPLOYED ON WEST COAST

It is to the credit of the I.W.W. that it was the first organized group to recognize the existence of an unemployment problem, call attention to the growing breadlines throughout the country and the increasing number of homeless men sleeping in doorways and cellars, and attempt to do something to relieve the suffering of men and women who were out of work through no fault of their own. Early in the winter of 1913–14, the I.W.W. called upon its members to conduct "revolutionary agitation among the unemployed." They were to impress upon the unemployed that they should not scab on their "fellow slaves" in the shops by taking jobs at lower wages. Rather, they should try to force prevailing rates up, and seek to convince those at work to divide the work that was available, and attempt to reduce the speed-up in the shops and cut down the length of the working day to six hours.* While impressing upon the

* About the same time, V. I. Lenin wrote: "America, along with other countries, is suffering from widespread unemployment and a constantly rising cost of living. Destitution among workers is becoming more intense and intolerable. American statistics show that approximately half of all workers are not fully employed. . . . The country is already immeasurably rich. It can treble its wealth in no time; it can treble the productivity of its social labor and thereby ensure for all its workers and their families a decent earning level worthy of a sensible human being, along with a reasonable working day period of six hours." He advocated that American

unemployed that it was impossible to really solve the problem of unemployment under capitalism, the Wobblies should convince them that they could not afford to wait until capitalism had passed out of existence, but must immediately do something for themselves to end their distress.[5] I.W.W. agitators began to publicize this program, distributing leaflets by January 1914, with the following message:

"Unemployed and Employed Workers Attention. Overwork for Some Means Out of Work For Others!

"Fellow workers: Let us look facts in the face.

"Men and women in want and misery are tramping the streets *Desperate . . . Starving Amid Plenty.* Are we to allow the condition to continue until we die? . . .

"Conditions right now demand a shorter work day. If those who are now working would take it easy and not work so many hours a day, or so many days a week, there would be plenty of work for all.

"We should divide the work of the world amongst the workers of the world, then we would be in a position to put the '*shirkers*' to work. . . . Let us unite and refuse to starve *now*."[6]

I.W.W. agitation among the unemployed started first on the West Coast. On December 26, 1913, 1,000 unemployed workers, both native Americans and foreign-born, including Mexicans, led by the I.W.W., demonstrated in the Los Angeles Plaza, denouncing "Starvation amid Plenty." The police, with drawn clubs and revolvers, broke up the demonstration, killing one worker, clubbing many others, and arresting 75. Councilman Fred C. Wheeler demanded an investigation of the "Cossack methods," but the police were exonerated on the ground that "the Industrial Workers of the World who were involved in the trouble stirred up the unemployed to violence." This in the face of newspaper reports that "the meeting yesterday in the Plaza was peaceful and orderly until the police arrived."[7]

A few weeks later, in San Francisco, unemployed workers led by the I.W.W. and with Lucy Parsons, widow of the Haymarket martyr, Albert R. Parsons, at the head of the unemployed men, clashed with the police. Mrs. Parsons was arrested, but not before the unemployed had voiced demands for work at $3 for an eight-hour day and called upon Governor Johnson to convene a special session of the legislature to pass

---

workers immediately raise the demand for an annual wage of "four thousand roubles [$2,000] for each working family and a six-hour working day." On January 13, 1912, Victor L. Berger stated in Congress that the average annual income of American workers was $476. (*Cong. Record,* 62nd Cong., 2nd Sess., p. 930.)

Lenin's article, entitled "4000 Roubles per Year and a Six-Hour Working Day," was published on January 1, 1914. I am indebted to Mr. Yuri Perfilyev for furnishing me a translation of the article from the Russian edition of Lenin's *Collected Works.*

a Right-to-Work bill.* The Progressive Governor denied that there was an unemployment problem, and blamed the demonstration on a "few leaders who preach the tenets of the I.W.W., who neither wish to work themselves nor desire employment for others, and who preach an anarchistic doctrine at variance with organized Government."[8]

About the same time, the idea of putting pressure upon the government at Washington by means of a march of the unemployed to the nation's capital was advanced by "General" Charles T. Kelly, one of the former leaders of the California delegation in "Coxey's Army." Although George Speed, West Coast I.W.W. leader, argued against the move, calling Kelly a faker and predicting that nothing would come of such a march, an I.W.W. contingent, led by W. A. Thorn and called the "Union Army of the Unemployed," joined Kelly's army as a separate unit. On February 12, 1914, 1,500 unemployed workers, including the I.W.W. contingent, left San Francisco. When the army arrived in Sacramento, they proceeded to camp on the Southern Pacific Railroad sandlots. Kelly, Thorn and several other leaders were arrested on charges of "vagrancy," and lodged in the county jail. But the army refused to leave, and further arrests were made. The Southern Pacific offered the men transportation back to San Francisco, but this was refused. District Attorney Wackhorst then appealed to Governor Johnson to call out the militia, but the Governor denied the request, observing that the police and sheriffs were quite capable of "handling the situation."

The Sacramento *Bee* kept up a steady assault upon the unemployed army which it labeled "a gang of thugs, deadbeats, bummers and vagrants," and called for vigilante tactics to drive them out of the city. On the morning of March 9, the police, members of the Fire Department, county sheriffs and deputies recruited from among Sacramento citizens, were given pick handles and ordered to attack the unemployed army and forcibly eject them from the city. What followed was described by an angry reporter who witnessed the events on what came to be known as "Bloody Monday":

"With drawn pick handles they charged the unarmed men, who refused to budge. Most of Kelly's adherents ran when they saw that the officers meant business, but many of the I.W.W. members showed fight. The police and sheriffs jumped upon these men, beat them mercilessly, drove them over the fence and set fire to their camp and belongings, thus showing their respect for 'the rights of private property.' The fugitives gathered bricks and stones and hurled them at the officers and a number were hurt.

---

* The I.W.W. press said nothing of the political nature of the demand for a special session of the legislature. A "Right to Work" bill meant legislation giving the unemployed the right to work by furnishing jobs. Today "right to work" laws ban the union shop.

"Some unemployed threw themselves on the ground with American flags in their hands and refused to budge, but these men were dislodged by the firemen, who turned powerful streams of water on the men. Others were taken up bodily by husky citizens and thrown over the fence into the street. . . . The men were hotly pursued by the sheriffs and finally driven over the M Street bridge. Most of them were dripping wet from the streams turned on them by the firemen."[9]

Eight of the unemployed were carted away in the Sacramento County Hospital ambulance. One Negro member of the I.W.W. was beaten so severely that reporters could clearly see the "several deep holes the blows had indented in his head." In a letter to President Woodrow Wilson and his Secretary of Labor, leaders of the unemployed army complained bitterly of the brutality against the unemployed, assured the federal officials that "proof of the death of at least one could be supplied," and called for an investigation by the federal government. The plea was ignored in Washington.[10]

When Helen Keller, who was in San Francisco and scheduled to lecture in Sacramento, heard of the barbarous treatment of the unemployed, she declared she would speak in their behalf from the platform. The authorities sent word that if she dared carry out her promise, she would be "hauled down and carried from the city in a cart." But Miss Keller was not so easily intimidated. "I think their treatment was outrageous," she told reporters. "It is not a crime to protest for your fellows. It is not a crime to be without bread. They say that these men are I.W.W.'s and that means, 'I Won't Work.' I honor these men for their protest, and I am going to say that in Sacramento tonight." She did, too, and during her lecture dared the police to arrest her. But the authorities knew better, and she was not molested.[11]

For two weeks the unemployed army remained near Sacramento, suffering intensely but determined to stay until their leaders were released. Even the Sacramento *Bee,* while headlining that there were "Many Drug Fiends in 'Unemployed Army'," grudgingly acknowledged that the men could not be beaten into submission. "Hunger stalks throughout the camp, but the more determined among the men say they will remain until they have to be taken to the hospital." Volunteer deputy sheriffs aided the police in patrolling the streets of Sacramento to prevent any demonstrations of sympathy for the unemployed army. In addition, five companies, one troop of cavalry, and the Stockton battery of the National Guard were encamped at the armory. Finally, after weeks of suffering, the unemployed army faded away. Seven of the leaders were given suspended sentences, but "General" Kelly was sentenced to serve a term of six months in the county jail.[12]

Oregon also had its "army of the unemployed." In January 1914, a group—called the "idle army" by the press—formed in Portland and began a march down the Willamette Valley in quest of jobs. Two-thirds of the recruits in the army were unemployed Wobblies under 25 years of age. At each town the army held meetings, sang songs, made speeches, and distributed literature demanding jobs, food, and shelter for the unemployed. In Portland itself, the Wobblies organized the unemployed into a league and petitioned the City Council for food and shelter. Knowing from past experience what would follow a rejection of the petition, the Council gave the unemployed permission to occupy an unused tabernacle and appropriated $500 for blankets; the men kept their own order. Food was obtained from Portland citizens with the assistance of the Oregon Civic League. By April 1914, when the Unemployed League was disbanded, hundreds of unemployed had been fed and sheltered at the tabernacle.[13]

EDMONTON, CANADA

Edmonton, Canada, was an important center for the railroad construction workers, and in the winter of 1913-14, thousands of these men were suffering from unemployment and were without funds to return to New York, Boston, Chicago, and other places from which they had been recruited. As early as December 10, 1913, the Edmonton *Journal* noted the seriousness of "the unemployed problem," observing: "There is no use in shutting our eyes to the fact that there are a good many men in the city at present who cannot obtain work and who are badly up against it." But it was one thing to acknowledge the existence of the problem and quite another to do something to remedy it. The I.W.W. offered a remedy. Through the Edmonton Unemployed League, which it had organized, it raised the demand that the city furnish work for all unemployed, regardless of race, color, and nationality, at a rate of not less than 30 cents an hour, and that during the time the men were waiting for work, the city furnish three 25-cent meal tickets for every man out of work which would be redeemable at any restaurant in the city. At first, this proposal horrified the "respectable elements" of Edmonton. "The Executive of the Unemployed League is trying to run the city," the Edmonton *Journal* fumed, and warned that if the I.W.W. proposals were adopted, "they will attract outsiders and those who don't want to work in the regular way will take advantage of the responsibility that the municipality has assumed."[14]

But the unemployed backed up the I.W.W.'s demands with parades, and neither police clubs nor arrests brought a halt to the demonstrations. James Rowan, I.W.W. leader of the unemployed in Edmonton, warned the authorities that arrests would not stop the movement, for if the leaders were jailed, "more would be ready to take their places and carry on the work."[15]

The unemployed movement produced results. On January 28, 1914, the Edmonton *Journal* headlined the news: "I.W.W. Triumphant!" The Mayor and the City Council had yielded. A large building was turned over to the unemployed for shelter, meal tickets of 25 cents, each redeemable in the city's restaurants, were distributed, and 400 men were put to work on public projects at 30 cents an hour. To the Edmonton *Journal's* disgust, Alderman Joseph Clarke "commenced an eulogy of the I.W.W.'s [in the City Council]," praising them for their work in behalf of the unemployed, and for "cooperating with the city." The *Journal* denounced the city's "peculiar and unwarranted procedure," arguing that it was "none of the city's business to look after them at all, except to take them into custody when they became a public nuisance." Fortunately, wiser heads had prevailed. As the Press Committee of the Edmonton Unemployed League pointed out a few weeks after the organization's proposals had been adopted: "Since this relief work has been started by the city there has been an almost total absence of crime in the city and before the winter is over, we think it will be conclusively proved that one dollar spent in feeding hungry men is better than ten dollars spent in the prosecution of criminals."[16]

BOSTON, DETROIT AND NEW YORK

But in many communities the authorities had a different response to the demands of the unemployed. In Calgary, Canada, the police arrested the Wobbly leaders of the unemployed movement, and William McConnell, I.W.W. spokesman, was convicted of sedition and sent to jail. In Boston, a group of unemployed, led by the I.W.W., invaded the Chamber of Commerce building demanding bread; they were clubbed and ejected. A protest meeting on historic Boston Common proclaimed, in the name of "the unemployed of Greater Boston," that since the rich "think more of their dogs and dog shows than they do of us," and were satisfied "to reduce us to the degradation of pauperism or to let us starve rather than open their full pocket books to give us work," the unemployed worker had no alternative but "to preserve life by his own efforts; that he must therefore take food, clothing and shelter where he can, regardless of social edicts against his doing so." A call was issued from Boston Common by the I.W.W. advising the unemployed everywhere "to steal food and whatever else they need to maintain their health and welfare, and we affirm that it is stealing only in name and not in fact. . . . The primal rights of man are supreme."[17]

On Lincoln's birthday, February 12, 1914, the Detroit locals of the I.W.W., in cooperation with several unions and Socialist organizations, staged a demonstration in which, with the temperature below zero, 8,000 unemployed workers gathered in front of an employment office. The depression of 1913 and 1914 was particularly severe in Detroit. Reports of high wages paid in the automobile industry, particularly that the Ford Motor Co. was employing men at a minimum of $5.00 a day, brought thousands of workers to Detroit, all of whom had been assured that they would find it easy to get work. An investigator for the Commission on Industrial Relations asked a group of unemployed workers in Detroit why they had come to the city. "His reason for coming to Detroit he states," the investigator reported as a typical response, "was on account of the announcement of Ford. He has been hanging around the plant since his arrival here without any results."[18]

Arthur Christ, I.W.W. leader in Detroit, pointed out that one reason for the demonstration on February 12 was "to spread news to all parts of the country that Henry Ford was not giving $5.00 jobs to everybody who comes to Detroit." It was decided that Lincoln's Birthday, when the idea of "with malice to none, with charity to all" prevailed, would be a good day for the demonstration. A committee had visited Police Commissioner Gillespie to request permission for the demonstration. The Commissioner refused to grant a permit, but, said Christ, "we went ahead and made it anyway." The demonstrators demanded a municipal lodging house for workers who were without shelter and work for all willing to work.

The demonstration never got started. "The army of the unemployed assembled in Bagley Avenue near Grand River, for a demonstration this morning, was routed by a hundred patrolmen and mounted police," the Detroit *News* reported that evening. Another paper described "the police charging with drawn revolvers, wielding their clubs right and left. A man in a gray overcoat with long hair almost covering his eyes was the particular object of several patrolmen. It was said he had raised the sign reading on one side—*Bread or Revolution—Which?*—and on the other—*We want Work—Not Charity, I.W.W.* In the first rush he was felled by a night stick and before he could get up and make off, he received several raps more."[19]

Although the Detroit press conceded that the demonstrators were victims of an unfortunate condition—unemployment—the fact that they had agreed to protest under the leadership of the I.W.W. was enough to justify the use of police clubs in place of effective relief measures. "The I.W.W. and its agents are public menaces, open enemies to the American nation and not to be tolerated." Since the demonstration was started by the distribution of circulars by the I.W.W., the press applauded the news that the "police put a ban on I.W.W. and the distribution of circulars by the organization."[20]

I.W.W. agitation among the unemployed in New York attracted nation-wide attention. The winter of 1913–14 was a hard one for the workers of the Empire City. It snowed continuously and was bitter cold.

According to a survey conducted by the Employment Bureau of the Society for Improving the Condition of the Poor, there were more than 300,000 unemployed men in the city in February 1914; conditions were reported to be the worst since the winter of 1907–08. Reformer John Purroy Mitchel was mayor of the city. He conceded late in January 1914, that "a greater number of unemployed exists right now than usual," and that "unemployment is a problem for the city administration." But his plan to solve the problem was totally ineffective. He advocated a day-of-rest law for all the people who were fortunate enough to hold jobs. Meanwhile, he appealed to businessmen to give work to the unemployed, and set up a committee to organize a central employment exchange, a public employment bureau under the Department of Licenses, for the purpose "of bringing the manless job and jobless man together." But the businessmen ignored the appeal. By the end of March 1914, the only concrete proposal for dealing with the problem of unemployment was the establishment of official employment bureaus. Up to March 27 these bureaus had helped a total of 3,973 persons get jobs, "3,646 as snow shovelers, 126 as farm hands, 70 as laborers, 17 as drivers, and so forth." "What a bloody satire," commented the New York *Call*.[21]

During these months the number of unemployed in the city mounted and the lines of hungry men waiting for hours at the doors of charitable institutions to get a cup of coffee and a slice of bread grew daily. But shelter from the cold was practically unobtainable. The Municipal Lodging House, sheltered 93,807 men in December 1913 and January 1914, compared with 37,780 in a similar period in the winter of 1912–13, but this scarcely took care of the need for shelter, and unemployed women were not even admitted. On the night of February 12, 1914, 600 unemployed workers slept on the recreation piers.[22]

On February 15, 1914, P. A. Speek, an investigator for the Commission on Industrial Relations, visited the Municipal Exchange in New York City. By 7:30 A.M., he found hundreds of unemployed waiting to register for any kind of work.

"Their appearance was a sorrowful sight. Probably ten per cent had adequate shoes—overshoes, rubbers, or boots. About 50 per cent had made rags and burlap serve as coverings for their feet. Several with whom I talked told that they had shoes, under rags and burlaps, while one told me he had only rags on his feet. Possibly 20 per cent had overcoats, gloves and warm caps. The majority were poorly clothed. 'Yes, sir, I suffer from cold, this scanty shoddy on me does not protect me very much,' was a typical comment."

Suddenly, Speek heard a loud cry in the crowd: "Brothers, let's go to the City Hall." Led by Harry Kleine, whom Speek described as "an I.W.W. man," a considerable number of the unemployed went to the City Hall where they were told by the Mayor's secretary that their complaints over inability to obtain work would be investigated. "It seemed to me," Speek concluded, "if their leader, Kleine, would say to them, 'Brothers, let's attack a store,' they undoubtedly would follow him."[23]

In late January 1914, a general meeting of all I.W.W. locals in New York City was held to discuss the problem of the unemployed and to devise methods for meeting their needs. At this meeting, a 21-year-old bus-boy, Frank Tannenbaum, a member of the Waiter's Industrial Union, proposed that the I.W.W. lead the unemployed to the churches to seek shelter and food. The proposal was approved, and Tannenbaum and a handful of Wobblies were assigned to carry the plan into operation. The unemployed responded to the I.W.W. appeal: "Let us get shelter in the house of Christ, in the churches." On February 27, 1914, 1,000 unemployed men, led by Tannenbaum, entered the Baptist Tabernacle during the services, demanding shelter. The following evening 600 entered the Labor Temple. On March 2, the Fifth Avenue First Presbyterian Church was invaded while the Reverend Howard Duffield was conducting the evening service. "We are hungry," Tannenbaum told the Reverend, "and we are homeless. We want something to eat and a place to sleep."[24]

In each invasion up to this point, the orderly army of unemployed had received food and lodging. It had also received widespread publicity in the press and had brought down an avalanche of criticism upon the I.W.W. *The New York Times* declared furiously on March 3: "The invasion of the churches while services are in progress, by bodies of men under the direction of the I.W.W., is an offense against property, and a defiance of law and order which ought not to be tolerated for any reason whatever. Whenever such an invasion occurs, police reserves should be summoned without delay and all attempts by the invaders to interrupt the services should be sternly discountenanced." The New York *World,* on the same day, referred to Tannenbaum's army of unemployed as "a criminal menace," and warned that "unless energetic measures are used, we may expect gangs of professional gunmen and thugs to join the professional unemployed in terrorizing public assemblies from the Battery to Harlem. The I.W.W. leaders, who are inviting the worst elements of a great city to plunder, do not want work—they seek a social revolution."

New York City and A.F. of L. officials joined the press in condemning I.W.W. activities in behalf of the unemployed. They charged that Tannenbaum and other Wobbly agitators were stirring up the workers needlessly since "the city is doing its duty." "The acts and statements of the I.W.W.," declared Herman Robinson, member of the New York State Federation of Labor Executive Committee, "are wholly insincere. It is true that at this season of the year the building trades are idle, and that thousands of capable men are out of work. But very many of these men can live on their savings or get assistance from their unions. The reputable laboring man out of work has no sympathy with the I.W.W. movement, and will not take part in the demonstrations. The I.W.W. is trying to make trouble, and is bent mostly on notoriety and profit for its leaders." Daniel Harris, president of the State Federation of Labor, was terser: "Too much publicity is given to the I.W.W. The agitators collect bums and toughs and go shouting through the streets attempting to fool the public." Ernest Bohm, secretary of the New York Central Federated Union, sneered that "among the homeless men who have been making demonstrations at the churches, are very few who are willing to work."[25]

It is true that some unions provided relief for their unemployed members through insurance premiums, levies upon employed members, and "share the work" programs, though trade union insurance against unemployment in the United States was only a drop in the bucket compared to what existed in Europe.* But on the very day that the statements of the A.F. of L. officials appeared in the press, the Charity Organization Society reported that the resources of the poor, already strained to the breaking point by the extreme cold weather of February, were giving way. "They have been able to withstand hard times for weeks," the Society declared, "but the pressure now has become too great. Their savings have already been exhausted."[26] How these workers and their families were supposed to survive when there was no relief supplied by the federal, state or city governments and when the resources of the charity societies were drained, the A.F. of L. leaders did not bother to answer. To these men, as to the city officials and the commercial press, the workers became "professional beggars," "bums," "loafers," and "toughs" when they decided to follow the I.W.W. advice to "do something for ourselves" to obtain food and shelter.[27]

On March 4, 1914, *The New York Times* reported that "the members of the little armies of church invaders, led by Frank Tannenbaum, received food, drink and shelter last night [from the Reverend W. Montague Geer] in the parish house behind St. Paul's Protestant Chapel, at Broadway and Vesey Street." Editorially the *Times* expressed its horror. "The riotous proceedings should have been suppressed by the police." (The news report had specifically emphasized that the unemployed had been orderly throughout the evening, but to the editors of the *Times* any activity by the unemployed was a "riotous proceeding.") The authorities were warned to take "immediate and decisive steps" in the future "to suppress the I.W.W. pest, which is, in effect, nothing more

* In 1910, the year before public insurance was adopted in England, 90 per cent of the members of all registered unions were insured against unemployment. (J. L. Cohen, *Insurance Against Unemployment*, London, 1921, p. 279.) In the United States, before 1910, only six unions adopted plans of insurance against unemployment. Between 1910 and 1919, 13 others joined in adopting insurance against unemployment. (*Unions Provide Against Unemployment*, A.F. of L. publication, Washington D.C., 1929, p. 99.)

than a cheap advertisement of the most abominable organization ever formed in this country." The New York *Sun* was even more explicit in its advice on how to deal with the unemployed. It was "better to club and shoot rioters" than to "allow the I.W.W. to continue uninterruptedly the organization of bands of idle men—some of them honest dupes, most of them vicious outcasts—and spur them on to violent demonstrations designed to disturb the peace." However, the *Sun* did express the hope that "the heads of rogues and vagabonds only may be broken, and the honest, if simple, gulls of the I.W.W. may escape injury."[28] The *Sun* neglected to inform the police how to distinguish the heads of "gulls" from those of "rogues and vagabonds." In any event, it was clear that the police were being encouraged to solve the problem of unemployment by means of their clubs.

That same night, March 4, Tannenbaum addressed a crowd of unemployed in Rutgers Square, warning them that the police and the courts were lining up, at the urging of the commercial press, to crush their demand for relief. After the meeting, he led some 300 men, walking in two's and three's, to the Roman Catholic Church of St. Alphonsus at 312 West Broadway. When they reached the church, they were met by police detectives who told Tannenbaum that he could not enter with his army unless he obtained permission from Father Schneider, the rector. Tannenbaum then went to see the rector and asked for food and shelter for the unemployed who had accompanied him. The priest refused, whereupon Tannenbaum declared: "Do you call that the spirit of Christ, to turn hungry and homeless men away?"

While Tannenbaum was meeting with the rector, the unemployed had entered the church and quietly taken seats. The I.W.W. leader told his followers to leave since they were not wanted. But when the unemployed attempted to leave, they were stopped by detectives, one of whom called police headquarters for reserves. The unemployed sat quietly in the church awaiting the arrival of the police. Twenty patrol wagons arrived, and Tannenbaum and 190 of his unemployed followers (including one woman) were arrested and taken to the magistrate's court. Tannenbaum was charged with "inciting to riot," the others with disorderly conduct. Tannenbaum's bail was set at the incredible figure of $5,000.[29]

The following morning the press was full of praise for the police. *The New York Times* conceded that the unemployed had been peaceful, but declared that the conduct of the police towards "the outlaws" was justified, for "there has been too much temporizing with so-called socialism and anarchy in the churches." Several newspapers were infuriated because Joseph O'Carroll, an I.W.W. leader, had told the arrested men: "Jesus Christ was a hobo. He, too, was arrested and persecuted as we have been. I tell you we unemployed men here tonight are 20th century replicas of Jesus Christ." This was denounced as "a gross perversion of the name and teachings of one sacred to many."[30]

The New York *Sun* felt that the community owed a debt of gratitude to the Catholic Church in general and to Father Schneider in particular. Other religious groups had been foolish enough to help the men led by the I.W.W. "because of the professedly philanthropic objects of its crusade." It had remained for the Catholic Church "to assert the rights of order against disorder," and for Father Schneider to act firmly against the "revolutionary" organization. "A priest has put into operation the machinery to suppress this portentous and carefully contrived onslaught on the institutions of law and order."[31] The "machinery to suppress" the demands of the unemployed went into full operation directly after the events at St. Alphonsus Church. From that day on, practically every day, I.W.W. meetings of the unemployed were disrupted, the speakers arrested, and the unemployed clubbed and arrested as vagrants. The police announced that "the I.W.W. leaders are to be suppressed" at all costs.[32]

The Free Speech League denounced police terror and suppression of unemployed meetings, and demanded their right to assemble and speak. The authorities yielded, and the I.W.W. was given the right to use Union Square for its meetings. The I.W.W. promptly announced that it would continue to rally the unemployed "to convince the city authorities that they have not settled the unemployment problem by imprisoning Frank Tannenbaum and 190 others. We want to let the people know that there are thousands of idle, starving men in the city. We want to show them that the cause of the present depression is the inevitable result of overproduction and improved machinery under the capitalistic order of society."[33]

A Ministers' Unemployment Committee was started, and a number of churches opened their doors to the unemployed led by the I.W.W. Relief stations were opened. A Fair Play Committee was organized in behalf of Tannenbaum and the 190 unemployed workers arrested in St. Alphonsus Church. All this infuriated the press. *The New York Times* wrote angrily: "The respectable defenders of riot and disorder, the churchmen who are weak enough to dally with anarchists; the ill-informed sentimentalists who are always ready with fair-sounding words on occasions like this, but who would be absolutely useless in the protection of themselves or others in case of dangerous riots, are really more dangerous to society than an army of hoboes."[34]

Meanwhile, the Socialist Party was becoming increasingly worried by the publicity received by the I.W.W., and on March 3 the New York State Executive Committee issued an appeal to all locals to become active on the unemployment front. Henry L. Slobodin, who was put in charge of arrangements for an unemployed demonstration, wrote angrily to Julius Gerber: "The Socialist party was inexcusably derelict, in not taking a strong hold of the unemployed problem and letting freaks to be the only ones to call public attention to it." An "unemployment protest meeting" was called by the Socialist Party at Cooper Union on March 19, and the unemployed were urged to come to the meeting and demand unemployment insurance. "Fellow Workers! our families must have food, clothing and homes, whether we work or are thrown out of work. We want the law to provide it."[35] At the meeting, a program for immediate relief measures was proposed. It included demands for an appropriation from the legislature for food and clothing for the needy; the building of schools and other public works; reduction of the workday to eight hours; the abolition of child labor; the payment of decent wages to workers, and, if these did not suffice, workmen's insurance against unemployment. On March 23, the Brooklyn Conference on Unemployment, composed of Socialists and A.F. of L. unionists, proposed that the legislature empower the Highway Department to hire the largest possible force of workers immediately, and put them to work on the state highways at prevailing rates of wages for an eight-hour day.* The press immediately denounced these proposals as catering to the "communistic spirit of the I.W.W."[36]

Of the 190 arrested with Tannenbaum, one was sentenced to 60 days, four to 30 days, and three to 15 days in jail; the others were released.[37] Although a reporter for the New York *Tribune* who was present at St. Alphonsus Church testified that "there was no disorder in the church," Tannenbaum was found guilty of participating in an unlawful assembly. Judge Wadhams immediately imposed the extreme penalty of one year in jail and a fine of $500. Tannenbaum was to remain in jail until the fine was paid, "one day for each dollar." Reverend Alexander Irvine, the Socialist preacher, said: "Fifty years from now, when the doings of 1914 have been forgotten, mostly the people will look back to this day—this day, when we jailed for a year a boy just reaching his majority, for leading an unemployed army into an American church in search of shelter."[38]

After Tannenbaum's imprisonment,† the Wobblies decided to abandon the practice of church invasions as a totally inadequate solution for the unemployment problem. In the spring of 1914, at Haywood's suggestion,

* A bill embodying this proposal was introduced in the legislature, but it was never acted on.

† After his release from prison, Tannenbaum played little role in the I.W.W. The last mention of him as a participant in an I.W.W. activity is in *The New York Times* of Sept. 2, 1915. He is listed along with Elizabeth Gurley Flynn and Alexander Berkman as having been prevented by the police of Bayonne, N.J., from addressing a meeting of 1,500 employees of the Standard Oil and Tidewater companies. Following this experience, Tannenbaum was helped to complete his education by several philanthropic-minded people. He abandoned the labor movement and later became a professor at Columbia University, specializing in labor relations, Latin America, and anti-radicalism.

the I.W.W. Unemployed Union of New York was formed, with a committee of ten in charge and with headquarters and a reading room at 64 East 4th Street. (Haywood proposed the formation of the Union under I.W.W. leadership after the anarchists had assumed a leading place in the general unemployed movement.) Membership was free. Actually, the Unemployed Union was not a component part of the I.W.W., the plan being to issue cards that would be honored as a transfer when the men obtained work and were able to pay dues in the local of their industry.[39] Red cards carrying the program of the Unemployed Union were distributed throughout the city. The message charged the Mayor's Committee with doing nothing for the unemployed, urged the workers to expect nothing from the city, the state or the bosses, and advised them to "get together and see if we can do something for ourselves." Specifically, the I.W.W. Unemployed Union called for:

"1. Organization of the Unemployed (In Union there is Strength).

"2. A Rent Strike (No wages, no rent).

"3. A Workers' Moratorium (Don't pay your debts till the jobs come around).

"4. Refuse to Work at Scab Wages (Don't let the boss use your misery to pull down the workers' standard of life).

"5. A Demand for Work or Bread (If the bosses won't let you earn a decent livelihood, then they must foot the bill for your keep). The workers make the wealth of the world. It's up to us to get our share!"

On the reverse side of the red card were quotations from Cardinal Manning, Father Vaughn, Oscar Wilde, and Jesus, justifying the right of a starving man to obtain food and shelter without having to beg for them. *Solidarity* reprinted these quotations and urged all I.W.W. Unemployed Leagues to make use of them. "They expose the irreligion of capitalism. The latter, based on private ownership, is hostile to the communism of the early church, which finds an echo in them."[40]

By the late spring and summer of 1914, I.W.W. activity on the unemployed front had considerably slackened. For one thing, there was a general feeling among many Wobblies that unemployed struggles produced little of real significance for the unemployed and weakened the I.W.W. by causing the beating, arrest and imprisonment of its most militant members, without adding anything to the growth of the organization. Another danger, it was pointed out, was that the unemployed movement attracted various elements who had little in common with the I.W.W., especially the anarchists, and who created incidents for which the Wobblies were not responsible but for which they were blamed. This was particularly true in New York where the anarchists induced unemployed workers to break up meetings sponsored by the Socialist Party and the A.F. of L.'s Central Federated Union. The I.W.W. took no part in these demonstrations, but it was, nevertheless, blamed for the riots that occurred, and the police justified their refusal to permit the Wobblies to hold public meetings on the ground that they broke up the gatherings of other groups. In short, as Joe Ettor put it in the summer of 1914, "Everybody is trying to make the I.W.W. the goat."[41]

Some Wobblies felt that the I.W.W. had made a sufficient contribution to the unemployed struggles by being the first to call attention to the plight of those out of work, and that other groups should carry on from this point. They noted that "the fear of I.W.W. agitation" was forcing the Socialists and even A.F. of L. unions to devote some attention to the unemployment problem, and the anti-eviction activities, sponsored by the Socialists, which were spreading throughout New York, could be traced directly "to the influence of the I.W.W."

In October 1914, *Solidarity* featured the warning released by the A.F. of L.'s Central Federated Union to the city authorities that if nothing was done soon, "more I.W.W. unemployed agitation will be the result."[42] That same month, the Socialist Party of New York convened a Labor Conference to discuss the unemployment problem and seek ways to cope with it. The conference heard spokesmen from a number of trade unions describe the widespread unemployment of their membership, and warn that these workers might turn to the I.W.W. if the "legitimate labor movement" did nothing to alleviate their suffering. It then called upon "all labor organizations to urge all members not to work overtime during the emergency period; that they should give one day's work in the week to some unemployed member of their organization," and called upon the city to increase the tax rates on lands "so as to compel the owners to build" thereby providing employment for the building trades' unionists, more than half of whom were out of work; to fix the maximum price on the chief necessities of life, and to encourage farmers to bring their produce to city markets and sell them at cost to the consumer.[43]

I.W.W. ACTIVITY IN WINTER OF 1914–15

The I.W.W. leadership was not satisfied with the decision of members to abandon the unemployed to other groups and content themselves with taking credit for whatever was accomplished for those out of work. At the I.W.W. national convention, held in Chicago, September 1914, the slim attendance at which reflected the acute effect of the economic crisis,* Haywood emphasized that the I.W.W. had to concern itself with the problems of the unemployed. He urged the necessity of bending all efforts "to ward off the impending suffering of the unemployed during the coming winter" when the number out of work would mount sharply.

---

* Brissenden, who attended the sessions of September 22, 23, and 24, reported that on the 22nd he counted ten delegates actually present, and on the 23rd and 24th about 16 delegates. (*op. cit.*, p. 326.)

Haywood presented a direct action program to meet the plight of the unemployed, which the delegates adopted. It condemned the food merchants and the government for shipping bread to warring countries while "no single thought is given to the Peaceful Army of Production. Millions are appropriated for the militia and the army of destruction, but not a cent to provide work for the wealth producers." The workers were told to meet the situation of rising unemployment "with grim determination" by going to the granaries and warehouses, armed with pickaxes and crowbars, and helping themselves. They were advised not to waste time on demonstrations before municipal, state or national legislative bodies "as nothing more substantial than hot air is to be found in these political centers." "Rather than congregate around City Halls, Capitols and empty squares, go to the market place and waterfronts where food is abundant. If food is being shipped, confiscate it, if you have the power. Where houses are vacant, occupy them. If machinery is idle use it, if practical to your purpose." Wobblies were urged to organize the unemployed into the I.W.W. The new members were to be given propaganda cards which were to be deposited in the industrial unions when they obtained work. Haywood predicted that if this plan was adopted, "the unemployed, as soon as industries resume operation, will become an integral part of One Big Union and through organization will be in a position to levy tribute on the prosperity that the privileged class is anticipating and the newspapers are promising as a result of the devastation of war."[44]

Haywood's prediction that the winter of 1914-15 would be a hard one for American workers proved to be accurate. Three independent investigations—by the Mayor's Committee on Unemployment, the Metropolitan Life Insurance Co., and the U.S. Department of Labor—showed that in the early months of 1915 from 400,000 to 440,000 wage earners in New York City were simultaneously unemployed, to say nothing of those workers who were kept on part-time or were employed irregularly. In short, 18 per cent of the 2,455,000 wage earners in the city were unemployed! In other cities estimates and surveys gave proof that unemployment existed in somewhat the same proportion as in New York. Sixty-five thousand in Cleveland were looking for work; 150,000 in Philadelphia (an increase of as much as 130,000 over the previous year); 40,000 in Rochester; 75,000 to 80,000 in St. Louis; 133,000 out of 1,113,000 wage earners in Chicago. In his study of unemployment during this period, Maxwell Bertch has estimated that the number of unemployed in the winter of 1914-1915 "reached as much as 4,000,000 and possibly higher." In addition, there were several million working only part-time.[45]*

* This is a good deal higher than the estimate of the National Progressive Service which stated that "at least 2,000,000 people" were out of work. (*American Labor Legislation Review,* vol. V, Nov. 1915, p. 483.) But, in the absence of truly accurate nation-wide statistics, it was impossible to do anything but guess at the actual

Reports from 36 charitable organizations located in 29 cities in the United States gave proof of the great increase of unemployment. Combined figures showed that from October 1, 1914, until April 1, 1915, a period of six months, in 29,039 or 48 per cent of the family cases handled by them, the chief wage earner held no job at the time of application, even though physically and mentally fit to work. In 1912–13 for the corresponding months, in only 7,760 or 23 per cent of the cases had the chief wage earner been out of work. The comparison shows that such applications in 1914–15 were more than double those of 1912–13.

The same was true of the number of homeless men. Forty-three charitable organizations in 30 cities reported that whereas during the six months preceding April 1, 1913, they had received applications from 35,311 homeless men, during the same period in 1914–15, the number had jumped to 77,735, an increase of 120 per cent.[46]

"From the Atlantic to the Pacific, hunger and cold stalk among the great armies of men and women without work," noted a newspaper in January 1915.[47] In Philadelphia, the sign "No More Applications Received" hung in the doors and windows of the Home Relief Emergency Committee. "A new phase of suffering throughout the city was brought to light yesterday," the Philadelphia *Public Ledger* reported on January 30, 1915, "when it was learned at the Committee's headquarters that hundreds of children are starving through lack of milk, a necessity which their parents have no money to buy." The European war had multiplied the cost of living and rising prices had sharpened the misery of the unemployed. Five-cent bread became a thing of the past. On February 13, 1915, Mayor John Purroy Mitchel wrote to President Wilson: "There is in immediate prospect much hardship and suffering in New York and other cities caused by the recent increase in the price of bread. In the last few days this increase has amounted to 20%, which is a very considerable burden on our poor people." "Six cent bread," Samuel Gompers noted, "meant tragedy to east side New York and similar localities where wage earners lived."[48]

But when an attempt was made to involve the A.F. of L. in mass demonstrations to assist the unemployed, the Executive Council rejected the idea. In January 1915, Chester M. Wright, managing editor of the New York *Call,* urged the Executive Council to endorse mass demonstrations of the unemployed, called by the Socialist Party for February 12, 1915, and to lend its support. Gompers reported the decision in a letter to Wright. He began with the usual words of sympathy for the plight of the unemployed: "The Executive Council of the A.F. of L. requests me

number. "Guesses are our chief source of information on this vital business of unemployment," Alvin Johnson wrote in the spring of 1915. (*The New Republic,* April 17, 1915, p. 12.)

to say that they, like all other thoughtful, humanity-loving men, feel keenly the unemployment of one man or woman and much more the unemployment of large numbers who suffer through no fault of their own. We realize the fact that to every unemployed man who is willing to work all the progress of the world is a hollow mockery." Then followed the usual "but":

"If demonstrations, as you propose, could meet the present situation and solve it there would be no hesitancy on the part of the Executive Council of the American Federation of Labor to co-operate, but to follow the leadership of any one or any body of men when the matter presented to us is for mere agitation purposes alone, without any practical results occurring, we must respectfully decline to permit our movement to be used for any such purpose."[49]

Since Gompers did not then or later propose any other way to achieve "practical purposes," it is clear that for all the words of sympathy for the unemployed, the A.F. of L. leadership simply did not want to concern itself with their problems.*

Although the Socialist Party and its local branches throughout the country became increasingly active in the unemployed struggles during the winter of 1914-15, especially the Cleveland Socialists led by Charles E. Ruthenberg,[50] the opportunity existed for the I.W.W. to fulfill the role assigned to it by the 1914 convention. "The Industrial Workers of the World is pre-eminently the organization to take the lead in the cause of the unemployed," an I.W.W. pamphlet issued in January 1915 stated boldly. "It is the representative of the unskilled and semiskilled workers, who are the first and greatest sufferers from work scarcity."[51] On January 9, 1915, *Solidarity* stressed the need for a special organizing drive among the unemployed. "Agitation among the unemployed appears to be all that the I.W.W. can do effectually at present; and every possible effort should be made in every locality to line them up in the I.W.W. without requiring dues or admission fees, and with a view toward keeping them permanently in the organization."

In New York, Portland, St. Louis, Sioux City, Des Moines, Detroit, Salt Lake City, Providence and other cities, the I.W.W. established Unemployed Leagues during the hard winter of 1914-15. All of them distributed "A Message to the Unemployed From the Industrial Workers of the World" calling upon the unemployed to join with the I.W.W. to

---

* The only concrete proposal offered by the A.F. of L. on the unemployment issue during the period 1913-15 was the action of the 1915 convention urging Congress and the states to enact laws providing for the erection of buildings in which the unemployed could find lodging and meals during the winter. (*Proceedings*, A.F. of L. Convention, 1915, p. 313. *See also* Barry M. Goldstone, "The American Federation of Labor Views Unemployment, 1881-1932," unpublished B.A. thesis, University of Pennsylvania, 1957, pp. 29-31.)

"force the employers to cut down the daily working hours to 6, 5 or 4 or any number that may be necessary to make room for all our unemployed fellow workers to make a living." Some Leagues demonstrated before City Councils demanding that they appropriate funds for relief and public works while others rejected this type of activity as a violation of the position adopted by the 1914 convention to depend primarily upon direct-action methods. A number set up kitchens in buildings furnished by friendly organizations and offered unemployed workers a combination of public forums and mulligan stew. Some sent volunteers daily to centers where old clothing collected for the unemployed during city-wide "Bundle Days" were distributed, and, after fitting themselves out in overcoats, shirts, shoes, and suits, would turn them over to the needy gathered at the Unemployed League. Others sent groups of hungry men to restaurants, instructing them to eat and charge the meals to the Mayor.[52] Some, as the following account in the Seattle *Post-Intelligencer* of December 18, 1914, reported, simply raided restaurants and food markets:

"Two hundred howling men, operating from a base on Washington Street, terrorized the patrons and proprietors of the New York lunch room on Second Avenue last night by marching into the dining room and forcibly taking all the food in sight, including the meals that were spread for the diners. Following this raid the mob paraded the downtown streets and within an hour made an onslaught on the Westlake market, seizing everything edible within reach."

To make sure the diners knew who was responsible for the raid, the men distributed I.W.W. literature among them.

Such stunts, the I.W.W. argued, accomplished two things: They gave hundreds of hungry men one or two meals, and they attracted attention to the plight of the unemployed. Unemployed Wobblies were urged to come to cities where restaurant visits were taking place and participate in "this form of direct action until it brings results."[53] Not all Wobblies, however, favored this method. James Larkin, addressing an I.W.W. mass meeting of the unemployed in New York City on February 1, 1915, declared that "while he did not blame the individual worker who went into a restaurant and ate his fill without paying, it was an ineffective way of solving the problem." He favored mass action, such as a rent strike by the unemployed, rather than the single act of the individual. However, like most I.W.W. spokesmen, he reminded the unemployed: "The only real and lasting cure for unemployment is to secure for the workers the full proceeds of their toil. Only when they owned the industries for themselves would they be guaranteed the right to live and to work."[54]*

---

* James Larkin, the militant leader of the Irish Transport and General Workers' Union in Dublin, left Ireland for the United States in October 1914. He was supposed to return to Ireland within a few weeks, but did not set foot in his native

Actually, this theme was also stressed in much of the I.W.W. literature addressed to the unemployed. In a leaflet announcing an unemployed mass meeting on March 21, 1915, in Union Square, New York City, the I.W.W. asked: "Why all this poverty, misery and starvation?" The answer was: "Unemployment is caused by the capitalist system under which one man is forced to work for another, and to give up the whole of his product for a part, whence it must inevitably result that masses of wealth accumulate in the hands of some." There was a solution: "The workers, employed and unemployed, must unite their forces, and with their combined economic power expropriate the exploiters of the working class and take possession of the means of production to continue production—not for profit—but for the use and well-being of all." In the pamphlet entitled, "The I.W.W. and Unemployment," the I.W.W. insisted "that no temporary expedient, no paltering palliatives can solve the problem. Unemployment is the biggest adjunct of capitalist industry. Only when the control of production is wrested from the profiteering employer can all the workers be certain of the means of life. The I.W.W. offers no solution. But it recognizes that the capitalist masters of society may be harassed and driven into an attempt to minimize the evils of worklessness."[55]

Most of the Unemployed Leagues were strictly I.W.W. organizations, a policy adopted to avoid the past mistake of allowing other groups to cooperate and then leave the Wobblies to be "the 'goat' of official persecution and head-hunting." However, in a number of communities, the I.W.W. cooperated with other organizations. The Unemployed League of Seattle, organized in November 1914 by a committee composed of members of the I.W.W., the A.F. of L., and some who were affiliated to no organization, registered over 4,000 members within a brief time, published its own news sheet to bring the facts about unemployment to the public, and obtained food and clothing through contributions from middle-class families and small businessmen. Every day members of the League pulled a wagon through the streets of Seattle on which was a sign reading: "12,000 Hungry Men and Women in Seattle. What Are You Going to Do About it?" Soon, however, the radical tone of the news

---

land again for nearly nine years. Soon after he arrived in the United States, he joined the I.W.W. and became active in its work among the unemployed.

Larkin's suggestion for a rent strike may have been influenced by a proposal made by Joe Hill. Writing from the County Jail of Salt Lake City, where he was a prisoner awaiting execution, Joe Hill suggested to Elizabeth Gurley Flynn the organization of a "Workers Moratorium League of New York" which would distribute a certificate among the unemployed. This would then be handed to landlords when they came to collect rent, and would entitle the unemployed worker "to shelter without the paying of rent until able to secure a position." (*See* Philip S. Foner, editor, *The Letters of Joe Hill*, New York, 1965, pp. 22–23.)

sheet frightened contributors, and donations practically ceased. By the end of January 1915, the Seattle Unemployed League had disappeared.[56]

SIOUX CITY FREE-SPEECH FIGHT

In Sioux City, Iowa, I.W.W. activity in behalf of the unemployed led to one of the great free-speech fights with which the organization was associated. In October 1914, several Wobblies arrived in Sioux City, organized an Unemployed League, and began speaking at street corners to the unemployed. Most of the unemployed were migratory workers from the wheat fields and railway construction camps who were in Sioux City trying to pick up work during the winter months when there were no fields to harvest and the construction jobs were shut down. This winter, however, there were few jobs in Sioux City, and the unemployed were starving. A number worked for the ice companies at 15 cents an hour with deductions from their pay for the food they consumed. Even though these men earned 45 or 50 cents a day for a ten-hour day, there were hundreds of hungry men clamoring for the work.

Using the Socialist Hall as headquarters, the Wobblies began to feed and shelter the hungry, soliciting food from the local merchants. They also provided benches for the unemployed to sleep on in the hall. But when they began to organize the men working for the ice companies and launched a campaign for better working conditions, the local merchants stopped their contributions of food. The I.W.W. Unemployed League responded with street-corner meetings, demanding that an investigation of unemployment being conducted by the Commercial Club produce concrete results. "We will have confidence in them only when they have done something, and they must not wait too long to do it," the League announced. Finally, the League led 150 hungry men to the Commercial Club and insisted that steps be taken immediately to feed and house the unemployed.[57]

The majority of the businessmen demanded that the city officials rid Sioux City of the I.W.W. agitators and their unemployed followers. In January 1915, the right to speak in the streets was denied the Wobblies, and a campaign of arrests for vagrancy was launched against members of the I.W.W. With most members of the Unemployed League in jail for vagrancy under sentences of six months to one year, a call went out for aid to all "footloose rebels to help us win free speech here." Three hundred and ten men from nearby locals of Kansas City and Minneapolis poured into Sioux City and held street meetings, and a committee went to the police commissioner and demanded the release of the Wobblies in jail. The authorities, surprised and frightened by the invasion and warned by several more enlightened citizens that hundreds of Wobblies would soon descend upon Sioux City, released the men in jail and revoked the ban on street meetings.[58]

The men released from jail went back to the street corners and revived their campaign for unemployment relief to last at least until the summer when the migratory workers could return to the harvests and construction camps. Once again the businessmen became frightened, and demanded that the city authorities act to get rid of "the I.W.W. menace," and this time without retreating. Once again arrests and jailings of Wobblies on the charge of vagrancy started, and street meetings were again banned. Every night, crowds of 600 to 1,000 watched a Wobbly mount his box and talk until arrested.

This time the authorities prepared for an invasion. They built a stockade, shipped in rock, and announced that anyone violating the ban against street meetings would not only be arrested but put to work breaking rock. But if they believed this would end their troubles, they soon learned differently. On April 10, *Solidarity* carried the headline: "*Quick Action Needed in Sioux City, Iowa. Many I.W.W. Men in Jail.*" Immediately, Wobblies began arriving in Sioux City, some from as far East as Boston and as far West as San Francisco. By April 15, 83 Wobblies were in jail, but the fight appeared to be only beginning.[59]

On April 16, the Sioux City *Journal* reported that the men in jail were "conducting a double strike against work and food." It went on to inform its astonished readers that when the prisoners were led out to work breaking rocks, they went peaceably, sat down passively on the rock pile, and informed the police that under no circumstances would they break up the rock pile. Led back to the vermin-infested jail, they refused to eat. This procedure, they informed the authorities, would continue until all the prisoners were released and their right to speak on the street corners in behalf of the unemployed protected.

For the next three days, the Sioux City *Journal* carried the headline: "*Work and Hunger Strike Still On.*" The prisoners had been beaten by the police to force them to work; several had been sent to the hospital with broken heads; fire hoses had been turned on them—but still they refused to break rock. Meanwhile, they were "living on water and cigarettes." As a further gesture of defiance, they had swept together in a heap the vermin-infested blankets and rags in the jail and set fire to them.[60]

Expressions of admiration for the free-speech fighters began to appear in letters to the Sioux City *Journal*. The local Socialist Party reprinted some of these in a circular entitled "Let us Right This Wrong," and distributed it throughout the city. It called for immediate release of the prisoners and restoration of their right to speak on the street corners. This position contrasted sharply with that adopted by the A.F. of L. in Sioux City. The *Union Advocate,* organ of the Trades and Labor Assembly, praised the authorities for jailing the Wobblies whom it described as "the same sort of irresponsible, lazy, good-for-nothing louts who formerly made an easy living as strikebreakers. . . . Within recent years organized labor has become so strongly entrenched, and has forced arbitration and conciliation on the employers, through the force of public opinion to such an extent that the strikebreaker, as such, finds his occupation gone, and needs must turn to some other method of making 'easy pickings' without work. And the I.W.W. has been his refuge."[61] Sioux City employers, who were behind the drive to jail the Wobblies, must have found this amusing.

As more free-speech fighters arrived, the city authorities were forced to retreat. They agreed to release the prisoners on condition that they promise to leave the town. These terms were rejected by the men in jail. On April 19, the authorities capitulated completely, agreed to release the men in jail, and restore the right to speak in the streets unmolested. In return, the Wobblies agreed to halt appeals for recruits in the fight from outside the city. Eighty-six Wobblies, weak from hunger, were released from jail.[62]

After permission was granted by the city authorities, 52 free-speech fighters who arrived in Sioux City the morning the prisoners were released joined their fellow Wobblies in "an I.W.W. banquet on the rockpile." Then the free-speech fighters from San Francisco, Kansas City, Minneapolis, Chicago and other cities departed. The original group remained in Sioux City, holding street-corner meetings, collecting food for the unemployed, and building an organizational spirit among the migratory workers which was to bear fruit in the following summer and fall. The final triumph of the Sioux City Unemployed League came in May when the city authorities appropriated funds for unemployment relief.[63]

ROLE OF GOVERNMENT

At the end of February 1915, the I.W.W. predicted that the need for its activity on the unemployment front would soon end. "To supply the markets that will be created by the present European war it is safe to assume that in the near future there will be an increase in industrial activity." The prediction proved to be accurate. By April 1915, the depression began to lift, as European war orders caused mills and factories to rehire workers. In the fall of 1915, a contemporary journal noted: "The trend toward a full resumption of industrial activity seems to have attained the dimensions almost of a wave of prosperity, although in some industries the movement has not reached the point where all pessimism is dispelled. Unemployment has reached probably the lowest point since 1907."[64]

The 18 months from December 1913 to April 1915 were exceedingly difficult ones for millions of American workers. The federal government did not concern itself in the slightest with the unemployment problem, not even bothering to appropriate funds to gather statistics on the number of unemployed in the country. Secretary of Labor Wilson was placed in the embarrassing position of having repeatedly to reply to inquiries: "I regret to have to advise you, in response to your letter . . . that this Department has no authentic information as to the number of idle workmen throughout the country nor as to the factories that have been closed down. I fully appreciate the importance of these statistics and deplore the fact that we have not as yet been provided with the machinery for gathering such information." Royal Meeker, Commissioner of the United States Bureau of Labor Statistics, admitted later that it was "humiliating to note that, in the vitally important matter of unemployment, the facts needed were not available, and that lack of funds rendered the Federal officials helpless to obtain the required information."[65]

Efforts to get President Wilson to take up the cause of the unemployed were futile. Telegrams and letters received at the White House from mass meetings of the unemployed or from various city committees on unemployment urging the government "to push actively all public work" to alleviate "so far as possible the situation of the unemployed" were ignored. Hundreds of letters from all over the country describing the serious plight of the unemployed were filed in a folder headed "Pessimistic Letters on Crisis" and forgotten.[66] Indeed, the only time President Wilson expressed himself publicly on the economic crisis was to deny the accuracy of a statement by Frank P. Walsh, chairman of the Industrial Relations Commission, estimating that between 250,000 to 300,000 workers were unemployed in New York City in February 1914. Secretary of Labor Wilson echoed the President when he informed a correspondent that "stories about the unemployed in the city of New York have been greatly exaggerated."[67] The only proposal by the federal government to deal with the severe economic crisis was advanced in July 1915 when the problem was over. And this was a plan for the federal government to finance workers desiring to take up farm land.[68]

In the report of the Industrial Relations Commission, signed by the labor commissioners and Frank P. Walsh, the federal government was sharply criticized for having ignored the problems of the unemployed during the crisis of 1913-15: "Surely there is no condition which more immediately demands the attention of Congress than that of unemployment, which is annually driving hundreds of otherwise productive citizens into poverty and bitter despair, sapping the very basis of our national efficiency, and germinating the seeds of revolution."[69] The same criticism could have been directed at the cities and states, for the measures adopted by them during this period were neither adequate nor systematically planned. "In almost every part of the country," concludes one student, "nothing was done until it was approaching a matter of life and death for those out of work."[70]

When the situation became so bad that something had to be done to relieve the suffering and distress, nearly every city resorted to what seemed the most expedient method, which usually amounted to the same thing as charity, even though disguised in many cases. One can understand this more clearly when it is realized that during these months of unemployment, Philadelphia was the only major city in the country to vote public funds for relief. All the others raised whatever funds they disbursed through private contributions. Generally, the unemployed had to depend on soup kitchens and shelters provided by municipal lodging houses which were taxed to capacity and furnished beds only for a few nights. Efforts of social agencies to find jobs for the unemployed were fruitless. "Odd jobs for a limited number of people might be found, but the great mass of the unemployed could not be helped even by frantic attempts to find every available work opportunity."[71]

SIGNIFICANCE OF WORK OF I.W.W.

Inadequate though these measures were, their existence was largely the result of protest movements by the unemployed. In these, A.F. of L. unions and Socialist Party locals became active as the crisis deepened. But it was the I.W.W. that first urged the unemployed to demonstrate their refusal to starve, repeatedly organized the unemployed to demand relief, and devoted major attention to the unemployment problem. Its methods were often bizarre, and, to many, even ridiculous as a solution to the problem. Confusion over the value of demonstrations and of applying pressure on government to obtain unemployment relief, weakened the effectiveness of its work, as did, of course, the limited number of members who were still associated with the organization and available to assume leadership of the unemployed struggles. Nevertheless, the I.W.W., with all these limitations, made a notable contribution to the unemployed movement of the period 1913–15. In March 1915, John Graham Brooks, president of the National Consumers League, startled the members of the Economic Club of New York by paying tribute to the I.W.W. for having stirred society into action on the unemployment question. He dismissed the I.W.W. solution for unemployment, which he described as a demand for "$2 a day or take it when you can find it" (an obvious distortion of the I.W.W. program), as "childishness." But he declared firmly: "I, for one, even thank the I.W.W. for stinging us and nagging us into some recognition of our duty, . . . [and for] their service of insisting that we have thus far merely fooled with these issues." Henry Bruere, New York City municipal reformer, declared in the winter of 1914–15, that "thanks to the activities of the I.W.W., the unemployed are no longer regarded as hoboes as they were last year."[72]

Looking back on its work on the unemployed front since the winter of 1913–14, the I.W.W. declared in March 1915 that it had made two significant contributions which "should cause it to receive the commendation of every thoughtful and progressive workingman and woman."

"First, it is anti-scab; the unemployed, in other words, are being taught to uphold present wage standards, and not to break them down. Second, it is anti-submissive; it is teaching the unemployed to refuse to submit to charity and to capitalist conditions, and to rebel against them instead. This tends to preserve the prevailing standards of decency and self-respect, the decline of which makes any advance in society impossible."[73]

With its limited membership the I.W.W. could hardly build an effective nation-wide unemployed movement. But in many communities, both through its own Unemployed Leagues and through participation in other organizations, the I.W.W. did succeed in calling attention to the plight of the unemployed, did stimulate the unemployed to do something for themselves rather than resign themselves to starvation, and did force the authorities to provide some relief for the men and women out of work. The activities of the Wobblies pointed the way for the militant mass struggles of the unemployed that were to take place during the greater economic crisis that began in 1929.

CHAPTER 20

"What's Wrong with the I.W.W.?"

On July 21, 1915, *Solidarity* issued a Special Number celebrating the tenth anniversary of the founding of the I.W.W. It featured articles evaluating a decade of contributions by the Wobblies to the American working class and the labor movement—even to the A.F. of L. "Not the least of the 'ten years of the I.W.W.' has been its educational influences. Many an A.F. of L. union owes its industrial tendencies, such as they are, to I.W.W. teachings and example." All in all, the I.W.W., after ten years of existence, was judged a success. B. H. Williams, editor of *Solidarity,* summed it up:

"No matter what may be the particular task engaged in by our organization, whether it be the carrying on of strikes of unskilled workers; the waging of fights for freedom of speech; the conducting of legal battles in the courts; the use of direct action tactics on the job; the lining up of the unemployed to demand rather than merely to beg for the chance to exist; or the many other forms of its activity—looking to the complete organization of the working class—the I.W.W. had demonstrated its efficiency as a fighting organization."

Yet for a movement that had "demonstrated its efficiency as a fighting organization," the I.W.W. had little concrete to show for it when it celebrated its tenth anniversary. It did not even hold a convention in 1915, and *Solidarity* itself teetered on the brink of extinction until an outright gift of $1,000, which one of the members had inherited, saved it.[1] Membership statistics show the declining fortunes of the I.W.W. from 1912 to 1915. For 1912: 18,387 (reflecting the gains of Eastern textile workers); for 1913: 14,851; for 1914: 11,365, and for 1915: 15,000.[2] And these official figures were probably exaggerated.

Even the activity among the unemployed during the economic crisis had yielded little in organizational growth. As one Wobbly pointed out in *Solidarity* on May 15, 1915: "Conditions were favorable to our purpose —discontent, high cost of living, unemployment due to capitalist mismanagement, were powerful allies to our cause; yet we were unable to crystallize them in the form of an industrial union. What's wrong with the I.W.W.?"

DISCUSSION IN I.W.W. PRESS

This was not the first time this question had been asked. As the I.W.W. descended rapidly from the "crest of power" achieved in 1912, the question was asked again and again in readers' letters to the Wobbly press. The letters described how the I.W.W. had struck a spark in the heart of the writers who had given unstintingly to advance the ideals of the "One Big Union." They told of the warmth and inspiration that came from the free-speech fights, and the heroic struggles at McKees Rocks, Lawrence, Paterson, Akron, Detroit, and other mass battles. Then came the disillusioning realization that none of these struggles had led to the creation of permanent unions in the industries involved. The letters not only pointed out the meager success of the I.W.W. in establishing revolutionary industrial unions in their natural habitat—the mass production industries—but stressed that all the major organizing drives in industries virtually unorganized by the A.F. of L. had collapsed after initial success. To be sure, the I.W.W., the writers conceded, listed a large number of independent local industrial unions and recruiting unions and even boasted of national industrial unions. But everyone knew that the local industrial unions (except for the longshoremen's union in Philadelphia) and the recruiting unions contained relatively few members, and the national industrial unions were largely paper unions.

"It is obvious from the present conditions of our locals," one correspondent wrote in *Solidarity* of February 6, 1914, "that we have failed to hold organizations which were effected during strikes at McKees Rocks, Lawrence, Paterson, Akron and other places. We enroll a large membership during a strike. We teach a solidarity that is sublime and infuse a militant spirit into the workers that is rare. . . . But in all this chain of revolutionary thinking there seems to be a weak link that gives way almost as soon as the last mass meeting is held and the strikers return to work."

"We have distributed literature," went a common complaint, "held meetings, hall and street, and taken advantage of various opportunities to advertise the fact of our being. But judging by our membership, revolutionary industrial unionism does not seem to 'take.'"[3] Some letters complained that in industries where the A.F. of L. was already established—shoe makers, hotel workers, barbers, piano makers, building-trades workers, and garment workers—the forays of the I.W.W. organizers, their attacks on the motives and philosophies of the A.F. of L. leaders, their efforts to promote dual unions, and their boast of the plan to drive the

A.F. of L. out of existence and emancipate the workers through revolutionary industrial unions, had produced nothing of consequence organizationally and had only made enemies of workers who had once been sympathetic to the Wobblies. Other letters pointed out that the I.W.W. had lost so much prestige that it was no longer a force to be reckoned with among the Italians, and stressed that this was a serious blow to the organization since in many I.W.W. strikes, the Italians had been the most numerous and militant of the strikers. Some readers, with pens dipped in irony, pointed to the less than 1,700 votes cast in the election for a secretary-treasurer, the highest office in the organization, early in 1914, and contrasted this with the 25,000 or more members the I.W.W. claimed publicly. Others, noting that Vincent St. John, who had been the previous secretary-treasurer, refused to become a candidate for reelection, cited this as evidence of the growing disillusionment of a veteran unionist with the possibility of building mass trade unions through the I.W.W.[4] It was all summed up by a letter in *Solidarity* of November 14, 1914, which asked: "If the principles of the I.W.W. are right, why has it failed to attract the workers or hold them when organized into locals?"

This bill of particulars against the I.W.W., compiled from readers' letters, was, as we have seen, mild in tone compared to what was published in the Socialist press during the same period. But even many Wobblies who attacked the Socialist critics admitted that by 1914, two years after the spectacular Lawrence victory, the I.W.W. seemed completely spent. "What's Wrong with the I.W.W.?" they asked.

Most of the I.W.W. leaders agreed that there was a value in raising this question. ("We must know the weak spots as well as the strong. . . . Disclosing and examining an obstacle seemingly hard to overcome, should not dampen our ardor or discourage us in the least; we'll meet with a lot of these in the course of our development. They should, and will, serve to make us more determined than ever to overcome every obstacle that hinders us in our sure and onward march to industrial freedom."[5]) But they insisted that there was nothing fundamentally wrong with the I.W.W., and that all talk of defeats suffered by the Wobblies was nonsense.

For one thing, the decline in membership meant nothing since the I.W.W. had always maintained that its influence was "immeasurably greater than its membership," and if it had been primarily interested in a large membership, it could easily have achieved this goal. Certainly the capitalists knew better than to regard the size of the I.W.W. membership as the measure of the organization's influence among the workers, and their fear and hatred of the organization was as great as ever.* Secondly,

---

* This statement was advanced in the face of *Solidarity's* admission that the capitalist press was stating "the I.W.W. is a waning menace following the retreat of the Paterson silk strikers back into the mills." (Aug. 16, 1913.)

the strikes at Paterson, Akron, and Detroit were not defeats since the workers went back to the plants and won concessions from the employers through sabotage—the strike on the job. No evidence was offered to prove this assertion. It was simply stated. Moreover, even if these strikes were defeats, "the low-paid slaves, under I.W.W. guidance, had put up fights that brought universal attention to the fighting qualities of unskilled workers and the I.W.W. which led their fights. The workers gained a wealth of experience for themselves, and for other slaves that would have been impossible without the application of the I.W.W. theory." The I.W.W. by teaching workers "the inspiration of defeat" was preparing them for future victories, for "only through such constant struggles can the working class finally be brought to sufficient unity to overthrow capitalism." Finally, the I.W.W. should not become involved in "petty insignificant sham battles" over the status of the organization and the correctness of Wobbly strategy and tactics. "What is the matter with us?" asked Matilda Rabinowitz. "Thousands are waiting to be educated and organized in fighting battalions. This is our work."[6]

REASONS FOR FAILURE TO GROW

Many members of the I.W.W. were not to be put off by such reassuring words. They felt that it was foolish to deny the validity of much of the criticism raised in the letters to the Wobbly press, and sought to provide explanations that might satisfy the critics. (They distinguished, however, between "honest criticism" by I.W.W. members and that by former disillusioned Wobblies and Socialists which they dismissed as the "howling of agents of the capitalists."[7]) They attributed the I.W.W.'s problems and difficulties to the following causes:

(1) The I.W.W. had done what no one had even dared to think of before—it had organized the migratory workers in the West into agricultural, construction, and lumber unions, and the unskilled workers in the mass-production industries of the East, including steel, rubber, textile, and auto. But this was no easy task. For one thing, it was difficult to build stable unions among the migratory workers.* Because of the very fact of their moving around they were not in continuous association with each other and hence difficult to keep organized. Then again, in the West, the law was still the law of the jungle, and the vigilantes had been brutal in hunting down, beating and murdering I.W.W. organizers who were without legal protection. The main power of the workers was concentrated in the East. But the power of the capitalist class was concen-

---

* "I suppose it is almost hopeless to try to maintain a permanent union of itinerant workers," John R. Commons, the noted labor historian, wrote in 1915. (Commons to Henry Parker, April 6, 1915, "Labor Collection, Miscellaneous Papers and Articles, folder marked 'Migratory Labor,'" U.S. MSS., 18 A, Box 3, *WSHS*.)

trated there too. The capitalists had fought the new revolutionary industrial unionism with all the power at their command. Against the program of the I.W.W. and its little band of agitators, they had brought up the heavy guns of their financial resources, public opinion molded in their favor by press and pulpit, their private armies of labor spies and detectives, and always and everywhere, the police and military power of the city and state governments. They had arrested I.W.W. leaders and members, usually on trumped-up charges, and forced the organization into long court battles which sapped its resources and vitality. They intimidated foreign-born workers with threats of deportation and denial of citizenship if they joined the I.W.W. Dependent on their jobs to support their families, and thus more easily subject to intimidation by the employers, the workers in the Eastern mass-production industries were hard to keep organized. Under these circumstances, no labor organization, no matter how correct its message of unionism, would be able to make rapid headway. It would take time to break down the fortified walls of the open-shop trusts in the East and the factories in the fields of the West. But the I.W.W. had made a beginning, and with continued effort and by avoiding past mistakes, it would yet succeed in achieving this objective.[8]

(2) In addition to this fundamental reason for the failure of the I.W.W. to win its battles and to grow, certain mistakes were committed that had made it easier for the capitalists to triumph. These were not mistakes in ideology so much as in an incorrect application. "In their zeal to obtain propaganda for their ideas, some members of the I.W.W. unfortunately employed means obnoxious in the eyes of a great part of the working class, and have been instrumental in increasing the prejudices towards the I.W.W." Too often, workers had been antagonized unnecessarily by anti-religious and anti-patriotic agitation, by organizers who had advocated that "a banner with the inscription 'No God! No Master!' should be carried by us into the shops and factories," and who had advised "making night shirts out of the American flag." Wobbly agitators had forgotten that the "workers who won the battles of McKees Rocks and Lawrence were not atheists." Too many Wobblies, in short, introduced "side issues" such as "religion and politics" and drove away potential members, instead of concentrating on discussion of job control. Then again, there had been too much loose talk about sabotage. Sabotage was a necessary weapon in the class struggle. But it had to be applied secretly and without giving the class enemy advance notice. And it had to be used when the workers were ready for it, as when they were forced to return to work after defeat in a strike. But by loudly talking about sabotage on all occasions, Wobbly agitators had frightened many workers at the same time that they had made it easier for the press to turn opinion against the organization and the police to railroad members to

jail. If the I.W.W. was to progress, it had "to make scientific use of sabotage and indulge in less unscientific talk about it."[9]

(3) Granted that migratory workers were exceedingly difficult to keep organized, the Wobbly organizers had compounded the difficulty by failing methodically to follow the same group of migrant laborers in order to promote stability among them. Instead, they traveled about in more or less random fashion, and failed to develop a conscious, systematic coordinated effort at building and especially maintaining organizations of the migratory workers. Then again, too many I.W.W. organizers had operated as stunt makers. They had arrived in a city, decided that they had to "start something," mounted the soapbox, pulled off "a few sensational stunts," got the workers excited, recruited them into unions, led them in strikes, "made a lot of noise and then went on their way to more virgin fields, leaving behind no organization and nothing but a depleted treasury as the sole evidence of their 'successful work.'" These men were undoubtedly zealous members of the I.W.W., but they were guilty of confusing a union organizing job with agitation for revolutionary ideals. They failed to realize that the work of organizing took patient skill. Many of them found street agitation and free-speech fights easier than union organization. "We have been very energetic in fighting free-speech fights but begrudge anything spent in the direct work of organizing."

The soapbox approach had to be abandoned. "Organization cannot be accomplished on a street corner." It was not enough to arouse exploited workers to a spectacular and sudden fight; it was also necessary in the future to carry the message of the I.W.W. to the workers in the shops, factories, mines, lumber camps, and the harvest fields the year 'round, and for this "persistent, patient, unending campaigns rather than spectacular stunts are required. A mushroom growth of an organization may be better than no organization at all, but it rarely accomplishes any lasting results."[10]

(4) Too many Wobblies had unnecessarily antagonized Socialists who were ready to lend support to the I.W.W. It was correct to condemn the Socialist leaders who were allied with the A.F. of L. bureaucracy and acted as spokesmen for the capitalists in denouncing direct action and revolutionary industrial unionism. But many Left-wing Socialists did appreciate the mission of the I.W.W. and did aid the Wobblies in their struggles. It did not help the cause of the I.W.W. when their work was not appreciated, and they themselves subjected to attack for believing in political action. The result was that when the I.W.W. called upon them again for help, they refused to cooperate, and the locals organized by the Wobblies suffered by reason of this inability to obtain support from their natural allies.

The same mistake had been made in relations with rank and file A.F.

of L. members. Often they had been antagonized unnecessarily because of a tendency on the part of Wobbly agitators to lump them with the bureaucrats. How could the I.W.W. succeed in attracting these A.F. of L. members to join with the Wobblies in building new industrial unions if it looked upon them as hopelessly attached to the labor bureaucracy? I.W.W. agitators often turned away potential members among craft unions "by denouncing ridiculing and anathemizing [sic]" the only unions they have known.

Moreover, no permanent organization would be built in a community unless organizers abandoned the attitude that the workers who were not ready to join the I.W.W. were hopelessly backward. These were the workers who would have to be recruited if the I.W.W. was to grow, and no headway could be made if organizers continued "to treat the non-class conscious workers as a hopeless 'block.' "[11]

(5) The loose form of organization in the I.W.W. had operated against its growth and stability. The whole concept of mixed locals and Propaganda Leagues had to be abandoned. Since the members of the former were not oriented to any particular job, shop, or industry they were rarely union-minded and spent their time philosophizing. "A mixed local will always remain a discussion club." The same was true of the Propaganda Leagues. One Wobbly complained that the Leagues were dominated by "spell-binders and professional spielers."

Another weakness of these two organizations was the opportunity afforded for all sorts of unreliable and unscrupulous characters to join the I.W.W. and worm their way into positions of leadership. They often did so for the purpose of absconding with what little funds the mixed unions or the Leagues had* or to spy on the I.W.W. for employers. As Mortimer Downing noted in a letter to Bill Haywood:

"We also had the misfortune to get Ben Wright here as secretary [of the mixed local]. Wright as you know was a full fledged detective. He had several men of the small membership of the local canned.

"Wright is a peculiar product of the times. He had a four-year card in the I.W.W. During those four years none ever knew when he had done a day's work. Yet he would blow into a town, loaf around the locals, spend money quietly, and gather his information. The same thing was true about F. W. Goebel. Goebel even [went] so far as to spend $150 of his money to organize the Ft. Bragg local. When will we reach the day that men without visible means of support will be suspected of the parasitism they openly practice?"[12]

(6) The I.W.W. conception of democracy and individual freedom had been so loose that all sorts of "ism peddlers," including the anarchists, had

* Since the stolen funds of the locals were often listed as $12.97 or even $2.80 it is clear that both the members and the organization were impoverished. (See Industrial Worker, May 28, 1910, July 13, Oct. 26, 1911.)

been able to preach their doctrines in the organization's halls and from its platforms. The result was that the I.W.W. was associated in the minds of the workers with principles which it neither upheld nor approved. The I.W.W. had to stop being "simply a clearing house for ideals and isms" which it did not endorse, to institute a firmer discipline within its local unions, particularly in the West, and cease "to worship the Great God 'individual freedom.'" This new policy would undoubtedly help open the door to many workers who had hesitated to join and keep them from leaving once they joined.[13]

There was a good deal of truth in the fundamental reason advanced by these I.W.W. spokesmen for the failure of the organization to grow or even to consolidate its victories. It is true that by attacking the great unorganized centers of industrial America, the I.W.W. brought down upon itself the implacable hatred of the employers and their powerful allies. As we have seen, all types of violence were unleashed to defeat the I.W.W. in its organizing drives, and no amount of endeavors by the Wobblies to keep the workers from resorting to violence in their struggles prevented it from being used against the organization and its followers. With its limited finances and resources, it is doubtful, even if it had not committed many errors, that it would have been possible for the I.W.W. in pre-World War I America to achieve great success in organizing the mass-production industries.

The largest percentage of the workers in the Eastern mass-production industries and a large percentage of the migratory workers in the West were, of course, the foreign-born. But an alien who was an I.W.W. member after 1912 found it difficult to obtain citizenship, and in the Northwest it became almost impossible. During 1912 and 1913, federal officials in the Northwest disqualified applicants for citizenship if there was the slightest proof that they had been associated with the I.W.W., even if they had simply joined during a strike to improve wages, hours or working conditions and left the organization after the battle. In fact, an alien who was no longer a Wobbly but had been a member of the I.W.W. at any time in the five years preceding his application could not become a citizen. The same applied to an alien who was married to an I.W.W. member or one who had an I.W.W. member as a witness. In Minnesota and Wisconsin, some judges even refused to issue first papers to I.W.W. members. In short, after 1912 it took special courage for an alien in Washington, Oregon, Minnesota or Wisconsin, who was desirous of becoming an American citizen or even of remaining longer in this country, to join the I.W.W.[14]

While this vicious practice was not widespread in the East, it was used to intimidate foreign-born workers from joining the I.W.W. or remaining in the organization. Wide publicity was given in 1913, for example, to a statement by the authorities in New Jersey that efforts would be made to debar applicants from citizenship who had taken part in the Paterson strike; indeed, Munson Force, Assistant Prosecutor of the county, announced that the "authorities will take good care that they do not become citizens."[15] It is not difficult to imagine that when this was brought to the attention of the immigrants in the basic industries through the foreign-language press, many of them would hesitate before joining the I.W.W. The foreign-language press also devoted considerable space to the debates and votes in Congress on an immigration bill which included a clause permitting the deportation of an alien "advocating or teaching the unlawful destruction of property," a law specifically aimed at members of the I.W.W. The bill, with its sabotage clause, passed Congress in 1913, but was twice vetoed by President Wilson. The first time the House lacked by five votes the necessary two-thirds majority to overrule the President; the second time it failed by only four votes.[16] But there is little doubt that the threat of passage of the law made immigrants chary of joining the I.W.W. or staying with the organization.

REASONS NOT MENTIONED BY WOBBLIES

A flow of letters to the I.W.W. press corroborated the correctness of the point that past mistakes had contributed to the organization's failure to grow. But there were areas which none of these correspondents would touch. No one mentioned such a basic error as the I.W.W.'s opposition to political action and how this mistaken position isolated the organization from many of the most significant struggles of the American working class. Nor was there reference to the policy of "dual unionism" on which the organization was founded and to which it continued to adhere. Linked to this was the fundamental mistake of combining a revolutionary propaganda group and a trade union, even an industrial union. Not only were the two functions often confused, but just as often activities that were logical and necessary on the trade union front had to be rejected because they conflicted with revolutionary aims. Thus the "no contract" practice of the I.W.W. made stability impossible. What protection could the I.W.W. give the worker if it could not control the job? And how could it control the job if it refused, on revolutionary principles, to enter into agreements with employers? To be sure, a powerful I.W.W. union like the Marine Transport Workers No. 8 of Philadelphia was able, for a time, to obtain "recognition" by force of numbers. But the weaker I.W.W. unions—and most of them were weak—usually lost job control as hostile employers, not bound by a "recognition" contract, resorted to hiring non-Wobblies. Thus, ironically, while the refusal to sign contracts was justified, in part, as a means of keeping the capitalists off balance, experience proved that it had the opposite effect of enabling the employers to use it to their own advantage.

Other examples of how the combination of revolutionary propaganda functions with trade union activities resulted in practices which made for instability of the I.W.W. were: (1) Its refusal to institute a dues check-off which would guarantee its unions a stable income and a hold on the job through steady membership; (2) its scorn for the common union practice of making provisions for unemployment, sickness and death benefits to members and their families; (3) its refusal, in most cases, to build a strike fund and provide strike benefits, and to rely almost exclusively on emotional appeals for relief funds; (4) its universal transfer system which kept its locals in constant flux; (5) its low initiation fees and dues which kept the treasury pitifully small and hampered its ability to conduct prolonged organizing drives.

Although some of these practices were recognized as harmful to the organization and resulted eventually in modifications in I.W.W. policies, in the period between 1913 and 1915, they were uniformly regarded as sacred and any suggestion to alter them was rejected as conflicting with basic I.W.W. values.* I.W.W. theorists conceded that the A.F. of L. was able to enroll new members because of its use of the contract, protocol, check-off and benefits, and then to hold on to these members. They conceded, too, that if the Wobblies adopted these practices the I.W.W. would also increase its membership and its stability. But they maintained that their use would only compromise the purity of the revolutionary unionists. The whole concept of higher dues and initiation fees, of strike funds, of unemployment, sickness and death benefits, of contracts with employers and dues check-offs was based, in the eyes of most Wobblies, on the idea that workers' organizations had to be held together by incentives other than class-consciousness. This was true for the craft unions, but then, as the Wobblies saw it, these were not real labor unions but only "coffin societies." They would collapse if their insurance features were removed, their contracts with employers ended, and compulsory membership abandoned. True class-conscious unionists (like the Wobblies) did not need all of these incentives to keep them in One Big Union. They were acting together to better the conditions of their class and to end the vicious capitalist system. Joseph J. Ettor summed it up neatly when he asked:

"Can there be any dispute that if the I.W.W. struck bargains with employers, compromised its principles, signed protocols, contracts, had the employers collect the dues and acted as 'good boys' generally, we should have a half million members? . . . But rather than sacrifice our principles,

* According to Elizabeth Gurley Flynn, Vincent St. John, unlike Haywood, realized the contradiction in trying to function as a revolutionary propaganda organization and a trade union, and his conviction that nothing could be done to convince the majority of the Wobblies that this was a fundamental reason for the organization's failure to grow and achieve stability led to his resignation as general secretary in 1914. Miss Flynn feels that this was the basic weakness of the I.W.W. (Interview with Elizabeth Gurley Flynn, Jan. 31, 1964.)

kow-tow to all sorts of freak notions, declare a practical truce with the enemy, and have a large number of dues-payers, we have preferred to be true to our own purpose in spite of all opposition. Our men have sweated blood in carrying on the propaganda for a revolutionary labor body—revolutionary in methods as well as final purpose."

The two major points in the I.W.W. program—education and organization—when correctly applied would be enough to enable the workers to achieve its revolutionary goal. Many mistakes had been made in applying the I.W.W. program, but once they were corrected, the decline of the I.W.W. would be checked and "the principles advocated by the Industrial Workers of the World will undoubtedly triumph."[17]

RESULTS OF THE DISCUSSION

The discussion of the question "What's Wrong with the I.W.W.?" prolonged though it was, failed to come to grips with many of the fundamental problems facing the organization. Yet the self-critical attitude in the I.W.W., reflected in letters to the Wobbly press, beginning with the defeat at Paterson and continuing into 1915, was not without its positive contributions. The fact that the I.W.W. had failed to hold its membership was at least publicly acknowledged, as was the growing demand for building a constructive and permanent organization, rather than a purely agitational apparatus—a demand that even the most uncritical leaders in the organization had to recognize as both correct and necessary.

Thus it was that despite its meager membership and despite a practically empty treasury at national headquarters, the I.W.W. appeared supremely confident as it celebrated a decade of existence. True, there had been many failures in the past, but from them the I.W.W. had gained valuable experience which it was now prepared to apply in such a manner as would "make 1915 the banner year in the history of the One Big Union."[18] Already in the spring of 1915, a development had occurred which proved that the I.W.W. was capable of learning from past mistakes and which promised to build it into a powerful economic organization of unskilled and semi-skilled workers. This was the emergence of the Agricultural Workers Organization 400—the famous A.W.O.

CHAPTER 21

The Agricultural Workers Organization

By the time of the harvest season of 1914, it was clear that I.W.W. agitational work among the harvest hands had reaped few permanent results, and that conditions in the Middle-Western grain belt—Oklahoma, Kansas, Iowa, Nebraska, Minnesota, the Dakotas, Montana, and parts of Canada—were still intolerable. Wages of $2 to $2.50 for a day's work which began at 5:30 A.M. and ended at 7:30 P.M., plus inadequate board, was the norm. Harvest workers noted ironically that they enjoyed an "eight-hour work day—eight in the morning and eight in the afternoon." An investigator for the Industrial Relations Commission reported that "fourteen hours a day was not unusual." Referring to living conditions in the grain belt, he noted: "They [the men] object to sleeping in granaries full of rats and mice, on the bare ground in tents or in barns where the odor of the stable is strong and where mattresses and blankets are infested with vermin." It was generally conceded that nine out of every ten workers left the harvest as poor as when they entered. Indeed, as one contemporary noted: "The best paying occupation in the harvest country is 'the harvesting of the harvester,' which is heavily indulged in by train crews, railroad 'bulls,' gamblers and hold-up men."[1]

"Living in Kansas is a perennial joy," editorialized the Emporia *Gazette*. But to the harvest workers, living in any of the states in the grain belt meant a perennial struggle to exist through the season, in the face of inadequate earnings, intolerable living conditions, tin-horn gamblers, hijackers, bootleggers, brutal policemen, and hostile townspeople. The latter's contempt for the workers in the grain belt was illustrated in an editorial entitled "The Harvest Hand," published in the Emporia *Gazette*: "The harvest hands are arriving, and, as usual, they are arriving hungry. But a harvest hand never gets so hungry that he forgets to be haughty and stick for higher wages when offered a job."[2]

In its earliest attempts at organizing the harvest hands, the I.W.W. had relied primarily upon soapboxers who addressed these workers as they passed through Kansas City and St. Joseph, Mo., Omaha, Neb., Sioux City, Iowa, Minneapolis, Minn., and other cities which bordered the grain belt. But by 1913 it was clear that street agitation not only reached a small percentage of the workers, but produced nothing concrete in an organizational sense. "Street and hall meetings are good in a way," *Solidarity* conceded in evaluating the poor organizational results of the 1913 harvest, "but work on the job among the slaves is the way, the only way to build up the I.W.W."[3]

Heeding this advice, in the spring of 1914, the local unions of the I.W.W. in the cities bordering on the grain belt began sending their delegates into the harvest fields in an effort to recruit members among thousands of migratory workers. Although this method of organizing was a vast improvement over soapboxing, it still had weaknesses. Delegates from locals in Kansas City, Omaha and Minneapolis competed with each other in recruiting drives; initiation fees and dues varied among the different locals, and, in general, the work was haphazard. In an article entitled, "After the Harvest," a Wobbly organizer wrote in the fall of 1914: "Our chief shortcoming this year was in insufficiency of trained job agitators to cope with the situation, and also a deplorable lack of the thing called *Co-operation* among locals conducting this particular kind of work which is positively inexcusable and which must be remedied."[4]

FORMATION OF A.W.O.

The need was obviously to establish cooperation among the different locals so that a united organizational drive could be conducted in the grain fields. During the ninth annual I.W.W. convention, in September 1914, Frank Little, the one-eyed, half-Indian organizer and member of the General Executive Board, suggested that "some means should be taken for concerted and efficient action in the harvest fields next year." It was proposed that a conference be called composed of members from different locals bordering the harvest district, and that this conference determine ways and means "for harmonious grouping of hitherto spasmodic efforts of harvest organization." A resolution embodying Little's proposal was carried, and a few months after the convention, Haywood announced the formation by the I.W.W. of a Bureau of Migratory Workers to set up the conference, coordinate information on jobs, and further organization among the harvest workers. One of its chief duties would be "to circumvent the schemes of the labor bureaus and employment sharks" whose exaggerated accounts of labor shortages produced a surplus of labor, driving down wages and forcing many unemployed harvest hands to resort to begging and stealing.[5]

Following intense discussion in every issue of *Solidarity* during the winter and early spring of 1915 on the best way to organize the harvest workers in the following summer, a conference of locals adjacent to the grain belt took place in Kansas City on April 21, 1915. Seven locals were represented at the conference—Des Moines, Fresno, Portland, Kansas City, Salt Lake City, San Francisco, and Minneapolis—and a fraternal delegate from the International Brotherhood Welfare Association. Delegate after delegate urged that street agitation or "soapboxing" in harvest towns be avoided, as it would dissipate energy in free-speech fights and conflict with a hostile public opinion. Such slogans as "Get on the Job!" and "Never Mind the Empty Street Corners: the Means of Life are Not Made There!" became the keynote of the Conference. After voting "that street speaking shall not be used in the harvest towns as a means of propaganda," the delegates established the Agricultural Workers Organization 400. A secretary-treasurer and an agitation committee, later to become the organization committee, were chosen. W. T. Nef was elected secretary-treasurer at a salary of $18 per week. Field delegates were to work without pay, and each local could nominate as many of them as they saw fit, and they were to report regularly to the secretary. The conference closed with the delegates singing the "Harvest Song 1915" to the tune of "I Didn't Raise My Boy to be a Soldier," part of which went:

> *The fields and jungles now are full*
> *of slaves*
> *They are waiting to be put wise,*
> *And One Big Union is the way*
> *That all workers should organize,*
> *Line them all up solid, union makes*
> *us strong;*
> *And better hours and wages is our song.*[6]

1915 ORGANIZING CAMPAIGN

Although the conference adopted resolutions calling for higher wages, shorter hours, and better food for harvest workers, no specific demands were set forth. Shortly afterwards, the agitation committee decided to advance the following set of demands for the 1915 harvest season: A minimum wage of $3 for not more than ten hours a day; 50 cents overtime for every hour worked above ten in one day; good, clean board; good clean places to sleep in, and plenty of clean bedding, and no discrimination against members of the I.W.W. Farmers of Kansas and

Oklahoma were notified: "The above demands are asked of you, and if granted, satisfactory work will be done."[7]

A shudder ran through the grain belt at this announcement. The Kansas City *Post,* which did not even report the organization of the A.W.O. in its own city, now carried a dispatch from Topeka, Kan., announcing that "the wheat growers of Kansas" were openly proclaiming in alarm that "they will be at the mercy of the I.W.W.'s this summer." At first they had dismissed the A.W.O. as "a wild-eyed plan." But it now appeared definite that "the I.W.W.'s intended to carry out their schemes." The farmers, the report continued, looked to the U.S. government to defeat the I.W.W. organizing drive. The government had established the National Farm Labor Exchange in December 1914 to recruit workers in anticipation of a labor shortage during wartime. The office in Kansas City primarily supplied workers for the wheat harvests in Oklahoma, Kansas, Nebraska, Missouri, and adjacent territory. I.W.W. spokesmen maintained, with considerable justification, that the office purposely recruited an oversupply of labor in various grain-growing sections by advertising in large metropolitan dailies in the East. They charged further, again with much justification, that the Employment Office refused to send members of the I.W.W. to any job.[8]

This forced the Wobblies to keep their union affiliation secret. Whenever an employer knew or suspected that certain workers were members of the I.W.W. and fired them for that reason, they were advised to go to any lengths, even to tearing up their union cards in front of the "boss," in order to hold their jobs. They were then to notify the A.W.O. office which would give them duplicate cards. The main thing was to get on the job and stay on the job, so as to be able to organize the harvest hands.[9] By the use of such methods, the A.W.O. became entrenched in the wheat belt, secured wage increases and better working conditions, and expanded its membership rapidly.

"The I.W.W. may not be able to do much this season except in a few localities," a Wobbly organizer wrote shortly after the formation of the A.W.O., "but we will have a good nucleus and better sentiment for next year's work." Actually, the first organizing campaign of the A.W.O. was very successful. It began in June in the wheat fields of Oklahoma and Kansas, and in October, the A.W.O. announced that it had netted shorter hours—"ten hours where formerly the harvesters worked from 12 to 16 hours a day"—and $3.50, to $4.50 a day instead of $2.50. Similar gains in wages were reported from the corn fields of the Dakotas: $3.50 a day and in some quarters $4. Hours, however, were still long, and the ten-hour day was a rarity.[10]

Less success was registered in ending the "stick-up" menace, and the agitation committee conceded that despite the efforts of the A.W.O., "over 10,000 workers have been relieved of their money, and many killed during stick-ups." As a temporary solution, the agitation committee cautioned all members against carrying too much money, and advised those wishing to protect themselves to send their money either to W. T. Nef or William D. Haywood.[11]

From July 1, 1915, to December 31, 1915, the A.W.O. initiated 2,280 members—mostly recruited between June and October—and accumulated $14,113.06 in its treasury. Branches had been established in Des Moines, Kansas City, Sioux City, Omaha, Minneapolis, and Duluth, and plans were under way to start one in Sacramento, Calif.[12]

The April 1915 conference had voted "if there is any surplus of finances at the end of the season in the treasury of the Agricultural Workers Organization, that it be used for organizing work among the migratory workers." But it is doubtful if the delegates believed there would be a surplus. Now at the end of the first organizing drive, A.W.O. 400 could actually boast of prosperity—a rare outcome for an I.W.W. organizing campaign. No wonder *Solidarity* boasted of "the new lease of life that the I.W.W. has taken on," and exulted that the A.W.O. had "demonstrated that the I.W.W. has capabilities of organization when it utilizes for that purpose men familiar with the conditions of a given industry, and determined to apply that knowledge in accordance with a given plan to the places where they work." *Solidarity* urged workers in all industries to take heart from the success of the drive in the harvest fields:*

"Look at what the migratory workers are doing in the harvest this year, under the banner of the I.W.W. The farmers of the middle west section declared before the season opened that they would not pay more than $3 a day for the harvest hands and would work them from dawn to dusk. But the I.W.W. started organizing, and as a result ran the wages up to $3.50 and $4 a day and brought down the hours in many places to ten or less.

"What these and others have done, you can do, if you only make up your minds to try."

All that the workers in auto, lumber, mining, steel and other industries had to do was to apply the methods of the A.W.O. "The A.W.O. conquers all things in its line."[13]

The A.W.O., in short, stimulated the resurgence of the I.W.W. Beginning in 1916, the I.W.W. launched determined campaigns to organize a number of industries. Indeed, a Detective Agency warned employers in the spring of 1916 that unless they launched a counter-offensive "the in-

* The A.W.O. appears to have been the main organizing wing of the I.W.W. in the summer and fall of 1915. Most of the issues of *Solidarity* for these months were filled with reports from the harvest fields, and rarely was there a report of activity in the industrial areas.

fluence of the I.W.W. propaganda will spread until it has covered every industry."[14] On April 1, 1916, the *Industrial Worker* began publication again, and, in keeping with the idea that there was practically a new I.W.W. in existence since the formation of the A.W.O., announced: "This is a new *Industrial Worker* not a revival of the old."

1916 ORGANIZING CAMPAIGN

Meanwhile, the A.W.O. was preparing to begin its 1916 organizing campaign in the harvest fields. Even before the new season opened, the agitation committee learned that in order to cope with the I.W.W., Midwest farmers were planning to import 30,000 Southern Negroes for the harvest fields. The committee broadcast a notice warning "John Farmer" that "the I.W.W. has some good Negro organizers, just itching for a chance of this kind. Thirty thousand Negroes will come and 30,000 I.W.W.'s will go back. The red card is cherished as much and its objects understood as well by a *black* man as by a white one."[15] This was the last heard of a mass importation of Negroes for the harvest!

On May 23, 1916, the first annual conference of the A.W.O. took place in Kansas City. Walter T. Nef was unanimously reelected secretary, and demands were drawn up for the forthcoming season: $4 a day for ten hours' work; 50 cents overtime for every hour worked after 10 hours; good, clean board and places to sleep in, with clean bedding. However, in place of the previous year's demand for no discrimination against members of the I.W.W., the A.W.O. now asked that all men be hired either at the I.W.W. halls or through the delegates on the job. This last demand was advanced with confidence, delegates voicing the opinion that "a closed shop and an open union in the harvest fields is [*sic*] practically assured." The conference closed with the singing of Richard Brazier's "Michael Shea of the A.W.O.," and the shouting of the slogan, "Come on 400!" The delegates then adjourned to the harvest fields.[16]

The organizing campaign in the summer of 1916 has been called "one of the most marvellous union organization jobs ever performed in the history of the world."[17] It was certainly brilliantly executed under the direction of the A.W.O. Organization Committee. Stationary delegates were located at principal points in the grain belt during the harvest season such as Enid, Okla.; Wichita and Ellis, Kan.; Fargo and Minot, N. Dak.; and Aberdeen, S. Dak. The actual organizing was carried on by about 300 delegates in the field who were given credentials by the stationary delegates or by members of the Organization Committee. Meetings were held in the towns, in box-cars, in the jungles; literature was distributed in vast quantities, and the message, oral and written, was always geared to the realities and conditions of the harvest worker's life.[18] A commission of

50 cents was paid to the organizers for every new member they brought into the union. And bring them in they did! Late in July, the *Industrial Worker* published the following dispatch from Kansas: "Cannot write any news just now. We are rushed to beat Hell. Lined up 500 members here in four days. So you can guess what it is like." The I.W.W. journal added: "This is only one of the branches of the A.W.O. and other branches and the numerous delegates in the field are sending in hundreds every day." By November 20, 1916, the A.W.O. received dues from 20,000 paid-up members.[19] This was one-third of the I.W.W.'s total enrollment.

The best picture of how the campaign of 1916 was conducted was furnished by a reporter for the Aberdeen (S. Dak.) *Daily News* in his story of an interview with a group of A.W.O. delegates at the organization's headquarters—three shacks in the railroad yards rented by the I.W.W.:

"'You can tell the readers of the Aberdeen *Daily News* that, in the main, we are aiming to do two things in your city. We want to run out all the hi-jacks, bootleggers and gamblers that would fleece the harvest workers and we want to establish and maintain a proper minimum wage for harvesting. . . .'

"'What do you do with these hi-jacks and bootleggers,' hazarded the reporter.

"'We take care of them in our own style and they never bother us any more. We don't call any bull or fly cop, but we give them our own brand of justice.'*

"'But recruiting members from transient men as you do you can't help but let some of them in.'"†

"'Sure we do. You'll find crooks in any organization. But we put ours out. We investigate an applicant with more strictness than you know. Inside of three days we can know an awful lot about him. Somebody in the crowd will know how he has worked and what he has done. And if we line up a man and he proved to be a hi-jack or stick-up man he only pulls his stuff once. He'll never do it again, until he gets a long ways away. . . .'

---

* In a separate column, the Aberdeen *Daily News* published the text of a leaflet distributed by the A.W.O. which read: "Warning to Hi-Jacks, Bootleggers, Gamblers, etc., in the Harvest Fields. To anyone who has any schemes of personal advancement to exploit where the wage-earners are calculated to be the victims, we wish to say, 'You Had Better Get Out of the Way. Your Game Won't Go.'" (Reprinted in *Industrial Worker*, Aug. 5, 1916.)

† Even members of the I.W.W. voiced such concern. A correspondent in *Solidarity* described the shooting and robbing of a member of the A.W.O. by a bandit who had "joined the organization merely as a shield and with the view of using the union as a means of self-protection." Nor was this an isolated case, he noted, for others had informed him of "tinhorns, hijacks and other undesirables" who had joined the I.W.W. as a cover for their criminal activities. (*Solidarity*, Dec. 22, 1916.)

" 'Are you going to establish a minimum wage in Brown County here?' inquired the reporter.

" 'We sure are.'

" 'What'll it be?'

" 'It'll be $4.50 a day and a ten-hour day. It was $4 here last year. . . .'

" 'Is this scale stationary now?'

" 'Hardly,' said another man. 'The wage varies in different localities. It doesn't depend on crops or number of demands either. The I.W.W. is never satisfied and never will be until it gets absolute control of the industrial world and turns the profits where they belong—the pockets of the men who labor. The wages will continue to go up! . . .'

" 'Do you let fellows ride who don't belong? They say you don't.'

" 'We put hi-jacks, bootleggers and gamblers off the trains and keep them off. . . !'

" 'Would you put off a union man who didn't belong to the I.W.W.?'

" 'No. But we wouldn't let him work in the harvest fields. Because the harvest fields are ours. They belong to the tradeless transients. A union plumber wouldn't think he could go into a union barber shop and work on his card. Why should a union barber or plumber think he should come into our harvest fields and work on his card? He can do it, only if he will line up. The I.W.W. will accept men, union or nonunion, Catholic or Protestant, deaf or dumb, just so they are wage-earners. They can all join, but they can't work in our fields unless they do join. . . .'

" 'I notice one thing this year . . . none of the I.W.W.'s seem to be going hungry.'

" 'You bet we don't. We have got $20,000 for organizing, and we have got plenty of money to see that no one starves. If they won't pay us our prices we won't go hungry, and that's where we have them. . . . No one around here looks hungry, nor do you see cannon sticking out of their pockets or black jacks. . . .'

" 'How many members have you got in Aberdeen now?'

" 'We did have six or seven hundred, but in the last two days hundreds have gone out to work. We have sent out a lot in this country and many into other districts. This is a distributing center here and more are coming in all the time.' "[20]

A.W.O. ORGANIZING METHODS

When the reporter for the Aberdeen *Daily News* asked, "Do you let fellows ride who don't belong? They say you don't"—he was being exceedingly polite. Most newspapers in the grain belt charged that a reign of terror had been unleashed by the A.W.O. to force the initiation of thousands of harvest workers. A.W.O. organizers and their aids were described as armed with clubs, pickhandles and guns, which they used to take over control of the freight cars entering the harvest fields and to compel everyone on board to sign up with the I.W.W. Men who refused to join were said to be kicked off the trains; indeed, no one was allowed to ride unless he showed a card issued by the A.W.O. 400 or another I.W.W. unit. "A lawless condition has been created on the freight trains entering North and South Dakota by these men who claim no country and no flag," raged a Midwest paper.[21]

The response of the A.W.O. delegates that "hi-jacks, bootleggers and gamblers" were the only ones put off the trains convinced none of the newspapers. And with good reason. There was considerable evidence that many A.W.O. delegates resorted to intimidating workers who could not be convinced to join by appeals. Complaints of terrorism, ranging from outright murder to crippling non-cooperative workers by leaving acid in their shoes, were recorded in the press.[22] How many of these complaints were true is difficult to determine. Certainly it was true that the harvest worker who wanted to ride the freight trains was well advised to carry an I.W.W. card.[23] One Wobbly even warned another member in the fall of 1916:

"Say Phil if you go to the Orange County don't go without your card because it is Damned unhealthy down there just now without a card as they are sapping hell out of those that have not got a card, they won't let them ride on the trains and they won't let them light in the jungles, and the winches [non-unionists] are catching particular Hell."[24]

Many of the older members of the I.W.W. were critical of some of the organizational methods of the A.W.O. They argued that joining the I.W.W. should always be a voluntary act based upon sympathy for, and understanding of, the principles of the One Big Union. Leaders of the agricultural drive conceded that to "oldtime I.W.W. men" the "methods of the '400'" seemed "too severe."[25] They conceded, too, that coercion was used to sign up members. But they insisted that stories of terrorist tactics were exaggerated, and that the majority of the new recruits among the harvest workers were organized by convincing arguments proving to them that only through the A.W.O. could they obtain higher wages, shorter hours and decent working conditions. Where argument failed, they noted, the A.W.O. organizers had no alternative but to apply pressure. Yet all they did was to prevent those who would not cooperate with the union from reaching the harvest fields just as union members in industrial centers kept scabs away from the struck plants. In organizing the harvest workers, every freight car, every freight yard, every jungle was a picket line. Since the non-cooperative harvesters rode the freight cars, they had to be kept off unless they joined up. This was legitimate trade-union procedure, and that it was acknowledged to be such was proven by the fact that the union railroaders cooperated by asking all free riders for their red membership cards.* Basically what the A.W.O. had done was to establish "a picket line over a thousand miles from the harvest fields of Northern Oklahoma to the Northern wheat fields of Canada." This "simply represented an effort to keep non-union men off the job."[26]†

The question of the A.W.O's organizational tactics was long a disputed issue in the I.W.W.[27] But there was no dispute over the fact that the agricultural drive of 1916 was exceedingly successful in spite of considerable opposition from the farm communities. This usually took the form of arresting A.W.O. members, or forcing them to leave the community, although brutal beatings and killings of Wobblies were also part of the pattern of opposition. However, these actions rarely halted the organizing drive. A.W.O. members, abandoning the "passive resistance" tactics of previous struggles with police and vigilantes, fought back, giving them blow for blow.‡ "Pitched Battles in South Dakota Towns with I.W.W. Armies," read the headline in the Sioux City (S. Dak.) *Daily Argus-Leader* of July 28, 1916. In Mitchell, S. Dak., the Wobblies fought back so vigorously against "two hundred citizens carrying big guns and boys with 22 rifles and revolvers [who] comprised the posse of vigilantes," that Sheriff E. E. Owens appealed to the Secretary of War in Washington, pointing out that the "vigilance committee . . . is now much exhausted," and requesting the services of Company F of Mitchell, members of the South Dakota National Guard, to help fight the I.W.W. In the end, the request was withdrawn and a truce worked out under which the authorities agreed to prevent the vigilantes from interfering with the I.W.W.

---

* The A.W.O. repaid this assistance by warning the railway companies, when the roads were threatened by a strike in the summer of 1916, that its members would go all out to assist the strikers. Officials of the Great Northern Railway Co. asked the Governor of North Dakota for protection, stating: "Because of the large number of I.W.W. members employed in the harvest fields of the state it is feared they may make sympathetic demonstrations should the railroad operate trains after the strike is called." (Duluth *News Tribune*, Aug. 31, 1916.)

† In his discussion of the 1916 organizing campaign, Philip Taft leaves the distinct impression that the only workers recruited by the A.W.O. were those forced into the organization by "the use of force" and "strong arm tactics." ("The I.W.W. in the Grain Belt," *Labor History*, vol. I, Winter, 1960, p. 59.) He cites no evidence to substantiate this claim. He repeats the charge, again without citing any evidence, in his *Organized Labor in American History*, New York, 1964, p. 296.

‡ No free-speech fights took place in communities which arrested A.W.O. members. Usually the problem was handled in the manner revealed by the following item in the Sioux City *Daily Argus-Leader* of July 29, 1916: "Letcher, July 29—Three hundred harvest hands, mostly I.W.W.'s, stormed the city jail here yesterday and forced the release of two of their number who had been arrested for disorderly conduct." The I.W.W. also called for a boycott of merchants in such towns so as to "hit them in the pocketbooks" (*Industrial Worker*, Aug. 26, 1916.)

organizing drive, and the Wobblies agreed to keep their followers from congregating in the vicinity of the town.[28]

So frightened of the I.W.W. were South Dakota communities by reports from Mitchell and other towns that the Princess Theatre in Sioux Falls felt it necessary to insert the following notice in the press, under the headline: "CHARLES CHAPLIN IS NOT AN I.W.W.":

"Charles Chaplin . . . arrived today with his cane, mustache and hat at the Princess Theatre where he will stop until midnight tomorrow.

"The half million dollar star is seen as 'The Vagabond,' but one of those happy, philosophical vags, not at all like those grouchy I.W.W. boys who have been shooting up Mitchell and other nice towns around here."[29]

The Duluth *News Tribune* had a simple explanation for the failure of the anti-A.W.O. offensive in the grain belt. "Big industry, if necessary, can provide its own protection. The farmers and isolated storekeepers cannot do this."[30] It was unfortunate, in other words, that the farmer and storekeeper, unlike "big industry," could not afford to hire gunmen to shoot down union workers and organizers!

Years later, a leader of the A.W.O. summed up the results of the 1916 drive: "The Four Hundred had scared most of the hi-jackers of the area. They had taught the local town clowns to respect the migratory workers, and to refrain from getting gay at his expense. They had cut the dawn-to-dusk working day into something resembling a civilized working period. They had taught the farmer wives how to cook and how to serve decent grub. They had more than doubled the 'going wages' so that a harvest hand remaining in the field for the 'run' (from Texas to Montana) had some hope of leaving the harvest with a few nickels in the poke. They had educated the threshers into the supplying of blankets with a few less than a million lice in each one. They had inculcated trust and friendship among the workers so that a man could rely upon and trust his fellow man.

"These conditions prevailed generally throughout the entire field. They had been gained and retained without any written agreement with any farmer or with any group of farmers."[31]

Newspapers in the grain belt conceded that wages were higher, hours shorter and conditions better for the harvest workers during the season of 1916 than ever before. But they attributed all this to the fact that the war in Europe had put a premium on agricultural products and a great demand for labor. Yet, at the same time, they blamed the agitation of the I.W.W. for the fact that the harvest workers dared to demand higher wages, shorter hours, and better working conditions. The Sioux Falls *Daily Argus-Leader* conceded in August 1916 that "the help question has been a very serious problem in many sections of the state because members of the Industrial Workers of the World have demanded from $4.50 to $5 per day and board and lodging for their services, and the farmers have been compelled to grant these demands to get their grain harvested."[32]

On June 10, 1916, the *Industrial Worker* predicted "15,000 new members in the A.W.O. this summer." In October, the A.W.O. reported that it had initiated 18,000 members since April 1915, indicating that close to 16,000 members had been recruited during the 1916 campaign in the harvest fields. Included in this membership, according to one former official, were such seasonal workers as miners, harvest hands, lumber jacks, railroad maintenance workers or "gandy-dancers," construction workers, and even some cottonpickers in Southern Louisiana.[33] There was likewise a sharp increase in the organization's income. This is reflected in the income received at the general headquarters of the I.W.W. For the year ending August 31, 1915, the income of the I.W.W. was $8,934.47; for the next fiscal year it reached $49,114.84. Small wonder that it was announced at the mass conference held by the A.W.O. in October 1916: "The A.W.O. delivers the goods!" The meeting decided to establish a permanent industrial union instead of the original idea of a temporary means for "organizing on the job" and improving farm-labor conditions for one harvest season.[34]

By the end of 1916, the Agricultural Workers Organization 400 had come to play a most important part in the I.W.W. Its momentum was such that it stimulated organization in other industries. On July 29, 1916, the *Industrial Worker* reported that it had just received a list of new unions organized since May 1: "It is almost as long as the list of all locals in the I.W.W. used to be a few years back." It was the funds provided by the A.W.O.,* in the main, that enabled the I.W.W. to establish its new headquarters in the four-story building in Chicago from which General Secretary Haywood issued his famous call for all Wobblies to emulate the A.W.O. organizers and get "out of the jungles and on to the job."[35]

The tenth annual convention of the I.W.W. held in Chicago, November 20 to December 1, 1916, heard a glowing report on the job delegate system on which the A.W.O. was based. "To the Delegate System," declared General Secretary Haywood in his report, "is largely due the thousands of new members, especially those initiated by A.W.O. No. 400 during the last year." The convention endorsed the job delegate system of organization with little discussion: "This method has proved to be the most effective system of organizing ever adopted."[36]

The influence of the A.W.O. in other industries was more than a moral one. Its organizers were sent into other fields, and it supported financially,

---

* The A.W.O. contributed 15 cents of a member's monthly dues of 50 cents to the general treasury. It gave 25 cents "of each initiation fee to *Solidarity* as a subscription card for the new members." (*Solidarity*, April 24, 1915, Dec. 2, 1916.)

as well as organizationally, campaigns in these industries.* This was especially felt, as we shall now see, among the metal miners and the lumber workers.

* Many of the non-agricultural members of the I.W.W. during this period first entered the organization through the A.W.O. In March 1917, I.W.W. general headquarters stripped the A.W.O. of its non-agricultural members and changed the name of the organization to the Agricultural Workers Industrial Union No. 110.

CHAPTER 22

The Mesabi Range Strike

THE WORKERS AND THE INDUSTRY

Located in Northeastern Minnesota and lying some 60 miles inland and Northwest of Duluth is the Mesabi Range, the greatest iron-ore mining center in the world. Iron ore was discovered on the Mesabi Range in 1890, and soon thereafter mining began in vast open-pit and underground operations. Soon, too, settlements sprang up in the wilderness surrounding the open-pits and mine shafts, and in time became villages and towns bearing the names of Mt. Iron, McKinley, Biwabik, Virginia, Eveleth, Hibbing, Nashwauk, Keewaitin, and Bovey. Into these early rough, frontier settlements and later into some twenty villages and towns, extending over a distance of 80 miles, poured an immigrant population of more than 30 nationalities. In the first wave of immigration to the Range came native Americans, English from Cornwall, English, Scotch, Irish and French from Canada, Scandinavians and Finns, as well as some Slovenians, Italians, Bohemians, Poles, and Lithuanians. After 1900, the Slovenians, Croatians, Serbians, Montenegrins, Italians, Bulgarians, Greeks, Poles, and Russians came in great numbers. By 1910, there were at least 35 different nationality groups on the Range of sufficient size to be easily identifiable, while scattered numbers were present from at least ten other nationalities.[1]

Each nationality group fitted into the mining activity on the Range according to the requirements for labor at the time of arrival. Since early mining activity on the Mesabi was predominantly in underground mines, the earliest arrivals usually secured mine jobs. After 1905, when pit and stripping activities increased, the new arrivals usually found employment in surface operations. Thus, the Carpatho-Russians, Montenegrins, Serbs, Bulgarians, Roumanians, Italians, Galician Poles, Lithuanians and Greeks, who arrived in these years, went into pit and stripping work, while the Finns, Slovenians, Croatians, and Italians, with smaller numbers of Poles, Slovaks, Bohemians, Lithuanians, and Bulgarians, worked underground. In any event, as one student points out: "Whatever work required hard, physical labor and back-breaking effort was performed by the foreign-born. The machine and skilled jobs continued to be handled by the English-speaking groups and Scandinavians with a gradual infiltration into their ranks of the native-born sons of the immigrants."[2] The English-speaking groups, particularly the Cornish (known on the Mesabi as the "Cousin Jacks") became the predominant group of mine captains and shift bosses. Others with previous experience on the Michigan or Vermilion ranges, such as the Irish and Scandinavians, were made bosses in smaller numbers. Later, some shift bosses were chosen from among the main nationality groups, such as the Finns, Slovenians, and Italians, but the bulk of the mine captains and the shift remained the English-speaking element.[3]

After 1900, the vast majority of the workers were employed by large and powerful companies. During the preceding decade, a vast consolidation had occurred among the ore properties on the Mesabi. John D. Rockefeller took over the Lake Superior Consolidated Iron Mines Co. (an empire in itself, controlling the largest deposit of ore in the Mesabi Range) when the Merritt brothers, with whom Rockefeller was associated, could not pay off loans he had extended them. The Carnegie-Oliver Co. took over the ore properties of small, independent operators who were forced to sell by the hard times of the depression of 1893. In 1898, the Federal Steel Co., organized as a holding company, absorbed the Minnesota Iron Co., which had already acquired huge ore properties in the Mesabi, the Duluth & Iron Range Railroad, and a fleet of lake vessels and barges. Then in 1901, with the organization of the U.S. Steel Corp., there occurred the greatest combination of all. The Oliver Iron Mining Co. was established as a subsidiary of U.S. Steel, and into it were absorbed three previous combinations—the Lake Superior Consolidated Iron Mines Co., the Carnegie-Oliver Co., and the Federal Steel Co. With this consolidation, "41 mines, nearly 1,000 miles of railroad, and a lake fleet of 112 vessels," more than half of the entire Mesabi ore properties, came into the control of U.S. Steel through the Oliver company. In 1902, Oliver mined 60 per cent of the total range production. This trend continued as Oliver acquired additional parcels of property. In 1908, Oliver (or U.S. Steel) controlled 912,768,830 tons out of a total reserve tonnage of 1,192,509,757 tons. The other concerns that owned mines and ore reserves were, like Oliver, subsidiaries of steel and furnace companies: Republic Iron & Steel Co., Pickands Mather Co., Jones & Laughlin, Union Steel Co., Corrigan & McKinney, and Todd, Stambraugh & Co.[4]

It was against these giant corporations, and particularly the greatest giant of all, U.S. Steel, that the I.W.W. in 1916, at the request of the exploited mine workers of the Mesabi Range, conducted one of the most militant struggles in American labor history.

The grievances of the workers were of long standing. Dominated by finance capitalists who lived in the East, the companies were concerned only with obtaining the highest profit at the lowest cost, regardless of what this meant to the workers whom they had enticed to the Range from European villages with promotional literature promising them plenty of work at high wages and an easy life in general.[5] Hours of work were gradually reduced from 12-hour shifts for a six-day week during the first years of operation after 1900 to eight hours in 1912. However, these were not portal-to-portal hours, but were reckoned only from the moment the picks were in the miners' hands, so that the day's work was considerably longer. Then again, with each reduction in the hours worked per day, the work was speeded up. "Now two of us must do the work that four of us did formerly," was the complaint soon after the ten-hour day was introduced. Likewise, after the eight-hour day was instituted, a miner wrote: "We are driven much more than we were before." Another complained: "The work which before was done in ten hours must now be finished in eight."[6]

The average daily wages of miners and laborers in 1909 were $2.40 and $2.12, and they remained at this level up to 1916. But for many miners, employment was seasonal so that annual earnings were far below what the figures might imply. The cold winters which prevailed on the Range and the freezing of the Lake ports virtually closed the open-pit mines for from three to five months during the year. To keep their families from starving, the open-pit miners were compelled to leave them for a winter spent in the lumber camps or at odd jobs in other parts of Minnesota or Michigan. But the immigrant press is full of letters telling of miners who could find no work during the winter months.[7]

Underground miners were able to work the entire year. But these miners had a special grievance—the contract system used for determining wages. The miners were paid according to the amount of ore they shoveled. This was basically a "speed-up" device to compel the miners to work at full speed. But, in addition, since prices for contracts were oral and never written, the mine captains simply lowered them when they thought a miner was earning too much. The files of the Federal Commissioners of Conciliation in the 1916 strike are full of affidavits by miners, sworn to before a notary public, stating that they never knew what their contract rate was; that they were neither consulted nor informed regarding the rate until the end of the month when they received their pay; that when a miner's tonnage for the week ran up to a figure that yielded high wages, the rate was cut. The Commissioners found that earnings for many contract miners "were often considerably less than Two ($2.00) Dollars per day."[8]

On top of this, the miner had to pay for powder, fuses, tools and spikes, and these were never itemized but merely deducted from his month's pay. Consequently the miners never knew in advance what their take-home pay would be. Since the miner was paid monthly only, if he was discharged or left before pay-day, he had to wait until the end of the month for his pay.[9]

Inasmuch as the cost of housing, food, clothing and fuel was higher in Northern Minnesota than anywhere else in the state, the real wages of the miners were a good deal less than their actual earnings. In fact, in order to make ends meet, many of the miners' wives, particularly among the Slovenians, Croatians, and Finns, took in boarders. The typical home of a Mesabi immigrant was a ". . . one room shack with bed along the wall constantly in use by day and night shifts of men. The typical family is the man, his wife, a few children, and the boarders."[10] Several of the leading towns on the Range—notably Hibbing, Virginia, and Chisholm—were modern communities with well-paved streets, lined with trees and illuminated with electric lights, and with excellent school houses and well-stocked libraries, all built with taxes wrung from the mining companies. But too many of the miners lived in miserable one-room tar-paper shacks.[11]

In broken English, a Chisholm miner described his living conditions: "I am a miner for fourteen years—over fourteen years, and I have eight children—I have seven living and one dead. I work now for last three years. I get $59 check, $61, $63, $67, up to $70—but a couple of times over $70 in three years,* and I send four kids to school, and the teacher would like to have the children dressed and clean and everything like that. I would like to do that myself. And the children go to church, the priest like to see the wife is dressed nice like the American ladies, and the children dressed nice like the American children. I like that too, but I can't. You fellows think—single man maybe gets $50 or $60 check for his own self, and we are nine of them. I get $60, $70, and I have extra—we pay coal, pay insurance, pay taxes, pay light, pay water—now, I think fellows, how I can live. . . . So here—a man have seven children. He needs every second week to get children stockings and shoes. You know that yourself, everyone. Where I am going to get money? I can't get it working, or nothing."[12]

The "insurance" referred to was in case of an accident. Mining iron ore was an extremely hazardous occupation. Accidents due to premature dynamite explosions, lack of proper timbering in drifts and raises, slides of soft ore and earth, and runaway ore trains, were weekly occurrences. To the operators safety regulations meant expenditures so that it is not surprising that they should have concluded early that it was more profitable to keep immigrants flowing into the Range than to inaugurate

* These, of course, were monthly checks.

safety devices to reduce accidents. "They figure what's the difference," a Finnish miner declared in describing the attitude of the operators when a miner was killed in an accident. "There's more Finlanders and Bohunks from where this one came."[13]

For a long time, the companies operated on the theory that they had fulfilled their responsibilities by providing hasty instructions in English to workers who could not understand the language. Eventually they instituted more elaborate safety campaigns, with safety signs posted in many languages. But the value of these precautions was largely nullified by the ever-increasing speed-up. As one miner complained: "How can a person look after his safety when everything is so arranged that he must drive himself if he wants to earn anything? If he only looked after his own safety . . . he would not earn anything."[14] Compensation for injuries was so small that an accident, with its period of hospitalization, brought real tragedy to the miner's family, living from month to month on the earnings of the father.[15]

The despotic tyranny of the bosses, mine captains and foremen was a complaint most frequently voiced by the miners. It started when the new immigrant applied for a job at the mines. It was not enough for the applicant to have a robust appearance; he frequently had to pay a bribe to the foreman to be hired as a laborer or trammer. To hold on to his job, and especially if he wanted a good spot from which he might be able to remove a large quantity of ore, the miner would have to keep paying bribes to the "boss" in regular gifts of money, compulsory Christmas gifts, sharing his moose or deer felled in the hunt, treating to drinks, and, in some cases, submitting to propositions made to his wife and daughters. An Eveleth miner even complained that he was not given a job because he refused to buy a home which the shift boss had for sale.[16]

But it was the callous, driving attitude of the bosses that the miners most resented. They pushed the men to the limit day in and day out. "Always they are driving us in all manners of way," protested an Eveleth miner. "We must work like former slaves in the South . . . until the sweat rolls off every hair on our head." A miner recalled years later that "mules used for tramming in the mines were treated better than the men."[17]

Is it any wonder that it was a common saying on the Range that five years in the mines was enough to ruin any man in body and spirit, however strong he was physically?[18] Little wonder, too, that an immigrant miner wrote bitterly in *Proletarec,* a Slovene paper, in February 1911: "We escaped the old-country tricksters in the hope of creating a better existence for ourselves on this continent. But we are convinced that this is not the land of liberty described by old-country newspapers and the American constitution but the land of humbug and big capital.

Thousands of Slovene workers are enslaved in the Minnesota mines and are exploited on all sides and to the limit." For many of these immigrants the bright hope that they would be able to save some money and return to their European villages quickly vanished. "I came over to the United States to work and earn money," a miner said. "I intended to go back to Galicia, yes. If you had told me I would still be in this country after thirty years when I left, I would have said you were crazy."[19]

EARLY ORGANIZATION AND STRIKES

Unable (or unwilling), in most cases, to return to their native lands and finding it impossible to advance on the job ladder in the mines, the majority of the workers had only one way in which to improve their working conditions—by concerted effort and action through unions. "Only through organization can the worker live like a man in freedom," a Slovenian miner wrote.[20] But this was difficult to achieve on the Range. The size and power of the companies, the control they exercised over the political and economic life of the Range village and towns, the support they received from the local newspapers, business and professional interests, and the many diverse nationality groups, each speaking its own language, discouraged the workers, and, for years, convinced many of them that unionism could not thrive in such surroundings.

The mining companies quickly stamped out the unions and strikes that were attempted in the 1890's and early 1900's. But the need for unionism remained, and it was kept alive by the growth of Socialist ideology among the foreign miners, especially the Finns. By 1903, Finnish societies and workers' clubs on the Range were becoming more and more Socialist-oriented, partly because the conditions in the mines forced the workers to conclude that socialism was fully justified, and partly because of the influence of Finnish intellectual radicals who preached the doctrines of socialism to the Finns, gathered in their temperance halls and workers' clubs. Soon the Socialist Finns established their own halls in opposition to those of the temperance group. These Socialist halls served as headquarters for whatever union organizing campaigns were started on the Range and for the strikes that followed.[21]

In the spring of 1907, as a result of an organizing drive by the Western Federation of Miners on the Range, led by Teofila Petriella, an Italian Socialist, who was assisted by Vincent St. John, approximately 2,500 miners were enrolled in the ranks of the union. On July 20, 1907, a strike began on the Mesabi Range.[22]

President Thomas F. Cole of Oliver received instructions from the New York offices of U.S. Steel "to make a stand," and use any methods necessary to break the strike.[23] This he proceeded to do. Special deputies were sworn in and additional special deputies brought in from Duluth,

Chicago, and New York. Professional strike breakers and gunmen were also imported to the Range. Pressure was applied to the local businessmen not to extend credit to the striking miners for their daily needs.[24]

Using the Finnish Socialist halls as headquarters, groups of striking miners marched each day from mine to mine notifying everyone in the mining towns that the strike was on. They were not intimidated by screaming headlines in the press: "Blood Red Flag Flaunted by the Federation Strikers. Finns March Through Streets of Sparta, Led by Amazon Bearing the Emblem of Anarchy." But the strikers found it difficult to hold out against the barrage of company power. "Mother" Mary Jones visited the Range on August 10, and shored up the strikers' confidence as she hurled defiance at the deputies and gunmen, challenging them to "Shoot and Be Damned."[25] But in mid-August carloads of strike-breakers—Serbians, Montenegrins, Croatians, and some Italians and Greeks—arrived to work in the mines, most of them new arrivals in this country who had no knowledge that a strike was under way. This, together with the use of strong-arm deputies and gunmen, broke the back of the strike. By the middle of September the strike was over. "Army of Deputies Overawe the Western Federation of Miners," was the Duluth *News-Tribune's* jubilant explanation for the failure of the strike.[26]

The mining companies were not satisfied with their victory. They blacklisted many of the strikers, especially the Finns who had been the most active unionists and strikers. Before the 1907 strike, 18 per cent of the miners employed by the Oliver Iron Mining Co. had been Finns. After 1907 only 8 per cent of the miners in its employ were Finns.[27]

The economic depression of 1907, following on the heels of the strike, added to the misery of the defeated workers. Thousands of miners were laid off, including the Montenegrin and Croatian strikebreakers imported to the Range during the strike, and starvation stalked through the mining towns, none of which furnished relief for the unemployed.[28]

The failure of the strike and the hard times put an end to the miners' organizations. By the end of 1908, The W.F. of M. had disappeared from the Range, and new organization was held back both by the feeling that it was futile to battle the powerful "Steel Trust" and by an espionage system used by the mining companies, particularly the Oliver, which used informers or "stool pigeons" among the various nationalities to check and report upon potential "trouble makers." The latter, when uncovered, were promptly fired and blacklisted from future employment.*

With the help of informers, intimidation, and the solid support of

---

* A vivid and detailed account of the espionage system at the Oliver is given in Frank L. Palmer, *Spies in Steel, An Expose of Industrial War* (Denver, Colo., 1928). Palmer, who had worked for the Oliver, published photostatic copies kept by the company and reports of "stool pigeons," naming persons, places and dates.

the businessmen of the mining communities, the companies had the workers completely under control. Nevertheless, a small core of miners, especially among the Socialist Finns, kept the idea of unionism alive. These workers continued to hold meetings and discussions in and around the workers' halls.

In order to achieve this goal, the union-conscious elements among the miners appealed several times to the A.F. of L. Minnesota State Federation of Labor to launch an organizing drive on the Range. They were repeatedly rebuffed.* The same result was produced by appeals to the Western Federation of Miners. The W.F. of M., its strength drained by a series of defeats on various fronts, including the severe and long-drawn out strike of 1913-14 on the Michigan ranges,† showed no interest in invading the Mesabi Range again.[29]

1916 STRIKE BEGINS

Under the headline, "Steel Slaves Awakening," the *Industrial Worker* of May 13, 1916, published an appeal from a Virginia (Minn.) Wobbly urging the I.W.W. to send organizers to the Range. "The spirit of revolt is growing among the workers on the Iron Range," he reported, and predicted that if the miners were "not soon organized, unorganized strikes will break out" which would be "easily defeated either by the power or the promises of the Steel Trust." The need was for "workers who have an understanding of the tactics and methods of the I.W.W. and who would go on the job, and agitate and organize on the job." The I.W.W., of course, was not unknown on the Range, especially among the Finns. After the strike of 1907, the issue of craft or industrial unionism, or more specifically the A.F. of L. or the I.W.W., was constantly debated by the Range Finns. In 1914, as we have seen, the supporters of the I.W.W. were either expelled or withdrew from the Finnish Socialist Federation and established their own headquarters in Duluth. Most of the Range Finns supported the new organization and backed the I.W.W. as the only labor organization capable of leading the workers in the struggle both for immediate demands and for socialism.[30]

But before the I.W.W. had a chance to consider the appeal from Virginia, the strike had already begun on the Mesabi Range. As M. E. Shusterich, one of the strike leaders, explained in an effort to put the

---

* In 1917 E. G. Hall, President of the Minnesota State Federation of Labor, denied that the organization had ever been asked to organize the Range prior to the 1916 strike. However, evidence produced during and after the strike indicates that Hall was trying to cover up for the Federation. Hall did make the following revelation in the same statement: "At one time I took the matter up with President Gompers, to ascertain if we might organize the Mesabi miners into Federal labor unions, but found it could not be done." (Eveleth *News,* Feb. 22, 1917.)

† The Michigan Copper Strike of 1913-14 will be discussed in the next volume.

record straight in the face of repeated charges by the companies and the press that the strike was instigated by "outside agitators" sent in by the I.W.W.: "This strike was not started by the I.W.W., but has been under way the past six years. We have appealed to every labor official in Minnesota to have the miners on the range organized, but we have been shuttled back and forth between the Western Federation of Miners and other organizations who passed us on again until finally the miners took things into their own hands and went out without organization."[31]

On June 2, 1916, an Italian miner, Joe Greeni, employed underground at the St. James mine near Aurora, opened his pay envelope and saw that his check was for a sum much less than he had understood his contract called for. "To hell with such wages," he cried; he threw down his pick, and decided to quit. To his surprise, the entire shift in the underground mine went along with him. Greeni and his coworkers went from stope to stope in Aurora, crying: "We've been robbed long enough. It's time to strike." By June 4 every mine in Aurora was shut down, and every miner was a striker. The strikers appointed a committee and sent an appeal to the mine owners to meet for the purpose of adjusting the miners' grievances. The request went unanswered.[32]

Thus began the great strike of 1916. The word "strike" began to reverberate out of Aurora as a group of Finnish and other Socialists spread the news throughout the Range. Parades were organized, and the striking Aurora miners marched over 75 miles of mountain road from town to town, passing the word "strike" from place to place. The processions, sometimes augmented by children and wives wheeling baby carriages, picked up recruits for the strike. Within a week, many of the mines throughout the Range were closed.[33]

Many of the strikers of 1916 had been the strikebreakers of 1907. Eleven years of exploitation by the mining companies had convinced the former strikebreakers that they had had more than enough. The Finns, who were the leaders and made up most of the strikers in 1907, were also actively involved. But, unlike its forerunner in 1907, the 1916 strike was not dominated by the Finns. This time, Italian, Russian, Croat, Bulgarian, and Roumanian miners were particularly active, and carried a large share of the strike activity. As in 1907, however, the Finnish Socialist halls in the Range towns became the headquarters for the strikers.[34]

Still unorganized and without experienced leadership, the strikers looked for assistance outside of the Range. Having already been rebuffed by the Minnesota State Federation of Labor and having little confidence in the Western Federation of Miners because of its failure during the Michigan copper strike and its growing conservatism, the strikers turned naturally to the I.W.W. Letters were sent to the headquarters in Chicago asking that I.W.W. organizers come to the Range and help the miners to organize and conduct the strike. The Wobblies responded to the call, and sent some of their most able organizers to assist the strikers.[35]

The first I.W.W. organizers to arrive were James Gilday, chairman of the organization committee of the A.W.O., Sam Scarlett, I.W.W. speaker and organizer, Arthur Boose, organizer, Joe Schmidt, Polish organizer, and Carlo Tresca, Italian organizer. (Scarlett was first in command of the strike and Tresca and Schmidt were second and third in command.) On June 24, Haywood informed Tresca that "Frank Little is leaving here [Chicago] tonight for the range. . . . There is a big territory there to cover. If you need more organizers after Little arrives, let me know, and I will send the best material we have got." Haywood enclosed a check of $36 to cover two weeks' organizing expenses.[36]

Although they pointed out that "the I.W.W. is acting only in an advisory capacity," the Wobbly organizers took over the direction of the strike. However, a number of local leaders played an important role in the early stages of the strike, especially George Andreytchine, a Bulgarian civil engineer working for the Oliver in Hibbing, who joined the I.W.W. and was an active participant until his arrest on a deportation warrant. William Wiertola, a Finnish Socialist miner, also emerged as a leader of his people during the strike.[37]

The I.W.W. leaders held meetings in the Finnish halls with speakers in several languages—Finnish, German, Croatian, English, Italian, etc.— and here the votes were taken by the miners to spread the strike to mines which were not yet closed down. Here, too, committees were elected by the strikers to carry through the struggle. (Usually, two representatives of each nationality were elected to each committee.) At Haywood's suggestion, a strike committee was established in each town and a general strike committee for the entire district. The Central Strike Committee consisted of 15 miners from the different towns of the Range, and was made up of Italian, Finnish, and Slavic nationalities. Tony Shragel, chairman, was from Virginia as was F. Pertinellie, secretary, while M. E. Shusterich, the treasurer, was from Chisholm.[38]

The finance committee was chosen with great care and publicity; first, because in the 1907 strike, money collected for initiation fees and dues had disappeared, and second, because the local press charged that for the I.W.W. the strike was "only a money-making proposition," and that "the I.W.W. strike agitators are here for the sole purpose of enriching themselves and when they secured sufficient funds will decamp and leave the miners to shift for themselves." In each town, therefore, a strikers' finance committee was elected to act as custodian of funds—initiation fees, dues, and contributions—taken in during the strike. The money was placed in the bank in the name of the I.W.W. local. By the third week of June, there were already five locals of the Metal Mine Workers'

Industrial Union 490 on the Range with an I.W.W. membership of 5,000 of the more than 10,000 strikers.[39]

At the beginning of the strike, the miners had not yet drawn up a list of demands, but when the I.W.W. organizers entered, they called upon the strikers to draw up a specific list of demands and to include only their major grievances. ("The demands of the men," Haywood wrote to Tresca, "should be reduced to the lowest proportions so that each striking miner can understand what he is fighting for.") For days on end, hundreds of strikers gathered in the Finnish halls and separated into seven or eight nationalities according to language, each with a fellow countryman as leader, discussing the demands of the miners. By June 24 the following list had been adopted by the strikers:

(1) An eight-hour working day throughout the Range to be timed from when the miners entered the mine until they were outside the mine.

(2) A scale of $2.75 per day for open-pit miners and $3 to $3.50 for underground miners, with the higher pay going to those who worked on wet ground.

(3) Pay day twice a month.

(4) Immediate payment when a miner quit.

(5) Abolition of the Saturday night shift.

(6) Abolition of the contract system.[40]

The demand for a wage increase was a modest one in view of the fact that the cost of living had increased by one-third in the first six months of 1916 as compared with 1915.[41] The demand for pay day twice a month would, of course, allow the miners to discontinue credit purchasing of their necessities which forced them to pay higher prices. But the crucial demand was for the elimination of the contract system of underground mining. The strikers insisted that this system made possible the tyranny and bribery by the mining officials, and that whatever wage increases had been granted in the past were not reflected in the miners' pay checks because of the manipulation of the contract system. John A. Keyes, the brilliant and courageous lawyer for the strikers, publicly exhibited checks received by men employed on the contract system. One check for eight cents represented an entire day's work for one man while others for 55 cents and 12 cents represented the pay received by several miners for a day's digging in the mines. No wonder the Central Strike Committee declared: "Our conditions are intolerable and inexcusable in these days of so-called prosperity when our employers have reaped fortunes on European war orders."[42]

The miners, it should be noted, did not ask for union recognition or a contract from the mining companies. As John A. Keyes pointed out: "They [the I.W.W. leaders] do not even ask that the union be recognized.

Simply that the men be given a reasonable wage and that certain forms of work be abolished."[43]

On June 28, committees representing the striking miners called on the superintendents of various companies on the Range and presented their demands. Those presented to the Oliver were forwarded by registered mail to the Duluth office of U.S. Steel Corp. Company officials of the Oliver on the Range, reported the Duluth *News Tribune,* "declined to hazard a guess as to what action would be taken there [in Duluth]."[44]

The Range was not left in the dark for long. Oliver's reply to the strikers' demands was given almost immediately when the company augmented its permanent private police with 1,000 special mine guards recruited in Duluth, St. Paul, Minneapolis—in fact, any place where men could be found willing to attack picket lines, attack strikers' parades, and browbeat strikers. These professional strikebreakers (mainly underworld characters) were equipped with carbines, revolvers, riot sticks, and deputy sheriff's badges, and sent to the Range to keep the mines working. At the Hull-Rust and Mahoning mines of Oliver in Hibbing, two armored cars guarded the entrances to prevent picketing. Each car contained 22 sharpshooters armed with rapid-fire Winchesters. Outside the Oliver mines at Virginia, which were guarded by company police armed with Winchesters, were posted signs warning: "Any Striker Who Steps on Mining Company Property Does So At the Risk of His Life."[45] On July 1, the Duluth *News Tribune* reported from Virginia: "Oliver police, armed with repeating Winchesters are tonight patrolling the mine properties prepared to shoot to kill if any striker steps on mining property."

Other mining companies followed suit and began hiring their own armed guards and hurried them to the Range to augment the number of company and municipal police. But it was Oliver, the U.S. Steel affiliate, which carried the brunt of the strikebreaking and set the pattern for the entire Range. This, of course, was in keeping with the general labor policy of U.S. Steel. In September 1914, the Preliminary Report of the U.S. Commission on Industrial Relations pointed out: "The most important setbacks encountered by collective bargaining on a national scale in the past fifteen years are directly traceable to the United States Steel Corporation and its subsidiary companies."[46] It was this tradition, set by the most powerful corporation in the United States, that the miners of the Mesabi Range were courageously seeking to break.

Although some strikebreakers were imported into the Range during the strike, their number was never large. Since the first World War had put a halt to the steady flow of unskilled hands to the United States and since unemployment, so widespread in the years 1913–15, had relatively ceased, it was not possible, as in 1907, to recruit large numbers of strikebreakers to take the place of the strikers.[47] Basically then, the strikers had to be intimidated, terrorized, and starved into returning to work.

This the mining companies set out to accomplish by enrolling thugs, hoods and strong-arm men into their force of armed guards, and, under the cover of the law, since these men were deputized by the sheriffs of St. Louis County, by having them break up strike meetings and terrorize individual workers. The press would do its part by distorting what the strikers demanded, vilifying the I.W.W. and blaming the Wobblies for any violence that occurred. The business community would withdraw all credit from the strikers as they had done in 1907; indeed, the companies were confident that "by cutting off the strikers' source of supplies . . . the agitation will be suddenly terminated."[48]

These tactics were applied early in the strike. Some local merchants, especially in Biwabik, began immediately to cut off credit to the strikers.[49] Simultaneously the press began a vicious attack on the strike. The Duluth *News Tribune,* which had played a similar role in the 1907 strike, was particularly useful to the companies. Here are some typical headlines: "I.W.W. Dynamiters Blow Up Houses"; "I.W.W. Agitators Pass Hat For Themselves"; "I.W.W. Resorts to Setting Bridges on Fire"; "I.W.W. On The Range Creates Trouble Where There Was None."[50] A typical comment appeared under the heading, "Revolution, Not A Labor Strike":

"The one thing that the people of St. Louis County must get out of their heads is that the trouble on the range and that threatened Duluth* is a labor strike and the I.W.W. is a labor union. The I.W.W. is not a labor union and the condition faced on the range is not a labor strike. The I.W.W. is a revolutionary organization whose sole aim is to overthrow government and take possession of all property for the uses of its members. What is faced on the ranges and threatened in Duluth is revolution, just that and nothing else."[51]

VIOLENCE AGAINST STRIKERS

On June 14, miners from Aurora, Biwabik, Eveleth, and Gilbert arrived in Virginia to help close down all the mines in the town. The following day, the businessmen of Virginia, acting at the behest of the mining companies, met and adopted a resolution denouncing the strike, condemning the I.W.W. as "Industrial Wreckers of the World," banning all parades and demonstrations, and asserting that all miners who were neither working nor living in Virginia had to be out of the town by noon

* The reference to Duluth was to the effort made by the I.W.W. to get the Duluth ore dock workers, employed by U.S. Steel, to join the striking miners on the Range and walk out for better conditions. Although this move won some support, the Duluth authorities prevented further steps by the I.W.W. to organize the dock workers by arresting all Wobblies. The City Council did its part by passing an emergency ordinance empowering the police to imprison the Wobblies for distributing handbills to the dock workers or to arouse public support and raise funds for the striking miners. (Duluth *News Tribune,* June 28, July 21, 27, 1916.)

the following day or they would be removed by officers and officials of the community. Precisely at the same time, 1,500 miners were meeting at the Finnish Socialist hall. Scarlett, Tresca, and Schmidt addressed the workers by turn in English, Italian and Polish, and their words "were translated into a half dozen languages in as many minutes." A special "strike" police, composed of 150 strikers, was set up to keep the peace and instructed to "arrest" anyone who attempted to interfere with the parades and other orderly demonstrations, and turn them over to the authorities. The strikers were advised "to keep their hands in their pockets," and avoid violence. But Scarlett won tremendous applause when he said that while the strikers advocated peaceful methods, there was a point at which these would cease. "If we are deported others will return. Then this strike becomes a violent strike. I want to say to those who are advocating the shanghaiing of the leaders of the movement and thus openly advocating violence, that if any committee or anyone else in Virginia starts violence, the strikers will finish it." Scarlett warned that for every striker shot down by a company gunman, summary vengeance would be meted out.

Before the meeting was over, the miners of Virginia had voted for a general walkout. From Virginia, the strikers marched through the Range towns, headed by Scarlett, Tresca, Schmidt, and other I.W.W. organizers, mobilizing striking miners along the way. On June 21, they joined the strikers in Hibbing and, several thousand strong, paraded through the streets, carrying banners with mottoes such as "Citizens, We Want Your Sympathy," "This Village Is Not Governed by the Steel Trust," "One Big Union, One Big Enemy," "Gunmen Beware—Keep Away." The peaceful demonstration turned into a riot when special guards, under the pretext of patriotism (the marchers were carrying a red flag), broke up the parade, and assaulted and bruised many of the strikers.[52]

On June 22, the same procedure was followed in Virginia, but when the strikers resisted, the guards opened fire and a Croatian miner, John Alar, the father of three children, was killed. No one was arrested or indicted for this brutal act.

Although the city officials banned all parades, the strikers marched along the sidewalks, two by two, to the home of Alar's widow. On every hat band was a red ribbon bearing the words, "We Never Forget." A committee of the strikers presented the bereaved widow with a purse of $68.75. On June 26, the largest and longest funeral procession ever held in the city of Virginia—3,000 in the line of march, including delegations of strikers from all the Range towns—moved through the principal streets to Calvary cemetery. In front of the hearse a contingent of women and children carried a red banner 12 feet wide on which were inscribed the words, "Murdered By Oliver Gunmen." No priest would perform the burial services for the slain striker. At the grave John G. Saltus, a Minneapolis Socialist, told how Alar had left his little town in Europe to come to the "land of the free" only to find working conditions on the Range worse than in Europe. "John Alar asked for bread and they gave him lead," he concluded. Scarlett declared that "although Alar is dead, his spirit, as that of John Brown, goes marching over the Range country." But it was Carlo Tresca who stirred the huge crowd most when he asked for a standing vote to carry out an "eye for an eye" policy. "Fellow workers, I want you to take the following oath: 'I solemnly swear that if any Oliver gunmen shoot or wound any miner, we will take a tooth for a tooth, an eye for an eye or a life for a life.'" Everyone in the audience took the oath.[53]

Despite this ultimatum, the I.W.W. leaders, as even the hostile press conceded, continued to urge the strikers "to keep their hands in their pockets." "Be peaceful brothers. Let the mining companies be the ones to incite disorder. We will put them to shame."[54]

But the companies had lost any understanding of the meaning of the word "shame" when it came to dealing with the strikers. As soon as the proceedings at Alar's grave were reported in the press, they rushed to Governor John A. W. Burnquist with the news that the law was being violated on the Range by the striking miners, that riot and bloodshed were widespread, and that life and property were in danger of destruction from the I.W.W.-led mob. Without bothering to ascertain the truth or falsity of the charges made against the strikers, Governor Burnquist, on June 30, sent the following telegram to Sheriff Meining:

"Arrest forthwith and take before magistrate, preferably at Duluth, all persons who have participated and are participating in riots in your county and make complaint against them. Prevent further breaches of the peace, riots and unlawful assemblies. Use all your powers, including the summoning of a posse, for the preservation of life and property. . . ."[55]

This telegram was generally accepted as an order to the sheriff and his deputies, including the deputized gunmen, to go the limit in breaking the strike. As the *Mesaba Ore,* a newspaper published at Hibbing, noted:

"Was there anything more likely to drench the range with human blood than this governor's order to the sheriff? It was just what the mining companies wanted to give their gunmen, their armed thugs, full authority to murder those opposed to the mining company—the authority of the State of Minnesota backing up the mining companies in the wanton killing of men who were only asking for an increase in wages, and the protection from the thugs with the bloody hands."[56]

ARREST OF I.W.W. LEADERS

Following the receipt of this telegram, the company gunmen became bolder. On July 3, a number of armed special deputies and armed guards, including a notorious character named Nick Dillon, a gunman in the employ of the companies and deputized by the sheriff, stormed into the home of Phillip Masonovitch, a striker in Biwabik, without warrants, ostensibly to investigate the existence of an illegal liquor still there. When they began to abuse Mrs. Masonovitch, a number of the Montenegrin boarders, all strikers, fought back, and in the general mêlée which followed, James C. Myron, a deputized mine guard from Duluth, and Thomas Ladvalla of Biwabik, a sodapop deliverer, were killed. All the occupants of the house were arrested. Many miles away, at Virginia, Scarlett, Tresca, Schmidt, Little, Gilday and other I.W.W. organizers were taken from their hotel at 3 A.M., manacled, and placed on a train for Duluth, where they were charged with murder in the first degree. The claim was made that even though they were not within 12 miles of the shooting, they were "accessories after the fact," since their speeches were designed to incite violence and thus caused the killing. Masonovitch, his wife, and three of the boarders remained in jail on charge of murder.[57]

The real reason for the arrest of the I.W.W. organizers, of course, was to leave the strikers without leaders. To further this aim, George Andreytchine was arrested on a deportation warrant on the ground that he was an anarchist, and that his activities in the strike "tended to incite violence." Like the other I.W.W. organizers, Andreytchine was transported to Duluth where he remained in jail.[58]*

Thus at a critical moment in the strike, the guidance and influence of practically all the I.W.W. leaders were lost to the strikers. The miners at once substituted local men, several of whom were Finnish Socialists, to continue the struggle, but they, too, were promptly arrested, and shipped to jail in Duluth, usually on charges of violating local ordinances prohibiting meetings or parades. On July 7, I.W.W. headquarters in Chicago began receiving calls for help from the Range: "All our organizers here have been arrested for free speech on charges of first degree murder. Send more speakers and organizers immediately as we need them badly. Our territory requires a large force. Yours for the Cause." Haywood immediately wired back: "Sending more men at once. You must appoint organizers from among the strikers. Keep up the good work."[59]†

* On July 25, Andreytchine was taken East by an Immigration officer and kept on Ellis Island to await deportation. After protests from all over the country, including those of Frank P. Walsh and Jane Addams, he was released. But by then the strike was practically over. (Duluth *News Tribune,* July 25, 1916; *Industrial Worker,* Aug. 12, 1916.)

† A number of the strikers were angered because Haywood did not himself immediately come to the Range even though Chicago was but a short trip away. But Haywood remained at I.W.W. headquarters throughout the entire strike, sending out wires, messages and appeals. Several I.W.W. leaders, especially Elizabeth Gurley Flynn and Joe Ettor, felt that Haywood should have come to the Range. (Interview with Elizabeth Gurley Flynn, Feb. 19, 1964.)

"Elizabeth Flynn Arrives to Stir Up Strife," screamed the Duluth *News Tribune* on July 12, reporting that she was *en route* to the Range. On the day she arrived in Duluth, big posters appeared on the streets headed "Declaration of War" and signed by William D. Haywood, announcing that "War has been declared against the Steel Trust and the independent mining companies of Minnesota by the Industrial Workers of the World," and calling for contributions of "food, clothing, shelter and organization work." The "Declaration of War" was also circulated throughout the country, and published in many labor papers as well as in the general press.[60]

While new I.W.W. organizers were preparing to enter the strike zone, homes of the strikers were still being entered without warrants, and partially dressed strikers hurried off to jail.[61] Strikers were still being kept in jails to await charges against them, and then sentenced to 40 and 90 days in Duluth prison on charges of picketing. Attorneys for the I.W.W. were forced to move from one Range town to the next, fruitlessly defending the arrested strikers.[62] In only one instance was an I.W.W. attorney successful in obtaining the release of an arrested striker. This was in the case of John Sarvardi, a miner arrested in Hibbing for unlawful assemblage. Attorney Harry Faber White proved to the jury that Sarvardi was the victim of an assault, "the most brutal, cowardly and disgraceful ever perpetrated against an innocent man outside the boundaries of Russia." Witnesses testified that Sarvardi, known as a militant striker, had been suddenly attacked by three deputies who struck him several times over the head with clubs, felling him to the ground. Sarvardi dragged himself home, and while his wife was dressing his wounds, several deputies kicked in the door, and after treating his wife roughly, seized the striker and threw him in the Hibbing jail. Dr. C. F. Morsman, Hibbing health officer, testified that as a result of the blows he had received, Sarvardi was totally deaf in the left ear. This was too much even for a Range jury, and, after being out two minutes, a record for local courts, it brought in a verdict of "Not Guilty." Sarvardi was released from jail.[63]

But this was the exception. After futilely trying to obtain the release of other arrested strikers, Attorney Christenson, who came to the Range from Chicago, declared in disgust that "if things that are happening here were pulled off in Cook County there would be a revolution. Organized labor down there wouldn't stand for it a minute."[64]

LOCAL SUPPORT OF STRIKERS

Even the mayors and local officials of Hibbing, Chisholm, Virginia, and Aurora and local businessmen were appalled by what was being "pulled off" by the mining companies. Apart from their concern over the violence of the mine guards, the local officials and merchants of the Range towns had been engaged in a series of tax fights with the mining companies since 1907 when both groups had helped the companies break the strike, and they had no great love for the arrogant company officials who refused to pay their fair share of taxes. Finally, while the local merchants had, in many cases, cooperated with the companies at the outset of the strike, most of them knew they would suffer from a prolonged battle and they were anxious to achieve a speedy settlement.[65] Consequently, unlike their practice in 1907 when they cut off credit sales to the miners as soon as the strike began, many merchants now allowed the strikers to purchase their necessities on credit until the Duluth wholesalers, pressured by U.S. Steel, curtailed their own credit. On July 3, 1916, the Duluth *News Tribune* reported: "Retail stores in some of the range cities and villages have been compelled to notify patrons that they will go on a cash basis if the strike continues. The action of wholesalers in curbing the credit of the retailers is responsible for the notice to customers."

The Range mayors refused to comply with the strikers' request that company guards and police be kept from the streets of their cities, claiming that they had no power to remove men who were now deputy sheriffs.[66] Nevertheless, they did try to achieve an early settlement of the strike. On June 25, Sam Scarlett appealed to the mayors and citizens of the Range towns to call a conference between the mine operators and representatives of the striking miners; he made it clear that it was not necessary for an I.W.W. spokesman to be present. The suggestion was hailed by a number of prominent citizens, but the mayors appealed to the strikers to first return to work and leave it to the officials to mediate the differences between the men and the companies.[67] When their proposal was rejected, they formed a Mesaba Range Municipal League with Michael Boylan, Mayor of Virginia, as chairman, "to protect the local interest in the towns and to guarantee that the strikers would receive a fair hearing." On July 7, an open meeting was held under the sponsorship of the League at which miner after miner voiced his grievances. The League went on record condemning the use of armed guards and protesting Governor Burnquist's order that arrested strikers be tried in Duluth rather than in the Range towns.* At the same time, the League voted to call the mining companies, the strikers, and businessmen into a conference to end the strike. The conference was set for July 11 in the City Hall of Virginia, and the mining companies, the strikers, and the businessmen were notified and urged to send representatives to the meeting.[68]

The meeting scheduled for July 11 never took place. The mining

* The Range officials also attacked Governor Burnquist's envoy, Gus Lindquist, who had been sent to the Range to investigate the strike. They pointed out that he had met only with the companies and ignored the municipal officials and the miners. (Duluth *News Tribune,* July 8, 1916.)

companies refused either to acknowledge the invitation or to send representatives to the meeting. Mayor Boylan called off the meeting, remarking bitterly that "the mining men are not desirous of taking any part in effecting a settlement and ending the strike, which has hampered the business of every interest on the range." This enraged the Duluth *News Tribune* which promptly leaped to the defense of the companies. "As the I.W.W. never settle a strike since they make no agreements with employers, and give no notice before ordering another strike, they cannot be useful in ending this one."[69] The paper ignored the fact, reported in its own news columns, that the Wobbly leaders had repeatedly emphasized that it was not necessary for I.W.W. spokesmen to be present at conferences with the mine owners, and that the strikers themselves would negotiate the settlement. It also ignored the fact, also reported in its news columns, that the invitation to the mine owners had made it clear that "the miners do not require the recognition of any union whatever or will not require the participation of any union or the organizers or officials of any union in the deliberation that may be had to reach a settlement of this strike."[70]

The anger of the Duluth *News Tribune* over the effort of the mayors to settle the strike was mild compared with its reaction to the news that the mayors of Hibbing, Chisholm, and Virginia had appealed to William B. Wilson, Secretary of Labor, requesting that he send mediators to the Range in an effort to settle the strike, which they viewed as "one of the most serious industrial situations that has arisen in recent months." "Why not ask the government to intervene with Carranza on behalf of Villa?" the Duluth daily asked angrily. "They would have the government put the stamp of approval on the I.W.W." When, late in July, Secretary Wilson notified the three mayors that he had named William B. Fairley and Hywell Davies to act as conciliators in the strike and instructed them to go to Hibbing immediately, the fury of the Duluth spokesman for the mine owners reached new heights. "The I.W.W. has won the most important victory in its history," it raged.[71]

This was too much even for the labor papers usually hostile to the I.W.W. *The Labor World,* organ of the Duluth Central Labor Council, A.F. of L., commented angrily:

"The aim of the *News Tribune,* speaking for the Steel Corporation, is to harp on the I.W.W. continually in the hope of blinding the people of the state to the depredations and lawlessness of the mining companies, and in doing that it cares not how malicious and barefaced be its lying effort to discredit the men of the range who stand for the rights of the people against corporate greed—who are trying to bring about a better condition on the range, a condition that can come only when the laboring men are paid the worth of their hire, a decent wage."[72]

ACTION OF STATE A.F. OF L.

Coincidentally with the appearance of this defense of the strikers, the State Convention of the A.F. of L. was being held in Hibbing. Over the opposition of the conservative delegates, the Socialist contingent succeeded in having one day set aside for a discussion of the Range strike. On that day, July 18, a communication from the Central Strike Committee was read to the delegates. It asked them to pledge "your support morally and with all ways in your power to our struggle against the greedy slave-driving, union-hating U.S. Steel Trust," and "in view of much misrepresentation of our cause," to listen to a spokesman for the strikers who would "give you all facts of our conditions and our struggle." M. E. Shusterich, a member of the Strike Committee, was allowed to address the convention after he had given assurances that he did "not represent the I.W.W." He praised the Wobblies for having accepted the invitation to organize the miners, but noted that it was not an I.W.W. strike and that it is "us, the striking miners," and not the I.W.W. that the delegates were being asked to assist.

Following this appeal, the delegates overwhelmingly adopted a resolution supporting the striking miners, endorsing their demands, and announcing that the State Federation of Labor would immediately appropriate all surplus funds in its treasury to organize the Range, and hire speakers in various tongues "to spread the principles of unionism among the different nationalities employed in production of ore." At the same time, the resolution made it clear that in the endorsement of the strike, there was "strictly no recognition of the Industrial Workers of the World."

A bitter battle broke out at the convention over a resolution calling for censure of Governor Burnquist for having "acted unjustly toward the working class in the strike on the range," and for having permitted "steel trust thugs to carry on a reign of terror on the range and invading the rights of the workers." The resolution also instructed the executive council to take steps to bring about the governor's impeachment. After heated discussion, with the conservative delegates denying that the governor was "a representative of the capitalist or corporation classes" and the Socialists denouncing him as a "tool of U.S. Steel," a substitute resolution was adopted. It provided for the appointment of a committee of delegates to go before the governor, acquaint him with the facts as to existing conditions on the Range, and urge him to send a member of the State Labor Bureau to investigate the strike.[73]

Although the Central Strike Committee welcomed the convention's action in supporting the strike and endorsing the strikers' demands, it quickly made it clear to the State Federation of Labor that it did not look with favor on the proposal to send organizers to the Range unless they came "to co-operate in a friendly way" with the strikers. It pointed out that while the Central Strike Committee represented the strikers and not the I.W.W., there were eight locals of that organization now on the Range, and that their total membership constituted a majority of the strikers. The I.W.W. organizers, the Committee reminded the Federation, had responded to the first plea for help that went out, and were now in jail charged with murder, "although their only crime is loyalty to us."

"We are honor bound to be loyal to them in their hour of need, and any action which contemplates desertion of these men will be overwhelmingly rejected by the striking miners. Any attempt at dual unionism on the range at this time is bound to cause dissension and division in our ranks to the end that the strike will be seriously injured. . . . If the State Federation would contribute their surplus funds to our strike fund, we would be assured of their sincerity in voting to support our demands."

The I.W.W., for its part, suggested that the Federation stay out of the strike, "and when the strike is over, we will put up to the miners, which union they desire to join."[74]

Actually, the whole issue was an academic one. The leadership of the State Federation of Labor had no intention of implementing the resolution by sending organizers to the range. In private conversations with E. G. Hall, president of the Federation, Mayor Power of Hibbing urged that the resolution be carried out and that the A.F. of L. take over the miners' strike. Hall replied that lack of jurisdiction prevented any official action by the Federation.[75] No explanation was ever given for the fact that none of the Federation's surplus funds were contributed to the strikers' treasury.

THE STRIKE CONTINUES

"Elizabeth Gurley Flynn, the most feared woman in the whole of the corporation world is now in the Hibbing District," the Duluth *Labor World* reported in the third week of July.[76] Miss Flynn was joined on July 27 by Joseph J. Ettor, Ed Rowan, and Joseph Gruni, and a few days later by Frank Little, Joseph Gilday, Leo Stark, and Frank Russell, all four of whom, because of the complete lack of any concrete evidence, had been released after the preliminary hearing on the death of Deputy Sheriff Myron.[77] (Tresca, Scarlett, Ahlgren, Schmidt, Essman and five others, including Mrs. Masonovitch, were held for the Grand Jury on a charge of first-degree murder. The second five were charged with the actual murder and the I.W.W. leaders were accused of having been accessories to the act.) Thus by the end of July, a number of the foremost organizers of the I.W.W. were again back on the Range. Unfortunately, the period of over three weeks when the strikers were without experienced leadership had seriously affected the entire struggle, and it is doubtful whether the early efficiency was ever entirely recaptured.

On July 27, to celebrate the return of I.W.W. organizers, close to 1,000 strikers, many with their wives and children, with Finnish women pushing their baby carriages along, marched for almost 12 hours in over 100° heat, from all part of the Range into Virginia and attended the largest meeting held since the beginning of the strike. The marchers carried banners reading, "Citizens, We Need Your Sympathy"; "The Cost of Living is Going Up, Wages Must Also"; "Higher Wages, Eight Hours and Abolishment of Contract Labor."

Because of the huge crowd, it was necessary to have two meetings, one inside the Socialist Opera House and the other in the streets surrounding the building. Miss Flynn, Ettor, Rowan, Gruni and others addressed the meeting.[78]

"The strike has just fairly begun," the Central Strike Committee announced after the Virginia mass meeting. However, lack of funds was creating a serious problem. The past two mining seasons had not been good ones, and many miners were in dire need early in the strike. To be sure, quite a number of strikers had left the Range to work in other mining areas and in the harvest fields, and, assisted by the A.W.O., they were able to get jobs on the farms and send money back to their families. But funds were still needed for many miners' families, now completely dependent on the $4 a week they received for strike relief or on the "Strikers Relief Store" set up in a number of towns which furnished groceries and other necessities. This problem was intensified when the companies began to evict the striking miners from their homes located on mine company property. When they resisted, the companies sent gunmen to drive them out.[79]

On July 28, the *Strikers' News*, the official strike bulletin,* appealed: "We will stick to the end; whether the end of the strike will bring victory or defeat will be decided, not by us, but by you who are on the outside and at work. The only enemy we fear is hunger and you can defeat that enemy for us. Do that and we will tame the Steel Trust." Some money came in as a result of such appeals, especially from the A.W.O., and some was brought in by Miss Flynn during speaking tours in Minneapolis and Duluth, specifically organized for the purpose of raising funds.[80]

While many of the strikers were in the harvest fields, their wives did the picketing of the struck mines. (Even the children did their part. They conducted processions carrying signs which read: "Our Fathers Strike For Us," "We Are Human Beans," "We Want Milk."[81]) Naturally, the

---

* The *Strikers' News* carried the notice that it was "Published by the Strikers of Mesaba Range, Editors: The Strikers Themselves." The only existing copies appear to be those in the Labor Department Files, 25/247, NA. The Library in Hibbing has no copies. (Letter of Lillian Sheehy, Reference Library to author, Nov. 30, 1963.)

Duluth *News Tribune* was furious. "Women are serving on the picket line and are giving more trouble than the men ever did," it reported angrily late in July. Day after day it carried news items like the following:

"Two automobile loads of deputies were confronted by more than 60 women and small children when the deputies tried to break through a picket line. The women shielded themselves against the deputies with their infants, several singling out a man whom they would beat until he fled with the screaming women after him. A number of women were arrested.

"The village jail was transformed into a kindergarten by the children whom the mothers, on advice of I.W.W. counsel, persisted in taking with them to their cells. Each of the mothers possessed from three to five children, ranging in age from nursing infants to six years."[82]

At first the deputies had been instructed not to use their guns and riot sticks on the women, but soon they were told to treat the wives of the strikers "just the same as if they were men." Early in August, the Duluth *News Tribune* reported from Hibbing that 150 deputies, "armed with repeating rifles, revolvers and riot sticks," had attacked a crowd of women pickets, beating them to the ground even when they "raised their infants as protection." Blaming the women for having used their children to protect themselves, a deputy told the *News Tribune:* "A mother dog has more consideration for her pups than have many of the miners' wives for their children." To this the I.W.W. replied: "Even the wolves respect motherhood, but not the cowardly, inhuman curs who wear the badges of the United States and the Steel Trust, both united in forcing the strikers back into slavery."[83]

Although facing privation, evictions, beatings, and imprisonment, the strikers' hopes for victory still remained high throughout much of August. The reason for this was that the two federal mediators, Fairley and Davies, were on the Range investigating the strike, and the Strike Committee felt that they might be able to get the mining companies to settle. "After we get all the facts on the situation we will attempt to prescribe a remedy," Fairley and Davies told the press at Hibbing on July 27, thus buoying the strikers' hopes. Even if they could not convince the companies to settle, the Strike Committee felt that if the federal mediators would hold public hearings, the strike would be publicized throughout the nation, "and in that manner more funds will be raised for our miners." William B. Colver, editor of the St. Paul *Daily News,* urged Secretary of Labor Wilson to instruct Fairley and Davies to hold public hearings in the strike region "so that a flood of publicity would be turned upon that section."[84]

But the suggestion was ignored, and the federal mediators not only did not hold public hearings but did not even issue a report during all of

August.* The strike, however, did receive publicity during this month as a result of a federal and state report. †August 3 saw the report on the strike submitted to the U.S. Commission on Industrial Relations by George P. West. Based on a field investigation, it ripped into Governor Burnquist, Sheriff Meining of Duluth, County Prosecutor Greene, and the Duluth Chief of Police, accusing them of being tools of the U.S. Steel Corp., and "playing at ducks and drakes with the most sacred rights of the foreign workmen." West reported how 1,000 gunmen had been imported, armed and deputized to break the strike, how the leading wholesalers of Duluth, "responding to the Steel Corporation's bidding," had stopped credit to the merchants on the Range, forcing them to require the strikers to pay cash. He noted that "while the miners of Minnesota and their families face want and suffering and endure the abuse and violence of a private army of gunmen, the United States Steel Corporation announces the largest earnings in the history of an American industrial corporation." After relating the conditions that led to the strike, quoting from testimony of the strikers themselves, and proving that it had not been started by the I.W.W., as charged by the companies and large sections of the press, West's report concluded:

"The story is not yet half told of the lengths to which the companies went in beating up, shooting and jailing and terrorizing their workmen; ... of how the Duluth newspapers, subservient to the company interest, exhorted the authorities to disregard every legal constitutional right of these organizers, and how the authorities responded. It is a story of tyrannical abuse, cruelty and persecution involving a hundred cases and a thousand details. And all to defeat any movement looking toward industrial democracy, living wages, a square deal for the men who mine the raw material for the country's prosperous and powerful corporation.

"The strikers have done and are doing their part in this battle for freedom, for the things America is supposed to stand for."[85]

As was to be expected, the Duluth *News Tribune* immediately charged that West's report had been "written by the I.W.W." But the officials of

---

* Davies submitted a preliminary report to Washington on July 29, stating that 15,000 workers were involved directly or indirectly in the strike, and commenting: "Absence of real organization among the strikers makes it slow work to get at facts that will help in conference with operating Co.'s." (Labor Department Files, 25/247, NA.) Fairley and Davies claimed that their failure to hold public hearings during August was due to the fact that the strikers were afraid to face the men they accused of exploiting them for fear of reprisals. ("Report of Federal Conciliators. . . ." *Ibid.*)

† The strike also received publicity during August in magazine articles: Mary Heaton Vorse's "The Mesabi Strike: From the Miner's Point of View" (*Outlook*, Aug. 1916, pp. 1044-46); Marion B. Cothren's "When Strike-Breakers Strike: The Demands of the Miners on the Mesaba Range" (*The Survey*, Aug. 26, 1916, p. 536), and Leslie H. Marcy's, "The Iron Heel on the Mesabi Range," *International Socialist Review*, Vol. XVII, Aug. 1916, pp. 74-80.)

the Range towns, led by Mayor Power of Hibbing, called the report "absolutely correct."[86]

Practically every statement in West's report and every charge brought against U.S. Steel by the strikers was confirmed in mid-August with the publication of the report submitted to Governor Burnquist by Minnesota's Deputy Labor Commissioners, Don D. Lescohier and Martin Cole, who had investigated the strike at the request of the State Labor Commissioner. To be sure, unlike every other investigator, Lescohier and Cole reported that while there was "dissatisfaction" among the miners with existing conditions, the strike was started and spread by the I.W.W. and was in no sense "a spontaneous outburst." (Federal Mediator W. R. Fairley promptly blasted this statement as inaccurate, stating: "Everything we have been able to learn leads us to believe that the strike started before the I.W.W. organizers came here.") But the report did point out that the miners had been exploited by the contract system, cheated, oppressed, forced to give bribes to their mine captains, arrested without warrants, given unfair trials, and subjected to "serious injustices" at the hands of the mine guards and police. The report made it clear that the mine guards employed by the companies, particularly the Oliver, deputized by Sheriff Meining without investigation, and supported by Governor Burnquist, were to blame for all disorder. The report put it bluntly:

"We are seriously impressed that the mine guards should have been compelled to remain on mine property or disarm when they left it. Every shooting affray that has occurred on the range has occurred on public property. In no case have the so-called riots occurred on or even near company property. The parades of the miners have been peaceful, the public police have had no trouble in maintaining order, and if the private mine guards had been compelled to remain on company property, we do not believe that there would ever have been any bloodshed on the range."[87]

The report of the State Labor Bureau investigators opened the lips of many Minnesotans who had heretofore remained silent. A police officer endorsed the report, declaring that the professional strikebreakers brought in by the companies were "outlaws who would as soon shoot a man as look at him. And to prolong their jobs, they caused riots, hijacked strikers, and caused most of the fighting and violence which occurred." Another informant said that much of the trouble in the Virginia section had been provoked by the Oliver police. "They were headed by a man who thought that the Oliver was God, and could do as it wanted. The Oliver cops indulged in high-handed lawlessness, and helped to provoke the men."[88]

Editorial comment on the report in the Minnesota press was overwhelmingly hostile to U.S. Steel. "We find," declared the St. Paul *Pioneer,* "that the Oliver Steel Company, in exploiting the miners of northern Minnesota, has torn to shreds the principles of the Constitution, has outraged the freedom of contract, has maintained a system of virtual slavery of white men in our state and has appropriated to itself the powers of government and the dispensation of public justice."[89] Even the Duluth *News Tribune,* though defending Oliver and maligning the strikers as "illiterate" and indifferent to "American affairs," conceded that the report proved that the miners might have had "legitimate grievances" when they decided to strike."[90]

END OF THE STRIKE

What did all the reports and articles accomplish? Not much so far as fundamentally helping the strikers achieve victory. To be sure, Governor Burnquist had been fully exposed for the part he had played in assisting the steel corporation to break the strike. But this did not cause him to cease playing this role. On August 26, he rejected a request from a committee of the State Federation of Labor that he order the withdrawal of the sheriffs and deputies, especially the deputized company gunmen, and replace them with the National Guard, and, at the same time, intervene personally to settle the strike. Moreover, while the unfavorable publicity caused Oliver to restrain its gunmen to a degree, the picket lines of the strikers continued to be attacked; strikers continued to be wounded and arrested. On August 28, Chief of Police Owen Gately of Virginia boasted that whenever striking miners "assemble to do picket duty, they are dispersed and those who cause any trouble arrested."[91]

The nation-wide publicity the strike received in August did bring in some much-needed funds from all over the country, the majority of the contributions still coming from local groups of the I.W.W. But the amount that came in was slight compared with the need, especially since, with the end of the harvest, many of the miners who had left the Range returned to join the others dependent on strike relief. On August 28, the "Strikers' Relief Store" in Hibbing was closed down, to be followed a few days later by stores in other towns. Mayors Webber of Chisholm, Boylan of Virginia, and Power of Hibbing had promised the strikers city jobs early in August, but there were not enough local funds to make good on this offer.[92]

The I.W.W. leaders kept urging the strikers not to "let anyone make you believe the strike is over."[93] But as the strike dragged to the end of its third month, more and more of the strikers, particularly those burdened by family responsibility, returned to work. Two factors seemed to have kept the Central Strike Committee from calling off the strike at the beginning of September. One was the hope of a large contribution to the strike fund from the A.W.O. The I.W.W. harvest workers' organization had already sent the strikers several sums of money directly, but Haywood objected to this and their later contributions had gone to Chicago where it was being held. Gurley Flynn traveled to national headquarters to ask that the funds be released to save the strike from collapse. But Haywood refused, probably convinced that the strike was lost anyway.[94] Now the only hope was that the two federal mediators would succeed in bringing about a conference between the strikers and the mine owners out of which a settlement might emerge. This hope also failed to materialize. For a month Fairley and Davies moved slowly to get at the main facts in the dispute, attributing the time required to achieve this to "the unorganized handling of the Mesabi Strike which had a spontaneous beginning and only recently developed into a concerted plan." By August 24, they were convinced that the strike was lost, "that the men are being whipped into an unconditional surrender," and hence there was no point in seeking a conference between the strikers and the companies.[95]

The strikers were understandably furious over the failure of the federal mediators to act. Calling Fairley and Davies "federal meditators" instead of mediators, they insisted that they do something to bring about the long-awaited conference. On September 10, the Central Strike Committee sent a desperate appeal to the federal mediators insisting that "as representatives of the federal government," Fairley and Davies arrange a conference, in the very near future, between the miners and the companies, setting a date for such meeting, and that they reply as to their willingness to pursue such a course so that "a just settlement between the miners and the companies might be arrived at." The appeal closed with the warning that "the causes for which these miners have rebelled still exist and if you fail at this time to bring about a reasonable settlement of the demands for which the men have struck and which are considered very just and fair, then in the not far distant future these differences will again be thrashed out by another industrial struggle."[96]

The appeal went unanswered. Fairley wrote to Davies that there was no point worrying about criticism of their conduct by "leaders of the I.W.W.'s." "Such men always seem to make goats for their lack of success."[97]

The failure of the federal mediators to act was the last straw. By this time more than half of the mining properties on the Mesabi Range were operating at a nearly normal rate. It was clear that the strike was lost. The militancy and courage of the strikers and their families, the financial support received from the I.W.W. locals and members, especially the "harvest stiffs" of the A.W.O., and the sympathy of local politicians were not enough to overcome the armed guards of the mining companies, the hostility of the state officials and most of the press, the arrest of the strikers and the imprisonment of many of their leaders, and the desperate needs of the miner and his family. On September 17, after the locals of all the Range towns had voted in favor, the Central Strike Committee called off the strike with a pledge that the struggle would be renewed next spring, "unless conditions are so improved that it becomes unnecessary."[98]

With the strike lost, the miners, except for a small number who found themselves barred by being blacklisted,* or those who decided to leave the Range, filed back to work at the same rate of wages and under the same conditions of employment that they had had prior to the strike. But the strike was not a complete failure. For one thing, the miners' organization, forged during the struggle, remained intact after the strike, and the companies were well aware of its existence.[99] Proof of this can be seen in the unpublished report sent to Secretary of Labor Wilson on October 28, 1916, by Fairley and Davies.† Based on the records of 21 mining companies in the strike zone, representing over 95 per cent of the production of the zone, the Commissioners were able to report an advance in day wages of 35 to 60 cents per day in the month after the strike and increases in the same period in contract rates. As a whole, wages had been "increased 15½ to 20 per cent" since the strike. Furthermore, the companies promised the Commissioners that the grievances of the strikers would gradually be eliminated. All this led Davies to conclude: "Our report will show some interesting phases of material improvements in wages and positive statements of policy which guarantees the elimination of most of the grievances complained, *so that the strike was not a failure because otherwise it is doubtful whether the position of the companies regarding their general policy and future assurances could have been so defined.*"[100]

Davies' conclusion was based on replies from the 21 companies to six recommendations proposed by the Commissioners. While these did not provide for the elimination of the contract system, they did recommend that the companies grant every contractor the right to select his own partner and fix the contract rate on the first of the month which should be the prevailing rate for the month "unless the conditions show that it will be impossible for a miner to make average wages." The Commissioners also recommended that monthly statements be furnished each worker, outlining in detail his credits and debits; semi-monthly pay; prompt dismissal of mine captains and shift bosses found guilty of exploiting the miners, and wage increases "to keep in line with the increased cost of living as compared with 1915." Most of the mining companies instituted all of the reforms proposed by the Commissioners except the one calling for semi-monthly pay.[101]

* The absence of large-scale blacklisting of strikers, as had followed the 1907 strike, was explained by the fact that the companies were reported to be "exceeding hard up for help." (*Strikers' News,* Sept. 22, 1916.)

† As late as 1920, H. L. Kerwin, Assistant Secretary of Labor, wrote to Amos Pinchot: "The report in this case has never been printed." Similar replies to queries appear as late as 1940. (Labor Department Files, 25/247, *NA.*) Although Fairley and Davies explained that they did not want the report published while they were engaged in correspondence with the mining companies, it is not clear why it was not published after their work was completed.

In November 1916, Oliver announced a ten per cent raise in wage rates to go into effect on December 15, and all the other mining companies followed suit. This was on top of the increases that had occurred in the month following the strike.[102] Although U.S. Steel attributed its decision to a desire to have the workers enjoy the fruits of wartime prosperity, the I.W.W. correctly claimed that it was due to the strike of the past summer and the threat of a new walkout in the spring. Fairley and Davies agreed with this conclusion, and even the Duluth *News Tribune* conceded that the wage increase was "the Steel Corporation's answer to the threat of a renewed I.W.W. strike on the ranges next spring."[103]

THE LEGAL AFTERMATH

On August 30, the Grand Jury indicted seven men and a woman for the murder of Deputy Sheriff Myron. Tresca, Scarlett and Schmidt were charged with being accessories to the murder while Joe Cernogovich, Joe Mikich, John Orlandich, Phillip Masonovitch and his wife Militza were charged with having actually committed the murder. (The same jury reported that the killing of John Alar, the striker, had been justified and refused to indict anyone, a finding, Ettor remarked, that "would have been no different had it come from the board of directors of the steel trust.")[104] Thus when the miners returned to work in September, three of their former organizers and five of their associates, including one woman, were still in jail in Duluth awaiting trial. The cases were handled by a group of capable lawyers which included John W. Keyes of Duluth, Mayor Victor L. Power of Hibbing, Arthur Le Seuer, a well-known Midwest Socialist, and the famous labor lawyer, Judge O. N. Hilton of Denver. "We will have plenty of talent," Joe Gilday proudly told the press.[105]

While the cases were awaiting trial, the I.W.W. tried to rally support for the defendants on the Range and to raise much-needed defense funds. Gurley Flynn, as usual, was indefatigable in this activity. She addressed mass meetings all over the Range, delivering an ultimatum wherever she spoke that "in the event justice is not meted out," the miners would lay down their tools and walk out for 24 hours in protest. In town after town, the miners voted to endorse this pledge. Fund-raising on the Range, however, was more difficult. The strike had drained the miners of their resources so they had little to contribute. Money, therefore, had to come from outside the Range, especially from the I.W.W. But Haywood, enraged over the selection of Judge Hilton, against whom he bore a personal grudge, as one of the defense attorneys, refused to release any money from the I.W.W. treasury. Miss Flynn went directly to Walter T. Nef, secretary-treasurer of the A.W.O., and obtained a contribution of $5,000 for the defense fund. The A.W.O. turned a deaf ear to Haywood's protest that the money should have been sent first to central headquarters. Apart from its growing dislike of Haywood's centralizing tactics, the A.W.O. feared its contribution might never be used for the defense fund.[106]

Support for the defendants and funds for their defense came also from other parts of the United States and even from Europe. Eugene V. Debs called upon all Socialists to rally to the defense of the prisoners regardless of their opinions about the I.W.W. The Brooklyn local of the Amalgamated Clothing Workers appealed to Secretary of Labor Wilson to intervene in behalf of the defendants. "Officials of the Steel Trust and their deputies should be in jail and not these workers," the union insisted. United Mine Workers locals in Colgate, Okla., and Panama, Ill., addressed resolutions to Wilson demanding "the release of the men imprisoned at the bidding of the Steel Trust." But the most sensational support came when thousands of coal miners in Scranton, Pa., members of the United Mine Workers, went on strike in sympathy with the prisoners being held in jail in Minnesota, "to show that the legal murder of workers, with the manhood to fight for themselves and their class, must cease."[107]

From Tom Mann, secretary of the Transport Workers of Liverpool, came a strongly-worded resolution in which the union condemned the "labor frame-up," and announced that it was their duty "to make it generally known in European countries from which the miners are drawn the treatment accorded them." All over Italy the story was made known as posters describing the case and playing up the part of Carlo Tresca, began to appear in leading industrial cities. The Executive Committee of the Italian Socialist Party condemned the imprisonment of the miners and the labor organizers, and Congressman Caroti of Rome even called upon the Italian government to register its protest.[108] "Through the efforts of Ettor money is coming in from Italy," the Duluth *News Tribune* reported on December 2, 1916, three days before the trial was scheduled to open.

But the cases never went to trial. On December 16, the *News Tribune* featured the following story on its first page:

"What the public had come to know as the I.W.W. murder cases reached a sudden end yesterday in District Judge Cant's court in this city. The state, represented by County Attorney Warren H. Greene, accepted pleas of guilty of manslaughter, first degree, by Phillip Masonovitch, Joseph Cernogovich, and Joseph Mikich, all Mesaba range miners."

Behind this story lay a confusing series of negotiations. There are two versions of these events. One, reported in the Duluth press, stated that defense attorneys, headed by Judge Hilton, approached the state and offered to have three of the men plead guilty to manslaughter, first degree, on condition that all of the other prisoners go free. County Attorney Greene, after consultation with the court "decided in the public interest to accept." The I.W.W. version emphasized that the state's attorney approached the defense to arrange a "possible disposition" of the cases. Realizing that the outcome of the trial was uncertain in an atmosphere hostile to the I.W.W., and hoping to avoid the heavy expenses involved, the defense attorneys agreed to discuss a settlement. However, they set the following conditions: No settlement could restrict the activities of the I.W.W. on the Range; it must meet with the approval of the committee representing the organization in Virginia; the court had to agree to the settlement, and the prisoners themselves had to agree to whatever arrangement was decided upon. On this basis, a settlement was worked out under which three miners would plead guilty to manslaughter, first degree, receive a sentence of about three years, and all the other defendants would go free. All of the conditions laid down by the defense were met, and the miners agreed to plead guilty, deciding among themselves who was to be freed. Masonovitch, delighted that his wife would be freed, voiced the sentiments of the others when he said that Scarlett, Schmidt, and Tresca "can do more good than we can."[109]

There seems to be substance to the I.W.W. version. The Duluth *News Tribune* reported that the state attorney had conceded he faced great difficulty in convicting Tresca, Scarlett, and Schmidt since they "bore no direct physical relation to the killing of Mr. Myron," and editorially it hailed the settlement on the ground that it was "doubtful if the I.W.W. leaders could have been convicted because of technical legal constructions," and thus the state had been saved needless expense.[110] This certainly left the impression that the state had initiated the settlement.

In any case, the three miners who pleaded guilty were given indeterminate sentences up to twenty years in the state penitentiary, making them eligible for parole at the end of one year.* Schmidt, Tresca, Scarlett, Mrs. Masonovitch and Orlandich were released by the court after the District Attorney noted that he had no evidence that would warrant their conviction. Harrison George, writing in the *Industrial Worker,* viewed this as a major achievement of the settlement, since it meant the "repudiation by the court of this state of the doctrine of conspiracy as cited in the Haymarket decision. . . . This outrageous precedent now can be considered broken to a greater degree than would have been possible had a verdict of 'not guilty' been returned, as this can be cited as the court's opinion in a question of legal definition. This means a great deal; a danger is removed from all organized labor and more evidence than speech-

---

* The miners were freed from prison in a little over three years after two appeals to the Parole Board. According to Miss Flynn there was an understanding with District Attorney Greene that the men would only stay in prison 1½ years. But Greene went off to war, and his successor denied any knowledge of the agreement. (*I Speak My Piece,* p. 103; interview with Elizabeth Gurley Flynn, Jan. 31, 1964.) Miss Flynn justifies the settlement on a number of grounds among them the need to concentrate defense activity on other labor cases, especially the Mooney-Billings Case (*ibid.*).

making and alleged incendiary utterances will have to be introduced in a labor case before a speaker or organizer can be held for crimes committed by other persons without their physical complicity in the deed."[111]

Although this was published as part of the I.W.W.'s justification of the settlement, it did not express Haywood's viewpoint. He was furious over the bargain with the authorities and viewed it as a sell-out of the miners. He criticized Miss Flynn and Ettor for having "allowed themselves to be entrapped by lawyers who would rather 'fix' a case than try it." Miss Flynn and Ettor, however, regarded it "as the best that could be done."[112]*

On December 18, a huge mass meeting took place in the Socialist Opera House in Virginia, scene of so many meetings during the great strike. Scarlett, Schmidt, Tresca, and Gurley Flynn made their farewell speeches to the miners before leaving the Range. Closing the meeting, Miss Flynn noted that wages and conditions on the Range were "satisfactory now" thanks to the militancy and heroism of the miners during the past summer. Although the I.W.W. organizers were leaving the Range, they would return in the spring and continue the work of organization. "We are all going home for Christmas and then to Everett, Wash., where they have 125 of our 'boys' in jail. Meanwhile, we wish you a fully organized New Year's."[113]

The I.W.W. pledge to continue the organization of the miners ran headlong into wartime hysteria and repression. The locals of the Metal Mine Workers' Industrial Union 490 were disrupted by illegal repressive acts against its members. Thereafter, the miners remained unorganized until the emergence of the C.I.O. when the International Union of Mine, Mill and Smelter Workers appeared on the Range and organized a number of local chapters. The first to join the C.I.O. union were the veterans of the 1916 strike.[114]

* There seems to have been a misunderstanding among the I.W.W. leaders as to the sentence imposed on the three miners. Harrison George reported it as an indeterminate sentence up to 20 years which made the men eligible for parole after one year. This is precisely what was reported in the Duluth press. Haywood, however, writes in his autobiography that the sentence was from five to 20 years. (*Bill Haywood's Book*, New York, 1929, p. 292.) Harrison George's report was correct.

CHAPTER 23

The Everett Massacre

On December 18, 1916, the I.W.W. leaders of the miners' strike left the Mesabi Range. The Duluth *News Tribune* could not restrain its joy. "The I.W.W. has gone from the Range. It is only a memory," it exulted.[1] The rejoicing was premature. Ten days later, the I.W.W. was back on the Range, this time leading the lumber workers.

BEGINNING A NEW PUSH IN LUMBER

For weeks, I.W.W. organizer, "Timber Beast" Jack Beaton, and Charles Jacobson, secretary of the Virginia I.W.W. local, had been meeting with workers employed in the sawmill and logging camps of the Virginia & Rainy Lumber Co. which operated two sawmills in Virginia and camps in the nearby woods. On December 26, 1916, a committee of I.W.W. members was elected to meet with company officials to discuss the grievances of the sawmill operatives and the lumberjacks. When the officials informed the committee that there was nothing to discuss, the workers held a mass meeting in Virginia's Finnish Socialist hall and voted to strike.[2] A red strike handbill was issued by the strike committee which listed the demands. The mill men demanded a wage raise of 25 cents, abolition of the Sunday night shift, an eight-hour day for Sunday day work, change of the day and night shift each week, and no discrimination against union men. The lumberjacks presented ten demands calling for a wage increase, reduction in hours, better conditions in the camps, no hospital fee, and again no discrimination against union men. The leaflet closed: "It is understood that the sawmill workers and lumberjacks are fighting together for these demands, and that neither the sawmill workers or [*sic*] the lumberjacks will go back to work until the demands of both the sawmill workers and the lumberjacks are recognized."[3]

Pickets were immediately stationed outside the two mills in Virginia and the camps, and they proceeded to distribute the strike handbill to those still at work. As hundreds joined the strike, the Virginia police and company guards began attacking, arresting, and jailing the pickets. "As soon as the pickets displayed the red bills they were arrested and jailed," a local reporter wrote on December 29, two days after the strike began.[4] The following day the City Council passed an ordinance prohibiting the distribution of handbills and strike literature, and this was followed by a decree by the police and fire commission ordering all members of the I.W.W. out of Virginia within 24 hours. This applied to Charles Jacobson, too, even though he had been born in Virginia.[5]

Defying the ordinance and the decree, the pickets succeeded in closing down the two mills and 11 company camps. By January 3, over 1,000 Virginia & Rainy's employees were on strike. Scores of them, however, were in jail, arrested on trumped-up charges. Unlike the situation during the miners' strike, the local officials and businessmen of Virginia were completely hostile to the strike, partly because they feared another prolonged struggle when they were still trying to recover from the economic effects of the previous strike, and partly because the city was greatly dependent upon the company's plant for power and shortages of power were already beginning to develop.[6]

A flying squad from Virginia brought news of the strike to the North woods' camps. On New Year's Day, 1917, the strike spread to other lumber firms. "More than 1,500 lumberjacks employed in the woods of Northern Minnesota went on strike yesterday under the leadership of I.W.W. organizers," the Duluth *News Tribune* reported on January 2. By the end of the week the strike was general throughout Northern Minnesota. Over 4,000 were now involved, most of them lumberjacks who were striking for the same demands as those employed by Virginia & Rainy.[7]

Now the employers' offensive began in earnest. Sheriff Meining rushed armed deputies to the camps from Duluth; the mining companies lent their gunmen to the lumber firms to help them break the strike. "The mining companies are as much interested as we are in smashing the I.W.W.," a lumber official joyfully told the press. I.W.W. organizers were arrested and deported from the lumber towns. "Wholesale Arrests," read the headlines in the local press in mid-January. As in the miners' strike, Governor Burnquist ordered that arrested strikers be taken to Duluth for trial rather than be tried where the arrests occurred.[8]

Despite the terror the strike lasted through the month of January. But by the third week of the month, the mills and camps were operating with reduced crews. The strike collapsed at the end of January.[9]

Although the uprising of the Mesabi Range lumber workers seemed to come as a complete surprise to the companies, they had had ample advance notice. A year before, the A.W.O. had warned the companies that just as it had "pitchforked" thousands of dollars into the pockets of the "harvest stiffs," it would soon heave "more thousands into the lumber-jacks' pockets." "After the harvest—what? Why the lumber camps of course!" was the common refrain among A.W.O. members.[10]

In February 1916, Lumber Workers Local No. 315 became part of the A.W.O. as Lumber Workers' Organization No. 400. As a consequence the A.W.O. gave financial and organizational support to a campaign in the lumber industry, and a number of new locals were established. On July 3, a big conference of delegates from these locals, plus loggers from a number of camps, was held in Seattle. The discussion dealt with the mistakes of the past in order that they might be avoided in future work, then got down to drafting a concrete plan of organization. Since the lumber industry divided itself into certain districts, it was decided to operate through a district form of organization under the supervision of an organization committee and general secretary. Seven members of the I.W.W. in any camp or mill were authorized to hold meetings under authority from district headquarters. Finally, several organizers were to be placed in the field immediately to begin the work of building "job power in the lumber industry."

The decisions taken at the conference revealed that the I.W.W. was at last ready to apply to the lumber industry the tactics that had proved so successful in the harvest fields. Instead of having the work done from the offices in the major cities, as formerly, they would be only centers of supply, collection, and correspondence. The local unions would do the chief work on the job wherever there were seven or more members in good standing. This would enable the members on the job to hold regular business meetings, recruit members, collect dues, and distribute literature. "We will have our union function where we work," James P. Thompson, a veteran of past organizing drives in lumber, declared at the conference in urging adoption of the plan.[11]

Following the June conference, a few Wobbly organizers moved into the lumber regions to investigate the possibilities of organization and to lay the groundwork for future activity. One of the organizers commissioned by Seattle Local 432, which had been assigned a key place in the drive in lumber, was James Rowan. Early in July 1916, Rowan was in Idaho holding meetings near the camps around Santa at which he emphasized the necessity of organization and outlined the benefits of industrial unionism.[12] On July 31, Rowan arrived in Everett, Wash., "the city of smokestacks," as it was sometimes called, located between 30 and 40 miles from Seattle. Here he planned to spend a day or two finding out what could be done in the neighboring timber industry and addressing the lumberjacks who had wandered in from the camps.[13] Soon Rowan and the entire I.W.W. was involved in an epic struggle that riveted the attention of the whole nation on Everett.

PROLOGUE TO EVERETT FREE-SPEECH FIGHT

Everett, a city of about 35,000 people in 1916, was a port on Puget Sound from which a considerable quantity of lumber was exported annually. Lumber, in fact, was the main reason for Everett's existence. In the surrounding countryside, the woods were dotted with logging camps. In and around the city were the sawmills. Lumbermen controlled the economic and political life of the city—its stores, banks, real estate, and its government. The city's power structure rested in the Everett Commercial Club, composed of mill owners and business and professional men, with Fred K. Baker of the F. K. Lumber Co. as president, and with representatives of the Weyerhaeuser and Jamison Mills, and the Clough-Hartley Lumber Co. on the Board of Directors. The Commercial Club's chief objective was the maintenance and perpetuation of the open shop at all costs.[14]*

The members of the Shingle Weavers' Union, for a long time a subdivision of the A.F. of L.'s International Timber Workers' Union, were among the most exploited and most militant of the workers in Everett. Again and again, between 1903 and 1913, they had struck to increase wages and end the ten-hour day, and although they had invariably been defeated, they still clung to their union. In 1915, in an effort to destroy the union once and for all, the Everett lumbermen declared war upon the shingle weavers, put into effect a 20 per cent wage cut, and posted open-shop notices. The Commercial Club endorsed the action as did the businessmen of Everett generally, convinced that if the shingle weavers could finally be crushed, other unions could be dealt with quite easily.[15]

The shingle weavers struck. The Superior Court of Snohomish County aided the mill owners by issuing an injunction against picketing. "The situation is extremely critical," E. P. Marsh, president of the Washington State Federation of Labor wrote to the Department of Labor on March 30, 1915. "There are over three hundred men involved. They have been out of work the better part of the winter, their credit is exhausted, the union funds are low as the union has been contributing to a dozen strikes throughout the state. Work is practically nil in all lines and there is nothing for the boys to do. . . . Mill men all over the state are watching the Everett struggle and should the union lose, ninety-five per cent of the mills operating throughout the State, will attempt to put the lowered scale into effect and declare war upon the union." The strike failed, and as Marsh predicted, wages were lowered throughout the entire state. However, the strikers did exact a vague promise from the mill owners

---

* The Commercial Club was organized in 1912 and reorganized on the stock-bureau plan in 1915, under the auspices of the Merchants' and Manufacturers' Association, itself a leading open-shop organization. Under the plan, each company and business purchased a certain number of stocks. ("Testimony of W. W. Blain," Everett *Tribune,* April 7, 1917.)

that the old wage scale would be restored when business conditions warranted.[16]

In the spring of 1916, due mainly to wartime demands, the price of shingles soared, and the weavers demanded fulfillment of the promise. By now they had formed a new union, the International Shingle Weavers' Union of America, also an A.F. of L. affiliate, and the organization announced from Seattle that the old wage scale would go into effect on May 1, 1916. This, of course, was a strike warning.

Most shingle mills in the state granted the raise in wages, but the Everett mill owners, the most influential in the shingle industry, refused. On May 1, over 400 shingle weavers in Everett left their jobs. Picket lines were set up outside the mills. For a time the strike seemed to be succeeding. Indeed, during the third week of June, the lumber mills in the Everett-Snohomish area went on a five-day week because of the strike. Then the Commercial Club, which had already denounced the strike as the work of "outside professional agitators,"[17] decided that there had been enough nonsense. The police and Sheriff Donald McRae and his deputies arrested the pickets and sent them to jail. But the longshoremen and tugboat laborers, who had themselves gone out on strike on June 1, helped the shingle weavers on the picket line. On July 22, *The Shingle Weaver* of Seattle published a letter from its correspondent in Everett which indicated that the situation was still well in hand:

"The strike has been on almost three months and local No. 2 of Everett has not lost a man that they depended upon when they went out—and that means nearly every shingle weaver there.

"A good crowd is continually on the picket line, including women when the weather is not stormy. The women have the men beat two to one doing picket duty. They succeed in getting the men out as fast as the scab herders bring them in."[18]

Directly after this dispatch was written, company gunmen fired into the homes of union pickets and the authorities stepped up the arrest of pickets. By the end of July there were only 60 on the picket line. The rest were in jail.[19]

This then was the situation in Everett late in July. The shingle weavers were holding on grimly against the scabs and gunmen imported by the mill companies and against the arrests and imprisonment of their pickets by the city and county authorities. Everett's tugboat laborers and longshoremen were also waging a desperate struggle for survival. The Commercial Club, bent on wiping out A.F. of L. unionism in Everett, was suddenly confronted by the activities of the I.W.W., of whom they were far more afraid. Some of the shingle weaver, longshore and tugboat strikers were Wobblies since dual membership in the I.W.W. and the A.F. of L. was not unusual in the Everett area. But they struck and manned the picket line as members of their A.F. of L. unions and not as I.W.W.'s[20]

The I.W.W.'s involvement in the sharpening conflict shaping up in Everett actually began on July 31 when James Rowan arrived in the city on his organizing tour for the Seattle local. "Fellow Worker Rowan," noted the *Industrial Worker*, "went to Everett with the purpose of filling in a day or so and getting a line on the work being done there, in the timber industry."[21] But so tense was the situation in Everett that Rowan clashed immediately with the Commercial Club and its henchmen, the law-enforcement authorities.

FREE-SPEECH FIGHT BEGINS

On the night of his arrival, Rowan held a small street meeting at Hewitt and Wetmore Avenues, in the center of the city. He denounced the lumber trust, distributed pamphlets describing an investigation of the industry made by the government, and read excerpts from the Report of the U.S. Commission on Industrial Relations. In the course of his harangue against the A.F. of L. and its craft form of organization, Jake Michel, Secretary of the Everett Building Trades Council (A.F. of L.) and an official of the Everett Labor Council, shouted indignantly that Rowan was a liar. Sheriff McRae of Snohomish County, watching the meeting in a parked automobile nearby, offered to arrest Rowan. Michel protested that Rowan had said nothing to warrant an arrest. Nevertheless, McRae pulled Rowan down from the soapbox and took him to the county jail. After an hour's grilling, Rowan was released. He immediately rushed back to the street corner and resumed his speech at the point he had been interrupted. He was arrested a second time and locked up in the city jail. The next morning the municipal court sentenced him to 30 days in jail for peddling without a license, but gave him the alternative of leaving town immediately. Rowan tried tenaciously to uphold his rights. He demanded counsel and was refused; demanded a jury trial and was refused; demanded a postponement and was refused. Finally, having exhausted his chances, Rowan chose to leave town. The same day, August 1, the Wobblies in Seattle, having learned of the incident, notified Mayor D. D. Merrill of Everett that they intended to look into Rowan's arrest "and find out if this has been a deliberate attempt to suppress free speech or not. . . . We are determined that we will speak on the streets of Everett and to this end if necessary will proceed immediately to do so."[22]

Rowan's minor skirmish rated several paragraphs on page 4 of the August 5 issue of the *Industrial Worker*. The account closed, however, with a warning: "The city of Everett needs a drastic dose of direct action, and, unless the officers there change their methods, the membership of the I.W.W. in this section will concentrate there and enforce free speech in ways not pleasant, but very educational for the Police Department of that town." The I.W.W. educational program was not immediately applied.

On August 4, Levi Remick, a "one-armed veteran of the industrial war," arrived in Everett. He interviewed the Shingle Weavers and sold some I.W.W. literature on the streets until the police ordered him to stop peddling without a license. After inquiring about the cost of a license, he journeyed to Seattle where he secured the necessary funds from the I.W.W. local and came back to Everett. Upon his return, Remick opened a small hall and paid a month's rent in advance. Then he placed a sign in the window, resumed the literature sales, and began to do some organizing work for the I.W.W.[23]

Throughout most of August, the police and the sheriff allowed the I.W.W. hall to function unmolested. But on August 19, a battle broke out between the Shingle Weavers' pickets, now down to only 18, and the gunmen imported to protect the strikebreakers. The scabs, protected by the police and gunmen, spirited the pickets away to a railroad trestle and beat them severely. When picket sympathizers joined the battle, gunfire broke out and one of the pickets was shot in the leg. The employers immediately cried "I.W.W. violence," but the Wobblies disclaimed any connection with the incident and were upheld by the A.F. of L. unionists.[24]

Following this battle, the I.W.W. sympathizers in Everett petitioned the Seattle office for an "ace" Wobbly speaker. James P. Thompson, national organizer, was dispatched, and Remick advertised a meeting on August 22 at which Thompson would be the featured speaker. When the Wobblies and their friends found they could not rent a hall for the meeting, they decided to hold it on the street at Hewitt and Wetmore. On the morning of the day before Thompson was to speak, Sheriff McRae, in an intoxicated condition, and several city policemen broke into the I.W.W. hall, tore up some of the posters and handbills advertising the meeting, and expelled Remick from the city. Remick hurried to Seattle and conferred with members of the I.W.W. local on the advisability of holding the meeting in Everett that evening. After hearing Remick's story, the Wobblies determined to hold the meeting.

On the same afternoon that Remick left, James Rowan returned to Everett, went to the I.W.W. hall, and finding it locked, reopened it for business. An hour later, McRae, still intoxicated, arrived with a policeman, tore up newly posted advertisements for the Thompson meeting, and ordered Rowan to leave town again or serve his 30-day jail sentence. Rowan followed Remick to Seattle and corroborated the latter's story of police interference. The Wobblies were now more determined than ever to hold the meeting in Everett.[25]

About 20 members accompanied Thompson to Everett that night, and he proceeded to mount the soapbox at Hewitt and Wetmore. He spoke to a large crowd for about 20 minutes when 15 police officers pushed through the crowd and arrested him. Rowan immediately took his place and the police promptly arrested him. Mrs. Edith Frenette, a Wobbly organizer from Seattle, called for the singing of "The Red Flag." While the crowd was singing, both she and Mrs. Lorna Mahler, wife of the secretary of the I.W.W. local, were arrested. Mrs. Letelsia Frey of Everett, who was not an I.W.W. member, then mounted the box and began to recite the Declaration of Independence, and she, too, was pulled down. Before being silenced, however, she shouted, "Is there a red-blooded man in the audience who will take the stand?" Jake Michel immediately responded, and the A.F. of L. official, too, was promptly arrested. Infuriated by the continuous replacements, the police joined hands and captured all the suspected Wobblies near the stand. They then marched their prisoners through the streets to the jail. About 500 persons in the audience followed the prisoners to the jail, demanding that they be released.

At the jail, the rank and file Wobblies were thrown into the drunk tank, but Thompson was told he would be released on condition that he left town and did no more speaking in Everett until the labor difficulties were over. When he refused, he was put in the cell with the other members. The following morning Thompson and the woman prisoners were deported from Everett on the Seattle-Everett Interurban. The rest were taken in wood carts to the City Dock and sent to Seattle by steamer, the authorities taking $13 from one of the Wobblies, James Orr, to pay for the passage.[26]

Upon arriving in Seattle, the Wobblies conferred with the Seattle members at a special meeting in the I.W.W. hall. A Free-Speech Committee was organized, general headquarters of the I.W.W., various branches, and the Wobbly press notified, and volunteers began immediately to conduct street meetings in Seattle to raise funds. At the same time, in Everett, the A.F. of L. Labor Council passed a resolution condemning Sheriff McRae and the city officials and asserting that the Everett unions endorsed "the battle for free speech." "The Free-Speech Fight was on!" notes Walker C. Smith in his book, *The Everett Massacre*, the official I.W.W. account of this great episode in labor history.[27]

The I.W.W. entered the Everett free-speech fight with some hesitation. Free-speech fights, as we have seen, were now regarded as a diversion from the main task of organizing the unorganized. In December 1915, J. A. McDonald had criticized this attitude in *Solidarity*, arguing that "Free-speech fights are important. They are a means to an end—Job Organization." But the response to his plea for new free-speech fights was extremely cold. Wobblies pointed out that had the A.W.O. followed McDonald's advice and become involved in free-speech fights whenever they met with opposition, the "harvest stiffs" would never have been organized.[28] A notice in the *Industrial Worker* of April 29, 1916, announcing a free-speech fight in Webb City, Mo., and calling for "all available members," went completely unanswered. Most Wobblies were not interested.

Still none of the Wobblies who were critical of the attention devoted in the past to free-speech fights hesitated to support the battle in Everett for the right to speak. This was different. The drive had just been initiated to organize the lumber workers, and if the I.W.W. retreated in the face of opposition from the lumber companies of Everett, its prestige among the workers in the industry would quickly decline. As the *Industrial Worker* put it tersely: "Everett is a strategic point for the organization of the Forest and Lumber Workers. Therefore, we must have free speech and full opportunity for organization in Everett." Yet as if to assure the skeptical Wobblies that Everett did not signify a return to the old pattern, it noted: "This is not a free-speech fight. It is a fight on the part of the bosses for the open shop and the destruction of all unionism on the Pacific Coast."[29] Finally, the I.W.W. was confident that the Everett fight would be brief and "won quickly." Said the *Industrial Worker* confidently on August 26, 1916: "Victory is but a question of a short time, and must be unconditional."

And it did seem for several weeks that this was precisely what would happen. On August 25, Harry Feinberg, son of a Jewish businessman in Peoria, Ill., but now a prominent I.W.W. member in Seattle, was allowed to speak at the corner of Hewitt and Wetmore, and the following day, the I.W.W. hall was reopened with F. W. Stead of Seattle as secretary. To celebrate the occasion, three Wobblies spoke on the streets that evening. One was pulled from the box, but by the I.W.W.'s not the police. George Reese, a Pinkerton in the employ of Snohomish County but posing as a Wobbly, began to call loudly for violence when Harry Feinberg silenced him. The evening passed without incident or arrests. Moreover, Rowan, after serving eight days in prison for his part in the Thompson meeting, conducted street meetings for several consecutive evenings without even seeing a deputy or policeman.[30]

"Everett Fight is an Easy Victory," exulted the *Industrial Worker* in its headline of September 2. "The city of Everett," it continued, "evidently measured its power and that of the I.W.W. movement, and decided that they could hope for nothing but defeat by the I.W.W." The Wobblies were deluding themselves! Later, the I.W.W. conceded that it had congratulated itself prematurely on an easy victory, and that the absence of official interference was because William Blackman, a federal labor mediator, was in Everett trying to settle the Shingle Weavers' strike, and the mill owners and other businessmen and the authorities were being careful.[31] *

---

* Another I.W.W. explanation was that no ordinance had yet been passed in Everett against speaking at the corner of Hewitt and Wetmore, and that the authorities were waiting for such a law which would give them "a cloak of more legality for their actions." (*Industrial Worker*, May 12, 1917.)

Actually, during the lull, the Everett Commercial Club had arranged to turn over real power of the county and city government to Sheriff McRae, bypassing Everett's mayor and police chief. Together the Club and the sheriff organized an army of several hundred deputies, divided into various groups with such objectives as guarding the entrances to the city, and patrolling the railroad yards, the streets, and the hobo jungles. The deputies were recruited from among Commercial Club members and the underworld, and were invariably drunk. They were instructed to drive the I.W.W. out of Everett and not to bother about the methods to accomplish this goal.[32]

REIGN OF TERROR

On the morning of September 7, William Blackman, the federal mediator, left Everett. That very evening the battle erupted again. Mrs. Frenette and five male I.W.W. members were arrested at a street meeting. She was released the next day, but the men were held for 30 days. The next evening, two more I.W.W. members were arrested for street-speaking, including the secretary of the I.W.W. hall, but a crowd followed the deputies and prisoners to the jail and demanded the release of all who had been arrested. Following these arrests, the Everett Free-Speech Committee of the Seattle local sent John Berg to Everett to secure a lawyer to effect the release of the prisoners. Berg hired E. C. Dailey, who had resigned from the Commercial Club in protest against its open-shop campaign, and then tried to get the keys to the I.W.W. hall from the secretary who was being held in jail. McRae promptly threw him into the same cell solely because he was an I.W.W. member. The next morning, the sheriff drove Berg out in the country in his car, ordered him to walk to Seattle under the threat of death, then knocked him down and kicked him in the groin as he lay prostrate, rupturing him severely.

The injured Wobbly made his way to Seattle. That night, he and a group of Wobblies, among whom was Mrs. Frenette, moved on to Mukilteo, a small town about four miles from Everett, and chartered a small launch, the *Wanderer,* to take them to the battle area. They hoped to smuggle themselves into Everett by avoiding the carefully watched inter-urban and public steamships. As they approached within a mile of the Weyerhaeuser dock, another launch carrying Sheriff McRae and 60 armed deputies pulled abreast. The deputies opened fire on the *Wanderer,* overtook the launch, and boarded it. The Wobblies, including Mrs. Frenette, were beaten. McRae beat Captain Jack Mitten of the *Wanderer* on the head and in the groin, rupturing him. Mrs. Frenette escaped, but 21 Wobblies and Captain Mitten were arrested and locked up. For over a week the prisoners waited in jail, sleeping on the bare floor without blankets, without a hearing or charges preferred against them. After being detained for nine days, most of the men were offered their freedom. "'All or none!' was their indignant demand." All were finally released. When Captain Mitten returned to the *Wanderer,* he found that 17 life preservers had been stolen.[33]

Meanwhile, the Wobblies still in Everett tried to hold street meetings, but each time they did, they were pulled down from the box by McRae's deputies and thrown into jail. On September 11, Harry Feinberg and William Roberts, having just been elected to serve on the Everett Free-Speech Committee,* went to Everett. Jack Michel met them; the A.F. of L. leader called Chief of Police Kelley and asked for permission to hold a street meeting at Hewitt and Wetmore. Kelley told Michel he did not object to the meeting, but they ought to check with the sheriff first. Unable to contact McRae, Feinberg mounted the box that evening.

After he had been speaking about 20 minutes, three companies of deputies, totaling 150 men, marched into the meeting, broke it up, pulled Feinberg from the stand and dragged him to the county jail. Instead of locking him up, they turned him over to vigilantes waiting on the steps of the jail who proceeded to beat him severely. When Feinberg broke away and fled down the street, the deputies fired wildly after him. Roberts, who replaced Feinberg on the box, received the same treatment. James Ovist, the third speaker, was knocked down and beaten on the street corner, and then forced to run a gauntlet outside the jail. At the street corner, the deputies attacked everyone in sight with fists and clubs. The deputies wore white handkerchiefs around their necks to identify themselves and to keep from hitting each other. But they did not bother to distinguish bystanders from Wobblies, and a number of Everett citizens were also beaten up. Frank Henig, a shingle weaver who was not on strike and not a Wobbly, was in the audience out of curiosity. McRae, drunk as usual, did not recognize Henig, and put him in jail in the custody of Chief of Police Kelley. Later, without provocation, McRae knocked Henig unconscious. When he finally recognized Henig, McRae let him out through the back door of the jail so that he would not have to run the gauntlet of deputies and vigilantes waiting for anyone released by the front door.[34]

Earlier the same day, James Rowan returned to Everett. He was arrested by McRae as soon as he left the inter-urban, and thrown into jail with the 30 other Wobblies who were being held and were undergoing repeated beatings. That evening, McRae, who had promised to teach Rowan a lesson so he would never return again, took him to the outskirts of the city, dumped him out of his car, and told him to "start toward Seattle." Rowan had walked about 100 yards when he was set

---

* The personnel of the Everett Free-Speech Committee had to be changed continually because of arrests.

upon by a mob of deputies who beat him on the head with clubs and gun butts. Then they dragged him into the woods, bent him over a log and beat his back to a bloody pulp with clubs. Rowan staggered to Seattle, his head and back bleeding, and had photographs made of his back showing severe lacerations.[35]

The bloody events of September 11 shocked the citizens of Everett who began to fear for their own safety in a city dominated by drunken, undisciplined deputies and vigilantes. On September 15, a protest meeting was held in the city park. Injured Wobblies and local citizens who had received beatings were on hand and voiced their indignation. James P. Thompson, the chief speaker, called for unity of all citizens, working people and middle class, I.W.W.'s, A.F. of L. members and others, to restore free speech to Everett and end the reign of terror.[36]

The deputies did not attempt to either break up the mass meeting or arrest the speakers. But the Commercial Club was not yielding to citizen pressure. It applied its own pressure on the city authorities. On September 16, the very next day, they issued an ordinance forbidding public speaking at the corner of Hewitt and Wetmore without permission, and Mayor Merrill signed it. Immediately Mrs. Frenette went to Everett and asked Chief of Police Kelley to protect her from the deputies so that she could take the box, defy the ordinance, be arrested, be imprisoned in the city jail, not the county prison, and be formally charged. The purpose of the proposed arrest was to make a test case of the ordinance. But Kelley replied that he could not guarantee protection because McRae had taken the authority out of his hands. Thus, a legal test of the ordinance was denied the I.W.W.[37]

The citizens did not take this lying down. Two thousand people gathered at the Everett Labor Temple and proposed another mass meeting for all citizens. The suggestion received a tremendous response. Ten thousand people—about a third of the entire population—attended the meeting in the city park. Speakers represented the citizens, I.W.W., A.F. of L., and Socialists, and they denounced McRae and his terrorist tactics. This time McRae promised that the I.W.W. would not be molested again. For several days no arrests were made on the streets of Everett, and though the Wobblies doubted that a "liar and drunkard" like McRae would keep his word, the I.W.W. reopened its hall.[38]

The truce lasted only a few days. On September 26, McRae and a contingent of deputies pushed into the hall, arrested the new secretary, Earl Osborn, drove him out of town and closed the hall. The I.W.W. did not try to reopen the hall until October 16 when Thomas H. Tracy took charge.[39]

During October there were so many beatings and deportations of Wobblies that it is impossible to compile a complete record. Mayor Merrill later estimated that between 300 and 400 were deported from

Everett during that month, but only a small minority of these deportations received notice in the city's newspapers. The pattern throughout the month was unvaried. The Wobblies daily made persistent efforts to enter the city. The deputies, guarding all entrances, turned them back with fists and clubs. They also enlisted the aid of railroad detectives. As a result, transients who had previously ridden empty freight cars into Everett with little interference, were now brutally beaten.[40]

On October 30, the I.W.W.–Commercial Club struggle reached a climax. Forty-one Wobblies, a contingent at least twice the size of any previous one, the majority fresh from the harvest fields of the Pacific Northwest, came up from Seattle on the regular passenger boat, *Verona*. Sheriff McRae, again intoxicated, and about 300 armed deputies, each with an identifying white handkerchief around his neck, met the steamer at the Everett dock. Each passenger was asked what his business was in Everett. The 41 Wobblies, all of whom acknowledged membership in the I.W.W., said they made the trip to hold a street meeting. They were separated from the other passengers. Then the deputies began to beat them with revolver butts and clubs, even hitting other passengers in their fury. Possemen forced the horrified passengers to stand still while the deputies loaded their battered prisoners into trucks and automobiles. The caravan drove to Beverly Park, an undeveloped suburb on the way to Seattle. Here, in the cold, driving rain, the deputies formed a gauntlet that ended in front of the cattle guard, with its sharp blades, at the inter-urban track. One by one the Wobblies were taken from the automobiles and trucks and started down the line. A deputy followed each victim and beat him furiously on the back to hurry him along. Just in front of the cattle guard, six deputies were lined, three on each side. Three clubbed the helpless Wobbly on the face and stomach and three on his back. The victim was then forced to run over the cattle guard. Some slipped on the blades, tearing their skin and spraining legs, ligaments and shoulders. C. H. Rice, whose shoulder was dislocated, described his experience:

"Two big fellows would hold a man until they were thru beating him and then turn him loose. I was turned loose and ran probably six or eight feet, something like that, and I was hit and knocked down. As I scrambled to my feet and ran a few feet again I was hit on the shoulder with a slingshot [a club made of sapling]. This time I went down and was dazed. I think I must have been unconscious for a moment because when I came to they were kicking me. . . . As I was going over the cattle guard several of them hit me and someone hollered 'Bring him back here, don't let him go over there'. . . . Then the fellow who was on the dock, and who had been drinking pretty heavily . . . shouted out 'Let's burn him!' About that time Sheriff McRae came over and got hold of my throat and said, 'Now, damn you, I will tell you I can kill you right here and there never would be nothing known about it, and you know it.' And some one said, 'Let's hang him,' and this other fellow kept hollering 'Burn him! Burn him!' McRae kept hitting me, first on one side and then the other, smacking me that way, and then he turned me loose again and hit me with one of those 'slingshots,' and he started me along, following behind and hitting me until I got over the cattle guard."[41]

So loud were the cries and moans of the wounded that the Ketchums, a family which lived a quarter of a mile away, were aroused from sleep. Roy Ketchum and his brother, Lew, went into the cold rain to investigate the cries and witnessed part of the beatings. Later they testified under oath that Rice's account was typical of what they had seen. After the deputies had left, the Ketchum brothers paid another visit to the scene with lanterns to render first aid to any of the Wobblies who might have been left lying in the brush. But eight of the most severely wounded men had managed to get on the inter-urban car, and the others staggered back to Seattle. Most of them went to the hospital the next day.[42]

On October 31, the Everett *Tribune* carried a story of how a "bunch" of I.W.W.'s had been taken off the steamer *Verona* by the sheriff and his deputies, driven to Beverly Park, and there "given a little talk" on the advisability of staying away from Everett, and "started toward Seattle." But the newspaper's effort to hide the real facts did not get far. Too many passengers had witnessed the beatings on the *Verona;* several of the deputies began to boast of what they had done to the Wobblies at Beverly Park, and the Ketchums talked about what they had seen. Everett seethed with indignation. An informal investigating committee was immediately formed, consisting of ministers, labor leaders, a city commissioner, two lawyers, and several prominent citizens. The delegation went to the scene, and although it had been raining, they found blood-soaked hats and hatbands, and large brown spots of blood on the pavement where the Wobblies were started down the gauntlet. A shoe sole and bits of skin, hair and clothing were found in the cattle guard. E. P. Marsh, President of the State Federation of Labor, a member of the delegation, declared: "The tale of the struggle was plainly written. The roadway was stained with blood. The blades of the cattle guard were so stained, and between the blades was a fresh imprint of a shoe where plainly one man in his hurry to escape the shower of blows, missed his footing in the dark and went down between the blades. . . . There can be no excuse for nor extenuation of such an inhuman method of punishment."[43]

TRAGIC VOYAGE OF THE "VERONA"

Although the Everett *Tribune* now conceded that it had played down the outrage, it declared in a front-page editorial headed, "I.W.W. Entitled To No Sympathy," that anything that was done to keep the Wobblies out of Everett was justified.[44] But the people of Everett violently disagreed. Businessmen even began to place signs in their stores reading: "Not a Member of the Commercial Club." A committee of clergymen, labor leaders, and citizens met to discuss how to get the city "out of Russia and back into the United States." It was decided to hold another mass meeting and present the facts to a public which had learned little of the true events at Beverly Park from the Everett press. Reverend Oscar McGill, a member of the committee, left for Seattle to get the cooperation of the I.W.W. He suggested to Herbert Mahler of the Seattle local that the meeting be held in a tabernacle in Everett. Mahler, however, proposed that it be a street meeting on the corner of Hewitt and Wetmore in order to make a test case of the constitutionality of the ordinance against street speaking. McGill agreed, and the date selected for the meeting was Sunday, November 5.[45]

All I.W.W. branches and locals in the region were notified of the intention to assemble in Everett "to establish the right of free speech. This fight must be won. All fighting members answer this call for action." Handbills were distributed headed, "Citizens of Everett, Attention":

"A meeting will be held at the corner of Hewitt and Wetmore Avenues, on Sunday, November 5th, 2 P.M. Come and help maintain your and our constitutional rights. Committee."[46]

The authorities of Everett were informed of the proposed meeting. All Seattle daily papers were also notified and requested to have their reporters on hand.

While the Wobbly organizers in Seattle were signing up recruits for an expedition to Everett, the authorities of Snohomish County and the Commercial Club were not idle. New deputies were sworn in daily, and by Sunday, 500 men were on the sheriff's force. "At a meeting of the Commercial Club," writes Robert L. Tyler, "the assembled deputies were issued weapons, were regaled with speeches on the 'open shop' and the 'I.W.W. menace,' and were told to report Sunday for instructions when they heard the mill whistles blow."[47]

At almost the last minute, the Wobbly leaders decided to make the journey from Seattle to Everett by boat. The inter-urban railway could not furnish enough extra coaches and the I.W.W. could not assemble enough trucks or automobiles. Finally, it was decided to leave on the regular passenger steamer, *Verona,* at 11 A.M., Sunday morning. The members and sympathizers pooled their money to pay the fares of all the free-speech fighters, and when the time of the steamer's departure was close at hand, 300 singing Wobblies paraded from the I.W.W. hall through the streets of Seattle to the Colman Dock. About 250 boarded the *Verona;* 38 others had to wait half an hour to board the *Calista,* another regular passenger boat. The funds for the passenger fares having been exhausted, the rest of the Wobblies returned to the I.W.W. hall.[48]

Someone, in all probability one of the two Pinkerton detectives in the departing group, slipped out and telephoned Lieutenant Hodges of the Seattle police force. Hodges, in turn, relayed the news of the Wobblies' departure to Everett officials. Although the I.W.W. had made its expedition public, news of its embarkation reached Everett in a garbled form. Now it seemed that a boatload of armed Wobblies had left Seattle bent on avenging the Beverly Park beatings and determined "to invade, pillage and burn the city."[49] At one o'clock in the afternoon the mill whistles blew, summoning the deputies to the Commercial Club. There they were plied with liquor and sent off to the city dock to wait for the *Verona*. Once there, they roped off the entrance to the dock, and assigned patrolmen to keep the curious away. Hundreds of Everett citizens, familiar with the plans for the meeting, came to the dock to witness the arrival of the Wobblies. Barred from the dock itself, they took up watch on the other docks and on the hill overlooking the harbor.

The armed deputies took up positions inside the warehouse at the end of the dock and on the dock itself, and in such a haphazard manner that those deputies on the open dock were actually in the line of fire of the others concealed in the warehouse. To compound the stupidity, a tugboat filled with deputies also directed its fire toward the men on the dock.[50]

As the *Verona* neared the dock, the 200 Wobblies and friends of the I.W.W. crowded the main deck. Several had scampered up on the cabin, and one Wobbly, Hugh Gerlot, had climbed the mast and waved at the crowd of spectators on the hill. All sang "Hold the Fort," the English Transport Workers' strike song, and as the boat cut through the harbor, the words came across clearly:

> *We meet today in Freedom's Cause,*
> *And raise our voices high;*
> *We'll join our hands in union strong,*
> *To battle or to die.*

A cheer went up from the people on the hill which was answered by the men on the ship. Cabin doors opened, and the passengers came out on deck prior to landing. As the vessel swung alongside the dock, the bowline was thrown and tied. At this point, the doors of the warehouse opened and deputies marched out in two lines and took up their places so as to block the passageway of the *Verona* and the exit from the dock. Sheriff McRae stepped forward, held up his hand for quiet:

"Who is your leader?" he shouted.

"We're all leaders," the men on the deck answered in one voice.

"You are coming here for an unlawful purpose, you can't land here," McRae announced.

"The hell we can't," the Wobblies shouted as they started to step forward toward the gangplank which had been partially lowered. At that instant a shot rang out, then two more in quick succession, and then a general fusillade followed which lasted between ten and 15 minutes. Many of the Wobblies crowded on the deck fell under the first volley. Those who were not dead or wounded or had not dropped to the deck to protect themselves, including the ordinary passengers, ran to the other side of the boat, seeking shelter behind the cabins and bulkheads. So rapidly was the weight of the passengers shifted that the *Verona* lurched crazily and would have capsized had it not been for the bowline which was tied to the wharf. Several of the men lost their balance on the decks made slippery by blood and fell into the water. The deputies turned their guns on these struggling men. Only one man who fell overboard regained the deck.

The deputies ran around wildly, inside and outside the warehouse, firing in all directions. Not only the defenseless men on the *Verona's* deck were now the target; the undisciplined deputies fired at each other, hitting some of their own number. "One of the deputies shot me in the ear," J. A. Ryman, himself a deputy, cried out as he ran from inside the warehouse. "They're crazy down there firing in all directions."

Meanwhile on the *Verona,* the Wobblies forced the engineer to back the boat away from the dock. With the deputies continuing to fire, the vessel started the two-hour trip back to Seattle with its cargo of dead and wounded. The Wobblies gave first aid to the wounded men on board, several of whom were regular passengers of the *Verona.* Almost four miles out, the *Verona* met her sister ship, the *Calista.* The *Verona* was stopped long enough for Captain Chauncey Wiman to tell the master of the *Calista* not to try to land at Everett.[51]

Two hours after the battle on the dock, three Everett Wobblies mounted the box and delivered speeches at the corner of Hewitt and Wetmore. Deputies arrested and jailed them immediately, but the Wobblies had the satisfaction of knowing that the meeting scheduled for the day, though decimated in number by the terror, had actually taken place.[52]

When the toll of the dead and wounded on the *Verona* was taken, it was found that four Wobblies had been killed instantly. One died later in the afternoon at the City Hospital in Seattle.* Six Wobblies were reported missing, all probably killed while in the water or drowned after

---

* They were Abraham Rabinowitz of New York City, Hugo Gerlot of Milwaukee, Gustav Johnson of Seattle, John Looney of Ayer, Mass., and Felix Baran of Brooklyn, N.Y. They were French, German, Swedish, Irish, and Jewish. The Jewish Wobbly, Rabinowitz, said the *Industrial Worker,* was "born of a race with-

having been wounded.* Twenty-seven Wobblies were wounded, the youngest a laborer of 18 and the oldest a longshoreman of 68.

The deputies reported one man, Lieutenant Charles O. Curtiss, a lumber company office manager, killed instantly. Deputy Sheriff Jefferson Beard died the next day. Twenty were wounded including Sheriff McRae, who was shot in his left leg and heel. Four persons, belonging to neither group, were wounded.[53]

MASS ARREST OF WOBBLIES

The Seattle police had been informed by Everett authorities of what had happened at the city dock. Captain D. D. Willard gathered a huge force to meet the *Verona*. "You are going up against the real thing now boys," he warned. "Every man draw his revolver." Revolvers drawn, 200 patrolman and 30 detectives marched to the dock. Reporters for the Seattle press followed. When the *Verona* reached the dock, scores of policemen and several reporters swarmed aboard. "Windows, rails and sides of the steamer *Verona* were riddled with bullets," wrote the reporter for the Seattle *Post-Intelligencer*. "The decks of the vessel were splattered with blood. . . . The windows were either entirely out or punctured in numerous places by bullet holes. Twenty-seven bullet holes were counted in the pilot house."[54]

The police arrested all the Wobblies and ordered them to the dock where each one was searched. To the surprise of police and reporters, "not a weapon, not even a jack knife was found on the men." The Wobblies put up no resistance, but they refused to be led away from the dock until their wounded had been cared for. After the dead had been taken to the morgue and the wounded to the hospitals, the Wobblies were marched to the city jail. Meanwhile, Governor Ernest Lister had ordered the Seattle units of the Washington Guard mobilized in the armories, and the soldiers arrived "with fixed bayonets and loaded rifles with twenty rounds of extra ammunition," ready for action in case Wobblies from the harvest fields should attempt, as rumored, to free the prisoners.[55]

Both the Seattle *Times* and the *Post-Intelligencer* blamed the city's officials for having failed "to halt the gang of thugs who went from this city to Everett with the deliberate intention of stirring up trouble." Mayor Gill promptly replied that "the whole tragedy would have been averted had the I.W.W. not been denied free speech, following the open shop in the Everett lumber mills. They speak here every night, and they

---

out a flag, a race oppressed by the intolerance and superstition of the ages, and died fighting for the brotherhood of man." (Nov. 25, 1916.)

* They were Fred Berger, William Colman, Peter Viberts, Tom Ellis, Charles E. Taylor, and Edward Raymond.

have given us no trouble." (The *Industrial Worker* commented that Gill's statement "touches the nerve center of the whole tragedy.") The Mayor went even further. In a speech before the Seattle Chamber of Commerce, Gill openly blamed Sheriff McRae and his deputies. "In the final analysis, it will be found that those cowards in Everett who, without right or justification, shot into the crowd on the boat were the murderers and not the I.W.W.'s. The men who met the I.W.W.'s at the boat were a bunch of cowards. They outnumbered the I.W.W.'s five to one, and in spite of this they stood there on the dock and fired into the boat, I.W.W.'s, innocent passengers and all." Mayor Merrill of Everett denounced Gill as an unwitting tool of the I.W.W. and was supported by business groups and newspapers of Seattle. There was even a move to recall Mayor Gill, but it quickly petered out.[56]

Without even calling a single I.W.W. witness or one friendly to the Wobblies, a hurriedly impaneled Coroner's jury handed down a verdict, after only two hours' deliberation, blaming the deaths of Curtiss and Beard on gunshot wounds "inflicted by a riotous mob on the Steamer Verona at the city dock." The Everett and Seattle press, having reached the same decision even before the inquest, naturally applauded the verdict. But the Seattle Central Labor Council passed a resolution branding the inquest as biased, charging that "only witnesses for the bosses" had been heard while those who would have testified in favor of the I.W.W. were systematically excluded. The Council demanded a new inquest, "free from control by the forces opposed to labor," a change of venue if necessary, and appropriated $100 for a complete investigation of the Everett massacre.[57]

While the Wobblies were being held in Seattle's jail, pending disposition of the case by Everett authorities, Everett itself was practically under martial law. So arrogant were the deputies that a report from Everett quoted citizens, "grey-haired women, mothers and wives . . . openly hoping the I.W.W.'s would come back and 'clean up' the city."[58] A few days after the massacre, the Shingle Weavers called off their seven-month-old strike in the interest of calming the atmosphere,* and with the assurance of Federal Mediator Blackman, State Labor Commissioner Younger, and a committee of ministers that they would recommend that

---

* "The officers of the International Shingle Weavers Union, the citizens' committee and even the strikers themselves in declaring the strike off felt that this would assist materially in bringing about industrial peace at Everett and thus allow the proper legal proceedings to be invoked and thus determine the guilt or innocence of the parties in question, namely, the I.W.W.'s and the citizens' committee or deputy sheriffs." (Henry M. White, Commissioner of Immigration, and William Blackman, Commissioner of Conciliation, to W. B. Wilson, Seattle, Nov. 18, 1916, "Labor Controversies at Everett and Seattle, Wash.," Labor Department Files, No. 33/312, *NA*.)

the employers reward the workers' "broad spirit" by granting some of their demands.[59]*

In the Seattle jail, two private detectives, who had for many weeks been paid *agent provocateurs* among the Wobblies, picked out 74 men from behind a peephole as the prisoners filed past. They were later charged with first degree murder of Deputy Jefferson Beard.† The initial charge mentioned both slain deputies, Curtiss and Beard, but later the District Attorney requested that the killing of Curtiss be dropped from the formal charge. The I.W.W. immediately pointed out that his name had been dropped because he had been killed by a rifle bullet, and only the deputies had been armed with rifles. They also offered to produce witnesses who would testify that Curtiss on his death bed had identified the fellow deputy who had shot him. The challenge was never taken up.

Heavily handcuffed, the 74 prisoners were transported to the Snohomish County jail in Everett. Of the others who had been arrested, 128 were released; a large number, between 70 and 113, were charged with unlawful assembly and freed under bail posted by the Seattle Labor Council and its paper, the *Union Record*.[60]

While in the Seattle jail, the prisoners had been relatively well treated. The chief of police sent a supply of tobacco at his own expense, and Mayor Gill distributed 300 blankets, and ordered the prisoners be given meat and potatoes instead of only coffee and bread. The conditions in the Snohomish County jail were very different. There were no mattresses and only one thin blanket for each prisoner to keep off the chill of a Puget Sound night in the cold, unheated cells. (In February, when the thermometer dropped to ten above zero, Sheriff McCulloch, who had replaced McRae, publicly conceded that the upper tank had no heat at all and that the whole heating system was inadequate and in poor repair.) Those in the lower cells were forced to sleep on the bare floors. There were five in each cell, and in order to keep from freezing, they had to sleep all huddled together in their clothing. Food consisted of coffee, stale bread and Mulligan stew made with withered vegetables and

---

* The employers coldly rejected this appeal, and the Shingle Weavers renewed their strike and returned to the picket line. The mill owners promptly imported gunmen from Seattle to break the new strike, an action which caused the Everett Trades and Labor Council to appoint a committee "to get prices on 500 rifles and 10,000 rounds of cartridges." Governor Lister was notified that unless he immediately took steps to oust the imported gunmen and tried to settle the strike, the guns and ammunition would be purchased and turned over to the pickets and sympathizers to enable them to defend themselves. (Seattle *Union Record*, Dec. 16, 1916.)

† Originally 73 men were held for trial. An I.W.W. member, Charles Adams, was promised his freedom if he would help identify the suspects and then take the witness stand against his comrades. Adams did help the private detectives select the prisoners to be held for first degree murder, but he was afraid to take the witness stand and so was held and charged with the rest of the men. (Everett *Tribune*, April 22, 1917.)

diseased beef. Free tobacco was out of the question; the prisoners were required to purchase it, and the defeated shingle weavers in a gesture of solidarity, took up a collection of $12 at a mass meeting and donated it to the I.W.W. prisoners for tobacco money.[61]

If the Snohomish County officials thought that barbarous treatment would destroy the morale of the prisoners, they quickly learned better. As the 74 prisoners later explained:

"When we first entered jail, true to the principles of the I.W.W., we proceeded to organize ourselves for the betterment of our conditions even in jail. A 'grub' committee, a sanitary committee and a floor committee were appointed. Certain rules and regulations were adopted. By the end of a week, instead of a growling, fighting crowd of men, such as one would expect to find where seventy-four men are thrown together, there was an orderly bunch of real I.W.W.'s, who got up at a certain hour every morning, and all of whose actions were part of a prearranged routine. Even though every man of the seventy-four was talking as loud as he might a few seconds before ten P.M., the instant the town clock struck ten all was hushed. If a sentence was unfinished, it remained unfinished until the following day."[62]

"The fact is, and that is proven anywhere a crowd of I.W.W. are arrested, that the I.W.W. is the same in jail as he is out," the Everett *Tribune* raged on January 23, 1917. By that time the prisoners had staged two hunger strikes and threatened others to obtain better food, mattresses, and blankets. The first, on November 21, was called off after nearly 36 hours when better conditions were promised. Another method used to obtain mattresses and blankets, when the demand was refused, was "building a battleship":

"With buckets and tins, and such strips of metal as could be wrenched loose, the men beat upon the walls, ceilings, and floors of the steel tanks. Those who found no other method either stamped on the steel floors in unison with their fellows, or else removed their shoes to use the heels to beat out a tattoo. To add to the unearthly noise they yelled concertedly with the full power of their lungs. . . . The townspeople turned out in numbers, thinking that the deputies were murdering the men within the jail. The battleship construction workers redoubled their efforts. Acknowledging defeat, the jail officials furnished the blankets and mattresses that had been demanded."[63]

On January 21, when the stew proved to be merely carrot juice, the prisoners "went on the war-path and almost demolished the building." After dumping the stew, the men ripped a piece of iron off one of the supporting beams and destroyed the locking system. They wound blankets around the bars and bent them out of shape, turned on the water and flooded the building, then soaked all the blankets and mattresses in the water. After getting out of their cells and into the jail corridors, they procured several cans of corned beef and cooked them with live steam from the radiators.[64]

These methods were denounced as "uncivilized" by the Everett press. But they produced results. When the thermometer dropped to ten degrees above zero on January 30, the prisoners demanded more heat and told Sheriff McCulloch that if they did not get it, they would stage another "battleship." McCulloch hastened to get in touch with County Commissioner Boyle, and seven oil stoves were rushed to the jail. Later, when the prisoners threatened another "battleship" because they had no fresh air and exercise, they were allowed the run of the corridors and to play ball on the jail lawn outside with only two guards to watch them. A group of women were even allowed to serve a dinner to the prisoners. Boiled halibut steak, gravy, potatoes, milk and coffee was the menu. A songfest was held afterward, and the prisoners entertained their hostesses with a round of Wobbly songs.[65]

DEFENSE CAMPAIGN

While the 74 free-speech prisoners awaited trial, the I.W.W. was organizing the defense campaign. The Everett Prisoners Defense Committee of Seattle, headed by Herbert Mahler, sought funds for the battery of lawyers. (Chief Counsel was Fred H. Moore, who had defended the Wobblies in several great free-speech cases and had served as attorney for Ettor and Giovannitti; assistant counsel were George F. Vanderveer of Seattle, former prosecuting attorney for King County and a prominent criminal lawyer for whom this was the first of many labor cases, and three other lawyers.) In Everett and Seattle, the committee organized numerous mass meetings to arouse public support. On December 24, a meeting was called by the committee and the Everett Trades and Labor Council to protest the fact that the sheriff had refused to allow Thanksgiving and Christmas dinners to be served to the men in jail. A group of Everett women, with the assistance of the Everett Cooks' and Waiters' Union, had prepared a meal, but when the delegation arrived at the jail on Thanksgiving Day, the group was denied admittance and the prisoners served mush for Thanksgiving Dinner. A request to serve a Christmas Dinner had also been rejected. Among those who spoke at the protest meeting were Robert Mills, business agent for the Shingle Weavers, Jake Michel, secretary of the Everett Building Trades Council, and James A. Duncan, secretary of the Seattle Central Labor Council. During his speech, Michel said, "If my son had been on the boat [*Verona*], and had been killed, I would have considered it an honor to have a son who gave his life for what he thought was right."[66]

In Seattle, a joint committee of the Central Labor Council and the I.W.W. sponsored several meetings in the giant Dreamland Rink. At the first meeting, on November 19, Hulet M. Wells of the Central Labor Council, set the tone of the whole defense campaign: "We of the American Federation of Labor and our friends of the Industrial Workers of the World do not always agree on methods or tactics. But we of the A.F. of L. never forget that these men are our brothers of the working-class and are with us in the great class struggle." James A. Duncan informed Secretary of Labor William B. Wilson that it was "the largest mass meeting that ever filled the Dreamland Rink of this city," and, like Wells, he stressed: "Of course as you are well aware, we, as members of the A.F. of L. have little in common with the I.W.W.'s and are irreconcilably apart so far as our idea of organization and the conduct of our affairs is concerned, nevertheless the principles underlying this whole affair are of most vital importance to all workers, and for that reason we have sunk our differences for the time being, and all parties are determined to bring the real culprits to justice."[67]

The second meeting at Dreamland Rink, January 21, was marked by the appearance of Elizabeth Gurley Flynn as principal speaker.* Heralded in advance as "the best labor speaker in America, the Joan of Arc of the Labor Movement, fresh from the great strike of 20,000 iron-ore miners in the Mesabi Range," she described the Everett struggle as primarily a fight to beat back an employers' offensive against all organized labor on the Pacific Coast and only secondarily as a free-speech fight. Miss Flynn reminded the 6,000 people that "now is the time to defend yourselves in the persons of those 74, for the heritage we leave to the next generation will be in the conditions that we make now." She was followed by Scott Bennett, an Australian who was touring the United States. Bennett made it clear that while he himself was not an I.W.W., "they are dear to me, for by God, they fight, they fight, *they fight!*"[68]

Speakers for the defense appeared all over the United States, many showing stereoptican slides of the massacre. In addition, Charles Ashleigh, Wobbly poet and publicity man, sent urgent appeals to most of the liberal and radical periodicals in the country, and, in a special appeal to every magazine in America, urged: "Send one of your best special writers to Everett and to Seattle. . . . Tell him to get the whole truth and nothing but the truth—and then print faithfully what he reports to you."[69]

The defense activities produced funds—about $38,000 was raised—numerous resolutions condemning the Everett authorities and the Com-

---

* Miss Flynn came to Seattle at the request of the Defense Committee despite Haywood's order that she stay out of the Everett case. (Interview with Elizabeth Gurley Flynn, Feb. 19, 1964.) In addition to speaking in Everett and Seattle, Miss Flynn went on a tour for the defense, covering Aberdeen, Hoquiam, Spokane, and parts of California. The funds she raised in California were divided equally between the Everett and Mooney-Billings Defense. (*Industrial Worker,* Jan. 27, April 14, 1917.)

mercial Club, and telegrams to Governor Lister demanding a fair trial for the men in jail. They came from across the country, from foreign countries,* and from A.F. of L. and Socialist, as well as I.W.W. locals.[70] So united were the labor and radical movements in the defense of the Everett prisoners that the *Industrial Worker* rhapsodized: "Over the dead bodies of labor's martyrs, tactical differences are forgotten; the oneness of labor has been visioned; a new solidarity is being grasped. Thus the murders which were intended to kill the labor movement have made it more united, more militant and more invulnerable."[71] This, of course, was carrying things too far. Most of the A.F. of L. unionists were careful to stress that they did not approve of the I.W.W. and its tactics, and that, as James Duncan noted, "we have sunk our differences for the time being." Nevertheless, the defense campaign for the Everett prisoners marked a high point in American labor unity.

Demands for a federal investigation of the terror against labor in Everett and especially of the events of November 5 were voiced at many of the defense meetings and by unions, Socialist locals, and women's organizations—even by businessmen of Seattle. Resolutions poured in on Secretary of Labor Wilson pointing out that a state investigation would not meet the need; first, because the state officials were under the thumb of the lumber companies, and, secondly, because the whole affair was of national not local importance. Wilson took the position that the Department of Labor "could not undertake a proper investigation . . . because it is not authorized by law to subpoena persons and papers and administer oaths, and, secondly, because it has no funds available which could be used to make such an investigation." He would, however, "gladly do anything within my power to secure a congressional investigation which will present to the people the facts as they actually occurred." But Congressmen whom he approached insisted that since it was "not an interstate matter," Congress would not order an investigating committee, and suggested that the Department of Labor conduct the inquiry and then propose legislation "that would be of assistance in preventing such occurrences." But Wilson refused to move, and the question of a federal investigation was allowed to die.[72]

The U.S. Committee of Industrial Relations, however, did issue a preliminary report based on an investigation by two Pacific Coast members of the National Labor Defense Counsel, Col. C. E. S. Wood and Austin Lewis. After reviewing the events leading up to the massacre, the report concluded:

"Not even the most vehement reactionist will argue that the men were

* The unions of Guadalajara, Mexico, wired Governor Lister demanding "that justice be done in the case of our murdered brothers and that exemplary punishment be meted out to those officials who have shown themselves to be the servile instruments of the lumber industry." (*Industrial Worker*, Jan. 6, 1917.)

not exercising a perfectly constitutional right in attempting to land at Everett. Nobody will deny, in fact it is cynically admitted, that the sheriff acted merely as the agent of the Commercial Club. The only defense made, and it is made with absolute effrontery and disdain, is that if the Commercial Club did not like these people to come into Everett, they had the right to prevent their entry into Everett by force of arms and in violation of constitutional authority."[73]

TRIAL OF THOMAS H. TRACY

The defense attorneys had their hands full preventing the prisoners from being railroaded to death. On December 28, all 74 Wobblies pleaded not guilty to first-degree murder charges. The same day, Attorney Fred H. Moore requested that the case be taken out of the hands of Judge Ralph C. Bell because he was a former Commercial Club member. The petition was referred to the State Supreme Court, but Judge Guy C. Alton was voluntarily substituted before a decision was handed down. Then Moore filed another affidavit of prejudice against Judge Alton and he was replaced by Judge T. T. Ronald.[74]

On January 26, Prosecutor Lloyd Black announced that Thomas H. Tracy would be the first prisoner to be tried on first-degree murder charges. The same day George F. Vanderveer presented an application asking for a change of venue on the grounds of prejudice in Snohomish County against the defendant. On February 9, Fred Moore again filed for a change of venue, this time submitting scores of affidavits gathered from all over the county, each ending with the statement: "It is impossible for the defendants to receive a fair and impartial trial in Snohomish County." The evidence was so overwhelming that the trial was moved to Seattle and set for March 5, 1917.[75] No dates were set for the others, it being understood that an acquittal for Tracy meant the release of all.

The State of Washington versus Thomas H. Tracy, or as the *Industrial Worker* put it, "the Clough-Hartley Mill Company, the Jamison Mill Company, the Weyerhaeusers and the others against Thomas H. Tracy," proved to be one of the longest and most important trials in American labor history. It was actually two trials, not one. One was a murder trial, the other a trial of the I.W.W. as a criminal organization and a test of the legality of its principles and methods. The I.W.W. recognized this fact even before the trial started, for the *Industrial Worker* noted on February 3: "To a great extent the future of Labor, the future of Free Speech, the future of the I.W.W. will depend upon the results of the Everett trial." That big business also recognized this is indicated by the large number of representatives of Eastern newspapers and periodicals present in the courtroom.[76]

Although a good deal of time was consumed by witnesses describing the story of the free-speech fight, the brutality of the deputies, and the events of "Bloody Sunday," it seemed at times as if the events in Everett during the summer and fall of 1916 were remote from the charges before the court. The prosecuting attorneys presented mountains of evidence in an effort to show that the I.W.W. was a society of conspirators advocating violence and sabotage. The jury heard excerpts read from I.W.W. pamphlets, newspapers and songs, and were shown cartoons picturing black cats, with appeals for sabotage.[77]

In his opening statement to the jury, the prosecuting attorney promised to prove that Tracy had fired the first shot from the *Verona,* "and that he was a persistent firer, continuing to shoot as the streamer backed away from the dock, firing through a window from the main deck."[78] Several witnesses, Sheriff McRae among them, identified Tracy as the Wobbly who had fired the first shot from the cabin window. But the defense had little difficulty in demolishing this testimony. At Vanderveer's request, the court adjourned to the Everett city dock and witnessed a reenactment of the November 5 battle. The defense then demonstrated that, given the places occupied by McRae and the other witnesses and the established position of the *Verona* at the dock, it would have been impossible for them to have seen Tracy or anyone else in the cabin window.[79] Vanderveer's strategy broke the back of the state's case against Tracy.

Vanderveer was brilliant in cross-examining prosecution witnesses. E. B. Hawes, a powerfully-built man weighing 260 pounds, mentioned on the witness stand that he had been one of the deputies at Beverly Park during the beatings of the Wobblies. Vanderveer asked him what he thought of the men who had been beaten up. Hawes replied that he thought they were "pretty big babies" who could take care of themselves. Vanderveer then asked Hawes to stand beside two of the men who had been beaten. Hawes himself outweighed both of them. The effect on the jury was immediately felt; they could see in an instant what the Wobblies had had to face at Beverly Park. Vanderveer also asked Hawes to define sabotage. Hawes said that it meant destroying property. Vanderveer then asked the witness where he got his information. Hawes replied that he had looked up the word in Webster's Unabridged Dictionary. Vanderveer then produced a copy. The word was not in the dictionary! Vanderveer also demolished Mayor Merrill's charge that the I.W.W. was responsible for a large number of incendiary fires in Everett and vicinity during the year 1916. He asked the mayor on what evidence his statement was based, and when Merrill cited the Everett fire department, Vanderveer submitted a report by the fire chief. It showed that there were fewer fires in 1916 than in any year previous and that there were only four of incendiary origin on the entire list. Vanderveer also showed great skill in handling evidence submitted by the defense. When Harry Feinberg said that George Reese was a Pinkerton detective, the prosecution objected to the statement on the ground that it had not been proven. Vanderveer immediately subpoenaed Phillip K. Ahern, the head of the Seattle branch of the Pinkerton Agency, who testified that Reese was employed to infiltrate the I.W.W. and act as an informer.[80]

Fred Moore, veteran of many I.W.W. cases, did brilliant work in proving that the prosecution's picture of I.W.W. ideals and beliefs was distorted. Time and again he proved that the prosecution witnesses did not even know what they were condemning. Moore was so familiar with I.W.W. literature that he could quote the page numbers of every pamphlet extract introduced as evidence by the state, and indicate where passages had been omitted which gave an entirely different impression from the one the prosecution was trying to convey. Moore also guided James B. Thompson in his appearance as a defense witness, as he explained the meaning of the pamphlets and documents submitted by the prosecution. Asked by Moore if the I.W.W. believed in murder, Thompson declared eloquently that the I.W.W. was organized to forever put a stop to murder—the murder of the child victims of industrial slavery, of women forced into prostitution by low wages, and men into beggary by unemployment. Thompson, as did Herbert Mahler before him, stated that while I.W.W.'s may have talked a good deal about sabotage, none of them practiced it. Asked about "Casey Jones" and "Ta-ra-ra-Boom-De-Ay," in the *Little Red Song Book,* with their references to sabotage, Thompson insisted that the *Song Book* was not the I.W.W.'s "Bible," that if anything were, it would be the Preamble and Constitution.[81]

From the cross-examination of the prosecution witnesses and the presentation of evidence by the defense, it became quite clear what actually had happened in Everett. The lumber companies in Everett, aided by other business and professional men, were determined to stop union organization, and especially the I.W.W., in the city. They knew that in Spokane, Fresno and other cities, the Wobblies had so filled the jails that the authorities had finally yielded and allowed them to speak and organize. To prevent such an outcome in Everett, the Commercial Club decided that the Wobblies should not be kept in jail but deported and prevented from returning to Everett by repeated brutal beatings. Mayor Merrill frankly explained the whole strategy to E. P. Marsh, president of the State Federation of Labor, J. E. Brown, president of the Shingle Weavers, and William Blackman, Federal Conciliator, when the three visited him at his office to protest the treatment of the I.W.W.'s by the citizen deputies:

"Well we got the idea of how to handle them from their own papers. We read in one of their newspapers a notice to the membership of the I.W.W.'s advising them to stay away from Minot, North Dakota because the citizens there had organized a bunch of vigilantes to beat up every I.W.W. who came into town.

"We figured that if that plan worked in Minot that it would work in Everett. Now we have it arranged in this way: we arrest them, take take them to jail. We don't charge them with anything but we release them and when we release them something always happens to them. Now when we want to release them they beg us not to release them because they know what is going to happen."[82]*

When, on November 5, it appeared that this open-shop conspiracy against constitutional rights was to be broken by aroused and indignant citizens and labor groups, a plan was worked out by the Commercial Club for a massacre. Sheriff McRae, the club's tool, executed the plan. He placed a number of armed men on the dock, inside the warehouse and adjacent docks and elsewhere so that the *Verona* could be covered from all angles. Then, after the bowline was tied and the boat secured to the dock, he ordered the men not to land. At the same time, he held up his hand. This was the prearranged signal for a shot which was probably the prearranged signal to open fire. At once the deputies poured lead into the boat and when several men fell into the bay, they aimed their fire on the Wobblies in the water. Undisciplined and disorganized, especially after McRae was wounded, the deputies fired helter-skelter even on each other. There were some Wobblies on the *Verona* armed with revolvers, but all the evidence at the trial proved that they had fired in self-defense and for a brief interval only. In short, the lengthy trial amply proved that the *Industrial Worker* was correct when it declared indignantly immediately after the battle on the Everett dock: "The most outrageous and most contemptible crime in the history of labor was not committed in the heat and excitement of passion. Every evidence shows a cold, deliberate murderous intent."[83]

In his summation, State Attorney H. D. Cooley conceded that there had been illegal action against the I.W.W. in Everett, but excused it on the ground that this was the only way to keep the city from being licked by the Wobblies as "Spokane was licked. . . . Is it any wonder that the citizens of Everett said: . . . 'We are going to keep you out of here.' Now that may not have been strictly legal, but it was human nature."[84] This may have been "human nature" for open-shop employers and sadistic deputies and sheriffs, but it was certainly not the "human nature" of the vast majority of Everett's citizens.

Attorney Fred Moore concluded the defense's case with a long and eloquent plea for social justice. After reviewing the long struggle of

---

* Mayor Merrill had not been talking abstractly. He himself had personally inflicted a cruel "third degree" upon one of the Wobbly prisoners, crushing his fingers under the legs of the jail cot and beating his head against the cement floor. (Seattle *Union Record*, Nov. 18, 1916; *Industrial Worker*, Nov. 18, 1916.)

organized labor against prosecution for criminal conspiracy simply because unions were organized to raise wages, and noting the significance of free speech in democratic society, he reminded the jury:

"Your verdict means much. The wires tonight will carry the word all over this land, into Australia, New Zealand, and throughout the world. Your verdict means much to the workers, their mothers, their children, who are interested in this great struggle. We are not in this courtroom as the representatives of one person, two persons or three persons. Our clients run into five or six hundred thousand. We are here as the mouthpiece of the workers of America, organized and unorganized, and they are behind our voices."[85]

TRACY'S ACQUITTAL AND ITS EFFECT

On May 4, 1917, the jury, after receiving instructions from Judge Ronald, retired for deliberation. After 22 ballots, the jury returned to the courtroom. The foreman pronounced the verdict. It was: "We the jury find the defendant, Thomas H. Tracy, not guilty!" A few days later, 73 I.W.W. prisoners were released from jail.[86]

The effect of Tracy's acquittal and the release of the other prisoners was far-reaching. To be sure, there were I.W.W. members and others who felt that until the deputies and leaders of the Commercial Club were convicted of the murder of the dead Wobblies, no real victory could be claimed.[87] But the Seattle *Union Record* put it correctly: "It is the first victory of the kind ever achieved by labor on the Pacific Coast, previous trials without exception having been decided against the workers."[88] For the I.W.W. it was a special triumph. The principles of the organization and the courage and militancy of its members had received publicity in the daily press of the entire nation. While the press had placed great emphasis on testimony involving sabotage, a fact which, as we shall see, was to influence the I.W.W.'s attitude toward this vexing subject, the reports of the trial and Tracy's acquittal proved that the employers were acting outside and the I.W.W. within the law, that the employers were using extra-legal methods to destroy unionism while the I.W.W. was using legitimate methods to organize workers in much need of this help.

In January, William Blackman had written to Secretary of Labor Wilson from Everett: "The Shingle Weavers' strike and the I.W.W. controversy which is now in the hands of the Court, in a way will be linked together, and the outcome largely depends upon the construction the Court will place upon the defendants' [the I.W.W.'s] actions." This proved to be an accurate prediction; shortly after Tracy's acquittal, the mill owners yielded to the Shingle Weavers' demands, raised wages and hauled down the open-shop flag. After a year, the strike had finally proven successful.[89]

To the loggers the Tracy verdict was "something like a Declaration of Independence . . . from the barons of lumber."[90] On March 5, the very day the trial had opened in Seattle, 13 delegates representing A.W.O. branches in Eastern Washington, Idaho, and Western Montana; the Middle-Western lumber states of Michigan, Minnesota and Wisconsin, and the lumber areas around Seattle and Tacoma, claiming to speak for 10,000 lumber workers, had met in Spokane and launched the Lumber Workers' Industrial Union, No. 500, I.W.W. With funds and manpower promised by the A.W.O., the delegates optimistically drew up a set of demands, centering on the eight-hour day, six-day week and a minimum wage of $60 a month with board and $5 a day for river drivers,* and made somewhat general plans for a general strike the following summer.[91]† But months before, loggers were leaving their jobs throughout the entire short log region—Eastern Washington, Idaho, and Western Montana where the trees are small—and in numerous spontaneous strikes were eliminating the 12-hour day and hiking wages from $3.50 to $5 a day for river drivers. The news of Tracy's acquittal stimulated a whole series of new walkouts and by the middle of June a strike epidemic was under way, sparked when several hundred loggers walked off their jobs near Sand Point, Idaho, in a "sort of instinctive protest" over living conditions.[92] As similar spontaneous outbursts broke out all over the region, the Wobblies issued a new strike call for June 20 and began to take control of the unorganized, runaway strikes. Out of the Seattle district moved the "job delegates" to assume leadership of what was to be the greatest labor upheaval in the history of the lumber industry. Within two weeks, the strikers had closed virtually all logging operations East of the Cascades.[93]

On November 5, 1916, the date of the *Verona* battle, the Seattle district had only two paid officials, Herbert Mahler, secretary of Local 432, and J. A. McDonald, editor of the *Industrial Worker*. By July 4, 1917, 30 people were employed by the district, and were working day and night to take care of the constantly increasing membership, especially the newly organized lumber workers.[94]

The 74 Wobblies released from jail reported to the Seattle I.W.W. hall for assignments as "job delegates," and left for the logging and construction camps. Wherever they went one was sure to hear workers reciting Charles Ashleigh's poem, "Everett, November Fifth":

* The other demands were for single beds with springs, clean mattresses and bedding, good lighting, not more than 12 to a bunkhouse, no double-tier beds, porcelain instead of enamel dishes, a drying room for wet clothes, a laundry room, showers, free hospital service, hiring on the job or from the union hall, free transportation to the job, and no discrimination against members of the I.W.W.

† The Spokane branch of the new union set the strike date for July 1.

Out of the dark they came; out of the night
Of poverty and injury and woe—
With flaming hope, their vision thrilled to light—
Song on their lips, and every heart aglow;

They came, that none should trample labor's right
To speak, and voice her centuries of pain.
Bare hands against the master's armed might!
A dream to match the tolls of sordid gain!

Refrain:
Song on his lips, he came;
Song on his lips, he went;
This is the token we bear of him—
Soldier of Discontent.[95]

CHAPTER 24

On the Eve of America's Entrance into World War I

The United States was already at war with Germany for a month when the verdict in the Tracy case was handed down. Thus we have come to the end of our study of the I.W.W. from its inception to America's entrance into World War I. (We will, of course, meet the organization in subsequent volumes.) Before taking leave of the Wobblies, let us have a look at the I.W.W. as the nation entered the war.

STATUS OF I.W.W.

On the eve of the war, the bulk of the I.W.W.'s membership and the main centers of its activities were West of Chicago. At this time, the I.W.W. was a flourishing organization and a power in the harvest fields and was becoming one in the lumber industry of the Northwest. It was also beginning to make headway among the construction workers, the metal miners, and the workers in the oil fields of the Southwest.[1]* In the East and Midwest, however, the picture was far different. The I.W.W.'s only center of strength here was among the waterfront workers of Philadelphia. In 1916, the Marine Transport Workers No. 8 had raised their wages from $1.25 to $4 a day, time-and-a-half for overtime and double time for Sundays. (The scale for longshoremen in February 1917 was 40 cents an hour for straight time, for men working on oil 50 cents an hour, and on powder 60 cents an hour.) Not only did the union, with its 4,000 members in and around the Philadelphia docks, unite Negroes, whites, Spanish and other workers of different nationalities, but it assisted

---

* In the fall of 1916 the I.W.W. initiated a vigorous campaign to organize Arizona's four metal-producing districts, which supplied 28 per cent of the nation's copper. The fruits of the campaign did not come, however, until June and July, 1917.

On March 6, 1916, the I.W.W. chartered the Construction Workers Industrial Union No. 573. It had originally been organized by the A.W.O.

workers in various industries in their strikes, refusing to handle products of the struck firms.[2]

But the Philadelphia union was the major exception.* Early in 1916, Haywood issued a call to the "harvest stiffs" to get out of the jungles and help unionize Gary, Detroit, and other large industrial centers. The campaign ended in failure. The situation in Detroit several months after the drive to organize the auto workers was launched was summarized in a report from that city: "The majority of the workers are still unorganized, but the work of education goes on. At present Local 16 is something like Micawber, 'waiting for something to turn up.' Many of the members have, or are getting ready to answer, 'The Call of the Wild,' and are going towards the harvest fields."[3] In general, the I.W.W. in the East and Midwest, apart from Philadelphia, was aptly characterized in the Wobbly press itself as composed of "locals, branches and propaganda leagues, but they are neither numerous, large in membership, nor of immense influence and prestige."[4]

The startling contrast between the I.W.W. in the far West and the Midwest and East caused considerable discussion in Wobbly circles. One group blamed it on overcentralization of the organization which had occurred at the 1916 convention and which Haywood had carried to ever-greater extremes.† By moving the publishing house and the offices of nearly all of the I.W.W. papers to the new four-story headquarters building in Chicago, Haywood had deprived the local regions of centers of activity.[5] (He had also increased the danger of a complete roundup of I.W.W. militants in case of a government raid.) Haywood's growing tendency to hand out edicts from Chicago without doing any organizational work on his own was also criticized. In the far West, these centralizing practices and Haywood's increasing personal control of the organization were resented, but since the Western locals practically operated independently, they simply ignored those edicts of which they disapproved.

* A small local of Italian bakers in New York City might also be included since it maintained a fairly permanent existence and succeeded in achieving job control.

† To give greater emphasis to the union aspects of the I.W.W. and to minimize the propaganda function, the 1916 Convention voted a radical change in the I.W.W. structure. Locals composed of members of one industrial classification were put under an industrial union of that class; the status of "member-at-large" was dropped, and all those who had that status were shifted into a new "industrial" union, the General Recruiting Union; the mixed local designation was abandoned and the existing mixed locals were put into the General Recruiting Union; Propaganda Leagues were dropped and their charters were to be exchanged for those of branches —the name "local" was dropped in favor of "branch"—of the General Recruiting Union. Financial centralization was drastic. Previously each local paid monthly only 15 cents per capita to Chicago (local industrial unions paid it to their national industrial union) and kept the rest of the members' dues and any assessments. After the reorganization, every branch paid all money collected to its industrial union, after deducting only immediate operating expenses. (*Proceedings, 10th I.W.W. Convention* (1916), p. 101.)

In the Midwest and East, however, where Haywood's influence was strong, they caused desertions from the ranks. Ettor quit in disgust over Haywood's policies and was soon followed by Tresca and Giovannitti. Elizabeth Gurley Flynn did not resign, but she was placed on the shelf. Haywood had never forgiven her for her role in the cases arising out of the Mesabi Range strike, and he had forbidden her to go to Everett to aid in the defense of the I.W.W. prisoners. She went anyway at the invitation of the local defense committee over Haywood's protest. When she returned from Everett, Miss Flynn suggested that her pamphlet on sabotage not be reprinted since the Tracy trial had clearly revealed how the question could be used against the I.W.W. Haywood accused her of losing her nerve and ordered a new edition "with a lurid cover designed by Ralph Chaplin, of black cats and wooden shoes."* Although the G.E.B. overruled Haywood and upheld Miss Flynn, the general secretary got back at her by refusing to assign her to any organizing work. Thus, several of the I.W.W.'s top organizers were no longer available for the necessary work to be done in the Midwest and East.[6]†

Basically, however, the difference in the status of the I.W.W. in the far West and Midwest and East can be attributed to the fact that in the grain fields and lumber and construction camps, it had developed over long experience an effective way to organize, the "job delegate" system, which was well suited to these special fields. But it had not yet developed a similarly effective form of organization to enable it to penetrate in a stable way the basic industries like steel, rubber, textile, and automobile, and it was clear that the migratory worker was not the figure around whom the I.W.W. could organize millions of steel workers, railroad men, textile weavers, coal miners—all of them with roots in a region and an industry. Fellow Worker George Hardy pointed this out in 1916: "We appreciate the A.W.O. method of organization. It is probably the most successful manner of organizing the migratory workers. There are, however, great stationary industries whose workers are home-guards who need

---

* Haywood, however, refused to go along with a Wobbly organizer who wrote to him urging him to use organization funds to further acts of sabotage, adding "the wobblies do not want every penny accounted for. If you put down so much for sabotage they will say 'good luck.'" Haywood replied: "Your suggestion is a poor one. There is nothing the enemy would like better than to see any entry on our accounts 'sabotage so much.'" (Pierce C. Wetter to Haywood, March 23, 1916, and Haywood to Pierce C. Wetter, both in PA File, 39/240, NA.) Apart from the stupidity of his suggestion, Haywood's correspondent was overly optimistic. Most Wobblies, particularly in the West, wanted "every penny accounted for," and there were frequent letters in the *Industrial Worker*, complaining that the leadership did not follow this practice to the most minute detail.

† A number of I.W.W. organizers who had previously been effective among Italian workers—Frank Bellanca, Aldo Cursi, Salvatore Ninfo, Arturo Caroti and others—also left the Wobblies and began to do organizing work for unions in the garment trades in the East. (Fenton, *op. cit.*, pp. 524–25.)

organization. These are by far the most important part of the working class, and a majority. If we want to walk steadily toward the goal of one big union we cannot afford to ignore these workers, and we must find the right way to build strong, permanent industrial unions among them."[7]

The truth is that the I.W.W. faced an important obstacle in organizing the "home guards" in the basic industries with which it did not have to cope among the migratory workers. Its attempts to organize the migrants prior to 1915–16 had not antagonized these workers, even though it had not produced much in the way of permanent results. Moreover, many new workers had entered the grain belt and the lumber camps who had had no previous contact with the Wobblies. They were not disillusioned with the I.W.W.; on the contrary, they looked upon the Wobblies as their only hope of achieving decent standards of living. But the same situation did not prevail in the basic industries of the East and Midwest. Here many workers had had previous experience with the I.W.W. and it had not been the kind to encourage them to renew their relationship with the organization. To be sure, McKees Rocks in steel, Lawrence, Little Falls and Paterson in textile, Akron in rubber, and Detroit in auto symbolized militant, heroic working-class struggles, and proved that the unskilled and semi-skilled, particularly the foreign-born, were ready for organization. But to the workers involved and to others who watched them, these struggles also symbolized deterioration of the unions after victory or loss of jobs and blacklists after defeat.* Many of the workers who had participated in the earlier strikes were still in the same factories and mills, and many had had their fill of the I.W.W. While the migratory workers welcomed Wobbly organizers, those in the basic industries now viewed their appeals with suspicion.

CREATING A NEW IMAGE

There is considerable evidence that the I.W.W. was beginning to understand this problem in the latter part of 1916 and was seeking ways to meet and overcome it by creating a new image of the organization. Despite the prominence given to events in Everett, I.W.W. publications now deemphasized free-speech fights as a method of organization, and, instead, continually urged members to "get on the job." Rather than glamorize

---

* Over the same period of time, 1909–16, the unions in the garment trades had succeeded in adding 200,000 workers to the ranks of organized labor, most of them also foreign-born. This record stood in sharp contrast to the meager total achievements of the I.W.W. among these workers. To be sure, it was a good deal less difficult to organize small employers such as those in the garment trades who lacked the capital to resist organizing drives for sustained periods of time than it was to organize gigantic corporations in steel, textile, auto, rubber and mining where the I.W.W. operated. Nevertheless, the achievements of the unions in the garment trades helped reduce I.W.W. influence among foreign-born workers.

workers who moved off the job the moment conditions did not suit them, they urged sticking to the work and organizing new members.

Instead of emphasizing swift, dramatic but ill-prepared and poorly financed strikes, they urged organizing slowly and systematically before calling a strike and even building a strike fund for those who walked out. And they particularly urged Wobbly organizers not to leave the scene when a strike was ended, but to help the new recruits to continue to build the local. Instead of treating middle-class citizens, especially small businessmen, as natural enemies of the workers, they pointed out that the small businessmen had aided the Mesabi Range strikers and that when the lumber companies and the criminal element had taken over the government in Everett, law-abiding citizens, including small businessmen, had not remained silent. This experience, they emphasized, should be kept in mind in all organizing campaigns.

They also played down sabotage—from May 1917 advocacy of sabotage ceased in the *Industrial Worker*—and such concepts as "Right or Wrong does not concern us!" In fact, they insisted that the organization could do with less propaganda and more activity. In January 1917, the *Industrial Worker* announced that "the revolution of talk had been displaced by the revolution of action, action on the job." Propaganda by itself was fine, but it only became "dangerous to the masters when it goes on the job done up in a pair of overalls." Only by linking propaganda with job activity could the I.W.W. become a power among workers in need of organization.[8]

So deep was the change in approach to problems in the winter and spring of 1916-17 that some Wobblies even accused the organization of "becoming respectable," and predicted that soon it would favor political action, union contracts, job control, high dues and high initiation fees, and "become transformed into another A.F. of L." The I.W.W. publications heatedly denied the charge. The organization would never cease to regard political action as a waste of time, and union contracts and written agreements as snares for the workers. The latter could be sure that the only agreement the I.W.W. would sign would be one for the capitalists "to take their places by the side of the workers in the production of the necessities of life." High dues and high initiation fees would always be considered obstacles to organization of the unorganized, while job control could only be meaningful when the workers "owned the job, the machinery of their work and the full product of their toil."

Moreover, while the Everett massacre had demonstrated that there were A.F. of L. officials and members who understood the class struggle, the Federation as a whole was still dominated by class-collaborationists and was still a burden upon the workers, and the I.W.W. could never become like it. As for "respectability," the I.W.W. had only one use for it: "To teach the working class to respect itself as the only useful class in society."[9] It is clear, then, that while the I.W.W. had learned many lessons from past experience, it still had not discovered how unrealistic and backward was its approach to political action and to such necessary instruments in building strong, stable unions as agreements and job control.

It is also clear, however, that in the opening months of 1917 the I.W.W. was supremely confident that it would soon succeed in creating a place for itself in the basic industries of the East and Midwest, as it had already done in the harvest fields and lumber camps. All that had happened since 1905, declared Haywood in March 1917, was "but preliminary to the greater work mapped out for the immediate future."[10] As one views the scene when Haywood was advancing this bright prospect, it did seem that his confidence had substance, and that the I.W.W. was on the way to becoming an effective and powerful economic organization of unskilled and semi-skilled workers. But these prospects did not materialize. Already a cloud had appeared on the horizon that was to grow in size and ultimately not only doom the I.W.W.'s great expectations but actually to destroy the organization. The I.W.W.'s plan to build a solid foundation in industry, applying the lessons it had learned from the past, ran head-on into the determination of the industrialists and financiers to reap the greatest profits from the war. Of course, the aspect of the I.W.W.'s activities that really alarmed big business was its drive to force them to share some of these profits with the workers. But it was the I.W.W.'s opposition to the war that was used as an excuse to justify the repression and practical destruction of the organization.

I.W.W. AND THE WAR, 1914–17

The usual picture of the I.W.W. as a militant and persistent fighter against America's entrance into World War I is based more on words than on deeds, and even these words have been frequently misinterpreted.[11] In truth, the I.W.W. took a fatalistic attitude that the United States was bound to enter the European conflict and that there was not much the Wobblies or any other sections of the American working class could do to prevent it.

A week after the war in Europe began in August 1914, the I.W.W. labeled it an imperialist war whose cause was the rivalry among the European countries for markets.[12] On October 31, in a "War Extra," *Solidarity* predicted that it would not be long before the United States joined the conflict. It was "imperialism that so plainly drove Europe to war, and it is imperialism that is now pushing American workers toward the battlefield." Nor was there much the American workers could do to halt the trend, for the "economic laws of the system" were "soon or late, bound to plunge America into war."

With this viewpoint prevailing throughout the rest of 1914 and all through 1915, it is hardly surprising that the I.W.W. leaders devoted little attention to the problem of mobilizing labor opposition to American entrance into the war. A report in the Toledo *Times* of a speech by Ettor under the title, "How to End the War," simply stated: "The speaker made but casual reference to the European war. He declared that a much more serious problem confronted this country in that of the unemployed." *Solidarity* reprinted this report as a guide to the correct I.W.W. attitude toward the war problem. To talk about the American workers, the way they were organized, as being able to halt the war drive was to indulge in sheer fantasy. "The capitalists will have their way." Of this there could not be the slightest doubt.[13] The same attitude was revealed by I.W.W. organizer C. L. Lambert, who wrote to Richard Ford on June 8, 1915: "This country is going to be mixed up in this war before long, they seem to be doing the best they can to get into it, and if it does come they will not have much trouble in getting all the cannon food they can use."[14]

Later that same year, in a speech in Detroit, B. H. Williams, editor of *Solidarity,* informed the audience that it should take it for granted that the United States would enter the war, and that the workers present, along with the rest of the American working class, should not waste their energy trying to prevent what was inevitable but should begin to prepare for the greater class struggle certain to emerge after the war. "Organize now in the One Big Union for the post-war struggle should be the watchword."[15] Criticized for this defeatist attitude by a subscriber to *Solidarity,* Williams explained that while the I.W.W. opposed war and militarism, it realized that until the One Big Union was a reality, talk of preventing war was just that—talk. "With the workers in control of industry, wars cannot take place against their will. On the other hand, without that control on the side of the workers, no proclamations, resolutions, or pledges, no matter how strongly worded, will avail to prevent them from shouldering arms, if their masters order them to do so."[16]

Thus, while many Socialists and trade unionists were mobilizing opposition to the mounting campaign to bring the United States into the war,* the I.W.W. was sitting on the sidelines, scoffing at the idea that it was possible to prevent this and holding out the prospect that only when the workers were fully organized could they stop the war makers.† It is true that at the tenth annual convention in the fall of 1916, the Wobblies put themselves on record as "determined opponents of all nationalistic

---

* This important subject will be discussed at length in the next volume.

† This was clearly illustrated in Rochester, N.Y., in the summer of 1915. Norman Thomas, Socialist, and Herbert W. Clyde, I.W.W., were both arrested on the same day for speaking at open-air meetings. Thomas was addressing an S.P. anti-war meeting while across the street, Clyde was speaking about the futility of anti-war activity and calling upon the workers to concentrate on preparing for the class struggle after the war. (New York *Call,* July 19, 1915.)

sectionalism, or patriotism, and the militarism preached by our enemy, the capitalist class," and called for "anti-militarist propaganda in time of peace" and "the General Strike in all industries" in time of war.[17] This was followed by a firm declaration by the General Executive Board which announced "opposition of the Industrial Workers of the World and its membership to all wars, and the participation therein of the membership," and notified the "capitalist masters" that the Wobblies would resist "any attempt upon their part to compel us—the disinherited to participate in a war that can only bring in its wake death and untold misery, privation and suffering to millions of workers."[18] But apart from publishing the statements of the convention and the G.E.B. in leaflet and pamphlet form, the I.W.W. still did nothing concrete to mobilize opposition to the pro-war forces. While it publicized the activities of the I.W.W.'s of Australia against conscription, it said nothing about what American workers should do in case they were conscripted.[19] It contented itself with publicizing the following warning that appeared in the *Industrial Worker* in February 1917: "Capitalists of America, we will fight against you, not for you! Conscription! There is not a power in the world that can make the working class fight if they refuse."[20]

Some Wobblies evidently felt that this was simply avoiding the issue. On February 4, 1917, Richard Brazier wrote to Haywood from Spokane: "What effect will war of this country and Germany have? Do you not think it advisable to mix a little anti-military dope with our organization talks to kill the virus of patriotism that will soon be sweeping the land? I wonder if we are going to face the same problem here that our Australian fellow-workers faced and defeated, and if we are, can we do as well as they, and what steps shall we take to get the results that they got? These are questions that have got to be answered, and it behooves us to get busy before the storm breaks and answer them."[21]*

Haywood replied on February 9: "We have not ceased to carry on the usual campaign against militarism. At the same time our members should also realize that they are in a bitter war, the class war, if they understand this they will realize their position when called on to battle for governments."[22]

In short, at a time when the United States had already broken diplomatic relations with Germany, the developing war crisis was still to Haywood and to many other I.W.W. leaders not really a major issue that required more than "the usual campaign against militarism." And the campaign against militarism, as we have seen, did not really go beyond

* At the I.W.W. convention of lumber workers held in Spokane on March 5, Brazier introduced a resolution urging the delegates to "go on record in favor of a general strike in case of conscription." The motion was tabled. (Pardon Attorney Files, 39/240, Department of Justice Records, *NA*.)

stating the I.W.W.'s opposition to war.* Many anti-war groups were now intensifying their activities to halt America's entrance into the conflict. But the I.W.W. was not among them. There was no hint in the Wobbly press even at this late date that the I.W.W. should participate, along with other organizations, in the struggle to prevent the United States from entering the war. J. A. McDonald, editor of the *Industrial Worker,* expressed the typical Wobbly contempt for the anti-war groups: "I attended a peace meeting the other day at which one of the strongest advocates of anti-militarism was a pudgy parasite given to waving a hand, carrying the two-year wages for a worker in diamonds. I said to myself, 'I am an anti-militarist because I am an internationalist, but you, damn you, peace or no peace, I am against you.' "[23]

FORESHADOWING WARTIME REPRESSION

If the I.W.W. thought that by relegating the struggle against the war to the background and bringing the class war to the front, it would have more leeway in which to conduct its organizing campaigns, it was soon to be disillusioned. Even before the United States declared war on Germany, the organizing activities of the Wobblies was considered serious enough to prompt the introduction of I.W.W.-control bills in the Minnesota and Idaho legislatures. Although the Minnesota bill did not pass, the arguments advanced by its proponents centered around the anti-war stand of the I.W.W., which was denounced as "treason." But, of course, they also made it clear that it was the I.W.W. agitation among the iron-ore miners and the lumber workers that really was treasonable.[24] The Idaho legislature's bill was drafted by the attorney for the lumber and mining industries. It stated, in part, that any person who "by word of mouth or writing, advocates or teaches the duty, necessity or propriety of crime, sabotage, violence or other unlawful methods of terrorism as a means of accomplishing industrial or political reform . . . is guilty of a felony and punishable by imprisonment in the State Prison for not more than ten years or by a fine of not more than five thousand dollars or both." The bill passed the legislature without serious debate, and Governor Moses Alexander signed it on March 14, 1917, making it the first of the state criminal syndicalism laws which, together with the federal Espionage Act, were to be used to round up and imprison most of the I.W.W.'s active leaders, hundreds of organizers and rank and file members. It is significant that when Governor Alexander signed the bill, he instructed newspapers throughout the state to publish its text as a warning to the Wobblies to cease their organizing operations in the lumber counties.[25]

* A few individual Wobblies did go beyond this. The Duluth *News Tribune* of March 28, 1917 carried a dispatch from Kansas City, Mo., describing the arrest of five members of the I.W.W. for "exhorting crowds of men not to enlist."

Thus it was that just as the I.W.W. was beginning to function as an effective labor organization, applying the lessons it had learned from the past and bringing the principles of industrial unionism to more and more American workers, it was at the same time confronting an alliance of big business and government that, taking advantage of wartime hysteria, would overwhelm and destroy the organization.

This is not to say that without this savage repression by the government, the I.W.W. would have moved forward to achieve its goals of organizing the unorganized and building a new society in the United States. The Wobblies had made improvements in their tactics. But they still clung to their opposition to political action and their syndicalist outlook; they still operated as a dual union, and they still opposed many trade union practices which the modern labor movement had learned, through bitter experience, were essential for growth and stability. It is difficult to see how with these serious flaws in its ideology, the I.W.W., despite its heroic militancy, could ever have fulfilled its mission.*

* Since this chapter was written, I have developed further the discussion of government repression of the I.W.W. *See* my article, "United States of America Et Al.: I.W.W. Indictment," *Labor History,* vol. XI, Fall, 1970.

REFERENCE NOTES

CHAPTER 1

1. *Proceedings of the First Convention of the Industrial Workers of the World*, New York, 1905, p. 82. (Hereinafter cited as *Proceedings*, First Convention, I.W.W.)
2. *Writings and Speeches of Eugene V. Debs*, New York, 1948, pp. 95–125.
3. *Proceedings*, W.F. of M. Convention, 1904, p. 77.
4. *Bill Haywood's Book: The Autobiography of William D. Haywood*, New York, 1929, p. 174.
5. *Proceedings*, First Convention, I.W.W., pp. 82, 89–90.
6. *Ibid.*, pp. 90–100; *Social-Democratic Herald*, Dec. 14, 1904.
7. *Miners' Magazine*, March 9, 1905, p. 6.
8. *Proceedings*, First Convention, I.W.W., pp. 3–6.
9. *Ibid.*, p. 7; Haywood, *op. cit.*, pp. 178–79.
10. Cincinnati *Post*, Jan. 9, 1905.
11. *Proceedings*, First Convention, I.W.W., pp. 82–90.
12. William Z. Foster, "Syndicalism in the United States," *The Communist*, July 1937, p. 1044.
13. Paris, 1901, pp. 59–60; Paris, 1921, pp. 27–67, 264.
14. Val R. Lorwin, *The French Labor Movement*, Cambridge, Mass., 1954, p. 35; G. D. H. Cole, *World of Labour*, London, 1913, pp. 75, 77, 95–97, 111–14.
15. Louis Levine, "The Development of Syndicalism in America," *Political Science Quarterly*, vol. XXVIII, Sept. 1913, p. 450. Emphasis mine. P.S.F.
16. William Z. Foster, *From Bryan to Stalin*, New York, 1936, pp. 42–46.
17. *Weekly People*, Feb. 18, May 27, June 13, 1905; *Miners' Magazine*, April 27, 1905, p. 12; *International Socialist Review*, vol. V, March 1905, pp. 496–99, 501. *Voice of Labor*, March 1905; Frank Morrison to A.F. of L. Executive Council, March 31, 1905, enclosing typed excerpts from New Jersey *Socialist Review* and Milwaukee *Social-Democratic Herald*, American Federation of Labor Cor-

respondence, Washington, D.C. (Hereinafter cited as *AFL Corr.*)
18. *Voice of Labor*, March 1905; *Proceedings*, W.F. of M. Convention, 1905, pp 21, 218–19, 234; *Miners' Magazine*, June 29, 1905, p. 4.
19. Report signed by Charles Noonan, R. A. Hunt and W. H. Eogty, Schenectady *Herald*, April 22, 1905.
20. E. W. Leonard to Gompers, Schenectady, N.Y., Apr. 16, 1905, *AFL Corr.*; Samuel Gompers, "The Trade Unions to Be Smashed Again," *American Federationist* March, April, May 1905, and reprinted as a pamphlet.
21. Gompers and Frank Morrison to A.F. of L. Executive Council, March 31, 1905, *AFL Corr.*
22. *Proceedings*, W.F. of M. Convention, 1905, p. 21; Paul F. Brissenden, *The I.W.W., A Study of American Syndicalism*, New York, 1919, pp. 65–66; *International Socialist Review*, vol. XII, March 1912, p. 670.
23. Gompers to A.F. of L. Executive Council, May 11, 1905, *AFL Corr.*; Gompers to Miss Guard, May 16, 1905; Gompers to Hugh Frayne, May 13, 1905, Samuel Gompers Letter-books, Washington, D.C. (Hereinafter cited as *GLB*.)
24. "To the Officers and Members of Affiliated Unions," March 21, 1905, *AFL Corr.*; *American Federationist*, May, 1905, p. 277; *Proceedings*, A.F. of L. Convention, 1905, pp. 28, 64, 252–56.
25. Haverhill Central Labor Union to Gompers, April 1, 1905; Local 183, Bridge and Structural Iron Workers' Union to Gompers, April 4, 1905, *AFL Corr.*; Boston *American*, April 2, 1905.
26. A. H. Casselman to Frank Morrison, April 5, 1905, *AFL Corr.*
27. John B. Lennon to Frank Morrison, May 1, 1905, *AFL Corr.*
28. Gompers to Lee Grant, July 20, 1905, *GLB*.
29. Lee Grant to Gompers, June 27, 1905, original in *AFL Corr.* and copy in *GLB*; *Proceedings*, First Convention, I.W.W., p. 18.
30. *Proceedings*, First Convention, I.W.W.,

pp. 80, 592–616; Lee Grant to Gompers, June 27, 1905, *AFL Corr.* and *GLB.*

31. *Proceedings,* First Convention, I.W.W., p. 18; Brissenden, *op. cit.,* pp. 73–74.

32. Lee Grant to Gompers, June 27, 28, 1905, *AFL Corr.* and *GLB; Proceedings,* First Convention, I.W.W., pp. 595–616; Vincent St. John, *The I.W.W.: Its History, Structure and Method,* Chicago, 1917, pp. 23–30; Brissenden, *op. cit.,* pp. 77–82, 105.

33. Lee Grant to Gompers, June 27, 28, 1905, *AFL Corr.* and *GLB.*

34. *Proceedings,* First Convention, I.W.W., pp. 68–70, 142–47, 148–51.

35. *Ibid.,* pp. 4–5, 143, 153, 359, 506, 577.

36. *Ibid.,* pp. 220, 247–48.

37. *Ibid.,* pp. 229, 232, 240.

38. *Ibid.,* pp. 230, 233, 244–46.

39. *Ibid.,* pp. 228–31.

40. Donald Kennedy McKee, "The Intellectual and Historical Influence Shaping the Political Theory of Daniel De Leon," unpublished Ph.D. thesis, Columbia University, 1955, p. 14.

41. *Proceedings,* First Convention, I.W.W., pp. 294–95; Lee Grant to Gompers, July 4, 1905, *AFL Corr.* and *GLB.*

42. *Proceedings,* First Convention, I.W.W., pp. 170, 180–85, 193, 197–98, 213–15, 248, 269, 569.

43. *Ibid.,* pp. 154, 298–99, 496, 534–35, 563, 575.

44. Lee Grant to Gompers, July 8, 1905, *AFL Corr.* and *GLB.*

CHAPTER 2

1. Vernon H. Jensen, *Heritage of Conflict: Labor Relations in the Nonferrous Metals Industry up to 1930,* Ithaca, N.Y., pp. 198–99.

2. *Miners' Magazine,* Jan. 11, 1906, p. 5; Jan. 18, 1906, pp. 6–7.

3. James McParland to Governor Gooding, Jan. 8, 1906, McParland Report, in Pinkerton Reports relating to the Western Federation of Miners, 1906–1907. From the Hawley and Borah Manuscripts, Idaho Historical Society. (Hereinafter cited as *Pinkerton Reports.*)

4. McParland Report, Jan. 10, 13, 1906, *Pinkerton Reports.*

5. McParland Report, Jan. 22, 1906, *Pinkerton Reports.*

6. McParland Report, Jan. 25, 1906, *Pinkerton Reports.*

7. *Ibid.*

8. "The Haywood Trial," *Outlook,* vol. LXXXVI, June 22, 1907, pp. 350–53.

9. McParland Report, March 16, 1907, *Pinkerton Reports.*

10. *Ibid.*

11. McParland Report, Feb. 3, 9, 1906, *Pinkerton Reports.*

12. McParland Report, Feb. 2, 1906, *Pinkerton Reports.*

13. James McParland to Hon. Luther M. Goddard, Feb. 9, 1906; McParland Report, Feb. 15, 1906, *Pinkerton Reports.*

14. McParland Report, Feb. 16, 1906, *Pinkerton Reports.*

15. *Ibid.*

16. McParland Report, Feb. 16, 17, 1906, *Pinkerton Reports.*

17. McParland Report, Feb. 18, 1906, *Pinkerton Reports.*

18. *Ibid.*

19. *Ibid.*

20. McParland Report, Feb. 20, 1906, *Pinkerton Reports.*

21. *Industrial Union Bulletin,* March 9, 1907.

22. McParland Report, March 12, 1907, *Pinkerton Reports.*

23. McParland to Joseph H. Hawley, Jan. 14, 1907; McParland to W. E. Borah, Aug. 14 1907; McParland Report, March 17, 1906, *Pinkerton Reports.*

24. U.S. 192 (1906); Arthur Weinberg, editor, *Attorney for the Damned,* New York, 1957, p. 412.

25. Copy of leaflet in *AFL Corr. See also* Chicago *Daily Socialist,* Feb. 24, 1906.

26. New York *Sun,* April 14, 1906; *Wilshire's Magazine,* May 1906.

27. Reprinted in Philip S. Foner, *Jack London: American Rebel,* New York, 1947, pp. 407–10.

28. Gompers to A.F. of L. Executive Council, Dec. 21, 1906, *AFL Corr.* and *GLB.*

29. Washington *Evening Star,* Jan. 21, 1907; New York *Evening Journal,* Jan. 21–22, 1907.

30. Letters to Gompers and Frank Morrison, Feb.–March 1907, *AFL Corr.; American Federationist,* May 1907, p. 334; Gompers to A.F. of L. Executive Council, March 30, 1907, *GLB.*

31. McParland Report, May 19, 1907, *Pinkerton Reports.*

32. *The Worker,* March 30, 1907.

33. New York *Tribune,* May 2, 1907; Chicago *Daily Socialist,* May 20, 1907; *Industrial Worker,* April–May 1907; "Will Papa Die?," in *Industrial Worker,* April 1907.

34. William A. Pinkerton to Gov. Gooding, enclosing report of G.S.D., New York, Jan. 20, 1907, *Pinkerton Reports.*

35. Roosevelt to Lawrence F. Abbott, April 28, 1906; Roosevelt to Lyman Abbott, July 10, 1906, Theodore Roosevelt Papers, Library of Congress. (Hereinafter cited as *TRP.*)

36. McParland Report, May 9, 1906, *Pinkerton Reports.*

37. New York *Tribune*, April 3, 8, 1907; *Miners' Magazine*, April 11, 1907, pp. 5–6; Chicago *Daily Socialist*, April 4, May 20, 1907; Chicago *Record-Herald*, May 20, 1907.

38. Washington *Herald*, April 25, 1907; Roosevelt to Honore Jaxon, April 22, 1907, *TRP*; Chicago *Record-Herald*, April 25–27, 1907.

39. *Industrial Union Bulletin*, March 16, 1907.

40. For an indication of the international attention aroused by the trial, *see Appeal to Reason*, June 22, 1907.

41. Terre Haute *Post*, in Eugene V. Debs Scrapbooks, vol. 8, Tamiment Institute Library, New York City. (Hereinafter cited as *TIL.*)

42. Irving Stone, *Clarence Darrow for the Defense*, Garden City, N.Y., 1941, p. 221; Opt. #19 Report, Aug. 26, 1907, *Pinkerton Reports.*

43. McParland to Gov. Gooding, March 5, 1907, *Pinkerton Reports.*

44. Gov. Gooding to Roosevelt, April 10, 1907, *TRP*. My emphasis, *P.S.F.*

45. McParland to Jas. H. Hawley, April 6, 1907; McParland Report, April 11, 1907, *Pinkerton Reports.*

46. Report of #21, April 14, 1907; McParland to Wm. A. Ernst, May 23, 1907; McParland Report, April 19, 1907; McParland to Jas. H. Hawley, Jan. 10, 1907, *Pinkerton Reports.*

47. McParland Report, April 26, 1906, *Pinkerton Reports*. My emphasis, *P.S.F.*

48. Fremont Wood, *The Introductory Chapter to the History of the Trials of Moyer, Haywood, and Pettibone*, Caldwell, Idaho, pp. 23–24.

49. Luke Grant, "Orchard's Testimony," *Outlook*, June 15, 1907, pp. 303–04; *Miners' Magazine*, May 9, 16, 23, 30, June 6, 13, 20, 1907; *Weekly People*, June 8, 15, 22, 1907; McParland Report, May 16, 1907, Pinkerton Reports.

50. Weinberg, *op. cit.*, pp. 443–87; Stone, *op. cit.*, pp. 236–37; Haywood, *op. cit.*, pp. 214–16; *Wilshire's Magazine*, Sept. 1907.

51. *The New York Times*, July 28–29, 1907.

52. *Appeal to Reason*, Aug. 17, 1907; Seattle *Socialist*, Aug. 31, 1907.

53. *Appeal to Reason*, Jan. 11, 1908.

54. Roosevelt to Whitelaw Reid, July 29, 1907, *TRP.*

CHAPTER 3

1. Gompers to John B. Lennon, July 14, 1905, *GLB; American Federationist*, Aug. 1905, pp. 514–16; Gompers to W. D. Ryan, July 6, 1905, *GLB.*

2. *International Socialist Review*, vol. VI, Sept. 1905, p. 182; Gompers to John B. Lennon, July 14, 1905, *GLB.*

3. *Voice of Labor*, June, 1905; *International Socialist Review*, vol. VI, Aug. 1905, pp. 65–67, 85–86.

4. *Writings and Speeches of Eugene V. Debs*, pp. 171–72.

5. *Social-Democratic Herald*, Aug. 7, 14, 1905; New York *Forward*, Aug. 25, 1905, Jan. 12, 1906; *The Worker*, May 12, 1906; Cleveland *Citizen*, Jan. 8, 16, 1906.

6. Chicago *Socialist*, Dec. 23, 1905; *Miners' Magazine*, Oct. 26, 1905, p. 13; Aug. 30, 1906, p. 9; *Social-Democratic Herald*, Aug. 12, 1905; Ray Ginger, *The Bending Cross: A Biography of Eugene Victor Debs*, New Brunswick, N.J., 1949, p. 240; *The Industrial Worker*, Sept. 1906.

7. Pittsburgh *Labor World*, Aug. 10, 1905.

8. Jas. O'Connell to Gompers, Oct. 26, 1905, *AFL Corr.*

9. *International Socialist Review*, vol. VI, Jan. 1906, pp. 434–35.

10. Thomas J. Sheridan to John Mitchell, Nov. 27, 1905, *AFL Corr.*

11. Gompers to David U. Williams, April 5, 1906; Gompers to John Mitchell, April 6, 1906; Gompers to Yonkers (N.Y.) Federation of Labor, Aug. 4, 1905; Jas. F. Valentine to Gompers, Dec. 23, 1905, *AFL Corr.*

12. John Golden to Gompers, Mar. 12, April 1, 1906; J. T. Windell to Gompers, Dec. 14, 1905, *AFL Corr.*

13. *Proceedings*, Second Convention, I.W.W., 1906, pp. 63, 71–72; Donald B. Robinson, *Spotlight on a Union: The Story of the United Hatters, Cap and Millinery Workers International Union*, New York, 1948, p. 183; Fred Thompson, *The I.W.W.: Its First Fifty Years, 1905–1955*, Chicago, 1955, p. 24.

14. Henry Fagin, "The Industrial Workers of the World in Detroit and Michigan

From the Period of Beginnings Through the World War," unpublished M.A. thesis, Wayne University, 1937, pp. 14–22; Detroit *Times*, Oct. 5, 12, Dec. 1, 21, 1905; Jan. 11, 18, 1906; *The Rule or Ruin Policy of the Industrial Workers*, pamphlet, n.d.; *The Deceit of the I.W.W. A Year's Record of the Activity of the I.W.W. in the Cloth Hat and Cap Trade*, pamphlet, New York, September 1906; *The Industrial Worker*, Jan.–Feb. 1906; *Daily People*, May 2, 23, 1906.

15. Louis Levine, *The Women Garment Workers*, New York, 1924, pp. 108–09; Martin A. Cohen, "Jewish Immigrants and American Trade Unions," unpublished Ph.D. thesis, University of Chicago, 1941, p. 109; Edwin Fenton, "Immigrants and Unions: A Case Study, Italians and American Labor, 1870–1920," unpublished Ph.D. thesis, Harvard University, 1957, p. 481.

16. Cohen, *op. cit.*, pp. 122–26, 142.

17. *The Industrial Worker*, Feb., March 1906; Chicago *Tribune*, Jan. 23, 1906.

18. *The Industrial Worker*, Jan. 1906.

19. *Ibid.*, Jan. Feb., March 1906.

20. *Ibid.*, May 1906.

21. *Ibid.*, Jan., April, Sept. 1906; Thompson, *op. cit.*, pp. 23–24.

22. *The Industrial Worker*, Aug. 1906.

23. *North American Times* reprinted in *Ibid.*, July 1906.

24. *Weekly People*, Sept. 2, 9, 1905; Brissenden, *op. cit.*, pp. 129–31, 181–82; *The Industrial Worker*, Jan.–Nov. 1906; *Proceedings*, Second Convention, I.W.W., 1906, p. 60; George Barnett, "Membership of American Trade Unions," *Quarterly Journal of Economics*, vol. XXX, Aug. 1916, p. 846.

25. Detroit *Times*, Feb. 18, 1907; Fagin, *op. cit.*, p. 36.

26. *The Industrial Worker*, Jan., Feb., July 1906.

27. *Miners' Magazine*, Sept. 6, 1906, pp. 7, 12; Thompson, *op. cit.*, pp. 25–26; *Industrial Union Bulletin*, March 16, 1907.

28. *Miners' Magazine*, Sept. 6, 1906, pp. 7, 12; Detroit *Times*, May 10, 1906; Fagin, *op. cit.*, pp. 26–27.

29. *Industrial Workers of the World Bulletin*, No. 4, Dec. 1, 1906; *Weekly People*, Dec. 25, 1920.

30. C. O. Sherman to Frank Morrison, April 17, Sept. 23, 1903, Nov. 7, 1904, Feb. 15, 1905; Frank Morrison to C. O. Sherman, Feb. 18, 1905, *AFL Corr.*

31. Thompson, *op. cit.*, pp. 24–25.

32. *Ibid.*, p. 26.

33. *Proceedings*, Second I.W.W. Convention, 1906, pp. 271, 610; *I.W.W. Bulletin*, No. 4, Dec. 1, 1906; Chicago *Socialist*, Jan. 5, 1907.

34. *Industrial Union News*, March 1914.

35. *The Industrial Worker*, Jan., March, May 1907; Brissenden, *op. cit.*, pp. 136–54; *Industrial Union Bulletin*, March 2, 1907.

36. *Proceedings*, Second I.W.W. Convention, 1906, pp. 304–06, 309–12.

37. *Ibid.*, p. 316.

38. *Miners' Magazine*, July 26, 1906, p. 13; *Proceedings*, Second I.W.W. Convention, 1906, pp. 421, 545, 557.

39. *Weekly People*, Nov. 17, 1906. Don K. McKee, "Daniel De Leon: A Reappraisal," *Labor History*, Fall, 1960, p. 277.

40. *Proceedings*, Second I.W.W. Convention, 1906, p. 589.

41. *Ibid.*, pp. 65–66, 68, 309.

42. *Ibid.*, pp. 609–11.

43. *The Industrial Worker*, Jan. 1907; *Proceedings*, W.F. of M. Convention, 1906, p. 132; Jensen, *Heritage of Conflict*, pp. 184–87.

44. Brissenden, *op. cit.*, p. 151; *Proceedings*, W.F. of M. Convention, 1907, pp. 788, 799.

45. *Industrial Union Bulletin*, July 13, 28, Aug. 24, Nov. 16, Dec. 14, 1907, Jan. 25, 1908; *Miners' Magazine*, Jan. 9, 1908, p. 5, July 23, 1908, pp. 5, 7, July 30, 1908, p. 5; *Proceedings*, W.F. of M. Convention, 1908, pp. 21–23.

46. *Proceedings*, Second I.W.W. Convention, 1906, p. 6; *International Socialist Review*, vol. VI, April 1906, p. 631; *Social-Democratic Herald*, June 9, 1906; *The Industrial Worker*, Jan. 1906.

47. *International Socialist Review*, vol. VII, Nov. 1906, pp. 311–12, Feb. 1907, p. 507, July 1907, p. 47, vol. VIII, March 1908, pp. 538–47; Chicago *Socialist*, Oct. 13, 1906; Detroit *Times*, Oct. 3, 1906.

CHAPTER 4

1. Brissenden, *op. cit.*, pp. 182–83, 207, 211; Gompers to John Mitchell, Aug. 8, 1907, GLB.

2. *Industrial Union Bulletin*, March 9, May 18, July 20, 1907, Feb. 29, April 11, July 13, 1908; Fenton, *op, cit.*, pp. 176–77.

3. *Industrial Union Bulletin*, July 13, 1907.
4. *Ibid.*, March 23, April 6, 13, 1907; *Solidarity*, March 26, 1910.
5. *Industrial Union Bulletin*, April 11, May 9, 16, 1908.
6. Brissenden, *op. cit.*, pp. 122–23; *Industrial Union Bulletin*, Sept. 14, 1907.
7. Bridgeport *Post*, July 16, 20, 1907.
8. *Ibid.*, July 16, 1907.
9. *Ibid.*, July 19, 1907.
10. *Ibid.*, July 20, 1907.
11. *Ibid.*, July 16, 1907.
12. *Ibid.*, July 22, 1907.
13. *Industrial Union Bulletin*, July 27, 1907.
14. Stewart Reed to Gompers, Aug. 18, 22, 1907, *AFL Corr.*
15. Bridgeport *Post*, Aug. 17-20, 1907; *Industrial Union Bulletin*, Aug. 31, 1907.
16. Somerset *Reporter*, Jan. 24, 1907; *Industrial Union Bulletin*, March 2, 1907; *Industrial Solidarity*, March 10, 1931.
17. Somerset *Reporter*, Jan. 31, Feb. 7, 1907.
18. *Ibid.*, Jan. 24, 1907.
19. *Ibid.*, Feb. 28, 1907.
20. *Ibid.*, April 30, May 8, 1907; *Industrial Union Bulletin*, April 27, Sept. 14, 1907; *Industrial Solidarity*, March 10, 1931.
21. F. W. Thompson in *Industrial Solidarity*, Feb. 17, 1931; *The Union* (Schenectady, N.Y.), Dec. 10, 11, 1906; *Weekly People*, Dec. 22, 1906; *Industrial Union Bulletin*, March 16, 1907.
22. R.D.G., "The First Sit-Down," *Industrial Worker*, Aug. 18, 1945.
23. *The Union* (Schenectady, N.Y.), Dec. 11, 1906.
24. *Ibid.*, Dec. 11, 1906.
25. *Ibid.*, Dec. 13, 1906.
26. *Ibid.*, Dec. 20, 21, 1906.
27. Portland *Oregonian*, March 10, 1907.
28. *Ibid.*, March 8, 1907; *Industrial Union Bulletin*, March 16, 1907.
29. Portland *Oregonian*, March 7, 1907.
30. *Cf.* Paul Abramson, "The Industrial Workers of the World in the Northwest Lumber Industry," unpublished B.A. thesis, Division of History and Social Science, Reed College, May 1952, *passim.*
31. Portland *Oregonian*, March 8, 9, 12, 1907.
32. *Ibid.*, March 7, 10, 1907; *Industrial Union Bulletin*, March 16, 30, 1907.
33. Portland *Oregonian*, March 12, 15, 1907; *Industrial Union Bulletin*, March 23, 1907.
34. C. H. Gram to Gompers, March 15,

1907, *AFL Corr.;* Portland *Oregonian*, March 15, 1907.
35. *Industrial Union Bulletin*, April 20, May 18, 1907.
36. Portland *Oregonian*, March 25, 1907; Vernon H. Jensen, "Labor Relations in the Northwest Lumber Industry," unpublished Ph.D. thesis, University of California, 1939, pp. 39–40.
37. *Industrial Union Bulletin*, April 13, 1908.
38. Vincent St. John, *op. cit.*, pp. 17-18; *Industrial Union Bulletin*, May 18, 1907.
39. Laura A. White, "Rise of the Industrial Workers of the World in Goldfield, Nevada," unpublished M.A. thesis, University of Nebraska, 1912, pp. 25–26.
40. *Ibid.*, pp. 15-16, 28-63; *Industrial Union Bulletin*, March 30, 1907; St. John, *op. cit.*, p. 18, *Appeal to Reason*, April 4, 1908.
41. *Miners' Magazine*, Jan. 31, 1907, p. 12; White, *op. cit.*, pp. 48-50.
42. Russel R. Elliot, "Labor Troubles in the Mining Camp at Goldfield, Nevada, 1906–1908," *Pacific Historical Review*, vol. IX, Nov. 1950, p. 374; White, *op. cit.*, pp. 98-100; Grant Hamilton to Gompers, March 2, 1907, *AFL Corr.*
43. Reprinted in *Industrial Union Bulletin*, March 30, 1907.
44. *Ibid.*
45. *Proceedings*, W.F. of M. Convention, 1907, pp. 33-35.
46. Reprinted in *Industrial Union Bulletin*, May 18, 1907.
47. *Ibid.*, April 6, May 25, 1907; *Proceedings*, W.F. of M. Convention, 1907, pp. 34, 214-17; White, *op. cit.*, 101-10; Elliot, *op. cit.*, p. 374.
48. *Miners' Magazine*, Jan. 16, 1908, p. 4; Elliot, *op. cit.*, p. 378; *House Doc. 607*, ser. 5374, 60th Cong., 1st Sess., p. 21.
49. John Sparks to Theodore Roosevelt, Dec. 3-4, 1907, *TRP.*
50. *House Doc. No. 607*, *op. cit.*, pp. 3-5; New York *Tribune*, Dec. 7, 1907; *Rocky Mountain News*, Dec. 12, 1907; Jensen, *Heritage of Conflict*, p. 230; *Engineering and Mining Journal*, Dec. 21, 1907, p. 1181; *Industrial Union Bulletin*, Dec. 21, 1907; *Cong. Record*, 60th Cong., 1st Sess., p. 1484; Edwin Anderson to Jonathan Dolliver, Dec. 16, 1907, Jonathan Dolliver Papers, Library of Congress; *Miners' Magazine*, Dec. 12, 1907, p. 6.
51. *House Doc. 607*, *op. cit.*, pp. 23-26; Lawrence O. Murray, Herbert Knox

Smith, and Charles P. Neill to Theodore Roosevelt, Dec. 20, 1907, *TRP.*

52. *Industrial Union Bulletin,* March 2, 1907.
53. Elliot, *op. cit.,* p. 383.
54. *Industrial Union Bulletin,* March 30, 1907.
55. *Proceedings of Third Convention of the Industrial Workers of the World, Official Report No. 3,* pp. 1–2.
56. Chicago *Tribune,* Sept. 4, 1907.
57. Daniel De Leon, *As To Politics,* New York, 1907; *Industrial Union Bulletin,* March 2, April 6, 13, May 4, 1907.
58. Brissenden, *op. cit.,* p. 188; *Proceedings,* Third Convention, I.W.W., p. 5.
59. *Industrial Union Bulletin,* Oct. 5, 1907.
60. *Solidarity,* vol. II, May 15, 1908, p. 16; Leah H. Feder, *Unemployment Relief in Periods of Depression. A Study of Measures Adopted in Certain American Cities, 1857 through 1912,* New York, 1936, pp. 197–98.
61. Fenton, *op. cit.,* pp. 180–81; *Solidarity,* Feb. 25, 1911; *Industrial Union Bulletin,* Oct. 24, 1908.
62. *Industrial Union Bulletin,* Feb. 22, May 23, 1908, Feb. 27, 1909, Fagin, *op. cit.,* p. 33.
63. *Industrial Union Bulletin,* Sept. 19, 1908, March 6, 1909.
64. St. Louis *Post-Dispatch,* Jan. 14–15, 1908; Boston *Herald,* Jan. 24–30, 1908; Chicago *Tribune,* Jan. 19, 1908.
65. Reprinted in *Industrial Union Bulletin,* Feb. 29, 1908.
66. *Industrial Union Bulletin,* Sept. 19, Dec. 12, 1908; Philadelphia *Press,* Aug. 25, 1908; Elizabeth Gurley Flynn, *I Speak My Own Piece: Autobiography of 'The Rebel Girl,'* New York, 1955, pp. 42–70.
67. *Industrial Union Bulletin,* March 14, 1908; Grace L. Stimson, *Rise of the Labor Movement in Los Angeles,* Berkeley and Los Angeles, 1955, pp. 308, 318.
68. Seattle *Times,* Jan. 21, 25, 1908.
69. *Industrial Union Bulletin,* May 16, 1908.
70. *Ibid.,* May 23, July 25, 1908.
71. *Industrial Union Bulletin,* March 2, 1907.
72. *Ibid.,* Sept. 7, 14, 28, 1907.
73. *Proceedings,* A.F. of L. Convention, 1907, pp. 218–19, 266; *Social-Democratic Herald,* Dec. 14, 1907; Socialist Party, *Proceedings of the National Convention, Held at Chicago, May 10–17,* 1908, pp. 94–102, 234–43, 324.
74. F. W. Thompson in *Industrial Solidarity,* April 14, 1931.

75. *Industrial Union Bulletin,* Nov. 9, 1907; Feb. 1 to April 25, 1908.
76. *Ibid.,* May 2, 23, June 27, 1908.
77. *Ibid.,* March 16, April 25, May 2, 23, 1908.
78. J. H. Walsh in *ibid.,* June 27, 1908; *Daily People,* March 13, 1908.
79. *Industrial Union Bulletin,* Oct. 10, 1908.
80. Brissenden, *op. cit.,* pp. 228–29.
81. *Industrial Union Bulletin,* Oct. 24, 1908.
82. *Ibid.,* Nov. 7, 1908.
83. *Ibid.,* Nov. 7, 1908; Feb. 27, 1909.
84. John B. Lennon to Gompers, Nov. 9, 1908, *AFL Corr.*
85. *Proceedings,* W.F. of M. Convention, 1908, p. 18.
86. Brissenden, *op. cit.,* p. 357.

CHAPTER 5

1. Reprinted in *Industrial Worker,* June 26, 1912.
2. *Solidarity,* Oct. 19, 1912.
3. Ralph Chaplin, *Wobbly: The Rough-and-Tumble Story of an American Radical,* Chicago, 1948, pp. 172, 180; *Solidarity,* Oct. 7, 1911; Fred W. Thompson, *The I.W.W.: Its First Fifty Years,* p. 40.
4. Vincent St. John, "How to Join the I.W.W.," *Industrial Worker,* Oct. 26, 1910.
5. *Industrial Union Bulletin,* Feb. 27, 1908; *Industrial Worker,* Feb. 26, 1910, Dec. 14, 1911.
6. Carleton Parker, *The Casual Laborer and Other Essays,* New York, 1920, p. 15; Rexford G. Tugwell, "The Casual of the Woods," *The Survey,* vol. XLIV, 1920, p. 472; Fred Bechdolt in San Francisco *Call,* March 2, 1911: *Solidarity,* Nov. 19, 1910.
7. Samuel Gompers, *Labor and the Employer,* New York, 1920, p. 42.
8. *Industrial Union Bulletin,* May 23, 1908; *Report of Commission on Industrial Relations,* vol. V, p. 4933.
9. *Industrial Worker,* Feb. 26, July 30, Aug. 6, Sept. 10, Oct. 15, Nov. 9, 1910, Jan. 19, July 20, 1911; Aug. 11, 22, Sept. 26, Nov. 7, Dec. 12, 19, 1912; June 5, 12, July 17, 1913, March 18, 1918; interview with Elizabeth Gurley Flynn, Feb. 10, 1964.
10. Robert L. Tyler, "Rebels of the Woods and Fields: A Study of the I.W.W. in the Pacific Northwest," Unpublished Ph.D. thesis, University of Oregon, 1953, p. 25.

11. *Solidarity*, Dec. 17, 1910; Nov. 28, 1914; Feb. 13, July 10, 1915.
12. *Ibid.*, Sept. 17, 1910; July 15, 1911; Nov. 2, 1914; Hyman Weintraub, "The I.W.W. in California, 1906–1931," unpublished Ph.D. thesis, University of California, Berkeley, 1947, pp. 64–65; *International Socialist Review*, vol. XII, Feb. 1912, p. 65.
13. Tyler, *op. cit.*, p. 18.
14. *Ibid.* For a contrary view, *see* Donald M. Barnes, "The Ideology of the Industrial Workers of the World," unpublished Ph.D. thesis, Washington State University, 1962, pp. 198–99.
15. *Solidarity*, June 4, 1910; April 11, 1914; *History of the I.W.W.*, Chicago, ca., 1913, p. 12; *Industrial Worker*, June 6, 1912.
16. Duluth *News Tribune*, July 4, 1916.
17. Carleton H. Parker, "The Economic Basis of the I.W.W.," *More Truth About the I.W.W.*, Chicago, 1918, pp. 10–11; Walter V. Woehlbe, *Truth About the I.W.W.*, Chicago, 1918, pp. 10–11; Walter V. Woehlbe, "The Red Rebels Declare War," *Sunset*, Sept. 1917, p. 33.
18. Weintraub, *op. cit.*, pp. 377–78; *Industrial Worker*, April 22, 1909.
19. *Industrial Worker*, Sept. 17, Nov. 24, 1910; May 8, 15, 29, 1913; *Solidarity*, May 28, 1910.
20. *See Solidarity*, May 14, 21, 1910; *Industrial Worker*, Sept. 10, 1910; Jan. 2, March 6, 27, 1913.
21. "Justice for the Negro—How Can He Get It," four-page leaflet, Wisconsin State Historical Society, Elizabeth Gurley Flynn Collection. (Hereinafter cited as *WSHS*.)
22. *The New Review*, Sept. 1913, pp. 747–48.
23. *Solidarity*, Nov. 26, 1910.
24. *Industrial Worker*, Dec. 26, 1912.
25. *Ibid.*, Aug. 1, 15, 1914.
26. *Ibid.*, June 4, 1910; *Solidarity*, June 8, 1912.
27. *Solidarity*, June 6, 1914; "To Colored Workingmen and Workingwomen," I.W.W. leaflet, Elizabeth Gurley Flynn Collection, *WSHS; Voice of Labor* reprinted in *Solidarity*, June 24, 1911.
28. Philadelphia *North American*, May 14–30, 1913; *Industrial Worker*, July 28, 1945.
29. Sterling D. Spero and Abram L. Harris, *The Black Worker: The Negro and the Labor Movement*, New York, 1931, p. 331; Barnes, *op. cit.*, p. 21.
30. *Industrial Worker*, Feb. 3, 1917; Sept. 19, 1919.
31. Elizabeth Gurley Flynn, "Women and Unionism," *Solidarity*, May 27, 1911.
32. *Solidarity*, Dec. 19, 1914.
33. *Industrial Worker*, May 4, 1918; *Solidarity*, Dec. 25, 1909; March 4, 1910; Feb. 11, 1911; *The Lumber Industry and its Workers*, no date or author given, third edition, p. 60; *Solidarity*, March 4, 1910.
34. *Industrial Worker*, July 31, 1912.
35. *Solidarity*, March 26, July 23, 1910; Duluth *News Tribune*, July 13, Aug. 3, 1916; Geo. Child to C. F. Lambert, Aug. 4, 1915, Department of Justice Files, Pardon Board, Appeals, National Archives. Hereinafter cited as *NA*.
36. New York *Call*, Jan. 28, 1912.
37. Quoted by John G. Brooks, *American Syndicalism: The I.W.W.*, New York, 1913, p. 103.
38. *Industrial Worker*, July 1, 1909; Feb. 22, 29, Sept. 19, 1912; *Solidarity*, Nov. 22, 1913; Oct. 16, 1915.
39. James Connell, "The Red Flag," *I.W.W. Songs*, p. 2; sentence order changed, *P.S.F.; Solidarity*, Dec. 18, 1909; May 11, 1912; July 3, 1915; mimeographed extract from *Industrial Worker*, in File, 54379/76, *NA*.
40. Spokane *Chronicle*, reprinted in *Industrial Worker*, July 24, 1913; Seattle *Post-Intelligencer*, July 19–21, 1913.
41. Quoted in Carleton H. Parker, *The Casual Laborer and Other Essays*, p. 102.
42. Vincent St. John, *The I.W.W.: Its History, Structure and Method*, pp, 2, 17; *Solidarity*, Feb 19, July 2, 1910; Dec. 23, 1911; March 30, 1912; Jan. 14, 1913; "B. Itso" in *Industrial Worker*, Aug. 22, 1917.
43. *I.W.W.—One Big Union for All the Workers: The Greatest Thing on Earth*, Chicago, n.d., p. 11; Brissenden, *op. cit.*, p. 98; Vincent St. John, *op. cit.*, pp. 2, 14.
44. Brissenden, *op. cit.*, p. 315; Barnes, *op. cit.*, p. 78.
45. *Industrial Worker*, April 17, 1913.
46. *Ibid.*, Nov. 2, 16, 1911; May 1, 1912.
47. *Solidarity*, July 2, 1910. *See also* issues of Dec. 23, 1911 and March 30, 1912.
48. *Report of Commission on Industrial Relations*, vol. V, p. 4241; Seattle *Post-Intelligencer*, April 7, 1912; Phillips Russell, "Strike Tactics," *The New Review*, March 29, 1913, pp. 406–07.
49. Mary Marcy, *Shop Talks on Economics*, Chicago, n.d., pp. 34–35; emphasis in original, *P.S.F.*; André Tridon, *The New*

Unionism, New York, 1913, p. 32; *Industrial Worker*, Sept. 19, 1923 and reprinted in Charlotte Todes, *Labor and Lumber*, New York, 1931, p. 181.

50. *Solidarity*, Sept. 10, 1910; *Industrial Worker*, Oct. 24, 1912.

51. New York *Sun*, April 14, 1912.

52. *Solidarity*, Feb. 5, 1910; Oct. 28, 1911; *Industrial Worker*, May 29, 1913.

53. *Solidarity*, Oct. 21, 1911.

54. *Ibid.*, Aug. 9, 1913; William E. Trautmann, *Industrial Unionism*, Chicago, 1909, p. 16.

55. Haywood in *The Industrial Syndicalist*, vol. I, Oct. 1910, copy in London School of Economics; *Solidarity*, Jan. 15, 1910; interview with Arthur Boose, Portland I.W.W. leader, quoted in Paul Abramson, *op. cit.*, p. 10; *Stenographic Report of the Eighth Convention of the Industrial Workers of the World*, Chicago, 1913, p. 79.

56. *Solidarity*, Sept. 28, 1912; Vincent St. John, *op. cit.*, p. 17; *Report of Commission on Industrial Relations*, vol. II, p. 1451.

57. Joseph J. Ettor, "I.W.W. vs. A.F. of L.," *The New Review*, May, 1914, pp. 277, 280; *Solidarity*, Sept. 18, 1915; *Industrial Worker*, June 24, July 1, 1909.

58. *I.W.W.—One Big Union for All the Workers, op. cit.; Solidarity*, Jan. 15, March 4, April 9, 23, July 30, 1910; Jan. 14, July 29, 1911.

59. *Industrial Worker*, June 20, July 4, 25, 1912; April 10, May 1, 1913.

60. *International Socialist Review*, vol. XI, Feb. 1911, p. 492; *Industrial Worker*, Jan. 15, July 27, 1911; *Emancipator*, Feb. 4, March 11, April 22, 29, 1911; Fagin, *op. cit.*, pp. 65–68.

61. *Industrial Worker*, Oct. 12, 1911.

62. *Solidarity*, Jan. 5, 1910; *Industrial Worker*, Sept. 5, 1912.

63. Wilfred H. Crook, *The General Strike*, Chapel Hill, N. Car., 1931, pp. 3–5, 11–12, 20–27; G. D. H. Cole, *A History of Socialist Thought, III, The Second International, 1880–1914*, London, 1956, Part I, pp. 329–30.

64. *Proceedings*, First Convention, I.W.W., pp. 170, 184.

65. William D. Haywood, *The General Strike*, Chicago, 1911, p. 2. *See also* Barnes, *op. cit.*, p. 34 and John E. Crow, "Ideology and Organization: A Case Study of the Industrial Workers of the World," unpublished M.A. thesis, University of Chicago, 1958, pp. 40, 41, 45, 108.

66. Grover H. Perry, *The Revolutionary I.W.W.*, Chicago, n.d., pp. 11–12.

67. *Industrial Worker*, May 15, 1913; Oakley Johnson, *The Day is Coming: Life and Work of Charles E. Ruthenberg*, New York, 1957, p. 147.

68. *Industrial Worker*, Feb. 5, 1910. Emphasis in the original. *P.S.F.*

69. *Ibid.*, Aug. 13, 1910; *Solidarity*, Oct. 24, 1914.

70. *Industrial Worker*, April 13, 1918; *What Is the I.W.W.? A Candid Statement of its Principles, Objects.*, n.p., n.d. Emphasis in original.

71. Perry, *op. cit.*, pp. 11–12; *Industrial Worker*, May 1, 1912.

72. Perry, *op. cit.*, pp. 11–12; *Industrial Worker*, Aug. 13, 1910.

73. *Cf.* Karl Marx, *Critique of the Gotha Programme*, New York, 1938.

74. *Industrial Worker*, Aug. 13, 1910; *The Lumber Industry and Its Workers, op. cit.*, pp. 84–88; Perry, *op. cit.*, p. 12; *International Socialist Review*, vol. XII, Feb. 1912, p. 136.

75. *Proceedings*, First Convention, I.W.W., p. 6.

76. Kansas City *Times*, reprinted in *Industrial Worker*, Nov. 9, 1911; Abner E. Woodruff, *Evolution of American Agriculture*, Chicago, n.d., p. 8.

77. *Report of Commission on Industrial Relations*, vol. XI, pp. 10, 582; Barnes, *op. cit.*, pp. 46–47; interview with Elizabeth Gurley Flynn, Jan. 31, 1964.

78. *Industrial Worker*, July 24, 1913; Todes, *op. cit.*, pp. 128–29.

79. *Industrial Worker*, Aug. 21, 1913.

80. *Industrial Worker*, Sept. 7, 1911.

81. *Ibid.*, Feb. 26, April 2, Nov. 21, 1910; Sept. 7, Oct. 12, 1911; Letter of John Pancner in *ibid.*, Sept. 14, 1911.

82. *Ibid.*, Feb. 23, 1911; Brissenden, *op. cit.*, pp. 311–12.

83. *Proceedings of the Eighth Convention of the Industrial Workers of the World*, Chicago, 1913, pp. 69–112; Robert L. Tyler, "The I.W.W. and the West," *American Quarterly*, vol. XII, Summer, 1960, p. 178.

CHAPTER 6

1. Vincent St. John, *op. cit.*, pp. 17–18; *Report of Commission on Industrial Relations*, vol. I, p. 29; *International Socialist Review*, vol. XIII, Sept. 1912, p. 247; *Solidarity*, Nov. 5, 12, 1910; *In-*

dustrial Worker, July 3, 1913; Voice of the People, Oct. 9, 1913.

2. Industrial Worker, March 12, 1910; July 3, 1913; Voice of the People, Oct. 9, 1913; Report of Commission on Industrial Relations, vol. II, p. 1440; What We Are and the Way Out, New Castle, Pa., no date, but marked "written, March 1911," p. 23; The Wooden Shoe, Jan. 2, 1914.

3. Solidarity, Dec. 18, 1909; March 16, 1912; Industrial Worker, April 25, 1912; Voice of the People, Oct. 16, 1913.

4. Sharon C. Smith, "Intellectuals and the Industrial Workers of the World," unpublished M.A. thesis, University of Wisconsin, pp. 52–53.

5. Fred Isler in Solidarity, Dec. 3, 1910, and ibid., Jan. 20, April 27, 1912.

6. Parker, The Casual Laborer, p. 101; Industrial Worker, May 6, 1916.

7. Industrial Worker, Aug. 1, 1912: Thomas Howard McEnroe, "The Industrial Workers of the World: Theories, Organizational Problems, and Appeals, as Revealed in the Industrial Worker," unpublished Ph.D. thesis, University of Minnesota, August 1960, pp. 62–63.

8. Cf. What We Are At and The Way Out, op. cit.

9. Seattle Post-Intelligencer, April 7, 1912.

10. Industrial Union Bulletin, Feb. 27, 1909.

11. Industrial Worker, March 12, 1910.

12. Ibid., Sept. 13, 1919.

13. Tyler, "Rebels of the Woods and Fields," op. cit., pp. 19–20.

14. D. D. Lescohier, "With the I.W.W. in the Wheat Lands," Harper's, vol. CXVII, Aug. 1923, p. 375; "A Day in A Country Library," Industrial Worker, Aug. 12, 1916.

15. Solidarity, Dec. 23, 1911, Jan. 13, 20, 1912, Dec. 19, 1914.

16. Industrial Union Bulletin, May 16, 1908.

17. Industrial Worker, June 6, 1912.

18. Barrie Stavis and Frank Harmon, The Songs of Joe Hill, New York, 1960, p. 3; Barrie Stavis, The Man Who Never Died: A Play About Joe Hill, With Notes on His Times, New York, 1954, pp. 3–114; Josh Dunson, "Songs of the American Labor Movement," Mainstream, Aug. 1962, pp. 44–48; Ralph Chaplin, "Joe Hill, A Biography," Industrial Pioneer, Nov. 1923, pp. 23–25; Archie Green, "John Neuhaus: Wobbly Folklorist," University of Illinois Bulletin, Institute of Labor and Industrial Relations, Reprint Series No. 88, Nov. 1960.

19. Marysville Democrat, Jan. 30, 1914; John D. Barry in San Francisco Bulletin, Jan. 31, 1914, both in "Scrapbooks of Clippings on the Wheatland Hop Field Riots, Wheatland, California, 1913–1915", University of California Library, Berkeley. (Hereinafter cited as WS.)

20. "I.W.W.," Outlook, July 6, 1912, p. 531: Industrial Worker, Feb. 8, 1912.

21. Sacramento Bee, Aug. 5, 1913, WS: Overland Monthly, Dec. 1924, p. 536; Duluth News Tribune, July 22, 1916.

22. Brissenden, op. cit., pp. 274–75; Parker, op. cit., pp. 105–06; Fred E. Hayes, Social Politics in the United States, New York, 1924, p. 235; Barnes, op. cit., pp. 174–81; William Z. Foster, American Trade Unionism, New York, 1947, p. 15; William English Walling, "Industrialism versus Socialism," International Socialist Review, vol. XIII, March 1913, p. 666; Ralph Edward Souers, "The Industrial Workers of the World," unpublished M.A. thesis, University of Chicago, 1913, pp. 31–33.

23. Solidarity, July 16, 1910; Industrial Union Bulletin, June 13, 1908; Feb. 27, 1909.

24. Solidarity, Feb. 15, 22, 29, 1913.

25. Ibid., April 29, Nov. 4, 1911, Nov. 1, 1913; Fenton, op. cit., pp. 183–85; Solidarity, July 1912; Industrial Worker, Jan. 9, 1913.

26. John Spargo, Syndicalism, Industrial Unionism and Socialism, New York, 1913, pp. 40–41.

27. Louis Levine, "Development of Syndicalism in the United States," op. cit., pp. 452–53; Solidarity, Sept. 14, 1912.

28. Industrial Worker, March 12, May 28, 1910; Solidarity, Oct. 28, 1911.

29. Industrial Worker, Jan. 1, 20, Feb. 6, 13, 20, 27, March 6, 13, 20, 27, April 3, 10, 24, 1913.

30. Brissenden, op. cit., p. 280; Solidarity, Sept. 11, 1915; Industrial Worker, May 29, Sept. 14, 1913.

31. Solidarity, Oct. 3, 1914.

32. Emil Pouget, Sabotage, Chicago, 1913, p. 14.

33. Industrial Worker, March 14, 1912, June 2, 1913.

34. William E. Walling, et. al., editors, The Socialism of Today, New York, 1916, pp. 382–83.

35. Solidarity, Feb. 25, 1911.

36. Industrial Worker, Sept. 5, 1912; Thompson, op. cit., p. 86.

37. Elizabeth Gurley Flynn, *Sabotage: The Conscious Withdrawal of the Workers' Efficiency*, Chicago, n.d., pp. 2–3; *Solidarity*, Feb. 25, 1911; *Industrial Worker*, Feb. 13, 1913; *The Wooden Shoe*, Jan. 22, 1914.

38. *Solidarity*, Aug. 10, 1912; Thompson, *op. cit.*, p. 86; Weintraub, *op. cit.*, p. 264.

39. Barnes, *op. cit.*, p. 146.

40. McEnroy, *op. cit.*, p. 190.

41. Eldridge F. Dowell, "A History of Criminal Syndicalism in the United States," *Johns Hopkins University Studies in Historical and Political and Social Science*, vol. LVII, Baltimore, 1939, p. 36. Emphasis in original. *P.S.F.*

42. *Cf.* Marion Dutton Savage, *Industrial Unionism in America*, New York, 1922, p. 97; Nelson Van Valen, "The Bolsheviki and the Orange Growers," *Pacific Historical Review*, vol. XXII, Feb. 1953, p. 41.

43. *Solidarity*, March 6, 1912; March 20, 1915.

44. *Industrial Worker*, March 12, 1910.

45. *Ibid.*, Oct. 19, 1912; *Solidarity*, July 25, 1914.

46. *An Open Letter from the I.W.W. to the State's Attorneys of California*, San Francisco, 1924, pp. 4–5; Justus Ebert, *The Trial of a New Society*, New York, 1912, p. 61; *Report of Commission on Industrial Relations*, vol. III, p. 2458; *Solidarity*, Dec. 24, 1910.

47. New York *Evening Post*, May 21, 1914; *Solidarity*, May 30, 1914.

48. M. E. Shusterich quoted in Duluth *News Tribune*, July 19, 1916.

49. *Twenty-Five Years of Industrial Unionism*, Chicago, n.d., p. 15.

50. *Industrial Worker*, May 20, 1909; Jan. 9, 1913; *Solidarity*, May 9, July 11, Nov. 28, 1914.

51. *Solidarity*, June 6, 1914.

52. *Industrial Worker*, May 20, 1909; Jan. 9, 1913; *Solidarity*, May 9, July 11, Nov. 28, 1914.

53. Elizabeth Gurley Flynn, "The Truth About the Paterson Strike," manuscript of a speech delivered January 31, 1914, p. 8. Copy in Labadie Collection, University of Michigan Library. For the complete text of Miss Flynn's speech, *see Rebel Voices: An I.W.W. Anthology*, edited, with introductions, by Joyce L. Kornbluh, Ann Arbor, Michigan, 1964, pp. 215–26.

54. Quoted in Thomas Taylor Hammond,

Lenin on Trade Unions and Revolution, 1893–1917, New York, 1957, p. 21.

55. *International Socialist Review*, vol. X, June 1910, p. 1120; *Solidarity*, June 17, 1911.

56. *Solidarity*, March 25, 1911; W. D. Haywood and J. J. Ettor in New York *World*, June 14, 1914. *See also Solidarity*, Aug. 20, 1910; May 24, 1913.

57. *Solidarity*, May 27, 1911; June 28, 1912; Elizabeth Gurley Flynn in *ibid.*, May 27, 1911 and in San Francisco *Bulletin*, Oct. 3, 1914, *WS*.

58. *Solidarity*, Dec. 6, 1913; Sept. 12, 1914; March 20, 1915; *The Wooden Shoe*, Jan. 22, 1914; *Report of Commission on Industrial Relations*, vol. XI, pp. 10, 576.

59. W. D. Haywood and W. E. Bohn, quoted in Cole, *World of Labour*, p. 129; *Solidarity*, Dec. 18, 1909; June 27, 1914; Abner E. Woodruff, *Solidarity*, Chicago, 1917, pp. 18–19; *Industrial Worker*, Jan. 25, 1912.

60. *Solidarity*, July 15, 1911; Nov. 2, 1912; Oct. 4, 1913.

61. Justus Ebert in *ibid.*, March 30, 1912; Justus Ebert, "Is the I.W.W. Anti-Political?" I.W.W. leaflet, 1912; J. E. in *Solidarity*, Dec. 9, 1911; *Industrial Union Bulletin*, May 25, 1907; *Industrial Union News*, Dec. 1913.

62. Quoted in Tyler, "*Rebels of the Woods and Fields*," *op. cit.*, p. 26.

63. *Bill Haywood's Book*, pp. 221–22.

64. I am indebted to Mr. Yuri Perfilyev for furnishing me with an English translation of this excerpt from Lenin's Collected Works in Russian.

65. *Industrial Worker*, April 11, 1912; Elizabeth Gurley Flynn in *Solidarity*, July 18, 1914.

66. *Solidarity*, July 25, 1914; Feb. 16, 1915.

67. *International Socialist Review*, vol. XIV, March 1914, p. 546.

CHAPTER 7

1. Grant S. Youmans in William D. Haywood, "Free Speech Fights, Letters Relating to," Commission of Industrial Relations File, Department of Labor, 413 Du P, *NA*.

2. *Industrial Worker*, Sept. 4, 1913.

3. *The Socialist* (Seattle), Sept. 7, 14, Oct. 12, 19, 26, 1907; Seattle *Times*, Oct. 13, 1907.

4. *Common Sense*, Feb. 15, March 14, 21, June 27, July 25, 1908; Grace Heilman

Stimson, *op. cit.*, p. 324; "A Notable Triumph for Free Speech in Los Angeles," *Arena*, vol. XI, Oct. 1908, pp. 350–51.

5. *Common Sense*, July 25, 1908.
6. *The New York Times*, May 9, 1912.
7. Kansas City *Star*, Oct. 24, 1911.
8. *Solidarity*, July 25, 1914.
9. *Industrial Worker*, July 13, 1913.
10. Elizabeth Gurley Flynn, *I Speak My Own Piece*, pp. 92–94; New York *Call*, Oct. 6, 1909.
11. Elizabeth Gurley Flynn, *I Speak My Own Piece*, p. 94.
12. C. O. Jones to Frank Morrison, Nov. 17, 1909, *AFL Corr.*
13. Testimony of William D. Haywood before Industrial Relations Commission, *Senate Documents*, vol. XX, No. 415, Washington, 1916, vol. XII, p. 10573; Elizabeth Gurley Flynn, *I Speak My Own Piece*, pp. 95–96; *Industrial Worker*, Feb. 12, 1910.
14. Fred W. Heslewood, "Barbarous Spokane," *International Socialist Review*, vol. X, Feb. 1910, p. 711.
15. "Barbarous Spokane," *Independent*, vol. LXVIII, Feb. 10, 1911, p. 330; Elizabeth Gurley Flynn, "The Free Speech Fight at Spokane," *International Socialist Review*, vol. X, Dec. 1909, p. 484.
16. Spokane *Spokesman-Review*, Nov. 3, 1909; Portland *Oregonian*, Nov. 3, 1909.
17. Portland *Oregonian*, Nov. 3, 1909; Spokane *Spokesman-Review*, Nov. 3, 1909.
18. Portland *Oregonian*, Nov. 4, 1909.
19. *Ibid.*
20. Spokane *Spokesman-Review*, Nov. 5, 12, 1909; Tyler, "Rebels of the Woods and Fields," *op. cit.*, p. 29.
21. Portland *Oregonian*, Nov. 11, 1909; Spokane *Chronicle*, Jan. 10, 1910.
22. Spokane *Spokesman-Review*, Nov. 12, 1909; Portland *Oregonian*, Nov. 7, 11, 1909.
23. William Z. Foster, *Pages From a Worker's Life*, New York, 1939, p. 145; Elizabeth Gurley Flynn, "The Shame of Spokane," *International Socialist Review*, vol. X, Jan. 1910, p. 613; Flynn, "Free-Speech Fight at Spokane," *op. cit.*, p. 485.
24. Robert Rose to the Industrial Relations Commission, Sept. 19, 1914, in "Letters, Etc. Addressed to Vincent St. John, by various writers," Department of Labor Files, MNC. 11–10–14, Serial No. 763, *NA*.
25. Portland *Oregonian*, Nov. 7, 14, 1909;

Flynn, "The Shame of Spokane," *op. cit.*, pp. 611–12; Flynn, *I Speak My Own Piece*, p. 97; Ralph Chaplin, *Wobbly*, p. 150; *Solidarity*, Dec. 18, 1909.
26. *Industrial Worker*, Jan. 8, 1910; Spokane *Spokesman-Review*, Jan. 3, 10, 1910; Ralph Chaplin, *Wobbly*, p. 150.
27. *Industrial Worker*, Jan. 8, 1910.
28. "From Foster in Jail," *The Workingman's Paper*, Jan. 22, 1910.
29. Flynn, *I Speak My Own Piece*, p. 97.
30. Portland *Oregonian*, Nov. 16, 1909.
31. Flynn, *I Speak My Own Piece*, p. 98.
32. I.W.W. Circular, copy in *AFL Corr.*; *Solidarity*, Feb. 26, 1910.
33. *Industrial Worker*, Feb. 5, 1910; Elizabeth Gurley Flynn, "Latest News from Spokane," *op. cit.*, pp. 828–29; Tyler, "Rebels of the Woods and Fields," *op. cit.*, p. 34.
34. *Industrial Worker*, Feb. 5, 1910.
35. Spokane *Inland Herald* reprinted in *The Workingman's Paper*, July 2, 1910; *Solidarity*, March 19, 1910; New York *Call*, Jan. 6. 1910.
36. I.W.W. Circular, *AFL Corr.*; Spokane Central Labor Council to Frank Morrison, Feb. 18, 1910; Frank Morrison to C. O. Young, March 5, 1910, *AFL Corr.*; *Solidarity*, Dec. 23, 1909.
37. *Industrial Worker*, June 19, 1913; C. O. Young to Frank Morrison, March 28, 1910; Frank Morrison to C. O. Young, April 2, 1910, *AFL Corr.*
38. *Industrial Worker*, May 28, June 4, 1910; *Solidarity*, Aug. 27, 1910; Weintraub, *op. cit.*, p. 25; Oakland *World*, Dec. 31, 1910.
39. *Solidarity*, Aug. 27, 1910.
40. *Ibid.*, Aug. 20, Sept. 5, 1910; *Industrial Worker*, Oct. 26, 1910.
41. *Industrial Worker*, Nov. 2, 9, Dec. 15, 1910; San Francisco *Call*, Dec. 10, 1910.
42. *Industrial Worker*, Oct. 15, 1910; San Francisco *Call*, Dec. 10, 1910.
43. San Francisco *Call*, Dec. 11, 1910.
44. *Ibid.*, Dec. 23–25, 1910; *Industrial Worker*, Jan. 5, 1911; Ed Delaney and M. T. Rice, *The Bloodstained Trail*, Seattle, 1927, p. 57; "I.W.W., Fresno Free Speech Fight," by H. Minderman, Labor Department files, C.M.E. 12–7–14, Serial No. 819, *NA*; William D. Haywood, "Testimony before Industrial Relations Commission," *op. cit.*, p. 10573; Denver *Post*, Feb. 20, 1911.
45. Kansas City *Star*, Oct. 24, 1911; Letter to Vincent St. John, unsigned, but dated Victorville, Cal., Sept. 21, 1914, "in

"Letters etc. addressed to Vincent St. John. . . ," *op. cit., NA.*

46. San Francisco *Call*, March 2, 1911; *Industrial Worker*, March 16, 1911; *The Agitator*, March 15, 1911.
47. *Solidarity*, April 29, 1911.
48. Weintraub, *op. cit.*, p. 274.

CHAPTER 8

1. Weintraub, *op. cit.*, p. 274; *Industrial Worker*, Nov. 30, 1911.
2. Tacoma *Times*, Aug. 7, 1911; Tacoma *Daily Tribune*, Aug. 7, 1911; Tacoma *News*, Aug. 8, 1911; *Industrial Worker*, Aug. 17, 1911.
3. Victoria *Colonist*, July 22, 1911; *Industrial Worker*, Aug. 3, 1911.
4. Quoted in Richard Connelly Miller, "Otis and His *Times*: The Career of Harrison Gray Otis of Los Angeles," unpublished Ph.D. thesis, University of California, Berkeley, 1961, p. 437.
5. Tyler, "Rebels of the Woods and Fields," *op. cit.*, p. 35; *Industrial Worker*, Nov. 23, 1911, Feb. 1, 1912.
6. Portland *Oregonian*, Nov. 23–24, 1911; Tyler, *op. cit.*, pp. 36–37; *Industrial Worker*, Dec. 14, 1911.
7. Portland *Oregonian*, Nov. 25, Dec. 4–5, 1911; *Solidarity*, Jan. 6, 1912; *Industrial Worker*, Nov. 23, 1911; *The Agitator*, Dec. 1, 1911.
8. Portland *Oregonian*, Dec. 4–5, 1911; *Solidarity*, Dec. 16, 1911; *Industrial Worker*, Dec. 14, 1911; Tyler, *op. cit.*, p. 35.
9. *Solidarity*, Jan. 6, 1912.
10. Seattle *Post-Intelligencer*, Dec. 27, 1911.
11. *Industrial Worker*, Feb. 1, 1912.
12. *Ibid.*, Jan. 25, Feb. 29, 1912.
13. *Ibid.*, Jan. 25, Feb. 29, 1912; New York *Call*, Feb. 11, 1912.
14. *Industrial Worker*, Aug. 27, Sept. 10, Dec. 8, 1910; *Solidarity*, Aug. 27, Nov. 5, Dec. 3, 1910; May 6, 1911; San Diego *Sun* reprinted in *Industrial Worker*, Dec. 8, 1910.
15. *Industrial Worker*, April 11, 1912.
16. Theodore Schroeder, *Free Speech for Radicals*, Riverside, Conn., 1916, pp. 116–18; Ernest Jerome Hopkins, "The San Diego Fight," *The Coming Nation*, May 4, 1912, pp. 8–9; *Solidarity*, Feb. 17, 1912; San Francisco *Call*, Feb. 10, 19, 1912; *Industrial Worker*, Feb. 29, 1912.
17. San Francisco *Call*, Feb. 10, 19, 1912; *Report of Harris Weinstock Commis-*

sioner to Investigate the Recent Disturbances in the City of San Diego and the County of San Diego, California to His Excellency Hiram W. Johnson, Governor of California, Sacramento, 1912, p. 9.
18. Reprinted in *Report of Weinstock*, pp. 17–19.
19. San Diego *Sun*, Feb. 15, 1912; *Solidarity*, March 16, 1912.
20. *Industrial Worker*, April 11, 1912; *San Diego Free Speech Controversy: Report to the San Francisco Labor Council by Special Investigating Committee*, San Francisco, Calif., April 25th, 1912, pp. 3–4.
21. *Industrial Worker*, March 7, 1912; Oakland *World*, March 23, 1912.
22. Hopkins, *op. cit.*, pp. 12–13.
23. San Diego *Herald* reprinted in *Industrial Worker*, May 1, 1912; *Solidarity*, June 1, 1912.
24. Fred H. Moore and Marcus W. Robbins to Gov. Hiram W. Johnson, April 3, 1912, Hiram Johnson Papers, University of California Library, Berkeley.
25. Chas. Hanson, "My Experiences During San Diego Free Speech Fight," in "Letters, Etc., Addressed to Vincent St. John. . . ," *op. cit., NA.*
26. "To Organized Labor and All Lovers of Liberty," signed by California Free Speech League, San Diego, California, copy in *AFL Corr.*
27. Report of Weinstock, *op. cit., passim; Report to the San Francisco Labor Council, op. cit.*, pp. 8–9; San Francisco *Call*, May 21, 1912.
28. *Report to the San Francisco Labor Council, op. cit.*, pp. 6–8.
29. *Industrial Worker*, May 16, 1912; San Francisco *Call*, May 21, 1912.
30. Emma Goldman in *Industrial Worker*, June 6, 1912.
31. Richard Drinnon, *Rebel in Paradise: A Biography of Emma Goldman*, Chicago, 1961, pp. 134–36; Emma Goldman, *Living My Life*, New York, 1931, pp. 500–01; statement by Ben Reitman in *Industrial Worker*, June 6, 1912.
32. San Francisco *Call*, June 3, 1912.
33. San Diego *Sun*, May 28, 1912.
34. *Industrial Worker*, June 13, Aug. 8, 1912; Weintraub, *op. cit.*, p. 38.
35. William Howard Taft to Attorney General George W. Wickersham, Sept. 7, 1912, Department of Justice File 150139–28, *NA.*
36. William Howard Taft to George W. Wickersham, Sept. 7, 1912, Department

of Justice File 150139–28; Assistant Attorney-General William R. Hart to George W. Wickersham, July 5, 1912, Department of Justice File 150139, *NA*.
37. San Diego *Sun*, April 13, 1912.
38. *Solidarity*, Dec. 17, 1910; *Industrial Worker*, Aug. 15, 1912; Schroeder, *op. cit.*, pp. 189–90; letter of Hiram W. Johnson quoted in J. Stilt Wilson to Hiram Johnson, Aug. 1, 1913, in Commission on Industrial Relations files, 565 Dup, Labor Department, *NA*.
39. *Industrial Worker*, Aug. 15, 1912.
40. *Industrial Worker*, June 5, 1913; Drinnon, *op. cit.*, p. 136.
41. *The Wooden Shoe*, Jan. 22, 1914; George Edwards, "Free Speech in San Diego," *Mother Earth*, vol. X, July 1915, pp. 182–85.
42. *Industrial Worker*, June 6, 1912; *Organized Labor* reprinted in *ibid.*, May 16, 1912.
43. *Solidarity*, May 18, 1912.
44. Frank Morrison to Paul Scharrenberg, June 4, 1912, *AFL Corr.*
45. British Columbia *Federationist*, Feb. 5, June 8, 1912; *Industrial Worker*, Feb. 8, 1912.
46. British Columbia *Federationist*, Feb. 5, 1912; *Industrial Worker*, Feb. 8, 1912.
47. British Columbia *Federationist*, Feb. 8, 1912; *Industrial Worker*, Feb. 8, 15, 1912.
48. *Industrial Worker*, Feb. 8, 1912.
49. British Columbia *Federationist*, March 14, 1912; *Industrial Worker*, Feb. 15, 22, 1912.
50. *Industrial Worker*, Feb. 1, March 28, 1912; *Solidarity*, March 23, 1912.
51. *Solidarity*, Feb. 10, 1912; San Francisco *Call*, June 25, Aug. 5–6, 1912; Weintraub, *op. cit.*, pp. 36–37.
52. *Industrial Worker*, May 29, June 5, 12, July 3, Sept. 4, 1913; *Solidarity*, June 4, Oct. 18, 1913, Jan. 31, 1914; Philadelphia *Public Ledger*, June 6, 1913.
53. *Industrial Worker*, Jan. 9, March 6, 1913.
54. *Ibid.*, March 27, 1913.
55. *Solidarity*, April 26, May 3, 1913.
56. *Industrial Worker*, May 8, 1913; *Solidarity*, June 7, 1913.
57. *Solidarity*, July 28, Aug. 8, Oct. 10, 24, 1914; *The Agitator*, Aug. 15, 1914.
58. Kansas City *Journal*, Oct. 30, 1911; *Industrial Worker*, Nov. 16, 1911; *Solidarity*, Oct. 28, Nov. 9, 1911.
59. Kansas City *Journal*, Dec. 12–13, 1913; *The Wooden Shoe*, Jan. 22, 1914.
60. *Solidarity*, Feb. 28, March 7, 1914.

61. Kansas City *Journal*, Feb. 18, 22, 1914.
62. *Solidarity*, March 14, 1914.
63. *Ibid.*, March 7, 1914.
64. *Industrial Worker*, Dec. 28, 1911.
65. Kansas City *Journal*, Feb. 18, 22, 1914.
66. W. I. Fisher, "Soap-Boxer or Organizer, Which?" *Industrial Worker*, June 6, 1912.
67. Grace V. Silver in New York *Call*, reprinted in *Solidarity*, March 25, 1911.
68. Reprinted in *Industrial Worker*, Jan. 25, 1912.
69. Selig Perlman and Philip Taft, *History of Labor in the United States, 1896–1932*, New York, 1935, p. 240.
70. Grant S. Youmans, "The Minot Free Speech Fight," in W. D. Haywood to C. McCarty, U.S. Commission on Industrial Relations, Oct. 10, 1914, Labor Department Files, 413 Dup, *NA*.
71. *Industrial Worker*, Feb. 1, 1912.
72. Reprinted in *Industrial Worker*, Dec. 9, 1916.

CHAPTER 9

1. Abramson, *op. cit.*, pp. 26–28; William Ogburn, "Causes and Remedies of the Labor Unrest in the Lumber Industry," University of Washington Forest *Annual*, Seattle, 1918, pp. 11–14.
2. I.W.W., *The Lumber Industry and Its Workers*, *op. cit.*, pp. 24–29.
3. Abramson, *op. cit.*, pp. 28–29.
4. *The Lumber Industry and Its Workers*, *op. cit.*, p. 56.
5. *Ibid.*, p. 50; "Labor Unrest in the Lumber Industry—Northern Idaho and Western Montana," Statement by District Forester F. A. Silcov, Department of Labor Files No. 20–473, *NA*; P. A. Speek, "Report on Conditions in Labor Camps, June 4, 1915," Department of Labor, Studies and Reports of Commission on Industrial Relations, original in *WSHS*, copy in *NA*.
6. British Columbia *Federationist*, Oct. 26, 1912.
7. *Solidarity*, March 2, 1910; *Industrial Worker*, June 5, 1913; Feb. 3, 1917; Ralph Winstead, "Evolution of Logging Conditions on the Northwest Coast," *One Big Union Monthly*, May 1920; Richard G. Lillard, *The Great Forest*, New York, 1948, p. 282.
8. Lillard, *op. cit.*, pp. 277–78.
9. *Industrial Union Bulletin*, June 15, 1907.
10. *The Lumber Industry and Its Workers*, *op. cit.*, p. 61.

11. *Industrial Union Bulletin,* June 15, 1907; *Industrial Worker,* Feb. 12, Sept. 17, Dec. 8, 1910.
12. *Industrial Worker,* Feb. 12, 1910.
13. *Solidarity,* July 23, 1910.
14. *Industrial Worker,* July 20, 1911.
15. *Industrial Worker,* Nov. 23, 1911; Cloice R. Howd, "Industrial Relations in the West Coast Lumber Industry," U.S. Department of Labor, Bureau of Labor Statistics, Bulletin No. 349, 1924, p. 65.
16. *Industrial Worker,* Feb. 1, 8, 15, 1912.
17. Ethel Elise Rasmusson, "Pacific Coast Timberland Frauds, 1891–1917," unpublished M.A. thesis, University of Chicago, 1947, pp. 25, 82–83.
18. Bruce Rogers, "The Mutiny of the Lumber Army," *The Coming Nation,* May 11, 1912, pp. 5–6.
19. Portland *Oregonian,* March 16, 1912.
20. Portland *Oregonian,* March 15, 16, 21, 1912.
21. *Industrial Worker,* March 28, 1912; *Solidarity,* March 30, 1912; Portland *Oregonian,* April 24, 1912.
22. Portland *Oregonian,* March 29, 30, 1912; Jensen, "Labor Relations in the Northwest Lumber Industry," *op. cit.,* p. 41.
23. Portland *Oregonian,* April 12, 1912.
24. *Ibid.,* March 31, April 1–12, May 3, 1912; Seattle *Post-Intelligencer,* March 31, April 1–2, May 3, 1912.
25. Portland *Oregonian,* April 1, 1912; Bruce Rogers, *op. cit.,* p. 6.
26. Portland *Oregonian,* April 6–8, May 7–10, 1912.
27. Reprinted in *Industrial Worker,* May 23, 1912.
28. *Ibid.,* June 20, 1912.
29. *Ibid.,* Nov. 28, 1912.
30. *Ibid.,* May 29, 1913; Portland *Oregonian,* June 26, 1913; New York *Call,* June 27, 1913; Tyler, *op. cit.,* pp. 53–54.
31. Portland *Oregonian,* Nov. 26, 1913; Abramson, *op. cit.,* pp. 64–65.
32. *Industrial Worker,* May 29, 1913.
33. *Ibid.,* July 10, 1913; *The Syndicalist,* Sept. 1–15, 1913.
34. Jensen, *op. cit.,* p. 43.
35. J. S. Biscay, "Job Organization in the West," *Solidarity,* Jan. 29, 1914.
36. *Ibid.*
37. *Industrial Worker,* Feb. 1, 1912, June 2, 1913; Howd, *op. cit.,* p. 67; Jensen, "Labor Relations in the Northwest Lumber Industry," *op. cit.,* p. 43.
38. British Columbia *Federationist,* June 22, 1912.

39. *Industrial Worker,* Aug. 8, 1912; British Columbia *Federationist,* July 25, 1913.
40. *Industrial Worker,* June 27, Aug. 8, 15, 22, 1912, July 17, 1913; *Solidarity,* June 15, Aug. 24, 1912; San Francisco *Bulletin,* Aug. 1, 1914; *Solidarity,* Oct. 2, 1915.
41. *Industrial Worker,* Aug. 31, Oct. 5, 19, 26, Nov. 2, 28, 1911.
42. *Solidarity,* Nov. 21, 1914.
43. British Columbia *Federationist,* June 22, 1912.
44. *Industrial Worker,* April 18, 1912.
45. Seattle *Post-Intelligencer,* April 2, 4, 1912; *Solidarity,* May 11, 1912; *Industrial Worker,* May 16, 1912; British Columbia *Federationist,* July 6, 1912; Agnes Lout, "Revolution Yawns," *International Socialist Review,* vol. XIII, Nov. 1912, pp. 426–27.
46. British Columbia *Federationist,* June 22, July 6, 1912; *Industrial Worker,* April 11, May 16, 1912; Lout, *op. cit.,* p. 428; Phillips Russell, "Strike Tactics," *The New Review,* March 29, 1913, p. 406.
47. *Industrial Worker,* May 9, 1912.
48. *Industrial Worker,* April 11, 18, 1912; British Columbia *Federationist,* June 8, 1912.
49. British Columbia *Federationist,* June 22, 1912.
50. *Industrial Worker,* Aug. 22, 29, Sept. 12, 1912; *Solidarity,* Aug. 24, 1912.
51. British Columbia *Federationist,* June 22, 29, 1912.
52. C. O. Young to Frank Morrison, Vancouver, B.C., Oct. 13, 1912, *AFL Corr.*
53. *Industrial Worker,* Jan. 23, 1913.

CHAPTER 10

1. Thompson, *op. cit.,* p. 67.
2. Ruth A. Allen, *East Texas Lumber Workers: An Economic and Social Picture, 1870–1950,* Austin, Texas, 1961, pp. 54, 58; Vernon H. Jensen, *Lumber and Labor,* New York, 1945, p. 76; *St. Louis Lumberman,* April 1, 1910, p. 65.
3. Hollie Hickman, *Mississippi Harvest: Lumbering in the Longleaf Pine Belt, 1840–1915,* University of Mississippi, 1962, pp. 142–43.
4. George Creel, "Feudal Towns of Texas," *Harper's Weekly,* vol. LX, Jan. 23, 1915, pp. 75–76; R. Lillard, *op. cit.,* p. 280.
5. Mary C. Terrell, "Peonage in the United States," *Nineteenth Century and After,* vol. LXII, 1907, pp. 202–05; Charles H.

McCord, "A Brief History of the Brotherhood of Timber Workers," unpublished M.A. thesis, University of Texas, May 1959, pp. 47–48.

6. Lillard, *op. cit.*, p. 280; Allen, *op. cit.*, p. 106; G. T. Starnes and F. T. De Vyver, *Labor in the Industrial South*, Charlottesville, Va., 1930, pp. 45, 51; Covington Hall, "The Southern Lumber War," *The Coming Nation*, June 22, 1912, p. 2; McCord, *op. cit.*, p. 43; New Orleans *Times Democrat*, July 28, 1912.

7. Allen, *op. cit.*, pp. 116–17; *Solidarity*, Aug. 17, 1912.

8. *Ninth Biennial Report of the Bureau of Statistics of Labor of the State of Louisiana, 1916–18*, pp. 96, 124–34; Allen, *op. cit.*, p. 156.

9. Frederic Myers, "The Knights of Labor in the South," *Southern Economic Journal*, vol. VI, April 1940, p. 485; Jensen, *Lumber and Labor*, pp. 86–87.

10. Wilson Compton, *The Organization of the Lumber Industry*, Chicago, 1916, p. 17; *The Lumber Industry and Its Workers*, *op. cit.*, p. 76; *Southwest*, Nov. 1907, p. 19; McCord, *op. cit.*, pp. 15–16.

11. Compton, *op. cit.*, p. 17.

12. H. G. Creel in *National Rip-Saw*, Nov. 1912.

13. *International Socialist Review*, vol. XIII, Aug. 1912, p. 108.

14. Thompson, *op. cit.*, p. 67; Covington Hall, "Louisiana Lumber War," *Industrial Worker*, July 14, 21, 1945.

15. *International Socialist Review*, vol. XIII, Sept. 1912, p. 223; *National Rip-Saw*, Nov. 1912.

16. McCord, *op. cit.*, pp. 19–20, 27.

17. New Orleans *Times-Democrat*, July 20, Aug. 8, 1911.

18. *Solidarity*, Oct. 28, 1911.

19. *Southwest*, Aug. 1911, p. 22; McCord, *op. cit.*, pp. 31–32; *Industrial Worker*, June 8, 1911.

20. New Orleans *Times-Democrat*, July 20, Aug. 8, 1911; *Solidarity*, Aug. 5, Sept. 2, 1911; *Industrial Worker*, Sept. 7, 1911.

21. James T. Bacon and others to Gompers, Aug. 12, 1911, *AFL Corr.*

22. New Orleans *Times-Democrat*, July 20–Aug. 8, 1911; McCord, *op. cit.*, p. 33.

23. New Orleans *Times-Democrat*, July 20, 1911; *Industrial Worker*, Dec. 26, 1912; *The Rebel* (Halletsville, Tex.), Feb. 8, 1913.

24. St. Louis *Lumberman*, Aug. 1, 1911, p. 69.

25. *National Rip-Saw*, June, 1912; McCord, *op. cit.*, p. 36.

26. *Southwest*, Aug. 1911, p. 33; McCord, *op. cit.*, p. 34.

27. Thompson, *op. cit.*, p. 76.

28. McCord, *op. cit.*, p. 36. Grady McWhiney, "Louisiana Socialists in the Early Twentieth Century: A Study of Rustic Radicalism," *Journal of Southern History*, vol. XXX, Aug. 1954, p. 328.

29. New Orleans *Times-Democrat*, Nov. 1, 1911.

30. *Solidarity*, Dec. 23, 1911.

31. McCord, *op. cit.*, p. 30.

32. *Voice of the People*, Dec. 25, 1913; Todes, *op. cit.*, p. 171; Jensen, *Lumber and Labor*, pp. 88–89; McCord, *op. cit.*, pp. 24–25, 30.

33. *Bill Haywood's Book*, pp. 241–42; McCord, *op. cit.*, pp. 51–52; *Solidarity*, May 25, Sept. 28, 1912; Chicago *World*, Sept. 23, 1912; *Industrial Worker*, May 30, 1912.

34. *Lumber Trade Journal*, May 15, 1912, pp. 1, 13, 34; June 1, 1912, p. 13; New Orleans *Times-Democrat*, May 17, 1912; McCord, *op. cit.*, pp. 53–54; *Industrial Worker*, Dec. 26, 1912.

35. *Industrial Worker*, Aug. 1, 1912.

36. *National Rip-Saw*, July, 1912.

37. *The Rebel*, Aug. 17, 1912; *Solidarity*, Aug. 1, 1912; New Orleans *Times-Democrat*, July 24, 1912.

38. New Orleans *Daily Picayune*, Aug. 12, 1912; *The Rebel*, Aug. 3, 1912.

39. *The Rebel*, July 20, 1912; *Solidarity*, Sept. 28, 1912; *Industrial Worker*, Sept. 26, 1912.

40. *The Coming Nation*, Oct. 19, 1912; *Industrial Worker*, July 28, 1945.

41. New Orleans *Times-Democrat*, Oct. 6, 1912.

42. *Industrial Worker*, Oct. 24, 1912; *International Socialist Review*, vol. XIII, Nov. 1912, p. 407.

43. New Orleans *Times-Democrat*, Oct. 6, 1912.

44. *The Rebel*, Oct. 26, 1912; New Orleans *Times-Democrat*, Oct. 24, 1912.

45. New Orleans *Times-Democrat*, Nov. 1, 1912.

46. *Ibid.*, Nov. 2–3, 1912; *Solidarity*, Nov. 9, 1912; *The Coming Nation*, Nov. 23, 1912.

47. New Orleans *Times-Democrat*, Nov. 3, 1912.

48. *Industrial Worker*, Aug. 15, 22, 1912; *Solidarity*, Aug. 7, 1912.

49. *Industrial Worker*, Dec. 26, 1912.

50. *Southwest*, Oct. 1912, p. 27.

51. *Industrial Worker*, Nov. 28, Dec. 26, 1912; Algernon Lee Scrapbooks, "Labor Struggles, 1912–13," *TIL*.
52. *The Rebel*, Nov. 16, 1912.
53. *Industrial Worker*, Dec. 26, 1912.
54. *The Crisis* (New York), Feb. 1913, p. 164; *Solidarity*, Dec. 21, 1912; New York *Call*, Feb. 5, 1913.
55. *Industrial Worker*, Dec. 26, 1912; Phineas Eastman, "The Southern Negro and One Big Union," *International Socialist Review*, vol. XIII, June 1913, pp. 890–91.
56. Covington Hall, "Labor Struggles in the Deep South," unpublished manuscript, Howard-Tilton Library, Tulane University, p. 149.
57. *Industrial Worker*, Jan. 30, 1913.
58. *Industrial Worker*, Feb. 27, March 6, 1913; New Orleans *Times-Democrat*, Feb. 17–20, 1913; New York *Call*, Feb. 20, 1913.
59. *Industrial Worker*, March 6, 1913; *Voice of the People*, Nov. 7, 1913.
60. *Ibid.*, June 19, 1913; McCord, *op. cit.*, p. 99.
61. *Voice of the People*, Jan. 1, 29, March 5, 1914.
62. *The Rebel*, May 3, 1913.
63. *Voice of the People*, Nov. 6, 20, 1913.
64. McCord, *op. cit.*, pp. 103–04; *Voice of the People*, Feb. 5, 1914.
65. Jensen, *Lumber and Labor*, p. 91; *The Lumber Industry and Its Workers*, *op. cit.*, pp. 27, 77.
66. Spero and Harris, *op. cit.*, p. 33; McCord, *op. cit.*, pp. 22–23.
67. New Orleans *Daily Picayune*, July 7, 1912.
68. Jensen, *Lumber and Labor*, pp. 91–94.

CHAPTER 11

1. *Industrial Worker*, Jan. 2, March 6, 1913.
2. *Industrial Worker*, Jan. 16, 23, 30, Feb. 6, 13, March 6, 20, 27, April 17, 1913.
3. *Ibid.*, Jan. 30, March 27, 1913.
4. *Solidarity*, Feb. 22, 1913.
5. *California Fruit Grower*, Jan. 17, 1903, p. 2, quoted in Weintraub, *op. cit.*, p. 71; Christina Krysto, "California Labor Camps," *The Survey*, Nov. 5, 1919, pp. 70–73.
6. Stuart Jamieson, *Labor Unionism in American Agriculture*, Washington, D.C., 1945, pp. 57–58; *Solidarity*, July 29, 1911.
7. Jamieson, *op. cit.*, p. 58.
8. *Solidarity*, March 4, May 21, July 2, 9,

23, 30, Aug. 6, 20, 27, Sept. 17, 1910; Oct. 7, 1911; *Industrial Worker*, Aug. 13, 1910.
9. *Industrial Worker*, July 2, 1910, July 20, 1911, Dec. 26, 1912.
10. Jamieson, *op. cit.*, p. 61.
11. *Hearings*, Industrial Commission, vol. V, 1915, p. 5000; Jamieson, *op. cit.*, p. 61.
12. Carleton H. Parker, *The Casual Laborer and Other Essays*, pp. 171–99; Carey McWilliams, *Factories in the Field*, Boston, 1939, pp. 158–69; Inez Haynes Gillmore, "The Marysville Strike," *Harper's Weekly*, April 4, 1914, pp. 18–19; Sacramento *Union*, Aug. 5, 1913; Sacramento *Bee*, Aug. 4, 1913, both in *WS*.
13. Parker, *op. cit.*, pp. 189–95; George L. Bell, "The Wheatland Hop Field Riots," *Outlook*, vol. CVII, May 16, 1914, p. 120; George L. Bell, "A California Labor Tragedy," *Literary Digest*, May 23, 1914, pp. 1239–40; San Francisco *Examiner*, Aug. 5–9, 1913; Marysville *Appeal*, Aug. 4, 1913, *WS*.
14. San Francisco *Bulletin*, Dec. 12, 1913, *WS*.
15. Sacramento *Bee*, Aug. 4, 1913; Marysville *Democrat*, Aug. 4, 1913, *WS*.
16. Marysville *Democrat*, Aug. 6, 1913, *WS*.
17. *Ibid.*, Aug. 8, 1913, *WS*.
18. Copy of notice for arrest of Ford and Suhr, in *WS*; Martinez *Gazette*, Sept. 22, 1913; Marysville *Democrat*, Sept. 22, 1913, *WS*.
19. San Francisco *Bulletin*, Dec. 23, 1913; Sacramento *Bee*, Jan. 16, 1914, *WS*.
20. Marysville *Appeal*, Nov. 18, 1913; Sacramento *Bee*, Dec. 1, 1913, *WS*.
21. San Francisco *Bulletin*, Oct. 16, 1913, *WS*; "Prosecution or Persecution," published by the California Branch, General Defense Committee, n.d., p. 3.
22. Marysville *Appeal*, Nov. 26, 1913; Sacramento *Bee*, Dec. 1913, *WS*.
23. San Francisco *Chronicle*, Sept. 26, 1913; Sacramento *Bee*, Dec. 13, 1913; Marysville *Democrat*, Dec. 15, 1913, *WS*; *Appeal to Reason*, Nov. 22, 1913; "Prosecution or Persecution," *op. cit.*, p. 4; Weintraub, *op. cit.*, p. 77; letter sent by Publicity Department, International Workers' Defense League, Oakland, Cal., Dec. 15, 1913, copy in *WSHS*; Woodrow C. Whitten, "The Wheatland Episode," *Pacific Historical Review*, vol. XVII, Feb. 1948, pp. 39–40.
24. San Francisco *Chronicle*, Dec. 11, 1913, *WS*.

25. Undated, unidentified clipping, around Nov. 1913, in *WS*.
26. Marysville *Appeal*, Dec. 13, 1913, *WS*.
27. Marysville *Democrat*, Dec. 9, 1913; Jan. 25, 1914, *WS*.
28. Marysville *Appeal*, Jan. 6, 7, 1914, *WS*.
29. Marysville *Democrat*, Dec. 14, 1913, Jan. 12, 1914, *WS*.
30. Marysville *Democrat*, Jan. 12, 1914; San Francisco *Star*, Jan. 28, 1914, *WS*; Weintraub, *op. cit.*, pp. 78–79.
31. San Francisco *Star*, Jan. 28, 1914. *See also* San Francisco *Bulletin*, Feb. 1, 1914, *WS*.
32. San Francisco *Bulletin*, Feb. 4, 1914; Marysville *Appeal*, Jan. 30, 1914, *WS*.
33. Sacramento *Bee*, Jan. 23, 1914 and *Bee* reprinted in Marysville *Democrat*, Feb. 5, 1914, *WS*.
34. Sacramento *Star*, Jan. 29, Feb. 6, 1914, *WS*; Gillmore, *op. cit.*, p. 20.
35. Sacramento *Star*, Feb. 5, 6, 7, 1914; Marysville *Democrat*, Feb. 10, 1914; Marysville *Appeal*, Feb. 26, 1914, *WS*.
36. Sacramento *Union*, Feb. 9, 1914; Sacramento *Bee*, May 30, 1914, WS; *Solidarity*, April 11, 1914.
37. Sacramento *Bee*, Aug. 29, 1914; San Francisco *Bulletin*, Aug. 28, 1914; San Francisco *Chronicle*, Aug. 29, 1914, *WS*; Whitten, *op. cit.*, p. 41n.
38. *The Wooden Shoe*, Jan. 22, 1914.
39. *Voice of the People*, April 23, 1914; *Solidarity*, Feb. 14, July 4, 1914.
40. *Solidarity*, June 20, July 18, Aug. 15, 1914.
41. Sacramento *Bee*, April 15, July 20, 1914; Marysville *Appeal*, June 28, July 26, 1914; San Francisco *Chronicle*, July 20, 1914; Marysville *Democrat*, July 18, 1914, *WS*.
42. *Solidarity*, Aug. 15, 22, 29, 1914; *Voice of the People*, Sept. 10, 1914; Sacramento *Bee*, Aug. 19, 26, Sept. 14, 1914, *WS*.
43. Marysville *Appeal*, Aug. 19, 26, 1914; Marysville *Democrat*, Sept. 2, 1914, *WS*: Headquarters Hop Pickers Defense Committee, *Bulletin*, September 22, 1914, in *Brief and Argument for Plaintiffs in Error, 9th Circuit Court of Appeals*, pp. 38–42, Pardon Attorney File, 39–241, *NA*; California *Outlook*, Sept. 12, 1914, *WS*.
44. Marysville *Democrat*, Sept. 11, Nov. 10, 25, 1914. *See also* Sacramento *Bee*, Dec. 21, 1914, *WS*.
45. "Prosecution or Persecution," *op. cit.*, p. 9; Weintraub, *op. cit.*, p. 79.
46. Marysville *Democrat*, Feb. 24, March 5, 1915, *WS*; *Solidarity*, March 20, 1915.
47. San Francisco *Bulletin*, March 6, 1915; Sacramento *Bee*, March 6, 1915, *WS*; *Solidarity*, March 20, 1915; Al Richmond, *Native Daughter*, San Francisco, 1942, pp. 62–63.
48. *International Socialist Review*, reprinted in Marysville *Democrat*, Dec. 7, 1914, *WS*.
49. Charles L. Lambert to Richard Ford, 6-18-15, Pardon Attorney File, 39–241, *NA*.
50. C. L. Lambert to Thomas Whitehead, 3-17-15; Lambert to Stackowitz Press, March 29, 1915, *ibid.*; *Solidarity*, March 6, Sept. 25, 1915.
51. C. L. Lambert to W. D. Haywood, 6-10-15, Pardon Attorney File, 39–241, *NA*; *Solidarity*, Sept. 25, 1915.
52. C. L. Lambert to Thomas Whitehead, 3-17-15; C. L. Lambert to John Pancner, 5-20-15, Pardon Attorney File, 39–241, *NA*; Simon J. Lubin to Thomas B. Gregory, Nov. 26, 1915, Department of Justice File, 150139-46, *NA*.
53. San Francisco *Examiner*, Sept. 12, 1915.
54. Harvey Duff, *The Silent Defenders, Courts and Capitalism*, Chicago, n.d., pp. 9–10; Tom Mooney to Frank P. Walsh, Sept. 23, 1915, enclosing statement of International Workers' Defense League, Frank P. Walsh Papers, New York Public Library.
55. J. H. Durst to George L. Bell, Nov. 8, 1915,; Governors Johnson, Withycombe, Lister, and Spry to Franklin K. Lane, confidential telegram of Oct. 5, 1915, Department of Justice File 150139-46 and 150139-48, *NA*.
56. Frank K. Lane to President Wilson, Oct. 6, 7, 1915; Woodrow Wilson to Attorney General, Oct. 7, 1915; Simon J. Lubin to Thomas B. Gregory, Nov. 26, 1915,; Report of Special Agent, Dec. 7, 1915, in Assistant Attorney-General William Wallace, Jr. to Hiram Johnson, Dec. 15, 1915, Department of Justice File 150139-47 and 150139-48, *NA*.
57. William Wallace, Jr. to Hiram Johnson, Dec. 15, 1915; Simon J. Lubin to Thomas B. Gregory, Nov. 26, 1915, Department of Justice File 150139-46 and 150139-47, *NA*.
58. William Preston, Jr., "The Ideology and Techniques of Repression: Government and Radicals, 1903–1933," unpublished Ph.D. thesis, University of Wisconsin, 1957, pp. 97–98.

59. George Child to Charles L. Lambert, Aug. 4, 1915; Joseph C. Williams to Philip Gordet, Nov. 26, 1916; Chris Luber to G. A. Roberts, Feb. 9, 1917; Chris Luber to H. C. Evans, Feb. 12, 1917, in Pardon Attorney File, 399–241, pp. 40, 43, 51–52, *NA.;* Report of Agent P. W. Kelly, San Francisco, Dec. 13, 1919, in Department of Justice File, 206462–1, *NA.*

60. Jamieson, *op. cit.,* p. 64; Weintraub, *op. cit.,* p. 107; *Industrial Worker,* Aug. 1, 1916; Austin Lewis, "Movements of Migratory Unskilled Labor in California," *The New Review,* Aug. 1914, pp. 464–65. Dr. Parker's report, "The Hop Fields Report," is reprinted in the appendix of his book, *The Casual Laborer and Other Essays.*

61. State Relief Administration of California, *Migratory Labor in California,* Sacramento, Calif., 1936, pp. 55–57; Sacramento *Bee,* Aug. 1, 1914, *WS.*

62. Labor Department Archives, Serial No. 734m B.11-1-14, *NA;* San Francisco *Bulletin,* Feb. 7, 1914, *WS.*

63. U.S. Commission on Industrial Relations, *op. cit.,* vol. II, p. 1462.

64. Report of Carleton H. Parker, March 30, 1914, in Record Group 174 General Records, Department of Labor, Studies and Reports of Commission on Industrial Relations, original in *WSHS,* copy in *NA.*

65. *Industrial Worker,* Feb. 3, 1917.

CHAPTER 12

1. *Cf.* "How Pierpont Morgan Kept His Word and 'Smashed the Union,'" Terre Haute *Post,* July 6, 1909, Eugene V. Debs Miscellaneous Papers, *TIL.*

2. New York *Call,* July 22, Aug. 30, 1909.

3. Paul U. Kellogg, "The McKees Rock Strike," *Survey,* Aug. 7, 1909, pp. 656–59; New York *Call,* July 16, 1909; New York *Tribune,* July 16, 1909.

4. Kellogg, *op. cit.,* pp. 656–59; New York *Tribune,* July 16, 1909; New York *Call,* July 16, 1909.

5. New York *Call,* July 16, Aug. 4, 1909; *Solidarity,* Dec. 18, 1909; April 30, 1910.

6. New York *Call,* July 17, 1909.

7. Felicia Fenton in Pittsburgh *Leader,* July 15, 1909.

8. New York *Call,* July 17, Aug. 3, 1909.

9. Pittsburgh *Leader,* July 15, 1909; New York *Call,* July 22, 1909.

10. Kellogg, *op. cit.,* p. 665; Pittsburgh *Leader,* July 15, 1909.

11. Pittsburgh *Leader,* July 17, 1909; New York *Call,* July 15, 1909; Kellogg, *op. cit.,* pp. 656–57.

12. Pittsburgh *Leader,* July 15, 1909; New York *Call,* July 15, 16, 1909; New York *Tribune,* July 16, 1909; Kellogg, *op. cit.,* pp. 656–57.

13. New York *Call,* July 15, 17, 1909.

14. Pittsburgh *Leader,* July 16, 1909; New York *Call,* July 16, 1909; New York *Tribune,* July 16, 1909; dispatch from Pittsburgh in unnamed paper, dated July 17, 1909, in Eugene V. Debs Clipping Book No. 2, 1909, *TIL.*

15. Pittsburgh *Leader,* July 16, 17, 1909; New York *Call,* July 20, 1909; Kellogg, *op. cit.,* pp. 657–58; dispatch from Pittsburgh, July 19, 1909, in Eugene V. Debs Clipping Book, No. 2, *TIL.*

16. Pittsburgh *Leader,* July 17, 1909.

17. *Ibid.,* July 17, 1909; New York *Call,* July 17, 1909.

18. Kellogg, *op. cit.,* pp. 657–59; New York *Tribune,* July 17, 1909.

19. Pittsburgh *Leader,* July 15–16, 1909; Kellogg, *op. cit.,* pp. 657–58; dispatch, July 17, 1909, Eugene V. Debs Clipping Book, No. 2, 1909, *TIL.*

20. Louis Duchez, "Victory at McKees Rock," *International Socialist Review,* vol. X, Oct. 1909, pp. 290–92.

21. New York *Tribune,* July 16–17, 1909; New York *Call,* July 27, 1909.

22. New York *Call,* July 19, 1909.

23. *Ibid.,* July 23–25, 1909.

24. *Ibid.,* July 21, 28, 1909.

25. *Ibid.,* July 29–Aug. 1, 1909.

26. Pittsburgh *Dispatch,* Aug. 14, 1909; New York *Call,* Aug. 7–12, 1909; New York *Tribune,* Aug. 10–12, 1909; Duchez, *op. cit.,* p. 292.

27. Duchez, *op. cit.,* p. 292; Haywood, testimony before U.S. Commission on Industrial Relations, 1915, *op. cit.,* p. 10573.

28. Pittsburgh *Dispatch,* Aug. 16, 1909.

29. Pittsburgh *Post,* Aug. 16, 1909; New York *Call,* Aug. 18, 1909; Pittsburgh *Dispatch,* Aug. 16–18, 1909.

30. New York *Call,* Aug. 29, 1909.

31. St. Louis *Labor,* Aug. 28, 1909, Eugene V. Debs Miscellaneous Papers, 1909, *TIL.*

32. New York *Call,* Aug. 24, 1909; New York *Tribune,* Aug. 24, 1909; Pittsburgh *Dispatch,* Aug. 23–24, 1909.

33. St. Louis *Labor,* Aug. 28, 1909, Eugene V. Debs Miscellaneous Papers, 1909,

TIL; New York *Tribune,* Aug. 25, 1909; New York *Call,* Aug. 24, 26, 1909; Pittsburgh *Dispatch* reprinted in *Industrial Worker,* Sept. 2, 1909.

34. New York *Call,* Aug. 25, 1909.

35. New York *Call,* Aug. 26, 1909; Pittsburgh *Leader,* Aug. 26, 1909.

36. Duchez, *op. cit.,* p. 296; New York *Call,* Aug. 24, 1909.

37. *The New York Times,* Aug. 29, 1909.

38. New York *Evening Post,* Aug. 29, 1909; New York *Sun,* Aug. 29, 1909; Pittsburgh *Leader,* Sept. 1–3, 1909; New York *Call,* Sept. 1, 3, 4, 1909; Rufus Smith, "Some Phases of the McKees Rocks Strike," *Survey,* Oct. 2, 1909, p. 41.

39. New York *Sun,* Aug. 29, 1909; Duchez, *op. cit.,* pp. 295–96.

40. Walter F. McCaleb, *Brotherhood of Railroad Trainmen,* New York, 1936, pp. 75–76.

41. Duchez, *op. cit.,* pp. 295–96; New York *Call,* Sept. 3, 1909.

42. Pittsburgh *Leader,* Sept. 2, 1909; Pittsburgh *Dispatch,* Sept. 3, 1909.

43. New York *Call,* Sept. 7–11, 1909; Rufus Smith, *op. cit.,* p. 41; Duchez, *op. cit.,* p. 290; Pittsburgh *Leader,* Sept. 8–9, 1909.

44. New York *Call,* Oct. 12, 1909.

45. W. W. Trautmann, *Why Strikes Are Lost: How to Win,* I.W.W. pamphlet, n.p., n.d., pp. 17–18.

46. *Solidarity,* Aug. 17, 1912; Pittsburgh *Dispatch,* Sept. 13, 1909.

47. Donald Griffith Adams, "Foreign-born Laborers in Indiana," unpublished M.A. thesis, 1911, pp. 15–16; *Solidarity,* Jan. 29, Feb. 5, 1910; Indianapolis *Star,* Jan. 16, 1910.

48. Lake County *Times,* Jan. 15, Feb. 5, 1910.

49. *Ibid.,* Jan. 18, 1910; *Solidarity,* Jan. 29, 1910.

50. Lake County *Times,* Jan. 19, 20, 27, 1910; *Solidarity,* Feb. 5, 1910.

51. Lake County *Times,* Jan. 26, Feb. 5, 1910; *Solidarity,* Jan. 29, 1910.

52. Lake County *Times,* Jan. 28, 1910; New York *Call,* Feb. 4, 1910; *Solidarity,* Feb. 1, 1910.

53. Lake County *Times,* Jan. 22, 24, 1910; *Solidarity,* Jan. 29, 1910.

54. Lake County *Times,* Jan. 26–28, 1910; Indianapolis *Star,* Jan. 27, 1910.

55. Lake County *Times,* Jan. 28, 29, 1910; Indianapolis *Star,* Feb. 1, 1910; *Solidarity,* Feb. 5, 1910; New York *Call,* Feb. 1, 1910.

56. New York *Call,* Feb. 1, 1910; Lake County *Times,* Jan. 31, Feb. 1910.

57. Lake County *Times,* Feb. 2, 4, 6, 16, 1910; New York *Call,* Feb. 4, 16, 1910.

58. Lake County *Times,* Feb. 4, 1910; *Solidarity,* Feb. 5, 1910; New York *Call,* Feb. 4, 1910.

59. Lake County *Times,* Feb. 2, 1910.

60. New York *Call,* July 17, 23, 1909; Duchez, *op. cit.,* pp. 295–96.

61. New York *Tribune,* July 2, 1909; John A. Garraty, "U.S. Steel Versus Labor: The Early Years," *Labor History,* vol. I, Winter, 1960, pp. 26–27.

62. *Amalgamated Journal,* July 1, 1909, p. 1.

63. Pittsburgh *Leader,* July 16, 1909; New York *Call,* July 15, 16, Oct. 12, 1909; Duchez, *op. cit.,* pp. 295–96.

64. New York *Tribune,* Aug. 12, 1909; New York *Call,* Aug. 13, 1909.

65. New York *Call,* Aug. 13, 1909.

66. *Ibid.; The Free Press,* New Castle, Nov. 6, 1909, Eugene V. Debs Miscellaneous Papers, *TIL.*

67. New York *Call,* Aug. 19, Oct. 12, 1909; April 15, 1910.

68. Reprinted in unnamed paper, dated Pittsburgh, Oct. 13, 1909, in Eugene V. Debs Miscellaneous Papers, *TIL.*

69. New York *Call,* Oct. 12, 1909.

70. P. J. McCardle to Frank Morrison, Oct. 15, 1909, *AFL Corr.*

71. Emmett Flood to Frank Morrison, Oct. 20, 1909, *AFL Corr.*

72. New York *Call,* Feb. 10–15, March 5, 1910; *Amalgamated Journal,* March 10, 1910, p. 1; *Solidarity,* May 25, 1912; *International Socialist Review,* vol. XVII, Jan. 1917, pp. 429–31; *Industrial Worker,* March 12, 1910; copy of leaflet, dated South Bethlehem, Pa., and signed by the I.W.W. and the Allentown Socialist Party, attached to John Fairley to Frank Morrison, March 1, 1910, *AFL Corr.*

73. New York *Call,* April 15, 1910; Pittsburgh *Gazette,* reprinted in *Solidarity,* Aug. 10, 1912; Petition to Joseph G. Steedle, Burgess of McKees Rocks, Pa., April 20, 1910, copied in circular letter issued by the Citizens' Association of Lawrence, Mass., 1912, copy in *AFL Corr.*

74. New York *Call,* Oct. 4, Dec. 16, 1909; Jan. 28, April 19–21, 1910; *Solidarity,* April 23, Aug. 6, 1910; *Industrial Worker,* Feb. 5, April 23, 1910.

75. *Solidarity,* July 9, 1910.

76. *Ibid.*

77. *Industrial Worker*, Sept. 17, 1910; *Solidarity*, Oct. 8, 1910.
78. *Industrial Worker*, Oct. 8, 1910; *Solidarity*, Oct. 8, 1910.
79. *Solidarity*, April 23, May 21, July 2, Sept. 24, 1910; Thompson, *op. cit.*, p. 45.
80. Circular letter issued by the Citizens' Association of Lawrence, Mass., 1912, copy in *AFL Corr.*

CHAPTER 13

1. Thompson, *op. cit.*, pp. 41–42.
2. Leo Wolman, *The Growth of American Trade Unions, 1880–1923*, New York, 1924, pp. 168–69, 182; Fenton, *op. cit.*, pp. 305–06; Horace B. Davis, *Shoes: The Workers and the Industry*, New York, 1940, pp. 180–82, 195; New York State, *Bureau of Labor Statistics*, 1898, pp. 1072–74; *Solidarity*, Nov. 5, 12, 19, Dec. 10, 1910; Jan. 18, 1911.
3. *Solidarity*, Nov. 26, Dec. 10, 1910; *Shoe Workers' Journal*, Jan. 1911, pp. 26–28.
4. *Solidarity*, Dec. 10, 17, 24, 1910; Feb. 11, 1911; Fenton, *op. cit.*, pp. 306–07.
5. *Solidarity*, Feb. 18, 1911; *Shoe Workers' Journal*, March, 1911, pp. 29–30.
6. *Solidarity*, March 11, 25, 1911; Fenton, *op. cit.*, pp. 306–07.
7. *Blue Book, Textile Directory of the United States and Canada*, 24th Annual Edition, 1911–12.
8. U.S. Bureau of Labor, *Report on Strike of Textile Workers in Lawrence, Massachusetts in 1912*, p. 9; Lawrence *Evening Tribune*, Jan. 24, 1912; Ray Stannard Baker, "The Revolutionary Strike," *American Magazine*, May 1912, pp. 26–27.
9. Hearings on Strike at Lawrence, Mass., 62nd Congress, 1st Session, *House Document No. 671*, Washington, 1912, pp. 458, 460; Maurice B. Dergan, *History of Lawrence, Massachusetts*, Lawrence, Mass., 1924, p. 44; Donald B. Cole, "Lawrence, Massachusetts: 1845–1912," unpublished Ph.D. thesis, Harvard University, 1956, p. 35; *Textile Manufacturers Journal*, March 9, 1912, p. 4; Fenton, *op. cit.*, pp. 320–21.
10. *Textile Manufacturers Journal*, March 16, 1912, pp. 1, 4; *Textile American*, March, 1912, pp. 13–14; Donald B. Cole, "Lawrence, Massachusetts: Model Town to Immigrant City, 1845–1912," *Essex Institute Historical Collections*, vol. XCII, Oct. 1956, p. 357.

11. *House Document No. 671, op. cit.*, pp. 37, 99; *Bulletin of the National Association of Wool Manufacturers*, June 1912, p. 141; *U.S. Bureau of Labor, op. cit.*, pp. 71, 72, 88, 94, 98, 108, 119.
12. *U.S. Bureau of Labor, op. cit.*, pp. 19, 76–78; U.S. Bureau of the Census, *Census Monographs*, vol. X, 1929; Paul F. Brissenden, *Earnings of Factory Workers 1899 to 1927*, Washington, D.C., 1929, pp. 45, 96, 104, 113, 114.
13. U.S. Bureau of Labor, *op. cit.*, pp. 28, 71, 120, 160, 205; Lewis E. Palmer, "A Strike for Four Loaves of Bread," *Survey*, Feb. 3, 1912, pp. 1695–99.
14. *House Document No. 671, op. cit.*, p. 9; Lawrence *Sun*, Jan. 21–22, 1912.
15. U.S. Bureau of Labor, *op. cit.*, pp. 22, 88, 119.
16. *House Document No. 671, op. cit.*, pp. 114–15; *Solidarity*, March 2, 1912; John B. McPherson, "The Lawrence Strike of 1912," *Bulletin of the National Association of Wool Manufacturers*, vol. XII, 1912, pp. 236–37.
17. U.S. Bureau of Labor, *op. cit.*, pp. 78–82.
18. *House Document No. 671, op. cit.*, pp. 118–21.
19. Lawrence, Mass., *Annual Report of the Inspector of Buildings for the Year December 31, 1912*, pp. 36, 194.
20. Lawrence, Mass., *Annual Report of the Director of the Department of Public Health and Charities for the Year 1912*, pp. 499–500; U.S. Bureau of Labor, *op. cit.*, pp. 178–80.
21. *House Document No. 671, op. cit.*, pp. 32, 145, 155; *U.S. Bureau of Labor, op. cit.*, pp. 178–80.
22. Irving J. Levine, "The Lawrence Strike," unpublished M.A. thesis, Columbia University, 1936, p. 35.
23. *House Document No. 671, op. cit.*, pp. 396–98, 402; Lawrence *Sun*, Feb. 2, 1912.
24. U.S. Bureau of Labor, *op. cit.*, pp. 191–204
25. *Lawrence City Documents*, Lawrence, Mass., 1913, p. 473; *The Report of the Lawrence Survey . . .*, Lawrence, Mass., 1912, p. 64.
26. "Appeal and Proclamation issued by the Strike Committee," New York *Call*, Jan. 24, 1912; Lawrence *Evening Tribune*, Feb. 27, 1912.
27. *House Document No. 671, op. cit.*, pp. 75, 85–87; *Annual Report of the (Massachusetts) State Board of Conciliation*

and Arbitration for the Year Ending December 31, 1912, 1913, p. 18.

28. John Golden to Frank Morrison, June 29, 1907, *AFL Corr.; House Documents No. 671, op. cit.,* pp. 75, 76, 87; M. K. O'Sullivan, "The Labor War at Lawrence," *Survey,* April 6, 1912, pp. 70–71. Massachusetts Bureau of Statistics, *44th Annual Report of the Statistics of Labor for the Year 1913,* 1913, p. 3.
29. *Solidarity,* Feb. 4, March 18, May 20, Oct. 21, 1911.
30. *Ibid.,* Oct. 21, Nov. 23, 1911; *Industrial Worker,* Nov. 23, 1911.
31. *Massachusetts Labor Bulletin,* vol. XIV, No. 6, Sept. 1909, p. 16; vol. XVI, No. 8, Oct. 1911, pp. 28–29; *Textile Manufacturers Journal,* Jan. 20, 1912, p. 4; U.S. Bureau of Labor, *op. cit.,* p. 9.
32. Lawrence *Evening Tribune,* Jan. 12, 1912.
33. *Ibid.,* Dec. 22, 23, 28, 1911; Jan. 4, 1912.
34. *Ibid.,* Jan. 5, 11, 1912; *House Document No. 671 ,op. cit.,* p. 34.
35. Lawrence *Evening Tribune,* Jan. 12, 1912; *Annual Report of the (Massachusetts) State Board of Conciliation and Arbitration for the Year Ending Dec. 31, 1912,* 1913, p. 19.
36. Levine, *op. cit.,* p. 47.
37. Lawrence *Evening Tribune,* Jan. 12, 1912; Lawrence *Daily American,* Jan. 12, 1912; Lawrence *Sun,* Jan. 12–13, 1912; Boston *Evening Transcript,* Jan. 13, 1912; Mary E. Marcy, "The Battle for Bread at Lawrence," *International Socialist Review,* vol. XII, March 1912, p. 534.
38. Lawrence *Evening Tribune,* Jan. 12–13, 1912; *House Document No. 671, op. cit.,* pp. 40, 112.
39. McPherson, *op. cit.,* p. 227; *Industrial Union Bulletin,* Nov. 7, Dec. 12, 1908; *Solidarity,* Jan. 15, 29, Nov. 12, 1910; May 25, June 8, 1912; *Industrial Worker,* March 14, 1912.
40. Lawrence *Evening Tribune,* Jan. 14–17, 1912; *Annual Report of the (Massachusetts) Board of Arbitration and Conciliation for 1912,* pp. 19–20.
41. O'Sullivan, *op. cit.,* p. 72; Lawrence *Evening Tribune,* Feb. 28, 1912.
42. Lawrence *Evening Tribune,* Feb. 29, March 5, 1912; New York *Sun,* Feb. 15, 1912; Levine, *op. cit.,* p. 80.
43. U.S. Bureau of Labor, *op. cit.,* p. 14; *Solidarity,* March 2, 1912; Lawrence, Mass., Citizens' Association, *A Reign of Terror in an American City,* March

1912, p. 1; *The Outlook,* June 1, 1912, p. 238.
44. New York *Sun,* Feb. 5, 1912; Lawrence *Evening Tribune,* March 5, 1912.
45. Lawrence *Evening Tribune,* Jan. 16, 1912.
46. *Ibid.*
47. *Ibid.,* Feb. 21, 1912.
48. Lawrence *Daily American,* Jan. 20, 1912.
49. *Ibid.,* Feb. 23, March 15, 1912; U.S. Bureau of Labor, *op. cit.,* p. 9; *Textile Manufacturers Journal,* March 16, 1912, p. 7; O'Sullivan, *op. cit.,* p. 73.
50. Massachusetts Bureau of Statistics, *13th Annual Report on Strikes and Lockouts for 1912,* 1913, p. 7.
51. Lawrence *Evening Tribune,* Jan. 17, 1912.
52. Lawrence *Sun,* Jan. 14, 20, Feb. 24, 1912; *Solidarity,* July 27, 1912; *House Document No. 671, op. cit.,* pp. 294–95, 387–88.
53. *House Document No. 671, op. cit.,* p. 300; Lawrence *Evening Tribune,* March 11, 1912; New York *Call,* March 12, 1912; Lawrence *Daily American,* March 10, 1912.
54. Lawrence *Evening Tribune,* Jan. 17, 1912; New York *Call,* Jan. 18, 1912; Lawrence, Mass., Citizens' Association, *A Reign of Terror in An American City,* March 1912, p. 3; W. M. Pratt, "The Lawrence Revolution," *New England Magazine,* March 1912, pp. 7–10.
55. Lawrence *Evening Tribune,* Jan. 30–Feb. 2, 1912; Lawrence *Daily American,* Jan. 30, 1912; *House Document No. 671, op. cit.,* p. 295.
56. New York *Call,* Feb. 24, 1912; *Bill Haywood's Book,* p. 249; Lawrence *Evening Tribune,* Feb. 24, 1912.
57. Lawrence *Evening Tribune,* Jan. 17, 1912; New York *Call,* Jan. 18, 1912.
58. Lawrence, Mass., Citizens' Association, *A Reign of Terror in An American City,* March 1912, p. 3.
59. Dudley Holman quoted in New York *Call,* Jan. 25, 1912.
60. New York *Call,* Feb. 2, 1912; leaflet of Textile Workers' Strike Committee, in Local New York, Socialist Party Papers, TIL.
61. *Solidarity,* Feb. 10, 1912.
62. *Ibid.,* July 19, Nov. 1, 1913; Lawrence *Daily American,* July 9, 1912.
63. Lawrence *Daily American,* Feb. 24, March 15, 1912; New York *Call,* Jan. 20, 1912; U.S. Bureau of Labor, *op. cit.,* p. 18.

64. Lawrence *Sun*, Jan. 18, 1912; New York *Call*, Feb. 6, 1912; *House Document, No. 671, op. cit.*, pp. 41-45.
65. New York *Call*, Feb. 9, 1912.
66. New York *Call*, March 6, 1912; Lawrence *Evening Tribune*, Feb. 10, 18, 1912; Margaret Sanger, *Autobiography*, New York, 1938, p. 81; *The Amalgamated Journal*, June 27, 1912.
67. New York *Call*, Feb. 8, 1912; Boston *American*, Feb. 15, 18, 1912.
68. Lawrence *Evening Tribune*, Feb. 22, 1912; *House Document No. 671, op. cit.*, pp. 275-76.
69. *House Document No. 671, op. cit.*, pp. 201-08, 249-53, 301-09; Lawrence *Evening Tribune*, Feb. 24, 1912; Lawrence *Sun*, Feb. 25, 1912; *Solidarity*, March 2, 1912; New York *Call*, March 6, 1912.
70. New York *Call*, Feb. 26, March 1, 1912; *Industrial Union News*, March, 1912, p. 3; *The Public*, March 1, 1912, p. 202.
71. New York *Call*, Feb. 25, 1912; *The Public*, March 1, 1912; p. 202; *Cong. Record*, 62nd Cong., 2nd Sess., pp. 2485-86.
72. New York *Call*, March 8, 1912; Lawrence *Evening Tribune*, March 25, 1912.
73. Lawrence *Sun*, March 31, 1912.

CHAPTER 14

1. Lawrence *Evening Tribune*, Feb. 10, 1912.
2. *The New York Times*, Jan. 16, 1912.
3. New York *Call*, Feb. 27, 1912; *Toledo Union Leader* reprinted in *Industrial Worker*, March 14, 1912.
4. R. W. Child, "Who's Violent?" *Collier's*, June 29, 1912, p. 13; *Bill Haywood's Book*, p. 252.
5. Lawrence *Evening Tribune*, Jan. 16, 1912; James P. Heaton, "The Legal Aftermath of the Lawrence Strike," *Survey*, July 6, 1912, p. 509.
6. New York *Call*, Jan. 24, 1912.
7. *House Document No. 671, op. cit.*, p. 278; *Survey*, Feb. 10, 1912, p. 1726; Lawrence *Evening Tribune*, Feb. 5, 1912; Lawrence *Sun*, March 18, 1912; *American Federationist*, April 1912, p. 283.
8. Lawrence *Evening Tribune*, Jan. 29, 1912; Lawrence *Daily American*, Jan. 29, 1912; *The New York Times*, Jan. 30, 1912.
9. Lawrence *Evening Tribune*, Jan. 30, 1912; Lawrence *Daily American*, Jan. 30, 1912.

10. Lawrence *Sun*, Jan. 15, 23, 24, 31, Feb. 14, 1912; *House Document No. 671, op. cit.*, p. 351.
11. W. M. Pratt, *op. cit.*, p. 9; Lawrence *Evening Tribune*, Jan. 30, 1912.
12. New York *Call*, Feb. 27, 1912.
13. Lawrence *Evening Tribune*, Jan. 20, 1912; Lawrence *Daily American*, Jan. 28, March 4, 1912; *Solidarity*, Oct. 19, 1912.
14. Lawrence *Sun*, Jan. 15, 1912; Lawrence *Evening Tribune*, Jan. 16, 1912; Lawrence *Daily American*, Jan. 16, 1912; *House Document No. 671, op. cit.*, p. 41.
15. Lawrence *Evening Tribune*, Feb. 2, 21, 1912; J. B. McPherson, *op. cit.*, p. 227.
16. Lawrence *Sun*, Jan. 19, 21, 23, 25, 1912.
17. Lawrence *Daily American*, Feb. 28, 1912; M. B. Dorgan, *op. cit.*, p. 157.
18. Citizens' Association, Circular, March 1912; No. 2, 1912; *A Reign of Terror in An American City*, March 1912.
19. Citizens' Association, Circular, Nos. 2, 3, 1912.
20. Lawrence *Sun*, Jan. 22, 29, 31, 1912; *American Wool and Cotton Reporter*, Jan. 18, 1912, p. 123; Lawrence *Evening Tribune*, Feb. 26, 1912; Boston *Globe*, Feb. 26, 1912.
21. Lawrence *Sun*, Feb. 26, 1912.
22. Lawrence *Evening Tribune*, Jan. 22, Feb. 17, 1912; Boston *American*, Jan. 21, 1912; New York *Call*, Jan. 22, March 2, 1912; Paul Stroh, "The Catholic Clergy and American Labor Disputes, 1900-1932," unpublished Ph.D. thesis, Catholic University of America, 1939, pp. 65-67.
23. New York *Call*, March 2, 1912.
24. Lawrence *Sun*, Jan. 20-21, 1912; *The New York Times*, Jan. 21, 1912.
25. Lawrence *Evening Tribune*, Jan. 27, 1912; Lawrence *Sun*, May 14-17, 1912; *Solidarity*, June 22, 1912.
26. *Survey*, Sept. 7, 1912, p. 693.
27. Lawrence *Telegram*, Aug. 28, 1912; Lawrence *Sun*, Aug. 28, 29, 31, 1912.
28. *Solidarity*, May 24, 1913; Commonwealth vs. William Wood et al., August 29, 1912; Commonwealth vs. Collins, December 27, 1913, Boston.
29. Lawrence *Daily American*, Jan. 13, 1912; Lawrence *Evening Tribune*, Jan. 16, 22, 1912; *Industrial Worker*, Feb. 8, 1912; New York *Call*, Jan. 20, 23, 1912; Irving J. Levine, *op. cit.*, p. 77.
30. Lawrence *Evening Tribune*, Jan. 30, 1912; New York *Call*, Feb. 1, 1912.

31. Lawrence *Daily American*, Feb. 13, 20, 21, 1912; *Solidarity*, Feb. 24, 1912.
32. *Solidarity*, July 27, 1912.
33. Lawrence *Evening Tribune*, Jan. 31, 1912; New York *Call*, Feb. 1, 1912.
34. Mary Heaton Vorse, *Footnote to Folly*, New York, 1935, pp. 8–9.
35. Lawrence *Daily American*, Jan. 24, 1912; Lorin F. Deland, "The Lawrence Strike: A Study," *Atlantic Monthly*, May 1912, p. 696; Ralph Chaplin, "How the I.W.W. Defends Labor," in *Twenty-Five Years of Industrial Unionism*, Chicago, 1930, p. 23.
36. Lawrence *Evening Tribune*, Jan. 16, 1912; *House Document No. 671, op. cit.*, p. 85.
37. New York *Call*, Feb. 15, 1912.
38. Lawrence *Sun*, Jan. 19–21, 28, Feb. 2, 4, 5, 7, 1912; New York *Call*, Feb. 7, 1912; Lawrence *Daily American*, Feb. 29, March 5, 1912; Lawrence *Evening Tribune*, March 1, 1912; *The New York Times*, March 1, 1912.
39. Robert R. Brooks, "The United Textile Workers of America," unpublished Ph.D. thesis, Yale University, 1938, pp. 227–28.
40. *House Document No. 671, op. cit.*, pp. 5, 11–16, 31–46, 261–72; New York *Call*, Feb. 27, 1912; May 3, 1913.
41. American Federation of Labor, *Weekly News Letter*, Feb. 10, 1912, p. 14; M. K. O'Sullivan, *op. cit.*, p. 74.
42. M. K. O'Sullivan, *op. cit.*, p. 72. See also Lawrence *Daily American*, Feb. 6, 1912.
43. New York *Call*, Jan. 17, 1912; *The New York Times*, Jan. 22, 1912; *Industrial Worker*, Feb. 1, 8, 1912.
44. *Annual Report of the Massachusetts Board of Conciliation and Arbitration for the Year Ending December 31, 1912*, Boston, 1913, p. 23.
45. Massachusetts Senate, Senate Documents, 1912, *No. 311*, Jan. 25, 1912; *No. 318*, Jan. 30, 1912; *The New York Times*, Jan. 30, 1912; Lawrence *Sun*, Jan. 30, Feb. 24, 1912; Massachusetts House of Representatives, *House Document No. 2294*, pp. 1–5.
46. Lawrence *Daily American*, Jan. 26, Feb. 28, 1912; *Textile American*, March 1912, pp. 13–14; *Textile Manufacturers Journal*, March 16, 1912, p. 4; Lawrence *Evening Tribune*, Feb. 2, 21, 1912; New York *Call*, Feb. 5, 16, 1912; *The New York Times*, Jan. 29, 1912.
47. Dudley M. Holman to Julius Gerber, Mar. 2, 1912, Local New York, Socialist Party Papers, *TIL*.
48. Massachusetts House of Representatives, *House Document No. 2294*, pp. 6–12; Lawrence *Sun*, March 1–5, 10, 13–14, 1912.
49. Lawrence *Sun*, March 14–15, 1912; New York *Call*, March 14–15, 1912.
50. Lawrence *Evening Tribune*, March 14–16, 25–26, 1912; *The New York Times*, March 25, 1912; *Solidarity*, March 23, 1912.
51. Lawrence *Evening Tribune*, April 2–3, 1912.
52. Massachusetts Bureau of Statistics, *13th Annual Report on Strikes and Lockouts for 1912*, 1913, pp. 6–9.
53. *The New York Times*, March 25, 1912; Lawrence *Evening Tribune*, March 25, 1912; *American Wool and Cotton Reporter*, March 21, 1912, p. 394; *Textile Manufacturer*, May 15, 1912, p. 146.
54. New York *Call*, March 15, 1912.
55. *Solidarity*, July 6, 1912; *The Agitator*, Aug. 15, 1912; *The New York Times*, Nov. 5, 1912; Donald B. Cole, *Immigrant City: Lawrence, Massachusetts, 1845–1921*, Chapel Hill, N. Car., 1963, p. 4.
56. Samuel Yellen, *American Labor Struggles*, New York, 1936, pp. 200–01.
57. *Solidarity*, July 20, Sept. 7, 1912.
58. *Ibid.*, April 6, 13, 20, 1912.
59. *Industrial Worker*, May 16, Oct. 3, 1912; Lawrence *Evening Tribune*, Sept. 14, 15, 21, 1912; Lawrence *Sun*, Sept. 26–30, 1912; Lawrence *Telegram*, Sept. 27–30, 1912; Phillips Russell, "The Second Battle of Lawrence," *International Socialist Review*, vol. XIII, Nov. 1912, p. 418.
60. Lawrence *Telegram*, Oct. 3, 1912.
61. *Ibid.*, Nov. 23, 1912; *Literary Digest*, vol. XLV, 1912, p. 1050.
62. *Current Opinion*, vol. LIV, Jan. 1913, p. 24.
63. James P. Heston, "The Salem Trial," *Survey*, Dec. 7, 1912, p. 304; Lawrence *Telegram*, Nov. 26, 1912; Boston *Evening Transcript*, Nov. 26, 1912.
64. New York *Call*, March 1, 1912.
65. *Survey*, April 6, 1912, pp. 1–2; John H. Conlin, "The Industrial Workers of the World and the Lawrence Strike," unpublished M.A. thesis, Dartmouth College, 1948, pp. 10–11; Joseph Casey, "The I.W.W. in Relation to the Lawrence Strike," unpublished Honors thesis, Harvard University, 1958, pp. 33–36.
66. Brissenden, *op. cit.*, p. 284.

67. New York *Call*, Jan. 22, March 14, 1912.
68. *Proceedings*, United Textile Workers Convention, 1912, pp. 66–67; *Bulletin of the National Association of Wool Manufacturers*, Sept. 1912, pp. 264–65; Lawrence *Sun*, March 17, 19, 21, 22, 23, 24, 25, 26, 27, 28, 29, 30, April 2, 8, 10, 24, 26, May 22, 24, 27, 28, 29, June 1, 3, 5, 7, 8, 10, 1912; Lawrence *Evening Tribune*, April 3, 8, 9, 10, 23, 24, 26, 1912; *Solidarity*, March 23, 1912.
69. Lawrence *Sun*, Oct. 1, 1912; Lawrence *Evening Tribune*, Oct. 1, 1912.
70. *Cf.* New Orleans *Times Democrat*, Oct. 1, 1912; Alice L. Walsh, *The Life and Labors of Rev. James T. O'Reilly, O.S.A.*, Lawrence, Mass., 1930, p. 50; Lawrence *Sun*, Oct. 7–11; 1912; Elizabeth Gurley Flynn, *I Speak My Own Piece*, p. 139.
71. Lawrence *Sun*, Oct. 12–13, 1912; Lawrence *Telegram*, Oct. 14, 1912; *Solidarity*, Oct. 19, 1912.
72. *Solidarity*, Feb. 6, 1915.
73. Brissenden, *op. cit.*, pp. 293–94.
74. *The New York Times*, July 12, Aug. 9, 1913; *Solidarity*, Nov. 23, 1912; Feb. 2, 1913.
75. R. F. Hoxie, "Truth About the Industrial Workers of the World," *Journal of Political Economy*, vol. XXI, Nov. 1913, p. 786; Conlin, *op. cit.*, p. 43.
76. Donald B. Cole, *Immigrant City . . .*, *op. cit.*, p. 192.
77. Mary E. McDowell to Mr. Leard (1912); Mary E. McDowell to Homer D. Call, (1912), and May 28, 1912, Mary E. McDowell Papers, Chicago Historical Society.
78. Homer D. Call to Mary E. McDowell, May 27, June 10, 1912, *ibid*.

CHAPTER 15

1. *Solidarity*, Nov. 9, 1912.
2. *Ibid.*, Nov. 16, 23, 30, Dec. 7, 14, 21, 28, 1912; New York *Call*, March 20, 21, 1913; *The Syndicalist*, Jan. 1, 1913; Phillips Russell, "The Strike at Little Falls," *International Socialist Review*, vol. XIII, Dec. 1912, pp. 455–60; Utica *Press*, Oct. 16, 1912.
3. *Industrial Worker*, Dec. 5, 1912, Jan. 9, 1913; *Solidarity*, Jan. 11, 1913; Utica *Press*, Jan. 2–3, 1913.
4. *Solidarity*, Jan. 18, 25, 1913.
5. *The New York Times*, Feb. 26, 1913;

Howard Levin, "The Paterson Silk workers' Strike of 1913," *King's Crown Essays*, Winter, 1961–62, p. 45; *Report of the Bureau of Statistics of Labor and Industry of New Jersey for 1913*, Camden, N.J., 1914, p. 188.
6. Gregory Mason, "Industrial War in Paterson," *Outlook*, vol. LIV, June 7, 1913, pp. 283–87; S. Matsu, *History of the Silk Industry in the United States*, New York, 1930, p. 183; *Report of the Bureau of Statistics of Labor and Industry of New Jersey for 1913*, p. 188; *Report . . . for 1914*, Camden, N.J., 1915, pp. 26, 127.
7. W. L. Kinkead, "Paterson Silk Strike," *Survey*, vol. XXX, June 31, 1913, p. 316; E. Koettgen, "Making Silk," *International Socialist Review*, vol. XIV, March 1914, pp. 553–54; *Report of the Bureau of Statistics of Labor and Industry of New Jersey for 1914*, pp. 158–59; Philip Charles Newman, "The I.W.W. in New Jersey, 1912–1913," unpublished M.A. thesis, Columbia University, p. 10; *Solidarity*, March 15, 1913; Grace Hutchins, *Labor and Silk*, New York, 1924, pp. 120–21.
8. U.S. Senate Commission on Industrial Relations, *Final Report and Testimony*, Washington, 1916, pp. 2142–46.
9. Matsu, *op. cit.*, pp. 208–11.
10. *Ibid.*, pp. 213–14; *Solidarity*, April 11, 1914.
11. Paterson *Evening News*, Nov. 11, 1912; M. B. Sumner, "Broad Silk Weavers of Paterson," *Survey*, vol. XXVII, March 16, 1912, pp. 1932–35; *Industrial Union News*, Jan. 1912.
12. Paterson *Call*, Feb. 22, 1912; Paterson *Press*, Feb. 23, 26, 1912; New York *Call*, Feb. 24, 27, 1912; Philip Newman, "The First I.W.W. Invasion of New Jersey," *Proceedings of the New Jersey Historical Society*, vol. LVIII, 1940, pp. 270–73.
13. St. Paul *Daily News*, March 31, 1912. See also Sumner, *op. cit.*, pp. 1932–37 and Newman, "The I.W.W. in New Jersey, 1912–1913," *op. cit.*, p. 18.
14. *Solidarity*, April 6, 1912.
15. Paterson *Evening News*, April 15, 22–May 2, 1912; Paterson *Press*, May 11, 13, 15, 22, 31, Aug. 12, 1912.
16. Paterson *Press*, May 31, 1912.
17. Harold B. Denn, "The History of the Silk Workers in Paterson, New Jersey, with special emphasis on strikes, 1910–1920," unpublished M.A. thesis, New York University, 1947, p. 49; *Industrial*

Union News, June 1912; Paterson *Press*, Aug. 12, Dec. 19, 23–27, 1912.

18. *Industrial Union News*, March–October 1912; *Weekly People*, Dec. 27, 1913; Jan. 22, 1916; *Solidarity*, April 6, 20, Oct. 6, 1912.

19. Philip Newman, "The First I.W.W. Invasion of New Jersey," *op. cit.*, p. 283.

20. Paterson *Press*, Jan. 27–28, 1913.

21. *Ibid.*, Feb. 7, 18, 1913.

22. Denn, *op. cit.*, p. 55; Paterson *Press*, Feb. 25, 1913; New York *Call*, Feb. 26, 1913; *Solidarity*, March 1, 1913.

23. Paterson *Press*, Feb. 26, March 4, 1913; *The New York Times*, Feb. 26, March 4, 1913; William D. Haywood, "The Rip in the Silk Industry," *International Socialist Review*, vol. XIII, May 1913, p. 783.

24. *Report of the Bureau of Statistics of Labor and Industry of New Jersey for 1913*, p. 185.

25. Paterson, 1914, p. 7. *See also* James E. Wood, "History of Labor in the Broad-Silk Industry of Paterson, New Jersey," unpublished Ph.D. thesis, University of California, 1941, p. 24.

26. Paterson *Press*, March 27, 1913; Silk Association of America, *Annual Report*, March 25, 1913, p. 35.

27. New York *Call*, Feb. 26, 1913; Paterson *Evening News*, March 6, 1913; Paterson *Morning Call*, March 14, 1913; *Solidarity*, April 11, 1913.

28. *The New York Times*, April 28, 1913.

29. Commission on Industrial Relations, *op. cit.*, vol. III, p. 2458. Testimony of Adolph Lessig.

30. L. Mannheimer, "Darkest New Jersey, How the Paterson Strike Looks to One in the Thick of the Conflict," *The Independent*, vol. LXXIV, April–June 1913, pp. 1191–92; *The New York Times*, May 5, 1913; Paterson *Press*, May 5, 1913.

31. Paterson *Press*, April 17–22, 1913; New York *Call*, April 17–19, 23, 1913.

32. Paterson *Call*, March 4, 1913; New York *Call*, Feb. 28, March 4, 1913.

33. *The New York Times*, March 11, 18, 31, April 20, 28, May 19, 1913.

34. Carl Sigrosser, "Sunday at Haledon," New York *Call*, June 11, 1913.

35. Haywood, "The Rip in the Silk Industry," *op. cit.*, p. 788.

36. Paterson *Press*, Feb. 26, 27, 1913; *The New York Times*, March 4, 1913.

37. Paterson *Press*, Feb. 27, 28, 1913.

38. Denn, *op. cit.*, pp. 69–70; "Possible Paterson," *Outlook*, vol. CIV, June 14,

1913, p. 319; Paterson *Press*, March 1, 1913; New York *Call*, March 3, 1913; *Industrial Worker*, March 27, 1913.

39. Paterson *Press*, April 5, 7, 8, 15, June 7, 1913; New York *Call*, June 2, 1913.

40. Commission on Industrial Relations, *op. cit.*, vol. II, pp. 2530–35; *The New York Times*, May 9, 28, July 6, 1913; Fenton, *op. cit.*, p. 371.

41. Paterson *Press*, March 31, April 5, 1913; Paterson *Evening News*, April 1, 1913; New York *Call*, April 3, 6, 1913; *The New York Times*, April 5, 1913.

42. Paterson *Press*, April 26, 1913; New York *Call*, April 27, 1913; John Reed, "War in Paterson," *International Socialist Review*, vol. XLIV, July 1913, p. 46; *The New York Times*, May 15, 1913; New York *Call*, May 11, July 4, 25, 1913; "Elizabeth Gurley Flynn's Contest with Paterson," *Survey*, vol. XXXV, Dec. 11, 1915, p. 283.

43. Paterson *Press*, June 7, 1913.

44. "The Conviction of Alexander Scott," *International Socialist Review*, vol. XIV, July 1913, pp. 10–11; New York *Call*, June 7, 1913; New York *World* quoted in *International Socialist Review*, vol. XIV, July 1913, pp. 10–11; New York *Tribune*, June 7, 1913; *The Outlook*, vol. CIV, June 7, 1913, pp. 283–87; *Solidarity*, June 21, 1913.

45. Paterson *Press*, March 6–14, 1913; New York *Call*, April 15, 1913.

46. Paterson *Press*, March 13–14, 19–20, 1913, New York *Call*, March 14, 1913; Cleveland *Socialist*, March 22, 1913.

47. Paterson *Press*, April 10, 11, 15, 16, 17, 21, 1913; New York *Call*, April 16–18, 1913; *Industrial Worker*, May 8, 1913; *Convention Proceedings*, United Textile Workers, 1913, pp. 22–27; Brooks, *op. cit.*, p. 229.

48. New York *Call*, April 21, May 7, 9, 1913; Brooks, *op. cit.*, p. 229.

49. New York *Call*, April 20, 22, May 7, 1913; Paterson *Press*, April 18, 19, 22, 1913; *The New York Times*, April 22, 1913; *Solidarity*, May 3, 1913; *International Socialist Review*, vol. XIII, May 1913, pp. 785–86; Mannheimer, *op. cit.*, p. 1192; Brooks, *op. cit.*, p. 229.

50. Leo Mannheimer to W. B. Wilson (April 1913); W. B. Wilson to Leo Mannheimer (April 1913), Labor Department File 3314, *NA*.

51. *The Education of John Reed*, Selected writings with a critical introduction by John Stuart, New York, 1955, p. 39.

52. Granville Hicks, *John Reed, The Mak-*

ing of a Revolutionary, New York, 1936, p. 100.

53. New York *Call*, April 30, 1913.
54. *Ibid.*, pp. 101–02; *The New York Times*, May 22, 1913.
55. *The Pageant of the Paterson Strike*, New York, 1913.
56. Grace Potter in *The New Review*, Sept. 1913, p. 795.
57. *The New York Times*, June 9, 1913; New York *Call*, June 9, 1913.
58. *The Independent*, vol. LXXXIV, June 19, 1913; p. 1406; *Survey*, vol. XXX, June 29, 1913, p. 428.
59. Hicks, *op. cit.*, p. 102.
60. *The New York Times*, June 8, 13, 1913; *International Socialist Review*, Vol. XIV, July 1913, pp. 7–9; Howard Levin, *op. cit.*, p. 57.
61. Elizabeth Gurley Flynn, "The Paterson Strike," *op. cit.*, p. 18. *See also* Elizabeth Gurley Flynn, *I Speak My Own Piece*, p. 156.
62. New York *Call*, June 20, 1913.
63. Paterson *Press*, June 20, 1913.
64. New York *Call*, June 6, 1913; *Survey*, June 14, 1913, p. 368.
65. Paterson *Press*, June 27, July 17, 18, 1913; New York *Call*, July 19, 1913.
66. Paterson *Press*, July 25, 1913.
67. "The End of the Paterson Strike," *The Outlook*, vol. CIV, 1913, p. 780; *Report of the Bureau of Statistics of Labor and Industry of New Jersey for 1913*, pp. 227, 230, 238.
68. New York *Call*, Aug. 4, 1913; *Solidarity*, Aug. 9, 1913.
69. Paterson *Press*, June 17, 1914, in "Scrapbooks of Commission on Industrial Relations, June 1914," Frank P. Walsh Papers, New York Public Library.
70. *Solidarity*, Aug. 9, 1913.
71. *Report of the Bureau of Statistics of Labor and Industry of New Jersey for 1913*, p. 227.
72. New York *Call*, June 20, Aug. 27, 1913; *The Syndicalist*, Sept. 1–15, 1913; "The Lesson of Paterson," *The Common Cause*, July 1913, p. 50; "Work of the I.W.W. in Paterson," *Literary Digest*, vol. XLVII, Aug. 9, 1913, p. 198.
73. Elizabeth Gurley Flynn, "The Truth About the Paterson Strike," *op. cit.*, p. 5.
74. *Ibid.*, pp. 6, 10.
75. *Report of the Bureau of Statistics of Labor and Industry of New Jersey for 1913*, p. 209; *Industrial Union News*, Jan. 1914.
76. Patrick L. Quinlan, "The Paterson Strike and After," *The New Review*, Jan. 1914, p. 33; *Solidarity*, Aug. 9, 1913.
77. Patrick F. Gill and Redmond S. Brennen, "Report on the Inferior Courts and Police of Paterson, N.J., Oct. 1914," C.M.I. 11–5–14, Serial No. 723, pp. 50–56, original in *WSHS*, copy in *NA*.
78. New York *Call*, July 2, 1913.
79. Crow, *op. cit.*, p. 72.
80. Paterson *Press* reprinted in *Solidarity*, Dec. 26, 1914.
81. Brooks, *op. cit.*, pp. 230–31.

CHAPTER 16

1. *Solidarity*, Aug. 17, 1912.
2. Akron *Press*, Sept. 20, 1912.
3. Harold S. Roberts, *The Rubber Workers*, New York, 1944, pp. 26–37.
4. New York *Call*, Feb. 21, 1913.
5. *Ohio Senate Journal*, vol. CIII, 1913, p. 208.
6. *Ibid.*, pp. 208, 211.
7. New York *Call*, Feb. 28, 1913.
8. *Solidarity*, Dec. 7, 1912; Akron *Beacon Journal*, Jan. 2, 1913.
9. *Solidarity*, June 15, 1912; *Industrial Worker*, Feb. 27, 1913; *Ohio Senate Journal*, vol. CIII, 1913, pp. 210–11.
10. Akron *Beacon Journal*, Feb. 12–14, 1913.
11. *Ibid.*, Feb. 15, 1913.
12. *Ibid.*, Feb. 15–16, 1913; *Industrial Worker*, March 6, 1913; Cleveland *Socialist*, Feb. 22, 1913; Akron *Press*, reprinted in Leslie H. Marcy, "800 Per Cent and the Akron Strike," *International Socialist Review*, vol. XIII, April 1913, pp. 719–20.
13. Cleveland *Socialist*, March 1, 1913; *Industrial Worker*, March 6, 1913.
14. Cleveland *Socialist*, March 1, 1913.
15. *Ibid.*
16. *Ibid.*, Feb. 22, 1913; New York *Call*, Feb. 28, 1913.
17. Akron *Beacon Journal*, Feb. 17, 1913.
18. *Ibid.*, Feb. 19, 1913.
19. *Ibid.*, Feb. 20, 25, 1913.
20. *Ibid.*, Feb. 13, 1913.
21. *Ibid.*, Feb. 17, 19, 21, 1913.
22. *Ibid.*, Feb. 18, 1913.
23. *Ibid.*, Feb. 22, 1913.
24. *Ibid.*, March 11, 1913.
25. *Ibid.*, March 15, 1913.
26. *Ibid.*, March 6, 1913.
27. *Ibid.*, March 13, 1913.
28. Roberts, *op. cit.*, p. 44.
29. Cleveland *Socialist*, March 1, 1913.
30. Akron *Beacon Journal*, Feb. 24, 25, 1913.

31. *Ibid.*, Feb. 26, 28, 1913.
32. *Ibid.*, March 6, 1913.
33. *Ibid.*, March 8, 1913.
34. *Ibid.*, March 11, 12, 1913; Cleveland *Socialist*, March 15, 1913.
35. Akron *Beacon Journal*, March 12, 1913.
36. *Ibid.*
37. *Ibid.*, March 13, 1913.
38. *Ibid.*; New York *Call*, March 15, 1913.
39. *India Rubber World*, April 1, 1913, pp. 365–66.
40. Cleveland *Socialist*, March 29, 1913.
41. *Ibid.*, March 13, 1913; *Industrial Worker*, April 10, 1913.
42. Robert H. Hoxie, *Trade Unionism in the United States*, New York, 1917, p. 141.
43. Cleveland *Socialist*, April 12, 1913; Akron *Beacon Journal*, March 1, 4, 1913.
44. *Ohio Senate Journal*, vol. CIII, 1913, pp. 205–06.
45. New York *Call*, June 16, 1913; Toledo *Unionist*, reprinted in *Solidarity*, April 19, 1913.
46. Akron *Beacon-Journal*, March 15, 1913; *Industrial Worker*, March 27, 1913; *Solidarity*, April 26, 1913.
47. Roberts, *op. cit.*, pp. 79–92.
48. *Solidarity*, April 26, 1913.
49. Robert W. Dunn, *Labor and Automobiles*, New York, 1928, pp. 14, 18, 20, 27, 117; *Solidarity*, May 27, 1911; John A. Fitch in *Survey*, reprinted in *Solidarity*, Feb. 14, 1914.
50. Detroit *Free Press*, June 21, 1913; Fagin, *op. cit.*, pp. 94–95; James O. Morris, *Conflict Within the A.F. of L.: A Study of Craft versus Industrial Unionism*, Ithaca, N.Y., 1958, pp. 22–24.
51. Allan Nevins (with the collaboration of Frank Ernest Hill), *Ford, The Times, The Man, the Company*, New York, 1954, pp. 377–79.
52. *Solidarity*, May 27, June 3, July 22, Aug. 5, Nov. 4, 1911.
53. *Ibid.*, May 4, 1912, June 14, Aug. 9, 1913.
54. Quoted in Nevins, *op. cit.*, p. 518.
55. *Ibid.*, p. 384.
56. Detroit *Free Press*, April 30, 1913; *Solidarity*, May 3, 1913; *Industrial Worker*, May 15, 1913; Keith Sward, *The Legend of Henry Ford*, New York, 1948, pp. 47–48.
57. *Industrial Worker*, May 15, 1913; Fagin, *op. cit.*, p. 73.
58. Detroit *Free Press*, June 10, 1913; *Solidarity*, July 12, 1913.

59. Detroit *Free Press*, June 17–19, 1913; New York *Call*, June 18, 1913.
60. Detroit *Free Press*, May 1, 1913.
61. Detroit *Times*, June 18, 1913; Detroit *News*, June 17, 1913.
62. Detroit *Free Press*, June 19, 1913; New York *Call*, June 19, 1913.
63. Detroit *Free Press*, June 20, 1913.
64. *Emancipator*, June 21, 1913; Detroit *Free Press*, June 21, 1913.
65. Detroit *Free Press*, June 18, 1913.
66. *Ibid.*, June 21, 22, 24, 1913.
67. *Proceedings*, A.F. of L. Convention, 1914, pp. 182, 240, 341; Dunn, *op. cit.*, p. 126.
68. Sward, *op. cit.*, p. 126.
69. *Solidarity*, Feb. 7, April 20, 1914; Joseph Galamb, Oral History interview, Oral History Collection, Columbia University. In his study of Ford, Allan Nevins questions this statement. (*op. cit.*, p. 537.)
70. *Solidarity*, July 12, 1913.
71. *Solidarity*, Feb. 7, April 20, 1914; July 24, 1915.
72. Detroit *News*, June 19, 1913.
73. Nevins, *Ford*, *op. cit.*, pp. 379, 522.
74. Detroit *Times*, June 21, 23, 1913.

CHAPTER 17

1. Chicago *Daily Socialist*, Oct. 20, 1906.
2. *Industrial Worker*, May 7, June 25, 1910; *Solidarity*, Oct. 15, 1910; May 4, 1912.
3. *Proceedings of the Fifth National Congress of the Socialist Party of the United States. Held at Chicago, Ill., May 15–21, 1910*, Chicago, 1910, pp. 277–89.
4. *Industrial Worker*, July 30, 1910; Carl D. Thompson, *The Rising Tide of Socialism*, Chicago, 1912, pp. 3–5.
5. Eugene V. Debs to William English Walling, Dec. 7, 1909, Archives of the National Office, Socialist Party, U.S.A., 1901–1938, Duke University Library; *International Socialist Review*, vol. XI, Jan. 1911, pp. 413–15.
6. *Solidarity*, April 29, June 17, Nov. 4, 1911; Fenton, *op. cit.*, pp. 183–84.
7. *Solidarity*, March 4, 1911; *Emancipator*, Feb. 25, 1911; Fagin, *op. cit.*, pp. 66–67.
8. Chicago *Daily Socialist*, July 14, 22, Aug. 25, 1906; *Appeal to Reason*, Jan. 18, 1908; *International Socialist Review*, vol. VIII, Feb. 1908, p. 506; *Solidarity*, Dec. 24, 1910, June 30, 1911.
9. William D. Haywood and Frank Bohn,

Industrial Socialism, Chicago, 1911, foreword, pp. 43–47, 55–59.
10. *International Socialist Review,* vol. XII,
Dec. 1911, p. 375.
11. Letter of W. D. Haywood in New York
Call, Nov. 29, 1911.
12. Ira Kipnis, *The American Socialist
Movement, 1897–1912,* New York, 1952,
p. 384; W. J. Ghent, "The Haywood
Vote," Chicago *Daily Socialist,* Feb. 2,
1912.
13. *Solidarity,* Dec. 9, 1911.
14. "Stenographic Report of the Hillquit-
Haywood Debate," New York *Call,* Jan.
14, 1912.
15. Haywood, *Bill Haywood's Book,* p. 246.
16. New York *Call,* Dec. 22, 23, 1911 and
letter in *ibid.,* Dec. 31, 1911; New York
Tribune, The New York Times, Dec.
22, 1911; Kipnis, *op. cit.,* pp. 386–87.
17. *International Socialist Review,* vol. XII,
Feb. 1912, pp. 461–71.
18. New York *Call,* Feb. 1, 1912.
19. *International Socialist Review,* vol. XII,
Feb. 1912, pp. 481–83.
20. *Solidarity,* Feb. 24, March 16, 23, 1912.
21. *Industrial Worker,* Feb. 22, March 7,
1912.
22. New York *Call,* Jan. 26, 30, March 14,
16, 1912; Leslie H. Marcy and Frederick
Summer Boyd, "One Big Union Wins,"
International Socialist Review, vol. XII,
April 1912, p. 627.
23. New York *Call,* May 18, 1912; *Solidarity,* Jan. 22, March 14, June 8, 1912.
24. *Solidarity,* April 20, 1912.
25. *National Socialist,* Feb. 10, Aug. 31,
1912, clippings in W. J. Ghent Papers,
Box 46, Library of Congress.
26. Kipnis, *op. cit.,* pp. 389–400; Carl D.
Thompson, "For a High Water Mark,"
Chicago *Daily Socialist,* April 26, 1912.
27. *Solidarity,* April 27, 1912.
28. New York *Call,* May 5, 1912; Kipnis,
op. cit., p. 397.
29. *International Socialist Review,* vol. XII,
June 1912, pp. 807–08; *Socialist Party
Bulletin,* May, June 1912; Kipnis, *op.
cit.,* p. 398.
30. *National Convention of the Socialist
Party, Held at Indianapolis, Ind., May
12 to 18, 1912, Stenographic Report,*
Chicago, 1912, pp. 60–63, hereinafter
cited as *Stenographic Report;* New York
Call, April 12, 14, 1912.
31. Samuel Gompers, *Seventy Years of Life
and Labor,* New York, 1924, vol. II,
p. 35; New York *Call,* April 17, 1912;
Solidarity, April 20, 1912; *Stenographic
Report,* pp. 59–60.

32. *Stenographic Report,* p. 195.
33. New York *Call,* May 18, 1912; *Solidarity,* May 25, 1912.
34. Letter of Martin Phelan in *Solidarity,*
May 25, 1912.
35. *Stenographic Report,* p. 100; "The National Socialist Convention of 1912,"
International Socialist Review, vol. XII,
June 1912, p. 823.
36. *Stenographic Report,* pp. 102–12; 196–
98; Kipnis, *op. cit.,* p. 401.
37. Letter of Martin Phelan in *Solidarity,*
May 25, 1912; *Stenographic Report,*
p. 130.
38. *Social-Democratic Herald,* May 25, 1912.
39. "The National Socialist Convention of
1912," *op. cit.,* p. 824; Kipnis, *op. cit.,*
pp. 402–03.
40. *Stenographic Report,* pp. 122, 134, 199.
41. *Ibid.,* p. 130.
42. *Ibid.,* pp. 128, 130–32, 136–37.
43. *National Socialist,* May 25, 1912, clipping in Box 46, W. J. Ghent Papers,
Library of Congress; W. J. Ghent to
Morris Hillquit, June 27, 1912, Morris
Hillquit Papers, *WSHS.*
44. *Solidarity,* May 25, June 8, Aug. 10,
1912.
45. New York *Call,* Aug. 13, 1912.
46. *Social-Democratic Herald,* Aug. 10, 17,
1912; New York *Call,* Dec. 3, 1912.
47. Kipnis, *op. cit.,* p. 415.
48. Copy of ballot in Socialist Party, U.S.,
New York County Local Papers, 1907–
14, *TIL.*
49. New York *Call,* Jan. 4, 1913; Cleveland
Socialist, Jan. 18, 1913; Wm. W. Shurt-
leff to John M. Work, secretary Socialist
Party, Schenectady, N.Y., Feb. 5, 1913,
and "Resolutions of Protest" in Socialist
Party, U.S., New York County Local
Papers, 1907–14.
50. *National Socialist,* clippings in Box 46,
W. J. Ghent Papers, Library of Congress; *Socialist Party Weekly Bulletin,*
March 1, 1913; Kipnis, *op. cit.,* p. 417.
51. *Survey,* vol. XXIX, March 29, 1913,
p. 909; Sacramento *Bee,* Aug. 5, 1913,
WS.
52. New York *Call,* March 23, 1913; *Industrial Worker,* March 20, 1913.
53. *The New Review,* April 12, 1913, pp.
450–53; May 1913, pp. 543–44; Aug.
1913, pp. 673–80, 701–06; *Solidarity,*
Aug. 16, 1913.
54. *Solidarity,* Oct. 18, 1913.
55. New York *Call,* May 3, 15, 31, June
12, Aug. 2, 12, 19, Sept. 5, 1913; Jan.
14, 1914; Milwaukee *Leader* in *ibid.,*

Sept. 14, 1913; New York *Forward*, June 1, 1913.

56. Letter of Arthur Le Seuer, in New York *Call*, Sept. 27, 1913; letter of Henry Slobodin in *ibid.*, June 13, 1913.

57. A. William Hoglund, *Finnish Immigrants in America, 1880–1920*, Madison, Wis., 1960, p. 75; *Who's Who in Socialist America for 1914*, Girard, Kan., 1914, original in Yale University Library, zerox copy in *TIL*.

58. *Solidarity*, Aug. 22, Sept. 26, 1914; Aug. 14, 1915.

59. *National Socialist*, June 1, 1912, clipping in Box 46, W. J. Ghent Papers, Library of Congress; *Solidarity*, Oct. 18, 1913.

60. Kipnis, *op. cit.*, pp. 416–20. For a contrary viewpoint, *see* James Weinstein, "The Socialist Party: Its Roots and Strength, 1912–1919," *Studies on the Left*, vol. I, Winter, 1960, pp. 5–27.

61. *The Syndicalist*, April 15, 1913.

62. Haywood, *op. cit.*, p. 259.

63. William Preston, Jr., *Aliens and Dissenters: Federal Suppression of the Radicals, 1903–1933*, Cambridge, Mass., 1963, p. 50.

CHAPTER 18

1. "Boring from Within," *Solidarity*, June 11, 1910. *See also ibid.*, Jan. 15, Feb. 1, April 2, 30, June 1, July 16, 23, 30, Aug. 20, 27, Oct. 1, Nov. 12, 19, Dec. 24, 1910; Jan. 21, 1911.

2. *Ibid.*, Dec. 24, 1910.

3. William Z. Foster, *From Bryan to Stalin*, New York, 1937, pp. 47–48.

4. *The Workingman's Paper* (Seattle), Sept. 17, 1910.

5. *Solidarity*, March 15, Sept. 16, 1911; *Industrial Worker*, Sept. 21, 1911; *American Federationist*, Oct. 1911, p. 827; New York *Call*, Sept. 5, 1911.

6. P. Monatte in *Solidarity*, March 18, 1911.

7. Foster, *op. cit.*, p. 49.

8. *Cf.* Vincent St. John, "Why the A.F. of L. Can Not Evolve into Industrial Union," in *Solidarity*, April 2, 1910.

9. Melvin Charles Shefftz, "British Labour, The General Strike, and the Constitution, 1910–1927," unpublished Ph.D. thesis, Harvard University, April 1962, p. 19; Henry Pelling, *America and the British Left: From Bright to Bevan*, New York, 1957, p. 101; Tom Mann, *Memoirs*, London, 1923, pp. 239–42.

10. Mann, *op. cit.*, pp. 251–56; Tom Mann, "Prepare for Action," *Industrial Syndicalist*, vol. I, July 1910, copy in London School of Economics Library; George Dangerfield, *The Strange Death of Liberal England*, New York, 1935, pp. 279–85; Sidney Webb, *History. of Trade Unionism*, London, 1920, pp. 482–501.

11. *Solidarity*, Sept. 30, 1911.

12. Foster, *op. cit.*, p. 55; *Solidarity*, Sept. 30, Oct. 7, 1911.

13. *Industrial Worker*, Nov. 2, 1911; *Solidarity*, Nov. 4, 1911.

14. *Solidarity*, Nov. 25, Dec. 2, 1911.

15. *Ibid.*, Nov. 8, Dec. 2, 9, 1911; *Industrial Worker*, Nov. 30, 1911.

16. *Industrial Worker*, Nov. 16, 1911; *Solidarity*, Dec. 2, 1911.

17. *Solidarity*, Jan. 27, 1912; *The Agitator*, Dec. 15, 1911, Feb. 15, April 15, 1912.

18. *The Agitator*, April 15, May 15, June 1, 15, July 1, 1912.

19. *Industrial Worker*, April 11, 1912; *The Agitator*, April 15, 1912.

20. *The Agitator*, Feb. 15, 1912; interview with William Z. Foster, New York City, Nov. 29, 1959.

21. William Z. Foster, *op. cit.*, p. 58.

22. *The Agitator*, June 15, July 15, 1912; interview with William Z. Foster, New York City, Nov. 29, 1959.

23. "A Call to Direct Actionists," *The Agitator*, Sept. 1, 1912.

24. *Solidarity*, Aug. 10, 1912; Foster, *op. cit.*, pp. 59–60; *The Syndicalist*, Feb. 1, 1913.

25. Foster, *op. cit.*, p. 60; *The Syndicalist*, Jan. 15, 1913.

26. *The Agitator*, Sept. 15, 1912.

27. Mann, *op. cit.*, 289–90.

28. New York *Call*, Aug. 4, 1913; *The Syndicalist*, Sept. 1–15, 1913; Mann, *op. cit.*, p. 320.

29. *Solidarity*, Nov. 22, 1913.

30. *Justice*, Nov. 29, 1913.

31. *International Socialist Review*, vol. XIV, Jan. 1914, pp. 391–94.

32. *Solidarity*, Nov. 22, 1913.

33. "I.W.W. Versus A.F. of L.," *The New Review*, April 1914, p. 283.

34. Tom Mann, "Impressions d'Amérique," Philadelphia, Dec. 1, 1913, in *La Vie Ouvrière* (Paris), vol. V. pp. 722–23. A brief excerpt appeared in *Solidarity*, Jan. 31, 1914.

35. *Solidarity*, Jan. 31, 1914.

36. *The Agitator*, July 15, 1912.

37. Elizabeth Gurley Flynn, *I Speak My Own Piece*, p. 161.

CHAPTER 19

1. H. D. Lamb to W. B. Wilson, April 20, 1913; W. B. Wilson to H. D. Lamb, (April 1913), Labor Department files, CC: 5420/39, *NA*.
2. E. D. Brough to W. B. Wilson, *Ibid.*, CC: 47/6, *NA*.
3. *Review of Economic Statistics*, January 1919, p. 66; Report of Dun's Commercial Agency in *Solidarity*, Feb. 14, 1914; Godfried Ritterskamp, "Unemployment and the Six-Hour Day," *International Socialist Review*, vol. XIV, Jan. 1914, p. 409.
4. New York Department of Labor, *Bulletin No. 69*, March 1915, p. 6; *Bulletin No. 73*, Aug. 1915, p. 2; *Massachusetts Industrial Review*, No. 7, March 1922.
5. *Solidarity*, March 7, 1914.
6. *The Wooden Shoe*, Jan. 22, 1914.
7. Los Angeles *Times*, Dec. 26–27, 1913; Sacramento *Union*, Dec. 27, 1913, *WS*.
8. San Francisco *Examiner*, Dec. 27, 1913; Sacramento *Bee*, Jan. 26, 1914, *WS*; J. Edward Morgan, "The Unemployed in San Francisco," *The New Review*, April 1914, pp. 193–99; *Solidarity*, Jan. 24, 1914.
9. Weintraub, *op. cit.*, p. 82; Sacramento *Star* Feb. 13, 1914, *WS*: San Francisco *Examiner*, March 9–10, 1914; New York *Call*, March 10, 1914; *International Socialist Review*, vol. XIV, May 1914, pp. 649–50.
10. Sacramento *Bee*, March 16, 1914; San Francisco *Bulletin*, reprinted in Woodland *Democrat*, March 16, 1914, both in *WS*; Deseret *Evening News*, March 14, 1914.
11. Sacramento *Star*, March 16, 1914, *WS*; *International Socialist Review*, vol. XIV, May 1914, pp. 649–50; San Francisco *Bulletin*, March 16, 1914.
12. Sacramento *Bee*, March 16, 17, 1914; Sacramento *Star*, March 18, 1914, both in *WS*; *Solidarity*, March 21, 28, 1914.
13. Portland *Oregonian*, Jan. 16, 1914; Tyler, *op. cit.*, pp. 45–46; Arthur Evans Wood, "A Study of the Unemployed in Portland, Oregon," *Reed College Social Service Bulletin*, No. 3, 1914, pp. 5, 21; "Notes on interviews with leaders of the Unemployed League, during the last winter (1914) in the City of Portland," Commission of Industrial Relations, Labor Department Files DVP/447, *NA*.

14. Edmonton *Journal*, Jan. 6, 7, 15, 1914; *The Wooden Shoe*, Jan. 22, 1914.
15. Edmonton *Journal*, Jan. 16–19, 1914.
16. *Ibid.*, Jan. 28, 29, Feb. 3–4, 25–26, 1914;` The Wooden Shoe*, Jan. 22, 29, Feb. 6, 1914.
17. Edmonton *Journal*, Jan. 28, 1914; Boston *American*, Jan. 16, March 15, 1914; Boston. *Herald*, March 16, 1914; *The Toiler*, April–May 1914.
18. P. A. Speek, "Life Histories of Unemployed," Commission of Industrial Relations, 189 Dup. Labor Dept. Files, *NA*.
19. Detroit *Times*, Feb. 12, 1914.
20. Detroit *News*, Feb. 12–14, 1914; Detroit *Free Press*, Dec. 12–14, 1914.
21. New York *Tribune*, Jan. 29, 30, 31, Feb. 11, 12, 14, 1914; New York *People*, Feb. 14, 1914; New York *Call*, March 27, 1914; *The New York Times*, Feb. 12, 25, 1914.
22. New York *Tribune*, Jan. 29, 31, Feb. 13, 1914.
23. P. A. Speek, "Report on Investigation of Congestion of the Unemployed People in the City of New York, Feb. 1914," Commission of Industrial Relations, 189 Dup. Labor Dept. Files, *NA*.
24. Jane A. Roulston, in *Solidarity*, Aug. 8, 1914.
25. New York *Call*, Feb. 28–March 3, 1914.
26. *Ibid.*, March 15, 1914; L. Feder., *op. cit.*, pp. 256–58.
27. New York *Call*, March 3, 1914.
28. *The New York Times*, March 4, 1914; New York *Sun*, March 4, 1914.
29. New York *Call*, March 5, 1914; Max Eastman, "The Tannenbaum Crime," *The Masses*, May 1914, pp. 6–8.
30. *The New York Times*, March 5, 1914; Gloucester (Mass.) *Times*, March 11, 1914, *WS*.
31. New York *Sun*, March 6, 1914.
32. New York *Call*, March 6, 1914; *Solidarity*, March 14, 1914.
33. New York *Call*, March 7, 9, 10, 11, 14, 1914; Carlo Tresca, "The Unemployed and the I.W.W.," *Retort*, vol. II, June 1944, p. 29.
34. *The New York Times*, March 6, 1914.
35. New York *Call*, March 6, 1914; Henry Slobodin to Julius Gerber, March 4, 1914, Local New York, Socialist Party Papers, *TIL*; copy of leaflet in *ibid.*
36. New York *Call*, March 20, 24, 1914; *The New York Times*, March 7, 26, 1914; New York *Sun*, March 8, 1914.
37. New York *Call*, March 27, 1914.

38. *The Masses*, May 1914, p. 5.
39. *Solidarity*, March 14, 1914; Elizabeth Gurley Flynn in *ibid.*, July 18, 1914.
40. *Solidarity*, Feb. 27, 1915.
41. *Ibid.*, March 21, April 11, 18, Aug. 18, Oct. 24, Dec. 12, 1914.
42. *Ibid.*, Oct. 24, 1914.
43. Proceedings of Labor Conference, October 1914, Local New York, Socialist Party Papers, *TIL*.
44. *Solidarity*, Oct. 31, 1914; Ralph Chaplin, *Wobbly*, pp. 166–67; Brissenden, *op. cit.*, p. 329.
45. *Report of the Mayor's Committee on Unemployment*, New York, 1916, pp. 12–15; U.S. Bureau of Labor, *Bulletin #195*, pp. 98, 108; *American Labor Legislation Review*, vol. V, November 1915, pp. 478, 480; Philadelphia *North American*, Jan. 31, 1915; Joseph H. Willits, *Philadelphia Unemployment with special reference to the Textile Industries*, Philadelphia, 1915, p. 52.
46. New York *Tribune*, Dec. 3, 1914; New York *Sun*, Jan. 15, 16, 17, 1915; New York *Call*, Jan. 11, 16, 1915; Max Bertch, "Unemployment, 1914–1915," unpublished M.A. thesis, Columbia University, Economics Division, 1928, p. 12; *American Labor Legislation Review*, vol. V, November, p. 476.
47. Cleveland *Socialist News*, Jan. 16, 1915.
48. John Purroy Mitchel to Woodrow Wilson, Feb. 13, 1915, Woodrow Wilson Papers, Library of Congress; Gompers in *Annals of the American Academy of Political and Social Science*, vol. XLI, Sept. 1915, p. 506.
49. Gompers to Chester M. Wright, Jan. 16, 1915, *GLB* and *AFL Corr.* in *WSHS*; New York *Call*, Jan. 10, 1915.
50. Cleveland *Socialist News*, Dec. 15, 19, 1914; Jan. 2, 9, 16, 23, 30, Feb. 6, 13, 20, 1915; Oakley Johnson, *The Day is Coming: Life and Work of Charles E. Ruthenberg*, New York, 1957, pp. 93–95.
51. Copy of leaflet, signed by Executive Committee, Conference of the Unemployed of Greater New York, in Amos Pinchot Papers, Library of Congress.
52. *Solidarity*, Dec. 12, 26, 1914; Jan. 9, 16, 23, Feb. 6, 13, 1915; Walter E. Kreusi, "Report upon unemployment in the Winter of 1914–1915 in Detroit, and the Institutions and Measures of Relief," Agnes Inglis *Notes*, Labadie Collection, University of Michigan Library.
53. *Solidarity*, Dec. 26, 1914.
54. New York *Call*, Feb. 2, 1915.
55. Both the leaflet and the pamphlet, the latter dated January, 1915, are in the Amos Pinchot Papers, Library of Congress.
56. *Solidarity*, Jan. 23, 1915. Seattle *Post-Intelligencer*, Dec. 12, 15, 1914; Jan. 12, 20, 1915; Seattle *Star*, Jan. 14, 16, 1915.
57. *Solidarity*, Jan. 23, 30, 1915; Wallace M. Short, "How One Town Learned a Lesson in Free Speech," *Survey*, Oct. 30, 1915, pp. 106–07; Sioux City *Journal*, Jan. 8–25, 1915.
58. Short, *op. cit.*, p. 107; Sioux City *Journal*, April 5–14, 1915.
59. Sioux City *Journal*, April 17–19, 1915; *Solidarity*, April 10, 17, 1915.
60. Short, *op. cit.*, p. 108; *Solidarity*, April 17, 1915.
61. *The Union Advocate*, April 15, 1915, reprinted in *Solidarity*, April 24, 1915.
62. Sioux City *Journal*, April 20, 1915; *Solidarity*, April 24, 1915.
63. Short, *op. cit.*, p. 108; Sioux City *Journal*, April 21–22, May 16, 17, 19, 1915.
64. *Solidarity*, Feb. 23, 1915.
65. W. B. Wilson to Secretary of Commerce, Dec. 13, 1913; W. B. Wilson to James H. Hunt, Nov. 9, 1914, Department of Labor Files CC47/16 and CC/45A, *NA*; Royal Meeker, "The Dependability and Meaning of Unemployment and Employment Statistics in the United States," *Harvard Business Review*, vol. VIII, July 1930, p. 387.
66. Executive Committee on Mayor's Committee on Unemployment to Woodrow Wilson, New York, Jan. 20, 1915, Woodrow Wilson Papers. For the folder, *see* Woodrow Wilson Papers, Box 435, Library of Congress.
67. *The New York Times*, Feb. 17, 1914; New York *Call*, Feb. 13, 1915; W. B. Wilson to Louis N. Hamerling, March 30, 1914, Department of Labor Files CC 20/145A, *NA*.
68. Deseret *Evening News*, July 7, 1915.
69. *Final Report of the Commission on Industrial Relations, Including the Report of Basil M. Manly*, Washington, 1916, p. 38.
70. Bertch, *op. cit.*, p. 44.
71. *American Labor Legislation Review*, vol. V, November 1915, pp. 500–15; Feder, *op. cit.*, p. 275.
72. John Graham Brooks, "The Challenge of Unemployment," *The Independent*,

vol. LXXXI, March 15, 1915, p. 385; New York *Tribune*, Dec. 19, 1914.
73. *Solidarity*, March 20, 1915.

CHAPTER 20

1. F. W. Thompson, "The I.W.W. Tells Its Own Story," *Industrial Worker*, Dec. 15, 1931.
2. Brissenden, *op. cit.*, p. 354.
3. *Solidarity*, Oct. 4, 1913.
4. *Ibid.*, Jan. 31, Feb. 21, 28, March 3, 10, 17, 24, 1914.
5. *Ibid.*, Oct. 4, 1913.
6. *Solidarity*, Aug. 2, 22, Nov. 22, 1913; March 7, 14, 21, 1914.
7. *Ibid.*, March 21, 1914.
8. *Ibid.*, July 5, Oct. 4, 1913; Jan. 24, 1914; Jan. 30, 1915.
9. *Industrial Worker*, June 6, 1912; "Some Mistakes of the I.W.W.," *Solidarity*, Sept. 13, 1913.
10. *Industrial Worker*, June 16, 1910; June 6, 1912; *Solidarity*, Aug. 23, 1913; Feb. 6, 21, May 2, 1914; Jan. 23, 1915.
11. *Industrial Worker*, June 6, 1912; *Solidarity*, Feb. 21, 1914; Jan. 23, 1915.
12. *Industrial Worker*, Aug. 17, 1911; June 5, 1913; Mortimer Downing to W. D. Haywood, July 7, 1916, Department of Justice Records, Appeals File, pp. 49–50, *NA*.
13. *Solidarity*, Jan. 24, Nov. 14, 1914; Jan. 30, 1915.
14. The Solicitor to the Secretary of Commerce and Labor, June 6, 1912, Department of Justice File 161250010; Henry B. Hazard to John Speed Smith, Report of June 28, 1913, in I & NS Files 53531/192-A, *NA*; Seattle *Post-Intelligencer*, June 15, 1912.
15. Paterson *Guardian*, Aug. 6, 1913.
16. Roy L. Garis, *Immigration Restriction*, New York, 1927, pp. 123–25; Preston Jr., *op. cit.*, pp. 125–28.
17. Joseph J. Ettor, "I.W.W. vs. A.F. of L.," *The New Review*, May 1914, p. 280; *Solidarity*, July 12, 1913; Feb. 21, May 2, Nov. 14, 1914; Sept. 18, 1915.
18. *Solidarity*, July 31, 1915.

CHAPTER 21

1. E. F. Dorree, "Gathering the Grain," *International Socialist Review*, vol. XV, June 1915, p. 742; P. A. Speek, "Labor Market Conditions in the Harvest Fields of the Middle West, Summer, 1914,"

Labor Department Files Wis I 45D, *NA*.
2. Emporia *Gazette*, March 18, June 5, 1916.
3. *Solidarity*, Oct. 4, 1913.
4. J. Gabriel Soltis in *ibid.*, Oct. 10, 1914.
5. *Solidarity*, Oct. 3, 1914; Feb. 13, 1915.
6. *Ibid.*, April 3, 24, 1915; E. Workman, *History of "400": Agricultural Workers*, Chicago, 1939, pp. 8–14.
7. *Solidarity*, June 26, 1915.
8. Kansas City *Post*, June 6, 1915; Deseret *Evening News*, Dec. 9, 1914; "Harvest Hands," Department of Labor file 20/166, June 22, 1914, *NA*.
9. Stuart Jamieson, "Labor Unionism in American Agriculture," unpublished Ph.D. thesis, University of Iowa, 1938, p. 1018; Workman, *op. cit.*, p. 11.
10. E. W. Latchem, South Dakota, in *Solidarity*, Oct 9, 1915; *Ibid.*, Sept. 18, Oct. 30, 1915; Jamieson, *op. cit.*, p. 1019.
11. *Solidarity*, July 10, Sept. 18, 25, Oct. 9, 1915.
12. *Ibid.*, Dec. 25, 1915; March 18, 1916.
13. *Ibid.*, Oct. 2, 14, 23, 1915.
14. *Ibid.*, Aug. 28, Dec. 18, 1915; letter of Shippy, Hunt, Dorman International Detective Agency, May 22, 1916, reproduced in *Industrial Worker*, May 3, 1916.
15. *Solidarity*, Oct. 10, 30, Nov. 13, 27, 1915.
16. *Industrial Worker*, May 27, 1916.
17. *Industrial Worker*, July 28, 1945.
18. *Ibid.*, June 10, 1916; Workman, *op. cit.*, p. 10.
19. *Industrial Worker*, July 29, 1916; Jamieson, *op. cit.*, p. 1016; *Solidarity*, Dec. 2, 1916.
20. Reprinted in *Industrial Worker*, Aug. 5, 1916.
21. Emporia *Gazette*, July 12, 1916; Duluth *News Tribune*, Aug. 7, 1916.
22. "Membership in the I.W.W., a Criminal Offense," *Monthly Labor Review*, Feb. 1923, p. 246; Cedrick Worth, "The Brotherhood of Man," *North American Review*, April 1929, pp. 487–92.
23. *Industrial Worker*, Feb. 17, 1945.
24. Joseph C. Williams to Phillip Gouaet, Nov. 26, 1916, Dept. of Justice files, Appeals file, p. 43, *NA*.
25. *Solidarity*, Aug. 19, 1916.
26. *Industrial Worker*, Aug. 12, 1916; *Solidarity*, Aug. 19, 1916.
27. *Industrial Worker*, July 21, 28, 1945. *See also* articles in issues of Aug. 4, 11, 18, 1945.
28. Sioux Falls *Daily Argus-Leader*, July 18, 28, 30, 31, Aug. 4, 1916; E. E. Owens

to Secretary of War, July 29, 30, 1916, Adjutant General's Office Records, 2439874, *NA*.

29. Sioux Falls *Daily Argus-Leader*, Aug. 4, 1916.

30. Duluth *News Tribune*, Aug. 7, 1916.

31. *Industrial Solidarity*, Aug. 4, 1945.

32. Minneapolis *Morning Tribune*, July 24, 1916; Hutchinson (Kan.) *Daily News*, reprinted in *Industrial Worker*, July 8, 1916; Sioux Falls *Daily Argus-Leader*, Aug. 4, 1916.

33. *Solidarity*, Nov. 18, 1916.

34. *Ibid.;* Workman, *op. cit.*, p. 14; *Proceedings of the Tenth Convention of the Industrial Workers of the World, November 10, 1916 to December 1, 1916*, Chicago, 1917, p. 32.

35. *Industrial Worker*, Oct. 7, 1916.

36. *Proceedings of the Tenth Convention of the Industrial Workers of the World, op. cit.*, p. 41.

CHAPTER 22

1. John Syrjamaki, "Mesabi Communities: A Study of their Development," unpublished Ph.D. thesis, Yale University, 1940, pp. 2–11; Hyman Berman, "Education for Work and Labor Solidarity: The Immigrant Miners and Radicalism in the Mesabi Range," unpublished paper in possession of author, pp. 2–3.

2. Syrjamaki, *op. cit.*, p. 115.

3. G. O. Virtue, "The Minnesota Iron Ranges," *Bulletin of the U.S. Bureau of Labor, No. 23*, Washington, D.C., 1909, p. 353.

4. Henry R. Mussey, *Consolidation in the Mining Industry: A Study of Concentration in Lake Superior Iron Ore Production*, New York, 1905, pp. 117–30; Abraham Berglund, *The United States Steel Corporation: A Study of the Growth and Influence of Combination in the Iron and Steel Industry*, New York, 1907, pp. 79–85; Syrjamaki, *op. cit.*, p. 57.

5. Syrjamaki, *op. cit.*, p. 184.

6. Letters in *Blas Svobode* and *Proletarec* quoted in Berman, *op. cit.*, pp. 12–13.

7. *Ibid.*, p. 5; A. William Hoglund, *Finnish Immigrants in America, 1880–1920*, Madison, Wis., 1960, p. 66.

8. "Strike of Miners of Mesaba Iron Range, Minnesota," Labor Department Files, 25/247, *NA*.

9. George P. West, "The Mesaba Range Strike," *New Republic*, Sept. 2, 1916, p. 108.

10. William J. Bell, Report, c. 1915, quoted in Berman, *op. cit.*, p. 11.

11. Syrjamaki, *op. cit.*, pp. 11–12; Mary Heaton Vorse, *A Footnote to Folly*, pp. 139–42; Duluth *News Tribune*, July 27, 1916.

12. Report of Mayors and Union Conference, in "Strike of Miners of Mesaba Iron Range, Minnesota," Labor Department Files, 25/247, *NA*.

13. Interview quoted in Syrjamaki, *op. cit.*, p. 187.

14. Quoted in Berman, *op. cit.*, p. 7.

15. Syrjamaki, *op. cit.*, pp. 192–93.

16. *United Mine Workers' Journal*, Aug. 10, 1916, pp. 12–14; Syrjamaki, *op. cit.*, p. 189; Mary Heaton Vorse, "The Mining Strike in Minnesota: From the Miners' Point of View," *The Outlook*, Aug. 30, 1916, pp. 1044–45; Berman, *op. cit.*, pp. 15–16; Mary Heaton Vorse, *A Footnote to Folly*, p. 133.

17. Interview cited in Syrjamaki, *op. cit.*, pp. 187, 190–91; letters to *Proletarec*, cited in Berman, *op. cit.*, pp. 12–13.

18. Syrjamaki, *op. cit.*, pp. 116, 186.

19. Letter in *Proletarec*, Feb. 28, 1911, quoted in Berman, *op. cit.*, p. 9, and -interview quoted in Syrjamaki, *op. cit.*, p. 139.

20. Letter in *Glas Svobode*, June 8, 1906, quoted in Berman, *op. cit.*, p. 37.

21. Syrjamaki, *op. cit.*, pp. 213–14; Hoglund, *op. cit.*, pp. 55–56; Arne Halonen, "The Role of the Finnish-Americans in the Political Labor Movement," unpublished M.A. thesis, University of Minnesota, 1945, pp. 32–33; "The Fighting Finns," *Industrial Worker*, June 30, 1945.

22. *Proceedings*, Fifteenth Convention, W.F. of M., 1907, pp. 186–87; "Report of Teofila Petriella"; Jensen, *Heritage of Conflict*, p. 247; Berman, *op. cit.*, pp. 38–39; Duluth *News Tribune*, July 20, 21, 1917.

23. Frank L. Palmer, *Spies in Steel, An Exposé of Industrial War*, Denver, 1928, pp. 58–64.

24. Duluth *News Tribune*, July 21, 1907.

25. *Ibid.*, July 22, 1907.

26. *Ibid.*, Aug. 10, 19, 1907.

27. *Ibid.*, Aug. 3, Sept. 17, 1907; Charles B. Cheny, "A Labor Crisis and a Governor," *The Outlook*, May 2, 1908, pp. 24–25; Syrjamaki, *op. cit.*, pp. 216–17; Berman, *op. cit.*, pp. 42–43.

28. Paul H. Landis, *Three Iron Mining Towns: A Study in Cultural Change*, Ann Arbor, Mich., 1930, p. 50; Berman, *op. cit.*, p. 44.

29. Berman, *op. cit.*, p. 451; *Miners' Magazine*, Nov. 15, 1908, p. 15; Jensen, *Heritage of Conflict*, pp. 247–49.

30. Syrjamaki, *op. cit.*, pp. 220–21; Halonen, *op. cit.*, pp. 114–16; Hoglund, *op. cit.*, pp. 56–57.

31. Duluth *News Tribune*, July 19, 1916.

32. Duluth *News Tribune*, June 4, 6, 8, 12, 22, 1916.

33. Marion B. Cothren, "When Strike-Breakers Strike," *Survey*, Aug. 26, 1916, p. 535; Eveleth *News*, June 15, 1916; *Strikers' News: Official Strike Bulletin of the Striking Iron Ore Miners of the Mesaba Range*, July 21, 1916; copy in Labor Department Files, 25/247, *NA*, hereinafter referred to as *Strikers' News*.

34. Syrjamaki, *op. cit.*, p. 221; Duluth *News Tribune*, June 20, 1912.

35. *Strikers' News*, July 21, 1916, copy in Labor Department Files, 25/247, *NA*; Duluth *News Tribune*, July 2, 1916.

36. *Industrial Worker*, June 17, 1916; Haywood to Tresca in Duluth *News Tribune*, July 2, 1916.

37. Duluth *News Tribune*, June 17, 22, 24, Aug. 2, 1916; *Strikers' News*, July 21, 1916, copy in Labor Department Files, 25/247, *NA*.

38. Duluth *News Tribune*, June 17, 21, 22, 1916; Haywood to Tresca in *ibid.*, July 19, 1916.

39. Duluth *News Tribune*, June 17, 21, 24, 1916.

40. *Ibid.*, June 16, 23, 1916; Haywood to Tresca in *ibid.*, July 2, 1916; Eveleth *News*, June 15, 1916.

41. Duluth *News Tribune*, June 22, 1916; "Report by U.S. Commissioners of Conciliation William R. Fairley of Alabama and Hywell Davies of Kentucky on the Mesaba Iron Miners' Strike in Minnesota, June 2 to September 17, 1916, submitted October 28, 1916," copy in Labor Department Files, 25/247, *NA*. (Hereinafter cited as "Report by U.S. Commissioners of Conciliation. . . .")

42. Duluth *News Tribune*, July 19, 1916.

43. *Ibid.*, July 2, 1916.

44. *Ibid.*, June 29, 30, 1916.

45. Berman, *op. cit.*, p. 49; Duluth *News Tribune*, June 27, July 1, 1916.

46. Original in University of Wisconsin, copy in *NA*.

47. Duluth *News Tribune*, June 28, July 27, 1916.

48. Report of George P. West to U.S. Commissioners on Industrial Relations, copy in Labor Department Files, 25/247, *NA; United Mine Workers' Journal*, Aug. 10, 1916, pp. 49–50; Berman, *op. cit.*, pp. 49–50; Duluth *News Tribune*, June 22, Aug. 17, 1916.

49. Duluth *News Tribune*, June 24, 1916.

50. *Ibid.*, July 1, 10, 12, 14, Aug. 18, 1916.

51. *Ibid.*, July 7, 1916.

52. *Ibid.*, June 16, 18, 19, 22, 23, 1916; *Industrial Worker*, June 24, 1916.

53. *Ibid.*, June 23, 24, 27, 1916; *Industrial Worker*, July 1, 1916.

54. Duluth *News Tribune*, June 27, 1916.

55. *Ibid.*, July 1, Aug. 27, 1916.

56. *Mesaba Ore*, July 22, 1916, quoted in Report of George P. West on the Strike of Miners of Mesaba Range, Minnesota, submitted to the United States Commission on Industrial Relations, copy in Labor Department Files, 25/247, *NA*.

57. Duluth *News Tribune*, July 4, 5, 1916.

58. *Ibid.*, July 1, 2, 8, 1916.

59. *Ibid.*, July 7, 1916.

60. *Ibid.*, July 12, 1916.

61. *Ibid.*, July 14, 1916; interview with Elizabeth Gurley Flynn, Feb. 19, 1964.

62. Duluth *News Tribune*, July 13, 15, 1916.

63. *Ibid.*, July 14, 1916.

64. *Ibid.*, July 30, 1916.

65. Berman, *op. cit.*, p. 51; Duluth *News Tribune*, July 22, 1916.

66. *Ibid.*, July 5, 1916.

67. *Ibid.*, June 26, July 12, 1916.

68. *Ibid.*, July 8, 12, 14, 1916; *Strikers' News*, July 28, 1916.

69. Duluth *News Tribune*, July 11, 1916.

70. *Ibid.*, June 26, July 8, 1916.

71. *Ibid.*, June 25, July 21, 22, 1916; James Lord to W. B. Wilson, July 21, 1916, Labor Department Files, 25/247, *NA*.

72. Undated clipping in Labor Department Files, 25/247, *NA*.

73. *Proceedings of the Thirty-Fourth Convention of the Minnesota State Federation of Labor*, Hibbing, Minn., July 17–19, 1916, pp. 3–60; Duluth *News Tribune*, July 18–21, 1916.

74. *Strikers' News*, July 21, 1916; *Industrial Worker*, July 29, 1916; Duluth *News Tribune*, July 21, 1916.

75. E. G. Hall, "Report to members of the Federation Council, 1916," E. G. Hall Papers, Box 1, Minnesota Historical Society; Berman, *op. cit.*, p. 53.

76. Undated clipping, Labor Department Files, 25/247, *NA*.
77. Duluth *News Tribune*, July 27, 29, 30, Aug. 3, 1916.
78. *Ibid.*, July 28, 29, 1916; *Solidarity*, Aug. 5, 1916.
79. Duluth *News Tribune*, July 13, 26, 29, Aug. 4, 5, 1916; Vorse, *op. cit.*, p. 135; Aberdeen *Daily Reporter*, reprinted in *Industrial Worker*, Aug. 5, 1916; Louis F. Post to W. B. Wilson, July 31, 1916, Labor Department Files, 25/247, *NA*. Eviction notes for strikers are reproduced in *Strikers' News*, Aug. 4, 1916. *See also* Duluth *News Tribune*, Aug. 22, 1916.
80. *Strikers' News*, July 28, 1916; Duluth *News Tribune*, July 26, Aug. 2, 1916.
81. Vorse, *op. cit.*, p. 142.
82. Duluth *News Tribune*, July 25, 27, Aug. 1, 2, 3, 1916.
83. Duluth *News Tribune*, Aug. 2, 3, 4, 29, 1916; *Industrial Worker*, Aug. 12, 1916.
84. Duluth *News Tribune*, July 28, 1916; W. B. Colver to W. B. Wilson, Aug. 3, 1916, Labor Department Files, 25/247, *NA*.
85. The complete text of West's report is in Labor Department Files, 25/247. *NA*. Excerpts were published in the *International Socialist Review*, vol. XVII, Sept. 1916, pp. 158–61; *United Mine Workers' Journal*, Aug. 10, 1916, pp. 12–14, and Duluth *News Tribune*, Aug. 2, 1916.
86. Duluth *News Tribune*, Aug. 2, 3, 1916.
87. The full text of the report was published in Duluth *News Tribune*, Aug. 17, 1916 and in *Industrial Worker*, Aug. 26, 1916. For Fairley's comment, see Duluth *News Tribune*, Aug. 17, 18, 1916.
88. Duluth *News Tribune*, Aug. 18, 19, 1916; Syrjamaki, *op. cit.*, pp. 224–25.
89. Reprinted in Duluth *News Tribune*, Aug. 19, 1916.
90. *Ibid.*, Aug. 18, 1916; *The Outlook*, Aug. 1916, pp. 1044–46; *Survey*, Aug. 26, 1916, p. 536; *International Socialist Review*, vol. XVII, Aug. 1916, pp. 74–80.
91. Duluth *News Tribune*, Aug. 27, 29, Sept. 12, 1916; Berman, *op. cit.*, p. 54.
92. Duluth *News Tribune*, Aug. 27, Sept. 12, 1916; Berman, *op. cit.*, p. 54.
93. Duluth *News Tribune*, Aug. 31, 1916.
94. Flynn, *I Speak My Own Piece*, p. 200; Interview with Elizabeth Gurley Flynn, Jan. 31, 1964.
95. Fairley and Davies to W. B. Wilson, Aug. 24, 1916, Labor Department Files, 25/247, *NA*.
96. Duluth *News Tribune*, Sept. 19, 1916; The Strikers Central Committee, Fulvio Ettinelli, sec'y, Tony Skragas, chairman, to the Representatives of the Secretary of Labor Sent to Investigate and Act as Mediators in the Strike of the Iron Mines of the Mesaba Range of Minnesota, Sept. 10, 1916, Labor Department Files, 25/247, *NA*.
97. Fairley to Davies, Sept. 19, 1916, Labor Department Files, 25/247, *NA*.
98. Duluth *News Tribune*, Sept. 18–20, 1916; Eveleth *News*, Sept. 21, 1916; *Strikers' News*, Sept. 22, 1916.
99. W. R. Fairley to W. B. Wilson, Sept. 19, 1916, Labor Department Files, 25/247, *NA;* Duluth *News Tribune*, Sept. 25, 1916.
100. "Report by U.S. Commissioners of Conciliation. . . . ," *op. cit.*, and Hywell Davies to W. B. Wilson, Oct. 17, 1916, Labor Department Files, 25/247, *NA*.
101. "Report of U.S. Commissioners of Conciliation . . . ," *op. cit.;* W. R. Fairley and Hywell Davies to W. B. Wilson, Jan. 8, 1917, Labor Department Files, 25/247, *NA*.
102. Eveleth *News*, Nov. 23, 1916; Duluth *News Tribune*, Dec. 17, 1916.
103. W. R. Fairley and Hywell Davies to W. B. Wilson, Jan. 8, 1917, Labor Department Files, 25/247, *NA;* Duluth *News Tribune*, Nov. 22, 23, 1916; *Industrial Worker*, Dec. 30, 1916.
104. Duluth *News Tribune*, Aug. 31, 1916.
105. *Ibid.*, Aug. 22, Sept. 22, Oct. 29, Dec. 2, 1916.
106. *Ibid.*, Oct. 19, Nov. 30, Dec. 4, 1916; Interview with Elizabeth Gurley Flynn, Jan. 31, 1964.
107. Eugene V. Debs, "Murder in the First Degree," *American Socialist*, Sept. 16, 1916; Resolutions adopted on Carlo Tresca and others on a charge of murder at the Mesaba Range, in "Iron Miners Strike, Mesaba Range, Minn.," Labor Department Files, 13/49, *NA; Industrial Worker*, Sept. 16, 1916.
108. *Industrial Worker*, Nov. 25, 1916; Duluth *News Tribune*, Sept. 10, Dec. 2, 3, 1916.
109. Duluth *News Tribune*, Dec. 16, 17, 1916; Harrison George in *Industrial Worker*, Dec. 30, 1916; Elizabeth Gurley Flynn quoted in Duluth *News Tribune*, Dec. 18, 1916.

110. Duluth *News Tribune*, Dec. 16, 19, 1916.
111. *Industrial Worker*, Dec. 30, 1916, Jan. 13, 1917, Duluth *News Tribune*, Dec. 16, 1916.
112. *Bill Haywood's Book*, pp. 291–92.
113. Duluth *News Tribune*, Dec. 18, 19, 1916.
114. Berman, *op. cit.*, pp. 56–58; Syrjamaki, *op. cit.*, p. 226.

CHAPTER 23

1. Duluth *News Tribune*, Dec. 19, 1916.
2. Ralph W. Hidy, Frank Ernest Hill, Allan Nevins, *Timber and Men, The Weyerhaeuser Story*, New York, 1963, pp. 144, 186, 187, 191, 195, 196, 338; *Solidarity*, Dec. 18, 1915; *Daily Virginian*, Dec. 26–30, 1916; Eveleth *News*, Dec. 28, 1916; Duluth *News Tribune*, Dec. 27–29, 1916.
3. Copy of the leaflet in Minnesota House of Representatives, Committee of Labor and Labor Legislation, Hearings, "Labor Troubles in Northern Minnesota, January 30, 1917," in John Lond Papers, Minnesota Historical Society, vol. I, pp. 81–87.
4. Duluth *News Tribune*, Dec. 29, 1916.
5. *Daily Virginian*, Dec. 30, 1916, Jan. 2, 3, 1917; Duluth *News Tribune*, Jan. 3, 8, 1917.
6. Testimony of Frank M. Gilmor, Superintendent of Logging for the Virginia and Rainey Lake Lumber Company, in Minnesota, "Labor Troubles," *op. cit.*, vol. I, p. 82; *Daily Virginian*, Dec. 28, 29, 30, 1916; Duluth *News Tribune*, Dec. 28, 30, 1916.
7. Duluth *News Tribune*, Jan. 2, 6, 7, 1917; George Barker Engberg, "Labor in the Lake States Lumber Industry 1830–1930," unpublished Ph.D. thesis, University of Minnesota, 1949, pp. 409–12.
8. Engberg, *op. cit.*, p. 412; Harrison George, "Hitting the Trail in the Lumber Camps," *International Socialist Review*, vol. XVII, Feb. 1917, pp. 455–57; Duluth *News Tribune*, Jan. 27, 10, 15, 17, 1917; *Industrial Worker*, Jan. 27, 1917.
9. Engberg, *op. cit.*, pp. 412–13; Duluth *News Tribune*, Jan. 20, 28, 1917.
10. *Solidarity*, Nov. 27, Dec. 25, 1915.
11. *Industrial Worker*, June 3, July 8, 29, 1916.
12. Robert Anthony Perrin, Jr., "Two Decades of Turbulence: A Study of the Great Lumber Strikes in Northern Idaho (1916–1936)," unpublished M.A. thesis, University of Idaho, 1961, p. 42; *Industrial Worker*, July 8, 1916.
13. *Industrial Worker*, Aug. 5, 1916.
14. Robert Edward Hull, "I.W.W. Activity in Everett, Washington, from May 1916 to June 1917," unpublished M.A. thesis, State College of Washington, 1938, pp. 12–15; Everett *Tribune*, May 15, 1916.
15. E. P. Marsh, "The Struggle in the Timber Industry," *Proceedings of the Fifteenth Annual Convention of the Washington State Federation of Labor, 1916, Supplemental Report*, Seattle, 1916, pp. 3–11.
16. Seattle *Union Record*, April 15, 1916; *The Shingle Weaver*, April 29, 1916.
17. Everett *Tribune*, May 2, 15, 1916; Seattle *Post-Intelligencer*, May 3, 1916; Hull, *op. cit.*, p. 10.
18. *The Shingle Weaver*, July 22, 1916.
19. Everett *Tribune*, July 22, 27, 1916.
20. Walker C. Smith, *The Everett Massacre: A History of the Class Struggle in the Lumber Industry*, Chicago, 1917, pp. 21, 32; Hull, *op. cit.*, p. 21; *Industrial Worker*, March 3, 1917; Barnes, *op. cit.*, pp. 150–51.
21. *Industrial Worker*, Aug. 5, 1916.
22. Everett *Tribune*, April 4, 1917; Smith, *op. cit.*, p. 35; Barnes, *op. cit.*, pp. 150–51.
23. Everett *Tribune*, April 20, 1917; Smith, *op. cit.*, pp. 35–36.
24. Everett *Tribune*, April 22, 1917; Seattle *Union Record*, Aug. 26, 1916.
25. Everett *Tribune*, April 3, 4, 10, 1917; Smith, *op. cit.*, pp. 37–38.
26. Everett *Tribune*, April 5, 6, 10, 13, 1917; *The Shingle Weaver*, Aug. 26, 1916; Smith, *op. cit.*, pp. 39–41; David C. Botting, Jr., "Bloody Sunday," *Pacific Northwest Quarterly*, vol. XLIX, Oct. 1958, pp. 164–65.
27. Smith, *op. cit.*, p. 41.
28. *Solidarity*, Dec. 21, 28, 1915; Jan. 4, 11, 1916.
29. *Industrial Worker*, Sept. 16, Oct. 21, 1916.
30. Everett *Tribune*, April 4, 6, 1917.
31. Everett *Tribune*, April 4, 1917.
32. Smith, *op. cit.*, p. 44; Botting, Jr., *op. cit.*, p. 165; Robert L. Tyler, "I.W.W. in the Pacific N.W.: Rebels of the Woods," *Oregon Historical Quarterly*, vol. LV, March 1954, p. 14.
33. Everett *Tribune*, April 10, 1917; *Industrial Worker*, Sept. 16, 1916; Seattle

Post-Intelligencer, Sept. 10, 1916; Smith, *op. cit.*, pp. 50–52.

34. Everett *Tribune*, April 6, 10, 1917; *Industrial Worker*, Sept. 16, 1916; Smith, *op. cit.*, pp. 51–62.

35. *Industrial Worker*, Sept. 16, 1916; Everett *Tribune*, April 4, 1917; Smith, *op. cit.*, pp. 53–56.

36. Everett *Tribune*, March 17, 1917; Smith, *op. cit.*, pp. 58–59.

37. Everett *Tribune*, April 13, 1917.

38. Everett *Tribune*, April 3, 6, 1917; *Industrial Worker*, Sept. 23, 1916; Smith, *op. cit.*, pp. 62–63, 67, 68.

39. Hull, *op. cit.*, pp. 33–34.

40. Everett *Tribune*, March 17, 1917. For the few references to deportations in the Everett *Tribune*, *see* issues of Oct. 3, 7, 10, 11, 12, 13, 25, 27, 1916.

41. Smith, *op. cit.*, pp. 72–77; Botting, Jr., *op. cit.*, p. 168; Everett *Tribune*, March 28, April 14, 15, 22, 1917.

42. Everett *Tribune*, April 15, 1917; Smith, *op. cit.*, pp. 76–77.

43. Smith, *op. cit.*, pp. 78–79; Everett *Tribune*, April 6, 1917.

44. Everett *Tribune*, Nov. 6, 1916.

45. Everett *Tribune*, April 17, 1917.

46. Smith, *op. cit.*, p. 80; Barnes, *op. cit.*, p. 151.

47. Captain Harry Ramwell, "History of Everett's Troubles with I.W.W.," Everett *Tribune*, Nov. 25, 1916; Tyler, "I.W.W. in the Pacific N.W.," *op. cit.*, p. 15. *See also* Everett *Tribune*, Nov. 4, 1916.

48. Everett *Tribune*, March 23, 1917; Smith, *op. cit.*, p. 84; *Industrial Worker*, Nov. 18, 1916.

49. Ramwell, *op. cit.*; Smith, *op. cit.*, p. 85.

50. Smith, *op. cit.*, pp. 85–87; Tyler, "Rebels of the Woods and Fields," *op. cit.*, pp. 69–70.

51. Walker C. Smith, "The Voyage of the *Verona*," *Militant*, 1916, pp. 340–46; Everett *Tribune*, March 23, 28, 29, April 24, 1917; Seattle *Post-Intelligencer*, Nov. 6, 1917.

52. Seattle *Union Record*, Nov. 18, 1916.

53. Everett *Tribune*, Nov. 6, 1916; Seattle *Post-Intelligencer*, Nov. 6, 1916.

54. Seattle *Post-Intelligencer*, Nov. 6, 1916.

55. *Ibid.*

56. *Ibid.*, Nov. 7, 12, 15, 1916; *Industrial Worker*, Nov. 11, 1916.

57. Smith, *op. cit.*, p. 101; Seattle *Union Record*, Nov. 11, 1916; Batting, Jr., *op. cit.*, p. 169.

58. *The Shingle Weaver*, Nov. 11, 1916.

59. Seattle *Union Record*, Nov. 9, 1916.

60. Smith, *op. cit.*, pp. 94, 110–14; Seattle *Post-Intelligencer*, Nov. 14, 1916; *Solidarity*, Jan. 13, 1917.

61. *Industrial Worker*, March 3, 1917; Smith, *op. cit.*, p. 130; Everett *Tribune*, Dec. 1, 1916; Feb. 2, 1917; Anna Louise Strong, "The Verdict at Everett," *The Survey*, vol. XXXVIII, 1917, p. 162; Robert L. Tyler, "The Everett Free Speech Fight," *Pacific Historical Review*, vol. XXIII, Feb. 1954, pp. 27–28.

62. *Industrial Worker*, March 3, 1917.

63. Smith, *op. cit.*, p. 122.

64. C. H. Younger, State Labor Commissioner, Olympia, Wash., to William Blackman, Jan. 25, 1917, "Labor Controversies at Everett and Seattle, Wash.," Labor Department Files, No. 33/288, *NA.;* Everett *Tribune*, Jan. 22, 23, 1917.

65. Smith, *op. cit.*, pp. 131–34, 138; Everett *Tribune*, Jan. 22, 23, March 6, 1917.

66. Everett *Tribune*, Dec. 26, 1916.

67. Seattle Post-Intelligencer, Nov. 20, 1916; James A. Duncan to William B. Wilson, Nov. 22, 1916, Records of U.S. Conciliation Service, No. 33/312, *NA*.

68. *Industrial Worker*, Jan. 20, 27, 1917; Seattle *Post-Intelligencer*, Jan. 22, 1917.

69. *Industrial Worker*, Dec. 23, 1916; *The Masses*, Feb. 1917, pp. 18–19.

70. *Industrial Worker*, Nov. 11, 25, Dec. 2, 1916; *Socialist World*, Nov. 18, 1916; *The Rebel*, Dec. 9, 1916.

71. *Industrial Worker*, Dec. 2, 1916.

72. *See* letters to W. B. Wilson, Nov.–Dec. 1916, in "Labor Controversies at Everett and Seattle, Wash.," Labor Department Files, 33/32, *NA*.

73. *Industrial Worker*, Dec. 23, 1916.

74. Everett *Tribune*, Dec. 21, 27, 29, 1916; Jan. 13, 17, 18, 23, 1917.

75. *Ibid.*, Jan. 27, Feb. 9, 10, 1917; Hull, *op. cit.*, pp. 100–01.

76. Everett *Tribune*, March 9, April 3, 13, 1917; *Industrial Worker*, April 7, 1917; Tyler, "Rebels of the Woods and Fields," *op. cit.*, pp. 75–76.

77. Everett *Tribune*, March 9, 1917.

78. *Ibid.*, Seattle *Post-Intelligencer*, March 9, 1917.

79. Everett *Tribune*, April 21, 1917.

80. *Ibid.*, March 20, 22, 30, May 1, 1917.

81. Everett *Tribune*, April 3, 1917; *Industrial Worker*, April 7, 1917.

82. Fred H. Moore to W. B. Wilson, March 24, 1917, "Labor Controversies at Everett and Seattle, Wash.," Labor Department Files, No. 33/312, *NA*.

83. *Industrial Worker*, Nov. 18, 1916.

84. Everett *Tribune*, May 4, 1917.

85. *Ibid.*, May 3, 4, 1917; Smith, *op. cit.*, pp. 270–76.
86. Seattle *Post-Intelligencer*, May 5–6, 1917; *Industrial Worker*, May 12, 1917.
87. *International Socialist Review*, vol. XVII, June 1917, p. 123.
88. Quoted in Harvey O'Connor, *Revolution in Seattle: A Memoir*, New York, 1964, p. 55.
89. William Blackman to W. B. Wilson, Jan. 19, 1917, "Labor Controversies at Everett and Seattle," Labor Department Files No. 33/288, *NA;* Hull, *op. cit.*, p. 112.
90. O'Connor, *op. cit.*, p. 55.
91. James Rowan, *The I.W.W. in the Lumber Industry*, n.p., n.d., pp. 25–31.
92. *Industrial Worker*, May 19, 1917; Perrin, Jr., *op. cit.*, pp. 3, 43–44; Tyler, "Rebels of the Woods and Fields," *op. cit.*, p. 85.
93. Rowan, *op. cit.*, pp. 30–32; *Industrial Worker*, July 14, 1917.
94. *Industrial Worker*, May 19, 1917; Smith, *op. cit.*, p. 291.
95. Smith, *op. cit.*, unpaged front section.

CHAPTER 24

1. *Industrial Worker*, Feb. 3, 1917.
2. *Ibid.*, Feb. 3, 24, 1917.
3. *Ibid.*, July 15, 1916.
4. *Ibid.*, April 1, 1916.
5. *Solidarity*, Oct. 1, 1916; *Industrial Worker*, Nov. 11, 1916.
6. Interview with Elizabeth Gurley Flynn, Jan. 31, Feb. 19, 1964; Flynn, *I Speak My Own Piece*, p. 214; Francis Russell, "The Last of the Anarchists: The Strange Story of Carlo Tresca," *Modern Age*, Winter 1963–64, p. 69.

7. George W. Hardy, "Some Urgent I.W.W. Problems," *Solidarity*, Oct. 21, 1916.
8. *Industrial Worker*, Jan. 13, 1917.
9. *Ibid.*, May 12, 19, 1917.
10. *Ibid.*, March 3, 1917.
11. *See* H. C. Peterson and Gilbert C. Fite, *Opponents of War, 1917–1918*, Madison, Wis., 1957, pp. 3–8; William Preston, Jr., *Aliens and Dissenters: Federal Suppression of Radicals, 1903–1933*, Cambridge, Mass., 1963, pp. 88–89.
12. *Solidarity*, Aug. 8, Sept. 5, 1914.
13. *Ibid.*, Feb. 13, 1915. *See also ibid.*, July 3, 1915.
14. Pardon Appeals, C. L. Lambert, p. 39, *NA.*
15. *Solidarity*, Oct. 16, 1915.
16. *Ibid.*, Nov. 13, 1915.
17. *Proceedings of the Tenth Convention of the Industrial Workers of the World, November 20 to December 1, 1916*, Chicago, 1917, p. 138.
18. G.E.B. Statement on War, P.A. Files, 39/240, Department of Justice Records, *NA.*, and I.W.W., *Pamphlet on War.*
19. *Industrial Worker*, Nov. 4, 1916.
20. *Ibid.*, Feb. 10, 1917.
21. Pardon file of Richard Brazier, No. 15/132, Department of Justice Records, *NA.*
22. *Ibid.*
23. J. A. McDonald to S. R. Darnelly, April 12, 1917, Pardon Attorney File, No. 39/240, Department of Justice Records, *NA.*
24. Dowell, *op. cit.*, pp. 171–79; Eveleth *News*, Feb. 1, 8, March 8, 15, 1917; Duluth *News Tribune*, Feb. 8, 12, 15, 1917; Berman, *op. cit.*, p. 56.
25. 18 Idaho Code 2001 (1948); Perrin, Jr., *op. cit.*, pp. 46–48; Dowell, *op. cit.*, p. 67.

INDEX

INDEX